THE ENCYCLOPEDIA
OF THE
ARAB-ISRAELI
CONFLICT

A Political, Social, and Military History

THE ENCYCLOPEDIA
OF THE
ARAB-ISRAELI
CONFLICT

A Political, Social, and Military History

VOLUME I: A–F

Dr. Spencer C. Tucker
Volume Editor

Dr. Priscilla Roberts
Editor, Documents Volume

Dr. Paul G. Pierpaoli Jr.
Associate Editor

Major General David Zabecki, USAR (retired)
Dr. Sherifa Zuhur
Assistant Editors

FOREWORD BY
General Anthony C. Zinni, USMC (retired)

Santa Barbara, California   Denver, Colorado   Oxford, England

Cataloging-in-Publication Data is on file with the Library of Congress

   ISBN 978-1-85109-841-5 (hard copy : alk. paper) — ISBN 978-1-85109-842-2 (ebook)

10 09 08 07 06 05 10 9 8 7 6 5 4 3 2 1

This book is also available on the World Wide Web as an ebook.
Visit abc-clio.com for details.

ABC-CLIO, Inc.
130 Cremona Drive, P.O. Box 1911
Santa Barbara, California 93116–1911

This book is printed on acid-free paper ⊗ .
Manufactured in the United States of America

For Dr. Eric H. Boehm

In recognition of his vision and pursuit of scholarly excellence

About the Editors

Spencer C. Tucker, PhD, held the John Biggs Chair of Military History at his alma mater, the Virginia Military Institute in Lexington, for 6 years until his retirement from teaching in 2003. Before that, he was professor of history for 30 years at Texas Christian University, Fort Worth. He has also been a Fulbright scholar and, as an army captain, an intelligence analyst in the Pentagon. Currently the senior fellow in military history at ABC-CLIO, he has written or edited 25 books, including the award-winning *Encyclopedia of World War I, Encyclopedia of World War II,* and *Encyclopedia of the Cold War,* all published by ABC-CLIO.

Priscilla Mary Roberts received her PhD from Cambridge University and is an associate professor of history and honorary director of the Centre of American Studies at the University of Hong Kong. Dr. Roberts has received numerous research awards and was assistant editor of the *Encyclopedia of World War II* and *Encyclopedia of the Vietnam War,* published by ABC-CLIO. She spent 2003 as a visiting Fulbright scholar at the Institute for European, Russian, and Eurasian Studies at the George Washington University in Washington, D.C.

Contents

List of Entries

List of Maps

Preface

The Arab-Israeli wars from 1947 collectively form one of the most important and long-running conflicts of modern times. They have had a major impact not only on the countries directly involved but also on the entire region and the world. For most of the second half of the 20th century, the Arab-Israeli conflict was bound up in the larger Cold War. Thereafter, the failure to resolve the conflict became a prime mover in the spread of worldwide terrorism. It has also impacted international money markets and the price of oil.

To the historian, the wars are important for the role that individual decisions have had on the course of events. The military historian finds much of interest in the conflicts, including tactical decisions such as the brilliant preemptive strike by the Israeli Air Force to begin the Six-Day War of June 1967 or the battles such as the Israeli struggle to retain the Golan Heights during the 1973 Yom Kippur War. The Arab-Israeli wars have also seen a number of firsts in military history, including the first sinking of a warship by a ship-launched missile and history's first ship-to-ship missile battle. As is always the case in military history, the wars are a useful laboratory for policy decisions gone awry, such as the Jordanian decision to participate in the 1967 Six-Day War and the 1982 and 2006 Israeli invasions of Lebanon. More recently, the wars have taught the world much about the continuing sway of religious fanaticism, about the power of civil disobedience, and about terrorism in the form of suicide bombings. Certainly, solving the Israeli-Palestinian problem would go a long way toward reducing the allure of terrorism throughout the world.

To a great extent we are prisoners of the past, and nowhere is that more obvious than in conflicts in the Middle East. The Fertile Crescent gave birth to one of the world's first civilizations, and animosities there are long-standing. It is simply impossible to examine the Arab-Israeli wars without a detailed look at this rich past,

which includes political, diplomatic, social, cultural, economic, and of course religious issues. Thus, we have included among the more than 750 entries herein a number of long essays of a broader historical context, such as overviews of the wars, as well as entries on the British Mandate for Palestine and the history of Palestine and the Ottoman Empire. We also have essays covering religious issues and Zionism and the Pan-Arab movement as well as a number of entries that treat cultural and social themes.

We have a large number of entries on specific military topics such as individual wars and campaigns, key battles, weapons systems (to include types of aircraft, tanks and tank warfare, artillery, antiaircraft guns, ships, missiles, and small arms). The encyclopedia also contains essays on the leading states of the region and separate entries on the most important national military establishments. We emphasize key individuals in a wide range of fields as well as diplomatic and political events, including conferences, policy pronouncements, and treaties. We believe that understanding different cultures is essential, and to that end we have included entries on art, music, and literature as well as key individuals in these areas. We also hope that the many maps and illustrations in the encyclopedia will add to an understanding of events. Spelling of names in English from Arabic and Hebrew differs widely, and we have tried to use more commonly employed forms without diacritical marks.

I have been ably assisted on this project by associate editor Dr. Paul P. Pierpaoli Jr. and assistant editors Major General Dr. David Zabecki and Dr. Sherifa Zuhur. It is a great privilege for me to work with Dr. Pierpaoli, and I have come to rely on him greatly. A distinguished diplomatic historian, he is especially knowledgeable about the Korean War and the Cold War but has wide-ranging interests.

General Zabecki is a much-respected military historian and author of important books in the field. A student of long standing of the Arab-Israeli wars who holds a doctorate in military history, he has also been personally involved in efforts to resolve the conflict as a member of the United States Coordinating and Monitoring Mission, part of the 2003 U.S. peace initiative known as the Roadmap to Peace in the Middle East. General Zabecki is extraordinarily knowledgeable about 20th-century military history and technology and is a fine editor, and I have the greatest respect for him and am pleased that we have been able to work together on a number of projects.

Sherifa Zuhur is a specialist in Muslim and Arab affairs. She is professor of Islamic and regional studies in the Regional Strategy and Planning Department of the Strategic Studies Institute of the U.S. Army War College at Carlisle, Pennsylvania. Dr. Zuhur has traveled widely in the Middle East. A native Arabic speaker, she is an expert on and has published widely in Middle Eastern politics, international affairs, and gender issues. I am grateful for her unique perspective. The views of Dr. Zuhur and Dr. General Zabecki are, however, entirely their own and do not reflect the position of the U.S. government.

I am also greatly honored that General Anthony Zinni, U.S. Marine Corps Retired, would consent to write the introduction. I first met General Zinni when he was a visiting professor at the Virginia Military Institute, and I was most impressed with his candid and blunt assessments of the world situation. His own wide experience in the Arab-Israeli conflict gives his opinions special voice.

This project began four years ago. I developed the initial entry list and then sought the input of the assistant editors and the Editorial Advisory Board. One topic always leads to another, and Dr. Pierpaoli and I have continued to add new entries throughout the project. We accomplished all preliminary editing, and the assistant editors each read the entire copy and made editorial suggestions, which I have incorporated.

I am especially pleased to be able to again work with Dr. Priscilla Roberts on the documents volume. We have been associated with a number of encyclopedia projects, and there is simply no more professional, reliable associate. A distinguished historian of the Cold War era, Dr. Roberts has an amazing grasp of documentary collections.

I am also appreciative of the work of the members of the Editorial Advisory Board. I have been able to go to them on a number of occasions for specialized assistance on often obscure topics. Finally, I am, as always, indebted to my wife Beverly for her patience and her unstinting support in this and all other projects.

SPENCER C. TUCKER

General Maps

MIDDLE EAST, 1920

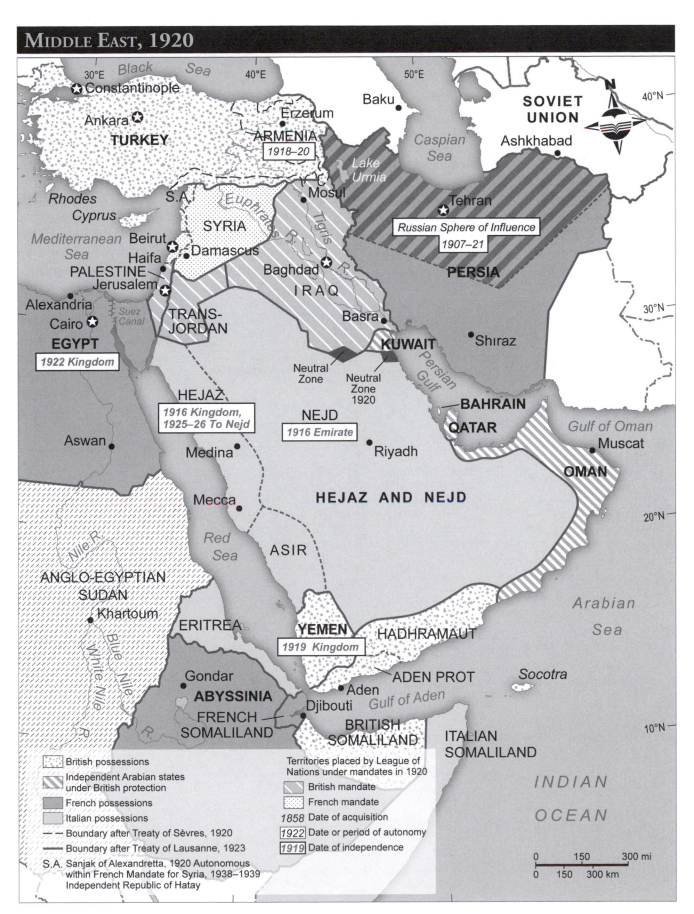

MIDDLE EAST, 1945 – 1990

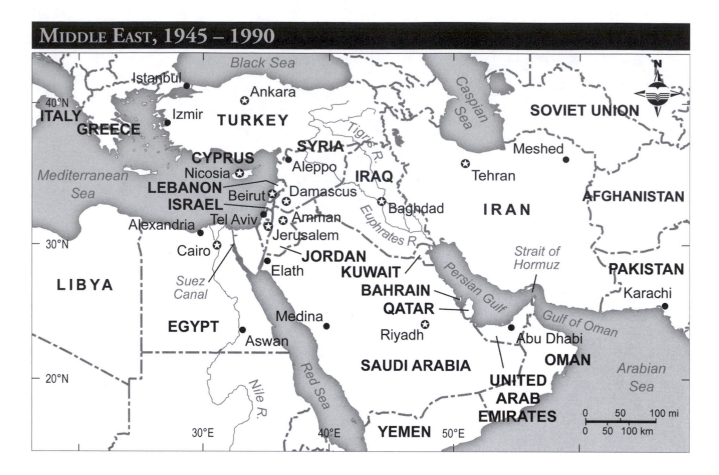

EUROPE, 1945 – 1990

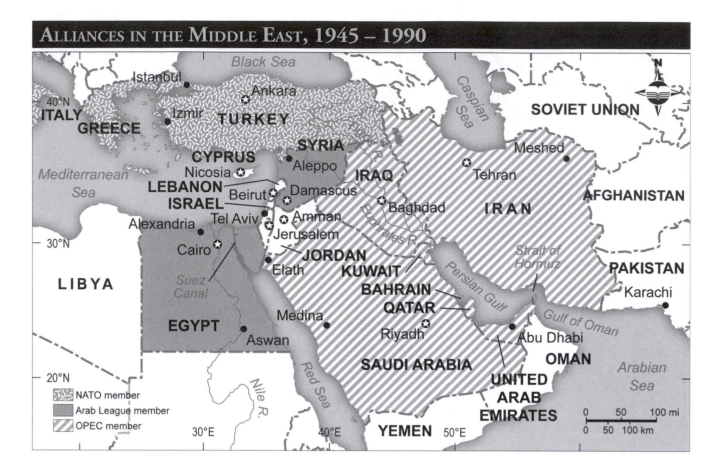

ALLIANCES IN THE MIDDLE EAST, 1945 – 1990

Black Sea

Istanbul
Ankara
40°N
ITALY
Izmir
TURKEY
GREECE
SYRIA
CYPRUS
Aleppo
Nicosia
IRAQ
Mediterranean
Sea
LEBANON
Damascus
ISRAEL
Beirut
Baghdad
Tel Aviv
Amman
Alexandria
Jerusalem
30°N
Cairo
JORDAN
KUWAIT
Elath
Suez
Canal
BAHRAIN
LIBYA
QATAR
EGYPT
Medina
Aswan
Riyadh
20°N
SAUDI ARABIA
NATO member
UNITED
Arab League member
ARAB
OPEC member
EMIRATES
30°E
40°E
YEMEN
50°E

Caspian
Sea

SOVIET UNION

Meshed

Tehran

AFGHANISTAN

IRAN

Strait of
Hormuz

PAKISTAN

Persian Gulf

Karachi

Gulf of Oman

Abu Dhabi

OMAN
Arabian
Sea

50   100 mi
0   50 100 km

Euphrates R.
Nile R.
Red Sea

General Essays

Introduction

My first real association with the continuing Arab-Israeli conflict was in 1991 during the Persian Gulf War. As the deputy director of operations for the United States European Command (USEUCOM), I was involved in the planning and execution of operations against Iraq that were based out of Turkey. Iraqi leader Saddam Hussein initiated Scud missile attacks against Israel immediately after the coalition commenced operations to remove his forces from Kuwait and attack targets inside Iraq. The USEUCOM attacked Scud launch sites in Iraq and deployed Patriot missile defense batteries into Israel to protect the targeted cities, and I was dispatched to Tel Aviv to coordinate the deployment with the leadership of the Israel Defense Forces (IDF). It was a touchy task for me, as the Israeli military leaders were chafing at the bit to join in the attacks against Iraq and did not like the political decision not to react. Their pride was deeply bruised by having someone else defend their homeland. In short order I received a rapid course on the history of the decades-old conflict and found myself getting a visceral sense of this history, particularly from the Israeli point of view, that I previously understood only from indirect academic and military studies of the conflict.

A few years later I was assigned to command I Marine Expeditionary Force, the principal Marine Corps operational organization responsible to the United States Central Command (CENTCOM) for military operations in the Middle East. This assignment added further to my education and understanding of the Arab-Israeli conflict. Although the Levant (Israel, Jordan, Syria, Lebanon, the Palestinian territories, and the Sinai Peninsula) was not in CENTCOM's area of responsibility, this conflict was clearly the most significant factor in dealing with relationships, tensions, and other conflicts in the region. In 1996 I became the deputy commander of CENTCOM, and

one year later I became the commander. By 2000 when I retired, I had six years of immersion in the region, which stretched from East Africa to Southwest Asia and included much of the Islamic world. I saw the depth of the effects of the Arab-Israeli conflict throughout this region and the visceral view from the other side.

I believed that I had a good and balanced understanding of the conflict from these experiences and from the readings, discussions, conferences, seminars, courses, and other efforts that I was also engaged in during the course of my time with CENTCOM. I was to learn that there was much more to know and that no amount of peripheral experience or study can match direct involvement.

Following my retirement in 2000, I was asked by Secretary of State Colin Powell to serve as his senior adviser on the Middle East. The true purpose of this assignment was to act as the envoy to the Israelis and Palestinians in order to restart the dormant Middle East peace process. My initial briefs from the State Department experts in this process, many of whom had decades of experience in the frustrating efforts to secure peace, were enlightening and humbling. I realized how complex this situation was and how much there was yet to know in order to effectively engage in this extremely complicated situation.

My time on the ground attempting to broker a series of incremental steps toward a comprehensive resolution of the final status issues and the establishment of a Palestinian state was frustrating. I was lectured at and scolded by the leadership on both sides as I bounced from Israeli prime minister Ariel Sharon to Palestine Liberation Organization (PLO) leader Yasser Arafat to try to seek agreements. However, I also saw a strong desire by the Israeli and Palestinian people for a solution and an end to the violence. It seemed as if history, politics, and distrust worked against the passion for peace that I experienced on the street and among the soldiers and security forces on both sides who had to deal with violence every day. I kept wondering how we got to this state.

To understand the Arab-Israeli conflict, it is important to begin with a basic understanding of the multimillennia's worth of religious evolution, wars, and conquests. The real focus, however, has to be on the period following World War I to the present when the issues and events framing the current conflict were forged. It is certainly critical to understand the political events and the attempts at peaceful resolution to this conflict during this era. But it is equally, if not more, important to understand the wars that shaped the current environment.

The stage was set when the Zionist movement of the late 1800s started a modest flow of Jews returning to biblical Israel. Initially this did not seem overly threatening to the rulers of the region, the Ottoman Empire, or to the Palestinian inhabitants of the region. The end of World War I, however, saw the defeat, collapse, and dismemberment of the Ottoman Empire and the subsequent granting of a mandate to govern Palestine by the League of Nations to Great Britain. This mandate was to last from 1920 to 1948. During that period, the persecution of the Jews in Europe by the Nazis created a growing flow of Jewish refugees into Palestine.

Through the 1930s and 1940s, this increasing influx of Jews sparked the Great Arab Revolt against the British and the growing Jewish population. This violence was followed by a Zionist guerrilla war against the British and attacks against the Arabs. With the British departure in 1948, the Israelis declared independence and set in motion the conditions for a series of conventional wars and a virtually continuous state of occupation, civil strife, guerrilla warfare, and terrorist violence during the past 60 years.

Arabs and Israelis have managed to engage each other in a conventional war every decade beginning in the 1940s. They have had the 1948–1949 War, the 1956 War, the 1967 Six-Day War, the 1973–1974 Yom Kippur War, the 1982 Lebanon War, the 1991 Gulf War, and the 2006 Lebanon War (known in Lebanon as the July War and in Israel as the Second Lebanon War). There has also been conflict on a lesser scale throughout these six decades, including the 1969–1970 War of Attrition, the two intifadas, terrorist campaigns, occupations, incursions, and retaliations. These conflicts drew in the superpowers during the Cold War, as both the United States and its allies came dangerously close to direct involvement with the Soviet Union as their clients waged war.

The clear early conventional dominance by the Israelis has led to a shift toward an asymmetrical approach by the Arabs. The use of terror and guerrilla-style tactics have proved much more problematic for the conventionally oriented Israel Defense Forces (IDF). In addition, the growing possibility of development of weapons of mass destruction (WMDs) by regional states creates another frightening dimension to this ongoing conflict.

In the up-and-down swings from hope to disappointment, there have been encouraging events during these decades of conflict. Some have lasted, and some were short-lived. The Camp David Accords that brought a peace agreement between Egypt and Jordan on one side and Israel on the other has lasted. This has required a continuous presence of multinational peacekeepers in the Sinai to maintain the peace. United Nations (UN) peacekeepers have tried for decades, with less success, to do the same on the Lebanon-Israel border. Following numerous promising peace negotiations, the Palestine Liberation Organization (PLO) transitioned, not without problems, from a terrorist organization to a political one. Agreements reached, or nearly reached, at Camp David, Oslo, Taba, and elsewhere offered promise. Although these have not resulted in a conclusive resolution of the conflict, they have framed the basis for a solution and have defined the issues. The Palestinian political leadership has regressed and fragmented after elections brought Hamas to power, but recent agreements may lead to establishing a credible political return to the peace table if further conditions can be met.

The Arab-Israeli conflict has been a painful experience for all those involved. Hatreds have deepened over the years, and sides have been taken by outsiders who have become involved. The conflict has drawn in virtually the whole world, not only in the conflict itself but also in the attempts at peaceful resolution. Currently, the Quartet (the United States, Russia, the UN, and the European Union) that works toward a plan for peace demonstrates the global involvement and concern over this situation. Today the conflict incites worldwide violence and engagement, as most current threats to global security and stability seem directly or indirectly connected to this conflict. As I have become more and more involved in this tragic dilemma, I have come to appreciate the deep complexity of the issues and events that form this conflict. These reflect views of history, religion, birthright, and justice that are tough to mediate and resolve. It is important to fully understand all of these in order to effectively engage in the process or hope to have credibility on any path to resolution.

A crucial part of this understanding is thorough knowledge of the wars that have been fought by these two societies as well as of their underlying causes and the history of the region. *The Encyclopedia of the Arab-Israeli Conflict* offers a comprehensive and important work to aid in that understanding. It is important for soldiers and those interested in military history to study these wars through excellent publications such as this encyclopedia for the valuable strategic, operational, and tactical lessons. It is equally important, in my view, for those seeking peace to study these wars to gain the understanding necessary to resolve the issues that underlie the conflict and have drawn blood.

ANTHONY C. ZINNI
GENERAL, UNITED STATES MARINE CORPS (RETIRED)

Overview of the Arab-Israeli Conflict

Establishing precise parameters for the Arab-Israeli conflict is difficult. The wars are usually given as beginning with the Arab-Jewish Communal War (1947–1948) or the Israeli War of Independence (1948–1949). These wars in effect extend to the present, for some of the Arab confrontation states, most notably Syria, have yet to sign peace treaties with Israel.

But beginning the conflict in 1948 or even 1947 gives a false impression, as there had long been episodes of violence and armed clashes between Arabs and Jews in Palestine, especially in the 1920s and 1930s. These events were sparked by Arab fears over significant Jewish immigration to Palestine and land purchases there. Animosity thus found expression in the Arab Riots of 1920 and the Arab Revolt of 1936–1939.

Of course, strife was hardly new to this region. Palestine had been a battleground since the beginning of recorded history. History's first reliably recorded battle took place in 1457 BC at Megiddo, at the head of present-day Israel's Jezreel Valley. When Egyptian forces under the command of Pharaoh Thutmose III decisively defeated a Canaanite coalition under the king of Kadesh, the Canaanites withdrew to the city of Megiddo, which the Egyptians then brought under siege. Certain fundamentalist Christians identify Megiddo as the site of Armageddon, where according to the Book of Revelation the final great battle between good and evil will take place.

With its location on the eastern Mediterranean coast, ancient Palestine formed an important communication route between larger empires such as Egypt, Assyria, Babylon, and Persia. As such, it was destined for a stormy existence. These empires as well as Alexander the Great, the Seleucid Empire, the Romans, the Byzantines, the Abbasid caliphate, the Tartars, the Mongols, the Mamluks, the Ottoman Turks, and finally the British all fought for control of Palestine. Sometime around 1200 BC the Jews established and then maintained an independent Jewish state there. Ultimately, more powerful states prevailed, and the Jews were largely expelled from their own land by the occupiers in what became known as the Diaspora. Jews settled in most of the world's countries and on almost every continent.

In the 19th century, nationalism swept Europe. Sentiment for a national state also touched the Jews, who longed for a state of their own, one that would be able to protect them from the persecutions (pogroms) that occurred in the late 19th and early 20th centuries, most notably in Russia. Zionism, or the effort to reestablish a Jewish state in Palestine, attracted a great many Jews—religious and nonreligious—and a number of them went to Palestine as immigrants.

During World War I, the British government endeavored to win the support of both Arabs and Jews in the war against the Central Powers, including the Ottoman Empire. While at the same time supporting the Arab Revolt against Ottoman Turkey, the British government in the Balfour Declaration of November 1917 promised to work for the establishment of a Jewish homeland in Palestine. In retrospect, British policies were at once shortsighted and contradictory and helped sow the seeds of even more Arab-Jewish enmity when the war ended in 1918. Britain and France both secured League of Nations mandates in the Middle East after the war. France obtained Syria and Lebanon, while Britain took control of Palestine (which included what is today Israel/Palestine and Jordan) and Iraq.

Increasing Jewish immigration, however, as well as ongoing Jewish purchases of Arab land increasingly inflamed Arab leaders in Palestine, who feared that if immigration could not be halted, the growing Jewish minority in Palestine would become a majority. In this position, the Arab leadership had the strong support of the Arab governments of the region. In what became an increasingly violent atmosphere, the British government found it impossible to please both sides. London, worried about its overall position in the Middle East with the approach of a new world war, increasingly tended to side with the Arabs. This meant restrictions on both Jewish immigration and land purchases in Palestine, but this came at precisely the time when German leader Adolf Hitler challenged the post–World War I status quo in Europe and was carrying out a fervent anti-Semite policy.

Finding it impossible to secure agreement between the two sides, London announced plans for the partition of Palestine. The Arabs rejected this partitioning, insisting on independence for Palestine as one state under majority (Arab) rule. Concerned about their overall position in the Middle East, the British then withdrew from their pro-Zionist policy and in May 1939 issued a White Paper that severely restricted the immigration of Jews to Palestine and forbade the purchase of Arab lands in Palestine by Jews.

Following World War II, Jews in Palestine conducted a campaign against the British policy there that mixed diplomatic campaign with armed struggle. Finding it more and more difficult to contain the growing violence in Palestine, coupled with the support of President Harry S. Truman's administration in the United States for the Jewish position, London turned the future of Palestine over to the new United Nations (UN). On November 29, 1947, The UN General Assembly voted to partition the British mandate into Jewish and Arab states. The Arabs of Palestine, supported by the Arab League, adamantly opposed the partition, and the first of four major wars began following news of the UN vote. The first war of 1947–1949 contains two identifiably separate conflicts: the Arab-Jewish communal war of November 30, 1947–May 14, 1948, which included volunteer forces from other Arab states as well as Palestinian Arabs, and the Israeli War of Independence, which began on May 15, 1948, a day after the ending of the British mandate and with the founding of the State of Israel. It ended with the last truce agreement with Syria on July 30, 1949. The three other conflicts ensued in 1956 (the Sinai War, or Suez Crisis), 1967 (the Six-Day War), and 1973 (the October War, Ramadan War, or Yom Kippur War). In these four conflicts, Israeli forces eventually triumphed. Each threatened to bring about superpower intervention, and the four wars also had profound implications throughout the Middle East and beyond. Beyond these wars, however, were ongoing terrorist attacks against Israel; cross-border raids, some of them quite large; a successful Israeli air strike on the Iraqi Osiraq nuclear reactor (1981); and large Israeli incursions into southern Lebanon (1982).

The 1948 war began following the announcement of the UN General Assembly's endorsement of Resolution 181 on November 29, 1947, calling for the partition of Palestine into Jewish and Arab states. While Jewish authorities in Palestine accepted the resolution, the Arabs—including the Palestinians and the Arab League—rejected it. In response to passage of the UN resolution, Arabs began attacking Jews throughout Palestine, and the incidents expanded so

that from December 1947 to April or May 1948 an intercommunal war raged between Jewish and Arab residents of Palestine.

The Jewish community in Palestine then numbered some 600,000 people, while the Palestinians consisted of more than 1.2 million. However, Palestinian numerical advantage counted for little on the battlefield. The Palestinians had no national institutions of any kind, let alone a cohesive military. They were fragmented with divided elites and were unprepared for the violence, expulsions, and loss of their property. Probably most of the Palestinians did not want to go to the war, hoping that their Jewish neighbors would retreat. Perhaps only 5,000 Palestinians took part in the fighting against the Jews. These essentially guerrilla forces were poorly trained, poorly equipped, and ineffectively organized.

The Arab League pledged support to the Palestinians but through its Military Committee actually usurped the conflict from the Palestinians. The Military Committee and the mufti Haj Amin al-Husseini argued over the conduct of the war as each sought to control operations. The Military Committee failed, however, to provide the Palestinians with the money and weapons that the Arab rulers had pledged and sent its own commanders to Palestine to oversee the war. Such internal conflicts further weakened the overall Arab effort.

The Jews, on the other hand, were much better equipped and more organized. Jewish society was both Western and industrialized, having all the institutions of a modern state. In fact, structurally the establishment of the Jewish state required only the formal transformation of the prestatehood institutions to government entities, parliament, political parties, banks, and a relatively well-developed military arm, known as the Haganah. The Haganah was organized during the civil war as a full-fledged army, with nine brigades with a total of some 25,000 conscripts. By May 1948 there were 11 brigades, with nearly 35,000 men. With the Jewish forces taking the offensive in early April 1948, the Palestinians had no chance but to counterattack and by early May had been defeated.

During this time, and even before the Jews' final campaign, hundreds of thousands of Palestinians were driven from or fled their homes and became refugees. By the end of the war, there would be 750,000–1 million or more Palestinian refugees. Many of them escaped from the battle zone, but others were forcibly expelled and deported by Jewish forces during the actual fighting.

On May 14, 1948, with the formal establishment of the State of Israel, Israeli forces secured control over all the territory allocated to it by the UN in addition to a corridor leading to Jerusalem and the Jewish part of Jerusalem, which according to the Partition Resolution was to have been internationalized. With the official termination of British rule in Palestine earlier that day, David Ben-Gurion, Israel's first elected prime minister, declared the establishment of the State of Israel. This declaration was followed by the advance of four Arab armies toward Palestine bent on a campaign to extinguish Israel.

The resulting war was, in many respects, primitive. Some 35,000 Israeli soldiers faced 35,000–40,000 Arab soldiers. Both sides were subjected to a UN Security Council arms embargo, but it was the Arabs who suffered the most from this. The Arab armies secured their weapons from Britain for Egypt, while Jordan and Iraq, which had no access to other markets, were forced into this arrangement under treaties with Britain. With the embargo in place, the Arabs were unable to replace damaged or destroyed weapons, and they had only limited access to ammunition. However, while the Jews received no military equipment from the West, they did manage in early 1948 to sign a major arms contract with the Czech government, thereby purchasing various weapons but mostly small arms and ammunition.

The strength of the Arab armies was in infantry. Their few tanks were mostly Egyptian. Even then, only a few dozen were operative. Despite an initial effort to create a unified command structure, the movements of the four Arab armies on Palestine were not coordinated. In April 1948 General Nur al-Din Mahmud, an Iraqi officer, was appointed by the Arab League to command the Arab forces. Mahmud submitted a plan that focused on northeastern Palestine, where the invading forces would try to sever eastern Galilee from the Hula Valley to Lake Kinneret (the Sea of Galilee) from Israel. That would be achieved through the coordinated advance of the Syrian, Lebanese, Iraqi, and Jordanian forces in the northern part of Palestine, while the Egyptian Army would move northward to Yibna, which was inside the designated Arab state. The Egyptians were not to advance into the Jewish state's territory, at least not in the first stage, but rather were to create a diversion that would lure Israeli forces into their sector and reduce Israeli pressure on the main Arab push in the north.

Jordan's King Abdullah had different plans for his army, however. He planned to occupy the area designated for the Palestinian Arab state, west of the Jordan River (the West Bank). For that reason he rebuffed Mahmud's plan and ordered the commander of the Arab Legion to act independently and occupy the West Bank. That was done, with the Arab Legion completing its mission in a few days. With that, each Arab army acted in isolation, while at the last minute Lebanon refrained from participation in the war. Syrian and Iraqi forces fought in the northern part of Israel, the Jordanian Arab League in the central sector, and the Egyptian Army in the southern sector.

The Egyptian government dispatched to Palestine 5,500 soldiers organized into two infantry brigades, accompanied by nearly 4,500 irregulars. Iraq dispatched to Palestine some 4,500 soldiers, while Syria sent 6,000. Jordan deployed almost all of its army, some 6,500 men. In addition, some 3,000 irregulars fought alongside the Arab armies.

At that time, Israel fielded more than 30,000 soldiers. The fighting was divided into two parts: the first from May 15 to June 10 and the second from July 9 to the end of the war. The first stage saw the Jews on the defensive, while in the second half of the war they took the offensive. In the indecisive first phase, small Iraqi and Syrian forces invaded Israel in the north but were repelled following a few days of fighting.

Jordanian forces concentrated on the occupation of the West Bank, while the main Egyptian expeditionary force moved northward along the coastline, reaching its final staging area near Yibna, within the area designated to the Arab state. Another part of the Egyptian force split from the main force. It crossed the Negev Desert from west to east and moved toward Samaria through Hebron up to the southern outskirts of Jerusalem. Neither Egyptian force encountered any Israeli forces during their movements.

In the north, the Syrian and the Iraqi armies tried to execute their part in Mahmud's plan, which was no longer valid. Acting in an uncoordinated manner, small forces of both armies invaded Israel in an area south of the Kinneret but were thwarted by the Israelis. The Syrian Army retreated, to return about a week later and attack two Israeli settlements near the Israeli-Syrian border and occupy them. Israeli counterattacks failed, and the Syrian forces withdrew only at the end of the war as part of the truce agreement between the two states. The Iraqi forces retreated too and returned to the Jordanian-occupied West Bank. The Iraqi troops acted in coordination with the Jordanian Army, allowing the Jordanian command to send troops from around Samaria, now held by the Iraqis, to the Israeli-Jordanian battlefield. Iraqi forces departed the West Bank at the end of the war, with Iraq refraining from signing a truce agreement with Israel.

In this initial stage, the Israelis were concentrated along the road to Jerusalem. Both the Jordanians and the Israelis completely misread the other's intentions. The Israelis assumed that the Arab Legion planned to invade Israel, and the Jordanians feared that the Israelis intended to drive the Arab Legion from the West Bank.

In fact, all the Israelis sought was to bring the Jewish part of Jerusalem under Israeli control and, toward that end, to gain control over the road from the coast to Jerusalem. The Israelis feared that the Arab Legion would cut the road to Jerusalem and occupy all of Jerusalem, and to prevent this from occurring they reinforced Jerusalem. The Jordanians interpreted the dispatch of Israeli troops to Jerusalem as an attempt to build up a force to take the offensive against them. This mutual misunderstanding was the cause of the fierce fighting between Israeli and Jordanian forces that ended with the Jordanians repulsing the Israeli troops and holding on to bases in the Latrun area, the strategic site along the Tel Aviv–Jerusalem road.

Israeli-Jordanian fighting ended when the Israeli government acknowledged its inability to drive out Jordanian forces that blocked the road to Jerusalem and when the two governments realized that the other posed no risk. In November 1948, Jewish and Jordanian military commanders in Jerusalem concluded an agreement that formalized the positions established with the de facto cease-fire of the previous July.

With the end of the fighting with Jordan, the Israelis launched the final phase of the war. In a two-stage operation in October and December 1948, the Israeli Army drove the Egyptian forces from the Negev. The Israeli effort to force out the Egyptians along the coast was only partially successful, however. The Egyptians remained in the Gaza Strip. Indeed, the Gaza Strip remained under Egyptian control until 1967.

Concurrent with the October operations in the south, other Israeli troops stormed the high ground in central Galilee, controlled by the Arab League's Arab Liberation Army. After brief fighting, the Israelis occupied all of Galilee. In early January 1949 a cease-fire came into effect, and shortly thereafter negotiations on armistice agreements began.

The second major confrontation between Israel and the Arabs was the Sinai War, or Suez Crisis, of October 1956. This time, France, Britain, Israel, and Egypt were involved in the fighting. The Israeli-Egyptian portion of the war, which in Israel was known as Operation KADESH, was part of a larger picture. During 1949–1956, there was constant unrest along the Israeli-Egyptian demarcation line as well as between Israel and Jordan. Infiltrators regularly crossed the border from the Egyptian-controlled Gaza Strip, from the Sinai, and from the West Bank. Some were Palestinian refugees seeking to return to their homes or to visit relatives who remained inside Israel; some hoped to harvest their fields on the Israeli side of the border; some came to steal; and a few went to launch terrorist attacks against Israeli targets.

These infiltrations had an enormous impact on Israel. Economic damage mounted, and border-area residents, many of them newly arrived immigrants, were unprepared for the challenge. Israel feared the political implications of the infiltrations, as estimates of their numbers were thousands per month. Consequently, Israeli security forces undertook harsh measures against the infiltrators, regardless of the motives for crossing the border. Israeli soldiers often ambushed infiltrators, killing them and launching reprisal attacks. As a result, tensions along the Israeli borders increased, chiefly along the frontiers with Jordan and Egypt.

While the cross-border tensions provided the background context, the war occurred for two main reasons. First, Egyptian president Gamal Abdel Nasser had absorbed a large number of Palestinian refugees into Egypt and was responsible in a legal sense for those in the Gaza Strip. Rather than allowing the Palestinians free rein to attack Israel, he sought to simultaneously support their cause yet limit the Israeli response to their actions in unspoken rules of engagement, which the Israelis hoped to overturn. Nasser was a fervent Arab nationalist who also aspired to lead and unite the Arab world, a potentiality that deeply troubled Prime Minister Ben-Gurion. Ben-Gurion attributed the Arab defeat in 1948 to a great extent to their divisions. Thus, he was fearful of a unified Arab world under Nasser's leadership. The third immediate reason for the war was the Egyptian-Soviet arms arrangement (normally referred to as the Czech Arms Deal), announced in September 1955. The agreement assured Nasser of the modern weapons that Ben-Gurion was certain Nasser intended to use in an all-out attack against Israel.

Israeli fears were mitigated by an Israeli-French arms agreement completed in June 1956 one month before Nasser nationalized the Suez Canal on July 26, provoking an acute international crisis that culminated with the 1956 war. Shortly after the beginning of the crisis, France invited Israel to take part in planning a joint military attack on Egypt.

For Israel, while there was no specific reason for such an offensive move, fear of Nasser's intentions seemed sufficient justification. Tensions between Israel and Egypt since 1949, and especially since 1954, had significantly diminished. In the summer of 1956 exchanges of fire along the armistice line had largely ceased. More importantly, Nasser, expecting a fierce Anglo-French reaction to the nationalization of the Suez Canal, reduced the Egyptian troop deployment along the Israeli-Egyptian border to reinforce the Suez Canal.

While Egypt had blockaded the Straits of Tiran, closing it to Israeli ships, that by itself could not be reason for war, as there was no Israeli commercial maritime transportation along that route. Nevertheless, Ben-Gurion feared that Nasser was planning to unite the Arab world against Israel, and thus the invitation from two major powers to take part in a combined military effort was too much to resist. In a meeting at Sèvres, France, during October 22–25, 1956, French, British, and Israeli negotiators worked out the details of the war.

According to the plan that was worked out, Israeli parachutists would land a few miles east of Suez. France and Britain would then issue an ultimatum to both parties to remove their military forces from the canal. Expecting an Egyptian refusal, French and British forces would then invade Egypt to enforce the ultimatum. In the meantime, Israeli forces would storm the Sinai Peninsula. Their goal was to join up with the parachutists in the heart of the Sinai and to open the Straits of Tiran.

Israel deployed the 7th Armored Brigade, with two tank battalions; the 27th and 37th Mechanized brigades; the 202nd Parachute Brigade; and the 1st, 4th, 9th, 10th, 11th, and 12th Infantry Brigades. The agreement with the British and French was the determining factor in the Israeli plan of attack. Instead of storming the Egyptian positions in front of them, a paratroop battalion was dropped on October 29, 1956, at the eastern gates of the Mitla Pass, some 30 miles east of the Suez Canal. Simultaneously, the paratroop brigade, commanded by Lieutenant Colonel Ariel Sharon, moved into the Sinai to join with the battalion waiting deep in the Sinai. The other Israeli forces had to wait until the Anglo-French attack on Egypt began.

Israeli commanders in the field were unaware of the agreement with the British and the French. Fearing for the parachute brigade and seeking a resolute and decisive victory over Egyptian forces, Major General Assaf Simhoni, commander of the southern command, ordered his forces to move ahead, with the armored brigade leading. The armored brigade stormed the Egyptian positions, with the remainder of the forces ensuring the defeat of the Egyptians. Israeli forces completed the occupation of the Sinai and the Gaza Strip within three days. During the fighting, nearly 170 Israeli soldiers were killed and 700 were wounded. The Egyptians suffered thousands of deaths, far more wounded, and more than 5,500 prisoners.

Israel did not enjoy for long the territorial achievements it gained in the war. Under enormous pressure from the United States and the Soviet Union, it was forced to remove its forces from the Sinai and the Gaza Strip. However, the terms of the Israeli evacuation of the Sinai aimed to provide it the security it was lacking: UN observers were deployed along the armistice demarcation lines to ensure that they would not be crossed by infiltrators. One result of the stationing of UN forces was the nearly complete cessation of infiltration from the Gaza Strip to Israel. It was also agreed that the Sinai would be demilitarized, removing with that the threat of an Egyptian surprise attack against Israel. The Dwight D. Eisenhower administration provided assurances that it would no longer allow closure of the Straits of Tiran. Finally, the performance of Israeli forces in the war marked a dramatic change in the history of the Israel Defense Forces (IDF). The IDF went from being an unsophisticated, infantry-based army to an efficient, modernized, and mechanized military force. The lessons of the Sinai War certainly paved the way toward the Israelis' impressive achievement in the Six-Day War of June 6–11, 1967.

While the immediate cause of the Six-Day War may be unclear, the long-term catalysts are more obvious. On May 15, 1967, Nasser sent his army into the Sinai. This set the stage for a dramatic three weeks that culminated in an Israeli attack and the total defeat of Egyptian, Jordanian, and Syrian forces. It also resulted in the loss of territories by these three Arab countries.

Tensions along the Israeli-Syrian and the Israeli-Jordanian borders formed the long-term cause of the war. There were three issues of contention. The first was the Israeli-Syrian struggle over the sovereignty of several pieces of land along their mutual border. According to the Israeli-Syrian armistice agreements, these areas were demilitarized. The Syrians insisted that sovereignty of the areas was undecided, while the Israelis believed that because the areas were on their side of the international border, they were under Israeli sovereignty. Consequently, Israel insisted that it had the right to cultivate the controversial pieces of land, to Syria's dismay. In a number of instances, the Syrians tried, by armed force, to prevent Israeli settlers from farming the land. The second point of controversy lay in Syrian attempts to prevent Israel from diverting water from the Jordan River. Encouraged by the Arab League, the Syrians had tried since 1964 to divert the headwaters of the Jordan River inside Syria. Israel reacted fiercely to this, and until the Syrians finally abandoned the project, many clashes took place between the two nations' armed forces. The third issue was the continuing grievances of the Palestinians. Their desire to regain their land and find a solution for their displaced refugees was an ever-present theme in the politics of the neighboring Arab states and the Palestinian refugee community.

In 1964, Palestinian engineer and nationalist Yasser Arafat established Fatah, a political organization dedicated to liberating Palestine within the rubric of the Palestine Liberation Organization (PLO), also established in that year by the Arab League to provide a political representative body for the Palestinians. Over the next few years, other militant, political, and representative Palestinian organizations were established. In January 1965, Fatah planted a bomb near an Israeli water-pumping station. The Israelis defused the bomb, but Fatah celebrated this as the first Palestinian terrorist attack. Palestinian attacks continued throughout 1965, 1966, and 1967. Despite the relatively low scale of the attacks, Israel responded aggressively, blaming Jordan for funding the terrorists and Syria for harboring and encouraging them.

The extent and ferocity of Israeli-Syrian clashes increased during 1967, culminating in an aerial battle between Israeli and Syrian forces that took place in April 1967. Israeli pilots shot down six Syrian planes during one of the dogfights. In the course of a public address, IDF chief of staff Lieutenant General Yitzhak Rabin threatened war against Syria.

A month later, in May 1967, Nasser ordered his forces into the Sinai. The reasons for this action are in dispute. The common assumption is that Moscow warned both the Egyptian and Syrian governments that Israel was massing military forces along the Israeli-Syrian border and planning to attack Syria. Because Egypt and Syria were bound by a military pact signed on November 4, 1966, Nasser sent his army into the Sinai to force the Israelis to dilute their forces in the north and to forestall what he assumed was an imminent attack on Syria.

The Israelis responded to the entry of Egyptian forces into the Sinai with the calling up of IDF reserve forces. Nasser subsequently increased Israeli concerns when he ordered the UN observers along the Israeli-Egyptian border to concentrate in one location. UN secretary-general U Thant responded by pulling UN forces out of the Sinai altogether. Next, Nasser again closed the Straits of Tiran, yet another violation of the agreements that had led to the Israeli withdrawal from the Sinai in 1957. Besides that, Jordan and Egypt signed a military pact on May 30, 1967. This further increased the Israeli sense of siege.

Israeli military doctrine called for preemptive strikes in case of a concentration of Arab forces along its borders. All that was necessary was U.S. permission, and the Lyndon B. Johnson administration gave that in early June. The war began at dawn on June 5, 1967, with preemptive Israeli air strikes on Egyptian and then Syrian, Jordanian, and Iraqi air bases. The purpose of the attack was to neutralize the Arab air forces and remove the threat of air strikes on Israel. This would also, at a later stage, allow the Israeli Air Force to provide close air support to its forces on the ground.

Catching the vast bulk of the Egyptian aircraft on the ground as their pilots were at breakfast, some 250 Israeli aircraft destroyed the backbone of the Arab air forces within an hour, and by the end of the day they had been almost completely wiped out. More than 300 of a total of 420 Egyptian combat aircraft were destroyed that day. The Israelis then turned to destroy the far smaller Jordanian and Syrian Air Forces.

About an hour after the start of the air raids against Egypt, at about 8:30 a.m. Israeli time, the IDF launched its ground offensive. Three Israeli divisions attacked Egyptian forces in the Sinai and within four days had destroyed the Egyptian army in the Sinai and occupied the Peninsula.

Israeli operational plans were initially restricted to the Egyptian front. The IDF high command had developed plans to take the fighting to the Jordanian and Syrian fronts, but on the morning of June 5 it had no wish to go to war with these two Arab states.

There were, however, unexpected developments. As the Israeli troops stormed into the Sinai, Jordanian artillery shelled the suburbs of Jerusalem and other targets in Israel. The Israeli government hoped that Jordan's King Hussein would stay out of the fray and refrain from engaging in serious fighting. That did not happen. Jordanian troops stormed the UN headquarters in Jerusalem, inducing fears that the next step would be an attempt to take over Israeli-held Mount Scopus, an enclave within eastern Jerusalem, a Jordanian-held territory. To prevent that, Israeli forces moved ahead to secure a road to Mount Scopus, and the Jerusalem area became a battlefield. In addition, Israeli troops moved in northern Samaria, from which long-range Jordanian artillery was shelling Israeli seaside cities. A full-fledged war was now in progress that lasted two days and ended with the complete Israeli victory over Jordanian forces. Israel then occupied the West Bank and eastern Jerusalem.

In the north, Syrian forces began to move westward toward the Israeli border but did not complete the deployment and, for unknown reasons, returned to their bases. For five long days the Syrians shelled Israeli settlements from the Golan Heights overlooking the Jordan River Valley. Hoping to avoid a three-front war, the Israelis took no action against the Syrians, despite the heavy pressure imposed on them by the settlers who had come under Syrian artillery fire. It was only in the last day of the war, with the fighting in the south and center firmly under control, that Israeli troops stormed the Golan Heights, taking it after only a few hours of fighting.

The end of the war saw a new Middle East in which Israel controlled an area three times as large as its pre-1967 territory. It had also firmly established itself as a major regional power. Israel also found itself in control of nearly 2 million Arabs in the West Bank, many of whom were refugees from the 1948–1949 war. The 1967 Six-Day War, known as the Naksa in the Arab world, was considered an utter defeat not only for the Arab armies but also for the principles of secular Arab nationalism as embodied in their governments. The defeat led to a religious revival.

Militarily, the 1967 Six-Day War marked a major military departure. First, it was a full-fledged armor war in which both sides, but chiefly the Egyptians and Israelis, deployed hundreds of tanks. Second, Cold War imperatives were clearly evident on the battlefield, with Israel equipped with sophisticated Western weapons and enjoying the full political support of the United States, while the Egyptians and the Syrians had the military and political support of the Soviet Union.

The next major Arab-Israeli conflict occurred six years later: the 1973 Yom Kippur War, also known as the War of Atonement and the Ramadan War. The years between 1967 and 1973 were not peaceful ones in the Middle East. Nasser refused to accept the results of the Six-Day War and rejected Israeli terms for negotiations of direct peace talks that would end in a peace agreement in return for giving up the Sinai. The Jordanians and the Syrians, as well as the rest of the Arab world, also rejected Israel's terms, instead demanding compliance with UN Resolution 242 (November 22, 1967) that called for the "withdrawal of Israeli armed forces from territories occupied in the recent conflict" and the "termination of all claims or states of belligerency and respect for and acknowledgement of the sovereignty, territorial integrity, and political independence of every state in the area."

UN Resolution 242 became the main reference for any agreement in the region, but it has never been enforced. The Israelis argue that it called for the withdrawal of Israeli armed forces from "territories occupied" and not from "the territories occupied," and thus it need not return to all the pre–June 6, 1967, lines as the UN has instead argued. Tel Aviv held that this was a matter for discussion with the Arab states involved. In addition, the resolution was not tied to any demand for the parties to begin direct peace talks, as Israel consistently required. The result was stalemate.

Israel launched settlement endeavors and placed Jewish settlers in the occupied territories, seeking to perpetuate with that its hold on the territories, while the Arab side again resorted to violence. The first to endorse violence were the Palestinians. Disappointed by the Arab defeat, some of the Palestinians changed their strategy, declaring a revolution or people's movement. Prior to 1967 they had used terror attacks as a trigger that might provoke war, which they hoped would end in an Arab victory. Now they decided to take their fate into their own hands and launch their own war of liberation against what they called the Zionist entity. The result was a sharp increase in the extent and ferocity of Palestinian terrorist attacks on Israel and in the level of tensions between the Arab states and the Palestinians.

In 1968 the Palestinians internationalized their struggle by launching terrorist attacks against Israeli and Jewish targets all over the world. Nasser now also decided to take a path of aggression. Frustrated by his inability to bring about a change in Israel's position, he began a campaign under the slogan of "what was taken by force would be returned by force." Following low-level skirmishes along the Suez Canal and adjoining areas, from June 1968 Egyptian forces began shelling and raiding Israeli troop deployments across the canal. The Israelis responded with artillery fire and retaliatory attacks. The violence escalated as Israel struck deep inside Egypt with its air force. Before long, this midlevel-intensity conflict became known as the War of Attrition and continued until 1970.

With the growing intensity of Israeli air attacks on Egypt, pilots from the Soviet Union took an active part in the defense of Egypt. The increased involvement of the Soviet military in the conflict deeply worried both the Israelis and the United States. Through the mediation of U.S. secretary of state William Rogers, a cease-fire agreement was concluded in August 1970, and the fighting subsided. However, shortly after the signing of the agreement, the

Egyptians began placing surface-to-air (SAM) batteries throughout the Suez Canal area.

During 1970–1973, Rogers and UN mediator Gunnar Jarring introduced peace plans that were rejected by both the Israelis and the Egyptians. Following Nasser's death in September 1970, his successor, Anwar Sadat, was determined to change the status quo. Toward that end, he acted on two fronts: he called for a gradual settlement that would lead to Israeli withdrawal from the Sinai without a full peace agreement, and he expelled the Soviet advisers brought in by Nasser and resumed negotiations with the United States, which Nasser had ended in 1955.

The failure of Sadat's diplomatic efforts in 1971 led him to begin planning a military operation that would break the political stalemate along the Israeli-Egyptian front. Sadat believed that even a minor Egyptian military success would change the military equilibrium and force a political settlement that would lead to a final settlement. In devising his plan, he carefully calculated Israeli and Egyptian strengths and weaknesses. He believed that Israel's strength lay in its air force and armored divisions, well trained for the conduct of maneuver warfare. Egyptian strengths were the ability to build a strong defense line and the new SAM batteries deployed all along the canal area and deep within Egypt. Sadat hoped to paralyze the Israeli Air Force with the SAMs and hoped to counter the Israelis' advantage in maneuver warfare by forcing them to attack well-fortified and defended Egyptian strongholds.

In an attempt to dilute the Israeli military forces on the Sinai front, Sadat brought in Syria. A coordinated surprise attack on both the Syrian and Egyptian fronts would place maximum stress on the IDF. But above anything else, the key to the plan's success lay in its secrecy. Were Israel to suspect that an attack was imminent, it would undoubtedly launch a preventive attack, as in 1967. This part of the plan was successful.

Israeli ignorance of effective deceptive measures undertaken by Egypt contributed to Israel's failure to comprehend what was happening. One deception consisted of repeated Egyptian drills along the canal that simulated a possible crossing. The Israelis thus became accustomed to large Egyptian troop concentrations at the canal and interpreted Egyptian preparations for the actual crossings as just another drill. Even the Egyptian soldiers were told that it was simply a drill. Only when the actual crossing was occurring were they informed of its true nature. Even with the actual attack, however, the real intent of Egyptian and Syrian forces remained unclear to the Israelis, and they initially refrained from action.

Beginning at 2:00 p.m. on October 6, 1973, Egyptian and Syrian artillery and aircraft, and later their ground forces, launched major attacks along the Suez Canal and the Golan Heights. On the Israeli-Egyptian front, Egypt amassed a force of nearly 800,000 soldiers, 2,200 tanks, 2,300 artillery pieces, 150 SAM batteries, and 550 aircraft. Egypt deployed along the canal five infantry divisions with accompanying armored elements supported by additional infantry and armored independent brigades. This force was backed by three mechanized divisions and two armored divisions. Opposing this force on the eastern bank of the Suez Canal was one Israeli division supported by 280 tanks.

This Israeli force was no match for the advancing Egyptian troops. The defenders lacked reinforcements, as reserves were called on duty only after the outbreak of the war. They also did not have air support, as Egyptian SAMs proved deadly effective against Israeli aircraft.

The attacking Egyptians got across the canal and swept over the defending Israelis. It took less than 48 hours for the Egyptians to establish a penetration three to five miles deep on the east bank of the Suez Canal. They then fortified the area with more troops. Two divisions held the seized area, which was defended also by the SAM batteries across the canal. With that, the Egyptians had achieved their principal aims and a psychological victory.

The Israelis rushed reinforcements southward and launched a quick counteroffensive on October 8 in an attempt to repel the invading Egyptians troops. Much to Israeli surprise, it was a failure. Undermanned, unorganized, and underequipped Israeli troops moved against a far bigger and more well-organized and well-equipped force protected by highly effective handheld antitank missiles. The Egyptians crushed the Israeli counteroffensive.

Following this setback, the Israeli General Staff decided to halt offensive actions on the Suez front and give priority to the fighting in the north on the Golan Heights, where in the first hours of the war little stood between massive numbers of invading Syrian armor and the Jewish settlements. Syria deployed two infantry divisions in the first line and two armored divisions in the second. This force had 1,500 tanks against only two Israeli armored brigades with 170 tanks. The Syrian forces swept the Golan Heights, crushing the small Israeli forces facing them. The few Israeli forces there fought desperately, knowing that they were the only force between the Syrians and numerous settlements. The Israeli forces slowed the Syrians and bought sufficient time for reserves of men and tanks to be brought forward. The Syrians also had an ineffective battle plan, which played to Israeli strengths in maneuver warfare. After seven days of fighting, Israeli troops thwarted the Syrian forces beyond the starting point of the war, across the pre–October 1973 Purple Line, and then drove a wedge into Syrian territory. Only then did the IDF again turn to the Egyptian front, where the goal remained driving Egyptian troops from the Sinai.

Sadat also overruled his ground commander and continued the advance. This took his forces out of their prepared defensive positions and removed them from the effective SAM cover on the other side of the canal, working to the Israelis' advantage. Israeli troops also located a gap between the two Egyptian divisions defending the occupied area that had gone unnoticed by the Egyptian command. Israeli forces drove through the gap and crossed the canal. The IDF hoped to achieve two goals. The first and most immediate goal was to create a SAM-free zone over which Israeli aircraft could maneuver free from the threat of missile attack. The second goal was to cut off Egyptian troops east of the canal from their bases west of the canal. After nearly a week of fighting, the Israelis accomplished almost all of their objectives. Nonetheless, Soviet and U.S. pressure led to a cease-fire before the Israelis could completely cut off the two Egyptian divisions in the east from their bases.

Neither the Soviets nor the Americans wanted to see the Egyptians completely defeated. They also assumed that the Egyptian achievement would allow progress in the political process, just as Sadat had wanted. As a result, the war ended with Israeli and Egyptian forces entangled, the latter on the eastern side of the canal and the former on Egyptian soil.

Syrian president Hafez al-Assad's chief motivation in joining Sadat in the war against Israel was to recapture the Golan Heights. Al-Assad had no diplomatic goals and no intention of using the war as leverage for a settlement with Israel. The fighting in the north with Syria ended with the IDF positioned only about 25 miles from Damascus, while no Syrian forces remained within Israeli-held territory. It was only in 1974, after a disengagement agreement, that Israeli forces withdrew from Syrian territory beyond the Purple Line.

The 1973 war in effect ended in 1977 when Sadat visited Israel and the consequent 1979 Israeli-Egyptian peace treaty was signed. Turmoil continued, however, chiefly from the unresolved Palestinian problem, which was at the root of the Arab-Israeli conflict. Militant Palestinians refused to recognize the existence of the State of Israel, while Israel refused to treat with the Palestinian leadership. Terrorist attacks against Israel continued, and with a sharp increase in such attacks against the northern settlements from Lebanon, the Israeli government ordered IDF invasions of southern Lebanon in 1978 and 1982. The first invasion of 1978 was extremely costly in terms of civilian loss of life for the Lebanese, who were unable to mount an armed response to the Israelis. The Israelis also began to involve themselves in the ongoing civil war in Lebanon in order to further their own objectives.

Following increasing Palestinian rocket attacks from southern Lebanon, the Israelis began a large-scale invasion there on June 6, 1982. The stated goals of the operation were halting rocket attacks from that area against northern Israel and eliminating the Palestinian fighters there. Ultimately, Israel committed some 76,000 men and a considerable numbers of tanks, artillery, and aircraft to the operation. Minister of Defense Ariel Sharon and Prime Minister Menachem Begin had more ambitious goals, however. They hoped to also destroy the PLO and other Palestinian resistance in Lebanon altogether and to dismantle its political power. They also sought to force Syria from Lebanon and to influence Lebanese politics.

Begin and Sharon informed the cabinet that their goal was merely to eradicate PLO bases in southern Lebanon and push back PLO and Syrian forces some 25 miles, beyond rocket range of Galilee. Once the operation began, however, Sharon changed the original plan by expanding the mission to incorporate Beirut. Within days, the IDF advanced to the outskirts of Beirut. The PLO merely withdrew ahead of the advancing IDF on West Beirut. Sharon now mounted a broader operation that would force the PLO from Beirut, and for some 10 weeks Israeli artillery shelled West

Beirut, killing both PLO members and scores of civilians. Fighting also occurred with Syrian forces in the Bekáa Valley area, but most of this combat was in the air. Not until June 2000 did Israel withdraw all its forces from southern Lebanon.

Israel achieved none of its goals in the invasion of Lebanon except for the eviction of the PLO from Beirut to Tunis and the deaths of many Palestinians and Lebanese. The Lebanese political scene was more turbulent than ever, and the PLO was certainly not eliminated. The Lebanese saw Israel as an implacable enemy, and an even more radical Islamic resistance took up hostilities against Israeli occupying troops and their Lebanese allies. That resistance eventually grew into Hezbollah, backed by Syria and Iran.

In December 1987 Palestinians began a protest movement, now known as the First Intifada, against Israeli rule in an effort to establish a Palestinian homeland through a series of demonstrations, improvised attacks, and riots. This intifada produced widespread destruction and human suffering, yet it also helped create a Palestinian national consciousness and made statehood a clear objective. It also cast much of Israeli policy in a negative light, especially with the deaths of Palestinian children, and thus helped rekindle international efforts to resolve the Arab-Israeli conflict. It also helped return the PLO from its Tunisian exile. Finally, it cost the Israeli economy hundreds of millions of dollars. The First Intifada ended in September 1993 with the signing of the historic Oslo Accords and the creation of the Palestinian Authority (PA).

Following torturous negotiations, the Israelis and Palestinians reached limited agreement at Oslo in September 1993 in the so-called Declaration of Principles. This eventually led to the establishment of the PA and limited Palestinian self-rule in the West Bank and the Gaza Strip. Nonetheless, the agreement was not fully implemented, and mutual Palestinian-Israeli violence continued, placing serious obstacles in the path of a general Arab-Israeli peace settlement.

With the advent of rightist Likud Party governments in Israel in the late 1990s, the Israeli-Palestinian peace process was essentially put on hold. Many politicians in Likud—but especially Prime Minister Benjamin Netanyahu—rejected the so-called land-for-peace formula. In the summer of 2000, U.S. president Bill Clinton hosted talks at Camp David between Israeli prime minister Ehud Barak and PLO chairman Yasser Arafat in an attempt to jump-start the moribund peace process. After 14 days of intense negotiations, the summit ended in an impasse. The failure of the talks disheartened Clinton in the waning days of his presidency and led to bitter recriminations on both sides that the other had not negotiated in good faith.

Not surprisingly, the Palestinians reacted with great negativity to the failure of the Camp David talks. Their frustration was heightened by Arafat's false contention that Israel—and not the Palestinian side—had sabotaged the peace process. A new dimension to Palestinian outrage was added when Likud Party chairman Ariel Sharon visited the Temple Mount (Haram al-Sharif) on September 28, 2000. His presence there ignited Palestinian anger that began as a stone-throwing demonstration. Before long, a full-blown Palestinian uprising, known as the Second (al-Aqsa) Intifada, was under way. The uprising resulted in the deaths of many Israelis and Palestinians.

In recent years, momentous changes within the PLO and the PA have wrought more uncertainty for both the Palestinians and the Israelis. Arafat's death in November 2004 resulted in a sea change within the Palestinian leadership. Mahmoud Abbas was chosen to succeed Arafat. Like Arafat, Abbas was a member of Fatah. In January 2005 Abbas was elected president of the PA. In the meantime, terror attacks against Israelis and Israeli interests continued, and Abbas seemed powerless to stop the violence. Just a year after he ascended to the presidency, he suffered a stinging reversal when the Islamist party and organization Hamas won a majority of seats in the January 2006 Palestinian legislative elections. This led to the appointment of a Hamas prime minister. Most of the West promptly shunned the Hamas-led government and cut off all funding to the Palestinians. As violence continued to occur and the lack of foreign aid hobbled the PA, Abbas threatened to call for early elections if Hamas would not submit to a coalition-led government. It was unclear, however, if he had that authority.

With increasing violence that included the kidnapping of an Israeli soldier in Gaza and a cross-border raid mounted by Hezbollah from Lebanon in July 2006 that killed three IDF soldiers and captured two others, the cabinet of Israeli prime minister Ehud Olmert again attacked southern Lebanon as well as Gaza. The fighting along the Israel-Lebanese border raged for 32 days between mid-July and mid-August. The incursion was largely limited to artillery and to air strikes that nonetheless included sections of Beirut and key bridges and lines of communication. Finally, some IDF ground troops were also sent in. Hezbollah responded by launching thousands of rockets into Israel. A great deal of Lebanese infrastructure that had been rebuilt since 1982 was destroyed in the countering Israeli strikes, and Israelis' hopes that it might influence Lebanese politics again proved illusory. Indeed, Hezbollah, whose ability to launch rockets into northern Israel appeared undiminished despite the strikes, appeared to have strengthened its position in Lebanese politics and also to have gained prestige in the Arab world for seemingly fighting toe-to-toe with the IDF.

In early 2007, there were renewed calls for a concerted effort to jump-start the peace process. There were, however, no indications that this would be any more successful than past attempts.

DAVID TAL AND SPENCER C. TUCKER

See also

Abdullah I, King of Jordan; Arab-Jewish Communal War; Arab League; Arafat, Yasser; Assad, Hafez al-; Begin, Menachem; Ben-Gurion, David; Egypt; Egypt, Armed Forces; Haganah; Hussein, King of Jordan; Iraq; Iraq, Armed Forces; Israel; Israel Defense Forces; Israeli War of Independence, Overview; Jordan; Jordan, Armed Forces; Lebanon; Lebanon, Armed Forces; Lebanon, Israeli Invasion of; Lebanon, Israeli Operations against; Nasser, Gamal Abdel; Ottoman Empire; Palestine, British Mandate for; Palestine, Pre-1918 History of; Rabin, Yitzhak; Rogers, William Pierce; Sadat, Anwar; Sharon, Ariel; Six-Day War; Suez Crisis; Syria; Syria, Armed Forces; U Thant; White Paper (1939); World War I, Impact of; World War II, Impact of; Yom Kippur War

References

Barker, A. J. *Arab-Israeli Wars.* New York: Hippocrene, 1980.

Bell, J. Bowyer. *The Long War: Israel and the Arabs since 1946.* Englewood Cliffs, NJ: Prentice Hall, 1969.

Hammel, Eric. *Six Days in June: How Israel Won the 1967 Arab-Israeli War.* New York: Scribner, 1992.

Herzog, Chaim. *The Arab-Israeli Wars: War and Peace in the Middle East from the War of Independence to Lebanon.* Westminster, MD: Random House, 1984.

———. *The War of Atonement: October, 1973.* Boston: Little, Brown, 1975.

Oren, Michael B. *Six Days of War: June 1967 and the Making of the Modern Middle East.* Novato, CA: Presidio, 2003.

Taylor, Alan R. *The Superpowers and the Middle East.* Syracuse, NY: Syracuse University Press, 1991.

THE ENCYCLOPEDIA
OF THE
ARAB-ISRAELI
CONFLICT

A

Aaronsohn, Aaron
Born: 1876
Died: May 15, 1919

Jewish agronomist and Zionist leader. Born in Bacau, Romania, in 1876, Aaronsohn immigrated with his parents to Turkish-controlled Palestine in 1882. His father was one of the founders of the Jewish agricultural settlement of Zikhron Ya'akov in northern Palestine and there established a successful farm. Following several years of study under agricultural experts sent by Baron de Rothschild to Palestine, Aaronsohn was invited by Rothschild to come to France and study at the agricultural college of Grignon. Aaronsohn spent two years there before returning to Palestine in 1895 to begin work as an agronomist at the newly established settlement of Metullah. Within a year, however, he clashed with Rothschild's administrators and was dismissed from his post.

Aaronsohn next found employment as the manager of a large Turkish farm in Anatolia. He returned to Palestine just before the end of the century and, with two other individuals, established a firm to identify land in Palestine for possible future Jewish settlement. Aaronsohn was now an expert in Palestinian geology and the leading authority on the region's flora. Encouraged by German botanists, in 1906 in Upper Galilee Aaronsohn discovered natural wild wheat, the predecessor of cultivated wheat. This discovery brought recognition among botanists worldwide.

In 1909 on the invitation of the U.S. Department of Agriculture, Aaronsohn traveled to the United States, where he worked on the development of wheat, especially in the western states, and was offered, but refused, a position with the University of California. With the assistance of influential Jewish philanthropists led by Julius Rosenwald, Aaronsohn secured funds to establish an agricultural experimental station, located at Athlit near Haifa. On his return to Palestine, he persuaded his younger brother Alexander to go to the United States and carry on his work there with the Department of Agriculture.

In 1915 Aaronsohn, his sister Sarah, and their friend Avshalom Feinberg founded Nili, a spy ring working for the British against the Turks. The term "Nili" was an acronym for words spoken by the prophet Samuel in anger at Saul for not having completely destroyed Amalek: *Netzach Yisrael lo yishaker* ("The Strength of Israel will not lie").

Feinberg died during a mission in the Negev in 1916. Aaronsohn relocated to Cairo that same year to assist the British in their plans to invade Palestine. Among others, he briefed British lieutenant general Sir Edmund Allenby, apprising him of the attitudes of the Palestinian population. Following 10 months there, Aaronsohn traveled to London, where he worked closely with British scientist and Zionist leader Chaim Weizmann to make creation of a Jewish homeland in Palestine part of British war aims. This found culmination in the 1917 Balfour Declaration. Aaronsohn urged his sister, who had gone to Cairo early in 1917, to remain there, but she returned to Palestine to continue spying activities and there was arrested and tortured by the Turkish authorities. She committed suicide while under arrest in October 1917.

Aaronsohn worked with the Zionist Commission in Palestine in 1918 and the next year was part of the Zionist delegation to the Paris Peace Conference, where he specialized in Palestinian boundary issues. He died on May 15, 1919, when the plane in which he was a passenger crashed into the English Channel. Much of Aaronsohn's research into Palestinian flora was published after his death. The Institute for Agriculture of Hebrew University of Jerusalem is named in his honor.

SPENCER C. TUCKER

See also

Aaronsohn, Sarah; Allenby, Sir Edmund Henry Hynman, 1st Viscount; Balfour Declaration; Weizmann, Chaim

References

Herzog, Chaim. *Heroes of Israel: Profiles of Jewish Courage*. New York: Little, Brown, 1989.

Sanders, Ronald. *The High Walls of Jerusalem: A History of the Balfour Declaration and the Birth of the British Mandate for Palestine*. New York: Holt, Rinehart and Winston, 1983.

Aaronsohn, Sarah
Born: 1890
Died: October 9, 1917

Jewish heroine. Born the daughter of a well-to-do farmer in Zichron Yaakov, in northern Turkish-controlled Palestine, in 1890, Sarah Aaronsohn lived briefly in Istanbul until 1915, when she returned to Palestine to end what was for her an unhappy marriage. Reportedly she decided to help the British against the Turks during World War I upon witnessing acts of genocide committed by the Turks against Armenians in Anatolia. She, her brother Aaron (later a noted agronomist and Jewish political leader), and their friend Avshalom Feinberg founded Nili, a spy ring operating against the Turks. Feinberg died during a mission in the Negev in 1916. The term "Nili" was an acronym for words spoken by the prophet Samuel in anger at Saul for not having completely destroyed Amalek: *Netzach Yisrael lo yishaker* ("The Strength of Israel will not lie").

Aaronsohn traveled throughout the Ottoman Empire gathering information that might be useful to the British. She was the chief courier, delivering the collected information to a British agent who would come ashore from a ship off the coast near their farm. In 1917 she traveled with her brother Aaron to British-controlled Egypt. Aaron went on from there to London and, fearing action by the Ottoman authorities against Nili, urged Sarah to remain in Cairo. She refused and returned to Zichron Yaakov in June, there to continue her spying activities. In September 1917 Turkish authorities caught a carrier pigeon and decrypted the Nili message it was carrying to the British. In early October 1917, the Turks traced the operation to the Aaronsohn farm at Zichron Yaachov and arrested and tortured Aaronsohn and her father. She was tortured for several days, during which time she reportedly did not reveal any secrets. The Turks were preparing to take her to Nazareth for further questioning when she convinced them to let her return home to change out of her bloody dress. There she located a concealed pistol and shot and mortally wounded herself with it on October 5. She died on October 9, 1917. In a last letter, Aaronsohn expressed the hope that a Jewish state would soon be created in Palestine. In 1991 Aaronsohn was honored with an Israeli postage stamp.

SPENCER C. TUCKER

See also

Aaronsohn, Aaron

References

Herzog, Chaim. *Heroes of Israel: Profiles of Jewish Courage*. New York: Little, Brown, 1989.

Sanders, Ronald. *The High Walls of Jerusalem: A History of the Balfour Declaration and the Birth of the British Mandate for Palestine*. New York: Holt, Rinehart and Winston, 1983.

Slater, Elinor, and Robert Slater. *Great Jewish Women*. Middle Village, NY: Jonathon David, 1996.

Abbas, Abu
Born: December 10, 1948
Died: March 8, 2004

Leader of the Palestine Liberation Front (PLF). Abu Abbas, the nom de guerre of Muhammad Zaidan, was born in Safed, Palestine, on December 10, 1948, and moved with his family to Syria that same year. In 1968 he joined the Popular Front for the Liberation of Palestine–General Command (PFLP-GC) led by Ahmad Jibril. Abbas disagreed with Jibril over the PFLP-GC's strong support for Syria and its failure to criticize Syrian support of the Phalange against the Palestine Liberation Organization (PLO) in Lebanon. In April 1977, Abbas and Talat Yaqub left the PFLP-GC to form the PLF.

During the 1980s, Abbas advocated armed struggle against Israel, chiefly in the form of terrorism mounted from southern Lebanon. He was wounded in fighting during the 1982 Israeli invasion of Lebanon. In 1983 when the PLF split into three factions, he led the largest pro-Iraqi group. In 1984 he became a member of the PLO's Executive Committee.

On October 7, 1985, Abbas masterminded the PLF's most dramatic terrorist action, the hijacking of the Italian cruise ship *Achille Lauro* that resulted in the death of American Jew Leon Klinghoffer. Although the Egyptian aircraft carrying Abbas and the other three hijackers to asylum in Tunisia was diverted by U.S. aircraft to a North Atlantic Treaty Organization (NATO) air base in Sicily, the Italian government let the passengers depart, and Abbas escaped among them. There was, however, much criticism of Abbas for the PLF attempted terrorist attack on Nizamim Beach near Tel Aviv on May 30, 1990, that was designed to torpedo the possibility of PLO-Israeli peace talks. Nonetheless, the PLF had regularly received funding from PLO chairman Yasser Arafat. Indeed, in January 1996 the PLO agreed to provide an undisclosed sum to finance the Leon and Marilyn Klinghoffer Memorial Foundation of the U.S. Anti-Defamation League, in return for which Klinghoffer's daughters dropped a lawsuit brought against the PLO. In 1989, Abbas supported the PLO's acceptance of United Nations (UN) Security Council Resolution 242.

Following the 1993 Oslo Accords, Abbas returned to the Gaza Strip. He then moved to Iraq. There was a U.S. warrant for his arrest, and in 2003 during the U.S.-led invasion of Iraq, he was taken by U.S. forces. He died in Iraq, reportedly of natural causes, on March 8, 2004, while in U.S. custody.

SPENCER C. TUCKER

See also

Achille Lauro Hijacking; Arafat, Yasser; Palestine Liberation Organization; Terrorism; United Nations Security Council Resolution 242

References

Alexander, Yonah. *Palestinian Secular Terrorism.* Ardsley, NY: Transnational Publishers, 2003.

Bohn, Michael K. *The Achille Lauro Hijacking: Lessons in the Politics and Prejudice of Terrorism.* Dulles, VA: Potomac Books, 2004.

Cassese, Antonio. *Terrorism, Politics and Law: The Achille Lauro Affair.* Princeton, NJ: Princeton University Press, 1989.

Nassar, Jamal R. *The Palestine Liberation Organization: From Armed Struggle to the Declaration of Independence.* New York: Praeger, 1991.

Abbas, Mahmoud
Born: March 26, 1935

First prime minister of the Palestinian Authority (PA) during March–October 2003 and president of the PA since January 2005. Mahmoud Abbas (Abu Mazen) was born on March 26, 1935, in Safed, British Mandatory Palestine. During the Israeli War of Independence (1948–1949), his family fled Palestine and settled in Syria. Abbas graduated from the University of Damascus and studied law in Egypt and Syria before earning a PhD in history in 1982 from the Oriental College, more often known as the People's Friendship University in Moscow.

Abbas was the civil service director of personnel for Qatar when he began his involvement in Palestinian politics in the mid-1950s. He was one of the founders of Fatah (1957) and was part of the leadership of Yasser Arafat's Palestine Liberation Organization (PLO) in exile in Jordan, Lebanon, and Tunisia during the 1960s through the 1980s. During this time, Abbas cultivated relationships with left-wing and pacifist Jewish groups. He joined the Palestinian National Council (PNC) in 1968. According to Mumamad Daod Awda, Abbas was the funding source for Black September's attack on Israeli athletes at the 1972 Summer Olympics in Munich, Germany. Abbas asserts that he was unaware of the intended use of the funds.

Abbas assumed the leadership of the PLO's Department for National and International Relations in 1980. He began his leadership of the PLO's Negotiations Affairs Department that same year. In May 1988 he assumed chairmanship of the division treating the occupied territories. When PLO support for Iraq's 1990 invasion of Kuwait harmed relationships with Arab states that joined the U.S.-led coalition in the 1991 Persian Gulf War, it was Abbas who repaired the damage. He was also the major architect of the 1993 Oslo Accords between the PLO and Israel. In 1996 he was elected

Mahmoud Abbas, chairman of the Executive Committee of the Palestine Liberation Organization (PLO) since November 2004 and president of the Palestinian Authority (PA) since January 2005. (European Community)

secretary-general of the PLO Executive Committee, headed the first session of the Israeli-Palestinian final status negotiations, led the Central Election Commission for the Palestinian Legislative Council (PLC), and then was elected to the PLC.

On March 19, 2003, Arafat appointed the more moderately and pragmatically perceived Abbas as the first prime minister of the PA. Arafat's unwillingness to share significant power, persistent conflicts with militant Palestinian groups such as Hamas and Islamic Jihad, Israeli targeted assassinations of Palestinian militants, and a perceived lack of support from the United States led Abbas to resign as prime minister on September 4, 2003, effective October 7, 2003.

Following Arafat's death, Abbas became chairman of the PLO on November 11, 2004. His authority and attempts to reengage the Road Map for Peace were challenged by most of the militant Palestinian groups, however. On January 15, 2005, he became president of the PA. A May 2005 pledge of $50 million and continued support of a free Palestinian state from the United States coupled with the Israeli withdrawal from Gaza on August 23, 2005, led Abbas to set PLC elections for January 25, 2006. However, when Hamas fared well in local elections in December 2005, Abbas sought to postpone the PLC elections. However, he proceeded with the scheduled January elections, in which Hamas won a majority of the seats in the PA Parliament and reduced Abbas's Fatah party to minority status.

Although Abbas remains as the PA president, Hamas controls the parliament, governmental services, and the security forces. Israel has made it clear that Abbas and the PA are expected to fulfill all agreements made prior to the 2006 elections, including the agreement to disarm Palestinian militants. The United States and many European countries withdrew their financial support of the PA in view of Hamas's refusal to disavow its commitment to the destruction of Israel. This financial crisis and Hamas's militancy continue to challenge Abbas's leadership and presidency.

On March 17, 2007, Abbas brokered a Palestinian unity government that included members of both Hamas and Fatah in which Hamas leader Ismail Haniyeh became prime minister. Yet beginning in May, violence between Hamas and Fatah escalated in the Gaza Strip. Following the Hamas takeover of Gaza on June 14, Abbas dissolved the Hamas-led unity government and declared a state of emergency. On June 18, having been assured of European Union support, he dissolved the National Security Council and swore in an emergency Palestinian government. That same day, the United States ended its 15-month embargo on the PA and resumed aid in an effort to strengthen Abbas's government, which was now limited to the West Bank. On June 19 Abbas cut off all ties and dialogue with Hamas, pending the return of Gaza. In a further move to strengthen the perceived moderate Abbas, on July 1 Israel restored financial ties to the PA.

RICHARD EDWARDS

See also

Al-Aqsa Martyrs Brigades; Arafat, Yasser; Black September; Fatah; Hamas; Intifada, Second; Islamic Jihad, Palestinian; Palestine Liberation Organization; Palestinian Authority

References

Abbas, Mahmoud. *Through Secret Channels: The Road to Oslo; Senior PLO Leader Abu Mazen's Revealing Story of the Negotiations with Israel.* Reading, UK: Garnet, 1997.

Daoud, Abu. *Memoirs of a Palestinian Terrorist.* New York: Arcade Publishing, 2002.

Gelvin, James L. *The Israel-Palestine Conflict: One Hundred Years of War.* New York: Cambridge University Press, 2005.

Makovsky, David. *Making Peace with the PLO: The Rabin Government's Road to the Oslo Accord.* Boulder, CO: Westview, 1996.

Pappe, Ilan. *A History of Modern Palestine: One Land, Two Peoples.* Cambridge: Cambridge University Press, 2003.

Rubin, Barry. *Revolution until Victory? The Politics and History of the PLO.* Reprint ed. Cambridge: Harvard University Press, 2003.

Abd al-Hadi, Awni

Born: 1889
Died: March 15, 1970

Palestinian lawyer and early Arab nationalist. Born in Nablus in 1889, Awni Abd al-Hadi was educated in Beirut and Istanbul before going to Paris to study law at the University of Paris. In 1911 he was one of the founders of the nationalist political society al-Fatat (Youth), and in 1913 he helped organize the Arab Nationalist Congress held in Paris. Following World War I, he served as the private secretary to King Faisal I of Iraq at the Paris Peace Conference in 1919. Later Abd al-Hadi was a paid adviser to Emir Abdullah of Transjordan.

Returning to Palestine in 1924, Abd al-Hadi became one of the principal spokesmen for the Palestinian Arab nationalist movement. He served as the elected representative to a number of congresses of the Arab Executive Committee. In 1930 he was a member of the Palestinian delegation that went to London to discuss British policy in Palestine. He then acted as a lawyer for the Supreme Muslim Council.

Abd al-Hadi was one of the founders of the Palestinian Istiqlal (Independence) Party, the first regularly constituted Palestinian political party, established on August 2, 1932. He was its general secretary and first president. In 1936 he represented the party on the Arab Higher Committee, for which he served as general secretary. In that capacity he worked to organize opposition to British policy and to restrict Jewish immigration to Palestine.

A moderate who was prepared to negotiate with the Jewish community in Palestine, Abd al-Hadi met with Jewish leader (later first prime minister of Israel) David Ben-Gurion in 1934. A supporter of the Arab Revolt of 1936–1939, Abd al-Hadi was arrested and then banned from Palestine when the British mandatory authorities decided to deport the Arab Higher Committee members in 1937. He was a member of the Palestinian delegation to the London Conference on Palestine in February 1939. Returning to Palestine in 1941, he was in 1948 minister for social affairs in the All-Palestine government established by Egypt in Gaza. During 1951–1955 Abd al-Hadi was Jordanian ambassador to Cairo, and in 1956 he was Jordan's minister of foreign affairs and justice. In 1958 he served on the Federal Council of the Jordan-Iraq Arab Federation. Abd al-Hadi died in Cairo on March 15, 1970.

SPENCER C. TUCKER

See also

Abdullah I, King of Jordan; Arab Nationalism; London Round Table Conference

References

Brinner, William M. *Like All the Nations: The Life and Legacy of Judah L. Magnes.* New York: SUNY Press, 1987.

Eisenberg, Laura Zittrain, and Neil Caplan. *Negotiating Arab-Israeli Peace: Patterns, Problems, Possibilities.* Bloomington: Indiana University Press, 1998.

Abdel-Rahman, Omar
Born: May 3, 1938

Egyptian religious leader. Omar Abdel-Rahman was born in Fayyum, Egypt, on May 3, 1938. He suffered from childhood diabetes, which resulted in blindness when he was 10 months old. By age 11 he had memorized the Koran and devoted himself to preaching the Muslim faith. He graduated in Koranic studies from Al-Azhar University in Cairo. As a professor at the Theological College in Asyut, he gained a large militant following in Cairo's southern slums and villages after speaking out against the government's violations of traditional Islamic sharia laws. Abdel-Rahman became the spiritual leader of the loosely knit, highly militant Al-Gama'a al-Islamiyya (Islamic Group) umbrella organization and the Egyptian Islamic Jihad. Both organizations opposed the Egyptian government's policies and preached militant jihad. Islamic Jihad was responsible for the 1981 assassination of Egyptian president Anwar Sadat.

In 1981, Abdel-Rahman and 23 other Islamic militants were arrested in connection with Sadat's assassination. Abdel-Rahman spent three years in Egyptian jails, where he was tortured. Although acquitted of conspiracy in the assassination of Sadat, Abdel-Rahman was expelled from Egypt and went to Afghanistan, where he reportedly made contact with Al Qaeda leader Osama bin Laden. Abdel-Rahman then traveled widely recruiting mujahideen for the Afghan War. Returning to Egypt, he was again arrested in 1989 for inciting antigovernment clashes in Fayyum but was again acquitted.

Abdel-Rahman fled Egypt after being linked to further terrorist attacks on Coptic Christians in northern Egypt and illegally entered the United States in 1990 on a tourist visa obtained in Sudan. He gained permanent U.S. residency as a religious worker in 1991, an action that the U.S. Immigration and Naturalization Service (INS) now says was erroneous. However, Abdel-Rahman's marriage to an American Muslim convert enabled him to avoid deportation despite Egypt's calls for his extradition and his status as a prominent figure on the official U.S. terrorist list.

Abdel-Rahman was discovered in January 1993 to be actively preaching militant Islamic fundamentalist sermons in New York's

Sheikh Omar Abdel-Rahman, Egyptian religious leader and alleged terrorist, photographed on February 20, 1993, in Jersey City, New Jersey. (Reuters/Corbis)

Muslim mosques to thousands of Egyptian, Yemeni, Sudanese, and other Muslim immigrants. The sheikh's messages, secretly recorded on tape cassettes and funneled to his followers in the Egyptian underground, advocated "the eradication of all those who stand in the way of Islam" because "the laws of God have been usurped by Crusaders' laws. The hand of a thief is not cut off, the drinker of liquor is not whipped, the adulterer is not stoned. Islamic holy law should be followed to the letter."

Abdel-Rahman was arrested in the United States in July 1993 for his suspected involvement in the World Trade Center bombing, but insufficient evidence forced the INS to hold him on lesser charges of illegal immigration and polygamy. He was held in a U.S. federal prison while he appealed the deportation order against him and was awarded limited preferential treatment because of his ill health and blindness.

On October 1, 1995, in the largest terrorism trial up to that point in U.S. history, Abdel-Rahman was convicted of 48 of 50 charges, including seditious conspiracy for leading a four-year terrorist campaign of bombings and assassinations intended to destroy the United Nations (UN) building and other landmarks in the New York area. He was also convicted of conspiring to assassinate Egyptian president Hosni Mubarak and of solicitation to attack U.S. military installations. Abdel-Rahman was sentenced to life imprisonment on January 17, 1996. He is currently serving his life sentence at the

Federal Administrative Maximum Penitentiary hospital in Florence, Colorado. Abdel-Rahman is also believed to have ordered the November 1990 assassination in New York of militant Zionist leader Rabbi Meir Kahane.

SPENCER C. TUCKER

See also
Egypt; Mubarak, Hosni; Sadat, Anwar

References
Fried, Joseph P. "Sheik Sentenced to Life in Prison in Bombing Plot." *New York Times,* January 18, 1996.
Lance, P. *1000 Years of Revenge: International Terrorism and the FBI.* New York: HarperCollins, 2003.
Macfarquhar, Neil. "In Jail or Out, Sheik Preaches Views of Islam." *New York Times,* October 2, 1995.

Abdulhamid II, Sultan
Born: September 21, 1842
Died: February 10, 1918

Ottoman sultan. The son of Sultan Abdulmecid, Abdulhamid was born on September 21, 1842. He succeeded to the throne on the deposition of his brother Murad on August 31, 1876, and ruled until April 27, 1909. Abdulhamid II enjoyed near absolutist rule. He attempted to carry out reforms, but these latter proved impossible. His reign came to be marked by war, internal violence, upheaval, and pressure on the empire from outside powers. A revolt occurred in Bosnia and Herzegovina in 1875, and war with Serbia and Montenegro followed, leading to Russian intervention and the Russo-Turkish War of 1877–1878. The latter was a disaster for the empire, although the harsh effects of the Treaty of San Stefano were somewhat mitigated by the 1878 Congress of Berlin. In gratitude for London's assistance at that conference, Turkey ceded Cyprus to Britain in 1878. In 1881 the French seized Tunis in North Africa, and in 1882 British forces occupied Egypt. Despite the Ottoman wartime victory over Greece in 1897, the Great Powers insisted that Turkey yield Crete.

Abdulhamid pursued a surprisingly liberal policy toward the Jews. In 1876 he allowed Jews of the empire full equality before the law. Jews were elected to the Ottoman Parliament, and Abdulhamid named two Jews as senators. Another Jew was made an admiral in the Turkish Navy. In Palestine, Abdulhamid introduced administrative reforms that improved the situation for the people there, and during his reign the Hejaz Railroad was constructed to Medina and Mecca.

Abdulhamid strongly opposed Zionist aspirations for a state in Palestine, however. This was at least in part because he feared that resulting increased immigration from the European states, especially from Turkey's historic enemy Russia, would lead to expanded European influence in the empire. Following expanded Jewish emigration from Russia after the 1881 pogroms, in 1882 Abdulhamid prohibited Jewish immigration to Palestine. He rescinded the order in 1883 but reinstated it in 1891. Nonetheless, the regulations against

Sultan Abdulhamid II, Ottoman ruler during 1876–1909. (Edwin Pears, *Life of Abdul Hamid,* New York: Henry Holt, 1917)

---

immigration were not stringently enforced, and Jews were still able to settle in Palestine.

In June 1896 Abdulhamid awarded Zionist leader Theodor Herzl the Commander's Cross of the Majidiyya Order. In May 1891 the sultan received Herzl in private audience, although this brought no tangible advantages to Zionism. Abdulhamid rejected Herzl's effort to secure a charter that would have established an autonomous Jewish settlement in Palestine in return for cash payments to help reduce the Turkish national debt. Abdulhamid suggested instead that Jewish immigrants settle in various parts of the Ottoman Empire.

Dissatisfaction with the continued deterioration of the Ottoman domestic situation coupled with crumbling frontiers brought the rise of the Young Turk movement and the Revolution of 1908. Suspected of sympathies with a counterrevolutionary coup attempt of April 23, 1909, Abdulhamid was deposed on April 27. Banished to Salonica, he was permitted to return to Istanbul in 1912 and passed his last years studying and working at his hobby of carpentry. Abdulhamid died in Istanbul on February 10, 1918.

SPENCER C. TUCKER

See also
Ottoman Empire; Palestine, Pre-1918 History of; World War I, Impact of; Zionism

References
Fromkin, David. *A Peace to End All Peace: The Fall of the Ottoman Empire and the Creation of the Modern Middle East.* New York: Avon, 1989.

Kent, Marian, ed. *The Great Powers and the End of the Ottoman Empire.* London: Routledge, 1996.

Palmer, Alan. *The Decline and Fall of the Ottoman Empire.* London: John Murray, 1992.

Abdullah, King of Saudi Arabia
Born: August 1, 1924

Saudi crown prince (1982–2005), acting ruler of Saudi Arabia (1995–2005), and king of Saudi Arabia (2005–present). Abdullah ibn Abd al-Aziz al-Saud was born in Riyadh, Saudi Arabia, in 1924. He was educated privately, chiefly at the Princes' School in the Royal Court. He became acquainted with governmental and administrative work at a young age and became mayor of Mecca in 1950.

In 1963 Abdullah assumed the post of deputy defense minister and commander of the National Guard. In 1975 he began serving as second deputy prime minister. He became the crown prince as well as first deputy prime minister in 1982 when Fahd ibn Abdul Aziz al-Saud became king.

Abdullah's power increased dramatically after Fahd was incapacitated by a stroke in 1995. Abdullah began his formal rule when he became king on August 1, 2005. A devout Muslim, he is known as a conservative and for leading a modest lifestyle. The challenges confronting him have not been easy ones, given both rising demands for reform and the activities of radical Islamic groups.

Abdullah sought to walk a diplomatic tightrope following the September 11, 2001, terrorist attacks on the United States. Although he strongly condemned the attacks, critics in the West pointed out that more of the September 11 terrorists were Saudis than any other nationality and that Saudi Arabia was a major funding source for terrorist networks and also supplies financial support for the madrassas, a number of which are extremist and are breeding grounds for Islamic fundamentalism, in many Islamic nations.

Abdullah was interested in making peace with Israel and devised a plan known as the Arab Peace Initiative in March 2002. It called for creation of a Palestinian state in the West Bank and Gaza with its capital in East Jerusalem. A peace treaty would then be signed with Israel, which would then receive diplomatic recognition from the Arab states. Both the hard-line Arab states and Israel criticized the plan. In January 2004, Abdullah produced an addendum to his plan that addressed the problem of Palestinian refugees.

Although probably less pro-Western than his predecessor, Abdullah has not fundamentally changed the foreign policy of Saudi Arabia, and he continues to maintain cordial relations with the United States in spite of occasional strains. Having visited the United States many times before becoming ruler, Abdullah enjoyed a solid personal relationship with President George W. Bush.

Since the September 11 attacks, the Saudi government has tracked down some terrorist cells operating inside Saudi Arabia that are themselves a threat to the survival of the Saudi regime. It has also eliminated from within the kingdom many sources of terrorist funding. Saudi Arabia itself has been the target of attacks by Islamic militants. In May 2003, some 100 people were killed in one such attack.

During the Iraq War, Abdullah did not permit U.S. forces to use Saudi air bases for coalition combat operations, but he did permit the use of Saudi Arabia's extensive command and control facilities, and tanker aircraft from these bases provided critical in-flight refueling for coalition fighter aircraft flying north. Despite ups and downs, the Saudi-U.S. relationship has remained largely unchanged under Abdullah.

PATIT PABAN MISHRA

See also
Bush, George Walker; Saudi Arabia

References
Al-Rasheed, Madawi. *A History of Saudi Arabia.* New York: Cambridge University Press, 2002.

Lippman, Thomas W. *Inside the Mirage: America's Fragile Partnership with Saudi Arabia.* New York: Westview, 2005.

Ménoret, Pascal. *The Saudi Enigma: A History.* London: Zed, 2005.

Teitelbaum, Joshua. *The Rise and Fall of the Hashemite Kingdom of Hejaz.* New York: New York University Press, 2001.

Abdullah I, King of Jordan
Born: 1882
Died: July 20, 1951

Emir of Transjordan under the British Mandate during 1921–1946 and, following Transjordan's independence in 1946, king of Transjordan (Jordan after April 1949) from 1946 until his assassination in 1951. Abdullah ibn Hussein was a 40th-generation direct descendant of the Prophet Muhammad, founder of the Muslim community. Abdullah was born in Mecca (now Saudi Arabia) sometime in 1882 and was the second son of Hussein ibn Ali, the sharif of Mecca and Medina (guardian of the two holy cities) during 1908–1917. The Arab revolt against the Ottomans began in June 1916. Sharif Hussein was the Supreme Commander, while Abdullah led the Eastern Army with Sharif Shakir ibn Zayd. In 1916 Hussein, a Hashemite, proclaimed himself king of the Hejaz. His eldest son Ali became king in 1924 but was defeated in 1925 in a power struggle with Abd al-Aziz al-Saud, who founded Saudi Arabia.

During World War I, Abdullah helped lead the Arab Revolt, which involved fighting the Ottomans on several fronts and fighting the French in Syria. Because of promises made in the Lord McMahon–Sharif Hussein correspondence and the fact that Abdullah had been elected the king of Iraq by the Arab National Congress and his brother, Faisal, became the king of Syria in 1920, in 1921 Abdullah was offered the throne of Transjordan, a political division of the British Mandate for Palestine. The British government recognized Transjordan as a state in May 1923 and agreed to limit British control to military, financial, and foreign policy concerns. At the same time, the British placed Faisal on the throne of Iraq. In

Abdullah I, king of Jordan from 1946 until his assassination in 1951. (Library of Congress)

1928, Abdullah promulgated a constitution for Transjordan, making him one of the first Arab leaders to establish a constitutional monarchy.

During World War II, Abdullah strongly opposed the Axis powers. This outlook reflected his overall stance on foreign policy, which was generally pro-Western and prodemocratic. On March 22, 1946, the British granted Transjordan complete independence, and on May 25, 1946, the Transjordanian Parliament proclaimed Abdullah king of the Hashemite Kingdom of Transjordan.

During the Israeli War of Independence (1948–1949), Transjordan's Arab Legion, which had been trained by the British and led by Lieutenant General John Bagot Glubb, was the most effective Arab fighting force, defeating the Israelis at Bab al-Wad, at Latroun, and at East Jerusalem. In April 1949, Abdullah changed his country's name to the Hashemite Kingdom of Jordan. In 1950, the Jordanian Parliament formally annexed the West Bank. Abdullah's neighbors, particularly the Saudis, opposed his goal of uniting Jordan, Iraq, and Syria under the Hashemite dynasty. Some also looked askance at his pro-Western positions and generally moderate foreign and domestic policies, viewing them as akin to subservience to colonialist nations.

On Friday July 20, 1951, Abdullah paid a visit to the al-Aqsa Mosque in Jerusalem. There he was assassinated by Mustafa Shukri Ushu, a Palestinian, who shot the king three times. The king was accompanied by his young grandson and future Jordanian King,

Hussein ibn Talal, who was also shot and wounded. Hussein survived because the bullet had been deflected by a medal that was pinned on his chest at Abdullah's insistence earlier in the day. The assassin, who was immediately shot by security guards, was part of a conspiracy led by Colonel Abdullah Tall, former military governor of Jerusalem and a hero of the Israeli War of Independence (1948–1949), and Dr. Musa Abdullah al-Husseini. A Jordanian court sentenced six men to death for the king's murder. The death sentence was in absentia for Tall and another accomplice, who had managed to flee to Egypt immediately after the shooting.

Abdullah was briefly succeeded by his son Talal, who suffered from mental illness. Talal abdicated the throne on August 11, 1952, whereupon Hussein became king.

Michael R. Hall

See also

Al-Aqsa Mosque; Arab Legion; Hussein, King of Jordan; Israeli War of Independence, Israeli-Jordanian Front; Israeli War of Independence, Overview; Jordan

References

El Edross, Syed Ali. *The Hashemite Arab Army, 1908–1979.* Amman, Jordan: Central Publishing House, 1986.

Milton-Edwards, Beverly, and Peter Hinchcliffe. *Jordan: A Hashemite Legacy.* London: Routledge, 2001.

Paris, Timothy. *Britain, the Hashemites, and Arab Rule, 1920–1925: The Sherifian Solution.* London: Frank Cass, 2003.

Abdullah II, King of Jordan
Born: January 30, 1962

King of Jordan. Born in Amman, Jordan, on January 30, 1962, Abdullah ibn al-Hussein was the eldest son of King Hussein and Princess Muna al-Hussein. Abdullah and his 10 brothers and sisters are 43rd-generation direct descendants of the Prophet Muhammad. Abdullah attended the Islamic Educational College in Amman and St. Edmund's School in Surrey, England. His secondary education occurred at Eaglebook School and Deerfield Academy in the United States.

In 1980 Abdullah entered the Royal Military Academy, Sandhurst. Commissioned a second lieutenant in the British Army upon his graduation in 1981, he served in West Germany and in Britain. During 1982–1983 he completed a course in Middle Eastern affairs at Oxford University. Returning to Jordan, he served as a junior officer in the 40th Armored Brigade of the Jordanian Army. In 1985 he attended the Armored Officers Advanced Course at Fort Knox, Kentucky, returning to Jordan to take command as captain of a tank company in the 91st Armored Brigade. He also served with the Anti-Tank Wing of the Jordanian Air Force, where he earned his wings as a helicopter pilot and also became a qualified parachutist.

During 1987–1988 Abdullah earned a master's degree in the School of Foreign Service at Georgetown University in Washington, D.C. Resuming his military career, he commanded the Jordanian Special Forces in 1989 and then was a tank company commander,

Abdullah II, king of Jordan since February 1999, shown here on April 5, 2001, during a visit to the United States. (U.S. Department of Defense)

attended the British Staff College at Camberley, and was promoted to major in 1990. He next served as the Armored Corps representative in the Office of the Inspector General of the Jordanian Armed Forces.

In 1992 Abdullah took command of a battalion in the 2nd Armored Cavalry Regiment. The next year he was promoted to colonel and served with the 40th Brigade. In 1994, as a brigadier general, he reorganized the Special Forces and other elite Jordanian units into the Special Operations Command. Promoted to major general in 1998, he attended a course in defense resources management at the U.S. Naval Postgraduate School at Monterey, California.

On occasion during the 1990s, Abdullah had acted as regent on the absence of King Hussein from Jordan, but for the most part this duty was performed by Hussein's younger brother, Crown Prince El Hassan bin Talal, whom Hussein had designated in 1965 as his successor. Hussein was diagnosed with cancer in 1992 and underwent several periods of medical treatment in the United States. Upon his return to Jordan after a six-month medical absence in late 1998, Hussein publicly criticized Hassan's management of Jordanian affairs and accused him of abusing his power as regent and crown prince. On January 24, 1999, to the surprise of many, Hussein shifted the line of succession to Abdullah, naming him crown prince and heir to the throne. Abdullah became king following the death of his father two weeks later on February 7, 1999.

Since his accession to the throne, Abdullah has sought to continue his father's work in finding a solution to the Arab-Israeli conflict. Toward that end, he has met frequently with world leaders, including U.S. president George W. Bush. Abdullah has also committed himself to the continued development of democratic institutions and pluralism in Jordan as well as to improving the

Current and Former Monarchs of Selected Middle Eastern and North African States

Current Monarchies			
Country	Type of Monarchy	Current Ruler	Ruling Since
Bahrain	Constitutional	Hamad bin Isa al-Khalifa	1999
Jordan	Constitutional	Abdullah II	1999
Kuwait	Constitutional	Sabah Al-Ahmad Al-Jaber Al-Sabah	2006
Morocco	Constitutional	Muhammad VI	1999
Oman	Absolute	Qabus ibn Said	1970
Qatar	Absolute	Sheik Hamad ibn Khalifa al-Thani	1995
Saudi Arabia	Absolute	Abdullah ibn Abd al-Aziz al-Saud	2005
United Arab Emirates	Absolute	Khalifa bin Zayed Al Nahayan	2004
Former Monarchies			
Country	Monarchy Until	Last Monarch	
Egypt	1953	Fuad II	
Iran	1979	Mohammad Reza Shah Pahlavi	
Iraq	1958	Faisal II	
Libya	1969	Sayyid Hasan ar-Rida al-Mahdi as-Sanussi	
Tunisia	1957	Muhammad VIII al-Amin	
Yemen	1962	Muhammad al-Badr	

lot of its citizens through economic development, to improving education, and to protecting and furthering civil liberties. During Abdullah's reign, Jordan has been admitted to the World Trade Organization (WTO) and has ratified free trade agreements with a number of countries, including the United States.

SPENCER C. TUCKER

See also
El Hassan bin Talal, Prince; Hussein, King of Jordan; Jordan

References
Robbins, Philip. *A History of Jordan.* Cambridge: Cambridge University Press, 2004.
Wagner, Heather Lehr. *King Abdullah II.* New York: Chelsea House, 2005.

Abed Rabbo, Yasser
Born: 1945

Prominent Palestinian Arab politician. Born in Jaffa in 1945, Abu Bashar later took the nom de guerre of Yasser Abed Rabbo. He earned a master's degree in economics and political science from the American University in Cairo, Egypt. Later he became a close associate of Yasser Arafat. In 1969 Abed Rabbo and Nayef Hawat-

Palestinian Arab politician Yasser Abed Rabbo during a visit to the European Community headquarters in Brussels, February 2004. (European Community)

meh cofounded the Democratic Front for the Liberation of Palestine (DFLP), a leftist group in Arafat's Palestine Liberation Organization (PLO). Abed Rabbo became the deputy secretary-general in 1973 and headed its Information and Culture Department during 1973–1994. He also served as a member of the PLO Executive Committee.

Abed Rabbo was a member of the Palestinian-Jordanian negotiating teams to U.S.-brokered peace talks. In 1991 he left the DFLP and formed his own organization, the Al-Ittihad al-Dimuqrati al-Filastini (Palestine Democratic Union), commonly known as FIDA. It supported Arafat and negotiations with the Israelis and also rejected the Marxist platform of the DFLP. Abed Rabbo was an active participant in and his organization strongly supported both the Madrid and Oslo peace negotiations. On the establishment of the Palestinian Authority (PA) in 1994, Arafat named Abed Rabbo the information minister. Appointed head of the PA's negotiating team to the Final Status talks, Abed Rabbo resigned in 2000 when he learned of secret negotiations going on with the Israelis in Sweden of which he had not been informed. He also resigned from FIDA in 2002 following disagreements within that organization.

In recent years, Abed Rabbo has been a visible spokesman for the Palestinian cause, writing articles in the American press and touring the United States with the Israeli-Palestinian Peace Coalition, which includes former Israeli minister of justice and peace advocate Yossef "Yossi" Beilin. He also served as PA minister of culture and information. Although he has demanded an end to Israeli settlements and an Israeli withdrawal from the West Bank, Abed Rabbo has been a strong supporter of negotiations rather than terrorist activities as the best means to secure lasting peace with Israel.

SPENCER C. TUCKER

See also
Arafat, Yasser; Democratic Front for the Liberation of Palestine; Hawatmeh, Nayef; Madrid Conference; Oslo Accords; Palestine Liberation Organization; Palestinian Authority

References
Nassar, Jamal R. *The Palestine Liberation Organization: From Armed Struggle to the Declaration of Independence.* New York: Praeger, 1991.
Rubin, Barry, and Judith Colp Rubin. *Yasir Arafat: A Political Biography.* New York: Oxford University Press, 2003.

Abu Daoud
See Daoud, Muhammad

Abu Iyad
See Khalaf, Salah

Abu Jihad
See Wazir, Khalil al-

Abu Nidal
Born: May 1937
Died: August 19, 2002

Radical Palestinian and founder of the Fatah Revolutionary Council (FRC), also known as the Abu Nidal Organization (ANO), a notorious international terrorist group. Abu Nidal, which translates as "the father of struggle," was the nom de guerre of Sabri Khalil al-Banna, who was born in May 1937 in Jaffa, Palestine (now Tel Aviv-Jaffa), which at the time was under the British Mandate. In 1948, the Arab nations in the region rejected the United Nations (UN) partition plan, which ultimately led to war between the Jews and Arabs. Jaffa soon became a battle zone. During the conflict, the new Israeli government confiscated Abu Nidal's father's expansive orange groves, and Abu Nidal and his family fled to refugee camps in Gaza. He later moved on to Nablus, which was under Jordanian governance.

While in Jordan, Abu Nidal joined the Arab nationalist Baath Party. He soon landed in a Jordanian prison for his political views. When Baathists were suppressed by Jordanian King Hussein in 1957, Abu Nidal fled to Saudi Arabia. There in 1967 he founded the Palestine Secret Organization (PSO). After the Israelis won the 1967 Six-Day War, he was jailed again, this time by the Saudis, for his radical views.

In Saudi Arabia, Abu Nidal joined Fatah, Yasser Arafat's faction within the Palestine Liberation Organization (PLO), whose stated objective was to free Palestine from Israeli control. Abu Nidal, apparently dissatisfied with certain members of Fatah who sought diplomatic solutions, including a two-state solution to the Jewish problem, left Fatah in 1973. He became enamored with the rejectionist position held by the Iraqi government, which opposed any solution to the Palestinian problem that allowed for the existence of a Jewish state. Abu Nidal soon accused the PLO of treason, formed the FRC, and became Arafat's bitter rival. Meanwhile, Fatah sentenced Abu Nidal to death in absentia.

The FRC, operating out of Iraq, burst onto the international scene on September 5, 1973, when FRC gunmen took control of the Saudi embassy in Paris. This was followed by a number of spectacular acts of violence that were remarkable primarily because they seemed to show no concern for their effect on innocent civilians. The FRC has also assassinated a number of key PLO diplomats.

In 1981, Abu Nidal switched bases from Iraq to Syria because Damascus was interested in utilizing his brand of terrorism. Just one year later, the FRC critically wounded Schlomo Argov, Israel's ambassador to the United Kingdom. The Israelis wasted no time in retaliating and, only three days later, used the failed assassination attempt as a justification to invade Lebanon and attempt to destroy the PLO there.

By the mid-1980s, Abu Nidal was considered the world's most lethal terrorist and was the top target of the U.S. Central Intelligence Agency (CIA) and other counterterrorist organizations. At the same

Radical Palestinian leader Abu Nidal (1937–2002), the nom de guerre of Sabri Khalil al-Banna, founder of a notorious international terrorist organization, shown here in Beirut, Lebanon, circa 1985. (Reuters/Corbis)

time, he became increasingly paranoid, subjecting his followers to endless security checks and bloody purges.

In 1985 Abu Nidal moved his base to Tripoli, Libya, where he became close friends with Libyan strongman Muammar Qaddafi. As with the Syrians, Qaddafi also found many ways to employ Abu Nidal's services. After American warplanes struck Tripoli in April 1986 as punishment for a West Berlin nightclub bombing, Qaddafi convinced Abu Nidal to strike the United States and Britain. The result was staggering. After a kidnapping that left 3 hostages dead, an FRC team hijacked Pan Am Flight 73 in Karachi, Pakistan, in September 1986, killing 22 people. The FRC also provided the explosives that brought down Pan Am Flight 103 en route to New York City over Lockerbie, Scotland, on December 21, 1988, killing 270 people.

The FRC was also responsible for the 1988 attack on the Greek cruise ship *City of Poros* that killed 9 people and left 80 others injured. The attack was roundly criticized in Arab circles because its savagery did not serve either the Palestinian or the Arab political cause. As a result, some theorists accused Abu Nidal of being a Mossad agent or at least being on the Israeli payroll. Some have even argued that the FRC was Arafat's supreme deception in that it allowed Arafat to pose as a moderate while Abu Nidal carried out all of the PLO's truly violent acts.

In 1999, after being expelled by Qaddafi when the Libyan leader began to mend relations with the United States, Abu Nidal returned to Iraq, where he lived in open defiance of the Jordanian government that had sentenced him to death in absentia. He was living in a Baghdad home owned by the Iraqi Mukhabarat (Secret Service) when on August 19, 2002, he allegedly committed suicide, suffering multiple gunshot wounds, after being detained by Iraq's internal security force.

From a Western perspective, Abu Nidal's violence may have seemed to be targeted at just Israeli interests. However, the bulk of his victims were Arabs. In fact, most of his killings were not even ideologically driven per se in that he served as a mercenary for such states as Iraq, Syria, and Libya, killing these nations' political enemies for financial gain. Abu Nidal's activities tended to put Palestinian demands in the worst possible light and diminish any hope of gaining broader international support. As a result, it should come as no surprise that the FRC was never popular among most Palestinians. Abu Nidal and the FRC were believed to have carried out some 90 terrorist attacks in 20 nations that may have killed as many as 1,000 people.

B. KEITH MURPHY

See also

Arafat, Yasser; Baathism; Fatah; Iraq; Israel; Jordan; Lebanon; Lebanon, Israeli Invasion of; Mossad; Palestine Liberation Organization; Qaddafi, Muammar; Syria; Terrorism

References

Melman, Yossi. *The Master Terrorist: The True Story of Abu Nidal.* Translated by Shmuel Himmelstein. New York: Adama, 1986.

Seale, Patrick. *Abu Nidal, a Gun for Hire: The Secret Life of the World's Most Notorious Arab Terrorist.* New York: Random House, 1992.

Tibi, Bassam. *Arab Nationalism: Between Islam and the Nation-State.* New York: St. Martin's, 1997.

Abu Sharah, Naif

Born: 1966
Died: June 29, 2004

Local commander of Fatah's al-Aqsa Martyrs Brigades in Nablus. Abu Sharah was born in 1966 and came to command the al-Aqsa Martyrs Brigades in the city of Nablus. A militant group closely linked to the Fatah political organization, it was one of the most active forces in the al-Aqsa (Second) Intifada that commenced in 2000. Allegedly a central figure in the Tanzim terrorist infrastructure in Nablus, Abu Sharah was the conduit for much of the funding and explosives for suicide bombings, reportedly some of it from Hezbollah. As such, he was involved in numerous terrorist operations against Israel, including suicide bombings. They included a suicide bombing in Tel Aviv in January 2003 that killed 23 civilians and injured dozens more and one in November 2002

that killed 2 Israeli civilians and injured another 30. Abu Sharah was one of 8 Palestinian militants killed by the Israel Defense Forces (IDF) during an antiterrorist raid in the Old City of Nablus on the West Bank on June 29, 2004.

SPENCER C. TUCKER

See also

Al-Aqsa Martyrs Brigades; Hezbollah; Intifada, Second; Suicide Bombings; Terrorism

References

Alexander, Yonah. *Palestinian Secular Terrorism.* Ardsley, NY: Transnational Publishers, 2003.

Kurz, Anat N. *Fatah and the Politics of Violence: The Institutionalization of a Popular Struggle.* Eastbourne, East Sussex, UK: Sussex Academic Press, 2006.

Acheson, Dean

Born: April 11, 1893
Died: October 12, 1971

U.S. secretary of state (1949–1953) and one of the chief architects of U.S. post–World War II foreign policy. Born in Middletown, Connecticut, on April 11, 1893, to British parents, Dean Acheson graduated from the Groton School and then from Yale University in 1915. After earning a law degree from Harvard University in 1918, he served as private secretary to Supreme Court justice Louis Brandeis during 1918–1921 and then joined a Washington, D.C., law firm.

Acheson began his public service career in 1933 when President Franklin D. Roosevelt appointed him undersecretary of the treasury. Acheson soon resigned in a policy dispute, however. In 1940 he authored a key legal opinion leading to the establishment of the Lend-Lease program, and in 1943 he became assistant secretary of state. In 1945, new president Harry S. Truman appointed Acheson undersecretary of state.

Acheson initially favored postwar cooperation with the Soviet Union but soon reversed his position. At Bretton Woods, he helped create the major postwar international financial institutions, and he played a major role in organizing the Marshall Plan to restore the economies of postwar Europe. He also helped draft the Truman Doctrine to contain Soviet advances into the Middle East and the Mediterranean, and he supported the 1949 creation of the North Atlantic Treaty Organization (NATO).

Acheson was also deeply involved in Middle Eastern affairs. He sharply disagreed with Truman on the disposition of Palestine. Truman, moved by the terrible suffering of the Jewish people in the wartime Nazi Holocaust and concerned about the Jewish vote in America, announced on Yom Kippur, October 4, 1946, his support for a viable Jewish state in Palestine. Acheson joined Truman's other chief foreign policy advisers in opposing recognition of a Jewish state in Palestine. These men believed that good relations with the Arab world would be critical in light of apparent Soviet interest

Dean Acheson, U.S. secretary of state from 1949 to 1953. (Library of Congress)

in Iran, Turkey, and Greece. Although Arab oil was not yet vital to the American economy, it was essential to the reconstruction of war-torn Western Europe.

With Secretary of State James Burns in Europe for extended periods negotiating postwar issues with the Soviets, Truman relied to a considerable extent on Acheson. Much to Acheson's consternation, Truman pressured the British government to relax the Jewish immigration quotas for entry into Palestine set by the White Paper of 1939. Truman also encouraged the United Kingdom to turn over the Palestine question to the United Nations (UN), which London did in February 1947 and announced its decision to withdraw from the mandate the next year. The new American secretary of state, George C. Marshall, was faced with escalating Arab violence in response to the UN partition plan, yet he was preoccupied with the crisis situation in Western Europe during 1947 and 1948.

In January 1949, on Marshall's departure, Truman named Acheson secretary of state. As with Marshall, Acheson found his time in office dominated by events in Europe and Asia as the Cold War became an international arena of confrontation with the Soviet Union and its allies: NATO, the Soviet atomic bomb, the Chinese communist revolution (he favored recognition of the communist regime once that side had won the civil war), the decision to create

a hydrogen bomb (he played a leading role in encouraging Truman to proceed with it), aid to the French in Indochina, and, finally, the Korean War of 1950–1953.

In the Middle East, in the wake of the creation of Israel and the Israeli War of Independence (1948–1949), Acheson sought to secure stability in order to thwart Soviet ambitions in the region. For two years he and the State Department sought a permanent peace settlement between Arabs and Israelis, but to no avail. In May 1950 Acheson joined with the foreign ministers of Britain and France to issue a Tripartite Declaration designed to further stabilize the armistice ending the war and to control the flow of arms to the Middle East by prohibiting sales to states harboring aggressive designs.

Acheson's last official involvement in Middle East affairs came in Iran in the spring of 1951, when Iranian nationalist prime minister Mohammad Mosaddeq moved against the British-controlled Anglo-Iranian Oil Company. Under Mosaddeq's leadership, the Majlis (parliament) nationalized Anglo-Iranian Oil. Fearing a British military response as well as an Iranian request for Soviet assistance, Acheson urged Truman to send ambassador-at-large W. Averell Harriman to Tehran to encourage negotiation, a policy that failed to resolve the crisis but nevertheless drew both sides back from the brink of war. The crisis dragged on though 1952 with Acheson unsuccessfully attempting to bring the parties together. When Mosaddeq broke diplomatic relations with London in October, the British suggested to the United States that they work together to mount a coup to overthrow him. Acheson rejected the proposal and continued to seek a solution of the impasse until President Dwight D. Eisenhower took office in January 1953. That August, Mosaddeq was overthrown in a coup assisted by the U.S. Central Intelligence Agency (CIA).

Acheson later admitted to "a feeling of dissatisfaction with everything we did in the Middle East." In prophetic testimony before the House Foreign Affairs Committee in 1957, the former secretary of state insisted that the United States needed "not more military intervention but a long-term program for economic development and some effort to alleviate Western dependence on Middle Eastern oil."

Acheson came under heavy pressure from the Republicans over Truman's policy in Korea, including the decision to remove General Douglas MacArthur from command in Korea (a step that Acheson fully supported) and the decision to settle for the status quo antebellum there. Acheson became a frequent whipping boy for right-wing Republicans, especially the red-baiting senator Joseph R. McCarthy.

Following Truman's decision not to run for reelection in 1952 and Eisenhower's victory that November, Acheson retired in early 1953 and returned to private law practice. He remained an influential figure, however, eventually becoming a highly valued unofficial adviser to presidents John F. Kennedy, Lyndon B. Johnson, and Richard M. Nixon. Acheson died on October 12, 1971, at Sandy Spring, Maryland.

Errol MacGregor Clauss

See also
Eisenhower, Dwight David; Iran

References
Acheson, Dean. *Present at the Creation: My Years in the State Department.* New York: Norton, 1969.

Beisner, Robert. *Dean Acheson: A Life in the Cold War.* New York: Oxford University Press, 2006.

Brinkley, Douglas. *Dean Acheson: The Cold War Years, 1953–71.* New Haven, CT: Yale University Press, 1992.

Chace, James. *Acheson: The Secretary of State Who Created the American World.* New York: Simon and Schuster, 1998.

Cohen, Michael. *Truman and Israel.* Berkeley: University of California Press, 1990.

McNay, John T. *Acheson and Empire: The British Accent in American Foreign Policy.* Columbia: University of Missouri Press, 2001.

Rubin, Barry. *Paved with Good Intentions: The American Experience and Iran.* New York: Oxford University Press, 1980.

Achille Lauro Hijacking
Start Date: October 7, 1985
End Date: October 10, 1985

The *Achille Lauro* was an Italian passenger liner hijacked by Palestinian terrorists in the eastern Mediterranean on October 7, 1985. Construction of the ship began at Vlissingen in the Netherlands in 1939 but was interrupted by World War II. Launched in 1946, the ship entered service in late 1947 as the *Willum Ruys*. Sold to the Italian Lauro Line in 1964, the ship was rebuilt and modernized and returned to service in 1966, named for the former mayor of Naples. Displacing about 21,100 tons, the *Achille Lauro* could accommodate 900 passengers.

On October 7, 1985, the *Achille Lauro* was steaming from Alexandria to Port Said off the Egyptian coast when four armed members of the Palestine Liberation Front (PLF) led by Abu Abbas seized control, apparently in retaliation for the Israeli destruction of the Palestine Liberation Organization (PLO) headquarters in Tunis on October 1.

The terrorists had been surprised by a crew member and were forced to act prematurely, but they demanded that the *Achille Lauro* steam to Tartus, Syria, and threatened to blow up the ship if Israel did not release 50 Palestinian prisoners held in Israel. The sole casualty of the affair was American Jewish passenger Leon Klinghoffer, who was confined to a wheelchair. Reportedly he confronted the hijackers and was shot by them, and his body was thrown overboard.

Syrian authorities refused to allow the ship to dock, and it returned to Port Said. Following two days of negotiations, the terrorists agreed to release the ship and its passengers in return for safe conduct aboard an Egyptian airliner to Tunis. On October 10, U.S. aircraft intercepted the Egyptian plane and forced it to fly to a North Atlantic Treaty Organization (NATO) base in Sicily. Disregarding U.S. government appeals, Italian authorities released the passengers, reportedly including Abbas, although he was subsequently sentenced in absentia by an Italian court to life in prison.

Following the surrender of their Palestinian hijackers, freed passengers disembark from the cruise ship *Achille Lauro* at Port Said, Egypt, on October 10, 1985. (Bernard Bisson/Corbis Sygma)

The close relationship between Abbas and the PLO caused the U.S. government to deny a visa to PLO chairman Yasser Arafat to enter the United State in order to speak to the United Nations (UN) General Assembly in November 1988. Abbas had been a member of the PLO Executive Committee during 1984–1991. Arrested in Iraq following the U.S.-led invasion of that country in 2003, he died, reportedly of natural causes, while in U.S. custody on March 8, 2004. The other three hijackers served varying terms in Italian prisons.

On November 29, 1994, the reflagged *Achille Lauro* was steaming off the coast of Somalia when a fire broke out. All 1,090 passengers and crew abandoned ship. Other ships were soon on the scene, but 2 people died in the lifeboat transfers. The fire totally consumed the ship, and it sank on December 2.

On January 19, 1996, the PLO agreed to provide an undisclosed sum to finance the Leon and Marilyn Klinghoffer Memorial Foundation of the U.S. Anti-Defamation League. The foundation is dedicated to combating terrorism through peaceful means. In return, Klinghoffer's daughters dropped a lawsuit brought against the PLO. The *Achille Lauro* hijacking has been the subject of a 1990 television docudrama and an opera, *The Death of Klinghofffer* (1991), that appeared as a film version in 2003.

SPENCER C. TUCKER

See also

Palestine Liberation Front; Palestine Liberation Organization; Terrorism

References

Bohn, Michael K. *The Achille Lauro Hijacking: Lessons in the Politics and Prejudice of Terrorism.* Dulles, VA: Potomac Books, 2004.

Cassese, Antonio. *Terrorism, Politics and Law: The Achille Lauro Affair.* Princeton, NJ: Princeton University Press, 1989.

Acre, Israel

See Akko, Israel

Acre Prison

See Akko Prison

Adan, Avraham
Born: 1926

Israel Defense Forces (IDF) general. Born in 1926 in Kfar Gileadi in the British Mandate for Palestine, Avraham "Bren" Adan was old enough to participate in all of the major Arab-Israeli conflicts that have marked the recent history of the Middle East. He joined the Palmach Jewish strike force in 1943. In the Israeli War of Independence (1948–1949), he was a captain in the Negev Brigade that captured the port of Eilat on the Red Sea.

Adan remained in the IDF after the war and, by the time of the Sinai Campaign during the Suez Crisis of 1956, was a lieutenant colonel in command of the 7th Armored Brigade in the Sinai. He remained in the Sinai as part of the Armored Corps. During the 1967 Six-Day War he was deputy commander of an armored division. By war's end, he was a major general.

The Six-Day War concluded with a cease-fire, but a permanent settlement between the Arabs and Israel proved elusive. The Israeli capture of the Sinai during the war was particularly galling to the Egyptians, who continued to engage in hostile actions along the frontier of the Suez Canal and the deserts of the Sinai. Thus, what became known as the War of Attrition gradually developed in this region and forced the IDF to devise a new defensive strategy.

Lieutenant General Chaim Bar-Lev appointed General Adan to preside over the military committee that would come up with this new policy. Until then, the most important element in Israeli strategy was that any war between Israel and an Arab state had to be short and fought on foreign soil. This strategy encouraged the armed forces to concentrate on the development of rapid offensive capabilities and a high degree of mobility, which had worked brilliantly during the 1967 conflict. Adan was now in charge of modifying these basic precepts.

The plan that Adan submitted to the General Staff required 35 small strong points located every seven miles along the east bank of the canal, between which IDF patrols would maintain constant observation of Egyptian forces on the other side. Strong armored formations were positioned in assembly areas some distance from the canal, ready to counterattack any Egyptian attempt to cross. The strong points were designed to prevent any surprise attack by the Egyptians crossing the canal while at the same time exposing only a small number of IDF troops to the danger of Egyptian artillery fire.

Although many Israeli generals, including Israel Tal and Ariel Sharon, disapproved of this plan because its static defensive line deviated so sharply from the traditional adherence to mobility, Bar-Lev approved the plan, and construction of what became known as the Bar-Lev Line was more or less complete by 1969.

In 1972, Adan became head of the Armored Corps and was thus a key commander in October 1973 when the armed forces of Egypt and Syria mounted their initially successful surprise attack on Israel to begin the Yom Kippur War. Caught off guard, the IDF stumbled badly at the beginning of the war. The standard strategy of the Armored Corps had been developed by General Tal and called for all-tank attacks without infantry. This was the Israeli operational doctrine in place as the IDF responded to the Egyptian crossing of the Suez Canal.

Adan's 162nd Armored Division with 250 tanks had the mission of relieving the Bar-Lev Line strong points that had been captured

Israeli general Avraham Adan, shown here on October 22, 1972. (Israeli Government Press Office)

by the Egyptians. On the morning of October 8, Adan's division started its attack but was surprised by unexpectedly effective Egyptian antitank guided missiles, supplied by the Soviets. Furthermore, Soviet-supplied surface-to-air missiles (SAMs) on the Egyptian side of the canal effectively prevented the Israeli Air Force from providing support to the tanks. Unprepared to deal with these weapons, the Israeli tank crews took heavy losses. Adan's division in the northern Sinai quickly lost three-quarters of its tanks and was not able to retake even one of the Israeli canal strong points.

After regrouping, Adan's division eventually crossed the Suez Canal, although significantly behind schedule. By October 14, however, the Israelis had recovered, and Adan's unit was engaged in heavy fighting on the Egyptian side of the canal, taking out many of the SAM sites that had caused such heavy damage earlier. At Suez City, his division cut off the Egyptian Third Army. A cease-fire took place shortly thereafter. Adan's division, on orders from the IDF Southern Command, violated the cease-fire by continuing to fight on until October 25.

Although the IDF emerged from the war with a tactical victory, it had suffered heavy losses in the first days of the fighting. Analysts evaluated the wisdom of the Bar-Lev Line, the emphasis on all-tank battalions, and the difficulties that Adan and others had encountered in trying to carry out their orders. Generally speaking, the official Agranat Commission report found that Adan had acquitted himself correctly on most specific counts and that in situations where a different approach was indicated, he had erred in a "good faith misinterpretation" of orders. He was absolved of any blame for the early setbacks.

During 1974–1977 Adan served as the Israeli military attaché in Washington, D.C. In 1980 he published his own account of the Yom Kippur War.

SPENCER C. TUCKER

See also

Agranat Commission; Attrition, War of; Bar-Lev, Chaim; Bar-Lev Line; Eilat, Israel; Israel Defense Forces; Israeli War of Independence, Overview; Palmach; Sharon, Ariel; Sinai Campaign; Six-Day War; Suez Crisis; Tal, Israel

References

Adan, Avraham. *On the Banks of the Suez: An Israeli General's Personal Account of the Yom Kippur War.* Novato, CA: Presidio, 1980.

El Shazly, Saad. *The Crossing of the Suez.* San Francisco: American Mideast Research, 1980.

Rabinovich, Abraham. *The Yom Kippur War: The Epic Encounter That Transformed the Middle East.* New York: Schocken, 2005.

Adenauer, Konrad

Born: January 5, 1876
Died: April 19, 1967

First chancellor of West Germany during 1949–1963. Born in Köln (Cologne) on January 5, 1876, the son of a minor civil servant, Konrad Adenauer was brought up a devout Roman Catholic. He stud-

ied law and politics at the universities of Freiburg, Munich, and Bonn and in 1901 entered the Cologne state prosecutor's office, later serving as assistant district court judge.

In 1906 Adenauer entered local politics, becoming leader of the Catholic Center Party and, in 1911, chief assistant to Cologne's lord mayor. In 1917 Adenauer was elected lord mayor, a position he held for 16 years, through Germany's defeat in World War I until the end of the Weimar Republic. In 1934 the Gestapo arrested Adenauer on trumped-up charges and held him for several months.

Narrowly escaping death at the hands of the Gestapo, Adenauer was restored to political activities by British forces in March 1945. He soon clashed with the British over priorities, and they dismissed him in October 1945. This, however, freed him to take a leading role in national politics, and he became one of the founders and the leader of the Christian Democratic Union (CDU). In September 1949 he was elected the first chancellor of West Germany by the Bundestag (lower house of parliament).

Adenauer closely identified himself and the new West Germany with the West. The new government still lacked authority over defense and foreign affairs, but Adenauer's pro-Western orientation reassured top U.S. officials that he could be trusted. Thus, even before West Germany regained full independence in 1955, the United States left many matters to his discretion.

Adenauer's overriding preoccupation was to restore his country's sovereignty and international standing while continuing its free market, democratic capitalist orientation and anchoring it firmly within the U.S.-led Western Cold War camp. In 1950 he worked closely with French leaders to create the European Coal and Steel Community (ECSC). Closer European integration remained central to Adenauer's vision of postwar German foreign policy, and he signed several further agreements whereby Germany became one of the key pillars of a united Europe, most notably the 1957–1958 Treaty of Rome creating the European Economic Community (EEC). The common market thereby created, together with adept German deployment of Marshall Plan aid and sheer hard work, contributed to West German industrial recovery and the *Wirtschaftswunder* (economic miracle) of the late 1950s and 1960s.

As early as 1948, Adenauer, who viewed the creation of a German military force as one means whereby his country could regain its sovereignty, began drafting plans for a German contribution to a common European army, which France, fearful of a German military resurgence, immediately vetoed. The outbreak of war in Korea in June 1950 caused the United States to treat West German rearmament as a distasteful necessity. In 1952 and 1953 Adenauer rejected overtures from Soviet leader Joseph Stalin and his successors that envisaged a peace settlement that would create a united but neutral Germany. Adenauer's decision, clearly demonstrating his commitment to the Western alliance even at the price of Germany's continuing division, contributed to the 1954 U.S. and British decision to make West Germany a full member of the North Atlantic Treaty Organization (NATO). In 1954 and 1955 the Western powers signed a series of peace treaties with Adenauer's gov-

Konrad Adenauer, first chancellor of West Germany, 1949–1963. (Library of Congress)

ernment restoring its sovereignty and also control of the Saar region, under French occupation since 1945. The Saarland was formally restored to Germany in 1957 after a plebiscite in 1955.

One of the more controversial questions facing Adenauer was how best to deal with the legacy of German persecution of German and European Jewry under Adolf Hitler and the Holocaust, in which some 6 million Jews died. Adenauer's stance may have owed something not just to political considerations but also to his own 1944 concentration camp experiences and those of his second wife Gussi, whose incarceration contributed to her death in 1948. As chancellor, Adenauer, who personally considered reparations for Jewish sufferings a moral issue, in 1951 admitted German guilt without any pressure from the West and decided that the new West Germany must take responsibility for the crimes of the Third Reich. In 1952 the Bundestag passed a Restitution Law providing for compensation to individual Jews who had suffered under the Nazi regime.

In 1952 Adenauer's government negotiated a Reparations Agreement with Israeli foreign minister Moshe Sharett under which West Germany agreed to supply goods worth 3.45 billion German marks ($845 million) to Israel in installments over the period 1953 to 1966. These funds were intended to represent compensation to Israel for the resettlement of 500,000 Jews left homeless after the war. The agreement was controversial in Israel, since some Israelis deplored

direct negotiations with Germany and condemned the accord as simply an expedient whereby Germany sought to regain credibility and acceptance in the West by buying off Jewish survivors of the Holocaust. Sharett only signed the agreement after the Israeli Knesset (parliament) voted to approve it. Threats of an Arab boycott also caused reservations within the German government, which only approved the accord in 1953.

West Germany carried out the agreement in full. Between 1953 and 1965, West Germany made collective restitution to the Israeli government in both goods and cash for property stolen from Jews during the Nazi era. Israel transferred 450 million marks ($110 million) to the Claims Conference, a body that represented the interests of Jewish Nazi victims living outside Israel. The bulk of reparations, however, were used by Israel itself, saving the new state from bankruptcy in its early years. Some 30 percent of the total was used to purchase crude oil shipments from British suppliers, and the remainder was used for capital goods that the Israeli government purchased directly. Israel used German reparations to build a 60-vessel merchant fleet, mechanize agriculture, renovate the equipment of 1,400 industrial concerns, and develop water resources, all major contributions to the economic strength of the Jewish state. West Germany and Israel did not, however, establish full diplomatic relations until 1965, the year reparations ended.

The reparations agreement notwithstanding, critics claimed that Adenauer was lukewarm on denazification and too lenient toward politically compromised individuals whose past treatment of Jews was at best questionable. Controversially, civil servant Hans Globke, author of a commentary on the anti-Jewish Nuremberg Laws, served under Adenauer as West German state secretary from 1953 to 1963, and Theodor Oberländer, who had sent Jews in occupied Poland to death camps, was minister of refugees from 1953 to 1960.

Although Adenauer acquiesced in U.S. actions during the Suez Crisis and sought to maintain good relations with those Arab states on which West Germany was increasingly dependent for oil, with his approval West Germany also helped to build up Israeli military strength. From 1957 the West German military covertly supplied Israel with weapons, on occasion breaking international sanctions. At the request of Israeli prime minister David Ben-Gurion, in 1960 Adenauer expanded this program to include submarines, antitank missiles, and helicopters, making West Germany one of Israel's most significant arms suppliers. Ben-Gurion and Adenauer became personal friends. In 1966, after both men had left office, Ben-Gurion invited Adenauer to visit Israel, a trip that sparked anti-German demonstrations but during which Adenauer predictably behaved impeccably.

In 1963, following the *Der Spiegel* Affair in which West German defense minister Franz Josef Strauss ordered the arrest of journalists for allegedly having published state secrets, Adenauer finally resigned, ironic proof that the democratic system he had reestablished genuinely worked. His was the longest incumbency as chancellor since Otto von Bismarck in the 19th century. "Der Alte" (the old man) remained head of the CDU until 1966 and wrote several volumes of memoirs in his final years. Adenauer died at Rhöndorf on April 19, 1967, at the age of 91.

PRISCILLA MARY ROBERTS

See also

Acheson, Dean; Ben-Gurion, David; Dulles, John Foster; Eisenhower, Dwight David; Holocaust; Israel; Israeli War of Independence, Overview; Kennedy, John Fitzgerald; Knesset; Sharett, Moshe; Six-Day War; Suez Crisis; Truman, Harry S.

References

Adenauer, Konrad. *Memoirs, 1945–1953.* Translated by Beate Ruhm von Oppen. London: Weidenfeld and Nicolson, 1966.

Alexander, Edgar. *Adenauer and the New Germany: The Chancellor of the Vanquished.* Translated by Thomas E. Goldstein. New York: Farrar, Straus and Cudahy, 1957.

Frei, Norbert. *Adenauer, Germany and the Nazi Past: The Politics of Amnesty and Integration.* Translated by Joel Golb. New York: Columbia University Press, 2002.

Irving, Ronald. *Adenauer.* New York: Longman, 2002.

Schwarz, Hans-Peter. *Konrad Adenauer: A German Politician and Statesman in a Period of War, Revolution, and Reconstruction.* Translated by Louise Willmott and Geoffrey Penny. 2 vols. Providence, RI: Berghahn, 1995–1997.

Weymar, Paul. *Konrad Adenauer: The Authorized Biography.* Translated by Peter de Mendelssohn. London: Andre Deutsch, 1957.

Williams, Charles. *Adenauer: The Father of the New Germany.* London: Little, Brown, 2000.

Administrative Detentions

The practice of holding individuals without charging them with specific crimes or putting them on trial. Israeli authorities have used administrative detentions since 1948, but some sources claim that they have been used more extensively since the beginning of the First Intifada in 1987. One reason for their use is to remove opposition leaders from the public arena. Another aim is to deter Palestinians from political activity. Indeed, Palestinian intellectuals, professors, lawyers, and journalists have been special targets of administrative detention. The practice of extending administrative detentions indefinitely without review by an outside authority has led to accusations of human rights violations on the part of the Israelis. For example, Jamal Farag, a Palestinian journalist, was held for three years in administrative detention, most of that time in solitary confinement. Neither he nor his lawyer were allowed to see the evidence against him.

Administrative detention is based on the concept that some individuals pose a threat to the public or the state. The legal basis for such detentions is the 1945 Emergency Decree of the British Mandate for Palestine. That decree was amended by the 1979 Law on Authority in States of Emergency. In practice, administrative detentions are used in cases in which little direct evidence of criminal activity exists. They are also used when the revelation of evidence would compromise sources, such as the identity of an informant or an infiltrator into a Palestinian organization. They are also employed when the person to be incarcerated is believed to pose a potential threat to public order without having committed a crime.

Authority for imposing administrative detentions varies according to the location. Within Israel proper, the defense minister can issue orders for up to six months' detention. The minister can also renew administrative detention orders for up to six months at a time. The chief of the General Staff can also order detention within Israel but for only 48 hours. Before that time period has expired, law enforcement officials must show cause for continued detention in a closed hearing. Anyone who is the subject of an administrative detention order may appeal to the District Court. If denied relief by the District Court, the detainee can then appeal to the Israeli Supreme Court. The courts have the right to dismiss any detention orders if they find that the orders were issued for reasons other than security. Some individuals have had no recourse to such appeals, however, and have been held for longer periods of time.

In the occupied territories, senior local military commanders can also issue administrative detention orders. The effective time period is limited to six months, but the orders can be renewed by the same commanders. Individuals have the right to appeal to a local military court, but only after six months. If denied relief, they can then appeal to the Israeli Supreme Court.

Many observers, including Amnesty International and Israeli peace activists, believe that administrative detentions are violations of generally recognized human rights. Individuals are sometimes arrested because of their opinions or their presence in a particular location or, in earlier periods, for being identified with any Palestinian political group, for wearing the colors of the Palestinian flag, or for holding such a flag and not for any overt actions they might have taken. The accused does not receive information about the crime for which he or she is arrested. In appeals hearings, detainees rarely receive any further information. Families of the accused cannot obtain any information about them. Witnesses are not required to answer questions that might compromise Israeli security, and hearings are held behind closed doors. Appeals are held only if the accused requests them. Since 1996, Palestinian prisoners have boycotted the Israeli courts, refusing to appeal their sentences. Detentions are frequently renewed at the end of six months and may be renewed without limit. These detentions are even less clear legally when they involve, as they have, Lebanese citizens, whether Hezbollah operatives or ordinary persons taken in Israeli raids.

During the First Intifada of 1987, when the Israeli military was not able to stop the violence, the government turned to administrative detentions to remove potential Palestinian leaders. The number of Palestinians in administrative detention peaked at around 2,000 in 1989, but many other Palestinians were actually charged, tried, and sentenced in that period for political crimes.

Over the next decade, the number declined. By 1999, only about 20 Palestinians remained in detention. After the September 11, 2001, terrorist attacks on the United States, however, the number steadily increased. By the time the United States invaded Iraq in March 2003, more than 1,000 Palestinians were being held. The number gradually declined to approximately 780 at the end of 2006. This number stands alongside about 10,000 Palestinian prisoners held for security reasons or for political crimes, and together with those in administrative detention, this is a fairly high proportion of the population. Most prisoners were held in camps in the Negev Desert. Until the middle of 2005, the Israeli military held most prisoners in administrative detention. Since that time, however, nearly all prisoners have been transferred to the custody of the Israel Prison Service. A small number of Jewish citizens have also been held under administrative detention, most for their support of peace initiatives.

TIM J. WATTS

See also

Intifada, First; Iraq War

References

Bucaille, Laetitia. *Growing Up Palestinian: Israeli Occupation and the Intifada Generation.* Princeton, NJ: Princeton University Press, 2004.

Carey, Roane. *The New Intifada: Resisting Israel's Apartheid.* New York: Verso, 2001.

Gross, Emanuel. *The Struggle of Democracy against Terrorism: Lessons from the United States, the United Kingdom, and Israel.* Charlottesville: University of Virginia Press, 2006.

Agranat, Shimon

Born: 1906
Died: 1992

Chief justice of the Israeli Supreme Court from 1950 to 1976. Born in Louisville, Kentucky, in 1906, Shimon Agranat graduated from the University of Chicago with a degree in law. An ardent Zionist, he had chaired the local chapter of Avukah, the Zionist student organization. He immigrated to the British Mandate for Palestine in 1930 and settled in Haifa, where he practiced law. During 1940–1948 he was a magistrate and then served as chief judge of the Haifa District Court.

Following the formation of the State of Israel in 1948, Agranat was named to the Supreme Court in 1950 and became its chief justice in March 1965. He is best known for having chaired the 1974 commission, which was named for him and charged with investigating the circumstances under which Israel had been caught by surprise by the 1973 Yom Kippur War. Agranat retired from his post when he reached the mandatory retirement age of 70 in 1976. He died in 1992.

SPENCER C. TUCKER

See also

Agranat Commission

References

Herzog, Chaim. *The War of Atonement: October, 1973.* Boston: Little, Brown, 1975.

Israeli Supreme Court judge Shimon Agranat, shown here during appeal proceedings of Nazi war criminal Adolf Eichmann at Beit Ha'am in Jerusalem, March 27, 1962. (Israeli Government Press Office)

Rabinovich, Abraham. *The Yom Kippur War: The Epic Encounter That Transformed the Middle East.* New York: Schocken, 2005.

Agranat Commission

Start Date: November 18, 1973
End Date: January 30, 1975

Israeli government commission appointed by Prime Minister Golda Meir to investigate the circumstances under which Israel Defense Forces (IDF) and the Israeli government were caught by surprise in the Egyptian-Syrian attacks that began the Yom Kippur War of October 1973. The commission was named for its chairman, chief justice of the Israeli Supreme Court Shimon Agranat. Other members were Justice Moshe Landau, State Comptroller Yitzchak Nebrmzahl, and former IDF chiefs of staff General Yigal Yadin and General Haim Laskov.

The committee, which held 140 sessions and heard 58 witnesses, issued an interim report on April 1, 1974, and its final report on

January 30, 1975. The report chiefly blamed a failure of Israeli military intelligence and basic operational assumptions that in order for a war to occur, the Arab states would first have to unite and Egypt would not attack without first achieving air superiority. The committee noted the failure to assess political motivations present in the Egyptian decision to initiate hostilities.

The committee report found fault with six individuals, including IDF chief of staff Lieutenant General David Elazar and chief of the Southern Command Major General Shmuel Gonen. The report held that Elazar, who had primary responsibility for the entire IDF, should be dismissed. It recommended that Gonen, who commanded the Egyptian Front and whose forces had been unable to prevent the Egyptians from crossing the Suez Canal, be relieved from active duty. It also recommended the same for the director of military intelligence Major General Eli Zeira and his deputy, Brigadier General Aryeh Shalev. The commission recommended that two other intelligence officers, the head of the Egyptian desk Lieutenant Colonel Bandman and the chief of Southern Command intelligence Lieutenant Colonel Gedelia, both be transferred from intelligence duties. Elazar subsequently resigned as chief of staff, and Gonen and Zeira were removed from active duty.

The report was controversial in that it absolved both Defense Minister Moshe Dayan and Prime Minister Meir of all responsibility. The commission held that it could not take into account Dayan's military background and should judge him only as a civilian defense minister acting in a political capacity. Dayan offered his resignation, but Meir refused to accept it. Strong adverse public opinion following publication of the interim report, however, forced Meir and her entire cabinet to resign on April 11, 1974, although she did not formally leave office until the formation of a new government on June 3.

SPENCER C. TUCKER

See also

Agranat, Shimon; Laskov, Haim; Meir, Golda; Yadin, Yigal; Yom Kippur War

References

Herzog, Chaim. *The War of Atonement: October, 1973*. Boston: Little, Brown, 1975.
Rabinovich, Abraham. *The Yom Kippur War: The Epic Encounter That Transformed the Middle East*. New York: Schocken, 2005.

Agriculture

Because of the Middle East's seemingly inhospitable environment, agriculture is a vitally important aspect of the economies, politics, and cultures of the region. In addition to providing food and products for local consumption and export, farming and the raising of livestock play a role in state security, international diplomacy, and even national identity. Although multinational cooperation would help maximize limited resources such as water, tensions within the Middle East continue to make agriculture a complex and volatile subject.

Although agriculture was an important facet of life in many traditional Middle Eastern societies, technological underdevelopment, territorial losses, lack of infrastructure, scarce water supplies, and the sometimes harsh climate have reduced the monetary importance of agriculture in many Arab nations today. In Jordan, for instance, employment in the agricultural sector dropped from 37 percent of the workforce to only 6 percent between the mid-1980s and mid-1990s. Currently, only about 3 percent of Jordan's land is being cultivated. In Lebanon, it is more difficult to estimate the impact of agriculture because no census has been taken since 1932, and thus the estimated 7 percent of the workforce in agriculture might actually be as high as 28–30 percent. It is clear that a large percentage of rural Lebanon is used as farmland.

Saudi Arabia, which must import much of its food, cultivates less than 2 percent of its land. This is largely because of the country's vast deserts and negligible freshwater supplies. Conversely, about 25 percent of Syria's workforce is employed in the agricultural sector, producing a third of the nation's gross domestic product (GDP). Half of this income comes from cash crops such as cotton. The Middle East, excluding Israel, is able to produce locally only about half of its food requirement. Billions of dollars of food must be imported.

Israel's agricultural situation is markedly different from those of most of its Arab neighbors. Like Lebanon and Jordan, the Israeli agricultural sector does not employ a large portion of the population. Although about 17 percent of Israelis were engaged in agriculture during the 1950s, this figure has since fallen to about 5 percent. Agricultural products account for less than 5 percent of Israel's GDP. In other ways, however, Israel's agricultural outlook has brightened over the last half century. From Israel's creation in 1948 until 1998, the amount of cultivated land increased from 408,000 acres to almost 1.1 million acres. At the end of the 20th century, Israel was producing approximately 1.2 million tons of vegetables and 869,000 tons of citrus fruit in addition to sizable crops of wheat and cotton. Israel's meat and dairy industries, which have made extensive use of computerized feeding and milking technologies, also produce high yields. Israeli agriculturalists have also worked to breed milk cows and other livestock that are resistant to both disease and the hot, dry environment. Israel produces sufficient food to feed its population and is even able to export some of its agricultural goods. Citrus fruit, including unique Israeli varieties that are highly prized for their superior appearance and flavor, are the country's primary agricultural export. Other exports include cotton, poultry, sunflower oil, and dairy products.

The productivity of Israeli agriculture is due in large part to a highly effective use of water resources. Israel's crops require more than 42 billion cubic feet of water each year, or about 60 percent of Israel's total water usage. Because the Negev Desert covers 65 percent of Israel, irrigation is essential. As Israeli prime minister David Ben-Gurion noted, for Israel to flourish it needed to "make the desert bloom." This was achieved largely through the National Water Carrier (NWC), an extensive series of pipelines created in 1964 to

Irrigated Land in the Middle East

Country	Irrigated Land (sq. mi.)	Total Area (sq. mi.)	% of Total Area Irrigated
Iran	27,799	630,575	4.41%
Iraq	13,514	169,236	7.99%
Israel	768	8,131	9.45%
Jordan	290	34,444	0.84%
Lebanon	452	4,015	11.26%
Saudi Arabia	6,178	829,996	0.74%
United Arab Emirates	278	71,498	0.39%

bring water from the Sea of Galilee to drier areas of the country. Today, the NWC irrigates more than 500,000 acres of land and has increased annual water output to the Negev by 75 percent. Water provided by the NWC is used in a variety of drip, spray, and buried irrigation systems, many of them fully computerized and automated. Subterranean water supplies have also been tapped to supply water to crops. At an estimated cost of $1–2 billion a year, desalinization has generally been ignored until recently.

Agriculture is, however, more than just a modest but important component of the Israeli economy. The history of Israeli agriculture is closely tied to Zionism, the creation of the State of Israel, and Israeli identity. The Zionist movement of the late 19th century, which called for the creation of a Jewish homeland in the Middle East, was concerned with agriculture for both practical and spiritual reasons. Farming in Palestine was a tangible way for Jewish immigrants to claim territory in the region. Agriculture also provided security for the growing Jewish population by providing food and even products for trade. Zionists also saw farming as a way to spiritually connect to their homeland, and many believed that only through physically working the land could an individual become a spiritual part of Israel. For many immigrants, the kibbutz, or communal farm, became the ideal institution by which to synthesize practical necessities and metaphysical ideology.

While many of the immigrants during the First Aliya (1882–1904) took up farming in Palestine, the creation of kibbutzim did not begin until the Second Aliya (1904–1914). Many of the 40,000

Irrigated fields on an Israeli kibbutz. (iStockPhoto.com)

Jews who immigrated to the Middle East during this period were young socialists who were attracted to the idea of creating farming communes. Owning, working, and sharing the profits of the kibbutz among its members fit nicely into the immigrants' worldview. And, because most of the money used to purchase kibbutz land was donated by Jews around the world, it did not seem appropriate to operate the settlements as individually owned private enterprises.

Degania, the first kibbutz, was founded in 1910 on the southern shore of the Sea of Galilee. Four years later, it had more than 50 members. By the beginning of World War II, more than 25,000 Jewish immigrants were living in kibbutzim. The Jewish Agency of the World Zionist Organization (WZO) facilitated the rapid growth of the kibbutz movement by providing land, seeds, equipment, and work animals at low costs. The first kibbutzim were largely secular, as many of the initial socialist-inspired kibbutniks rejected orthodox Judaism. In fact, the first religious kibbutz, Ein Tzurim, was not created until 1946. Both secular and religious kibbutzim operated on communal principles, with members sharing work and child-rearing duties and dividing proceeds based on contribution. A kibbutz could have anywhere from 100 to 2,000 members.

Today there are 130,000 people (2.5 percent of Israel's population) living in some 270 kibbutzim. Some kibbutzim continue to engage in agriculture, while others engage in industries such as food processing, quarrying, and tourism. Although the kibbutz movement has been declining, many kibbutzim are so successful that they must hire non-Jewish seasonal workers. Kibbutzim have also attracted a large number of both Israeli and non-Israeli volunteers, and today less than 40 percent of kibbutz workers are actually permanent members.

In addition to the kibbutzim, there are several other agricultural institutions in Israel. The moshavot were the initial form of late 19th-century settlement. They were rural establishments based on the concepts of private enterprise, and today many have become urbanized and industrialized. Moshavim are cooperatives, but plots of land are owned and worked by individuals. Moshavim shitufiyim are economic organizations that combine the communal nature of kibbutzim with the more private living arrangements of the moshavim.

In addition to laying claim to territory for Israel, kibbutzniks and other agricultural workers have helped to defend that territory during Israel's many wars with its Arab neighbors. In addition to taking up arms, their communities have served as communication and supply relays for the Israeli government and military. During the 1950s and 1960s, the Israel Defense Forces (IDF) group Nahal established kibbutzim in sensitive border areas. The distribution of kibbutzim continues to be a sensitive defense issue in Israel today.

Agriculture, and more specifically access to water, has had a dramatic impact on the military, diplomatic, and geostrategic policies of Middle Eastern countries. Water resources obviously serve as a prime target for military and terrorist sabotage because of their essential nature and short supply. The poisoning of wells has been perpetrated by both Arabs and Israelis during times of war. During the 1960s, the new Israeli NWC and its counterpart irrigation systems in various Arab nations were attacked because they were seen as extensions of national aggression. In January 1966, the first act of the Palestinian terrorist organization Fatah targeted the Israelis' NWC.

The 1967 Six-Day War vastly increased Israel's access to water, to the detriment of its Arab opponents. By occupying the West Bank, Israel denied Jordan about half of its agricultural land, including 70 percent of its fruit production, 40 percent of its vegetable production, and 25 percent of its grain production. Once in possession of the West Bank, the Israelis implemented measures to maintain tight control over the area's water, including the Jordan River. Approximately 95.5 percent of the area's water went to nourish Israeli agriculture, while only 4.5 percent remained in the West Bank. The Israeli government limited water access for Arabs living in the West Bank and prohibited them from digging wells without government permission.

Later, in 1982, Israel invaded Lebanon, ostensibly for national security reasons. To many observers, however, it was clear that the country had ulterior economic motives. Israel wished to secure the waters of the Litani River. Even when Israel was forced to withdraw from Lebanon, the Israelis were able to establish a security zone that allowed them to siphon off some of the Litani's waters. In fact, Israel's efforts to gain control over the region's limited water supply were so successful that by the early 1990s, about 55 percent of Israel's water came from occupied territories or other countries. Israel had vastly changed the region's landscape, rechanneling 50–75 percent of the Jordan River's waters.

Conflict over water is not, however, limited to fighting between Arabs and Israelis. The Arab nations of the Middle East, while more inclined to work together than with Israel, have often put national interests before multinational cooperation. In the early 1990s, for instance, Jordan accused Syria of attempting to channel 40 percent of the Yarmuk River's waters into the latter's national boundaries. Although control over water resources has often led to contentious struggles in the Middle East, it has also inspired numerous, although usually unsuccessful, attempts at cooperation. Initial cooperation proposals during the 1950s were hampered by military hostility between Israel and the Arab states and by the sensitive diplomatic issue of the recognition of Israel's sovereignty. During the 1978 Camp David Accords, Israel tried to negotiate a diversion of 1 percent of the Nile River's waters to the Negev, but this attempt ultimately failed because of opposition in Egypt. In 1987, Turkey's proposal for a so-called peace pipeline to divert its excess waters to the Middle East was blocked by several Arab states. During the early 1990s, with the end of the Cold War, the prospects for cooperation on water issues improved somewhat. For example, the October 1994 peace agreement between Israel and Jordan includes annexes to address both water and environmental issues.

Although still a politically charged subject, countries in the Middle East continue to tentatively explore multinational cooperation, including proposals to create regional pipelines and desalinization plants. In the future, Israel and the Arab states may also be required to collaborate to solve other environmental problems that affect agricultural production such as erosion, deforestation, desertification and pollution.

PAUL G. PIERPAOLI JR.

See also

Climate of the Middle East; Geography of the Middle East; Jordan River; Kibbutz Movement; Moshavim; Negev Desert; Water Rights and Resources

References

Keyder, Caglar, and Faruk Tabak. *Landholding and Commercial Agriculture in the Middle East.* Ithaca, NY: SUNY Press, 1991.

Mort, Jo-Ann, and Gary Brenner. *Our Hearts Invented a Place: Can Kibbutzim Survive in Today's Israel?* Ithaca, NY: Cornell University Press, 2003.

Salman, Edel, ed. *Agriculture in the Middle East: Challenged and Possibilities.* New York: Paragon House, 1990.

Agudat Israel Party

A minority political party in Israel that maintains an ultraorthodox viewpoint within the Israeli political spectrum. Agudat Israel (Union of Israel) has never elected more than a handful of representatives to the Knesset (Israeli parliament), but it has utilized its political power effectively, joining ruling coalitions on a regular basis for the passage of orthodox legislation. Despite its importance to ruling coalitions, Agudat Israel has never received more than 12.2 percent of the votes cast in a national election. The high point was reached in 1949, when the party held 16 Knesset seats. More typically, Agudat Israel has received less than 5 percent of votes cast nationwide, resulting in only a handful of seats.

Agudat Israel was founded in 1912 in Katowice, Poland. Under the guidance of the Council of Torah Sages, Agudat Israel directly opposed the World Zionist Organization (WZO) and the cause of Zionism in general. In part, this was due to events at the Tenth World Zionist Conference, where adherents of the Mizrahi orthodox Zionists proposed a resolution calling for the WZO to fund religious schools. When the resolution was defeated, many Mizrahi supporters rejected Zionism and created Agudat Israel. The heart of the movement soon shifted to Frankfurt, Germany, where the goals of the party coalesced into support of yeshivas (orthodox schools) and the creation of agricultural settlements in Palestine. Despite supporting the immigration of Jews to the Holy Land, Agudat Israel opposed the creation of a Jewish nation. Rather, the leadership of Agudat Israel argued that Jews comprise solely a religious community that should not be compromised or distracted by the formation of a secular state.

In the 1920s, Agudat Israel became vehemently anti-Zionist, refusing to cooperate even with religious Zionists. To many observers this stance seemed contradictory, as many argued that orthodox Judaism is inherently Zionist. However, the Council of Torah Sages argued that the pursuit of orthodoxy was the prime directive of the

organization and should not be diluted by secular pursuits. Certain pragmatic factions of Agudat Israel pushed for involvement in Palestine despite remaining opposed to the creation of a Zionist state. During the British Mandate period, Agudat Israel opted out of Knesset Israel, an organization that chose an Elected Assembly, which subsequently chose the National Council to serve as a local representative body under the mandate government.

Despite consistent opposition to the creation of a Zionist state, Agudat Israel entered an agreement with the Jewish Agency to receive 6.5 percent of the immigration permits issued under the British Mandate government in Palestine. This ensured that members of Agudat Israel would be present for the proclamation of the independent state of Israel on May 15, 1948. The party was included in the initial government founded by Prime Minister David Ben-Gurion, although it refused to accept any formal cabinet posts. The refusal of cabinet positions established a tradition of participating in the secular government without holding formal authoritative positions.

From 1948 until 1961, Agudat Israel joined an orthodox-based political coalition, the Torah Religious Front (TRF). This served to increase the number of orthodox representatives in the Knesset and allowed Agudat Israel to push for its primary political objectives. In addition to state funding for yeshivas, Agudat Israel and the TRF successfully pushed for orthodox legislation, including mandatory public observance of the Sabbath and formal dietary (kosher) laws. Furthermore, the TRF advocated that Israel's Law of Return would not define nonorthodox conversions as Jews. Beginning in 1961, the labor faction of the party was represented separately in the Knesset, remaining associated with the cabinet, while the main body departed the coalition led by Ben-Gurion in protest of the issue of female conscription.

Throughout its existence, Agudat Israel has been very socially conservative. It pushed for the government of Israel to rescind the right of women to vote, argued that no violator of the Sabbath should be permitted membership on the National Council, and demanded that the Torah be acknowledged as the supreme legal and spiritual authority in Israel.

Repeatedly throughout Agudat Israel's history, factions have split from the main body of the party, continually eroding its support. Most of the splits have occurred after compromises between the party and Zionist organizations. The most extreme factions of Agudat Israel continue to reject the existence of the State of Israel and believe that any political participation constitutes heresy. At the opposite end of the party's political spectrum, the workers' section has pushed for increased cooperation with the Israeli government.

In 1988, an internal division led to a formal schism within Agudat Israel. Rabbi Elazar Shach led a significant portion of the party's non-Hasidic members to form Degel HaTorah (Flag of Torah), a competing orthodox party. Despite the definitive split, the two organizations have often partnered together to maximize orthodox representation in the Knesset. In 1992, Agudat Israel, Degel HaTorah, and Moriah formed Yahadut HaTorah (United Torah Judaism), an electoral coalition that has split and re-formed repeatedly, most recently uniting for the 2006 elections of the Seventeenth Knesset.

Agudat Israel has continually pushed for the creation and expansion of yeshivas in Europe and Israel. These schools include Beis Yakov girls' schools and institutions dedicated to adult education in the orthodox tradition. Within Israel, the party has maintained an independent system of schools, called Hinnukh Atzmai, that are entirely separate from the public education system. Among the graduates of Agudat Israel's schools was Yigal Amir, who assassinated Yitzhak Rabin in 1995, citing his personal opposition to the 1993 Oslo Peace Accords.

Agudat Israel's ability to join diverse ruling coalitions, including cabinets under both Likud and Labor Party leadership, is in large part due to its intense focus on domestic issues. Agudat Israel remains flexible in its approach to security and foreign policy, a vestige of the original opposition to the establishment of the State of Israel. In the past two decades, increasing Palestinian terrorism has led Agudat Israel's leadership to adopt a more security-conscious stance, including support for the West Bank settler movement and endorsement of Prime Minister Ariel Sharon's 2005 unilateral disengagement from the Gaza Strip.

PAUL J. SPRINGER

See also

Ben-Gurion, David; Labor Party; Likud Party; Mizrahic Judaism; Oslo Accords; World Zionist Organization; Zionism

References

Beilin, Yossi. *Israel: A Concise Political History.* New York: St. Martin's, 1992.

Laqueur, Walter. *A History of Zionism: From the French Revolution to the Establishment of the State of Israel.* Reprint ed. New York: Schocken, 2003.

Peretz, Don. *The Government and Politics of Israel.* Boulder, CO: Westview, 1979.

Reich, Bernard. *A Brief History of Israel.* New York: Facts on File, 2005.

Air-to-Air Missiles

See Missiles, Air-to-Air

Air-to-Surface Missiles

See Missiles, Air-to-Surface

Aircraft, Bombers

Bomber aircraft played a relatively minor role in the Arab-Israeli wars. The combatants were close enough geographically that the long range of a bomber was not needed, and none of the combatants seriously envisioned a strategic bombing campaign. The principal role of airpower in the Arab-Israeli wars was tactical in nature (close air support and interdiction), for which multirole fighters were far more suitable than bombers. The combatants had limited financial resources and thus preferred less-expensive fighters to expensive bombers for this reason as well. The combatants depended on foreign suppliers—primarily the United States, France, the United Kingdom, and the Soviet Union—for their combat aircraft, and these suppliers were either unwilling or unable to provide significant bomber forces. Despite all these constraints, Egypt and Israel briefly operated a small number of surplus World War II bombers. After 1955, Egypt, Syria, and Iraq operated Soviet-built medium bomber aircraft.

Israeli Bombers

Boeing B-17G Flying Fortress. In 1948, Israel obtained three American Boeing B-17 Flying Fortresses via Czechoslovakia, despite an American embargo on arms shipments to the Middle East. The aircraft were in poor shape, lacking armor, turrets, guns, and oxygen equipment. Nevertheless, they raided Cairo and attacked Egyptian forces during the Israeli War of Independence (1948–1949). They flew only a few sorties during the 1956 Suez Crisis and were scrapped in 1958. From then on, Israel employed multirole fighters rather than bombers to conduct long-range strikes.

With four Wright Cyclone engines, B-17G maximum speed was 302 miles per hour (mph), with a 160-mph cruise speed and a 35,600-foot ceiling. Maximum ferry range was 3,400 miles, with operational radius usually 800 miles. The B-17G had a crew of 10 and was armed with 13 .50-caliber machine guns and up to 17,600 pounds of bombs. It weighed 36,135 pounds empty and 72,000 pounds loaded.

Egyptian Bombers

Short Stirling. The Short Stirling was Britain's first four-engine bomber and was employed after 1943 primarily as a glider tug and transport. In 1948 Egypt purchased 12 Mark V Stirlings, a variant that was purpose-built as an unarmed transport. Egypt installed makeshift bomb racks and employed them as bombers. During the Israeli War of Independence, the Stirlings attacked Israeli cities, airfields, and fielded forces, to no great effect. They were scrapped in 1951. With four Bristol Hercules engines, the Stirling's maximum speed was 280 mph, with a 233-mph cruise speed and an 18,000-foot ceiling. Maximum range was 3,000 miles as a transport, but operational radius as a bomber was around 600 miles. The Stirling Mark V had a crew of five and was unarmed. It weighed 43,500 pounds empty and 70,000 pounds loaded.

Handley Page Halifax. The Handley Page Halifax was a British four-engine bomber employed in World War II as a glider tug, troop transport, and electronic warfare aircraft as well as a bomber. Egypt bought nine Halifax A.IX transports in 1948 and converted them to bombers. They had little effect, if any, on Israel in the Israeli War of Independence. Some were destroyed on the ground during the Suez Crisis, and the remainder were scrapped afterward. Maximum speed was 304 mph, with a 200-mph cruising speed and a 25,000-foot ceiling. Maximum range was 2,710 miles as a transport (much

Israeli Air Force B-17 bombers, shown in flight in January 1950. (Israeli Government Press Office)

less as a bomber). The Halifax had a crew of 5 and could carry 16 passengers and 8,000 pounds of cargo. Armament consisted of two .50-caliber machine guns in a tail turret. The aircraft weighed 37,600 pounds empty and 65,000 pounds loaded.

Avro Lancaster. The Avro Lancaster was Britain's most famous four-engine World War II bomber and one of the best strategic bombers of the war. Egypt acquired nine demilitarized Mk. I models in 1948 and converted them to bombers. As with Egypt's Halifaxes, they achieved little success against Israeli targets during the Israeli War of Independence in 1948. Some were destroyed on the ground during the Suez Crisis, with the rest scrapped afterward. The Lancaster's maximum speed was 287 mph, with a 210-mph cruise speed and a 24,500-foot ceiling. Maximum range was 2,530 miles with a bomb load of 7,000 pounds. It had a crew of seven. Armament consisted of eight .303-caliber machine guns (two in the nose turret, two in the dorsal turret, and four in the tail turret) and up to 14,000 pounds of bombs. Exact armament and bomb loads of the Egyptian Lancasters are unclear. The Lancaster weighed 36,900 pounds empty and 70,000 pounds loaded.

In 1955, Egyptian president Gamal Abdel Nasser turned to the Soviet bloc to obtain advanced weapons. These included Ilyushin and Tupolev jet bombers, which were superior to anything in Israel's arsenal. However, Egypt never enjoyed air superiority over Israel, and as a result these bombers accomplished very little.

Ilyushin Il-28. The twin-engine, straight-wing Soviet medium Ilyushin IL-28 bomber used Soviet copies of the Rolls Royce Nene turbojet engine, which Britain sold to the Soviet Union in 1946. The engines were contained in nacelles under each wing. The Il-28 was sturdy and reliable, handled easily, and was equipped with both optical and radar bombsights. Egypt operated Il-28s from 1955 into the 1990s. Forty-eight arrived before and during the 1956 Suez Crisis and flew some sorties against Israeli airfields. At least 26 were destroyed, mainly on the ground, and another 16 flew to safety in Syria. The Soviets quickly replaced these losses, and by June 1967 Egypt had 40 Il-28s. The Israelis, determined to neutralize this threat to their cities, destroyed 29 Il-28s in their preemptive air strikes at the start of the Six-Day War on June 5, 1967. Again the Soviets replaced these losses, and by late 1968 Egypt had 40 Il-28s to use for hit-and-run attacks on Israeli forces in the Sinai. The aircraft played only a marginal role in the October 1973 Yom Kippur War. After 1973, they were mainly employed for reconnaissance and maritime patrol. The Il-28 had a maximum speed of 560 mph, and its ceiling was 40,350 feet. Maximum range was 1,490 miles. The Il-28 carried a crew of three and was armed with three 23-mm cannon (two in the nose and one in the tail) and 2,200 pounds of bombs carried internally. It weighed 28,420 pounds empty and 46,300 pounds loaded.

Tupolev Tu-16. Egypt received 30 Tupolev Tu-16 bombers in 1967, just in time for Israel to destroy them all on the ground in its preemptive air strike of June 5, 1967. The Soviets replaced 25 of them the following year. In the opening phase of the Yom Kippur War, Egyptian Tu-16KSR-2–11s launched 25 cruise missiles against Israeli targets in the Sinai, destroying some radar stations. Egypt operated Tu-16s into the late 1990s. The Tu-16 had a maximum speed of 615 mph and a 49,200-foot ceiling. Maximum range was 3,680 miles. The Tu-16 had four crew members. Armament consisted of six 23-mm cannon (two each in dorsal and ventral turrets and two in the tail turret). It also carried up to 24 250-pound or 18 500-pound bombs internally or 2 KSR-2 supersonic air-to-surface cruise missiles carried under the wing. The aircraft weighed 82,000 pounds empty and 167,100 pounds loaded.

Two Egyptian Air Force Tu-16 bombers, photographed on November 1, 1980. (U.S. Department of Defense)

Syrian Bombers

Ilyushin Il-28. Syria received 6 Il-28s from 1959 to 1967. It had trouble keeping them operational, and most crashed or were stripped for parts. Only 2 were available in June 1967, and they were destroyed at the outset of the Six-Day War. The Soviets did not replace them. Instead, the Soviets provided Syria with 200 MiG-21 fighters, 80 MiG-17 fighters, and 30 Su-7B fighter-bombers for use in the Yom Kippur War.

Iraqi Bombers

Ilyushin Il-28. Iraq received its first Il-28s in 1958 and had perhaps 10 in June 1967, but they played no role in the Six-Day War or the Yom Kippur War. They were used successfully against Kurdish rebels in the 1970s. Iraqi Il-28s struck Iranian air bases, rear-area targets, and industrial facilities during the Iran-Iraq War of 1980–1988. In the 1990s, derelict Il-28s were parked on runways as decoys to lure American air strikes away from more important targets.

Tupolev Tu-16. Iraq received eight Tu-16s in 1962, of which six remained operational by June 1967. Two bombed Israel on June 6, and one was shot down. Iraq received six more in 1972, but Iraqi Tu-16s did not participate in the Yom Kippur War. They were used against the Kurds in the 1970s. Against Iran in the 1980s, Tu-16s carried out long-range bombing strikes, cruise missile attacks, and electronic warfare. Iraq bought four H-6D bombers (a Chinese-

built Tu-16) equipped with C-601 antiship missiles in 1987. The U.S. Air Force destroyed three Iraqi Tu-16s on the ground in 1991, and the few remaining Tu-16s never flew again.

Tupolev Tu-22. This swept-wing supersonic Soviet bomber had two engines mounted on the rear fuselage on either side of the tail fin. Designed in 1954 and intended to replace the Tu-16, the Tupolev Tu-22 entered Soviet service in 1962. The Tu-22 was difficult to fly and maintain, and the aircraft had a history of frequent crashes. Iraq ordered 16 Tu-22s in 1973 and had received 10 Tu-22B bombers and 2 Tu-22U trainers by 1979. They were employed against the Kurds in 1974. They flew deep strikes against the Iranians in the

Estimated Combat Aircraft in Selected Middle Eastern and North African Countries (1972, 1982)

Country	1972	1982
Algeria	181	306
Egypt	768	429
Iran	160	90
Iraq	189	330
Israel	432	634
Jordan	50	94
Lebanon	18	8
Libya	22	555
Saudi Arabia	71	128
Syria	210	450

Aircraft Used by Israel and Various Arab Nations during the Arab-Israeli Wars

Name	Type	Chiefly Used by	First Developed in
Avro Anson Mk.I	reconnaissance	Egypt	Britain
Avro Lancaster	bomber	Egypt	Britain
De Havilland Dove	reconnaissance	Egypt	Britain
Fiat G.55	fighter	Egypt	Italy
Handley Page Halifax	bomber	Egypt	Britain
Macchi C.205	fighter	Egypt	Italy
Mikoyan-Gurevich MiG-15	fighter	Egypt	Soviet Union
Mikoyan-Gurevich MiG-17	fighter	Egypt	Soviet Union
Mikoyan-Gurevich MiG-19	fighter	Egypt	Soviet Union
Short Stirling	bomber	Egypt	Britain
De Havilland Vampire	fighter	Egypt, Iraq	Britain
Tupolev Tu-16	bomber	Egypt, Iraq	Soviet Union
Mikoyan-Gurevich MiG-21	fighter	Egypt, Syria	Soviet Union
Ilyushin Il-14	transport	Egypt, Syria, Iraq	Soviet Union
Ilyushin Il-28	bomber	Egypt, Syria, Iraq	Soviet Union
Tupolev Tu-22	bomber	Iraq	Soviet Union
Avia S-199	fighter	Israel	Czechoslovakia
Boeing 377 Stratocruiser	transport	Israel	United States
Boeing 707	transport	Israel	United States
Boeing B-17G Flying Fortress	bomber	Israel	United States
Dassault Mirage IIICJ	fighter	Israel	France
Dassault Mystère IVA	fighter	Israel	France
Dassault Ouragan	fighter	Israel	France
Dassault Super Mystère	fighter	Israel	France
De Havilland Mosquito	reconnaissance	Israel	Britain
Douglas C-47 Skytrain	transport	Israel	United States
General Dynamics F-16 Fighting Falcon	fighter	Israel	United States
Israel Aircraft Industries Arava	transport	Israel	Israel
Israel Aircraft Industries Kfir	fighter	Israel	Israel
Israel Aircraft Industries Nesher	fighter	Israel	Israel
Lockheed C-130 Hercules	transport	Israel	United States
McDonnell Douglas F-15 Eagle	fighter	Israel	United States
McDonnell Douglas Phantom II	fighter	Israel	United States
Noorduyn Norseman	transport	Israel	Canada
Nord N.2501 Noratlas	transport	Israel	France
North American P-51D Mustang	fighter	Israel	United States
Sud Aviation Vautour II	fighter	Israel	France
Gloster Meteor	fighter	Israel, Egypt	Britain
Supermarine Spitfire	fighter	Israel, Egypt	Britain
Hawker Hunter	fighter	Jordan, Iraq	Britain
Mikoyan-Gurevich MiG-23	fighter	Syria	Soviet Union
Yakovlev Yak-40	transport	Syria	Soviet Union
Antonov An-12	transport	Syria, Iraq	Soviet Union

1980s, but at least 7 aircraft were lost. In the 1980s, Iraq received 4 Tu-22K bombers equipped with Kh-22 air-to-surface missiles. They proved ineffective, and 3 were lost in combat. Coalition forces destroyed the surviving Iraqi Tu-22s during the Persian Gulf War of 1991. The Tu-22B had a crew of three. Cruise speed was 516 mph, and maximum speed was 1,000 mph. Its combat radius was 1,522 miles unrefueled, and its ceiling was 48,228 feet. Its armament consisted of one 23-mm cannon in the tail and up to 20,000 pounds of bombs or one Kh-22 missile. The Tu-22 weighed 86,000 pounds empty and 188,495 pounds loaded.

British Bombers during the Suez Crisis

British bombers were major participants in the 1956 Suez Crisis. Egypt's Soviet-built Mikoyan-Gurevich MiG-15 jet fighters were intrinsically superior to British, French, and Israeli fighters, although Egyptian pilots were decidedly lacking in training and experience. The British thus decided to eliminate the Egyptian Air Force with surprise high-altitude bombing raids. The Royal Air Force based 61 Canberra bombers on Cyprus and 24 Canberra and 24 Valiant bombers on Malta. On the night of November 1, 1956, these bombers attacked Egyptian air bases but did little damage. Low-altitude fighter and fighter-bomber attacks the following morning proved far more effective, essentially eliminating the Egyptian Air Force.

English Electric Canberra. The Canberra was designed in 1944 and first flew in 1949. With two Rolls Royce Avon engines in nacelles on the large wings, the Canberra set many altitude and speed records in the 1950s. Unarmed reconnaissance Canberras flew a number of long-endurance covert missions over the Soviet Union in the 1950s, relying on high altitude for protection from Soviet fighters. During the Suez Crisis, the British deployed the B.Mk.2 and PR.Mk.7 variants on Cyprus and the B.Mk.6 variant on Malta. The B.Mk.2 was the initial production version, and the B.Mk.6 had longer range and more powerful engines. The unarmed PR.Mk.9 had a stretched fuselage, increased wingspan, and other improvements for high-altitude photo reconnaissance. The B.Mk.6 had a 580-mph maximum speed, a 48,000-foot ceiling, and an 810-mile combat range. It carried three crew members. Its armament consisted of up to 6,000 pounds of bombs internally carried, up to 2,000 pounds of externally carried stores, and an optional gun pack in the bomb bay with four 20-mm cannon. The bomber weighed 21,650 pounds empty and 55,000 pounds loaded. In American service the Canberra was designated the B-57 and served in Vietnam.

Vickers Valiant. The Valiant was one of three British post–World War II nuclear-capable jet bombers. The Vickers Valiant was designed in 1948 and entered service in 1955. With two Rolls Royce Avon engines in each wing root, Valiants had a very clean appearance. Vickers built 107 Valiants in bomber, tanker, and reconnaissance variants. In light of the threat from Soviet air-defense missiles, Valiants began practicing low-level flight in 1962. Unfortunately, this caused excessive metal fatigue, and Valiants had to be withdrawn from service in 1965. During the Suez Crisis, Valiants attacked seven Egyptian airfields but damaged only three, a disappointing performance that partly resulted from inexperienced crews. Valiants had a 567-mph maximum speed and a 54,000-foot ceiling. Maximum range was 4,500 miles with external tanks. The aircraft had a crew of five. Armament consisted of a single 10,000-pound nuclear weapon or 21 1,000-pound conventional bombs carried internally. The aircraft had no defensive armament. The Valiant weighed 75,880 pounds empty and 175,000 pounds loaded.

JAMES D. PERRY

See also

Attrition, War of; Egypt, Armed Forces; Iraq, Armed Forces; Israel Defense Forces; Israeli War of Independence, Overview; Six-Day War; Suez Crisis; Yom Kippur War

References

Angelucci, Enzo. *The Rand McNally Encyclopedia of Military Aircraft, 1914–1980.* New York: Military Press, 1983.

Fredriksen, John C. *International Warbirds: An Illustrated Guide to World Military Aircraft, 1914–2000.* Santa Barbara, CA: ABC-CLIO, 2001.

———. *Warbirds: An Illustrated Guide to U.S. Military Aircraft, 1915–2000.* Santa Barbara, CA: ABC-CLIO, 1999.

Nordeen, Lon O. *Air Warfare in the Missile Age.* Washington, DC: Smithsonian Institution Press, 1985.

Aircraft, Electronic Warfare

The advent of radar in World War II gave rise to a new type of warfare centered on dominating the electronic spectrum. Known as electronic warfare (EW), it was initially focused on defeating enemy radars or protecting one's own radars from enemy electronic attack. Since the Korean War (1950–1953), EW has come to encompass any measures or activities intended to ensure one's own use of the electronic spectrum while denying it to an enemy. The introduction of missiles in warfare has made defeating the missiles' guidance components (radars and data links) an increasingly important aspect of EW.

Electronic warfare had little application during the early Arab-Israeli wars, but the 1967 Six-Day War saw Israel conducting extensive prewar tactical electronic surveillance to map out the Arab nations' radar coverage and their air defense systems' electronic order of battle. The primary platform for that surveillance was a specially modified Sud Aviation Vautour jet fighter, which previously had been relegated to a ground-attack role. The intelligence they gathered proved critical to Israel's surprise air strikes that opened the fighting of that war. However, Egypt, the primary victim of that opening-day attack, learned from the experience and was better prepared for the October 1973 Yom Kippur War.

Because air defense systems rely most heavily on the electronic spectrum, aircraft have become the most important assets in any EW operation. With their altitude extending the onboard electronic signals' reach, EW aircraft are the ideal platform. In addition to the Vautour aircraft employed so effectively in 1967, Israel also modified a pair of Rockwell Jet Commander aircraft for electronic reconnaissance. They were supplemented by American-made OV-1D and RV-1D reconnaissance aircraft. The Vautours remained in service until the 1973 war, by which point they were rapidly becoming obsolete against increasing Arab capabilities.

Prior to the 1973 Yom Kippur War, Israeli aircraft used low-level flight tactics to counter Arab surveillance and surface-to-air missiles (SAMs), which were optimized against medium- to high-level aircraft. EW aircraft only accompanied deep-strike targets or those going into the most heavily defended areas. However, Egypt's employment of the mobile SA-6 SAM and ZSU-23/4 AAA systems, with their robust electronic countermeasures (ECM) capabilities, made that an expensive tactic. Israel added the McDonnell-Douglas F-4G Phantom Wild Weasel EW aircraft to its inventory after the 1973 war. Fortunately for the Israelis, Egypt's airborne EW assets in that war were limited to a handful of modified Mil Mi-6 Hook helicopters that were capable only of limited standoff electronic surveillance.

The 1980–1988 Iran-Iraq War saw very little EW because neither side had extensive air defense systems and neither air force conducted a significant aerial campaign. However, the American-led EW effort during operations DESERT STORM (Iraq, 1991), ENDURING FREEDOM (Afghanistan, 2001) and IRAQI FREEDOM (Iraq, 2003) rendered enemy air defense and command and control systems ineffective. The primary jamming platforms in those operations were the U.S. Air Force's General Dynamics EF-111 Raven and the U.S. Navy and U.S. Marine Corps Grumman EA-6B Prowler electronic jamming aircraft. The EF-111 and EA-6B (based on heavily modified F-111 and A-6 airframes, respectively) carried the same EW equipment and variable electronic sensor and jamming pods. F-4G Wild Weasels complemented the EW mission. The United

Israeli Air Force Vautour jet aircraft, photographed on August 12, 1958. The Vautour jet fighter was modified in the 1960s for electronic surveillance missions. (David Eldan/Israeli Government Press Office)

States also operated RC-135 and EP-3 electronic surveillance aircraft to map out enemy radars and command and control systems. Enemy radars and command headquarters were destroyed only when absolutely required. Instead, the Americans left those systems operational so they could be exploited for intelligence purposes and used jamming and other EW techniques to deny the enemy's use of those systems at times and locations as needed to facilitate operations. In effect, coalition forces controlled the electronic spectrum during these conflicts and determined whose military forces could use it and when. Their success coined a new phrase, "information dominance," to characterize superiority in the movement and use of battlefield information.

CARL OTIS SCHUSTER

See also

Aircraft, Bombers; Aircraft, Fighters; Aircraft, Helicopters; Aircraft, Reconnaissance; Six-Day War; Yom Kippur War

References

Aloni, Shlomo. *Arab-Israeli Air Wars, 1947–1982*. London: Osprey, 2001.

Church, Jimmy H. *The Battle for Air Superiority during the 1973 Arab-Israeli War*. Quantico, VA: Marine Corps Command and Staff College, 1983.

Finlan, Alastair. *The Gulf War, 1991*. Oxford, UK: Osprey, 2004.

Gunston, Bill. *An Illustrated Guide to Spy Planes & Electronic Warfare Aircraft*. New York: Arco, 1983.

Hammel, Eric. *Six Days in June: How Israel Won the 1967 Arab-Israeli War*. New York: Scribner, 1992.

Hewson, Robert. *Jane's Air-Launched Weapons, 2001*. London: Jane's, 2002.

Jackson, Paul, et al. *Jane's All the World's Aircraft, 2005–06*. London: Jane's, 2005.

Jane, Fred T. *Jane's All the World's Aircraft, 1974–75*. London: Jane's, 1974.

Knight, Michael, ed. *Operation Iraqi Freedom and the New Iraq*. Washington, DC: Washington Institute for Near East Policy, 2004.

Nordeen, Lon, and David Nicolle. *Phoenix over the Nile: A History of Egyptian Air Power, 1932–1994*. Washington, DC: Smithsonian Books, 1996.

Olsen, John. *Strategic Air Power in Desert Storm*. London: Frank Cass, 2003.

Tripp, Robert. *Lessons Learned from Operation Enduring Freedom*. Santa Monica, CA: RAND, 2004.

Aircraft, Fighters

Fighter aircraft and their ability to secure air superiority were of decisive importance to the course and outcome of the Arab-Israeli wars. Initially, Israel and the Arabs employed surplus World War II fighters, but both sides quickly sought modern jets. Israel bought fighters mainly from Britain and France until 1967 and then afterward from the United States. The Arabs principally obtained their fighters from Britain until 1955 and thereafter from the Soviet Union.

Arab and Israeli fighter technology largely depended on the willingness of external suppliers—Britain, France, the United States, and the Soviet Union—to provide their clients with the latest systems. Airframes, engines, avionics, sensors, and weapons improved continuously over the course of the Arab-Israeli wars. Initial jet aircraft such as the Meteor, Ouragan, and Vampire were straight-winged aircraft aerodynamically similar to propeller-driven fighters. They operated at high subsonic speeds with optical gunsights and mechanical control systems. The next development was the swept-wing transonic fighter—such as the MiG-15/17, Mystère, and Hunter—that operated close to the speed of sound. These were quickly superseded by fighters such as the Super Mystère and MiG-19 that were capable of level supersonic flight. Next appeared the truly supersonic fighters, such as the Mirage III and the MiG-21, typically armed with air-to-air missiles. Then, supersonic fighters such as the Phantom, Mirage V, MiG-23, and the later model MiG-21 appeared with greatly improved avionics, sensors, heads-up displays, and a wide range of air-to-air and air-to-surface munitions. The final generation consisted of agile supersonic fighters such as the F-15 and F-16, which were capable of both great speed and high maneuverability. These aircraft had advanced radars and flight controls and employed diverse precision air-to-surface weapons.

Fighter technology, though not unimportant, was less critical to Israeli success in air combat than superior leadership, organization, training, and individual initiative. Israeli pilots continuously practiced their close-quarters air-to-air combat skills (dogfighting), and that training repeatedly proved its value.

Israeli Fighters

During the 1948 War of Independence, an international arms embargo forced Israel to obtain aircraft surreptitiously. Israel procured a mix of surplus propeller-driven World War II aircraft, primarily of British and American origin.

Supermarine Spitfire. The Supermarine Spitfire was the most famous British fighter of World War II. More than 20,000 Spitfires were manufactured in 24 variants, or Marks. Israel obtained 50 Spitfires from Czechoslovakia in 1948 and another 30 from Italy in 1953. All were retired in 1955. Israel chiefly used the Spitfire LF Mark IX, which was modified for low-altitude work. Spitfires were maneuverable and easy to fly but were limited in range and thus most effective as defensive interceptors. Another advantage was that many early Israeli pilots were Royal Air Force veterans with prior Spitfire experience. The LF Mark IX was powered by a Rolls Royce Merlin 66 engine that produced a maximum speed of 407 miles per hour (mph). It had a ceiling of 42,500 feet. Range was 434 miles on internal fuel. Armament consisted of two 20-mm cannon,

Two Israeli Air Force F-15D Eagle aircraft, photographed on August 25, 2004. (U.S. Department of Defense)

two .50-caliber machine guns, and up to 1,000 pounds of bombs. It weighed 5,634 pounds empty and 9,500 pounds loaded.

North American P-51D Mustang. The Mustang was the best U.S. fighter of World War II. Early model P-51s were underpowered, but the P-51D achieved great success using Rolls Royce Merlin 61 engines built under license in the United States as the Packard V-1650. The P-51D's bubble canopy gave the pilot excellent all-round visibility. With their long range, high speed, and high ceiling, Mustangs were suitable for reconnaissance work but also had sufficiently heavy payload for ground-attack missions. Israel obtained 30 Mustangs from the United States during 1948–1953, 25 from Sweden in 1952, and 30 from Italy in 1954. All were retired in 1957. P-51Ds had a maximum speed of 437 mph and a ceiling of 41,900 feet. Range was 1,650 miles with external tanks. Armament consisted of six .50-caliber machine guns and up to 2,000 pounds of bombs. The P-51D weighed 7,635 pounds empty and 12,100 pounds loaded.

Avia S-199. The Czechoslovakian Avia S-199 was built in the former German Messerschmitt factory in Prague. The Czechs lacked access to Daimler-Benz engines, and thus the S-199s combined Bf-109G airframes with Junkers Jumo 211F engines. The aircraft was very difficult to fly, particularly on takeoff and landing, and had poor visibility to the rear. Israel used 25 S-199s from 1948 to 1949, and they played a critical role in defending the Jewish state against early Arab air raids. S-199s had a maximum speed of 368 mph and a ceiling of 28,500 feet. Range was 530 miles on internal fuel. Armament consisted of two 20-mm cannon and two 13-mm machine guns. The airplane weighed 6,305 pounds empty and 8,236 pounds loaded.

Fighters developed rapidly after 1945, and Israel needed jets to counter its enemies. Although Israel's first jets were British Gloster Meteors, France supplied most of Israel's jets until 1967. During the 1956 Suez Crisis, Israel's jet fighter force consisted of 16 Meteors, 22 Dassault Ouragans, and 16 Dassault Mystère IVAs. Israel still operated 29 P-51Ds for ground-attack missions.

Gloster Meteor. Britain's first operational jet fighter, the straight-winged Meteor, was the only Allied jet aircraft to fly in combat in World War II. Israel acquired 34 Meteors: 11 F.8 interceptors in 1952, 10 T.7 trainers from 1953 to 1957, 7 FR.9 reconnaissance aircraft in 1954, and 6 NF.13 night fighters in 1956. Israeli Meteors served only briefly as air superiority fighters because they were no match for Egypt's faster and more maneuverable MiG-15s. Israeli Meteors provided ground support during the Suez Crisis and then served as trainers until they were retired in 1964. The F.8, powered with twin Derwent 8 engines, had a maximum speed of 598 mph and a ceiling of 43,000 feet. Range was 600 miles on internal fuel. Armament consisted of four 20-mm cannon and two 1,000-pound bombs or eight rockets. The aircraft weighed 10,684 pounds empty and 15,700 pounds loaded. The FR.9 was an F.8 with an extended nose to house a camera. The T.7 was an unarmed two-seat training variant of the F.4 interceptor (discussed below under Egyptian fighters). The NF.13, a two-seat night fighter, was a stretched ver-

sion of the T.7, equipped with SCR-720 radar and modified for tropical operation. It was armed with four 20-mm cannon. The NF.13 had a maximum speed of 541 mph, a 43,000-foot ceiling, and a 950-mile range on internal fuel. It weighed 19,788 pounds fully loaded.

Dassault Ouragan. In 1949, the Ouragan became France's first jet fighter to enter series production. The Ouragans had straight wings and employed the used Rolls Royce Nene jet engine. Israel bought 75 Ouragans and operated them from 1955 to 1973. Like the Meteor, the Ouragan was slower and less maneuverable than the MiG-15, but Israeli Ouragan pilots nevertheless did well in air combat. After 1956, Ouragans were largely used for ground attack and could survive considerable damage from enemy ground fire. The Ouragan had a maximum speed of 503 mph, a ceiling of 49,000 feet, and a 520-mile range with wing-tip tanks. Armament consisted of 4 20-mm cannon and 2 1,000-pound bombs or 16 rockets. It weighed 10,582 pounds empty and 15,322 pounds loaded.

Dassault Mystère IVA. This French swept-wing fighter entered series production in 1954. Israel bought 60 Mystère IVAs in 1956 and operated them until 1971. The Mystère, which had power-assisted controls, was more agile than the MiG-15, which did not. Mystères proved extremely robust and survivable during ground-attack missions, which was their principal role in the 1960s. With a Hispano-Suiza Verdon 30 engine, the Mystère IVA had a 662-mph maximum speed and a 49,200-foot ceiling. Range was 570 miles on internal fuel and 1,417 miles with external tanks. Armament consisted of two 30-mm cannon and usually two drop tanks plus two 1,000-pound bombs or two 68-mm rocket packs. The aircraft weighed 12,919 pounds empty and 18,100 pounds loaded.

Following the Suez Crisis, Israel procured additional French jets in order to match Arab procurement of Soviet fighters. By the time of the June 1967 Six-Day War, Israel had 72 Mirage IIICJs, 18 Super Mystères, 50 Mystère IVAs, 40 Ouragans, and 25 Vautour IIs. These aircraft executed a devastating low-altitude strike that annihilated the Arab air forces in the opening hours of the war.

Sud Aviation Vautour II. This twin-engine multirole fighter entered French service in 1957. Israel operated 31 Vautours from 1958 to 1971: 19 single-seat interceptors, 4 two-seat reconnaissance aircraft, and 8 two-seat night fighters. Somewhat underpowered and difficult to fly, Israeli Vautours nevertheless performed well in air combat. They were valued for their long range and heavy payload. Vautour IIA interceptors had a 721-mph maximum speed and a 50,000-foot ceiling. Range was 3,375 miles on external tanks. Armament consisted of 4 30-mm cannon and up to 14 250-kilogram (kg) bombs (6 internally and 8 externally). The aircraft weighed 32,850 pounds empty and 45,635 pounds loaded.

Dassault Super Mystère. France's first aircraft capable of level supersonic flight, the Super Mystère entered production in 1957. Israel operated 36 from 1958 to 1976, mainly in an attack role after 1960. Super Mystères had flying qualities similar to the MiG-17, and when these aircraft met, pilot skill usually decided the issue. In Israeli hands, Super Mystères could sometimes beat the MiG-21, which was much faster but could not turn as tightly. Super Mystères, with Rolls Royce Avon engines, had a maximum speed of 745 mph and a 55,750-foot ceiling. Range was 1,112 miles on external tanks. Armament consisted of two 30-mm cannon and two 1,000-pound bombs. The aircraft weighed 15,282 pounds empty and 20,558 pounds loaded.

Dassault Mirage IIICJ. This low-cost delta-wing supersonic French fighter first flew in 1960 and was widely exported. Israel bought 72 Mirage IIICJ interceptors, 2 photo-reconnaissance models, and 4 trainers. They operated from 1961 until 1980 and were the first Israeli fighters equipped with air-to-air missiles, although pilots tended to prefer the more reliable and effective cannon. Their speed, acceleration, and climb rate were slightly inferior to the MiG-21. Nevertheless, Israeli Mirage pilots achieved highly favorable kill ratios against the MiG-21. The Mirage IIICJ had a maximum speed of 1,386 mph, a 59,055-foot ceiling, and a 745-mile range on internal fuel. Armament included two 30-mm cannon and up to 5,000 pounds of external stores on five pylons. The aircraft weighed 13,055 pounds empty and 21,444 pounds loaded.

After June 1967, the United States became Israel's primary supplier of combat aircraft. In 1969, Israel received its first McDonnell Phantom fighters and Douglas Skyhawk attack jets. American electronics countermeasures equipment, jammers, chaff dispensers, and AIM-9 Sidewinder missiles enhanced Israeli fighter survivability and lethality. Israel began the Yom Kippur War with 127 Phantoms, 162 Skyhawks, 35 Mirage IIICs, 40 Israeli-built Neshers, and 15 Super Mystères.

McDonnell Douglas Phantom II. This large two-seat supersonic fighter had a powerful radar for engagements beyond visual range. Originally designed for the U.S. Navy but later adopted by the U.S. Air Force, the Phantom first flew in 1958. Israel received 204 F-4Es after 1969, retiring them in 2003. The Phantoms saw heavy combat from 1969 to 1973, when they were especially prized for their ability to conduct long-range strikes and suppress enemy air defenses. Phantoms also achieved more than 70 air-to-air victories, primarily against MiG-21s. Israeli Phantoms were extensively modified over time, including structural upgrades, new avionics, new electronic countermeasures (ECMs), and a new radar suite in the mid-1980s. The F-4E had a 1,472-mph maximum speed and a 54,400-foot ceiling. The two General Electric J79 engines had an unfortunate tendency to emit highly visible smoke trails. Range was 1,613 miles with external tanks. Armament consisted of one 20-mm cannon and up to 16,000 pounds of bombs, rockets, and/or air-to-air missiles. The F-4E weighed 30,328 pounds empty and 61,795 pounds loaded.

Israel Aircraft Industries Nesher. This unlicensed Israeli copy of the delta-winged French Mirage V first flew in 1969 and was retired in 1981. Israel built 51 Nesher fighters plus 10 trainers. They achieved more than 70 confirmed air-to-air victories in 1973. The Nesher had a maximum speed of 1,451, a 58,000-foot ceiling, and a 777-mile range with external tanks. Armament consisted of two 30-mm cannon and up to 8,818 pounds of bombs, rockets, and air-to-air missiles mounted on seven pylons. The aircraft weighed 15,763 pounds empty and 30,200 pounds loaded.

After the Yom Kippur War, Israel continued building modified Mirages and received American F-15 and F-16 fighters. These aircraft skirmished with Syrian fighters over Lebanon and conducted long-range strikes against Israel's enemies.

Israel Aircraft Industries Kfir. This was a Mirage/Nesher airframe with improved aerodynamics and a J79 engine. First introduced in 1974, Kfirs were improved incrementally until their retirement in 1999. Their primary role from 1976 onward was ground attack, although they did achieve one air-to-air victory over Lebanon. Israel built 27 Kfir C.1 models and 185 C.2 models. Israel fielded the C.7 (which was a C.2 with improved strike capabilities) in the late 1980s. Kfirs had a 1,516-mph maximum speed, a 58,000-foot ceiling, and a 548-mile range. Armament consisted of two 30-mm cannon and up to 13,415 pounds of bombs, rockets, and air-to-air missiles on seven pylons (nine on the C.7). The aircraft weighed 16,072 pounds empty and 36,376 pounds loaded.

McDonnell Douglas F-15 Eagle. Israel began receiving this U.S.-built fighter in 1976. The F-15 had a powerful air-search radar and twin Pratt & Whitney F100 engines. With a high thrust-to-weight ratio and low wing loading, F-15s had outstanding acceleration, climb rate, and agility. Superior radars and good cockpit visibility allowed F-15 pilots to detect enemy aircraft and deliver undetected attacks. Israel acquired 80 F-15s: 23 F-15As and 2 F-15Bs in 1976, 9 F-15Cs and 6 F-15Ds in 1981, 9 F-15Cs and 2 F-15Ds in 1984, 18 F-15As and 6 F-15Bs in 1991–1992, and 5 F-15Ds in 1992. Furthermore, Israel received 25 F-15I variants of the F-15E Strike Eagle in 1993. The F-15 A and C are single-seat models, and the B, D, and E are two-seat models. Vastly superior to Syrian MiG-21s and MiG-23s in every respect, Israeli F-15s shot down some 58 Syrian aircraft from 1979 to 1982 with no friendly losses. The Eagle has a 1,650-mph maximum speed and a 65,000-foot ceiling. Range on an interception mission is 1,222 miles with external tanks. Typical armament includes one 20-mm cannon, four AIM-7 Sparrow and four AIM-9 Sidewinder missiles, and 15,000 pounds of external ordnance. Empty weight is 28,600 pounds, and loaded weight is 54,400 pounds.

General Dynamics F-16 Fighting Falcon. This single-seat, lightweight, multirole fighter entered U.S. service in 1979. Widely exported, the F-16 has a high thrust-to-weight ratio and low wing loading. The F-16 is extremely fast and agile, and its bubble canopy allows excellent visibility. The F-16 has fly-by-wire controls and a reclined seat to reduce the impact of high G forces. Israel acquired 255 F-16s: 67 F-16As and 8 F-16Bs in 1980–1981, 45 F-16Cs and 24 F-16Ds in 1987–1988, 30 F-16Cs and 30 F-16Ds in 1991–1993, and 36 F-16As and 15 F-16Bs in 1994. In 1999 and 2001, Israel also ordered 102 F-16I aircraft that are currently being delivered.

Clearly superior to Syrian MiG-21s and MiG-23s in every respect, Israeli F-16s shot down 53 Syrian aircraft during 1981–1982 with no friendly losses. With a single Pratt & Whitney F100 engine, the F-16 has a 1,500-mph maximum speed, a 50,000-foot ceiling, and an 851-mile range. The aircraft carries two AIM-9 missiles, two 2,000-pound bombs, and two 1,000-gallon fuel tanks. Armament includes one 20-mm cannon and 20,450 pounds of external ordnance on nine pylons. Empty weight is 19,100 pounds, and loaded weight is 37,500 pounds.

Egyptian Fighters

Egypt began the 1948 war flying surplus World War II British aircraft and obtained additional aircraft after the war began, including surplus Italian wartime fighters. Egypt's seemingly large inventory masked serious problems keeping aircraft operational, problems that persisted throughout the Arab-Israeli wars.

Supermarine Spitfire. Egypt operated 26 Mark V Spitfires from 1943 to 1949 and 38 Mark IX models (described above) from 1946 to 1955. With a Merlin 45 engine, the Mark V had a maximum speed of 378 mph and a ceiling of 37,000 feet. Range was 470 miles on internal fuel. Armament consisted of two 20-mm cannon, four .303-caliber machine guns, and one 500-pound bomb. The aircraft weighed 5,100 pounds empty and 6,785 pounds loaded.

Macchi C.205. This excellent Italian fighter, comparable to the P-51, entered service in mid-1943 and was produced in small numbers before Italy surrendered. Egypt operated 42 C.205s from 1948 to 1952. A Daimler-Benz DB 605 engine powered the C.205, which had a maximum speed of 400 mph and a ceiling of 37,650 feet. Range was 530 miles on internal fuel. Armament consisted of two 20-mm cannon and two 12.7-mm machine guns. The aircraft weighed 5,690 pounds empty and 7,513 pounds loaded.

Fiat G.55. This was another fine Italian fighter that entered service in small numbers in 1943. Designed to combat Allied bombers, the G.55 had a large wing area for high-altitude performance and heavy armament. Egypt operated 30 G.55s from 1948 to 1955. With a Daimler-Benz DB 605 engine, the G.55 had a maximum speed of 385 mph and a ceiling of 41,830 feet. Range was 746 miles on internal fuel and 1,025 miles with external tanks. Armament consisted of three 20-mm cannon and two 12.7-mm machine guns. It weighed 5,798 pounds empty and 7,760 pounds loaded.

In the early 1950s, Egypt transitioned from propeller-driven to jet fighters. Britain sold some Gloster Meteors and de Havilland Vampires to Egypt, but Britain and the United States refused to sell Egypt advanced weapons. Egyptian president Gamal Abdel Nasser then turned to the Soviet bloc. In 1955, the Soviets agreed to supply Egypt with Mikoyan-Gurevich fighters and Ilyushin bombers, which were superior to anything in Israel's arsenal. When the October 1956 Suez Crisis began, Egypt had 120 MiG-15s, some MiG-17s, 50 Il-28s, and 87 Meteors and Vampires. Egyptian MiG pilots were not yet fully trained, and the combined British, French, and Israeli Air Forces were superior in numbers and quality. Nasser decided

A formation of Egyptian and U.S. Navy aircraft fly over one of the Great Pyramids near Cairo. Unless indicated, all are Egyptian Air Force aircraft. From left to right are the F-4 Phantom, F-16 Falcon, Mirage 2000, U.S. Navy F-14 Tomcat, MiG-21 Fishbed, MiG-19, U.S. Navy A7D Corsair, and U.S. Navy A-6E Intruder. July 1988. (U.S. Department of Defense)

to withhold his pilots from combat, and as a result, his air force was largely destroyed on the ground.

Gloster Meteor. Egypt operated 12 F.4, 6 T.7, 12 F.8, and 6 NF.13 British Meteors. Egypt bought the F.4s and T.7s in 1949 and the F.8s and NF.13s in 1952. All were retired in 1958. (The T.7, F.8, and NF.13 are described above under Israeli fighters.) The F.4, powered with twin Derwent 5 engines, had a maximum speed of 580 mph and a ceiling of 40,000 feet. Range was 610 miles on internal fuel. Armament was four 20-mm cannon. The aircraft weighed 11,217 pounds empty and 14,545 pounds loaded.

De Havilland Vampire. The twin-boom de Havilland Vampire was Britain's second operational jet fighter. Simple and cheap, the Vampires were popular exports. They were agile and easy to fly, but the Goblin engine provided insufficient power to climb quickly and perform well at altitude. Egypt bought 108 Vampires starting in 1949 and retired them in 1958. Egypt's FB.52 models had a strengthened airframe for ground-attack duties. The FB.52 had a 482-mph maximum speed and a 44,000-foot ceiling. Range was 1,145 miles on internal fuel. Armament consisted of four 20-mm cannon, two 500-pound bombs, and four 7.62-cm rockets. The Vampire weighed 7,253 pounds empty and 12,360 pounds loaded.

Mikoyan-Gurevich MiG-15. The swept-wing Soviet MiG-15 was still relatively new in 1956. It had excellent acceleration and rate of climb but poor control at high speed, poor stall characteristics, and an outmoded gunsight. Egypt operated the MiG-15 and MiG-15bis as well as the two-seat MiG-15UTI trainer from 1955 until 1982. A Soviet copy of the Rolls Royce Nene engine, provided by Britain to the Soviets in 1946, powered the MiG-15, which had a 688-mph maximum speed and a 50,900-foot ceiling. Range was 826 miles on internal fuel. The aircraft weighed 8,115 pounds empty and 11,861 pounds loaded. Originally designed to intercept American bombers, the MiG-15 was heavily armed with two 23-mm cannon and one 37-mm cannon. The MiG-15 (and its successors, the MiG-17 and MiG-19) rarely carried bombs.

Mikoyan-Gurevich MiG-17. This was essentially an improved MiG-15 with better wings and more power. Extremely agile and with excellent turning abilities, the MiG-17 proved a tricky adversary for ostensibly superior U.S. aircraft such as the F-100, F-105, and F-4 over North Vietnam in the 1960s. Egypt operated MiG-17F and PF models from 1956 to 1982. The MiG-17F had a 710-mph maximum speed and a 54,500-foot ceiling. Range was 913 miles on external tanks. Armament consisted of two 23-mm cannon and one 37-mm cannon. The MiG-17 weighed 8,664 pounds empty and 11,773 pounds loaded. The MiG-17PF incorporated an afterburner and radar.

Egypt's air force was destroyed during the Suez Crisis, but the Soviets quickly replaced it. In June 1967, Egypt had 120 MiG-21s, 80 MiG-19s, and 150 MiG-15/17s. Readiness was poor, however, with only about 60 percent of aircraft operational.

Mikoyan-Gurevich MiG-19. The MiG-19 was the first Soviet fighter capable of supersonic level flight. These aircraft were difficult to fly and prone to hydraulic failures and engine fires. During the Arab-Israeli wars, Egypt flew the MiG-19F, the MiG-19PF, the MiG-19S, and the MiG-19SF variants. Egypt received 80 in 1961 and another 50–60 after June 1967 (when they were apparently restricted to providing air defense over Egypt). Egypt bought 40 Chinese-built MiG-19 variants (the F-6) in the 1980s. The MiG-19S had a 903-mph maximum speed and a 56,145-foot ceiling. Range was 430 miles on internal fuel. Armament was three 30-mm cannon. The MiG-19 weighed 11,399 pounds empty and 19,470 pounds loaded.

Mikoyan-Gurevich MiG-21. First flown in 1955 and extensively exported, the delta-wing Soviet MiG-21 was superior to anything in Israel's inventory in 1967. High thrust-to-weight gave it good acceleration and rate of climb. The MiG-21 could not turn as tightly as the MiG-17, which some pilots preferred even though the MiG-17 was subsonic and the MiG-21 supersonic. Skillful Israeli pilots could beat the MiG-21 even while flying greatly inferior aircraft such as the Ouragan or Super Mystère. During the Arab-Israeli wars, Egypt operated hundreds of MiG-21F-13, MiG-21FL, MiG-21M, MiG-21MF, MiG-21PF, and MiG-21PFM interceptors as well as training and reconnaissance versions. Egypt bought 100 Chinese-built MiG-21F-13 fighters (the F-7) in the 1980s. The MiG-21F-13 had a 1,350-mph maximum speed and a 50,000-foot ceiling. Range was 808 miles on internal fuel. Armament consisted of one 20-mm cannon and two Vympel K-13 air-to-air missiles (a Soviet copy of the American AIM-9 Sidewinder). The MiG-21 weighed 10,979 pounds empty and 19,014 pounds loaded.

The MiG-21PF had a 1,350-mph maximum speed and a 50,000-foot ceiling. Range was 963 miles on internal fuel. Armament was the same as the MiG-21F-13. The aircraft weighed 11,587 pounds empty and 20,018 pounds loaded.

Most Egyptian aircraft were destroyed on the ground in June 1967, but again the Soviets replaced them. By October 1973, Egypt had 210 MiG-21s, 100 MiG-17s, and 110 bomber and ground-attack aircraft, although many were unserviceable. After the Yom Kippur War, Egypt and Israel reached a peace agreement and have not met in aerial combat since then.

Syrian Fighters

During the Israeli War of Independence (1948–1949), Syria operated no fighters per se. It bought several dozen Fiat G.55s, 10 Macchi C.205s, 20 Supermarine Spitfires, and 23 Gloster Meteors (T.7, F.8, FR.9, and NF.13 models) in the 1950s. These never saw combat. After Egypt obtained Soviet arms in 1955, Syria requested Soviet military assistance. Syria operated the MiG-15bis from 1955 to 1976 as well as the two-seat MiG-15UTI trainer. Syria began receiving the MiG-17F in 1957, the MiG-17PF in 1967, and the MiG-19S and MiG-19SF in 1963. Accidents and maintenance problems kept Syria's operational inventory low.

Syria flew hundreds of MiG-21 interceptors during the Arab-Israeli wars. It received the MiG-21MF, the MiG-21F-13, and the MiG-21PF in the 1960s; the MiG-21PFM in the 1970s; and the MiG-21SMT in 1983. It also operated training and reconnaissance versions. Syria still flies the MiG-21 today.

A MiG-23 fighter, which had been flown to Israel by a Syrian defector, photographed during the annual Israeli Air Force Day demonstration on July 19, 1990. (Nathan Alpert/Israeli Government Press Office)

Syria had 36 MiG-21s, 90 MiG-15/17s, and some MiG-19s at the beginning of the Six-Day War. Few aircraft were operational, and few pilots were well trained. At least 58 Syrian fighters were destroyed, mostly on the ground. The Soviets quickly replaced these losses. Syria began the Yom Kippur War with 200 MiG-21s and 120 MiG-17s and lost 179 aircraft during 19 days of intense combat. After the war Syria remained Israel's enemy, and again the Soviets replaced lost Syrian equipment. Prior to the final major clash with Israel in 1982, Syria received Soviet MiG-23 and MiG-25 fighters.

Mikoyan-Gurevich MiG-23. The swing-wing MiG-23 entered Soviet service in 1971. More than 4,000 were built, and the MiG-23 was widely exported. The MiG-23 had good acceleration, but export models often lacked radars and ECMs that enhanced survivability and effectiveness. Syria received the MiG-23MS in 1975, the MiG-23MLD in 1982, the MiG-23MF in 1986, and the MiG-23ML in 1988. Syria also operated ground-attack and training versions. The MiG-23MLD had a 1,550-mph maximum speed and a 60,695-foot ceiling. Range was 715 miles with six air-to-air missiles. Armament consisted of one 23-mm cannon and up to six air-to-air missiles or bombs. The MiG-23 weighed 21,153 pounds empty and 34,612 pounds loaded.

Mikoyan-Gurevich MiG-25. This high-speed, high-altitude Soviet fighter was originally designed in the late 1950s to intercept U.S. bombers. The aircraft handled poorly at low altitudes and had terrible dogfighting characteristics. The MiG-25 entered Soviet service in 1969. Syria received 30 MiG-25PD models in 1979 and also operated five trainers and eight reconnaissance models. The MiG-25PD had a 1,865-mph maximum speed and a 67,915-foot ceiling with combat payload. Range was 1,075 miles (subsonic) and 775 miles (supersonic) with internal fuel. Armament consisted of four air-to-air missiles (two radar-guided and two infrared-guided). The aircraft weighed 44,080 pounds empty and 80,952 pounds loaded.

Jordanian Fighters

Jordan created its air force in 1955. Its first fighters were 20 British Vampires (10 FB.9 and 7 F.52 fighters and 3 T.11 trainers), but they never saw combat. Before the Six-Day War, Jordan acquired British Hawker Hunters and had taken delivery of U.S. F-104 Lockheed Starfighters. However, the American F-104 pilots flew them to Turkey before the war began. After 1967, Jordan played no further direct role in Arab-Israeli air combat.

Hawker Hunter. The Hunter, Britain's first transonic fighter, first flew in 1951 and was widely exported to Middle Eastern air forces. Hunters had excellent flying qualities and were very agile and ruggedly built. From 1958 to 1968, Jordan bought 15 F.6 interceptors, 16 FGA.9, and 23 FGA.73 ground-attack aircraft; 2 FR.10 reconnaissance aircraft; and 3 T.66 trainers. It retired them all by 1975. In June 1967, Jordan's 22 Hunters were destroyed, after which Jordanian pilots flew Iraqi Hunters. The F.6, with Rolls Royce Avon engines, had a 623-mph maximum speed and a 51,500-foot ceiling. Range was 1,840 miles with external tanks. Armament consisted of four 30-mm cannon and up to 7,400 pounds of ordnance on four pylons. Hunters could carry four air-to-air missiles, but Jordan did not have these weapons in 1967. Hunters weighed 14,122 pounds empty and 17,750 pounds loaded.

Iraqi Fighters

The Iraqi Air Force played a minor role in the Yom Kippur War. Four British-built Hawker Fury fighters flew a few armed reconnaissance sorties over Israel from Syria before hostilities ended. In the 1950s, Iraq obtained British Vampires, 12 FB.52 fighters, and 10 T.55 trainers. All were retired in 1966. Iraq began buying British Hawker Hunters in 1958 and ultimately obtained 15 F.6 interceptors, 42 FGA.59/59A ground-attack aircraft, 5 T.69 trainers, and 4 FR.59B reconnaissance aircraft. (The FGA.59 and FR.59B were F.6 airframes modified for ground-attack and reconnaissance, respectively.)

In 1958, a postcoup Iraqi regime requested Soviet military assistance. As a result, Iraq received perhaps 20 MiG-15bis, 30 MiG-15UTI trainers, and 20 MiG-17F in 1958–1959. Iraq also received 50 MiG-19S in 1960. Starting in 1963, Iraq received MiG-21F-13s, MiG-21PFs, MiG-21PFMs, MiG-21MFs, and MiG-21UTIs, although exact numbers are unclear. The Iraqi Air Force frequently led coup attempts from 1958 to 1973, and the resulting purges of its pilots reduced Iraqi Air Force effectiveness. An Iraqi pilot with his MiG-21 defected to Israel in 1966, allowing the Israelis to analyze the aircraft's capabilities.

Iraq had 88 fighters when the Six-Day War began but suffered from severe readiness problems. Iraq's participation in the war was modest and involved a bombing raid launched against Israel. Hunters in western Iraq managed to shoot down 3 Israeli aircraft. In the 1973 Yom Kippur War, Iraq deployed 12 Hunters to Egypt along with 20 Hunters, 18 Sukhoi Su-7BMK attack aircraft, 18 MiG-21PF, and 11 MiG-21MF fighters to Syria. Iraq lost 21 aircraft but shot down 3 Israeli aircraft.

British and French Fighters during the Suez Crisis

The British and French armed forces directly participated in the Arab-Israeli wars during the 1956 Suez Crisis. Britain, France, and Israel invaded Egypt in order to overthrow President Nasser and reverse his nationalization of the Suez Canal. Britain and France stationed fighter forces on Cyprus and on aircraft carriers at sea as well as bombers on Cyprus and Malta in order to support the invasion. These aircraft quickly destroyed the Egyptian Air Force and supported Anglo-French ground forces.

On Cyprus, Britain deployed 8 Gloster Meteor NF.13 and 24 Hawker Hunter F.5 fighters, similar to those described above (although the Hunter F.5 had a less powerful engine than the F.6). Britain also based 47 de Havilland FB.4 Venom fighters on Cyprus. The Royal Navy operated 50 Hawker Sea Hawks from the carriers HMS *Eagle,* HMS *Albion,* and HMS *Bulwark* and 28 de Havilland FAW.21 Sea Venoms aboard the *Eagle* and the *Albion.*

De Havilland Venom. Venoms resembled de Havilland Vampires, although Venoms had thinner wings and had wing fences and wingtip fuel tanks. Venoms also had more powerful engines, giving them a 640-mph maximum speed and a 45,000-foot ceiling. For all these improvements, Venoms were inferior to the MiG-15. Range and armament were similar to those of Vampires. Venoms weighed 8,100 pounds empty and 15,310 pounds loaded. Sea Venoms were the carrier-capable variant. At Suez, Venoms and Sea Venoms were chiefly employed for attack missions rather than aerial combat.

Hawker Sea Hawk. Britain's carrier-based Hawker Sea Hawk entered frontline service in 1953. In 1956, the aircraft was clearly obsolescent and chiefly flew surface attack missions. The Sea Hawk FGA.6 had a 560-mph maximum speed and a 44,500-foot ceiling. Range was 480 miles on internal fuel. Armament consisted of 4 20-mm cannon, 2 500-pound bombs, and 20 7.62-mm rockets. The aircraft weighed 9,728 pounds empty and 16,153 pounds loaded.

France based 60 American-built F-84F and 16 RF-84F fighters in Cyprus and 36 Mystère IVA and 18 F-84F fighters in Israel. France also deployed 36 American-built F4U-7 Corsairs aboard the aircraft carriers *Arromanches* and *Lafayette.*

Republic F-84F Thunderstreak. The U.S.-built Thunderstreak was an effort to improve the performance of the F-84 Thunderjet to match that of the F-86 Sabre. They were the first U.S. fighters designed to deliver tactical nuclear weapons. Many Thunderstreaks were exported to North Atlantic Treaty Organization (NATO) countries, including 355 to France. French F-84Fs were the only ones that ever flew in combat. The F-84F had a 685-mph maximum speed and a 44,450-foot ceiling. Range was 810 miles. Armament consisted of 6 .50-caliber machine guns, 24 rockets, and 6,000 pounds of bombs externally carried. It weighed 15,608 pounds empty and 21,200 pounds loaded.

Vought F4U-7 Corsair. The U.S.-built F4U-7 Corsair was a variant of the famous World War II U.S. Navy fighter. Vought delivered 94 to France in 1952–1953. (These were the last piston-engine fighters built in the United States.) French Corsairs flew ground-attack missions in Indochina and Algeria and at Suez. The Corsair had a 440-mph maximum speed and a 41,500-foot ceiling. Range was 1,120 miles. Armament consisted of 4 20-mm cannon and either 10 rockets, 1 1,000-pound bomb, or 2 500-pound bombs. The F4U-7 weighed 9,835 pounds empty and 17,600 pounds loaded.

Other Nations

The Soviet Union not only supplied vast quantities of equipment to the Arab states but also directly participated in combat during the War of Attrition. In 1970, Soviets manned Egyptian air defenses, and two regiments with 36 Soviet-piloted MiG-21MF interceptors each defended Egyptian airspace. The Israel Air Force tried to avoid combat with the Soviets for a time, but the Soviets began firing on Israeli aircraft. In response, in July 1970 the Israelis ambushed the Soviets and shot down 5 MiGs. Soviet pilots using MiG-25R reconnaissance aircraft based in Egypt flew high-altitude missions over Israeli-controlled territory in 1971, 1972, and 1973. Israel sought to intercept these fast aircraft without success.

Libya did not participate in the Arab-Israeli wars until after Muammar Qaddafi seized power in September 1969. Libya had only a handful of aircraft in 1969 but immediately ordered 110 Mirage V fighters (which had the same capabilities as the Israeli Nesher described above). Fifteen of these were two-seat trainers, and 10 were reconnaissance models. Libya received its first Mirages in 1971 and transferred 42 to the Egyptian Air Force. Thirty-eight Libyan Mirages were still operational during the Yom Kippur War and flew 495 sorties with Egyptian pilots. Nine were lost in combat and 5 to noncombat causes.

Algeria deployed two squadrons of MiG-21 fighters and a squadron of Su-7B fighter-bombers to Egypt in 1973. These aircraft were incorporated into Egyptian units. Morocco deployed a dozen American Northrop F-5A fighters to Egypt in mid-1973. These fighters defended Egypt and never engaged the Israelis. Pakistan sent 16 pilots to fly Egyptian aircraft, and North Korea sent 20 pilots.

JAMES D. PERRY

See also

Attrition, War of; Egypt, Armed Forces; Iraq, Armed Forces; Israel Defense Forces; Israeli War of Independence, Overview; Jordan, Armed Forces; Lebanon, Israeli Invasion of; Missiles, Surface-to-Air; Six-Day War; Suez Crisis; Syria, Armed Forces; Yom Kippur War

References

Angelucci, Enzo. *The Rand McNally Encyclopedia of Military Aircraft, 1914–1980.* New York: Military Press, 1983.

Fredriksen, John C. *International Warbirds: An Illustrated Guide to World Military Aircraft, 1914–2000.* Santa Barbara, CA: ABC-CLIO, 2001.

———. *Warbirds: An Illustrated Guide to U.S. Military Aircraft, 1915–2000.* Santa Barbara, CA: ABC-CLIO, 1999.

Green, William, and Gordon Swanborough. *The Complete Book of Fighters.* New York: Smithmark, 1994.

Nordeen, Lon O. *Air Warfare in the Missile Age.* Washington, DC: Smithsonian Institution Press, 1985.

Aircraft, Helicopters

Helicopters are aircraft powered by rotating horizontal blades and are commonly called rotary-wing aircraft to distinguish them from traditional fixed-wing airplanes. Although the concept of rotary aircraft can be traced back to the drawings of Leonardo da Vinci (1452–1519), the first functional models were not created until the 20th century and did not go into full-scale production until after World War II (1939–1945). In the Korean War (1950–1953), helicopters served in a variety of support roles, including reconnaissance, resupply, and battlefield medical evacuation.

During the Vietnam War (1957–1975), helicopters were employed as infantry assault vehicles, facilitating the deployment of lightly armed troops at high speed over intermediate distances. The Vietnam War also heralded the development of the attack helicopter, an aircraft designed for ground attack and aerial close-fire support. The Soviet Union made similar uses of helicopters during its invasion of Afghanistan (1979–1989).

Modern military helicopters are divided into three primary classes: transport, ground attack, and observation and command and control. Transport helicopters, such as the U.S. UH-1 Iroquois, CH-47 Chinook, and UH-60 Black Hawk or the Russian Mi-26 Halo, are primarily used to ferry troops to and from the battlefield. Although they may mount weapons, their armament serves primarily a defensive function. Attack helicopters are designed specifically to engage ground targets. The majority of their payload capacity is devoted to weapons, and they are designed for greater speed and maneuverability than transport helicopters. Many attack helicopters, such as the U.S. AH-64 Apache or the Russian Mi-24 Hind, have an antitank capability. Both are capable of engaging and destroying multiple armored vehicles with antitank rockets or missiles or specially designed Gatling guns.

Helicopters played only a very limited role in the first three decades of Arab-Israeli warfare. During the Israeli War of Independence (1948–1949), the helicopter was an emerging technology, not possessed in significant numbers by any of the belligerents. The Israel Defense Forces (IDF) began the war without a single combat aircraft, and the warplanes acquired during the fighting were of fixed-wing design. None of the Arab participants deployed helicopters in a combat capacity during this war. Likewise, during the 1956 Suez Crisis, helicopters were not used by the IDF or its Egyptian enemies in any attack or transport role.

During the June 1967 Six-Day War, helicopters started to play a role in IDF and Arab operational planning. When the Israeli Air Force launched a preemptive strike against Egyptian airfields beginning on June 5, most of Egypt's military helicopters were destroyed on the ground. Subsequent aerial attacks on Syrian, Jordanian, and Iraqi airfields similarly destroyed virtually all other Arab military helicopters. These attacks guaranteed that the IDF would enjoy air supremacy for the entire war. During the Six-Day War the IDF used helicopters primarily for reconnaissance and evacuation of wounded troops.

During the War of Attrition (1967–1970) between Israel and Egypt, helicopters became a major element of Israeli operations. Although no formal state of war existed between the two nations, the uneasy cease-fire declared in 1967 was punctured by a series of raids and artillery exchanges across the Suez Canal. Egyptian

An Israeli Air Force AH-64 Apache helicopter during an Independence Day demonstration on April 26, 1993. (Tsvika Israeli/Israeli Government Press Office)

artillery greatly outnumbered and generally outclassed the Israeli guns, and Egyptian shelling was typically more effective than Israeli counterbattery fire. Both sides occasionally mounted raids across the canal, sending troops in rubber dinghies to probe enemy forces for weaknesses.

On the night of October 31, 1968, Israeli commandos flown on French-built transport helicopters moved more than 200 miles into Egyptian territory and assaulted three sites in the Nile River Valley. The targets included two Nile bridges, at Qena and Najh Hamadi, and an electrical generating station, also at Najh Hamadi. The bridges and power station were all destroyed, and the commandos successfully returned via helicopter to their base in the Sinai Peninsula.

The raid was not only an economic attack upon the Egyptian infrastructure but also demonstrated the range and capability of Israeli helicopter-borne commando units. The Egyptians initially halted their own raids and artillery strikes across the Suez Canal, but they also initiated a nationwide militia system to counter similar raids in the future.

During the same period as the War of Attrition, Israel also faced a series of attacks along its eastern borders, carried out by elements

of the Jordanian Army, the Iraqi Army, and the Palestine Liberation Organization (PLO). Much like the combat actions across the Suez Canal, operations along the eastern border consisted of raids and intermittent shelling of Israeli positions. On March 21, 1968, IDF armored units crossed the Jordan River and attacked Karameh, a primary staging and headquarters area of the PLO. IDF transport helicopters inserted Israeli paratroopers into blocking positions outside Karameh to prevent the withdrawal of PLO troops. The mobility of Israel's helicopter-borne infantry surprised the PLO, but the blocking force was too small to stop PLO units from escaping and consequently isolating the blocking force.

Back on the Egyptian front, the IDF on September 11, 1969, launched a commando raid on the Egyptian radar station at Ras-Arab. Helicopter troops attacked the installation, dismantled the Soviet-supplied radar equipment, and transported it back to Israeli-occupied territory. The successful raid gave Israel and its Western allies an important intelligence exploitation opportunity to examine state-of-the-art Soviet radar equipment.

During the 1973 Yom Kippur War, Arab forces attacked the Israelis by helicopter for the first time. On the Egyptian front, most of the fighting involved direct engagements between armored forces.

Neither side used a significant number of helicopters, primarily because of the prohibitive air defense environment. On the Israeli northern front, however, the initial Syrian assault on Mount Hermon launched on October 6 included a helicopter-borne attack that succeeded in capturing key elevated terrain that overlooked the entire battlefield. On October 21, however, Israeli paratroopers mounted a helicopter assault and retook the same position.

Both Syria and Israel eventually intervened in the Lebanese Civil War that started in 1975. On April 25, 1981, Syrian helicopters launched devastating missile attacks against Lebanese Christian positions on Mount Lebanon with the intent of annihilating the Christian defenders and opening the area to assault by Syrian infantry units. A year of intermittent fighting between Israeli and Syrian units followed, and on June 6, 1982, Israeli ground troops invaded Lebanon. Israel too used ground-attack helicopters in its assault. After three weeks of intense fighting, Israel and Syria agreed to a cease-fire.

Since the 1982 invasion of Lebanon, attack helicopters have played an increasingly important role in Israeli operational planning. IDF attack helicopters have been used increasingly against terrorist targets, both in Lebanon and in the occupied territories. In many cases, the Israelis have used attack helicopters to carry out targeted killings against individual extremist leaders. Israel has been criticized in the world press for such attacks, and the so-called precision strikes more often than not result in civilian casualties.

A U.S. UH-60 Black Hawk helicopter (*top*) and an Egyptian H-3 Sea King helicopter (*bottom*) during a joint exercise in Egypt on November 9, 1980. (U.S. Department of Defense)

Most of Israel's helicopter fleet consists of American-built UH-1s, UH-60s, CH-47s, and AH-64s. The venerable Vietnam War–era UH-1 Hueys are aging but will probably remain in service for many years to come. The largest Arab helicopter fleets in the region are maintained by Egypt, Syria, and Saudi Arabia. Egypt and Saudi Arabia primarily use American aircraft, including AH-64s, UH-60s, and CH-47s. Prior to 1990 almost all of Syria's helicopters were supplied by the Soviet Union, but in the post-Soviet era the Syrians have had difficulty procuring modern equipment and maintaining their helicopter fleet. Other military forces in the region, including Bahrain, Kuwait, and the United Arab Emirates, maintain smaller fleets of attack and transport helicopters. The United States is by far the largest current exporter of military helicopters to the region.

PAUL J. SPRINGER

See also

Attrition, War of; Egypt, Armed Forces; Israel Defense Forces; Israeli War of Independence, Overview; Iraq, Armed Forces; Jordan, Armed Forces; Lebanon, Armed Forces; Lebanon, Civil War in; Lebanon, Israeli Invasion of; Saudi Arabia, Armed Forces; Six-Day War; Syria, Armed Forces; Yom Kippur War

References

Dorr, Robert F. *Chopper: Firsthand Accounts of Helicopter Warfare, World War II to Iraq.* New York: Berkeley Books, 2005.

Everett-Heath, John. *Helicopters in Combat: The First Fifty Years.* New York: Sterling, 1992.

McKinney, Mike, and Mike Ryan. *Chariots of the Damned: Helicopter Special Operations from Vietnam to Kosovo.* New York: St. Martin's, 2002.

Schliefer, Jay. *Combat Helicopters.* Minneapolis, MN: Capstone, 1996.

Wragg, David W. *Helicopters at War: A Pictorial History.* New York: St. Martin's, 1983.

Aircraft, Kfir Fighter

Multiuse Israeli-built jet combat aircraft. The Israeli Kfir (lion cub) owes its existence to an angry President Charles de Gaulle of France terminating the French defense relationship with Israel following the latter's decision for a preventive war with its Arab neighbors in 1967. France terminated its contract to supply Israel with Dassault Mirage V fighters in 1968 even though Israel had already paid for the aircraft. Covertly acquiring blueprints and key components from a French Mirage coproduction facility in Switzerland, Israel Aircraft Industries (IAI) initiated a high priority program to produce an indigenous Israeli fighter based on the acquired materials and the past Israeli experience and collaboration with Dassault. The Kfir was the result.

Essentially a Mirage V modified to incorporate Israeli avionics and the U.S. Pratt & Whitney J-79 turbojet engine, the Kfir employs a forward canard mounted above the air intake to enhance its low-speed maneuverability. First flown in June 1973, the initial C-1 model saw only limited production (27 aircraft) that year. The improved C-2 entered service in 1976. It had superior electronics, including better electronic countermeasures equipment, improved

Israeli-manufactured Kfir single-seat Mach 2.3 combat aircraft, shown in 1975. (Moshe Milner/Israeli Government Press Office)

maneuverability, and a better thrust-to-weigh ratio and lift body design. The final version, the C-7 variant, has a more powerful engine, smart-weapons capability, provision for in-flight refueling, heads-up display (HUD), and hands-on throttle and stick (HOTAS) controls. Significantly, despite an increase in takeoff weight, it enjoys an even better thrust-to-weight ratio over its predecessors. Top speed remains at Mach 2.3. Equally adept at air-to-air and air-to-surface missions, the Kfir was a key element in Israel's ability to maintain air superiority over its Arab opponents during the limited conflicts and aerial engagements, particularly against Syria, during the 1980s and early 1990s.

Equipped with a pair of 30-mm cannon and carrying a mix of infrared air-to-air and surface-to-air missiles, the single-seat, multirole-capable Kfir C-7 is one of the 20th century's most versatile and effective combat aircraft. It can carry up to 13,415 pounds of ordnance and has a combat radius of some 800 miles and a service ceiling of 59,000 feet.

The Kfir saw service as an opposition aircraft with the U.S. Navy and the U.S. Marine Corps in the 1990s. The TC-2 Kfir is a two-seater trainer. In all, more than 100 Kfirs were manufactured. Still in service with Israeli forces, the Kfir has gradually given way to the more modern and effective General Dynamics F-16 Fighting Falcon and

McDonnell-Douglas F-15 Eagle aircraft provided by the United States. However, the Kfir's canard design can now be seen in late-model French, Swedish, and Russian aircraft designs. Israel has exported the Kfir to Colombia, Ecuador, and the United States.

CARL OTIS SCHUSTER

See also

Airpower, Role in the Arab-Israeli Wars; Israel; Israel, Defense Industry; Israel Defense Forces

References

Cohen, Eliezer. *Israel's Best Defense: The First Full Story of the Israeli Air Force.* New York: Orion, 1993.
Jackson, Paul, ed. *Jane's All World Aircraft, 2001–2002.* London: Jane's, 2002.
Jackson, Robert. *The Israeli Air Force Story: The Struggle for Middle East Aircraft Supremacy since 1948.* London: Tom Stacey, 1994.
Sharpe, Michael. *Attack and Interceptor Jets.* London: Friedman, 1999.
Weiss, Raanan, and Yoav Efrati. *Israel Aircraft Industries Kfir.* Geneva: Books International Militaria, 2000.

Aircraft, Lavi Fighter-Bomber

Israeli fighter-bomber aircraft. The Lavi was part of an ambitious Israeli attempt to end its dependency on foreign-built attack air-

Aircraft mechanics work on the prototype model of the Lavi fighter-bomber at the Israel Aircraft Industries facility at Lod on February 2, 1985. (Herard Reogorodetzki/Israeli Government Press Office)

craft. Planned and preliminarily developed by Israel Aircraft Industries (IAI) during the 1970s, the Israelis formally launched the Lavi project in February 1980. The first prototype aircraft flew in December 1986.

The Lavi was a single-passenger aircraft designed principally to replace the U.S.-supplied Douglas A-4 Skyhawk. A two-seat version was also built in prototype and could be used for training purposes. A small but highly advanced jet, the Lavi was designed as a multipurpose aircraft to conduct a variety of short- to medium-range ground support missions and to serve as a fighter. The plane's avionics were among the most advanced in the world, and the jet was capable of carrying a wide array of weapons systems.

On August 30, 1987, however, the Israeli government, with Defense Minister Yitzhak Rabin in the lead, scuttled the Lavi project in a narrow cabinet vote. The government opted for the less-expensive solution of continuing to purchase needed aircraft from the United States.

In addition to concerns over runaway costs, the decision to abandon the Lavi project also stemmed from increasing diplomatic friction between Israel and the United States. Through intense lobbying efforts during the early 1980s, Israel and its associated interest groups managed to convince politicians in Washington to approve modifications to the policies directing the flow of U.S. aid to the country. Funds usually earmarked for the purchase of American-manufactured military hardware were instead diverted to finance the construction of the Lavi and the procurement of sensitive U.S. technologies for completion of the project. Such unprecedented support for Israel, a country that had invaded Lebanon in 1982, damaged the image of the United States throughout the Middle East.

More seriously, Israel's access to cutting-edge technology and its plans to market the Lavi internationally to cover the spiraling costs raised serious concerns that U.S. advancements in aeronautic and avionics might fall into the hands of unfriendly governments.

JONAS KAUFFELDT

See also

Aircraft, Bombers; Aircraft, Fighters; Israel Defense Forces; Rabin, Yitzhak

References

DeLoughry, James P. "The United States and the Lavi." *Airpower Journal* 4(3) (1990): 34–43.

Zakheim, Dov S. *Flight of the Lavi: Inside a U.S.-Israeli Crisis.* Washington, DC, and London: Brassey's, 1996.

Aircraft, Reconnaissance

Israel and opposing Arab states have employed three types of manned aerial reconnaissance techniques since 1947. The first is visual reconnaissance and involves the use of aircraft immediately over the battlefield to provide real-time observation of friendly and enemy force movements. Such aircraft typically fly at slow speeds to allow pilots to physically observe the battlefield.

The second type is electronic and signals reconnaissance aircraft. These planes carry sophisticated equipment to gather the electronic emissions from enemy communications and surveillance hardware. The third type is represented by aircraft equipped for tactical photographic reconnaissance. These are the most common type of reconnaissance aircraft that have been employed in the Arab-Israeli wars. Such aircraft are usually fighters or light bombers that have been specially modified to carry cameras to photograph enemy troop dispositions, fortifications, and other fixed sites. In addition to manned aircraft, both Israel and Egypt have also flown unmanned remotely piloted aircraft, or unmanned aerial vehicles (UAVs), for tactical photo reconnaissance.

Arab Reconnaissance Aircraft

Egypt was the only Arab nation to fly dedicated reconnaissance aircraft during the War of Israeli Independence (1948–1949). The Egyptians flew three types of aircraft in a reconnaissance role. For general visual reconnaissance missions, they operated British aircraft, the Avro Anson Mk.I and the de Havilland Dove. The two-engine Anson was a World War II–era British maritime reconnaissance aircraft. It had a maximum speed of 188 miles per hour (mph), a ceiling of 19,000 feet, and a range of 790 miles. The Dove, a small two-engine transport aircraft, entered Egyptian service at the end of the war. It had a top speed of 202 mph, a ceiling of 20,000 feet, and a range of 1,070 miles. For tactical photographic reconnaissance, Egypt used the Supermarine Spitfire. This aircraft, originally provided to Egypt by the British during World War II, was the Spitfire Mark IX. It had a maximum speed of 408 mph, a ceiling of 44,000 feet, and a range of 434 miles.

The Egyptian Air Force underwent major transformation between 1949 and 1956. The Egyptians could have employed any of their aircraft in the visual reconnaissance role. However, it is not clear if any of their planes had been modified for tactical photo duties. The Egyptian order of battle included Gloster Meteor fighters, which were used for photo reconnaissance by other countries. The twin-engine Meteor had a maximum speed of 598 mph, a ceiling of 43,000 feet, and a range of 980 miles. Israel flew them in reconnaissance missions during the 1956 Suez Crisis.

During the 1967 Six-Day War, the Soviet-built Mikoyen-Gurevich MiG-21 (NATO designation Fishbed) was the most advanced fighter of the Egyptian, Syrian, and Iraqi Air Forces. The MiG-21 had a maximum speed of 1,385 mph, a ceiling of 62,336 feet, and a range of 600 miles. The Israeli Air Force carried out a preemptive strike to begin the war, in the process destroying more than 75 percent of opposing Arab aircraft in the opening days. Very few Arab fighters managed to penetrate Israeli fighter defenses, and it is not known if any of these were MiG-21 photo-reconnaissance aircraft.

The MiG-21 continued as the primary Egyptian photo-reconnaissance aircraft during the 1970s so-called War of Attrition between Israel and Egypt and for Egypt and Syria in the 1973 Yom Kippur War. It carried its cameras in an external pod. Later, these aircraft were specifically modified to house an internal camera array. In October 1971, Soviet MiG-25s (NATO designation Foxbat) arrived in Egypt, and these flew photo-reconnaissance missions over Israeli-controlled territory until 1972. Israeli fighters were unable to catch this fast Soviet aircraft. It had a top speed of 1,849 mph, a ceiling of 80,000 feet, and a range of 901 miles. The MiG-25s were officially on loan to Egypt. They carried Egyptian markings but were flown by Soviet pilots.

In 1982 Israeli and Syrian forces fought one another during Operation PEACE FOR GALILEE, Israel's invasion of southern Lebanon. Syrian pilots flew the Mig-25R, acquired in 1975, for photo reconnaissance.

Israeli Reconnaissance Aircraft

The fledgling Israeli Air Force flew a greater variety of aircraft than its Arab neighbors during its War for Independence. In the visual reconnaissance role, Israel tasked many types of aircraft, including the Autocrat RWD series, Taylorcraft J-2, and Auster AOP-5. All three of these aircraft types were small transport planes that were also used for light bombing. The Israelis used a single ex-British de Havilland Mosquito as their principal tactical photographic reconnaissance aircraft. The twin-engine Mosquito had a crew of two, a maximum speed of 425 mph, a ceiling of 36,000 feet, and a range of 3,500 miles. Israel acquired additional Mosquito aircraft after the war. The Mosquito remained Israel's primary long-range tactical reconnaissance aircraft until the acquisition of British Gloster Meteor jets after 1953.

The British and French operated their own reconnaissance aircraft during the brief Suez Crisis. The British flew the excellent two-jet engine English Electric Canberra aircraft from their bases on Cyprus. It had a maximum speed of 541 mph, a ceiling of 48,000 feet, and a range of 806 miles. Syrian fighters (some sources claim they were flown by Soviet pilots) downed a Canberra operating over Syrian territory during the campaign. France flew the American Republic RF-84 from Cyprus as its reconnaissance aircraft. This single-engine jet aircraft was a modified Republic F-84 Thunderstreak. It had a maximum speed of 620 mph, a ceiling of 46,000 feet, and a range of 2,200 miles.

In the 1967 war, the French Sud Aviation Vautour was the primary Israeli photo-reconnaissance aircraft. Israel acquired these from France in 1957. The twin-engine Vautour had a maximum speed of 660 mph, a ceiling of 50,000 feet, and a range of 1,800 miles. Although primarily a light bomber, it performed well in the photo-reconnaissance role until phased out of service in 1971.

The Israeli Air Force began converting from the Vautour to the delta-wing Dassault Mirage III during this period. The latter was the photo-reconnaissance version of the French Mirage III fighter/light bomber. It had a maximum speed of 1,460 mph, a ceiling of 75,460 feet, and a range of 746 miles. Also, in 1969 Israel acquired its first 6 McDonnell Douglas RF-4E Phantom photo-reconnaissance aircraft and immediately began using them over Egyptian airspace. The Phantom had a maximum speed of 1,450 mph, a ceiling of 71,000 feet, and a range of 1,841 miles. Between 1970 and 1971, the U.S. Air Force loaned Israel 2 RF-4C photo-reconnaissance aircraft to augment the other planes. Israel flew these planes during the 1973 Yom Kippur War. The success of this plane was evident by Israel's order for 6 additional RF-4C aircraft in 1977. Israel eventually operated 21 of these reconnaissance aircraft. During Operation PEACE FOR GALILEE, Israel's 1982 invasion of southern Lebanon, Syrian pilots reportedly downed an RF-4E over Lebanon. Israel also operated an electronics and signals reconnaissance unit with Grumman twin-turboprop OV-1 Mohawks, which had a speed of 289 mph, a ceiling of 25,000 feet, and a range of 1,200 miles; Beechcraft RU-21J Utes; and Lockheed turboprop four-engine EC-130E Hercules aircraft, which had a speed of 374 mph, a ceiling of 33,000 feet, and a range of 4,894 miles. Israel has employed a modified Boeing 707 airliner as a signals-reconnaissance asset against the Syrians since the early 1980s.

TERRY MAYS AND SPENCER C. TUCKER

See also

Attrition, War of; Lebanon, Israeli Invasion of; Sinai Campaign; Six-Day War; Yom Kippur War

References

Cohen, Eliezer. *Israel's Best Defense: The First Full Story of the Israeli Air Force.* New York: Orion, 1993.

Nordeen, Lon, and David Nicolle. *Phoenix over the Nile: A History of Egyptian Air Power, 1932–1994.* Washington, DC: Smithsonian Books, 1996.

Stevenson, William. *Zanek! A Chronicle of the Israeli Air Force.* New York: Viking, 1971.

Yonay, Ehud. *No Margin for Error: The Making of the Israeli Air Force.* New York: Pantheon, 1993.

Aircraft, Transport

Transport aircraft move personnel, supplies, and weapons when speed is required or when ground or sea transport is difficult or impossible. Strategic airlift uses large aircraft to move troops and cargo over intercontinental distances. Tactical airlift employs smaller aircraft to move troops and cargo within a theater of operations. In the Arab-Israeli wars, the United States and the Soviet Union used strategic transports to resupply their client states. Israel and its Arab opponents primarily employed tactical airlift because of the relatively small area of operations.

Airlift is essential to U.S. power projection. For example, in October 1973 during the Yom Kippur War, U.S. Air Force C-5 and C-141 transports flew 566 missions to Israel and delivered 22,305 tons of critically needed tanks, ammunition, and supplies. The Arabs used American-made transports for some time after 1948 but generally procured Soviet transports after 1955. Israel has primarily used American-manufactured transports. A plethora of American-made transport aircraft have been used in the Arab-Israeli wars since 1948.

Boeing 707. The four-turbofan 707-320 carries up to 215 passengers or 63,380 pounds of cargo. It cruises at 605 miles per hour (mph) and has a 39,000-foot ceiling and a 5,755-mile range. Israel purchased 29 707-320 airliners beginning in 1973 and converted them to transports, tankers, and intelligence aircraft.

Lockheed C-5 Galaxy. The U.S. Air Force operated 126 C-5 acquired between 1969 and 1989. Each carried 270,000 pounds of cargo, including 73 passengers and a tank or armored fighting vehicle. They have four turbofans, a 500-mph cruising speed, a 41,000-foot ceiling, and a 2,473-mile unrefueled range.

Lockheed C-130 Hercules. Lockheed built more than 8,000 of these four-turboprop tactical transports in more than 40 variants from 1956 onward. Many foreign nations operate the C-130. Israel acquired 13 C-130E and 11 C-130H Hercules from 1971 to 1976. Four C-130H serve as tankers, and 2 C-130E serve as electronic intelligence aircraft. The C-130E has a cruising speed of 368 mph, a ceiling of 23,000 feet, and a range with a 45,000-pound maximum payload of 2,422 miles. The C-130H has a cruising speed of 374 mph, a ceiling of 33,000 feet, and a range with a 36,000-pound maximum payload of 2,356 miles.

The following American-built transports are no longer in U.S. service, but some still operate in Middle Eastern air forces.

Beech C-45 Expeditor. Beech produced this twin-engine transport from 1937 to 1970, including 4,000 C-45 models from 1940 to 1945. The Expeditor carried eight passengers and cruised at 185 mph with a 21,400-foot ceiling and 1,530-mile range. Syria used four from 1949 to 1974.

Boeing 377 Stratocruiser. This late-1940s' design served as an airliner, military transport, and tanker (377/C-97/KC-97). Israel purchased five Stratocruisers from Pan Am Airlines in 1962 and converted them to military transports. Some were later converted into tankers. All were retired in 1978. Stratocruisers had four piston engines. They carried 96 troops or 20,000 pounds of cargo. Cruise speed was 300 mph with a 30,200-foot ceiling and 4,300-mile range.

Curtiss C-46 Commando. Curtiss built 3,182 Commandos from 1942 to 1945. The C-46 had two piston engines. It carried 50 passengers and had a 173-mph cruising speed, a 24,500-foot ceiling, and a 3,150-mile range. Israel operated 5 from 1948 to 1949. Egypt operated 10 from 1945 to 1957.

Douglas DC-5. Douglas built only five DC-5 airliners. Israel used one during 1948–1949. The DC-5 had two piston engines and carried 22 passengers. It cruised at 202 mph and had a 23,700-foot ceiling and a 1,600-mile range.

Douglas C-47 Skytrain. Douglas built 10,123 Skytrains after 1935. Some still remain in service today. The commercial version of the

A U.S. C-141 Starlifter aircraft in flight on October 22, 1973. (Fritz Cohen/Israeli Government Press Office)

C-47 was the widely used DC-3. The C-47, with two piston engines, carried 28 troops or 6,000 pounds of cargo. Cruising speed was 207 mph with a 23,200-foot ceiling and 2,125-mile range. Israel acquired 34 of these aircraft from 1948 to 1960 and retired them in 2001. Egypt operated 20 from 1945 to 1972. Syria used 6 from 1949 into the 1970s. Jordan owned 4 from 1966 to 1977.

Douglas C-54 Skymaster. Douglas manufactured 1,170 Skymasters during World War II. The C-54 had four piston engines and carried 50 passengers. It had a 227-mph cruising speed, a 22,300-foot ceiling, and a 2,500-mile range. Israel used one from 1948 to 1949.

Lockheed Lodestar. Lockheed built only a few hundred Lodestars during World War II. Lodestars had two piston engines and carried 14 passengers. They had a 218-mph maximum speed, a 20,400-foot ceiling, and an 1,800-mile range. Israel used one during 1948–1949, and Egypt used one during 1950–1951.

Lockheed Hudson. Lockheed began building this variant of the Super Electra for Britain in 1939. Israel operated two during 1948–1949. Hudsons carried 12 passengers. They had two piston engines, a 246-mph maximum speed, a 25,000-foot ceiling, and a 1,960-mile range.

Lockheed Constellation. Lockheed built 846 Constellations from 1943 to 1956. In military service they were designated the C-121. They were quickly superseded by jet airliners in the early 1950s. They carried 60–100 passengers. They had four turbo-compound engines, a 354-mph cruising speed, a 25,000-foot ceiling, and a 5,400-mile range. Israel used three in 1948 and gave them to El Al, the Israeli-owned airline, in 1951.

Lockheed C-141 Starlifter. The U.S. Air Force acquired 284 Starlifters from 1964 to 1982, retiring the last in 2006. The C-141B carried 200 troops, 155 paratroops, 103 litters, or 68,725 pounds of cargo. With four turbofans, C-141 cruising speed was 500 mph, ceiling was 41,000 feet, and unrefueled range was 2,500 miles.

Antonov An-2. The Soviet Union and Poland built more than 17,000 of these single-engine transports from 1947 to 1992. The An-2 carried 12 passengers or 2,733 pounds of cargo and had a 115-mph cruising speed, a 14,425-foot ceiling, and a 560-mile range. Egypt operated 10 from 1955 to 1999, and Iraq used 20 from 1959 to 1990.

Antonov An-12. The Soviets produced some 900 An-12 aircraft between 1957 and 1973. The An-12 somewhat resembled the C-130. With four turboprops, it carried 90 troops or 44,000 pounds of cargo. It had a 342-mph cruising speed, a 33,465-foot ceiling, and a 2,113-mile range. Egypt operated 34 from 1956 to 1997, Syria flew 6 from 1975 to 1991, Iraq used 12 from 1962 to 1990.

Antonov An-22. The An-22 is an enlarged twin-tail An-12. Sixty-five were produced between 1965 and 1976. Some remain in service in Russia today. It has four turboprops and carries 180,000 pounds of cargo and 29 passengers. The An-22 has a maximum speed of 460 mph, a ceiling of 24,600 feet, and a range of 3,100 miles.

Antonov An-24. The twin-turboprop An-24 carried 44 troops. Its cruise speed was 280 mph, and it had a 27,560-foot ceiling and a 342-mile range. Egypt operated 3 from 1971 to 1994, Syria flew 5 from 1979 to 1998, and Iraq used 11 from 1969 to 1990.

Antonov An-26. The twin-turboprop An-26 carried 40 troops. Its cruise speed was 270 mph, and it had a 26,575-foot ceiling and a 559-mile range. Syria used 6 from 1979 onward, and Iraq flew 10 from 1973 to 1990.

Ilyushin Il-14. This twin piston engine transport carried 25 passengers. Maximum speed was 259 mph, and it had a 24,280-foot ceiling and an 811-mile range. Egypt operated 70 of these planes from 1955 to 1994, Syria used 16 from 1957 to 1998, and Iraq operated 13 from 1958 to 1990.

Ilyushin Il-18. The Il-18 had four turboprops and carried 75 passengers. It cruised at 419 mph and had a 25,250-foot ceiling and a 2,299-mile range. Syria operated 5 from 1972 to 1998.

Ilyushin Il-76. Still in production, the Il-76 somewhat resembles the C-141. It has four turbofans and carries 88,185 pounds of cargo. Cruising speed is 497 mph, and the aircraft has a 50,850-foot ceil-

ing and a 2,265-mile range. Syria purchased four in 1980 and still flies them.

Yakovlev Yak-40. The Yak-40 has three turbofans and carries 32 passengers. It cruises at 342 mph and has a 22,965-foot ceiling and a 901-mile range. Syria operated eight from 1976 onward.

Tupolev Tu-124. The twin-turbofan Tu-124 carried 44 passengers. It had a 603 mph maximum speed, a 38,285-foot ceiling, and a 758-mile range. Iraq operated two from 1965 to 1990.

Tupolev Tu-143. The twin-turbofan Tu-143B-3 carries 72 passengers. It has a cruising speed of 550 mph, a ceiling of 39,010 feet, and a range of 1,174 miles. Syria operated five from 1983 onward.

Other transports not built specifically by the Americans and Soviets were also employed during the Arab-Israeli wars and included the following.

Airspeed Ambassador. British-based Airspeed built only 20 of these twin-piston-engine transports in 1947. They carried 47 passengers and had a cruising speed of 312 mph, a ceiling of 36,089 feet, and a range of 550 miles. Jordan used three from 1959 to 1963.

Dornier Do-28D Skyservant. Israel purchased six of these twin-piston-engine transports from West Germany in 1975 and retired them in 1997. Skyservants carried 13 passengers or 2,205 pounds

A Soviet AN-12 transport aircraft, photographed on December 23, 1985. (U.S. Department of Defense)

of cargo. They cruised at 202 mph and had a 25,195-foot ceiling and a 399-mile range.

Handley Page Hastings. Britain operated 147 Hastings from 1947 to 1968. Each plane carried 30 paratroops or 50 troops. With four radial engines, cruising speed was 302 mph. The ceiling was 26,500 feet, and the range was 1,690 miles. During the 1956 Suez Crisis, they dropped British paratroops on Port Said.

Israel Aircraft Industries Arava. The Israeli Air Force operated 10 Aravas from 1973 to 1997. Twin-piston-engine Aravas carried 19 passengers or 5,184 pounds of cargo. They cruised at 193 mph and had a 25,000-foot ceiling and a 161-mile range.

Junkers Ju-52. Syria acquired seven examples of this workhorse German transport of World War II in 1949, using them until 1953. The Ju-52, with three piston engines, carried 18 troops. It had a 171-mph maximum speed, a 19,360-foot ceiling, and a 808-mile range.

Noorduyn Norseman. Israel used 20 Canadian-built Norsemen in 1948 and retired them in 1950. With a single piston engine, the Norseman carried 8 passengers. It had a 155-mph cruising speed, a 17,000-foot ceiling, and a 1,150-mile range.

Nord N.2501 Noratlas. France's Nord Aviation built 425 Noratlas transports from 1951 to 1961. Israel bought 24 in 1955 and retired them in 1976. They carried 15,000 pounds of cargo or 45 paratroops. The Noratlas had two piston engines, cruised at 273 mph, and had a 24,605-foot ceiling and an 1,864-mile range. During the Suez Crisis, Israeli Noratlas dropped Israeli paratroops in the Sinai, while French Noratlas based in Cyprus dropped French paratroopers on Port Said.

Vickers Valetta. Britain operated 211 Valetta C.1 aircraft, 11 C.2 aircraft, and 40 T.3 twin-engine transports from 1947 to 1968. Valettas carried 34 troops, 20 paratroops, or 12,050 pounds of cargo. They had a maximum speed of 258 mph, a 21,500-foot ceiling, and a 1,460-mile range. During the Suez Crisis, they dropped British paratroops on Port Said.

JAMES D. PERRY

See also

Aircraft, Bombers; Aircraft, Electronic Warfare; Aircraft, Fighters; Aircraft, Reconnaissance; Suez Crisis; Yom Kippur War

References

Angelucci, Enzo. *The Rand McNally Encyclopedia of Military Aircraft, 1914–1980.* New York: Military Press, 1983.

Lema Publications. *Transport Aircraft and Specialized Carriers.* New York: Lema Publications, 1999.

Stroud, John. *Soviet Transport Aircraft since 1945.* New York: Funk and Wagnalls, 1968.

Williams, Nicholas M. *Aircraft of the United States' Military Air Transport Service.* Minneapolis, MN: Voyageur, 1999.

Airpower, Role in the Arab-Israeli Wars

Airpower played an exceptionally important role in the Arab-Israeli wars during 1948–1982. Israel, a small country surrounded by much more populous and territorially larger enemies, could not afford to maintain large military forces, allow wars to be fought on its soil, or engage in long wars. Israel relied on rapid mobilization, offensive action with armored forces, and fighting short, decisive campaigns on enemy soil. Air superiority was essential to this strategy, for it shielded both the Israeli population and armed forces from enemy attack. Air superiority also permitted Israeli Air Force (IAF) aircraft to support friendly ground forces and interdict enemy rear areas while at the same denying these capabilities to enemy air forces. Throughout this period, the IAF consistently stressed high levels of training for pilots and ground crews. In the opinion of many impartial observers, IAF personnel were the best trained in the world.

Before 1967, Israel primarily used British and French aircraft, but afterward it increasingly relied on U.S. aircraft. Generally speaking, the IAF preferred multirole fighters rather than specialized aircraft for different tasks such as air superiority and close air support.

Egypt, Syria, and Iraq employed Soviet equipment and doctrine. In consequence, Arab air forces emphasized air support of friendly ground operations. Arab pilots were not as well trained as those of Israel and could not compete with Israeli pilots in aerial combat or in delivering ordnance against enemy ground targets. The Soviet Union did provide the Arab states with large numbers of excellent fighter aircraft. Indeed, Arab fighter aircraft were not notably inferior to Israeli aircraft until Israel received advanced U.S. fighter aircraft in 1969.

Airpower played only a marginal role in 1948. When Israel proclaimed its independence, Egypt, Syria, Jordan, Iraq, Saudi Arabia, and Lebanon immediately invaded. Their forces greatly outnumbered those of Israel and were much better equipped. Initially Israel had only light training aircraft adapted for ground attack and transports. However, despite an arms embargo, Israel obtained about 150 aircraft by the end of 1948. Israeli aircraft included the Supermarine Spitfire IX, the North American P-51D Mustang, the Avia S-199 (a Czech variant of the Messerschmitt Bf-109G), the Bristol Beaufighter, and the Boeing B-17G Flying Fortress.

Egypt began the war with about 130 aircraft but could not keep many aircraft operational. Egypt primarily employed Fiat G.55, Macchi C.205, and Spitfire V and IX fighters; Douglas C-47 transports; and Avro Anson bombers.

Initially Egypt enjoyed air superiority, and its aircraft constantly attacked Tel Aviv. Israel checked the Arab advance on the ground, with Israeli air attacks against ground forces behind Arab front lines playing a minor role. Israeli aircraft began shooting down intruding Arab aircraft and launched small raids on Amman and Damascus.

In October 1948, Israel attacked Egyptian forces in the Negev Desert. IAF surprise strikes on Egyptian air bases in the Sinai destroyed a number of Egyptian planes on the ground and gave Israel control of the air. The IAF primarily flew air superiority and interdiction missions rather than providing close air support to friendly troops in contact with the enemy. A truce was declared in January 1949.

In 1953, Major General Dan Tolkovsky assumed command of the IAF. Tolkovsky believed that given its limited resources, Israel

Israeli Air Force pilot Mordechai Hod and his navigator in front of their Canadian-built Noorduyn Norseman aircraft, July 1, 1949. (Zoltan Kluger/Israeli Government Press Office)

needed multipurpose aircraft and pilots who could perform every kind of mission. This philosophy guided IAF aircraft purchases for more than 50 years. Tolkovsky introduced highly rigorous pilot standards and emphasized fluid tactics, dogfighting, and individual initiative. Israeli pilots frequently practiced dogfighting and ground-attack skills. Tolkovsky demanded that ground crews maintain high aircraft serviceability levels, and he insisted on constant practice in refueling and arming aircraft. As a result, Israeli aircraft could typically fly more than four times as many sorties per day as each Arab aircraft.

Beginning in the mid-1950s, the Soviets trained and equipped the Arab air forces. Soviet doctrine relied on ground controllers vectoring interceptors to make a single hit-and-run pass at an enemy. Arab pilots received very little flying training hours per month, participated in few realistic exercises, and were untrained in the dynamic, close-quarters dogfighting in which the Israelis excelled.

The fighting in October 1956 during the Suez Crisis emerged from an Anglo-French-Israeli conspiracy that would see Israeli forces strike deep into the Sinai, allowing the United Kingdom and France to intervene militarily to protect the Suez Canal. Israel proposed a surprise low-altitude attack on the Egyptian Air Force, but the British and French rejected this plan. While Israeli ground forces invaded the Sinai, Israeli pilots defended Israel, supported the army, and remained well clear of the canal.

In 1956 Egypt had hundreds of aircraft capable of reaching Israel, including 120 Soviet Mikoyan-Gurevich MiG-15 and MiG-17 jet fighters (which were superior to most Israeli fighters at the time), 50 Soviet Ilyushin Il-28 jet bombers, and 84 British Gloster Meteor and de Havilland Vampire fighters. Unfortunately, only about 80 of these aircraft were operational, including 30 MiGs and 12 Il-28s, partly because pilots were still in training but mainly because of maintenance and repair problems.

Israel had 136 operational aircraft. Its jet fighter force consisted of 16 Dassault Mystère IVAs, 22 Dassault Ouragans and 16 Gloster Meteors. Israel used 29 P-51D Mustangs and 13 de Havilland Mosquitos for ground-attack missions. Fearing that Egypt might bomb its cities, Israel convinced the French to station 36 Mystère IVA and 18 Republic F-84F Thunderchief interceptors in Israel. However, this fear proved groundless.

The campaign began with an Israeli paradrop in the Sinai. Egyptian fighters did not intercept it but later attacked the paratroops on the ground to no great effect. With superior Israeli pilots, even obsolete Ouragan fighters bested Egyptian MiG-15s in aerial combat. Egyptian aircraft generally avoided combat, and air-to-air encounters were few. In total, the Israelis lost a single Piper Cub liaison aircraft to enemy aircraft and 14 other aircraft to ground fire while shooting down 10 Egyptian jets. The IAF conducted few close air support missions, but Israeli air interdiction caused numerous Egyptian crews to abandon their vehicles intact.

Soon after Israel attacked, British and French aircraft struck Egyptian air bases, and British and French forces invaded Egypt. Egyptian aircraft did not contest these actions, but American pressure forced Britain, France, and Israel to withdraw.

After the Suez Crisis, the Soviets replaced destroyed Egyptian equipment. By 1967, Egypt had some 450 jet aircraft, including 120 MiG-21s, 80 MiG-19s, 150 MiG-15/17s, 30 Sukhoi Su-7B fighter-bombers, 30 Tupolev Tu-16 bombers, and 40 Ilyushin Il-28 bombers. In addition, Egypt had more than 1,000 antiaircraft guns and 160 SA-2 surface-to-air missiles (SAMs). Syria had 150 aircraft, including 36 MiG-21s, 90 MiG-17s, and 6 Il-28s, while Jordan had 22 Hawker Hunter and 6 Lockheed F-104 Starfighter fighters. The delta-wing MiG-21, an advanced Soviet fighter, was superior to anything in Israel's inventory, but Israeli pilots' skill enabled them to defeat MiG-21s while flying inferior aircraft. Israel also benefited from the flight by an Iraqi defector of his MiG-21 to Israel in 1966, allowing the IAF to analyze its strengths and weaknesses.

In June 1967, Israel had 72 Dassault Mirage IIICs, 18 Dassault Super Mystères, 50 Mystère IVAs, 40 Ouragans, 25 Vautour IIAs, and 76 Fouga Magister trainers (which could also be used for ground attack). Only the Mirages and Super Mystères were truly modern fighters, although the Vautours, considered underpowered and obsolete in 1967, performed effectively in the hands of skilled pilots.

Israel's plan entailed preemptive destruction of the Egyptian and Syrian Air Forces and occupation of the Sinai, Gaza Strip, West Bank, and Golan Heights. The IAF sought to destroy Egyptian aircraft on the ground and to destroy runways using surprise low-altitude daylight attacks. To destroy runways, the IAF developed special rocket-propelled bombs that plunged deep into the earth

MiG-21 jet fighter flown to Israel by an Iraqi Air Force captain who had taken off near Baghdad and defected; photographed on August 16, 1966. (Moshe Milner/Israeli Government Press Office)

and cratered the concrete from beneath. The Israelis decided to crush the stronger Egyptians first with an all-out effort and then turn on Syria rather than splitting the IAF for two weaker simultaneous blows.

On June 5, 1967, virtually the entire IAF struck Egypt as the Egyptian pilots were having breakfast. The Israeli aircraft flew below radar coverage and approached from an unexpected direction. For three hours, Israeli fighters pounded Egyptian air bases and other installations. The first targets were the MiG-21s, to ensure air superiority, and Tu-16 and Il-28 bombers that might strike Israel. Rapid sortie generation was crucial, and Israeli ground crews got aircraft back in the air within 10–15 minutes. Most of Egypt's aircraft were destroyed on the ground. The few aircraft that managed to take off were quickly shot down or crashed when they could not find an undamaged base at which to land. The Israelis suffered no losses.

In the early afternoon, Syrian and Jordanian aircraft raided Israel, inflicting little damage. The IAF responded with strikes on airfields in Jordan and Syria. In one day, the Egyptian and Syrian air forces were crippled, and Jordan's small air force was annihilated. The three Arab states lost nearly 400 aircraft, while 25 air bases were put out of action. Israel lost 19 aircraft, mainly to ground fire, and it maintained air superiority for the remainder of the war.

The Israeli Army quickly advanced into the Sinai, routing the Egyptian Army and securing the peninsula within four days. The IAF supported the ground campaign primarily with interdiction attacks on enemy logistical nets, rear-area formations, and retreating Arab forces. The Israeli Army, not the IAF, destroyed most of Egypt's combat vehicles. The value of Israeli air superiority in the 1967 Six-Day War was clear. Egyptian aircraft flew 150 ground-attack sorties but had little effect on the Israeli Army, while Israeli aircraft punished Egyptian forces with 965 ground-attack sorties.

The Israeli Army also defeated Jordanian troops in the West Bank. Again, the IAF's principal role was interdiction. Relatively few sorties struck Jordanian units in contact with Israeli forces, and aircraft caused only 3 percent of Jordanian tank losses. The IAF prevented Jordanian aircraft from attacking the Israeli Army and Jordanian units from reinforcing Jerusalem and mauled Jordanian units as they retreated.

After defeating Egypt and Jordan, Israel turned on Syria. Intense IAF attacks—amounting to more than 1,000 sorties—against Syrian ground forces on June 9 enabled the Israeli Army to evict a numerically superior Syrian force from excellent defensive terrain on the Golan Heights while suffering only minimal casualties itself. In total, in June 1967 the Arabs probably lost more than 450 aircraft, 58 of them in aerial combat. Israel lost perhaps 45 aircraft (35 to ground fire and 10 to aerial combat).

Egypt prosecuted the War of Attrition from 1967 to 1970. Egyptian forces avoided major ground combat while inflicting continual Israeli casualties with commando raids, artillery fire, and air strikes. Meanwhile, the Soviet Union rebuilt the shattered Arab forces, and the Israelis received American aircraft.

By June 1968, Egyptian strength reached 110 MiG-21s, 80 MiG-19s, 120 MiG-15/17s, 40 Su-7Bs, and 50 Il-28 and Tu-16 bombers. Syrian strength increased to 60 MiG-21s, 70 MiG-15/17s, and 20 Su-7Bs. Soviet instructors trained both Egyptian and Syrian pilots. Meanwhile, the Israelis received 48 Douglas A-4H Skyhawk attack aircraft in 1968 and 50 McDonnell F-4E and 6 RF-4 Phantom fighters in 1969. Low-level aerial clashes frequently occurred in this period. From July to September 1969, Israel tried to suppress dug-in Egyptian artillery and air defense sites. The Israelis flew 1,000 sorties and lost 3 aircraft, while the Egyptians flew 110 sorties and lost 21 aircraft. The Egyptians used about 70 aircraft to attack Israeli positions in the Sinai on September 11 but lost 11 aircraft in the process.

The United States enhanced Israeli fighter survivability in late 1969 with electronic countermeasures (ECM) equipment, jammers, and chaff dispensers. The United States also supplied AIM-9 Sidewinder air-to-air missiles and new engines for older Super Mystère aircraft. (France had ceased to be a major Israeli arms supplier with the 1967 Six-Day War.) The Phantoms enabled Israel to conduct long-range strikes throughout Egypt, infuriating the Egyptians. In response, the Soviets supplied mobile SA-3 SAMs, which could intercept low-altitude aircraft. Soviet crews manned many of Egypt's air defenses, and Soviet pilots flew MiG-21 air defense sorties over Egypt. In mid-1970, the Egyptians and Soviets began gradually moving an interlocking missile screen closer to the Suez Canal, raising the specter that Egypt could cross the canal and control both banks. Despite an American-brokered cease-fire in August, the Soviets moved 45 SAM launchers within range of the canal. To counter this threat, the United States provided Israel ECM equipment and Shrike and Walleye air-to-surface guided munitions. The increasing density and sophistication of Egyptian air defenses was an ominous sign, however.

Egypt recognized that total defeat of Israel was unattainable but planned to cross the Suez Canal and defend a bridgehead on the eastern shore. Egypt hoped to use this victory to bring about an international peace conference and secure the return of the Sinai at the bargaining table. Egyptian generals understood that engaging the IAF in air-to-air combat would be a futile exercise, but they planned to use SAMs to protect the crossing of the canal from IAF interference. The target date for the offensive was October 1973, during the Israeli holiday of Yom Kippur.

In October 1973, Egypt possessed 210 MiG-21s, 100 MiG-17s, 80 Su-7Bs, and 30 Tu-16 bombers. Algeria, Libya, and Iraq operated 105 fighters under Egyptian command. More importantly, Egypt established an overlapping air defense system near the canal that consisted of 175 SA-2, SA-3, and SA-6 SAM batteries; 2,100 anti-aircraft guns; and ZSU 23/4 radar-guided air defense guns. Egyptian soldiers carried 5,000 man-portable SA-7 air defense missiles. The Syrian Air Force included 200 MiG-21s, 80 MiG-17s, and 30 Su-7Bs. Syrian air defenses employed SA-2, SA-3, SA-6, and SA-7 missiles and many air defense guns.

Both Egypt and Syria had also expanded their pilot training programs and trained them more realistically, although they were still not up to Israeli standards. Israel had 127 Phantoms, 162 Skyhawks, 35 Mirage IIICs, 15 Super Mystères, and 40 Neshers (an Israeli copy of the French Mirage V).

Egypt and Syria achieved tactical surprise on October 6. Egypt quickly got 90,000 men and 850 tanks across the canal. IAF efforts to attack bridges and Egyptian forces met heavy air defense fire. After Israel lost 14 fighters in 48 hours, the IAF stayed clear of the canal. The Israeli Army went into a defensive posture against Egypt while focusing first on defeating the more immediate threat from Syria. Israel's successful counterattack against the Syrians on October 10 forced the Egyptians to open a new offensive in order to draw off Israeli resources. This Egyptian attack failed catastrophically, partly because the IAF provided highly effective close air support once the Egyptian Army ventured beyond its SAM umbrella. After having defeated the Syrian offensive in the north and regaining lost ground, Israel counterattacked the Egyptians, crossing the Suez Canal and threatening to isolate Egyptian forces on the eastern shore. Heavy air battles ensued as both sides flew thousands of sorties to support their ground forces. Meanwhile, Israeli ground attacks crippled Egypt's SAM screen, allowing the IAF to operate more freely. The Israelis had encircled the Egyptian Third Army near Suez City when the superpowers imposed a cease-fire on October 28.

Egypt generally relied on artillery rather than close air support, and its aircraft had little effect on the ground battle. Egyptian pilots soon learned not to venture beyond the range of Egyptian SAM protection to interdict Israeli reinforcements. In aerial combat, the Israelis lost at most 8 aircraft and the Egyptians 162 in 52 major dogfights. Egyptian air defenses accounted for 35–45 Israeli aircraft but also shot down 45–60 Egyptian aircraft. Aircraft availability was crucial. The Egyptians averaged 0.6 sorties per day per aircraft, while the IAF managed 4.0 sorties per day per aircraft. Israeli centralized command and control was another important advantage.

Against Syria, Israeli aircraft at first achieved only limited success. The IAF focused its main effort on Syrian air defenses and brushed aside Syrian fighter interference. Israeli aircraft deliberately provoked so many SAM launches that Syrian missile supplies were soon exhausted. By October 10, Israel had air superiority over the Golan Heights, and the Israeli Army had begun its counterattack. Israel retook the Golan Heights and then drove to within 25 miles of Damascus. Israeli aircraft interdicted Syrian forces as they retreated and struck targets throughout Syria. The Syrian Air Force flew a number of relatively ineffective ground-attack sorties. In aerial combat the Israelis lost 6–10 aircraft, while the Syrians lost 162 in 65 major dogfights. Syrian air defenses were more successful, shooting down 27 Israeli aircraft but also at the same time shooting down several dozen Syrian aircraft.

In total, in the Yom Kippur War, Egypt and Syria probably lost more than 400 jet aircraft, mainly in aerial combat. (Because Egypt and Syria had built hardened shelters after 1967, very few of their aircraft were destroyed on the ground.) The Israelis lost about 100 aircraft, 87 of which were to ground fire. Each side flew around 10,000 sorties. While the Arab states had the advantages of numbers and surprise, the Israelis employed superior pilots in superior aircraft.

Egypt and Israel reached a peace agreement, but Syria and Israel remained at loggerheads. Syrian and Israeli fighters clashed over Lebanon in the late 1970s and early 1980s, with the last major clash in June 1982. In 1974, Israel fielded the Israeli-built Kfir (a modified Mirage). Israel soon received the American-built McDonnell-Douglas F-15 Eagle and General Dynamics F-16 Fighting Falcon fighters. In 1977–1978, Israel acquired four Grumman E-2C airborne early warning aircraft (AWACs), which could detect enemy aircraft at long range and guide friendly interceptors to them. Meanwhile, Syria received the MiG-23 fighter and the high-speed, high-altitude MiG-25 interceptor.

In July 1979, eight Syrian MiG-21s engaged Israeli aircraft that were striking Palestine Liberation Organization (PLO) targets in Lebanon. Israeli F-15s flying top cover shot down five MiGs. F-15s downed four Syrian MiGs in September 1979 and three more in late 1980. In February 1981, an F-15 shot down a Syrian MiG-25—the first time a MiG-25 had ever been downed in combat—and F-15s killed two more MiG-25s in 1982. In June 1981, eight F-16s with two F-15 escorts flew more than 600 miles to destroy the nuclear reactor at Osiraq, where Iraq was processing plutonium for nuclear weapons.

In June 1982, Israel invaded Lebanon in response to persistent attacks from the PLO. The Syrians reinforced Lebanon, where their forces included 2 SA-2, 2 SA-3, and 15 SA-6 batteries with 200 missiles and numerous antiaircraft guns. Israel employed electronic warfare and unmanned aircraft to convince Syrian SAM operators that real Israeli aircraft were overhead. When the Syrians activated their radars and fired at the unmanned aircraft, Israeli fighters launched antiradiation missiles that destroyed the radars. The Israelis then systematically killed the SAM batteries without losing a single aircraft. The Syrian Air Force sent 100 MiG-21s, MiG-23s, MiG-25s, and Su-7s to protect the SAM batteries, which encountered some 20 Israeli F-15s and F-16s directed by E-2Cs. Israel jammed the communications links between the Syrian aircraft and their ground controllers and shot down 29 Syrian planes. Syria repeated the performance for two more days, losing 53 more aircraft. Ultimately Syria lost 86 aircraft, while the Israelis lost none.

Airpower decisively affected the Arab-Israeli wars. Israeli air superiority prevented Arab aircraft from effectively attacking Israel or its army and permitted Israeli aircraft to punish Arab armies severely. Airpower allowed the Israeli armed forces to fight short, victorious campaigns at a relatively low cost in Israeli lives. Israel's lopsided aerial victories were only in part the result of technological advantage. They primarily emerged from superior leadership, organization, training, and initiative.

JAMES D. PERRY

See also

Artillery, Antiaircraft; Attrition, War of; Egypt, Armed Forces; Iraq, Armed Forces; Israel Defense Forces; Israeli Air Strikes Beginning the

Six-Day War; Israeli War of Independence, Overview; Jordan, Armed Forces; Lebanon, Israeli Invasion of; Missiles, Surface-to-Air; Osiraq Raid; Six-Day War; Suez Crisis; Syria, Armed Forces; Yom Kippur War

References

Cohen, Eliezer. *Israel's Best Defense: The First Full Story of the Israeli Air Force.* New York: Orion, 1993.

Cooling, Benjamin Franklin. *Case Studies in the Achievement of Air Superiority.* Washington, DC: U.S. Government Printing Office, 1994.

Nordeen, Lon O. *Air Warfare in the Missile Age.* Washington, DC: Smithsonian Institution Press, 1985.

Pollack, Kenneth M. *Arabs at War: Military Effectiveness, 1948–1991.* Lincoln: University of Nebraska Press, 2002.

Weizman, Ezer. *On Eagles' Wings: The Personal Story of the Leading Command of the Israeli Air Force.* New York: Macmillan 1977.

Akko, Israel

City located in northern Israel (western Galilee region). With a population of approximately 45,000 people, Akko (Acre, Akka) lies along the northern part of Haifa Bay on the Mediterranean Sea. Akko has a high population of Arabs. About one-quarter of the population is made up of Christians, Muslims, Druze, and those who follow the Baha'i faith.

Akko is one of the oldest continually inhabited places on Earth and dates back to the time of the Egyptian pharaohs (1500 BC).

Akko came under Persian rule and was controlled for a time by Alexander the Great. After the Roman-Jewish War (AD 66–77) and the destruction of the Second Temple in AD 70, Akko became home to a large population of Jews. Muslims finally wrested control of Akko from Christian Crusaders in AD 1291, in the process destroying much of the city. In the 18th and 19th centuries, Akko became an important trade and shipping center under the Turks and the Ottoman Empire.

In more modern times, Akko housed the notorious Akko Prison, operated by the British during the British Mandate for Palestine (1917–1948). Well-known Zionist leader Vladimir Jabotinsky was among those who spent time there. In 1947, Irgun Tsvai Leumi (National Military Organization) members launched a daring assault on the facility and freed numerous prisoners. After 1948, at which time the British Mandate ceased to exist, Akko Prison was converted into a hospital for the mentally ill.

Because of the age and important history that is part of Akko, the town and surrounding areas are home to numerous archaeological sites and ancient ruins. In addition to ancient sites, Akko boasts a number of edifices dating to the Middle Ages such as the Church of St. George. Akko also contains several shrines and holy places for the Baha'i religion, including the Baha'i holy place, the shrine to Bahji. Israel claimed Akko during the Israeli War of Independence (1948–1949) when Haganah fighters seized the

Contemporary photo of the coastline of Akko, Israel. (iStockPhoto.com)

town on May 17, 1948. The town was largely deserted by then, as the Arab citizens had already fled. The Israelis slowly began to resettle Akko, building several large communal apartment buildings and establishing manufacturing plants in and around it. Among the industries that call Akko home are chemicals, textiles, iron, and steel. Indeed, Akko is known as the center of Israel's steel industry.

Akko has also become a tourist attraction. Besides its seaside location, tourists flock to Akko because of its rich history and archaeological sites. Also attractive to the sightseer is the Old Arab Market, the crypt of St. John, and a centuries-old tower that overlooks Haifa Bay. An elaborate series of double-sided walls dating to the 18th century and the al-Jazzar Mosque of the same century attract tourists as well.

PAUL G. PIERPAOLI JR.

See also

Galilee; Haganah; Irgun Tsvai Leumi; Jabotinsky, Vladimir Yevgenyevich

References

Sachar, Howard M. *A History of Israel: From the Rise of Zionism to Our Time*. 3rd ed. New York: Knopf, 2007.

Shepherd, Naomi. *Ploughing Sand: British Rule in Palestine, 1917–1948*. New Brunswick, NJ: Rutgers University Press, 1999.

Akko Prison

Prison in the coastal city of Akko (Acre, Akka), located in the British Mandate for Palestine. During much of the period of British rule, political prisoners as well as common criminals were held in the former fortress renovated under Jazzar Pasha of Akko. Among the early political prisoners were Vladimir Jabotinsky and 19 of his followers, who were held there for their activities in the Arab riots in Jerusalem in April 1920. Over the years, hundreds of Jewish underground members were held in the prison, and a number of members of the Irgun Tsvai Leumi (National Military Organization) were executed there.

On May 4, 1947, members of the Irgun Tsvai Leumi carried out one of their most spectacular actions against the British Mandate authorities. On that day, they stormed the prison and managed to free a number of the prisoners held there.

With the proclamation of Israeli independence in May 1948, Akko Prison was converted into a mental hospital. Some years later the death cell and Jabotinsky's prison cell were dedicated as a national shrine.

SPENCER C. TUCKER

See also

Arab Riots, Jerusalem; Irgun Tsvai Leumi; Jabotinsky, Vladimir Yevgenyevich; Palestine, British Mandate for

References

Sachar, Howard M. *A History of Israel: From the Rise of Zionism to Our Time*. 3rd ed. New York: Knopf, 2007.

Shepherd, Naomi. *Ploughing Sand: British Rule in Palestine, 1917–1948*. New Brunswick, NJ: Rutgers University Press, 1999.

Al-Aqsa Intifada

See Intifada, Second

Al-Aqsa Martyrs Brigades

An amalgamation of militias in the West Bank, sometimes affiliated with the late Palestinian leader Yasser Arafat's Fatah movement. The al-Aqsa Martyrs Brigades consists of Palestinian nationalist groups formed in 2002 to force Israel from the West Bank and Gaza Strip through militant action, including suicide bombings. Unlike Hamas and the Palestinian Islamic Jihad, the brigade is not rooted in political Islam. It is a secular organization the primary goal of which is the creation of an autonomous Palestinian state (but not necessarily an Islamic state).

The al-Aqsa Martyrs Brigades was born out of the turbulent violence of the Second Intifada (also known as the al-Aqsa Intifada). The intifada (or uprising) was triggered partly by the breakdown in the Arab-Israeli peace process in the late 1990s. The actual fuse was lighted, however, by Likud Party leader Ariel Sharon's controversial visit to a site in Jerusalem held sacred by both Jews and Muslims in September 2000. (Sharon would become Israel's prime minister in February 2001.) The Haram al-Sharif (the Noble Sanctuary), known to Jews as the Temple Mount, is the site of the Prophet Muhammad's ascension to heaven as well as the site of both King Solomon's (First) Temple and Zerubbabel's (Second) Temple and the Mosque of Omar and the al-Aqsa Mosque. At the base of the Temple Mount is the Western Wall, a retaining wall built about the time of King Herod the Great (around 19 BC). The only physical remnant that connects to the biblical Jewish temples, the Wailing Wall as it is called, is the holiest site in Judaism today. Sharon's actions enraged Palestinians, and the al-Aqsa Martyrs Brigades arose from this outrage. The brigade took its name indirectly from the al-Aqsa Mosque and to symbolize their commitment to the Second Intifada and resistance to Israeli oppression. The brigade became one of the most active players in the intifada, which erupted shortly after Sharon's visit.

Initially, the group's strategy was to target Israeli military outposts and Jewish settlers within the West Bank and the Gaza Strip. However, in response to increased Israeli retaliation, the al-Aqsa Martyrs Brigades stepped up its activities to include targets in Israel itself. The organization cites Lebanon's militant Hezbollah group as the inspiration for its style of violence. And although the brigade does not have any documented links to Al Qaeda, it sometimes mirrored the actions of other militant organizations. The brigade does not exclusively target Israelis but has been known to attack Palestinians of differing factions and likewise has been targeted by them. For more than a year they fought Palestinian Authority (PA) leaders who attacked them, and some of these were associated with Fatah. For example, Fatah PA authorities captured and tortured brigade members in Jericho in June 2005. In some cities the brigade,

Three young women from the suicide bomber unit of the al-Aqsa Martyrs Brigades in the Gaza Strip in 2004. (Jean Chung/Corbis)

or certain brigade leaders, are regarded in a positive light for their attacks on criminals and gangs. Zakaria Zbaydi was very popular and not associated with suicide bombings. The same was true of Abdullah al-Qarawi of Jericho.

The al-Aqsa Martyrs Brigades has also fought with Palestinians over rights to establish launching sites of attacks near their homes. In July 2004, for example, militants reportedly shot and killed a 15-year-old Palestinian Arab after he and his family had tried to stop the erection of Qassam rocket launchers in their neighborhood. Most attacks have come from Gaza into places such as Sderot and were led by the Izz al-Din al-Qassam Brigade.

Israeli sources claim that many members of the al-Aqsa Martyrs Brigades are known to have come from Fatah's militant youth group Tanzim. The term "Tanzim" (Organization) is originally an Israeli identification for Fatah's militias and a means of asserting that these militias may pursue tactics other than the negotiations sought by the PN's leadership. Subsequently, Tanzim was identified by Israeli authorities as a youth organization and attributed to Marwan Barghuti after Yasser Arafat's death. Israelis also accused Barghuti of organizing the al-Aqsa Martyrs Brigades. Indeed, one of the local brigades acknowledged him as their leader, which his defenders took to mean as their source of inspiration but earned him a prison sentence. Some brigade members have been active in

the resistance, meaning Fatah's armed body, for 10–11 years and since they were 12 or 13 years old. This dates back several years past the formation of the brigades to about 1995.

In November 2003, reporters for the British Broadcasting Company (BBC) investigated the PA looking for some solid proof of a link to the al-Aqsa Martyrs Brigades. The BBC soon unearthed documents authorizing monthly payments of $50,000 from the PA to the militant group. The United States and Israel promptly denounced the PA for sponsoring terrorism. PA officials, however, insisted that the money—roughly $250 per group member—was actually intended to deter potential suicide bombers by providing them with financial assistance, thus reducing the lucrative appeal of terrorism.

On December 18, 2003, following the BBC investigation and resultant criticism, Fatah officially recognized its connection to the al-Aqsa Martyrs Brigades by inviting the group to join the Fatah Council. Arafat's personal involvement with planning the group's activities is open to conjecture. Some acknowledged him as the head of the group who directly ordered its movements, while others maintained that he was not involved in day-to-day planning or operations.

Typically, al-Aqsa Martyrs Brigades attacks have been carried out via shootings and suicide bombings. The bombings have included female suicide bombers, and several children have also been involved. In addition, the brigade has resorted to Qassam rocket attacks on Israel launched from Palestinian territory. Among the worst of the attacks charged to the brigade have been twin suicide bombings in downtown Tel Aviv in January 2003 that killed 23 and wounded 100, a March 2002 suicide bombing of a Jerusalem café that killed 11 and wounded 50, and a sniper assault at an Israeli checkpoint in the West Bank that killed 10 Israelis in March 2002. However, the al-Aqsa Martyrs Brigades is not committed to the destruction of Israel. Rather, its goal is that Israel should recognize the 1967 borders, and the brigade is loyal to Fatah's two-state solution.

Arafat died on November 11, 2004, and in commemoration of his passing, the al-Aqsa Martyrs Brigades changed its name to al-Shahid Yasser Arafat (the Martyr Yasser Arafat) Brigade, although it is still widely known as the al-Aqsa Martyrs Brigades. The group is reportedly being integrated into the PA's official security forces and supported Fatah candidate Mahmoud Abbas in the January 2005 Palestinian presidential election, although had Marwan Barghuti not withdrawn the brigade probably would have supported him. Brigade spokesmen have said that they would honor the PA's plan to disarm the organization and integrate members into officially sanctioned police duties. It remains to be seen whether the group will be integrated into security forces under Abbas's government in light of their repression at the hands of his faction and their competition with Hamas fighters.

SHERIFA ZUHUR

See also

Abbas, Mahmoud; Arafat, Yasser; Barghuti, Marwan; Hamas; Haram al-Sharif; Hezbollah; Intifada, Second; Israel; Palestinian Authority; Sharon, Ariel; Western Wall

References

Jones, Clive. *Between Terrorism and Civil War: The Al-Aqsa Intifada.* London: Routledge, 2005.

Parsons, Nigel Craig. *The Politics of the Palestinian Authority: From Oslo to Al-Aqsa.* London: Routledge, 2003.

Al-Aqsa Mosque

The al-Aqsa Mosque (literally, "farthest mosque") is both a building and a complex of religious buildings in Jerusalem. It is known to Muslims as al-Haram al-Sharif (the Noble Sanctuary) and to Jews and Christians as the Har ha-Bayit or Temple Mount. The whole area of the Noble Sanctuary is considered by Muslims to be the al-Aqsa Mosque, and the entire precinct is inviolable according to Islamic law. It is considered specifically part of the waqf (endowment) land that had included the Western Wall (Wailing Wall), property of an Algerian family, and more generally a waqf of all of Islam.

When viewed as a complex of buildings, the al-Aqsa Mosque is dominated and bounded by two major structures: the al-Aqsa Mosque building on the east and the Dome of the Rock (or the Mosque of Omar) on the west. The Dome of the Rock is the oldest holy building in Islam. Dating from AD 690, it surrounds a large rock from which Islamic tradition believes that the Prophet Muhammad

ascended to heaven at the end of his Night Journey in 621. The rock is also considered in Jewish tradition to be the place at which Abraham bound Isaac for sacrifice.

Additional structures that compose the al-Aqsa Mosque complex include the Dome of the Chain, east of the Dome of the Rock in the center of the complex; the Dome of the Prophet; the Dome of the Mi'raj; the Dome of al-Nahawiyah; the Dome of the Hebronite; the Minbar of Burhan al-Din; the Golden Gate; the Musalla Marwan; the Ancient Aqsa; and the Islamic Museum. As a complex, the al-Aqsa Mosque is the third most holy shrine in Islam.

The Umayyad caliph Abd al-Malik ibn Marwan commissioned the building of both the Dome of the Rock and the original wooden al-Aqsa Mosque building, with the latter being completed in 710 by his son al-Walid. The al-Aqsa Mosque building became a center of Islamic learning and worship.

The site of the compound is also holy to the Jews, who believe that a portion of the complex is built over the ruins of the biblical Jewish temples. At the base of the Temple Mount sits the Western Wall, a retaining wall built by King Herod the Great around 19 BC to reinforce his reconstruction of the Second Temple. Although not a direct structural part of any of the original buildings, it remains the only surviving physical connection to the biblical temples and therefore remains the most sacred site in Judaism today. Although some believe that a new Jewish temple can be built without disturbing the Noble Sanctuary, others, such as the Temple Mount Faithful, assert the right to rebuild the temple regardless of the impact on the mosque complex.

The war that ensued upon the Israeli declaration of independence left Israel with access to only West Jerusalem. Located in the Old City (which itself lies in East Jerusalem), the Western Wall, the Temple Mount, and the al-Aqsa Mosque complex remained under the control of the Jordanians and the Palestinians until the capture of East Jerusalem by the Israelis in the Six-Day War (1967). The Israelis cleared the area in front of the wall, creating a plaza used for prayer.

Muslims have at times showered the plaza area with rocks from the Temple Mount above, and the al-Aqsa complex has also been the target of Jewish extremists, most notably when it was set on fire by a delusional Australian tourist in 1969. Additionally, ancient tunnels running underneath the complex were discovered in 1981, 1988, and 1996. In the latter year, Israeli prime minister Benjamin Netanyahu and Jerusalem mayor Ehud Olmert opened an exit for the Western Wall tunnel, sparking three days of Palestinian riots in which more than a dozen Israelis and approximately a hundred Palestinians died.

When Israeli prime minister Ariel Sharon staged his provocative visit to the Temple Mount complex on September 28, 2000, he did not enter any of the complex's buildings. However, the Palestinian faithful saw the visit as a violation of the sacred environs. Sharon was also accompanied by troops, and up to that point, Palestinian security personnel had controlled entry to the Haram al-Sharif by agreement between Israelis and Palestinians. Sharon's

The al-Aqsa Mosque, among the holiest of Muslim sites, is situated in the Old City of Jerusalem. It is part of a complex of structures with historical and religious significance for Christians and Jews as well. (Dmitry Bomshtein/iStockphoto.com)

34-minute visit and the ensuing civil violence, the worst in contemporary Israel's history, began what is popularly known as the Second Intifada or the al-Aqsa Intifada, a sequel to the First Intifada (1988–1992). The Palestinian militia known as the al-Aqsa Martyrs Brigades is part of this continuing intifada.

RICHARD EDWARDS

See also

Intifada, First; Intifada, Second; Netanyahu, Benjamin; Olmert, Ehud; Sharon, Ariel

References

Duncan, Alistair. *The Noble Sanctuary: Portrait of a Holy Place in Arab Jerusalem.* London: Longman, 1972.

Hamilton, Robert William. *The Structural History of the Aqsa Mosque: A Record of Archaeological Gleanings from the Repairs of 1938–1942.* London: Oxford University Press, 1949.

Nuseibeh, Said. *The Dome of the Rock.* New York: Rizzoli, 1996.

Al-Aqsa Mosque Massacre
Event Date: October 8, 1990

The killing of Palestinian Arabs in and around the al-Aqsa Mosque on the Temple Mount (Haram al-Sharif) by Israeli troops on October 8, 1990. In the attack, some 23 Palestinians died and another 850 were injured. The Temple Mount is considered the third holiest site in Islam. The confrontation emerged from the activities of a Jewish organization that called itself the Temple Trustees. The organization sought to occupy the Temple Mount and to begin construction on the Third Temple there. Quite naturally, Arabs and Palestinians were outraged by what they viewed as the potential desecration of a significant holy shrine.

In the days leading up to October 8, the Temple Trustees announced plans for a mass march to the Temple Mount, the objective of which would be the laying of a cornerstone for a new temple. The march was very well publicized and began drawing a large Jewish contingent. The Israeli government did little to prevent the march, so the demonstration went forward despite the obvious threats it might pose to civil order. To make matters worse, the leader of the Temple Trustees, Ghershon Salomon, publicly exhorted Israelis to rally to the cause, reestablish their "sacred ties" to the Temple Mount, and terminate Arab claims to the area, including the al-Aqsa Mosque. Such rhetoric served only to stoke Arab enmity toward the marchers and the Israeli government.

By the time the march had reached its peak, as many as 200,000 Israelis may have joined the fray. (Israeli estimates are lower.)

A wounded Palestinian is taken to the hospital from the al-Aqsa Mosque in Jerusalem's Old City after serious rioting led Israeli police to fire on the crowd, October 8, 1990. The incident left 23 Palestinians dead and 850 wounded. (Sven Nackstrand/AFP/Getty Images)

Israeli security forces, in an attempt to keep Palestinians and Jews separated during the march, began cordoning off roads leading to Jerusalem and Haram al-Sharif. The idea was to prevent Palestinians from assembling their own counterdemonstrations. Furthermore, Israeli officials closed the doors to the al-Aqsa Mosque to prevent even more people from entering. Unfortunately, this was a move that came too late, for already assembled in the mosque were perhaps 2,000–3,000 Muslims, convened there by the imam in a show of force to prevent any Jews from entering the sanctuary.

When the marchers began to converge on the Temple Mount and efforts were afoot to lay the foundation stone of the Third Temple, mayhem ensued, and Israeli security forces lost control of the situation. Trapped in the al-Aqsa Mosque and with nowhere to go, the Arabs there attempted to leave. As they did so, at approximately 10:00 a.m. an Israeli soldier opened fire on the crowd. The result was utter chaos. For almost 30 minutes, the Israelis attempted to quell the crowd by firing indiscriminately with machine guns and tear gas. The ultimate—and tragic—result was the deaths of 23 Palestinians and the wounding of 850 others, some Israelis but mostly Palestinians.

Massacres in the Middle East

Name	Date	Location	Committed By	Committed Against	Number Killed
al-Aqsa Mosque Massacre	October 8, 1990	Jerusalem, Israel	Israeli soldiers	Arab protesters	23
Baldat al-Shaikh Massacre	January 30–31, 1947	Baldat al-Shaikh, Palestine	Israeli paramilitary forces	Arab civilians	60
Hebron Massacre	August 23–24, 1929	Hebron, West Bank	Arab mob	Jewish civilians	68
Hebron Mosque Massacre	February 25, 1994	Hebron, West Bank	Israeli gunman	Arab worshippers	29
Kafr-Qasim Massacre	October 29, 1956	Kafr-Qasim, Israel	Israeli soldiers	Arab civilians	49
Lod Airport Massacre	May 30, 1972	Tel Aviv, Israel	Japanese terrorists	passengers (various nationalities)	26
Qibya Massacre	October 14, 1953	Qibya, West Bank	Israeli soldiers	Arab civilians	60
Sabra and Shatila Massacre	September 16–18, 1982	Sabra and Shatila, Lebanon	Phalangists	Arab refugees	350–3,500

Internal and international pressure on the government in Tel Aviv compelled Israeli prime minister Yitzhak Shamir to form a fact-finding committee, headed by former Mossad director Tu'fi Zamir. After months of investigations, the Zamir Committee found no specific fault with the Israeli security forces present at the al-Aqsa Mosque that day. Instead, the committee found fault with extremists on both sides, although the implication was that Arab extremism had largely contributed to the showdown. This begs the question, however, as to why the Israelis had not anticipated such violence and why they had not attempted to stop the march in the first place. Since the massacre, Haram al-Sharif has witnessed increased security to prevent another show of mass violence.

PAUL G. PIERPAOLI JR.

See also

Al-Aqsa Mosque; Haram al-Sharif; Jerusalem; Jerusalem, Old City of; Shamir, Yitzhak

References

Journalists of Reuters. *The Israeli-Palestinian Conflict: Crisis in the Middle East.* New York: Reuters/Prentice Hall, 2002.

Qumsiyeh, Mazin B. *Sharing the Land of Canaan: Human Rights and the Israeli-Palestinian Struggle.* London: Pluto, 2004.

Tessler, Mark. *A History of the Israeli-Palestinian Conflict.* Bloomington: Indiana University Press, 1994.

Al Arish

See El Arish; El Arish Scheme

Al-Bireh

West Bank town in the Palestinian territories. Al-Bireh, meaning "water well" for its numerous springs and wells, is some 10 miles north of Jerusalem and 35 miles inland from the Mediterranean. Located among mountains about 3,000 feet above sea level, it is in a watershed area. The climate is moderate, and there is adequate rainfall. Al-Bireh constitutes with nearby Ramallah a single constituency for elections to the Palestinian Authority (PA). The twin cities constitute one area of population as well, as there is no distinct border.

A Canaanite community originally known as Ba-irut the town is thought to have been established around 3500 BC and owed its importance to its location. It is a major crossroads astride the main north-south road from Lebanon to Egypt and an east-west road running from Jaffa (Yafo) to Jericho. Tradition holds that Abraham passed through the town on his way to Egypt.

During the Arab-Jewish Communal War of 1947–1948, many Arab refugees crowded into al-Bireh, more than doubling its population. The Jordanian Arab Legion took control of the Ramallah/al-Bireh area during the Israeli War of Independence (1948–1949), preventing Israeli forces from capturing the cities and also preventing an exodus of civilians from the area. A number of refugee

camps were also established in the area. Al-Jalazon, Kalandia, al-Amari, and Kadura today house some 30,000 refugees.

Following the war, Jordan annexed the entire West Bank of the Jordan River. Al-Bireh was relatively tranquil during the years of Jordanian control (1948–1967), but that changed with the Six-Day War in June 1967. Following Jordan's entry into the war, Israel Defense Forces (IDF) captured al-Bireh on June 7, 1967. Under the terms of the 1993 Oslo Agreement, al-Bireh was turned over to the PA in 1994. Al-Bireh is currently the second-largest Palestinian town housing PA offices and as a result has seen considerable new construction. The city has a population of about 40,000 people.

SPENCER C. TUCKER

See also

Oslo Accords; Palestinian Authority; Ramallah

References

Beck, John A. *The Land of Milk and Honey: An Introduction to the Geography of Israel.* St. Louis: Concordia, 2006.

Orni, Ephraim. *Geography of Israel.* Philadelphia: Jewish Publication Society of America, 1977.

Shaheen, Azeez. *Ramallah: Its History and Genealogies.* Birzeit, Palestine: Birzeit University Press, 1982.

al-Gama'a al-Islamiyya

See Gamaat Islamiya

Al Jazeera

The most popular news agency in the Arab world and its first large non-government-operated news network. Founded in 1996, Al Jazeera (Jazira) has become well known for its willingness to report on topics that are controversial in both the Middle East and in the Western media. Al Jazeera is based in Qatar but is staffed by an international body of reporters. It claims to be the only uncensored news agency in the Middle East. However, its commitment to presenting material and interviews that countered U.S. foreign policy in the Middle East and at times were sharply critical of Middle Eastern leaders or governments made it a focus of displeasure for the U.S. government, which banned its reporters from Iraq.

The Arabic term *al-Jazeera* (meaning "the island") is a colloquial reference to the Arabian Peninsula. Its origins are rooted in a response to the censorship and control in the Arab media on the part of political commentators and reporters and the recognition of the new market available through satellite television.

Although popular with many in the region, the British Broadcasting Corporation (BBC) has discontinued much of its programming there in recent years. Many of the journalists employed by the BBC were eager to continue broadcasting and, together with Sheikh Hamad bin Thamer al-Thani, approached the emir of Qatar for money to establish a new network. Al-Thani, a cousin of Emir Sheikh Hamad ibn Khalifa al-Thani, convinced the Qatari ruler to provide a grant of $150 million. This became the start-up money for Al Jazeera. The network continues to receive financial assistance from Qatar and is further funded by advertising revenue and by distributing its exclusive news feeds.

Despite the subsidy from Qatar, Al Jazeera set out to maintain a strict independence from censorship, which was previously almost unknown in the region. Al Jazeera chose as its corporate motto "the right to speak up." It also proclaimed to the world that it sought in its reporting "objectivity, accuracy, and a passion for truth."

Broadcasting via satellite since November 1996, Al Jazeera quickly became the most-watched media outlet in the Arab world. Unfettered by the official censorship of government-sponsored news reporting, Al Jazeera has earned a reputation among its audience as a network committed to presenting multiple sides of any debate.

Al Jazeera became the first major news outlet in the Arabic-speaking Middle East to regularly present interviews with official Israeli spokesmen as well as with banned Islamist organizations and feminist groups. Al Jazeera has also been open in its critique of events that illustrate dictatorial or authoritarian actions by the governments of Saudi Arabia, Egypt, Syria, and Iraq. Such diversity of

opinion and outspoken criticism of oppression made Al Jazeera a popular force in the latter part of the 1990s. It was in 2001, however, that Al Jazeera captured the attention of news audiences far beyond the Arabic-speaking world.

When the dramatic terror attacks of September 11, 2001, were carried out against the United States, Al Jazeera broadcast footage of Osama bin Laden and Sulayman Abu Ghaith praising the carnage. For many in the West who were otherwise unfamiliar with Al Jazeera, the network was now immediately seen as a mouthpiece for Al Qaeda. Al Jazeera vehemently rejected this charge, stating that it had merely presented news footage obtained in the interest of showing all sides in a major story. Nevertheless, the broadcast initiated a new barrage of attacks, particularly by the U.S. government, against Al Jazeera. These were exacerbated by Al Jazeera's coverage of Iraqi resistance activities to the American military presence, which the U.S. government presented as an insurgency carried out mainly by foreign elements.

Although news organizations around the world have purchased the rights to broadcast the footage from Al Jazeera, the George W. Bush administration has been extremely critical of the network. The administration was outraged when Al Jazeera broadcast scenes of

Osama bin Laden appearing on Al Jazeera television on October 17, 2001, praising the September 11 attacks on the United States. (Maher Attar/Corbis Sygma)

suffering experienced by Afghan civilians in the wake of the November 2001 invasion of their country by U.S. military forces, claiming that it sponsored the perpetuation of terrorist ideals. News organizations throughout the world, however, were impressed with the unparalleled quality of the Afghan war coverage by Al Jazeera. Indeed, its feeds were widely purchased for rebroadcast.

The stakes against Al Jazeera in the United States were raised even higher in early 2003. In the run-up to the March 2003 invasion of Iraq, Al Jazeera was accused of being connected to Iraqi spies by a former Iraqi opposition organization known as the Iraqi National Congress. As a consequence, the U.S. Central Intelligence Agency (CIA) declared Al Jazeera to be an organ of anti-American propaganda. Al Jazeera's stock was banned from the New York Stock Exchange, and its reporters were ejected from the trading floor. Ironically, the Saddam Hussein regime also tossed out of Iraq Al Jazeera's main reporter at the time, claiming that he was a spy for the United States. In response, Al Jazeera launched a searing editorial attack on an Iraqi government that tried at every turn to thwart free reporting from the country. Under attack from both the United States and Iraq in the days before the launch of the Iraq War, Al Jazeera became a symbol for what some see as hypocrisy in both Iraq and the United States in regard to a free press.

As the invasion of Iraq progressed in 2003 and the occupation of Iraq took hold, Al Jazeera continued to provide some of the world's most controversial and in-depth reporting, and its feeds were rebroadcast on every continent. Despite its headquarters in Baghdad and Kabul being bombed by U.S. forces and pressure being exerted by Washington on the Qatari government to shut it down, Al Jazeera's reporting on Afghanistan and Iraq continues to be the most comprehensive in the world. In fact, it is often the only reporting to focus on the heart-wrenching experiences of local people coping with disaster. Al Jazeera continued to broadcast controversial missives from insurgents, including footage of Westerners held hostage, until the Iraqi interim government, with U.S. encouragement, banned the network from the country in September 2004.

The 2003 launch of Arabic- and English-language Web sites for Al Jazeera was plagued with controversy. Hackers repeatedly interrupted service on the English-language site, and several Internet service providers cancelled contracts with Al Jazeera when the network refused to remove controversial content. In 2005 an undeterred Al Jazeera planned to launch an international English-language satellite network based in Kuala Lumpur. Through extreme adversity and international controversy, Al Jazeera continues to be one of the most-watched news networks in the world, promoting itself as one of the only truly free voices in the Middle East.

NANCY STOCKDALE

See also

Iraq; Terrorism; United States, Middle East Policy

References

El-Nawawy, Mohammed, and Adel Iskander. *Al Jazeera: The Story of the Network That Is Rattling Governments and Redefining Journalism.* Boulder, CO: Westview, 2003.

Miles, Hugh. *Al Jazeera: How Arab TV News Challenges America.* New York: Grove, 2005.

Al-Mawasi

A Palestinian enclave located along the coast on the Gaza Strip, which prior to the Israeli withdrawal in 2005 was almost entirely surrounded by the Jewish settlement of Gush Katif to the east. Al-Mawasi (meaning "gardens") and commonly known as Mawasi, is a strip of coastal land measuring .62 miles (1 km) wide by 8.7 miles (14 km) long. It is divided administratively into the Khan Yunis and Rafah Mawasi. Al-Mawasi is classified under the 1994 Oslo Agreement I as a yellow area, with Israel controlling security and Palestine holding civil jurisdiction. Some 760 families (5,300 people) currently inhabit the Khan Yunis Mawasi. Of that number, 220 families are Palestinian refugees who fled to al-Mawasi in 1948. The residents of Malhala are Bedouin refugees, primarily from the Beersheba area. Approximately 430 families (3,000 persons) live in the Rafah Mawasi, including refugees from the Ashdod area who live in the so-called Swedish Village, part of the Rafah refugee camp.

At least 15 Israeli settlements were established on al-Mawasi including Katif, Ganei Tal, Kfar Yam, Neve Dekalim, Gan Or, Bedolah, Rafih Yam, and Morag. In 2005 al-Mawasi was the site of Israeli demonstrations protesting the Israeli government's withdrawal from Gaza. Demonstrators seized empty buildings and threw stones at Palestinian homes.

After the June 1967 Six-Day Way, the al-Mawasi Palestinians were not allowed to travel to Khan Yunis or Rafah, where some had families and property. Later, they were increasingly restricted because of their proximity to the Israeli Gush Katif settlement to the east. The Gush Katif central administration was based at Neve Dekalim, and the area was subjected to special security arrangements. The Palestinians used to fish to make a living but were forbidden to do so. Instead, they relied on agriculture. However, since 2000 agricultural output suffered from land-razing and Israeli-imposed transport restrictions. Electricity was available only at night for five to six hours through a temporary generator. The Rafah Khan Yunis school lacks electricity, water, and sufficient teachers, and its clinic has electricity for only two hours a day. The Khan Yunis Mawasi has only one private well for water and no sewage system.

Israeli settlers' standard of living in the area was considerably higher than the Palestinians' because the Israeli settlers enjoyed state subsidies and adequate services, well-maintained roads, better residences, and easier access to schools, clinics, and supermarkets. Until 2005 there were approximately 3,900 Israeli settlers in the area.

Palestinian truck drivers used to wait for hours to drive through checkpoints. Only men are allowed to walk through checkpoints on foot, and carrying metal including coins through the checkpoint was not allowed. Restrictions on gas for cooking and heating were also imposed. Of additional concern to Palestinians were incidents

An Israeli security guard fires his weapon into the air to warn a Palestinian crowd (*unseen*) at al-Mawasi during clashes outside an abandoned Palestinian house recently occupied by Jewish settlers, June 28, 2005. (AFP/Getty Images)

of the dumping of toxic waste in the area by Israel and the presence of four sewage treatment plants that serve Israeli settlements but pollute Palestinian areas. Since the 2005 Israeli pullout, a Red Cross project has restored some of the Shanshola boats used to fish sardines.

Sherifa Zuhur

See also

Expellees and Refugees, Palestinian; Gaza Strip; Gaza Strip Disengagement; Khan Yunis; Palestinian Refugee Camps

References

B'tselem, with Shlomi Swisa, Najib Kokaya, et al. "Al-Mawasi, Gaza Strip: Impossible Life in an Isolated Enclave." Status Report. Jerusalem: B'tselem (Israeli Information Center for Human Rights in the Occupied Territories), March 2003.

Palestinian Centre for Human Rights. *Suffering in Isolation: A Report on Life Under Occupation in the Mawasi Areas in the Gaza Strip.* Gaza City: Palestinian Centre for Human Rights, 2003.

Al-Muntada al-Adabi

See Literary Club

Al Qaeda

International radical Islamic organization, the hallmark of which is the perpetration of terrorist attacks against Western interests in the name of Islam. In the late 1980s Al Qaeda (Arabic for "base" or "foundation") fought with the mujahideen against the Soviet occupation of Afghanistan. The organization is, however, best known for the September 11, 2001, terrorist attacks in the United States, the worst such attacks in the history of that nation. The founding of Al Qaeda, which is comprised of salafi (purist) Sunni Muslims, is shrouded in controversy.

Al Qaeda was created sometime between 1987 or 1988 by Sheikh Abdullah Azzam, a mentor to Osama bin Laden, the current head of the group. Azzam was a professor at King Abd al-Aziz University in Jidda, Saudi Arabia. Bin Laden attended that university, where he met and was strongly influenced by Azzam.

Al Qaeda grew out of the Mujahideen Services Bureau that Azzam established in Peshawar. Bin Laden funded the organization and was considered the deputy director. This organization recruited, trained, and transported Muslim volunteers from any Muslim nation into Afghanistan to fight the jihad (holy war) against the Soviet armies in the 1980s. Radical groups such as the Gamaat Islamiya and the Egyptian Islamic Jihad developed the credo for Al Qaeda, basing their beliefs in turn on many ideas including those of Sayyid Qutb, an executed member of the Muslim Brotherhood, and Abd al-Salam al-Faraj whose influential pamphlet *al-Farida al-Gha'iba* (The Missing Duty) asserted the primacy of armed jihad to overthrow apostate Muslim governments. Azzam adopted and expanded on these arguments, and bin Laden applied them to the government of Saudi Arabia, which he believed was too closely allied with the West. Thus, armed struggle should combat the far as well as the near enemy in order to create a new Islamic society. Following the mysterious death of Sheikh Azzam in November 1989, perhaps at bin Laden's behest, bin Laden took over the leadership of Al Qaeda. He has continued to work toward Azzam's goal of creating an international organization comprised of mujahideen (soldiers) who will fight the oppression of Muslims throughout the world. Al Qaeda actually has several goals: to destroy Israel, to rid the Islamic world of the influence of Western civilization, to reestablish an authentic form of government throughout the world, to fight against any government viewed as contrary to the ideals of Islamic law and religion, and to aid Islamic groups trying to establish an Islamic form of government in their countries.

The organization of Al Qaeda has a *majlis al-shura,* or consultative council form of leadership. The *emir al-mu'minin* (commander of the faithful) is bin Laden, followed by several other generals, and then additional leaders of related groups. Some sources say there are 24 related groups as part of the consultative council. The council consists of four committees: military, religious-legal, finance, and media. Each leader of these committees has been selected personally by bin Laden and reports directly to him. All levels of Al Qaeda are highly compartmentalized, and secrecy is the key to all operations.

Al Qaeda's ideology has appealed to both Middle Eastern and non–Middle Eastern Muslim groups. There are also a number of radical Islamic terrorist groups who initiated an association with Al Qaeda via public declarations, such as Al Qaeda fi Bilad al-Rafidhayn (in the land of the two rivers, meaning Iraq) and Al Qaeda fi Jazirat al-Arabiyya (of the Arabian Peninsula). Nevertheless, Al Qaeda continues to be the central force of world terrorism because of the media attention given to its occasional pronouncements.

The genesis of Al Qaeda's great antipathy toward the West—in particular the United States—can be traced back to the Persian Gulf War (1991), precipitated by the Iraqi invasion of Kuwait in August 1990. Bin Laden, originally a well-to-do Saudi Arabian, allegedly offered to commit Al Qaeda mujahideen fighters to the defense of Saudi Arabia in case of an Iraqi move on that nation. The Saudi government declined the offer and instead decided to permit the stationing of thousands of U.S. and coalition soldiers in Saudi Arabia during the run-up to the war. This move enraged bin Laden, who perceived the presence of foreign troops in Saudi Arabia as a blatant acknowledgment of the political linkage between his govern-

ment and the United States. He portrayed this as a religious failing. Saudi Arabia is home to both Mecca and Medina, the holiest of places in all of Islam. When he condemned the stationing of troops in Saudi Arabia, bin Laden was expelled from the kingdom and had his citizenship revoked. He then took up temporary residence in the Sudan.

Once in Sudan, bin Laden began training Al Qaeda fighters and is believed to have carried out an abortive assassination attempt against Egyptian president Hosni Mubarak in 1994. Under intense international pressure led by the United States, Sudan expelled bin Laden and Al Qaeda leadership in late 1996. From Sudan, they traveled directly to Afghanistan, where the Islamic fundamentalist Taliban regime had already ensconced itself. The Taliban not only protected Al Qaeda but in all probability helped arm it and by doing so gave to it an air of legitimacy, at least in Afghanistan. In 1998 bin Laden joined forces with leaders from the Egyptian Islamic Jihad and several other radical organizations, all of whom vowed to wage a holy war against Israel and its allies. In August of that year, Al Qaeda carried out what are thought to be its first overseas attacks against Western interests. That month saw the car bombing of the U.S. embassies in Dar es Salaam, Tanzania, and Nairobi, Kenya. More than 200 people died in the attacks, and another 4,000 were wounded. In October 2000 Al Qaeda also carried out an attack on the U.S. Navy guided missile destroyer *Cole* in the Yemeni port of Aden in which 17 sailors perished.

No attacks by Al Qaeda are known to have occurred against Israel, but the group's most horrific deed was the September 11, 2001, attacks on the United States that killed an estimated 2,976 people. The attacks were carried out by the hijacking of four jetliners, two of which were flown into New York City's World Trade Center, destroying both towers. A third jetliner was crashed into the Pentagon outside Washington, D.C., while a fourth, supposedly bound for the White House, crashed in a western Pennsylvania field, killing all onboard.

The war on terror, so-called by U.S. president George W. Bush, has had Al Qaeda on the run since the September 11 attacks. Some of the leadership has been killed, but bin Laden has thus far apparently eluded capture or death. Since the 2003 Anglo-American invasion of Iraq, Al Qaeda is thought to be supporting the growing insurgency in Iraq, which became a full-blown civil war during 2006. While most Arab and Muslim governments have tried to distance themselves from Al Qaeda and its operations, there can be little doubt that the group enjoys support among significant elements of the populations of these countries.

Bin Laden has been able to put most of the radical Islamic terrorist groups under the umbrella of Al Qaeda. Indeed, its leadership has spread throughout the world, and its influence penetrates many religious, social, and economical structures in most Muslim communities. Today, the leadership of Al Qaeda continues to elude American intelligence and Western armies in Afghanistan and Pakistan. The membership of Al Qaeda remains difficult to determine because of its decentralized organizational structure.

Harry Raymond Hueston

See also
Mubarak, Hosni; Muslim Brotherhood; Terrorism

References
Bergen, Peter L. *Holy War, Inc.* New York: Touchstone, 2002.
Gunaratna, Rohan. *Inside Al Qaeda.* New York: Columbia University Press, 2002.
Hueston, Harry R., and B. Vizzin. *Terrorism 101.* 2nd ed. Ann Arbor, MI: XanEdu, 2004.
Zuhur, Sherifa. *A Hundred Osamas: Islamist Threats and the Future of Counterinsurgency.* Carlisle Barracks, PA: Strategic Studies Institute, U.S. Army War College, 2006.

Al-Saiqa

A small Palestinian guerrilla organization with close ties to the Baathist regime in Syria. Palestinian refugees and members of the Palestinian faction of the Syrian Baath Party founded al-Saiqa (Thunderbolt) in December 1968. The group is officially known as the Organization of the Vanguards of the Popular Liberation War. Al-Saiqa's membership peaked at about 5,000 in the early 1970s, but the group's credibility as a legitimate Palestinian organization has since declined because of its inability to act independently from Syria.

From its inception, al-Saiqa's central purpose was to serve Syrian interests and exercise considerable influence within the Palestinian national movement. In February 1969 the group joined the Palestine Liberation Organization (PLO). Already by 1970, al-Saiqa constituted an armed force second in size only to Yasser Arafat's Fatah. With hundreds of fighters under arms and as the first Palestinian group to directly receive both Soviet weapons and training, al-Saiqa seemed poised to assume a permanent leadership role within the PLO. By 1971, however, the domestic situation in Syria had changed significantly, and President Hafez al-Assad, the air force general who seized control of the country in a 1970 military coup, purged al-Saiqa's leadership. The group's operations now fell entirely under the control of the Syrian Ministry of Defense, and al-Saiqa's new leader, Zuhayr Muhsin, secured his position based largely on his loyalty to the new regime.

The outbreak of the Lebanese Civil War served to further discredit al-Saiqa as an organization dedicated to Palestinian interests. Its open support of Syria's 1976 invasion of Lebanon and its ambitions of regional hegemony led to mass defections, and the group became embroiled in clashes with fellow Palestinian groups in the streets of Lebanese cities. Al-Saiqa's fortunes further plummeted on July 26, 1979, when its capable leader, Muhsin, was assassinated in Nice, France, a murder attributed variously to the Israelis and the Arab Liberation Front, a Palestinian group supported by Iraq's Baath Party. The incident revealed al-Saiqa's growing isolation and the ever-widening gaps dividing the Palestinian national movement across the Middle East.

In the 1980s after the group's expulsion from Beirut, al-Saiqa drifted toward outright confrontation with Arafat's Fatah movement when it became a founding member of the Damascus-based organization known as the Palestinian National Salvation Front. Intent on blocking Arafat's efforts to improve relations with Jordan and Egypt, al-Saiqa worked to promote Syrian interests in the ongoing armed struggle of the Palestinians and the rejection of peace talks with Israel.

The future prospects for al-Saiqa as an organization are very much linked to the fate of the Syrian Baathist regime. With the withdrawal of Syrian forces from Lebanon in 2005, the Lebanese government moved quickly to arrest the local commander of al-Saiqa in accordance with the United Nations (UN) resolution to disarm militant groups in the country. In the absence of Syrian military protection, the group has been exposed as rather defenseless. It is likely doomed altogether if the Baath Party is ousted from power in Damascus.

JONAS KAUFFELDT

See also
Arafat, Yasser; Assad, Hafez al-; Baathism; Fatah; Lebanon, Civil War in; Palestine Liberation Organization; Popular Front for the Liberation of Palestine–General Command; Syria; Syria, Armed Forces

References
O'Neill, Bard E. *Armed Struggle in Palestine: A Political-Military Analysis.* Boulder, CO: Westview, 1978.
Quandt, William B., et al. *The Politics of Palestinian Nationalism.* Berkeley: University of California Press, 1973.
Rubin, Barry. *Revolution until Victory? The Politics and History of the PLO.* Reprint ed. Cambridge: Harvard University Press, 2003.

Albright, Madeleine
Born: May 15, 1937

Democratic Party foreign policy adviser, U.S. ambassador to the United Nations (UN) during 1993–1997, and secretary of state during 1997–2001. Madeleine Albright was born Marie Jana Korbel in Prague, Czechoslovakia, on May 15, 1937. Her father, Josef Korbel, was a diplomat, and he and his wife had converted to Catholicism from Judaism. In 1939 when the Germans took over Czechoslovakia, the Korbel family fled to Britain. Following the defeat of Germany, the family returned to Prague, where Korbel was appointed Czechoslovak ambassador to Yugoslavia and Albania. A few months after the February 1948 communist coup in Czechoslovakia, the family again sought asylum, this time in the United States. In 1949 they settled in Denver, Colorado, where Korbel became a professor at the University of Colorado and developed an acclaimed program in international relations. He would become an adviser to two U.S. secretaries of state and his own daughter.

An excellent student, Madeleine Albright graduated from Wellesley College in Massachusetts in 1959 and married Joseph Albright, a journalist from a distinguished family. Later they divorced. While rearing three daughters, Albright earned a PhD in government and public law from Columbia University, where she worked with Professor Zbigniew Brzezinski, later the national security adviser to President Jimmy Carter.

U.S. secretary of state Madeleine Albright at a press conference regarding the Middle East peace talks, September 19, 1997. (Najlah Feanny/Corbis Saba)

Following extensive volunteer work for the Democratic Party, in 1976 Albright became chief legislative assistant to Maine senator Edmund Muskie. In 1982 she became a professor of international affairs and director of the Women in Foreign Service Program at Georgetown University's School of Foreign Service. She was active in the presidential campaigns of Walter Mondale (1984) and Michael Dukakis (1988), serving as chief foreign policy adviser to both candidates. Meanwhile, she built her reputation as an authority on foreign policy and women's issues while forming close personal ties with fellow Wellesley alumna Hillary Rodham Clinton. Upon his 1993 election to the presidency, William Jefferson Clinton appointed Albright U.S. ambassador to the UN, a post she took up in February 1994. Her extensive knowledge of foreign languages and Balkan ethnic politics served her well at the UN.

In January 1997 Clinton chose Albright to be secretary of state, the highest government post held to that time by an American woman. Her charm, sense of humor, and sharp wit garnered wide press attention. The exhilaration of her first days in office were clouded by a journalist's revelation that three of her grandparents had perished in Nazi concentration camps and that Albright's immediate family had purposefully obscured their Jewish background. Albright, who had been baptized Roman Catholic at the age of five and had joined the Episcopal Church upon her marriage, knew nothing of her Jewish ancestry.

Early in Albright's term, questions were raised about the effectiveness of a woman, especially one with a Jewish heritage, negotiating with Middle Eastern heads of state, but Albright soon established effective ties with Saudi Arabian officials and forged a strong friendship with King Hussein of Jordan. Still, the Israeli-Palestinian conflict proved intractable. The Clinton administration had made numerous efforts to bring both parties to the negotiating table, beginning with the 1993 Oslo Accords. In January 1998, Israeli prime minister Benjamin Netanyahu and Palestine Liberation Organization (PLO) chairman Yasser Arafat traveled to Washington for talks but showed little willingness to compromise on the status of Jerusalem, a release of prisoners, and Jewish settlements.

Albright and the administration persisted, however, sponsoring talks again in October 1998 at Wye River in Maryland. She was able to bring in King Hussein and his wife, Queen Noor, as intermediaries. These talks ultimately resulted in the Wye River Memorandum, which pledged more cooperation in security for the Israelis and additional land rights for the Palestinians.

Any expectations that Albright and Clinton may have had for settling disputes in the Middle East were dashed in September 2000 when Israeli hard-line politician Ariel Sharon made a provocative visit to the al-Aqsa Mosque at Haram al-Sharif, the Muslim holy site in Jerusalem. The visit not only dashed hopes of Palestinian-Israeli peace but also sparked a new wave of violence, known as the Second (al-Aqsa) Intifada. Albright's experience alerted her to the importance of understanding religious passions in framing global policy. After she left office in 2001, her writings and speeches stressed the importance of educating policy makers in the tenets of major world religions.

Albright also played a central role in the Balkans, which had descended into chaos and spasms of genocidal violence. She was influential in shaping policy during the Kosovo Conflict (1996–1999), which ultimately resulted in the North Atlantic Treaty Organization (NATO) bombing campaign against Serbian-Yugoslavian targets during March–June 1999. The campaign forced Serbian strongman Slobodan Milosevic to the negotiating table. Albright also helped bring to an end the Bosnian War, which culminated in the December 1995 Dayton Agreement.

By the end of her four-year term, Albright's critics charged that she dealt with problems on a case-by-case basis and lacked a coherent foreign policy doctrine. Many in the Republican Party also believed that the Clinton administration, basking in prosperous times and relative world peace, had neglected the growing problems of terrorism and collapsing economies in a world no longer held in check by the communist-capitalist rivalry.

Albright, however, could cite solid achievements. Her strong personality had generated wide public interest in foreign affairs, while her presence in high office had advanced women worldwide. As a refugee from European oppression, she had been an unquestioned American patriot and a strong proponent of worldwide democracy and human rights. She had pointedly warned of American smugness at the beginning of the new millennium, had identified a new world order, and had faced down aggression in the Balkans while maintaining cordial relations with Russia. And despite disappointments, she had kept Israeli-Palestinian peace negotiations from collapsing completely during the difficult tenures of Netanyahu and Arafat.

ALLENE PHY-OLSEN

See also

Arafat, Yasser; Clinton, William Jefferson; Haram al-Sharif; Hussein, King of Jordan; Intifada, Second; Netanyahu, Benjamin; Sharon, Ariel; United Nations, Role of; Wye River Agreement

References

Albright, Madeleine. *Madam Secretary: A Memoir.* New York: Miramax, 2003.
———. *The Mighty and the Almighty: Reflections on America, God, and World Affairs.* New York: HarperCollins, 2006.
Blackman, Ann. *Seasons of Her Life: A Biography of Madeleine Korbel Albright.* New York: Scribner, 1998.
Dobbs, Michael. *Madeleine Albright: A Twentieth-Century Odyssey.* New York: Henry Holt, 1999.
Lippman, Thomas W. *Madeleine Albright and the New American Diplomacy.* Boulder, CO: Westview, 2000.

Algeria

Northwest African nation, almost 920,000 square miles in area. Algeria is bordered to the west by Morocco and Mauritania, to the north by the Mediterranean Sea, to the east by Tunisia and Libya, and to the south by Niger and Mali. Algeria was originally peopled by Berbers (who still make up a sizable national minority) but is now predominantly Arab. In 1830 France seized Algiers, and from then until 1847 it expanded its North African holdings to the interior in a protracted war that created modern Algeria, which was absorbed into France's metropolitan administrative structure in 1848.

French colonizers and their descendants (known as colons) dispossessed native Algerians of the best arable lands and monopolized political power. The non-European population worked the colons' lands or eked out a meager living in the less hospitable areas. By 1945, Algeria's population included approximately 900,000 colons. Arabs totaled perhaps eight times that number.

The postwar era saw the rapid growth of a militant nationalist movement opposed adamantly by the colons, who were determined that Algeria should remain part of France. In May 1945, Muslims throughout Algeria demonstrated against colonial rule. When French colonial police fired on the protesters in Sétif, they responded by attacking Europeans. In retaliation, the military carried out reprisals that killed thousands of Algerian Muslims. This massacre accelerated the conflict that culminated in the brutal Algerian War during 1954–1962.

From the beginning of the war, the Front de Libération Nationale (FLN) appealed to the United Nations (UN) for support of the nationalist cause, while France appealed to the United States and its European allies for assistance in its colonial claim. The Americans initially urged a negotiated peace, hoping to avoid a confrontation with France without antagonizing Arab nations. Convinced that Egypt was providing substantial assistance to the FLN, the French government joined with the governments of Britain and Israel in an attempt to overthrow Egyptian president Gamal Abdel Nasser in 1956. The ensuing Suez Crisis miscarried, thanks to U.S. government opposition. Exercised over the French role in the Suez Crisis, the United States then adopted a less compromising line with France, determined to prevent a wider conflict between Arab nationalists and France (and Britain). The Algerian War also split the communist bloc, with the People's Republic of China (PRC) supporting the Algerian nationalists and the Soviet Union keeping its distance.

The war actively influenced French politics and led to social and political turmoil in metropolitan France that toppled the Fourth French Republic in May 1958 and brought to power General Charles de Gaulle, who created the Fifth French Republic. De Gaulle, then president of France, having exhausted other options, signed the Evian Agreements of March 1962 that granted Algeria its independence effective July 3. Within the span of a few months, most of

View of the city of Algiers, Algeria. (iStockPhoto.com)

the more than 1 million colons as well as some 91,000 harkis, pro-French Muslims who had served in the French Army, immigrated to France.

The FLN-led Algerian government, headed by Prime Minister Muhammad Ben Bella, promptly confiscated the colons' abandoned property and established a decentralized socialist economy and a one-party state. The government collectivized land and began an aggressive campaign to industrialize the country.

Ben Bella's attempt to consolidate his power, combined with popular discontent with an inefficient economy, sparked a bloodless military coup by Defense Minister Houari Boumédienne in June 1965. In 1971, the government endeavored to stimulate economic growth by nationalizing the oil industry and investing the revenues in centrally orchestrated industrial development. In the years that followed his seizure of power, Boumédienne's military-dominated government took on an increasingly authoritarian cast. The military expanded rapidly during the 1970s and 1980s, and by 1985 the army numbered 110,000, the air force 12,000, and the navy 8,000 men.

Algeria's leaders sought to retain their autonomy, joining their country to the Non-Aligned Movement. Boumédienne phased out French military bases. Although Algeria denounced perceived American imperialism and supported Cuba, the communists in South Vietnam, Palestinian nationalists, and African anticolonial fighters, it maintained a strong trading relationship with the United States. At the same time, Algeria cultivated economic ties with the Soviet Union, which provided Algeria with important military material and training. When the Spanish relinquished control of Western Sahara in 1976, Morocco attempted to annex the region. This led to a 12-year war with Algeria, which supported the guerrilla move-

ment fighting for the region's independence. Diplomatic relations with the United States warmed after Algeria negotiated the release of American hostages in Iran in 1980 and Morocco fell out of U.S. favor by allying with Libya in 1984.

In 1976, a long-promised constitution that provided for elections was enacted, although Algeria remained a one-party state. When Boumédienne died in December 1978, power passed to Chadli Bendjedid, the army-backed candidate. Bendjedid retreated from Boumédienne's increasingly ineffective economic policies, privatizing much of the economy and encouraging entrepreneurship. However, accumulated debt continued to retard economic expansion. Growing public protests from labor unions, students, and Islamic fundamentalists forced the government to end restrictions on political expression in 1988.

The Islamic Salvation Front (Front Islamique du Salut, FIS) proved the most successful of the host of new political parties founded. Bendjedid resigned after large victories by the FIS in local elections in June 1990 and national elections in December 1991, and a new regime under Mohamed Boudiaf imposed martial law, banning the FIS in March 1992. In response, Islamist radicals began a guerrilla war in which more than 160,000 people perished during 1992–2002, most of them innocent civilians. By 2002 the fighting was largely over, thanks to government action and an amnesty program, although some violence continued thereafter.

Elections resumed in 1995, and in April 1999, following several short-term leaders representing the military, Abdelaziz Bouteflika was elected president. Linguistic rights became a major issue thereafter, and the government recognized Tamazight (Berber) as a national language and permitted it to be taught in schools. Meanwhile, the government sought to take advantage of the substantial increases in the price of oil and natural gas to invest in economic development projects.

During this period, Algeria was too absorbed in its own internal problems to take much interest or participate actively in the Arab-Israeli conflict, although as an Arab state it did lend strong verbal support to the Palestinians. During the 1973 Yom Kippur War, Algeria did not commit ground troops, but it did supply two squadrons of MiG-21 fighters and a squadron of Su-7B fighter-bombers to Egypt. These aircraft were simply incorporated into Egyptian units.

ELUN GABRIEL AND SPENCER C. TUCKER

See also

Morocco; Nasser, Gamal Abdel; Suez Crisis; Tunisia; Yom Kippur War

References

Ruedy, John. *Modern Algeria: The Origins and Development of a Nation.* Bloomington: Indiana University Press, 1992.

Stora, Benjamin. *Algeria, 1830–2000: A Short History.* Translated by Jane Marie Todd. Ithaca, NY: Cornell University Press, 2001.

Algiers Agreement
Event Date: March 6, 1975

Diplomatic accord between Iraq and Iran designed to settle outstanding issues between the two nations and avert war. The Algiers Agreement of March 6, 1975, known also as the Algiers Accord, was an agreement mediated by Algerian president Houari Boumédienne at a March 1975 meeting of the Organization of Petroleum Exporting Countries (OPEC). The accord was approved by Shah Reza Pahlavi II of Iran and President Saddam Hussein of Iraq.

Essentially, the agreement attempted to resolve territorial disputes between the two countries involving common borders as well as water and navigation rights. It provided for continuing Algerian participation in an ongoing Iranian-Iraqi dialogue that would occur at alternating meetings in Tehran and Baghdad. The Algiers Agreement also established a joint Iraqi-Iranian commission intended to refine and monitor the agreement's provisions and resolve any further disputes.

The agreement resulted in a formal treaty signed on June 13, 1975, that was based on the Constantinople Protocol of 1913 and the Proceedings of the Border Delimitation Commission of 1914 as the basis of the determination of the Iranian-Iraqi border. Iran and Iraq agreed that the thalweg, or the median course of the Shatt al Arab River, Iraq's only outlet to the sea, formed the river border between the two countries even though the shifting course of the Shatt al Arab had given rise to some of the original disputes. They further consented to resolve ownership of disputed islands and other territories related to the waterway, to end subversive infiltrations of each other's country, and to resolve issues related to other

President Houari Boumédienne (*center*) is flanked by Shah Reza Pahlavi II of Iran (*left*) and Iraq's Saddam Hussein (*right*) on March 3, 1975 (three days before the signing of the Algiers Agreement) at the Salle de Honour at Algiers Airport. (Bettmann/Corbis)

border disputes such as Khuzestan. Although not formally part of the agreement, the shah used the agreement's termination of subversive activities clause to withdraw Iranian support for the Kurdish rebellion against Iraq.

In the end, both parties failed to comply with the terms of the accord, and the festering, unresolved territorial issues that it was designed to address led in part to the destructive Iran-Iraq War (1980–1988). This in turn led to a general destabilization in the Middle East.

RICHARD M. EDWARDS

See also

Hussein, Saddam; Iran; Iran-Iraq War; Iraq; Reza Pahlavi, Mohammad, Shah of Iran

References

Coughlin, Con. *Saddam: His Rise and Fall.* New York: HarperCollins, 2002.

Hiro, Dilip. *The Longest War: The Iran-Iraq Military Conflict.* London: Routledge, 1991.

Karsh, Efraim. *The Iran-Iraq War, 1980–1988.* London: Osprey, 2002.

Algiers Declaration
Event Date: November 15, 1988

Formal proclamation of a Palestinian state made by Palestine Liberation Organization (PLO) chairman Yasser Arafat in Algiers, Algeria, on November 15, 1988. The declaration was made in conjunction with a meeting of the Palestinian National Council (PNC). Contrary to popular perception, Arafat's declaration was not the first such proclamation. A similar declaration of the existence of a Palestinian nation was made on October 1, 1948, in Gaza. This had occurred in the throes of the Israeli War of Independence (1948–1949). Despite the considerable press coverage that the proclamation engendered, Arafat's move was largely symbolic, as the PLO did not then control any of the territory it hoped to govern. Yet the Algiers Declaration was well-timed in that it coincided with the outbreak of the First Intifada (in 1987), came on the heels of Jordan's renouncement of its claims in the West Bank, and clearly signaled the future intent of the PLO.

Based on the 1947 United Nations (UN) General Assembly Resolution 181 (which codified the 1947 UN partition plan), the PNC's 1988 proclamation was risky. By basing its declaration on Resolution 181, the PNC—and thus the PLO and Fatah—were accepting what the Arab states had overwhelmingly rejected in 1947–1948. Even more risky was the tacit acceptance of the State of Israel, for the 1948 resolution had called for a Jewish and a Palestinian state. Thus, in cleaving to Resolution 181, Arafat and the PNC were essentially recognizing Israel's existence. This was a marked turn of events, for the PLO had never before been willing to make such a concession. Not surprisingly, Palestinian hard-liners balked at this approach.

Nevertheless, on December 15, 1988, the PLO's permanent representative to the UN presented the Algiers Declaration to the UN General Assembly for a vote. The body enthusiastically adopted the

Palestine Liberation Organization (PLO) leader Yasser Arafat speaking to a meeting of the Palestinian National Council on November 15, 1988, at Algiers, Algeria, during which Arafat proclaimed the State of Palestine. (Patrick Robert/Sygma/Corbis)

declaration by a vote of 104–2 (with Israel and the United States voting no and with 36 abstentions). In so doing, the UN specifically affirmed that the Palestinians had the right to form their own nation, per Resolution 181. All UN references to the Palestinians would now read "Palestine" in lieu of "Palestine Liberation Organization," thereby strengthening their UN observer status.

Over the months that followed, 89 countries moved to formally recognize the state of Palestine, if in theory only. Although the Algiers Declaration did not, of course, create a bona fide Palestinian nation, it was an important leap of faith for the PLO. Since its inception in the early 1960s, the organization had steadfastly refused to abandon its goal of the destruction of Israel. The United States, in turn, refused to enter into any talks with the PLO. Thus, the PNC's and Arafat's move toward greater accommodation was clearly an effort to court U.S. favor. It was also, no doubt, an attempt by the PLO to break out of its doldrums dating back to its banishment from Lebanon in 1982. In relative isolation in Tunisia since then, the organization sought to make itself relevant again by jump-starting efforts to secure a Palestinian homeland by nonviolent means.

PAUL G. PIERPAOLI JR.

See also

Arafat, Yasser; Intifada, First; Palestine Liberation Organization; United Nations, Role of; United Nations Palestine Partition Plan

References

Aburish, Said K. *Arafat: From Defender to Dictator.* New York: Bloomsbury, 1998.

Nassar, Jamal R. *The Palestine Liberation Organization: From Armed Struggle to the Declaration of Independence.* New York: Praeger, 1991.

Norton, Augustus Richard, and Martin H. Greenberg, eds. *The International Relations of the Palestine Liberation Organization.* Carbondale: Southern Illinois University Press, 1989.

ALI BABA, **Operation**

See EZRA AND NEHEMIA, Operation

Aliya, First
Start Date: 1882
End Date: 1904

The first of the large Jewish immigration movements to Palestine prior to the creation of the State of Israel in May 1948, lasting from 1882 to 1904. The First Aliya was also the first wave of immigration specifically associated with the Zionist movement, which had just begun to gain momentum.

The word *aliya* is Hebrew for "going up" or "ascending" and became associated with the Zionist-inspired movement of Jews of the Diaspora to Palestine beginning with the First Aliya. Aliya was an integral part of the Zionist philosophy that held that any Jew had the right of return to Palestine. This continued to be the case under Israeli law, which holds that any Jew may legally establish residency in and attain citizenship rights from Israel.

Jews who participate in an aliya to Israel are known as *olim* (immigrants) in Hebrew. Jewish emigration out of Palestine (or, later, Israel) is known as *yerida* (going down or descending). The population of Jews living in Palestine prior to 1948 was known collectively as the Yishuv (Settlement).

The First Aliya established the cultural and economic tenor of the Yishuv for nearly a generation. Furthermore, First Aliya pioneers introduced many uniquely Jewish experiments to Palestine, such as the *moshavim* (cooperative farms). Most of the immigrants to Palestine came from Russia, with smaller numbers also coming from Romania and Austria. The great impulse of Russian immigration occurred after Czar Alexander II's 1881 assassination, which many Russians blamed on a Jewish conspiracy. This event set off a

Members of Hashomer, a Jewish security organization dedicated to protecting pioneering Zionist settlements, pose with their weapons in the Jewish community of Rehovat in Palestine, October 1, 1900. (Getty Images)

spasm of violence against Jews through pogroms aimed mainly at the large Jewish population in the Pale of Settlement, a Jewish ghetto of sorts in western Russia where most Russian Jews were forced to live. Thus, beginning in 1882, Russian Jews began seeking refuge in Palestine, which was not met with much enthusiasm by Ottoman Turk authorities, who would rule Palestine until 1917.

The First Aliya can be divided into two peaks of immigration: the first during 1882–1884 and the second during 1890–1892. In all, about 35,000 Jewish immigrants came during the First Aliya. Those among the first wave were largely Jews of little means, with little or no education and with few skills. Many of them came as entire families. Those *olim* from the second major immigration wave had more skills—particularly in agriculture—and tended to have more money. After their arrival (almost all hailed from Russia), Palestine witnessed a land-buying campaign on the part of Palestinian and European Jews.

Because the first group of immigrants was ill-prepared to begin a new life in a strange new land, the Yishuv fell on hard times. Already-existing settlements were taxed to the limit with new people who lacked even the most basic farming prowess, while some new immigrants teetered on starvation. In the mid-1880s, however, Baron Edmond de Rothschild, a wealthy French Jew and supporter of Zionism, dispatched a small army of knowledgeable farm supervisors and financial administrators to Palestine to rescue the besieged Jewish settlements there. Rothschild also purchased large tracts of land that were suitable for agricultural endeavors. Not surprisingly, Rothschild's advisers encouraged the cultivation of grapes and the production of wine. For quite a while thereafter, Baron de Rothschild exerted considerable power among the Yishuv, which viewed him with great thanksgiving but also chafed under his administrative mandates.

The second major group of immigrants arriving in Palestine during this time was well-versed in agriculture and anxious to found new agricultural settlements. They soon busied themselves with putting Rothschild's land tracts under cultivation and created new settlements at Hadera, Mishmar Hayarden, and Rehovat.

Toward the end of the First Aliya, Jewish agricultural endeavors began to take off. In places such as Judea, grape cultivation had advanced to the point at which Jews were hiring Arab workers to help in the vineyards. Arabs were hired not only because of a shortage of Jewish workers but also because they could be paid less than Jews. Citrus cultivation also took off during this time. Jews planted thousands of citrus trees, and with proper irrigation these orchards became quite profitable. In fact, it was in the citrus and wine-making industries that the first *moshavim* took hold. Also under cultivation were olives and almonds.

By 1904, thousands of acres of Palestinian land had been purchased by Jews, and at least 20 separate farming settlements had been created. Some 6,000 Jews inhabited the villages. In that year, it is estimated that the Jewish population in Palestine was 50,000, with significant populations of Jews in Haifa, Jaffa, and Jerusalem. The first settlements of what would become Tel Aviv also sprang up

during the First Aliya, and much of Jaffa had been developed prior to 1904. By any measure and despite their rocky start, the Jews of the First Aliya had built vibrant and self-sustaining communities.

From a cultural vantage point, the First Aliya also set the example for all succeeding Jews in Palestine. Schools were created, and the decision was made early on to use Hebrew as the language of instruction. Before long, Hebrew had become the de facto language of exchange among all in the Yishuv. Medical clinics, local law enforcement, and even real estate transactions were supervised by the Jewish settlements at this time. The early settlements would also become the model of self-government, which would serve the Jews well in the years to come.

PAUL G. PIERPAOLI JR.

See also

Aliya Bet; Immigration to Palestine/Israel; Kibbutz Movement; Moshavim; Pale of Settlement; Pogroms; Rothschild, Edmond de; Zionism

References

Pappe, Ilan. *A History of Modern Palestine: One Land, Two Peoples.* Cambridge: Cambridge University Press, 2003.
Sachar, Howard M. *A History of Israel: From the Rise of Zionism to Our Time.* 3rd ed. New York: Knopf, 2007.
Segev, Tom. *One Palestine, Complete: Jews and Arabs under the British Mandate.* New York: Owl Books, 2001.
Smith, Charles D. *Palestine and the Arab-Israeli Conflict: A History with Documents.* 6th ed. New York: Bedford/St. Martin's, 2006.

Aliya, Second
Start Date: 1904
End Date: 1914

The second of the large Jewish immigration movements to Palestine prior to the creation of the State of Israel in May 1948. The Second Aliya lasted from 1904 to 1914 and all but ended with the beginning of World War I in 1914. The word *aliya* is Hebrew for "going up" or "ascending" and became associated with the Zionist-inspired movement of Jews of the Diaspora to Palestine beginning with the First Aliya (1882–1904). Aliya was an integral part of the Zionist philosophy that held that any Jew had the right of return to Palestine. This continued to be the case under Israeli law, which holds that any Jew may legally establish residency in and attain citizenship rights from Israel.

Jews who participate in an aliya to Israel are known as *olim* (immigrants) in Hebrew. Jewish emigration out of Palestine (or later Israel) is known as *yerida* (going down or descending). The population of Jews living in Palestine prior to 1948 was known collectively as the Yishuv (Settlement).

The Second Aliya saw the immigration of approximately 40,000 Jews to Palestine. Most of the *olim* came from czarist Russia and had left because of pogroms, rising anti-Semitism, and the abortive Russian Revolution of 1905. A sizable number of them were socialists seeking the overthrow of the capitalist-imperialist world order.

Because of depressed economic conditions in Palestine, however, almost half of the Jews who immigrated between 1904 and 1914 later left. The Jews of the Second Aliya were social as well as cultural pioneers, and under them the glimmer of an autonomous Jewish nation-state first took hold. Indeed, the Second Aliya saw the formation of the first kibbutz (Degania), the beginnings of the first all-Jewish city (Tel Aviv, near Jaffa), the creation of Jewish self-defense forces, the adoption of Hebrew as the de facto language of the Yishuv (although the First Aliya had set the precedent here), and the advancement of education.

Contrary to the *olim* of the First Aliya, those of the Second Aliya were not focused on traditional agricultural pursuits alone. Rather, they sought to explore new forms of agricultural settlements (such as kibbutzim), industrial formation, and even urban development. They also began to conceive of the Yishuv as a national polity. In this instance, they advanced the instruction of Hebrew in Yishuv schools, began to assemble defensive mechanisms, and encouraged the creation of political parties to advance democratic self-government. All of these activities were designed to foster the feel and look of an independent Jewish state.

In 1909, Second Aliya settlers began to construct the first modern city in Palestine (and the first all-Jewish city in the world) near the site of the ancient city of Jaffa. This urbanization effort would give birth to Tel Aviv, which by 1914 boasted a population of some 1,500 people. The city had also begun to serve as the political and cultural linchpin of the Jewish population in Palestine. The first real indigenous labor union was formed in 1907 (the Printers' Union), and between 1911 and 1912 the Yishuv had set up an industrial foundry outside Tel Aviv (at Jaffa) and an oil refinery in Haifa. The Haifa facility later became one of Israel's most important such endeavors and remains a productive refinery today.

What made the Jews of the Second Aliya so noteworthy was not just their efforts to improve the Yishuv through education, industry, self-government, and urbanization. Their desire to create an entirely new social structure in Palestine was equally revolutionary. The great majority were well educated and politically inclined. They were steeped in socialist thought and had been widely exposed to the various schools of socialist and Zionist philosophy. Yet they had little money and were not well-organized as a group. Nevertheless, they were anxious to go to work and begin building the workers' ideal in Palestine.

Upon their arrival, many of the Second Aliya's *olim* sought work in farming settlements established by the First Aliya. They were not always well-received, and established settlements had rather pay Arabs than Jews to do excess work because Jews expected more money than Arabs. Perhaps 1,500 or so Jews did manage to settle down in an established farming community shortly after their arrival. However, there was a generational and philosophical gap so large between the First and Second Aliyas that those of the Second Aliya eschewed work in the established settlements and instead sought to forge their own social and work arrangements. Before long, cooperative agricultural communities (moshavim) had begun to

spring up. At Merhavya, founded in 1911, cooperative farming began that stressed the hiring of no outside labor, no outside interference, and the freedom of those in the community to choose the type of settlement they desired.

By 1908, several self-defense organizations had become operational, the most notable of which was Hashomer, a male Jewish watchdog group. Some scholars view this organization as the forerunner of Haganah. Besides these many accomplishments, newspapers and other literature—almost always published in Hebrew—were funded and organized by members of the Second Aliya. It is indeed hard to overemphasize the importance of the Second Aliya to the eventual establishment of the Jewish state. The Second Aliya created nearly all of the institutions necessary to organize and run a modern nation and provided much of the philosophical and political constructs of modern Zionism.

PAUL G. PIERPAOLI JR.

See also

Aliya, First; Aliya, Third; Aliya, Fourth; Aliya, Fifth; Haganah; Kibbutz Movement; Moshavim; Tel Aviv–Jaffa; Zionism

References

Pappe, Ilan. *A History of Modern Palestine: One Land, Two Peoples.* Cambridge: Cambridge University Press, 2003.

Sachar, Howard M. *A History of Israel: From the Rise of Zionism to Our Time.* 3rd ed. New York: Knopf, 2007.

Segev, Tom. *One Palestine, Complete: Jews and Arabs under the British Mandate.* New York: Owl Books, 2001.

Smith, Charles D. *Palestine and the Arab-Israeli Conflict: A History with Documents.* 6th ed. New York: Bedford/St. Martin's, 2006.

Aliya, Third
Start Date: 1919
End Date: 1923

Third major wave of Jewish immigration to Palestine lasting from 1919 to 1923. The word *aliya* is Hebrew for "going up" or "ascending." It became associated with the Zionist-inspired movement of Jews of the Diaspora to Palestine beginning with the First Aliya (1882–1904). Aliya was an integral part of the Zionist philosophy that held that any Jew had the right of return to Palestine. This continued to be the case under Israeli law, which holds that any Jew may legally establish residency in and attain citizenship rights from Israel.

Jews who participate in an aliya to Israel are known as *olim* (immigrants). Jewish emigration out of Palestine (or, later, Israel) is known as *yerida* (going down or descending). The population of Jews living in Palestine prior to 1948 was known collectively as the Yishuv, or settlement.

The Third Aliya, which saw an influx of about 35,000 Jewish immigrants to Palestine, had several unique qualities. First, it was the first significant wave of immigration in more than five years, as World War I (1914–1918) had all but curtailed such movement. Second, it was the last aliya prior to restrictive U.S. immigration laws that went into effect in 1924. From 1919 to 1923, some 250,000 Jews had immigrated to America, meaning that those going to Palestine concurrently decided to go voluntarily, and many saw it as a fulfillment of the Zionist vision. Third, many of the Jews going to Palestine at this time had been greatly heartened by several key developments. These included the 1917 Balfour Declaration, signaling British support for a Jewish Palestine, the creation of the British Mandate, and the naming of Sir Hebert Samuel, a Jew, as the first high commissioner of Palestine. Fourth, immigrants from the Second Aliya (1904–1914) reached out to the newly arriving immigrants in unprecedented ways, making the transition to a new life in Palestine far easier than it had been for those who had come before.

Of the newly arriving immigrants at this time, 53 percent came from Russia, and 36 percent hailed from Poland. Their departure had been hastened by resurgent anti-Semitism in Poland and the 1917 Revolution in Russia, which plunged that nation into economic, political, and social chaos for several years. Anti-Semitism in Ukraine and Hungary also forced many Jews to leave, some of whom made their way to Palestine. There were also smaller contingents from Lithuania, Latvia, Romania, Austria, Germany, the Netherlands, and Czechoslovakia. Better than 50 percent of the Third Aliya comprised young unmarried women and men, many of whom had been part of Zionist youth groups.

The immigration influx into Palestine from 1919 to 1923 made many key contributions to the Yishuv in Palestine. Not only did it augment the Jewish population there by some 60 percent, but its youth, vitality, and pioneering spirit lent new purpose and urgency to the Zionist ideal. These immigrants helped form kibbutzim and moshavim, made important contributions to the organized labor movement, and in 1920 founded and staffed Haganah, a Jewish defense group in Palestine. And during the Arab uprising in 1921, many members of the Third Aliya played crucial roles in protecting Jewish lives and property. In addition, the sheer number of moshavim and kibbutzim that they founded greatly advanced Jewish settlement in the region.

Despite their many contributions, members of this aliya faced numerous—and serious—obstacles. Perhaps the greatest challenge for them was finding work. Seeing that unemployment among newly arrived immigrants was very high, High Commissioner Samuel convinced several labor parties to help fund the building of a road network in northern Palestine. The funding would be provided by various Zionist organizations. The roads were constructed largely by hand, so the work crews were considerable. Several of the labor organizations that helped fund the construction went on to become permanent establishments, including Hashomer Hatzair kibbutzim and the Trumpeldor Labor Battalion. This work brought together Third Aliya immigrants in various roadside work camps, which increased the cohesiveness of the group as a whole.

Yet these public works projects could not go on indefinitely, and by 1923 or so the Third Aliya was in a full-blown economic crisis that was driven by high unemployment. Many workers had only sporadic employment amounting to just two days a week on average. The rapid influx of immigrants had simply overwhelmed the labor market, and Zionist groups such as the World Zionist Organization (WZO) did not have enough money to sponsor work projects to keep the Third Aliya fully employed. Histadrut, the Jewish labor federation, founded in 1920, was marginally successful in pressuring privately owned companies to hire Jewish workers (as opposed to Arab workers, whom they could pay less). As such, a number of newly arrived Jews found work at the ports in Jaffa and Haifa. Yet this still was not enough to absorb the many unemployed or underemployed workers, and by the end of 1923 Jewish emigration out of Palestine began to rise.

Besides helping to found Histadrut in 1920, some members of the Third Aliya also engaged in agricultural endeavors. These tended to reflect their progressive and socialist-minded outlook, so their efforts came mainly in the formation of communal or cooperative farms (kibbutzim and moshavim). After 1921 or so, a good number of immigrants made their way to the Jezreel Valley, where they formed numerous kibbutzim and moshavim. In September 1921 the first moshav was founded in the western Jezreel Valley, and in the eastern portion of the valley the 'En Harod kibbutz was formally established just a few weeks later. In toto, some 1,000 Jews of the Third Aliya made these agricultural settlements their home. So popular was the Jezreel Valley for agricultural settlement that there was a waiting list of five years or longer for new settlements there. It is certainly no exaggeration to say that the Third Aliya fundamentally altered the Yishuv's outlook and character with its youthful enthusiasm, pioneering spirit, and dutiful work habits.

PAUL G. PIERPAOLI JR.

See also

Aliya, First; Aliya, Second; Aliya, Fourth; Aliya, Fifth; Balfour Declaration; Haganah; Histadrut; Kibbutz Movement; Moshavim

References

Pappe, Ilan. *A History of Modern Palestine: One Land, Two Peoples.* Cambridge: Cambridge University Press, 2003.

Sachar, Howard M. *A History of Israel: From the Rise of Zionism to Our Time.* 3rd ed. New York: Knopf, 2007.

Segev, Tom. *One Palestine, Complete: Jews and Arabs under the British Mandate.* New York: Owl Books, 2001.

Smith, Charles D. *Palestine and the Arab-Israeli Conflict: A History with Documents.* 6th ed. New York: Bedford/St. Martin's, 2006.

Aliya, Fourth
Start Date: 1924
End Date: 1928

Fourth major impulse of Jewish immigration to Palestine (1924–1928). The word *aliya* is Hebrew for "going up" or "ascending" and became associated with the Zionist-inspired movement of Jews of the Diaspora to Palestine beginning with the First Aliya. Aliya was an integral part of the Zionist philosophy that held that any Jew had the right of return to Palestine. This continued to be the case under

An immigrant from Poland poses on a farm in the Sharon region of Palestine around 1933. (Library of Congress)

Israeli law, which holds that any Jew may legally establish residency in and attain citizenship rights from Israel.

Jews who participate in an aliya to Israel are known as *olim* (immigrants) in Hebrew. Jewish emigration out of Palestine (or later, Israel) is known as *yerida* (going down or descending). The population of Jews living in Palestine prior to 1948 was known collectively as the Yishuv (Settlement).

The Fourth Aliya is associated most directly with a political and economic crisis in Poland, from which the majority in the group came, and restrictive new immigration policies passed by the U.S. Congress in 1924. A sizable number of Jews who immigrated during this time were also from Hungary, where anti-Semitism was on the increase. In Poland, rampant inflation and growing unemployment had thrown the economy into a virtual free-fall. What's worse, the Polish government pursued tax policies that placed a great burden on middle-income Jews. Looking to escape the economic chaos and leave anti-Semitism behind, thousands of Polish Jews now sought to leave the country. For many, moving to the United States made the most sense. But a nativist backlash in the United States after World War I compelled Congress to severely restrict immigration beginning in 1924. Thus, most Poles went to Palestine instead.

In total, the number of Jews who went to Palestine in this period is estimated at about 60,000. A sizable number of the *olim* were businessmen and craftsmen of modest means, and many were not well versed in agriculture. The vast majority of the immigrants arrived between 1924 and 1926, a time that was marked by economic well-being for the Yishuv in Palestine. However, during 1926–1928, which witnessed a marked economic downturn in Palestine, Jewish immigration plummeted. In fact, for the first time the number of Jews leaving Palestine (7,200) was higher than the number of Jews arriving (only 5,000).

From 1924 to 1926, a housing boom in Palestine's urban areas drove the economy to new heights. It was, in fact, in the urban areas where most of the Jews in the Fourth Aliya were settling. In the mid and late 1920s, the number of Jews living in Tel Aviv and Jaffa had grown by 30,000, and the number of Jews residing in Haifa had more than doubled to 15,000. The population of the entire Yishuv went from 90,000 in 1923 to better than 150,000 in 1928. This increased the percentage of Jews in Palestine from 13.2 percent to 17.8 percent in less than a decade. Many of the newly arriving immigrants opened up shops, restaurants, and other small business establishments. A number of small hotels, apartment buildings, and offices went up as well. Indeed, during the 1920s newly arriving Jews helped develop Palestine's fledgling light and medium industry and set the stage for the eventual rise of the textile industry there.

Nevertheless, the flush times did not last for very long. By late 1926, a serious economic downturn affected the Yishuv in Palestine. The contraction was mainly the result of such a large and concentrated influx of immigrants, who overwhelmed the existing economic system and overtaxed social services. An aggravating factor to this was Polish fiscal policies, which made it very difficult for departing immigrants to take with them all of their monetary assets. This in turn sharply reduced the amount of new capital going into Palestine. Things became so dire that several thousand *olim* had to be aided financially by the Zionist Executive. This convergence of economic bad news brought with it high employment that forced a good number of *olim* to leave. It also discouraged further immigration. To make ends meet, a number of urbanized Jews tried to join already-established agricultural settlements. Others formed their own, which would become the basis of a number of kibbutzim and moshavim.

Although the construction sector sagged badly during the economic depression, growth in agriculture continued apace. The amount of land dedicated to citrus production increased almost fourfold between 1924 and 1928. Also, many of the established agricultural settlements were able to absorb some of the unemployed and were able to produce enough foodstuffs to prevent any widespread hunger. During the Fourth Aliya, Zionists began to debate the best policies for future settlement in Palestine. Some argued for the continued focus on rural agricultural endeavors. Others, however, especially those in the middle class, urged a shift in focus to mainly urban communities funded privately and not created along the lines of labor Zionism.

PAUL G. PIERPAOLI JR.

See also

Aliya Bet; Immigration to Palestine/Israel; Kibbutz Movement; Moshavim; Palestine, British Mandate for; World Zionist Organization Executive; Zionism

References

Pappe, Ilan. *A History of Modern Palestine: One Land, Two Peoples.* Cambridge: Cambridge University Press, 2003.

Sachar, Howard M. *A History of Israel: From the Rise of Zionism to Our Time.* 3rd ed. New York: Knopf, 2007.

Segev, Tom. *One Palestine, Complete: Jews and Arabs under the British Mandate.* New York: Owl Books, 2001.

Smith, Charles D. *Palestine and the Arab-Israeli Conflict: A History with Documents.* 6th ed. New York: Bedford/St. Martin's, 2006.

Aliya, Fifth
Start Date: 1929
End Date: 1939

The last of the major Jewish immigration movements to Palestine prior to the creation of the State of Israel in May 1948, lasting from 1929 to 1939. The word *aliya* is Hebrew for "going up" or "ascending" and became associated with the Zionist-inspired movement of Jews of the Diaspora to Palestine beginning in the later years of the 19th century.

Aliya was an integral part of the Zionist philosophy that held that any Jew in the world had the right of return to Palestine. This continues to be the case under Israeli law, which holds that any Jew may legally establish residency in and attain citizenship rights from Israel. This policy is intended to increase the numbers of Jews in Israel. Jews who participate in an aliya to Israel are known as *olim* in Hebrew. Jewish emigration out of Palestine (or, later, Israel) is known as *yerida* (going down or descending). The population of Jews living in Palestine prior to 1948 was known collectively as the Yishuv (Settlement).

Although the statistics are inexact, it is estimated that as many as 250,000 Jews poured into Palestine during the Fifth Aliya, making it the largest by far of the pre-1948 Aliyas. About 230,000 Jews arrived in Palestine legally, while some 20,000 went illegally either by falsifying documents, staying beyond the term of their tourist visas, or slipping into the region clandestinely. The Fifth Aliya came on the immediate heels of a sharp economic downturn in Europe, lasting from 1926 to 1928. From 1929 to 1931 the influx of immigrants was relatively small, just 15,000 or so. The majority of these were part of the Zionist youth movement. By 1933, however, the aliya took on dramatically new urgency that saw the trickle of *olim* turn into a flood.

The stock market crash and deep depression that first hit the United States in late 1929 and 1930 sent economic shock waves across the Atlantic. By 1932, the economies of all the major European powers were in a downward spiral. The economic turmoil also coincided with a marked increase in anti-Semitism in Europe, especially in Germany and Eastern Europe. Several European nations such as Poland were placing great pressure on Jews to emigrate by using economic and social policies as weapons. That prompted many to leave beginning in 1933. Of course, the rise of Adolf Hitler and the Nazi Party to power in Germany in January 1933 precipitated a huge aliya from that nation. Between 1933 and 1936 alone, about 170,000 Jews poured into Palestine. Many were German Jews, while most of the remaining Jews hailed from Poland, Lithuania, Hungary, Romania, and other areas in Central and Eastern Europe. Beginning in 1936, the British tightened restrictions on Jewish immigration to Palestine, so the number of *olim* dropped precipitously.

Many of the immigrants in this last wave of immigration were from the middle and upper-middle classes. A good number of immigrants were lawyers, physicians, academics, and other professionals who had fled the Nazi onslaught. As a result, the Fifth Aliya brought with it a major influx of capital to Palestine. Also, almost all of these newly arrived *olim* had lived in large towns and cities, so there was a distinct urban component to this migration.

Two German children of the Fifth Aliya, on the train from Haifa to Kibbutz Ein Haron on February 19, 1934. (Zoltan Kluger/Israeli Government Press Office)

Many thus settled in Palestine's urban areas, leading to astronomical increases in the population of such cities as Tel Aviv and Haifa.

Because of the sheer number of newly arriving immigrants who needed housing, the Fifth Aliya precipitated a major construction and housing boom. Much of this was made possible by the huge influx of money into Palestine. Indeed, it is estimated that approximately 50 percent of this newly arriving capital was put toward home and industrial construction, and the construction sector kept the entire economy in Palestine on an upward trajectory for several years. In fewer than 10 years, the population of Tel Aviv tripled, so that by 1939 it had more than 150,000 inhabitants. Jerusalem's population also skyrocketed, and the percentage of Jews living in this city increased by some 50 percent. The port city of Haifa, whose modern port facilities opened in 1933 (funded and built in large measure by the Yishuv), also grew tremendously.

Industrial output increased too, with the addition of new plants and new industries. From 1929 to 1939, the number of Jews working in the industrial sector was three times what it had been before the aliya began. New industries, such as potash production, proved highly profitable and saw the relocation of more than 1,000 Jewish laborers to the Dead Sea and Negev areas.

Because of the very urban nature of the Fifth Aliya (and depressed prices for agricultural products), Palestine's agricultural enterprises suffered accordingly. Many of these latest immigrants had little interest in joining or working in a kibbutz or moshav. The only part of the agricultural economy that saw major increases during this time was the production of citrus fruit. Driven by earlier Jewish immigrants who had planted citrus groves and mastered the art of irrigation techniques, the number of crates of citrus fruit exported out of Palestine increased from 2.5 million in 1931 to an astounding 15.3 million in 1939, an increase of more than 600 percent.

The Fifth Aliya was equally transformative in terms of the demographic profile of Palestine. By 1939, Jews now comprised about 60 percent of working-age individuals (15–49 years of age) in Palestine compared to the Arabs' 40 percent. And for the first time, in the major cities and settlements along the immediate Mediterranean coast, Jews outnumbered Arabs and owned a greater percentage of the land. These developments did not go unnoticed by the Arabs, who by the mid-1930s were agitating for new immigration restrictions for the Jews. In 1936, a three-year-long Arab Revolt ensued in which the Arabs sought to end both British domination and Jewish plans for a Palestinian homeland. It was, in fact, the outbreak of the Arab Revolt that led the British to limit Jewish immigration, which slowed the Fifth Aliya to a mere trickle by 1937–1938.

After this last immigration wave, the Yishuv in Palestine remained largely stable until after the 1948 creation of Israel, which precipitated a massive aliya that commenced in 1949. The more upscale profile of the Fifth Aliya led to the creation of several important fine arts outlets, such as the Palestine Philharmonic Orchestra; several museums; and the importation of Germanic industrial practices and architectural patterns. In Tel Aviv, dozens of buildings were erected in the Bauhaus style, an import from Germany that presaged architectural modernism.

PAUL G. PIERPAOLI JR.

See also

Aliya Bet; Arab Revolt of 1936–1939; Immigration to Palestine/Israel; Kibbutz Movement; Moshavim; Palestine, British Mandate for; Zionism

References

Pappe, Ilan. *A History of Modern Palestine: One Land, Two Peoples.* Cambridge: Cambridge University Press, 2003.

Sachar, Howard M. *A History of Israel: From the Rise of Zionism to Our Time.* 3rd ed. New York: Knopf, 2007.

Segev, Tom. *One Palestine, Complete: Jews and Arabs under the British Mandate.* New York: Owl Books, 2001.

Smith, Charles D. *Palestine and the Arab-Israeli Conflict: A History with Documents.* 6th ed. New York: Bedford/St. Martin's, 2006.

Aliya Bet

The illegal immigration of Jews from Europe to the British Mandate for Palestine. The word *aliya* means "immigration" in Hebrew, while *Bet* is "B." Immigration B implied nonofficial immigration. The operation was a part of the Beri'hah (Hebrew for "flight" or "escape") underground operation during 1944–1948 that moved Jews from the displaced persons' (DP) camps in Europe to the British Mandate for Palestine, chiefly through illegal immigration. Jews were not supposed to leave the DP camps, and the British sought to prevent illegal immigration into Palestine, even to the point of stationing warships off the coast to intercept ships carrying the immigrants. At times American authorities provided unofficial support, allowing the Jews to cross through their occupation zones, but there was never any U.S. government official recognition. The British government had unofficially upped the immigration limits set by the White Paper and allowed a yearly total of 18,000 Jewish immigrants into Palestine. While this was a significant increase according to prewar standards, Jewish leaders were not impressed, given the suffering of the Holocaust and the hundreds of thousands of Jews in DP camps in Europe who wished to immigrate to Israel.

Berihah (the organized effort to help Jews escape to Palestine), led by Abba Kovner, had been established in Warsaw, Poland, in late 1944 and early 1945. It soon merged with similar undertakings by Haganah, led by Shaul Avigur, and the Jewish Brigade. The illegal immigration effort accelerated in 1946, with some 100,000 Jews leaving Europe in a three-month span. Operating primarily in Czechoslovakia, Hungary, Poland, Romania, and Yugoslavia, through 1948 more than 250,000 Holocaust survivors were moved over extensive smuggling networks into Austria, Germany, and then to Italy and France. The Italians had great sympathy for the plight of the DPs and some resentment against the British who were

Illegal immigrants to Palestine aboard the *Knesset Israel* being searched by British soldiers and members of the Arab Legion before transfer to camps on Cyprus on November 26, 1946. (Israeli Government Press Office)

in occupation. The French were especially helpful, in part because of anger at being pushed out of the Levant by the British during the war and the influence of highly placed French Jews such as Léon Blum, Jules Moch, and Daniel Mayer in the government. The French Ministry of the Interior worked closely with Avigur in securing transit facilities.

Jews sailed in the acquired ships from Italian and French Mediterranean ports to Palestine through the British naval cordon. Even during World War II and the height of the Holocaust the British had turned back illegal immigrants, but after the war the British increased their naval and air presence off the coast and often intercepted the ships and transported the refugees to Cyprus. Not infrequently there were armed clashes and deaths on both sides. By 1946–1947, the British also had 80,000 troops patrolling in Palestine. Haganah intelligence managed to secure copies of the British interception plans, and it also monitored radio messages by the patrol forces. Often Haganah would attempt to decoy the British away from the actual landing sites. During the autumn and early winter of 1945–1946, half a dozen small ships managed to bring 4,000 Jewish refugees to Palestine. These successes led the British to inten-

sify their coastal blockade, and between 1945 and 1948 the British intercepted most of the 65 ships employed, interning 28,000 DPs on them in Cyprus. Photographs of confrontations between the British and the refugees, however, appeared in European and U.S. newspapers and elicited widespread sympathy for the refugees.

Despite daunting odds, the illegal immigration operation continued until the establishment of the State of Israel, when immigration became legal. Nonetheless, a number of states continued to block immigration to Israel from their countries, including the Arab countries and the Soviet Union and its Eastern bloc satellites.

SPENCER C. TUCKER

See also

Haganah; Jewish Brigade

References

Hadari, Ze'ev V. *Second Exodus: The Full Story of Jewish Illegal Immigration to Palestine, 1945–1948.* London: Valentine Mitchell, 1991.

Lucas, Noah. *The Modern History of Israel.* New York: Praeger, 1975.

Sachar, Howard M. *A History of Israel: From the Rise of Zionism to Our Time.* 3rd ed. New York: Knopf, 2007.

JEWS IN EUROPE, 1937 – 1941

ATLANTIC OCEAN

SWEDEN 10,000 (0.16%)

FINLAND 2,000 (0.04%)

CENTRAL RUSSIA 900,000

NORWAY 2,000 (0.05%)

ESTONIA 5,000 (0.4%)

MEMEL TERR. 3,000

LATVIA 94,000 (5.4%)

UNITED KINGDOM 340,000 (0.7%)

DENMARK 7,000 (0.17%)

IRELAND 5,000

LITHUANIA 160,000 (7.6%)

NETHERLANDS 115,000 (2.2%)

DANZIG 7,000

POLAND 3,275,000 (10.5%)

BELARUS 400,000

BELGIUM 44,000 (0.8%)

GERMANY 365,000 (0.8%)

SOVIET UNION

LUXEMBOURG 3,000 (0.6%)

CZECHOSLOVAKIA 360,000 (2.5%)

UKRAINE 1,700,000 (2.8%)

FRANCE 270,000 (0.4%)

AUSTRIA 180,000 (2.5%)

HUNGARY 440,000 (5.6%)

ROMANIA 800,000 (4.8%)

PORTUGAL 3,000 (0.02%)

SWITZERLAND 20,000 (1.6%)

YUGOSLAVIA 75,000 (0.6%)

ITALY 50,000 (0.12%)

BULGARIA 50,000 (0.8%)

Black Sea

SPAIN 5,000 (0.02%)

GIBRALTAR 1,000 (8.1%)

ALBANIA

GREECE 75,000 (1.2%)

TURKEY 75,000 (4.0%)

Mediterranean Sea

AFRICA

Germany in 1937

Under German control 1938 – 1941

Not under German control 1939 – 1945

SWEDEN — Country
10,000 — Jewish population in 1937
(0.16%) — Jewish population as a percent of country population

PALESTINE
After May 1939, Britain essentially prohibits Jewish immigration

0   200   400 mi

0   200   400 km

Aliya Hadasha

A political party formed of recent German and Austrian immigrants to Palestine in October 1942. The organizers recognized that the cultural differences between these immigrants and those from other countries were so great that the German and Austrians had trouble adjusting. Aliya Hadasha (New Immigration) favored unlimited immigration but did not support a sovereign Jewish state. Instead, it hoped for more Arab-Israeli cooperation and a binational state. Aliya Hadasha merged with similar-minded parties in the summer of 1948 to create the Progressive Party.

Jewish immigration into Palestine consisted of a number of waves, or aliyas. The Zionists who encouraged the first settlements hoped to establish agricultural settlements where Jews could undergo a spiritual rebirth. They would develop strength and self-reliance. Most Jews who made aliya during these early years were lower- or working-class Jews from Europe who left little behind.

During the 1930s, a new type of Jewish immigrants made their way to Palestine. These were refugees from the anti-Semitism of Adolf Hitler's Europe. Many of these Jews were members of the wealthier classes, and they came not from a desire to found a Jewish homeland but rather for their own safety. These members of the middle class often came from an urban background and were less likely to settle in a kibbutz. Under terms of the agreement with the National Socialists, known as Ha-Avara, they were allowed to transfer most of their wealth to Palestine. To a certain extent, they could move their factories and other capitalist wealth to an undeveloped country. The education, wealth, and attitudes of these immigrants did not fit in with the Jewish society that had already developed in Palestine.

Known as yekkes, these refugees from Germany and Austria made up their own group, which resisted assimilation. The popular image of the yekkes included a sense of duty, lawfulness, and efficiency; a lack of ingenuity; and a taste for highbrow culture. Older groups both admired and disliked them.

By the late 1930s, the Jewish community in Palestine had a well-organized political system in place. Various parties with their own goals and programs existed, and local elections were held at regular intervals to elect representatives who made up an elected assembly. A governing council known as the Va'ad Leumi was drawn from the assembly. The Jewish Agency formed a virtual government bureaucracy for the Jewish community, providing social and other services. In this atmosphere, the German and Austrian immigrants decided to form their own political party to represent their special needs and outlooks.

In October 1942, the Aliya Hadasha party was formed at K'far Sh'maryahu in Palestine. Its founders were members of the Association of Immigrants from Germany and Austria, a nonpolitical organization. The leader was Georg Landauer, a German Jew who had been active in Zionist groups in Germany. Landauer had been managing director of the Palestine Office and of the Zionist Feder-

ation in Germany until 1933. In 1934 he immigrated to Palestine, where he headed the Jewish Agency's Central Bureau for the Settlement of German Jews. He helped work out the arrangements for the Ha-Avara and oversaw the transfer of capital and agricultural products to and from Germany before World War II broke out. Aliya Hadasha's goals included the struggle against Hitler and national socialism in all ways possible. It also opposed the Biltmore Program, which called for a separate Jewish state in Palestine. Instead, Aliya Hadasha and its members took a moderate stand that called for a Jewish national home. The party also called for open immigration of European Jews to Palestine, the lifting of restrictions on Jewish ownership of land, and cooperation and goodwill between Jews and Arabs.

Older groups of immigrants were opposed to Aliya Hadasha and its program. Even so, the 1943 communal elections saw considerable gains by the new party. A national meeting in Haifa that year demonstrated a large increase in membership and a growing consolidation of the party's internal organization. At the conference, Aliya Hadasha added to its platform. It called for a strengthening of the Va'ad Leumi's power, greater efficiency and integrity among civil servants, and a public labor exchange. The party also called for national elections to the Elected Assembly. Felix Rosenbluth was elected as chairman of the party.

The next few years saw an increase in Aliya Hadasha's power. Both a Hebrew-language and a German-language newspaper were published beginning in 1943. The party also initiated a demand for claims against Germany for the loss of Jewish lives and property once peace was made. Separate groups were formed in 1944 for workers, women, and youths.

In the election for the Elected Assembly held on August 1, 1944, Aliya Hadasha's candidates campaigned on a platform that called for internal reform, more planning for integration of new immigrants, and a halt to terrorism and violence by Jews against the British Mandate authorities. Aliya Hadasha placed second among the voting and received four seats on the Va'ad Leumi.

After the war, Aliya Hadasha remained opposed to the British restrictions on Jewish immigration. Even so, the party also continued to oppose acts of terrorism. Party leaders supported Chaim Weizmann's call for a British Palestine conference that included both Jewish and Arab representatives. The opposition of the majority of the representatives at the 1946 Zionist Congress to that plan caused Weizmann's resignation and the isolation of the party.

In 1947, the leadership of Aliya Hadasha split over the question of partition of Palestine. Rosenbluth supported the petition, while Landauer called for a binational state of both Jews and Arabs. The Rosenbluth faction won out. As a result, the provisional government of Israel formed by David Ben-Gurion included representatives of Aliya Hadasha, and Rosenbluth served as minister of justice.

In the summer of 1948, the Central Committee of Aliya Hadasha held conferences with leaders of the labor organization Ha'Oved Hatzioni and the progressive wing of the General Zionist Party. The groups realized that they held similar goals and decided to merge to form the Progressive Party. The last nationwide conference of Aliya Hadasha was held during September 17–18, 1948. At the conference, the party members assented to the merger, and the Progressive Party was formally proclaimed.

TIM J. WATTS

See also

Aliya Bet; Ben-Gurion, David; Biltmore Program; Ha-Avara; Weizmann, Chaim; Zionism

References

Landauer, Georg. *Aliya Hadasha, a New Political Grouping.* Tel Aviv: Bitaon, 1944.

Loewenstein, Kurt. *Georg Landauer als Erzieher.* Tel Aviv: Irgun Olej Merkas Europa, 1961.

Zohar, David M. *Political Parties in Israel: The Evolution of Israeli Democracy.* New York: Praeger, 1974.

All Palestine Government

Arab government of Palestine formed at the Arab League's meeting in Alexandria, Egypt, during September 6–16, 1948, and formally announced by the Arab Higher Committee (AHC) of Palestine in Gaza on September 23, 1948. The All Palestine Government (APG) was dissolved in 1959. The APG was an attempt by the Palestinian leadership to fill the expected vacuum that would result from the projected end of the British Mandate for Palestine. It was also meant to strengthen the Palestinians' position in the aftermath of the expected formation of the State of Israel.

The Palestinian leadership, using the cover of the AHC, had been disbanded because of the arrest and exile of its leaders by British authorities in the immediate wake of the 1936–1939 Arab Revolt. However, in 1946 the Arab League re-formed the AHC, which now fell under the Arab League's influence and thereby lost the independence it had enjoyed in the 1930s. Thus, inter-Arab rivalry influenced to a large extent the decisions of the Arab League regarding the Palestine question, and the AHC found itself in a difficult situation.

Pioneered by the Mufti of Jerusalem and the head of the AHC, Haj Amin al-Husseini, the idea of forming an Arab government of Palestine began to unfold after the British decision in September 1947 to leave Palestine by the autumn of 1948. The first proposal of the AHC to form a government in exile was rejected at the Arab League's Lebanon meeting in October 1947. Inter-Arab rivalry and Jordanian attempts to take over parts of Palestine were the chief reasons for this failure.

Initially, al-Husseini's continuous appeals to the Arab League to declare a Palestinian government met with stubborn resistance despite the United Nations (UN) adoption of the November 29, 1947, partition plan for Palestine and Israel's declaration of independence on May 14, 1948. However, on July 8, 1948, the political committee of the Arab League decided to set up a temporary civil Palestinian administration rather than a government that would be supervised by the Arab League. The civil administration did not survive the initial stages of the Israeli War of Independence (1948–1949) and was very short-lived.

Nevertheless, an Arab government of Palestine was a necessity for both Palestinians as well as Arab states. On the one hand, the UN 1948 autumn meeting was approaching, so the need for formal Palestinian representation intensified. On the other hand, Arab regimes were facing popular pressure and criticism for their poor performance in the ongoing war. The Arab governments had to demonstrate to their people some effort to wrest the initiative from Israel. Therefore, the Arab League accepted the AHC request and approved the formation of the APG at its September 6–16, 1948, meeting.

The initial September 1948 announcement of the formation of the APG spoke primarily of Palestinian natural rights of self-determination and the formation of a Palestinian state based on democratic principles. On October 1, 1948, the Palestinian National Convention, held in Gaza under the chairmanship of al-Husseini, ratified the declaration and set the formal agenda for the APG, thus providing the necessary legitimacy and popular support for the government. Ahmad Hilmy Abd al-Baqi was named prime minister, and his government included representatives of many political Palestinian parties at the time despite the overwhelming representation of the followers of al-Husseini. Jamal al-Husseini was named foreign minister.

However, King Abdullah of Jordan, who was engaged in secret negotiations with Zionist leaders to partition Palestine, strongly resisted the formation of the APG. Among other things, the Jordanian monarch initiated a campaign intended to undermine the APG and its legitimacy. To challenge the legitimacy of the APG, Jordan sponsored counter APG meetings—three in Amman, one in Jordan, one in Jericho in the West Bank, and one in Ramallah—between October and December 1, 1948. By December, the participants had declared their support for the king's rule over the West Bank. Thus, the conferences tried to legitimize unifying the West and East Banks of the Jordan River under King Abdullah.

The Jordanian challenge was not the only one that the APG faced in its formative phase. The Arab Legion, commanded by King Abdullah, took control of the West Bank and East Jerusalem during the 1948–1949 war, forcing the APG to operate primarily in the Gaza Strip under the direction of Egypt.

The APG's Holy War Army operating in the West Bank was forcibly disarmed by British officers of the Arab Legion after Arab officers had refused to carry out orders. This blow to APG forces was followed by a fierce Israeli offensive in Gaza on October 15, 1948. The Egyptians then forcibly brought al-Husseini to Cairo after his refusal to leave Gaza. Shortly afterward, the APG prime minister and the rest of the cabinet were called to Egypt and remained in Cairo. The much-needed Arab recognition of the APG came late, and it was more a product of inter-Arab rivalry directed against Jordan's King Abdullah than de facto support for the Palestinians. The UN, however, never recognized the APG.

Following the relocation of its headquarters to Cairo, the APG fell completely under Egyptian influence. The APG was essentially a shadow government relying on the Egyptian-controlled Arab

League for its finances and the approval of its agenda. In 1959 President Gamal Abdel Nasser of Egypt closed the APG offices in Cairo, thus ending a chapter in Palestinian history.

SEIF DA'NA

See also

Abdullah I, King of Jordan; Arab League; Arab Revolt of 1936–1939; Gaza Strip; Husseini, Haj Amin al-; Israeli War of Independence, Overview; Palestine, British Mandate for; United Nations, Role of; West Bank

References

Pappe, Ilan. *Britain and the Arab-Israeli Conflict, 1948–51*. Basingstoke, UK: Palgrave, 1988.

Shlaim, Avi. *The Politics of Partition: King Abdullah, the Zionists and Palestine, 1921–1951*. New York: Columbia University Press, 1990.

———. "The Rise and Fall of the All-Palestine Government in Gaza." *Journal of Palestine Studies* 20(1) (1990): 37–53.

Smith, Charles D. *Palestine and the Arab-Israeli Conflict: A History with Documents*. 6th ed. New York: Bedford/St. Martin's, 2006.

Allenby, Sir Edmund Henry Hynman
Born: April 23, 1861
Died: May 14, 1936

British Army field marshal and First Viscount of Megiddo and Felixstowe who secured Palestine during World War I. Born on April 23, 1861, at Brackenhurst, Nottinghamshire, Edmund Allenby received a classical education in public schools and graduated from the Royal Military College, Sandhurst, as a cavalry officer in 1882. He first served in the Inniskilling Dragoons, and this cavalry experience led him to develop an appreciation for the tactical advantages of rapid movement and maneuver.

Allenby first saw action in the Bechuanaland Expedition of 1884–1885 and in the Boer War, first on General Horatio Kitchener's staff followed by field duty (1900–1902). Recognized as a promising officer, Colonel Allenby commanded the 5th Lancers (1902–1905) followed by promotions to brigadier general (1905) and major general and the post of inspector of cavalry (1910). In the early stages of World War I, Allenby received ever-increasing responsibility from initial command of the British Expeditionary Force (BEF) cavalry division (August–November 1914) to V Corps and finally to the Third Army (October 1915). His troops performed particularly well at the Battle of Arras in April 1917. However, his aggressive style upset more cautious and conservative senior officers.

Allenby's leadership and battlefield skills fit perfectly with the dynamics of the desert theater in Egypt and Palestine. Replacing Sir Archibald Murray as commander of British and imperial forces in Egypt in June 1917, the War Office charged Lieutenant General Allenby with capturing Jerusalem by Christmas. His bold and proactive leadership instantly buoyed sagging morale as operations commenced against the Turks and their German advisers, notably generals Erich von Falkenhayn and Otto Liman von Sanders. The capture of Beersheba (October 31, 1917) by surprise attack made

British field marshal Edmund Allenby, who commanded troops conquering Palestine from the Ottoman Empire during World War I, photographed around 1921. (Library of Congress)

---

possible by artful operational deception broke the stalemate on the Gaza-Beersheba Line that had so stymied Murray.

Allenby's aggressive attacks in 1917 on Ottoman forces resulted in victories at Junction Station (November 13–15) and the eventual occupation of Jerusalem (December 10), all despite water and logistics problems complicated by stiffening Turkish defenses. The loss of troops for western front service handicapped offensive operations through the spring of 1918, but reinforcements allowed Allenby to resume vigorous summer actions. Rapid attacks coordinated with the forces of Emir Faisal in the Arab Revolt in September and October 1918 resulted in smashing the Turkish defensive lines at Megiddo (September 19–21) and the occupation of the key cities of Damascus (October 1), Homs (October 16), and Aleppo (October 25). Faced with the collapse of their southern imperial front, the Ottomans withdrew from the war on October 30, which further stimulated the armistice of November. As a theater commander, Allenby's qualities of bold, aggressive leadership resulted in rapid and overwhelming victory with relatively few casualties, making him among the most successful of all British major commanders of the war.

Created Viscount Allenby of Megiddo and Felixstowe (October 1918) and field marshal (1919), Allenby remained in the Middle East as British high commissioner for Egypt during 1919–1925, overseeing a trying transition to a nominally sovereign state. Returning to Britain, he died in London on May 14, 1936.

STANLEY D. M. CARPENTER

See also
Arab Revolt of 1916–1918; Jerusalem; Lawrence, Thomas Edward; World War I, Impact of

References
Bullock, David L. *Allenby's War: The Palestine-Arabian Campaigns, 1916–1918.* New York: Blandford, 1988.
Gardner, Brian M. *Allenby.* London: Cassell, 1965.
Hughes, Matthew. *Allenby and British Strategy in the Middle East, 1917–1919.* London: Frank Cass, 1999.
War Office, Great Britain. *Brief Record of the Egyptian Force under the Command of General Sir Edmund H. H. Allenby: July 1917 to October 1918, Egyptian Expeditionary Force.* 2nd ed. London: His Majesty's Stationery Office, 1919.

Allon, Yigal
Born: October 10, 1918
Died: February 29, 1980

Israeli politician, military officer, and foreign minister (1974–1977). Yigal Allon was born at Kfar Tavor in Galilee on October 10, 1918. In 1936 he joined the Haganah defense forces. He gained valuable military training while serving with Orde Wingate's Special Night Squads, organized in 1938. In 1941, Yitzhak Sadeh, the founder of the new elite commando unit, the Palmach, personally selected Allon for command of its 1st Company. In 1943 Sadeh promoted Allon to deputy command of Palmach, and in 1945 Allon assumed command of the strike force.

During World War II, Allon led Allied-sponsored Palmach raids into Syria and Lebanon. Following the war, he organized Palmach operations against Arab guerrillas and subverted attempts by the British Mandate forces to restrict the flow of Jews into Palestine. He was promoted to major general in 1948.

A bold and imaginative leader, Allon ranks among the best field commanders during the Israeli War of Independence (1948–1949). In May 1948, after Palmach was absorbed into the newly organized Israel Defense Forces (IDF), Allon led military operations that captured Upper Galilee. In June 1948 he planned the operations that captured Lydda and Ramla. In October, Allon, now commanding the southern front, forced the Egyptian Army to retreat into the Sinai, a success that ultimately gave Israel control of the Negev Desert and the port city of Eilat after the final armistice. In 1950 after Prime Minister David Ben-Gurion had dissolved the Palmach and passed Allon over as IDF chief of staff, he decided to retire from the military.

Allon subsequently helped found the Zionist Socialist Workers political party and won a seat in the Knesset in 1954. Joining the

Israeli deputy prime minister Yigal Allon in Jerusalem on February 26, 1969. Allon was also foreign minister during 1974–1977. (Israeli Government Press Office)

Labor government of Ben-Gurion in 1961 as minister of labor, Allon remained in the cabinet until 1977. He rose to deputy prime minister and minister for immigration absorption in 1967. He remained deputy prime minister until 1977. When Levi Eshkol died in 1969, Allon served for a brief time as acting prime minister. After Labor chose Golda Meir as Eshkol's replacement, Allon accepted the post of minister of education and culture. When Yitzhak Rabin became prime minister in 1974, he named Allon foreign minister.

Among his accomplishments while in the Israeli government, Allon was a member of the war cabinet that planned the dramatic victory of the Six-Day War in 1967. In 1972 he developed the so-called Allon Plan for the occupied West Bank. It offered a return of most of a demilitarized Judea and Samaria to Jordanian rule, while a series of protective Jewish paramilitary settlements would be built along the River Jordan. Although the plan was never instituted, it showed the flexibility with which Allon was prepared to engage the Arabs. He also served as a member of the Israeli delegation that negotiated the separation of forces with Egypt and Syria in 1974.

Leaving government in 1977 when the Likud Party won control of the Knesset, Allon maintained an active public life, remaining in the Knesset and chairing the World Labor Zionist Movement. He died at Afula, Israel, on February 29, 1980.

THOMAS VEVE

See also

Ben-Gurion, David; Haganah; Israeli War of Independence, Overview; Labor Party; Palmach; Sadeh, Yitzhak; Six-Day War; Wingate, Orde Charles

References

Allon, Yigal. *Shield of David: The Story of Israel's Armed Forces.* New York: Random House, 1970.

Herzog, Chaim. *Heroes of Israel: Profiles of Jewish Courage.* London: Little, Brown, 1989.

Rosenblum, Morris. *Heroes of Israel.* New York: Fleet, 1972.

Allon Plan
Event Date: July 26, 1967

Peace plan authored by Israeli military officer and politician Yigal Allon, initially presented to the Israeli cabinet in July 1967. At the time Allon was serving as deputy prime minister, and he would subsequently serve as foreign minister (1974–1977). The Allon Plan was a proposal to negotiate the partitioning of West Bank territories between Israel and Jordan in the immediate aftermath of the June 1967 Six-Day War. It was also aimed at providing Israel safe and defensible borders against potential future attacks from the east through the West Bank and the Jordan River Valley. A brilliant and well-respected military strategist whose experience dated back to the Palmach, Allon hoped to define and establish secure borders while at the same time extending an olive branch of sorts to the Jordanians.

Under the terms of the plan, the Israelis would turn over to the Jordanians those areas in Judea and Samaria that encompassed Arab majority populations. Meanwhile, Israel was to control a thin strip of relatively unpopulated territory along the Jordan River for defensive purposes. This piece of land would begin near the Syrian border to the north and run south through the Jordan River Valley and the Judean Desert and eventually converge with the Negev. Included in this was a sliver of territory along the western shore of the Dead Sea and a large area surrounding Jerusalem.

Allon reasoned that this barrier territory in the eastern part of the West Bank would provide the Israelis with enough space to buy time in the event of a concerted Arab attack. Under the proposed plan, Israel would ultimately retain control over some 700 square miles in the West Bank, or approximately 35 percent of the entire land mass. For the Israeli-controlled areas, Allon proposed the building of settlements and military installations. In other areas, local leaders would be involved in the creation of a semiautonomous Palestinian-Jordanian region that would maintain close economic ties to the State of Israel. The Israelis would retain sole control of Jerusalem with the possibility of a Jordanian-administered Muslim section within the Old City of Jerusalem.

The Allon Plan, submitted to several Israeli cabinets, was never formally adopted as a plan of action, but nor was it fully rejected. Indeed, it shaped to a significant extent Israeli settlement policies until 1977 and was the basis of Israeli negotiations with the Egyptians in 1978 and 1979 and during the Oslo Accords in 1993. In September 1968, Israeli officials entered into secret talks with King Hussein of Jordan during which they unveiled the Allon Plan to him. Hussein politely rejected the plan because he believed that it presented an infringement of Jordan's sovereignty. The Israelis still allowed for the construction of settlements beyond the confines of the Allon-proposed West Bank territories, and modern military analysts have argued that control of the area would afford virtually no protection from attack in the age of ballistic missiles and rockets.

PAUL G. PIERPAOLI JR.

See also

Allon, Yigal; Hussein, King of Jordan; Jordan; Settlements, Israeli; Six-Day War; West Bank

References

Hillel, Frisch. *Countdown to Statehood: Palestinian State Formation in the West Bank and Gaza.* Ithaca, NY: SUNY Press, 1998.

Parker, Richard B., ed. *The Six-Day War: A Retrospective.* Gainesville: University Press of Florida, 1996.

Roth, Stephen J. *The Impact of the Six-Day War: A Twenty-Year Assessment.* London: Palgrave Macmillan, 1988.

Altalena Incident
Event Date: June 23, 1948

The intentional shelling by Israel Defense Forces (IDF) of the *Altalena,* a ship carrying Irgun Tsvai Leumi (National Military Organization) troops and arms, off the coast of Tel Aviv on June 23, 1948. The *Altalena* Incident brought the infant State of Israel to the brink of civil war and remained a festering wound in Israeli politics for years to come. The incident must be understood in the related contexts of the military exigencies of the Israeli War of Independence (1948–1949) and the long-standing struggle for supremacy between the right and left within the Yishuv (Zionist settlement in Palestine).

The *Altalena* bore the pen name of Irgun founder Vladimir Jabotinsky. It was a World War II landing ship tank (LST) of 4,500 tons, purchased in New York in 1947 by American Irgunists and was expected to make a number of trips to Israel bearing arms for the new Jewish state. Originally scheduled to arrive in Palestine by the end of the British Mandate, it belatedly sailed from Port-de-Bouc (near Marseille, France) with 940 militia fighters under the command of Eliahu Lankin in early June 1948. This, however, coincided with the beginning of the first truce on June 11. The timing would prove to be fateful.

David Ben-Gurion, acting as both prime minister and defense minister, had ordered the dissolution of all militias and their subordination to a single command, that of the IDF. On the one hand, the IDF was exhausted and desperately needed the arms aboard the

The *Altalena,* shown burning off Tel Aviv on June 6, 1948. (Israeli Government Press Office)

Altalena, which French premier Georges Bidault had insisted be provided to Israel free of charge. These weapons were sufficient to equip 8 to 10 battalions and included several hundred machine guns, 5,000 rifles, 4 million rounds of ammunition, thousands of grenades and bombs, 5 Bren carriers, and several tons of other war matériel. On the other hand, their importation would be a visible violation of the truce. Of even greater concern to Ben-Gurion was the proposition that the arms would be under Irgun control, which was unthinkable.

Unable to halt or delay the arrival of the ship, Irgun leader Menachem Begin won government permission for it to dock in Israel. Negotiations faltered, however, over demands that a portion of the weapons go to Irgun troops within the IDF and to autonomous units in Jerusalem. The cabinet authorized the use of force as a last resort if negotiations could not bring the arms under effective IDF control.

Following sporadic fighting during June 20–21 around the first landing site at isolated Kfar Vitkin, Begin ordered the *Altalena* to Tel Aviv, where it attracted Irgun supporters, some of whom deserted IDF units. As crews attempted to unload the ship there, fighting broke out anew on June 22. Now no longer able to seize the ship, IDF forces shelled and destroyed it on June 23. In the process 3 IDF soldiers died, while the Irgun side suffered 16 killed and 70 others wounded. On June 28, all members of the armed forces took an oath of allegiance, and the Irgun ceased to exist as a separate entity.

Irgunists uniformly depicted themselves as blameless victims in the confrontation. Although it is true that Begin himself planned no revolt and that Ben-Gurion's tactics and timing made compromise impossible and violence inevitable, the threat posed by Irgun was not entirely fanciful. More than likely, a showdown would have come sooner or later. Ben-Gurion was unrepentant, often declaring that the cannon that sank the *Altalena* belonged in a museum exhibition. Whether because he had to or simply because he knew he could, Ben-Gurion followed other revolutionary leaders including Vladimir Lenin (whom he admired) by striking out against both rightists and leftists in order to consolidate power. He subsequently arrested some 250 Irgunists, and the assassination of United Nations (UN) mediator Folke Bernadotte by Lehi (the Stern Gang) provided Ben-Gurion with an excuse to complete the purge. He also broke the power of the Palmach.

Begin claimed that the arrival of the ship in May would have ended the war by enabling Israel to advance to the Jordan River and that its unloading in June would have lowered Israeli casualties and increased territorial gains. Principal IDF officers in the affair—Yigal Yadin, Moshe Dayan, and Yitzhak Rabin—went on to play leading roles in Israeli military and political life. After years of bitter rivalry, Begin was among those who implored Ben-Gurion to lead the government before the 1967 Six-Day War, which, under Defense Minister Dayan and Chief of Staff Rabin, resulted in Israeli control of eastern Jerusalem and the West Bank.

Because the *Altalena* Incident was the closest Israel came to civil war, it figured prominently in the discourse of those trying either to foment or prevent one. For the Right, it represented betrayal. Months before the Rabin assassination in November 1995, Ariel Sharon recalled the *Altalena* while accusing the government of abandoning the settlers in disputed territories. A decade later, the same allusion was applied to Sharon's government when he withdrew from Gaza. For the Left, the ship's arms were lost, but the battle for principle was won, as prompt and vigorous action was taken against extremists.

JAMES WALD

See also

Begin, Menachem; Ben-Gurion, David; Bernadotte, Folke; Dayan, Moshe; Eshkol, Levi; France, Middle East Policy; Haganah; Irgun Tsvai Leumi; Israel Defense Forces; Israeli War of Independence, Overview; Lohamei Herut Israel; Rabin, Yitzhak; Sharon, Ariel; Yadin, Yigal

References

Begin, Menachem. *The Revolt.* Los Angeles: Nash Publishing, 1972.

Kurzman, Dan. *Ben-Gurion: Prophet of Fire.* New York: Simon and Schuster, 1983.

Lankin, Eliahu. *To Win the Promised Land: Story of a Freedom Fighter.* Translated by Artziah Hershberg. Walnut Creek, CA: Benmir Books, 1992.

Sprinzak, Ehud. *Brother against Brother: Violence and Extremism in Israeli Politics from Altalena to the Rabin Assassination.* New York: Free Press, 1999.

Amer, Abdel Hakim
Born: December 11, 1919
Died: September 14, 1967

Egyptian Army field marshal and leading figure in the Gamal Abdel Nasser government from 1952 to 1967. Abdel Hakim Amer was born in the Minya Province of Egypt on December 11, 1919. He graduated from the Egyptian Military Academy in 1938. At the academy, he became acquainted with Nasser. Following graduation, both officers served briefly in the Egyptian town of Mankabad in the district of Asyut. Both Amer and Nasser were later transferred to Khartoum and then Jabal al-Awliyya, Sudan, where they served in an infantry unit together. There they became especially close friends.

Following service in the Sudan, Amer returned to Egypt and served as a military instructor at the Army School of Administra-

Field Marshal Abdel Hakim Amer, vice president of the United Arab Republic (UAR), addresses troops and pilots during a visit to UAR military outposts near the Israeli border on May 20, 1967. (Bettmann/Corbis)

tion. Both Amer and Nasser also served in the Israeli War of Independence (1948–1949) and were equally appalled by Egypt's lack of preparedness for this conflict. Later, Amer helped Nasser form the Free Officers Movement, which overthrew King Faruq in July 1952. Amer's warm and jovial nature complemented the personality of the often dour Nasser.

In June 1953, Amer was promoted directly from major to major general and became commander of the Egyptian Armed Forces. In 1954 he became minister of defense with the rank of full general. He is widely reported to have quarreled with Nasser over strategy during the 1956 Suez Crisis and Sinai Campaign but nevertheless remained in office. Amer was appointed to the rank of field marshal in 1958 and became head of the Joint Military Command established by Egypt and Syria when the two countries merged as the United Arab Republic (1958–1961). In March 1964 Amer was appointed first vice president of Egypt and deputy supreme commander of the Armed Forces (under Nasser). In May 1964 both Nasser and Amer were awarded the Soviet Union's Order of Lenin for their roles in improving Egyptian-Soviet relations. In May 1966

Amer was named to head the Committee for the Liquidation of Feudalism, an investigative body that was designed to discipline wealthy landholders deemed to be exploiting the peasantry by appropriating their landholdings. He gave up the position of minister of defense but arranged to have his protégé, Shams Badran, appointed to that position in the summer of 1966. Badran continued to function as one of Amer's most loyal subordinates.

Throughout his time in office, Amer was known for ensuring that only officers of complete loyalty to the regime were retained and promoted. His brilliance at political maneuvering was nevertheless not matched by even the most basic understanding of modern warfare. He displayed exceptional confidence during Cairo's buildup to the 1967 Six-Day War and by most accounts believed that Egypt would score an easy victory against the Israelis. In the aftermath of the massively successful preemptive Israeli air strike against Egyptian airfields on June 5, 1967, Amer went from supreme confidence to a state of almost total despair and ordered an immediate withdrawal of Egyptian units from the Sinai. It is not clear if he issued the order on his own authority or if the order had originated with Nasser, but Amer alone is usually blamed for this decision, which proved disastrous. Egyptian units did not retreat in an organized military withdrawal with some units covering others but instead made a mad scramble for the Suez Canal while being continually mauled by Israeli airpower. The Egyptian Armed Forces therefore suffered the most humiliating defeat in its modern history under Amer's leadership. In the aftermath of the war, Nasser sent word to Amer through Anwar Sadat that he would not be permitted to remain in Egypt but would not be pursued were he to go into exile. Amer chose to stay in Egypt and was later accused of attempting to seize control of the government.

Arrested by Egyptian authorities along with some 50 other officers, Amer was reported to have committed suicide on September 14, 1967 while in custody. The precise location of this event is not clear. Widespread speculation persists that he was either executed in prison or was told that his conviction and execution for treason were inevitable. In that case, he may have seen suicide as his only option. A subsequent investigation suggests that Amer died by poison, which may indicate the involvement of Egyptian security forces in his death.

W. Andrew Terrill

See also

Egypt; Egypt, Armed Forces; Israeli War of Independence, Israeli-Egyptian Front; Nasser, Gamal Abdel; Sinai Campaign; Six-Day War; Suez Crisis

References

Aburish, Said K. *Arafat: From Defender to Dictator.* New York: Bloomsbury, 1998.

El-Gamasy, Mohamed Abdel Ghani. *The October War: Memoirs of Field Marshal El-Gamasy of Egypt.* Cairo: American University in Cairo Press, 1989.

Nutting, Anthony. *Nasser.* New York: Dutton, 1972.

Oren, Michael B. *Six Days of War: June 1967 and the Making of the Modern Middle East.* Novato, CA: Presidio, 2003.

American Israel Public Affairs Committee

Large pro-Israeli political lobby located in the United States. The American Israel Public Affairs Committee (AIPAC) was founded in 1953 by I. L. "Si" Kenen and was initially called the American Zionist Committee for Public Affairs. The main thrust of AIPAC's efforts is to lobby members of the U.S. Congress with the goal of influencing legislation and policymaking that affect Israel and Israeli-American relations and the larger Middle East region. AIPAC is believed to be among the top political lobbying organizations in the United States. The group also closely monitors and compiles voting records of U.S. representatives and senators in order to better monitor its effectiveness with key politicians.

At the time of this writing, AIPAC boasted a membership of 100,000 (Jewish and non-Jewish alike) living in all 50 states. Through more than 2,000 meetings with members of the U.S. Congress, the organization helps to ensure the passage of some 100 legislative bills each year that affect U.S.-Israeli relations. AIPAC has a high-profile public relations function as well that interacts with journalists and other opinion makers. The group has regional offices all across the United States that monitor politics and public opinion at the local level and sponsor a variety of political and educational functions.

In the early years of AIPAC, the group had rather strained relations with President Dwight D. Eisenhower's administration, particularly after the 1956 Suez Crisis and resulting Sinai Campaign that saw Eisenhower exert great pressure on Britain, France, and Israel to withdraw their forces. Rumors at the time—which are more than likely untrue—suggested that the Eisenhower administration was sufficiently frustrated with the actions and rhetoric of AIPAC to have ordered an official investigation of the group.

Over the years, AIPAC has boasted many successes. These include successful lobbying for strengthened antiterrorism legislation, increased U.S.-Israeli cooperation on defense issues, arms sales to the Israelis, and direct and indirect aid to Israel worth billions of dollars.

AIPAC has also attracted its share of controversy. In 1982, the group managed to convince the majority in Congress and President Ronald Reagan's administration to veto the proposed United Nations (UN) resolution condemning Israel's invasion of Lebanon that same year. This brought much criticism that the United States was unwilling to take appropriate measures to halt the violence in Lebanon. In 1992, David Steiner, AIPAC's president, landed in hot water when he was recorded bragging that he had "cut a deal" with President George H. W. Bush's administration for major new aid initiatives to Israel. Steiner also claimed that he was already lobbying the incoming administration of President Bill Clinton for the same thing. The resultant firestorm of public exposure led to charges that AIPAC was too influential in Washington. In 2005, allegations surfaced that a U.S. Department of Defense employee had knowingly divulged top-secret information to several AIPAC members. A few months later, two top-level AIPAC employees were accused of having conspired to receive top-secret information to be passed to the Israelis.

AIPAC enjoys fairly broad bipartisan support, having attracted the interest of both Democratic and Republican legislators. On the other hand, a number of politicians have complained that the organization has torpedoed the reelection efforts of several legislators whose voting records were deemed anti-Israel. Others have charged that AIPAC tends to support the political Right in Israel (such as the Likud Party) while it often ignores the Israeli Left (such as the Labor Party). Some allege that the group has become so powerful that its influence may be detrimental to U.S. interests in the Middle East.

PAUL G. PIERPAOLI JR.

See also
Israel; Israel Defense Forces; Labor Party; Lebanon, Israeli Invasion of; Likud Party; Lobbies, Jewish; Suez Crisis

References
Ben-Zvi, Abraham. *Alliance Politics and the Limits of Influence: The Case of the U.S. and Israel, 1975–1983*. Boulder, CO: Westview, 1984.
Chomsky, Noam. *Fateful Triangle: The United States, Israel, and the Palestinians*. Cambridge, MA: South End Press, 2002.
Dershowitz, Alan M. *The Case for Israel*. New York: Wiley, 2004.
Terry, Janice. *U.S. Foreign Policy in the Middle East: The Role of Lobbies and Special Interest Groups*. London: Pluto, 2005.

American Jewish Committee

Jewish advocacy organization founded in New York City in 1906. When the American Jewish Committee (AJC) was formed, anti-Semitism was of great concern to American Jews. They were not only concerned with anti-Semitism in Europe (and the pogroms in Russia particularly) but were also determined to cleanse American society of anti-Semitism, which was particularly pronounced in the first decades of the 20th century.

Most of the AJC's charter members were Jews of German ancestry. The first elected president of the organization was Mayer Sulzberger, a judge in Philadelphia who played a key role in early Jewish education and who established the Jewish Museum in New York City. By 1908, the AJC's executive committee included a number of prominent American Jews including Cyrus Adler, the curator of the Smithsonian Institution.

Throughout its existence, the AJC has labored to foster democracy and pluralism through which minority populations of all kinds will be respected and safeguarded. The AJC also serves as a think tank that takes up a diverse set of issues and problems including discrimination, church-state relations, the Arab-Israeli peace process, and even the U.S. dependence on foreign oil supplies. In recent times, the AJC has also taken a prominent role in the effort to counter groups and individuals who insist that the World War II–era Holocaust never happened. The committee concentrates on five basic issues: fighting anti-Semitism and all forms of bigotry, advocating pluralism and civic ideals, protecting basic human rights,

protecting Israel's right to exist in peace, and promoting and reinforcing Jewish life. One of the oldest Jewish advocacy organizations in the United States, the AJC has tended to be more conservative than some of its counterparts and has never embraced militancy to achieve its ends.

The AJC maintains 2 primary offices. Its headquarters is located in New York City, and its Office of Governmental and Legislative Affairs is located in Washington, D.C. In addition to that, there are 33 other offices scattered throughout the United States and 18 foreign offices. Some of the AJC's affiliated think tanks and institutes include the Blaustein Institute for the Advancement of Human Rights, the Office of Domestic Policy and Legal Affairs, the Office of Inter-religious Affairs, and the Belfer Center for American Pluralism. In addition, the AJC publishes a magazine titled *Commentary* as well as the *American Jewish Yearbook*.

The AJC is particularly concerned with hate crimes in the United States. As such, it has consistently backed hate crime legislation at the local, state, and federal levels and has actively advocated for the lengthening of prison sentences for those who are convicted of hate crimes. In addition, the AJC has lobbied Congress to enact legislation mandating that each state compile yearly hate crimes statistics in order to better track the phenomenon. For years, the AJC's official response to racist organizations holding protests or marches has been not to respond at all, with the rationale that a response would only draw attention to the hatemongers. Over the years, especially early on, AJC members have lobbied Congress to lift or raise immigration quotas to allow more foreign Jews to enter the country. This was especially important in the 1930s. While some activist Jewish American organizations have criticized the AJC for its conservative and quiet approach to issues, the organization has nevertheless performed inestimable good for the Jewish community. The AJC remains one of the most respected agents of Jewish advocacy in the United States.

PAUL G. PIERPAOLI JR.

See also
American Jewish Congress; Anti-Semitism; Pogroms

References
Ben-Sasson, Haim Hillel. *A History of the Jewish People*. Cambridge: Harvard University Press, 1985.
Farber, Roberta Rosenberg, and Chaim I. Waxman, eds. *Jews in America: A Contemporary Reader*. Waltham, MA: Brandeis University Press, 1999.
Sachar, Howard M. *A History of Israel: From the Rise of Zionism to Our Time*. 3rd ed. New York: Knopf, 2007.
———. *A History of the Jews in America*. New York: Knopf, 1992.

American Jewish Conference
Event Date: August 1943

Congress and organization held in New York City in August 1943 to unite American Jews and to address current and future problems of worldwide Jewry, including the formation of a Jewish state in

Palestine. Nazi dictator Adolf Hitler's persecution of the Jewish population of Germany greatly alarmed Jews in Western Europe and the Americas. Despite the Nuremberg Laws and the 1938 Kristallnacht riots and the creation of Jewish ghettos, the West did little to try to rescue the Jews. Even with the creation of the Einsatzgruppen death squads and the extermination camps, many failed to take eyewitness reports seriously. For instance, the British government began receiving reports about mass killings and Germans targeting Jews in 1941, and British prime minister Winston Churchill began speaking of these incidents in public. During the summer of 1942 the Allies received information from a Jewish labor organization that suggested that upwards of 700,000 European Jews had already perished. The British, being privy to previous intelligence reports, took this information seriously, but the U.S. State Department did not.

However, when an eyewitness account became public in December 1942, the Allies finally issued a joint declaration condemning Nazi policies. But for six months this knowledge led to little action, for although the Allies knew the locations of the death camps, for a variety of military reasons they refused to strike them specifically. Many viewed this as shameful inaction, so much so that Szmul Zygielbojm committed suicide in London as a form of protest.

Amid this turmoil, in January 1943 representatives from 32 American Jewish organizations met to organize a conference they intended to hold later that year. Over the next six months, they created an agenda that was to include the rescue of European Jews, Jewish rights after the war, and the Jewish right to settle in Palestine. Finally, in August 1943 the American Jewish Organization was formed to unite American Jewry for postwar planning purposes. Later that month the American Jewish Conference was convened in New York City to address these issues.

The highlight of this meeting was a fiery speech by Stephen Wise of the World Jewish Congress about the creation of a Jewish state in Palestine. This speech compelled the non-Zionist American Jewish Committee to withdraw from the conference. In November 1942, Wise had publicized a telegram detailing Hitler's plans for the European Jewry in an effort to put pressure on President Franklin D. Roosevelt to act on the behalf of the European Jews. Wise's effort, however, was in vain.

Despite Wise's best efforts and a broad base of support for his motion, the American Jewish Conference failed to unify American Jews, nor did it gain the recognition of the U.S. government as the single American Jewish authority on rescue, Palestine, or postwar matters. The conference was dissolved, with little fanfare, in 1949.

PAUL G. PIERPAOLI JR.

See also

American Jewish Committee; Holocaust; World Jewish Congress; Zionism

References

Dimont, Max. *The Jews in America: The Roots, History and Destiny of American Jews*. New York: Simon and Schuster, 1978.

Penkower, Monty N. "American Jewry and the Holocaust: From Biltmore to the American Jewish Conference." *Jewish Social Studies* 47(2) (1985): 95–114.

American Jewish Congress

Jewish American civic and advocacy organization founded in 1918 and also dedicated to the creation and security of the State of Israel. Formally convened in 1918, just a month after the signing of the armistice agreement that ended World War I, the chief and immediate goal of the American Jewish Congress was to provide U.S. Jews a united voice at the upcoming Paris Peace Conference (1919) and to advocate on behalf of Jews in Europe. Designed for unified and democratic decision making, the first American Jewish Congress held in Philadelphia in December 1918 comprised a delegation that had been elected by some 350,000 Jews from all across the United States. Among the delegates at the inaugural congress were such Jewish luminaries as Louis D. Brandeis, Felix Frankfurter, Golda Meyerson (future Israeli prime minister Golda Meir, then living in Milwaukee, Wisconsin), and Rabbi Stephen Wise, the latter of whom wrote virtually all of the congress's agenda.

Bold and sure in his vision, Wise established that Jews were entitled to social and legal justice and that all peoples had the inalienable right to practice their religion freely. His agenda, which still holds the core of the American Jewish Congress's beliefs, also called for full civic participation in American society by all Jews and advocated for the creation of a Jewish state in Palestine. As such, it was the first Jewish group to publicly advocate a Zionist position in the United States. Today, the congress has five principal concerns: ensuring the security of Israel and of Jews worldwide, fighting anti-Semitism, preserving religious freedom in the United States and ensuring the separation of church and state, advocating American independence from Middle Eastern oil, and supporting moderate Muslim nations and individuals who oppose radical Islam.

The American Jewish Congress claims that it was the first organization in the United States to embrace Zionism as a goal and the first to call for a boycott of products made in Nazi Germany in the 1930s. The congress also proudly states that it was the first Jewish group to advocate for Jewish rights using the American court system (in the 1940s), paving the way for other groups to ultimately do the same. In 1936, the American Jewish Congress played a key role in organizing the World Jewish Congress, which met amid the pall of Nazi oppression. The American Jewish Congress also worked with U.S. government officials during World War II and the Nazi-inspired Holocaust in an attempt to safeguard Jews in Central and Eastern Europe.

Today, the American Jewish Congress has about 50,000 members. It is headquartered in New York City and maintains a permanent office in Jerusalem and has also had offices in several other nations over the years. In keeping to the congress's democratic ideals, delegates for the at-large membership meet as a congress every two

Dr. Stephen S. Wise, president of the American Jewish Congress, speaks to a crowd at Madison Square Park in New York City on July 31, 1945, regarding the plight facing Jews in Europe. (Bettmann/Corbis)

years to elect a president, who serves a two-year term. There the organization's goals and agenda are established for the two-year hiatus. Policies and implementation designed to conform to the agenda are carried out by the Executive Committee and the Governing Council. Beyond the core goals of the congress, over the years it has taken up other issues of national importance. For example, in recent years the American Jewish Congress has embarked on a major gun-control campaign.

PAUL G. PIERPAOLI JR.

See also

American Jewish Committee; Brandeis, Louis Dembitz; Holocaust; Lobbies, Jewish; Meir, Golda; Zionism

References

Farber, Roberta Rosenberg, and Chaim I. Waxman, eds. *Jews in America: A Contemporary Reader.* Waltham, MA: Brandeis University Press, 1999.

Sachar, Howard Morley. *A History of Jews in America.* New York: Knopf, 1992.

American Jewish Joint Distribution Committee

Founded in November 1914, the American Jewish Joint Distribution Committee (JDC) was originally established to ease the suffering of Palestinian Jews, then under the rule of the Ottoman Empire, at the outbreak of World War I. In the years since, the JDC has helped needy Jews in more than 85 countries. In the fall of 1914, U.S. ambassador to Turkey Henry Morgenthau cabled Louis Marshall and Jacob H. Schiff in New York requesting $50,000 to help the Palestinian Jewish population. Marshall and Schiff raised the funds by November of that year, and the JDC was created to help distribute the money to Palestinian Jews as well as those suffering in Europe.

Although World War I ended in 1918, the plight of Eurasian Jews did not. In the aftermath of the Russian Bolshevik Revolution of 1917 and the dissolution of the Austro-Hungarian Empire, pogroms

Leaders of the Jewish community unload a C-54 Skymaster that has brought a special shipment of Passover food for the Jews of the blockaded German capital on March 29, 1949. The food and wine were provided under the supervision and with the aid of the American Jewish Joint Distribution Committee. (Bettmann/Corbis)

occurred in Russia and in Poland. Additionally, thousands of Jews died of famine and starvation, and many of those who survived were without homes or social institutions.

When Adolf Hitler came into power in Germany in 1933, the JDC was utilized to help German Jews in an increasingly dire plight. It helped 250,000 Jews flee Germany and an additional 125,000 escape from Austria. As World War II progressed, the JDC also sent aid to Tehran, Yugoslavia, and Shanghai.

When World War II drew to a close in 1945, the JDC began a massive relief program. By the end of 1947, 700,000 Jews had received aid from the organization. It also began a project in Argentina for Holocaust survivors immigrating to South America and helped some 115,000 reach Palestine by 1948. When in May 1948 Israel declared its independence, the JDC helped 440,000 Jews from all over the world immigrate to Israel. The organization set up aid programs for Jews in North Africa and Europe and, with the onset

of the Cold War, assisted East European Jews expelled from their Soviet satellites to immigrate to Israel.

In the 1960s the JDC initiated aid programs in India and Romania, and in 1969 the organization began the Association for Planning and Developing Services for the Aged (ESHEL) in Israel. ESHEL developed comprehensive services for the elderly that were to serve as models for Jewish communities around the world. In 1975 the JDC began the JDC-Brookdale Institute for research on aging, health, disability, and children. And when the barriers of the Soviet Union began to loosen in the mid-1970s, the JDC helped escaping Soviet Jews immigrate to Israel or to the West.

During the 1980s, the JDC furthered its work around the world. It entered Ethiopia to provide aid to the Jews residing there. In 1986 the organization created the International Development Program that set up disaster relief and development aid in nearly every continent. At the close of the decade the JDC was able to reenter the

Soviet Union and its satellites to provide aid for the Jews living there.

Currently, the JDC continues to aid Jewish children and the elderly in addition to aiding vulnerable immigrant populations and researching and developing other social services. Recently the JDC provided aid to Argentinian Jews amid Argentina's economic crisis.

PAUL G. PIERPAOLI JR.

See also

Holocaust; Immigration to Palestine/Israel; Pogroms; Soviet Jews, Immigration to Israel; World War I, Impact of; World War II, Impact of; Zionism

References

Bauer, Yehuda. *American Jewry and the Holocaust: The American Jewish Joint Distribution Committee, 1939–1945.* Detroit: Wayne State University Press, 1981.

Hacochen, Dvora. *Immigrants in Turmoil: Mass Immigration to Israel.* Syracuse, NY: Syracuse University Press, 2003.

American Palestine Committee

Organization committed to promoting Zionism in the United States. Emanuel Neumann established the American Palestine Committee (APC) in 1932 as a means of promoting the goals of Zionism among the non-Jewish population of the United States. He believed that non-Jews, in particular Christian political leaders, would see the inherent value in the establishment of an independent Jewish state in the territory of Palestine, ruled as a British mandate in the decades after World War I.

Despite a rapid and positive response to initial calls for support by the APC, Neumann chose to immigrate to Palestine in 1932, virtually destroying his nascent organization, which was quite unable to function effectively without his charismatic leadership. After living in British-controlled Palestine for several years, he returned to the United States and was hired in 1941 as the public relations director of the Emergency Committee for Zionist Affairs, a wartime organization that had assumed worldwide leadership in the push for the establishment of a Jewish state.

In his new position, Neumann revived the now-defunct APC and also formed the Christian Council on Palestine (CCP), an organization designed to draw support for the Zionist cause from Christian clergy. The APC again quickly gathered support from national and state politicians as well as academics. It raised awareness of the Zionist cause and served as a fund-raising organ for other Zionist organizations. However, the efforts of the APC were hampered during the first few years of its revival because of World War II.

In the United States, particularly among the Jewish community, there existed a distinct unwillingness to criticize British policies in Palestine. Because Great Britain was locked in a life-and-death struggle with Nazi Germany, it was believed that all Zionist aspirations should be effectively shelved for the duration of the conflict. On November 2, 1942, the APC released a statement calling for the establishment of an independent Jewish national home. The statement included the signatures of 68 U.S. senators and 194 congressional representatives. Although nonbinding, the statement demonstrated the widespread support that Neumann had managed to develop in a very short period of intense wartime lobbying efforts.

When the war ended in 1945, the APC and the CCP merged into a single new entity, the American Christian Palestine Committee (ACPC), as a means of streamlining fund-raising and enhancing the ties between pro-Zionist clergy and laypersons. When the Zionist dream was realized in May 1948 with the proclamation of the State of Israel, the fundamental purpose of the ACPC shifted from the creation of a Zionist state to the preservation and assistance of Israel. However, the impetus for the creation of the ACPC was gone, and interest in the group rapidly declined. It was quickly superseded by other pro-Israeli organizations in the United States. The ACPC was formally disbanded in 1961.

PAUL J. SPRINGER

See also

Emergency Committee for Zionist Affairs; Zionism

References

Cohn-Sherbok, Dan, and Dawoud El-Alami. *The Palestine-Israeli Conflict: A Beginner's Guide.* Oxford, UK: Oneworld, 2001.

Laqueur, Walter. *A History of Zionism: From the French Revolution to the Establishment of the State of Israel.* Reprint ed. New York: Schocken, 2003.

Anglo-American Committee of Inquiry
Event Date: 1946

Committee composed of American and British delegates that recommended the creation of a single Arab-Jewish state under the trusteeship of the United Nations (UN) and the admission of 100,000 Jewish refugees to Palestine.

The conclusion of World War II presented new difficulties for Great Britain in the Middle East. Long considered the dominant colonial power in the Arab world, Britain's stabilizing influence in the region rapidly dissipated with the depletion of its economic resources from the war. Compounding the problem was the fierce nationalistic sentiment of its former wards. Both Egypt and Iraq were far less receptive to their prewar alliances. Transjordan soon became independent, fueling the debate among Arabs in Palestine regarding their own freedom. Britain's divergent past promises to both Zionists and Arabs quickly came unraveled when the U.S. government called for displaced Jews to live in Palestine. The Arabs outnumbered the Jews about two to one in Palestine and relied on Britain to honor its established immigration quotas.

U.S. president Harry S. Truman was sympathetic toward the Jews in light of their terrible losses in the World War II Holocaust. But politics may have played a larger role than Truman's humanitarianism. Apart from the fact that the United States wanted to secure Middle Eastern oil for the West as well as bases in the Middle East to check Soviet expansionism, Truman was very much

Members of the Anglo-American Committee of Inquiry, shown at the railroad station in Jerusalem in March 1946. (Tarlton Law Library)

concerned about securing the Jewish American vote, particularly in New York, for the forthcoming presidential election of 1948. The front-runner for the Republican nomination and the eventual nominee was New York governor Thomas E. Dewey. Toward that end, Truman began urging British prime minister Winston Churchill and his successor Clement Attlee to admit as many Jews to Palestine as possible.

Arabs living in the region were determined to keep the Jewish refugees out. Truman had notified the British that he had no intention of using American military forces to suppress any violence that might result from unrestricted immigration. Knowing that U.S. assistance would be minimal and understanding the volatility of the situation, in a speech to the House of Commons on October 26, 1945, and in remarks in a letter to Truman on November 13, Attlee proposed creation of a joint Anglo-American committee to investigate the immigration matter. The committee was actually a British attempt to deflect American pressure to admit refugees into Palestine. Truman accepted the idea of a joint committee but with the qualification that immigration into Palestine alone be the focus of the inquiry. The British grudgingly agreed.

The Anglo-American Committee of Inquiry first met in Washington and then heard from both Jewish and Arab representatives in New York. Neither side was willing to compromise. The Arabs claimed that U.S. interest in Jewish immigration to Palestine was driven solely by politics, while Jews savagely attacked British immigration policies, almost to the point of making the British government appear to have been responsible for the Holocaust. The committee moved on to London in January 1946. There it heard dire predictions from representatives of the British Colonial and Foreign Offices of a bloodbath in Palestine should large numbers of Jewish immigrants be admitted there.

After its stay in London and a trip to Vienna, in February 1946 committee members visited several displaced persons camps in Europe. No doubt this had a powerful influence. Commission member and Labour Party member of Parliament Richard Crossman later wrote that the visits to the camps made arguments about Zionism abstract and that a Jewish state seemed "curiously remote after this experience of human degradation."

The committee also traveled to Cairo and Jerusalem. It then proceeded to Lausanne, Switzerland, where it drafted its recommendations. On May 1, 1946, the committee issued a unanimous report of less than 100 pages. The report called for the admission of 100,000 Jewish refugees and the creation of a single Arab-Jewish state under the trusteeship of the UN. To maximize the possibility for the success of its recommendations, the commission rejected partition for Palestine. Despite the committee's conclusion that there was little or no evidence of cooperation between Jews and Arabs and its failure to make any recommendations as to how this might be achieved, it recommended that Jews and Arabs continue to live in a single state in which neither would dominate the other.

The commission did express concerns. Among these was the belief, later proven false, that Palestine could not support a much larger population. This was based on the belief that the amount of water in the area could not be increased by pumping water from the Jordan River. The commission also noted the economic imbalance between Arab and Jew. Although during the years of the British Mandate there had been an unprecedented growth in the size and prosperity of the Arab population in Palestine, generally speaking economic conditions for the Arabs were inferior to those for the Jews.

Extremists on both sides rejected the commission's recommendations, and subsequent attempts by the UN at partition failed. On May 14, 1947, Israel declared its independence, and that same day Arab forces invaded, beginning Israel's War for Independence (May 14, 1948–January 7, 1949).

CHARLES F. HOWLETT AND SPENCER C. TUCKER

See also

Attlee, Clement Richard; Israeli War of Independence, Overview; Palestine, British Mandate for; Truman, Harry S.; United Nations, Role of; United Nations Special Commission on Palestine

References

Donovan, Robert J. *Conflict and Crisis: The Presidency of Harry S. Truman, 1945–1948.* New York: Norton, 1977.

Goodwin, Geoffrey L. *Britain and the United Nations.* London: Oxford University Press, 1957.

Hurewitz, J. C. *The Struggle for Palestine.* New York: Schocken, 1976.

Manuel, Frank E. *The Realities of American-Palestine Relations.* Washington, DC: PublicAffairs, 1949.

Ryan, Stephen. *The United Nations and International Politics.* New York: St. Martin's, 2000.

Sachar, Howard M. *A History of Israel: From the Rise of Zionism to Our Time.* 3rd ed. New York: Knopf, 2007.

Safran, Nadav. *The United States and Israel.* Cambridge: Harvard University Press, 1963.

Anglo-Egyptian Treaty
Event Date: August 26, 1936

Treaty signed in London that spelled out the relationship between Britain and Egypt. Driven by strategic and economic interests in the Suez Canal as well as economic interests in cotton production, the British took over Egypt in 1882. The British government had promised to withdraw "once order had been restored," but they remained in Egypt. In December 1914 after the Ottoman Empire had entered World War I on the side of the Central Powers, Britain declared Egypt a protectorate.

In response to anti-British riots after the war, the British in February 1922 ended the protectorate and declared Egypt to be a sovereign, independent kingdom. This was mere window dressing, however, for Britain continued to dominate Egyptian affairs through its advisers who controlled the key organs of state, including internal security. Nonetheless, the threat posed to the security of the region by Italy's invasion of Ethiopia in September 1935 led to negotiations between London and Cairo and a treaty between the two nations, signed in London on August 26, 1936.

According to this treaty, Britain and Egypt entered into an alliance whereby Britain pledged to defend Egypt against outside aggression and Egypt promised to place its facilities at Britain's disposal in case of war. Recognizing the vital importance of the Suez Canal to Britain, Egypt allowed Britain to garrison 10,000 troops and 400 pilots in the Canal Zone and to provide for their barracks at Egyptian expense. In return, Britain would evacuate all other Egyptian bases except the naval base at Alexandria, which it would be allowed to maintain for eight more years.

All British personnel in the Egyptian Army and police were to be withdrawn, but a British military mission would remain to advise the Egyptian Army to the exclusion of any other foreigners. Also, Egyptian officers were to train abroad only in Britain. Egypt had the full right to expand the size of its armed forces.

On the thorny matter of the Sudan, Britain promised to allow unrestricted immigration of Egyptians into the Sudan. Egyptian troops were also allowed to return there. Britain agreed to work for the removal of the capitulations and for the admission of Egypt to the League of Nations. The British high commissioner would be replaced by an ambassador. The treaty was to be of indefinite duration, but negotiations for any changes would be permitted after a 20-year period.

In effect, Britain retained its right to protect security through the canal and compromised on a number of other issues, including that of the protection of British citizens and foreigners. Left unresolved was the question of the future status of the Sudan. Despite some criticism of it, the Egyptian parliament ratified the treaty on December 11, 1936. Although many Egyptians thought of this treaty as marking their independence because the action of 1922 had been a unilateral one by Britain alone, in fact the British continued to exercise considerable control over the Egyptian government.

In May 1937, the powers that had enjoyed capitulatory privileges in Egypt agreed to renounce these treaties, with the proviso that the mixed courts in Cairo and Alexandria were to remain in effect for another 12 years. That same month, Egypt was officially admitted to the League of Nations.

Relations with Britain dominated post–World War II Egyptian foreign policy, with Cairo determined to revise the 1936 treaty. The chief points of grievance for the Egyptians were the continued presence of British troops in the country; the matter of the future of the Sudan, which Egypt sought to regain; and the sovereignty of the Egyptian government. Egyptian leaders were determined that all British troops be withdrawn from Egyptian territory.

In October 1946, Egyptian prime minister Sidqi Pasha concluded an agreement with British foreign secretary Ernest Bevin. This provided for the withdrawal of British forces from the Canal Zone and for a formula regarding the Sudan. The Sudanese would themselves determine their own future government and decide whether they would be independent or part of Egypt. In the winter of 1950–1951, there were further talks over modification of the 1936 treaty. The arrival of the Cold War produced British intransigence on the matter of treaty revision, however, for the West came to regard Egypt as the most suitable military base in the Middle East.

Following the Egyptian Revolution of July 1952, however, on October 19, 1954, Egyptian strongman Gamal Abdel Nasser concluded a new treaty with Britain whereby the British gave up all rights to the Suez Canal base and agreed to evacuate the Canal Zone entirely within 20 months. In return, Egypt promised to keep the base in combat readiness and allow the British to return in case of an attack by an outside power against Turkey or any Arab state. The British right of defense of the canal under the treaty was, of course, London's justification for its attempt to intervene militarily in Egypt following Nasser's nationalization of the Suez Canal and the Israeli invasion of the Sinai (mounted with British collusion) during the 1956 Suez Crisis.

SPENCER C. TUCKER

See also

Egypt; Nasser, Gamal Abdel; Pan-Arabism; Suez Canal; Suez Crisis; United Kingdom, Middle East Policy

References

Dawisha, A. I. *Egypt in the Arab World.* New York: Wiley, 1976.

Gorst, Anthony, and Lewis Johnman. *The Suez Crisis.* London: Routledge, 1997.

Jankowski, James P. *Nasser's Egypt, Arab Nationalism, and the United Arab Republic.* Boulder, CO: Lynne Rienner, 2001.

Waterbury, John. *The Egypt of Nasser and Sadat: Political Economy of Two Regimes.* Princeton, NJ: Princeton University Press, 1983.

Anglo-Jordanian Defense Treaty
Event Date: March 15, 1948

Mutual defense agreement between the British and Jordanian governments signed on March 15, 1948. The 20-year accord bound each country to come to the other's aid if attacked, permitted British air bases on Jordanian soil, provided British military officers for Jordan's Arab Legion, and granted Jordan a £10 million annual subsidy.

Although independent from British mandatory rule in 1946, Jordan remained a functional British colony. The defense treaty, which built on the 1923, 1928, and 1946 Anglo-Transjordanian Agreements, fully codified Jordan's military and financial dependence on Great Britain.

Most importantly, John Bagot Glubb (Glubb Pasha), an Arabic-speaking British officer, commanded the Arab Legion, which protected British interests by defending the Hashemite monarchy from external and internal threats. The annual subsidy was paid directly to Glubb, while British officers held all Arab Legion command positions and made all decisions regarding financing, training, equipping, and expanding the Jordanian military.

In spite of the treaty, Britain remained aloof during the Israeli War of Independence (1948–1949). However, the British did support the Jordanian annexation of the West Bank in 1950. This move doubled Jordan's population, but the predominantly Palestinian newcomers upset the kingdom's delicate ethnic balance. From 1952 to 1956, Israeli attacks on the West Bank, mounted in retaliation for infiltration and fedayeen raids, did not activate the treaty, and Britain turned down numerous Jordanian requests for offensive military assistance.

Jordan became more strategically vital to Britain following the withdrawal of the latter's troops from Egypt in 1954. The success of Egyptian president Gamal Abdel Nasser in negotiating this withdrawal prompted King Hussein of Jordan to seek a similar agreement. This desire became embroiled in 1955 negotiations urging Jordan to join the Baghdad Pact, a British-inspired regional defense alliance. Accession to the pact contained the promise of revising the increasingly unpopular defense treaty.

In January 1956, however, the Jordanian parliament publicly declared its opposition to the kingdom joining the Baghdad Pact. Pressure from Egypt, Saudi Arabia, and Syria along with Palestinian and nationalist domestic opinion instead provoked calls to repeal the Anglo-Jordanian treaty and remove British officers and influence. Egyptian propaganda reminded the Jordanian people of the loss of much of Palestine, the Arab Legion's weak response to Israeli retaliatory attacks, and Britain's behind-the-scenes control of Jordan.

To protect his position, Hussein dismissed Glubb and 11 other British officers on March 1, 1956. The Jordanian Army then began a process of Arabization. On October 25, 1956, Jordan allied itself with Egypt and Syria.

March 1957 brought Jordan's official abrogation of the Anglo-Jordanian Defense Treaty. The British evacuated their forces, Jordan officially purchased their bases, and the Egyptians and Saudis replaced the annual subsidy. Following the 1958 coup in Iraq, British soldiers temporarily returned to Jordan at the king's request, but the other Arab countries and the United States soon superseded Britain as Jordan's benefactors.

ANDREW THEOBALD

See also

Arab Legion; Baghdad Pact; Fedayeen; Glubb, Sir John Bagot; Israeli War of Independence, Israeli-Jordanian Front; Jordan; Jordan, Armed Forces; United Kingdom, Middle East Policy

References

Faddah, Mohammed Ibrahim. *The Middle East in Transition: A Study of Jordan's Foreign Policy.* London: Asia Publishing House, 1974.

Glubb, John Bagot. *A Soldier with the Arabs.* New York: Harper and Brothers, 1959.

Oren, Michael B. "A Winter of Discontent: Britain's Crisis in Jordan, December 1955-March 1956." *International Journal of Middle East Studies* 22(2) (1990): 171–184.

Satloff, Robert B. *From Abdullah to Hussein: Jordan in Transition.* New York: Oxford University Press, 1993.

Anielwicz, Mordecai
Born: 1919 or 1920
Died: May 8, 1943

Commander of the Warsaw Ghetto Uprising in 1943. Mordecai Anielwicz (also given as Mordechai Anilewicz or Anielewicz) was born in a poor neighborhood in Warsaw in 1919 or 1920. He studied at the Warsaw Hebrew High School and was a member of the Hashomer Hatzair, the Jewish youth organization of Poland. Shortly after the September 1, 1939, German Army invasion of Poland, Anielwicz and some of his youth movement friends escaped to eastern Poland. He hoped to open up a route from there through Romania to Palestine. In mid-September, acting in accordance with secret provisions of the German-Soviet Non-Aggression Pact, Soviet armies invaded eastern Poland, and Anielwicz was arrested by Soviet authorities while attempting to make his way to Palestine. Upon his release, he voluntarily returned to German-occupied Warsaw to continue underground Hashomer Hatzair activities.

A natural leader, Anielwicz organized cells and worked at various educational activities for Jewish youths, but the focus of his activities changed when he and other Jews learned of the mass killings of Jews by the Germans. Anielwicz helped organize the

Jewish Fighting Organization (ZOB for its Polish initials) in the Warsaw Ghetto and was then selected as its commander. When the Germans began the second large deportation of Jews from the ghetto on January 18, 1943, they were surprised when Jews resisted with what arms they had and those smuggled in from the Polish Underground Army. The Germans then withdrew, and Anielwicz and his followers did what they could to prepare for the inevitable final German assault.

On April 19, 1943, the Germans began their drive against the ghetto. The Jews raised two large flags: one the white and red flag of Poland and the other a white and blue banner with the Star of David over the ghetto. The fighting was fierce and raged for four weeks until May 16, when a few Jewish fighters managed to escape through the sewers to continue resistance against the Germans. Anielwicz died a week earlier on May 8 in the resistance command center. His last message to his deputy, then outside the ghetto, was "The dream of my life has been fulfilled. I have lived to see Jewish defense in all its greatness and glory." Kibbutz Yad Mordechai in Israel was named in Anielwicz's memory, and a monument was erected there in his honor.

SPENCER C. TUCKER

See also
Hashomer; Holocaust

References
Callahan, Kerry P. *Mordechai Anielewicz: Hero of the Warsaw Ghetto Uprising.* New York: Rosen, 2001.
Gulman, Israel. *Resistance: The Warsaw Ghetto Uprising.* Wilmington, MA: Houghton Mifflin, 1994.
Kurzman, Dan. *The Bravest Battle: The Twenty-Eight Days of the Warsaw Ghetto Uprising.* New York: Putnam, 1976.

Antiaircraft Artillery

See Artillery, Antiaircraft

Anti-Arab Attitudes and Discrimination

Anti-Arab attitudes, especially toward Muslim Arabs, as well as formal and informal policies and codes of conduct that unfairly target Arabs and are sometimes known as anti-Arabism have been especially virulent in Israel since 1948. However, such prejudice against Arabs has certainly manifested itself in other areas of the world and has seen a widespread expansion in the West since 1973 that intensified following the Iranian Revolution and then again after September 11, 2001. People with anti-Arab attitudes often stereotype Arabs as uneducated, dirty, brutal, untrustworthy, and fanatical terrorists or supporters of terrorism.

In Israel, anti-Arabism dates to 1948 when the country was first established. But anti-Arab discrimination among Jews certainly predates the modern State of Israel, as Arabs and Jews had been in conflict since at least the early part of the 20th century. On May 15, 1948, the Arab League declared a jihad (holy war) against Israel that led to even stronger enmity of Israelis toward Arabs. Israelis tend to view Arabs as religious fanatics who insist on war with an internationally recognized country that favors peace. After numerous Arab-Israeli wars in the 20th century, anti-Arab attitudes now exist at both the personal and political levels in Israel. This bias is directed toward Arab citizens of Israel as well as those living in other Middle Eastern and North African countries.

In recent years, the most notable public manifestations in Israel that showcased anti-Arab attitudes were the October 2000 riots. During the riots, Israeli Jews assaulted Arabs by stone throwing, property destruction, and chants of "Death to Arabs." The worst of the rioting occurred in Tel Aviv and Nazareth. Two Arabs were killed and many more were injured in the attacks.

At the political level in Israel, anti-Arab attitudes include discriminatory language frequently used by politicians or party leaders and by government policies that are clearly discriminatory in nature. For example, Yehiel Hazan, a Knesset (Israeli parliament) member, spoke on the floor of that body and bluntly stated that "the Arabs are worms." Another example of anti-Arabism can be found in the rightist political party Yisrael Beytenu (Our Home). The party dedicates itself chiefly to the purpose of redrawing the Israeli border, which would force many Arab citizens of Israel to lose their citizenship.

The Israeli government also shows hostility toward Arabs. The 2005 U.S. State Department Country Reports on Human Rights Practices noted that the 2003 report of the Orr Commission, which was established following the police killing of 12 Israeli-Arab demonstrators and a Palestinian in October 2000, stated that government handling of the Arab sector was "primarily neglectful and discriminatory" and was not sufficiently sensitive to Arab needs and that the government did not allocate state resources equally. As a result, "serious distress prevailed in the Arab sector," including poverty, unemployment, land shortages, an inadequate educational system, and a substantially defective infrastructure.

Problems also exist in the health and social services sectors. According to 2004 reports by Mossawa (Advocacy Center for Arab Citizens of Israel) and the Arab Association for Human Rights, racist violence against Arab citizens of Israel has been on the increase, and the government has not acted to prevent this problem.

Today, anti-Arab attitudes in Israel continue to grow in scale and scope. According to a recent Israeli poll, more than two-thirds of Jews would refuse to live in the same building with an Arab, 41 percent were in favor of segregation, and 63 percent believed Arabs to be a "security and demographic threat" to Israel. Such attitudes, it should be noted, are fueled by terrorist attacks made by a small minority of Arabs.

Anti-Arab bias is not, of course, confined to Israel. A significant amount of Arab discrimination exists in Iran, for example, in which Arabs are an ethnic minority. Some critics of the hard-line fundamentalist regime there assert that the Iranian government is actively pursuing an anti-Arab campaign that smacks of ethnic cleansing.

Throughout the West there also exists considerable anti-Arab bias. In Western Europe these anti-Arab attitudes vary from country to country, as some were former colonial powers over Arab lands. Nevertheless, even in those nations anti-Arab bias is troublesome at best and dangerous at worst. Examples of this were the widespread riots in France in 2005 that virtually paralyzed the country. Suffering from extreme poverty, segregation, poor health services, and unemployment rates of 25 percent or more, thousands of French Muslims—Arab and non-Arab alike—demonstrated in French cities.

Anti-Arab attitudes and discrimination also widely exist in the United States and have grown in recent years. The primary reason for such attitudes in the West is considered to be the terrorist attacks carried out by or related to Arabs or Muslims. After the terrorist attacks on September 11, 2001, in the United States and the London subway bombings on July 7, 2005, anti-Arab attitudes became more widespread in the United States, Britain, and other Western countries. According to a poll of Arab Americans conducted by the Arab American Institute in 2001, 32 percent of Arab Americans reported being subjected to some form of ethnic-based discrimination during their lifetimes, and 20 percent reported having experienced ethnic-based discrimination since September 11, 2001.

Anti-Arabism in the United States takes many forms, including hate crimes and discrimination in schools and company hiring policies. Sometimes, non-Muslim Americans have blamed Arabs or Muslims for attacks in which they had no involvement. This was clearly the case in the immediate aftermath of the April 19, 1995, bombing of the Alfred P. Murrah Federal Building in Oklahoma City. Several supposed eyewitnesses claimed to have seen an Arab lurking about the scene before the attack, and the national media quickly picked up on this. As it turned out, there were no such persons on the scene that day, and the bombing was carried out by a white American citizen.

The Western media—and Hollywood in particular—has often resorted to ethnic stereotypes when depicting Arabs. Most Arabs in U.S. films are portrayed in a negative light, and most play the role of villain. The 2000 film *Rules of Engagement* has been heavily criticized for its anti-Arab slant. In a recent review of more than 900 Hollywood films released over a long time span, just 12 of them depicted Arabs in positive terms, and only 50 were considered balanced portrayals of Arabs.

YUANYUAN DING AND PAUL G. PIERPAOLI JR.

See also

Film and the Arab-Israeli Conflict; Terrorism

References

Herzog, Chaim. *The Arab-Israeli Wars: War and Peace in the Middle East from the War of Independence to Lebanon.* Westminster, MD: Random House, 1984.

Rabinovich, Itamar. *Waging Peace: Israel and the Arabs, 1948–2003.* Princeton, NJ: Princeton University Press, 2004.

Salaita, Steven. *Anti-Arab Racism in the USA: Where It Comes from and What It Means for Politics Today.* London: Pluto, 2006.

Anti-Semitism

Anti-Semitism, defined as hostility toward the Jewish people, has played a significant role in the history of the State of Israel and its relations with surrounding Muslim nations. European anti-Semitism, rooted in medieval culture, served as one of the principal motivations for the Zionist movement in the early 20th century and the initial migration of European Jews to Palestine.

The murder of 6 million Jews during World War II represents the most heinous expression of European antipathy toward Judaism. Revulsion at the atrocities of the Nazis and sympathy for the victims of the Holocaust contributed significantly to international support for the founding of the State of Israel in 1948. However, the end of the Holocaust did not mean an end to anti-Jewish feelings in the world. The establishment of Israel resulted in the growth of anti-Jewish sentiment throughout the Arab world and the global Muslim community, sentiments that remain strong today. Cold War anti-Zionism, the rejection of the Jewish claim to Israel/Palestine, often included elements of anti-Semitism, including attacks on the Jewish people themselves. The Arab-Israeli conflicts of the second half of the century involved significant use of anti-Semitic policy, rhetoric, and images as Arab states sought to define their struggle and motivate their people by denigrating their Jewish enemies. However, it is important to point out the difference between anti-Semitism and anti-Israeli language and policies on the part of Arab states and militant groups, even if the distinction is often blurred.

Some of the roots of European anti-Semitism lie in Late Antiquity. Early Christian texts may be interpreted as placing blame on the Jews for the death of Christ. However, most of the familiar manifestations of anti-Semitism in Europe originated in the Middle Ages. A significant decline in European acceptance of Judaism took place in the second half of the 11th century as increasing centralization in the Roman Church reduced the religious autonomy of local authorities. The Gregorian reforms of the period and the writings of St. Peter Damian attacked the practice of Judaism in Central Europe as a danger to the Christian community. The Crusades also had disastrous implications for European Jews, as the pursuit of Christian orthodoxy was combined with the use of force (military or otherwise) in a systematic way. Following Pope Urban II's call in 1095 for a holy war to wrest Jerusalem from Muslim control, a number of riots and massacres aimed at the Jewish communities of Europe took place. Both the People's Crusade of 1096 and the more formal military expedition (the First Crusade) that followed engaged in numerous pogroms on the way to their objectives in the Middle East. In short, crusading zeal was directed against non-Christians in general. Following the conquest of Jerusalem in 1099, the entire Jewish community of the city was killed by the victorious crusading army.

After the 11th century, anti-Semitism occupied a permanent place in medieval Christian culture. During the pontificate of Innocent III (1198–1216), such sentiments acquired an institutional character.

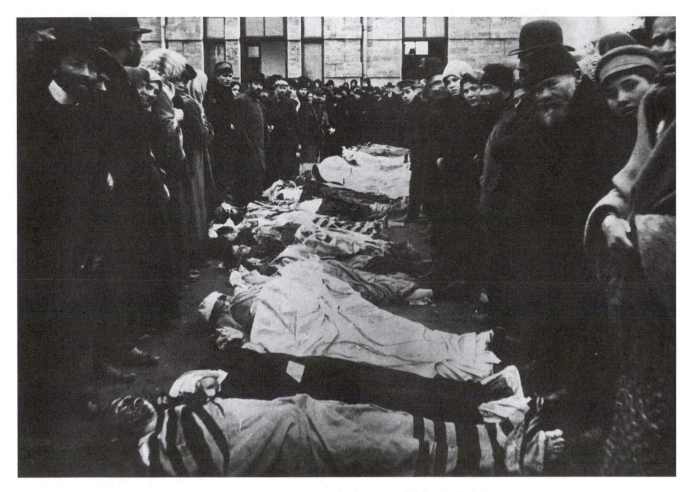

Bodies of the victims of an anti-Jewish riot (pogrom) in Russia, circa 1905. (Hulton-Deutsch Collection/Corbis)

Pope Innocent viewed Judaism and Christian heretical thought as significant threats to the orthodoxy of the Roman Church. The Fourth Lateran Council (1215), presided over by Innocent, required that Jewish communities be separated from those of Christians, thus creating Jewish ghettos. In addition, Jews were required to wear yellow labels and were denied participation in various professional and commercial enterprises. Jewish customs also contributed to separation of peoples. These policies formed the foundation for centuries of anti-Jewish behavior on the European continent.

The crowned heads of Europe also adopted measures directed against the Jewish population during the High Middle Ages. Rulers often charged high taxes in return for granting protection to Jewish communities. Ultimately, Edward I of England and Philip IV of France expelled the Jewish populations from their kingdoms in the late 13th century, confiscating property in the process. These expulsions contributed to the concentration of Jews in Central and Eastern Europe. Widespread vilification of the Jews accompanied physical violence and forced isolation. Jews were accused of complicity in the death of Christ, of using the blood of Christians in their rituals, and of slaughtering Christian children. During the Black Death of the 14th century, accusations of Jewish well-poisoning led to a series of anti-Jewish riots. Geoffrey Chaucer's *The Canterbury*

Tales serves as a case in point. In "The Prioress' Tale," a young Christian boy is killed by Jews as he walks home singing hymns.

The Jewish community of the medieval Iberian Peninsula had a more complex experience. While Jews suffered persecution in the Visigothic kingdom of the Early Middle Ages, they were quite well treated under the Arab Muslim rule that began in the early 8th century. Positive attitudes toward Jewish monotheism allowed for significant Jewish participation in the political and cultural life of the Arab state in the 10th and 11th centuries. However, later Berber-dominated governments adopted a more hostile view of Judaism, and this prompted Jewish migrations to the Christian kingdoms of northern Iberia, which accepted the new migrants. The Iberian Jewish population played a significant role in the economic and intellectual revival of Christian Europe after the 12th century.

Conditions for the Jews of Iberia changed in the Late Middle Ages. After 1391 they came under significant pressure to convert to Christianity. Many did, although converts were often viewed with suspicion. The Spanish Inquisition, founded by King Ferdinand and Queen Isabella in 1478, viewed the enforcement of Christian orthodoxy among converts as one of its principal roles and inflicted considerable suffering on Jews and Jewish converts through the first half of the 16th century. In 1492, Spanish tolerance of the Jews waned altogether. Ferdinand and Isabella ordered them expelled from the kingdom, and Portugal followed suit in 1497. These expulsions ultimately led to the establishment of Jewish communities across the Mediterranean and in North Africa. Medieval anti-Semitism established patterns and policies that would persist into the 20th century: vilification, physical separation, exclusion from economic activity, stigmatization, forced conversion, and periodic violence, including riots, pogroms, and inquisitions.

Ultimately, the European Enlightenment of the 18th century and the liberal political agendas of the 19th century reduced the role of Christianity in European public life and produced a more secular society. In this atmosphere, many European Jews gradually began to assimilate into the economic, political, and cultural lives of the nations in which they lived. In England, France, the Low Countries, and Germany, optimistic members of the Jewish community came to see themselves as Jewish citizens with strong allegiance to their countries.

However, the rise of modern European secular culture in the 18th and 19th centuries did not result in the disappearance of anti-Semitism. It remained an ugly part of the European cultural landscape. In the 1890s, the Dreyfus Affair revealed significant anti-Jewish sentiment in Republican France. Alfred Dreyfus, a Jewish captain in the French Army, was accused of treason and was convicted and imprisoned. When the shaky grounds of his conviction were openly challenged, great controversy erupted. The French Left supported acquittal for Dreyfus while the French Right, bolstered by the Catholic Church, opposed it. Dreyfus was ultimately pardoned, but the conflict led some European Jews to doubt the potential for cultural and political assimilation. Among them was Theodor Herzl, the founder of the Zionist movement.

Herzl's Zionist movement grew as a response to the continued exclusion of Jews from late-19th-century European culture, an exclusion rooted in medieval tradition. He was working as a correspondent in Paris at the time of the Dreyfus Affair, and it had a profound effect upon him. His arguments for a separate Jewish state proceeded from his realization that Jews would always be regarded as alien in Europe. In *Der Judenstaat,* he argued that Jews would never be assimilated in European nations despite their service and patriotism. Only a state of their own would free the Jews from oppression and persecution. Herzl suggested Palestine (then part of Ottoman Turkey) as a possible site for a Jewish homeland, and he also considered parts of Argentina. Many European Jews viewed Herzl's ideas as alarmist and maintained their varied national loyalties. The service of German Jews in the kaiser's armies during World War I serves as an excellent example of such thinking. Thirty years later, the horrors of the Nazi Holocaust gave renewed force to Herzl's Zionist ideas.

While Zionism provided an ideological basis for Jewish immigration to Palestine in the early 20th century, such immigration also proceeded from the harshly anti-Semitic policies adopted by Czar Alexander III in his Russian and Polish territories after 1881. Alexander's use of violent pogroms led to the departure of many of his

Jewish storefront during a boycott of Jewish goods launched on April 1, 1933, several months after Adolf Hitler came to power in Germany. The placard reads "Germans defend yourselves do not buy from Jews!" (National Archives and Records Administration)

Jewish subjects. While most fled to the United States or Western Europe, some proceeded to Palestine. Significant Jewish migration to the Middle East began while the region was still controlled by the Ottoman Turks. Local Arab nobility exercised significant authority in Palestine itself. The initial reaction of Palestinian Arabs to Jewish settlement was mixed: resentment on the one hand, economic cooperation and land sales on the other. The Jewish population grew and acquired a distinctly Zionist character. By the early 20th century, Palestinians began to pressure Turkish authorities to restrict Jewish immigration, with limited effectiveness. It is important to point out that Arab political action against Jewish ambitions did not necessarily have an anti-Semitic nature. However, as Jewish socialist agricultural collectives proliferated and largely ended the hiring of Arab farmworkers, the increasing tensions resulted in mutual bitterness.

World War I had a profound effect on Arab-Jewish relations in Palestine. In an effort to secure local support for its war against the Ottoman Turks, the British government made conflicting promises of autonomy or outright independence to the Jewish and Arab inhabitants of Palestine. When the British gained control of the region in 1918 at the end of World War I, they soon found themselves mediating an increasingly acrid dispute. The figure of Haj Amin al-Husseini, grand mufti of Jerusalem, serves as an excellent indication of growing anti-Jewish sentiment during this period. A significant leader of the Palestinian Arabs, al-Husseini moved incrementally toward anti-Semitism as he opposed Jewish ambitions in the region. While he had economic dealings with the Jewish population, he also inspired and organized the growth of Arab paramilitary groups intent on thwarting the growth of Jewish power. When disputes over access to the holy places in Jerusalem led to open conflict in 1929, he proved unable to control his followers and ultimately gave assent to their actions. Violent riots spread across the region, with hundreds of Jews and Arabs killed. Conspicuous among the Jewish dead were urban clerics and scholars, members of some of the oldest Jewish communities in Palestine. A significant consequence of the riots was the formation of the irregular Jewish defense force, the Hagana.

Unrest erupted again in 1936 as Arab attempts at economic and political action against the Jewish population turned violent. The 1936 Arab Revolt involved conflict among all three groups in the region: British, Arab, Jewish. The outbreaks of 1929 and 1936 resulted in severe limitations on Jewish immigration to Palestine as the British responded to Arab pressure. In addition, the violence undermined efforts at Arab-Jewish cooperation and led to mutual vilification and recrimination. Arab political resistance to Zionist aims came to include anti-Semitic policy and rhetoric.

The rise of Nazism in Germany and the ensuing World War II forever changed the destiny of the Jewish people. Nazi ideology drew upon the anti-Semitic elements of European culture that originated in the medieval period and amplified them through German ultranationalism, Social Darwinist rhetoric, and industrial technology. The systematic killing of 6 million Jews apparently confirmed Herzl's ideas about the illusory nature of Jewish assimilation in Europe. The Arab-Jewish conflict in Palestine was also affected by the war. The grand mufti of Jerusalem gained notoriety for his active courting of the Axis powers. However, his motivations also involved significant anti-British sentiment, for he viewed the Germans as the likely victors in the war and sought to gain influence with them. His efforts ended in failure, and his German sympathies resulted in his marginalization after the Allied victory.

Before and after the war, Zionists from the Middle East, eager to attract additional Jewish immigrants, depicted Palestine as an obvious refuge for European Jews. On the other hand, Palestinian Arabs continued to oppose any increase in Jewish migration. The British supported the Arab position and continued to severely restrict Jewish entry to Palestine after the war's end. British policy may be explained by the importance of their relations with the newly independent Arab oil states coupled with their ties to the Arabs of Palestine. However, the horrors of the Holocaust resulted in an increase in global support for a Jewish homeland in the Middle East. In 1947, the British agreed to refer the fate of Palestine to the newly formed

United Nations (UN). The UN resolution partitioning Palestine and creating a Jewish state was bitterly opposed by the Arab states, which considered it as an unjust seizure of Arab territory by the Western powers on behalf of Zionism. Arabs questioned why European atrocities against the Jews should result in a loss of Arab sovereignty over Arab land. When the new nation of Israel was proclaimed in May 1948, five of the newly formed Arab states—Egypt, Syria, Iraq, Transjordan, and Lebanon—immediately invaded, initiating half a century of Arab-Israeli warfare.

As Israel fought successfully in the various conflicts of 1948, 1956, 1967, 1973, 1982, and 2006, anti-Jewish feeling among the Arabs increased. Anti-Zionism represented the core of the Arab position. Indeed, none of the Arab nations of the Middle East recognized the right of Israel to exist until the Israel-Egypt Peace Treaty of 1979, and they vowed to destroy the Jewish state. Anti-Zionism, however, was often combined with anti-Semitism, as Arab rhetoric attacked Judaism and the Jewish people. For example, Lebanese and Syrian cartoons at the time of the 1967 Six-Day War depicted caricatured Jews being expelled from Israel and mounds of Jewish skulls in the streets of Tel Aviv. At the same time, some Israeli rhetoric vilified the Arab people. The existence of Arab refugees fanned the flames. Such refugees, mostly Palestinian Arabs who had fled Israel during the Israeli War of Independence (1948–1949), lived in a number of large camps located in Syria, Gaza, Jordan, and the West Bank. Dispossessed by the Israelis and not accepted by any of the Arab states, the refugees seethed with anti-Jewish sentiment. The Palestine Liberation Organization (PLO), founded in 1964, drew its members largely from their ranks.

During the Cold War, varied forms of Arab nationalism dominated the viewpoints of many Arab governments. Socialist and anti-colonialist in tone, Arab nationalism attacked Zionism and Judaism as racist and imperialist and denounced Israel as part of an American plot for global domination. With the Israeli victory in the 1967 war and the seizure and occupation of Arab territories in the Sinai, the West Bank, and the Gaza Strip, such charges intensified. Much of the developing world, recently liberated from European colonialism, responded to such Arab views. Muslim nations already had an obvious reason to sympathize with the Palestinian refugees and with the Arab cause in general. The Soviet Union cleverly fostered such anti-imperialist arguments as a way to reduce American influence among developing nations. The trend resulted in a global isolation of Israel, best illustrated by the UN General Assembly's resolution defining Zionism as a form of racism (1975) and its recognition of Yasser Arafat and the PLO. Global anti-Zionism and anti-Semitism continued to grow, and the Israeli invasion of Lebanon in 1982 accelerated its pace.

The Arab-Israeli struggle changed significantly in the 1980s as low-intensity local insurgency largely replaced large-scale confrontations between national armies. Islamist paramilitary groups— Hamas, Hezbollah, and Islamic Jihad—played a central role in this new conflict. In addition, the collapse of the Soviet Union in 1990 and the defeat of the Baathist regime in Iraq in 1991 resulted in a decline in the status of Arab nationalism. As a result, radical Islam has become an increasingly important ideological basis for Arab resistance to Israel. Anti-Zionist views in the Middle East and around the world have acquired a more religious character in the years since the end of the Cold War and often involve anti-Semitic rhetoric. Indeed, the conflict between Israel and Islamist groups has led to significant mutual vilification.

ROBERT S. KIELY

See also

Arab Revolt of 1936–1939; Dreyfus Affair; Haganah; Hamas; Hezbollah; Husseini, Haj Amin al-; Israeli War of Independence, Overview; Jihad; Palestine, British Mandate for; Palestine Liberation Organization; World War I, Impact of; World War II, Impact of; Zionism

References

Cantor, Norman. *Civilization of the Middle Ages.* New York: Harper Perennial, 1994.
Dimont, Max. *Jews, God and History.* New York: Simon and Schuster, 1962.
Lewis, Bernard. *The Middle East.* New York: Scribner, 1995.
Pappe, Ilan. *A History of Modern Palestine: One Land, Two Peoples.* Cambridge: Cambridge University Press, 2003.
Perry, Marvin, and Frederick Schweitzer. *Anti-Semitism: Myths and Hate from Antiquity to the Present.* New York: Palgrave Macmillan, 2005.

Antitank Weapons

Because of the importance of tanks and armored vehicles in the Arab-Israeli wars, antitank weapons came to play a critical role. Specialized antitank weapons—as opposed to armored vehicles, artillery, and self-propelled guns that serve in an antitank role against enemy armor—are those that may be carried by individual soldiers or are capable of being mounted on thin-skinned vehicles or even tanks.

The antitank rifle was first introduced in World War I. Today it is known as the antimaterial (antimateriél or equipment) rifle. Essentially a large-caliber, high-velocity rifle firing special armor-piercing ammunition, it is designed to operate against enemy equipment, such as thin-skinned and lightly armored vehicles. The weapon may also be used for long-range sniping. Antimaterial rifles are often favored by special operations military units.

The U.S. Army Browning M-2 .50-caliber machine gun, which may be fired single-shot, fits in this category. The Austrian Steyr 25-mm antimaterial rifle, with a claimed effective range of 1.2 miles, features both a muzzle brake and a hydropneumatic sleeve to lessen recoil. It has a bipod, and the weapon may be broken down for ease of transport by its crew. Among other such weapons is the South African Mechem NTW-20. This 20-mm bolt-action rifle features a three-round side-mounted box magazine. There is also a 14.5-mm model. To reduce recoil, the NTW-20 uses a hydraulic double-action damper along with a double baffle muzzle brake. Among other such weapons are the U.S. Armalite AR-50 and Barrett M-82A1, both of which fire the 12.7-mm .50-caliber round; the British Accuracy International AW50F, firing the 12.7-mm NATO (.50 caliber) round;

the Hungarian Gerpard M-1(B) and M-2(B) 12.7-mm rifles, which with changed barrel may also fire the .50-caliber round; and the Russian KSVK 12.7-mm rifle. A number of these or similar weapons were employed in the Arab-Israeli wars.

Missiles, at first unguided and then guided, came to dominate antitank weaponry. The first of these used in the Arab-Israeli wars were those remaining from World War II. The German Panzerfaust may have been the world's first expendable antitank weapon. An inexpensive, single-shot, lightweight weapon, it used a shaped charge warhead and could be operated by one man. The Panzerfaust consisted of a very simple small-diameter disposable launcher preloaded with a 3-foot-long finned projectile with an oversized warhead. The hollow tube concentrated the escaping gasses away from the user and made the firing recoilless. Pulling the trigger ignited a small charge of black powder inside the tube, driving the projectile toward its target. The projectile exploded on impact. The warhead was a hollow or shaped charge utilizing the Munro effect, whereby the detonation of a shaped explosive charge around an open-ended cavity concentrated that blast in that direction. The resulting plasma jet penetrated the armor and killed the tank crew. All subsequent antitank missiles operate on this basic principle.

The Panzerfaust 60, introduced beginning in August 1944, was the most common version. It had a practical range of 60 yards and could penetrate 140 mm of armor. Although lightweight, the Panzerfaust was a short-range weapon that required considerable courage to employ, as firing it and other similar weapons immediately telegraphed the user's location. The Germans produced millions of these weapons in the course of the war, and the Soviet Union subsequently manufactured a number of copies. Such weapons may well have found their way into the Israeli War of Independence (1948–1949).

The U.S. antitank rocket was the 2.36-inch bazooka. The bazooka consisted of a rocket and launcher operated by a two-man crew of operator and loader. The launcher was a tube with a shoulder stock. The hand grip contained a trigger assembly that had an electric generator to send a current along a wire. Each rocket had two wires extending from the nozzle at its rear. When the rocket was packed, the wires were tucked along the body and grounded with a shorting cap. The loader pulled off the shorting cap before he placed the rocket in the rear of the launcher, then individually tied off the wires against electrical posts at the back of the launch tube. When the operator squeezed the trigger, it generated an electric current through the wires to ignite the solid fuel in the rocket.

The rocket was 2.36 inches in diameter. The 2.36-inch rocket proved ineffective against the better-armored Soviet T-34 tank in the Korean War (1950–1953) and was replaced by the 3.5-inch M-20 Super Bazooka. Bazookas may or may not have seen service in the Arab-Israeli wars. The Germans copied the 2.36-inch bazooka at the end of World War II in their Panzerschreck.

The British PIAT (Projector Infantry Anti-Tank) definitely saw service in the Israeli War of Independence and was used by Israeli ground forces to knock out the far more numerous Arab tanks.

An Israeli infantryman aims a bazooka during summer maneuvers in the Negev Desert on July 5, 1960. (Moshe Pridan/Israeli Government Press Office)

Entering service in July 1943, it consisted of a hollow-charge 3-pound projectile that was pushed by a powerful metal spring and rod from a small trough or barrel. When the rod struck the rear of the projectile, it also set off its small propellant charge. The warhead was capable of penetrating about 100 mm of armor. The PIAT was more compact than the bazooka or Panzerschreck and thus more useful in urban warfare. Loaded, the PIAT weighed about 34 pounds. Although rated at 100 yards' range, it typically was fired at far shorter ranges to score a hit. It was often used against buildings prior to an infantry assault. Panzerfausts, bazookas, and PIATs all suffered from the great disadvantage of not having guidance systems. To ensure a hit, operators had to approach close to the target before firing. They were then likely subject to counterfire.

Antitank guided missiles (ATGMs), widely used by both the Arab and Israeli armies, represented a vast improvement on the early unguided antitank weapons. They were a key component of the Egyptian plan to defeat Israeli armor in the early period of the Yom Kippur War in 1973. Such missiles vary widely in size and type, ranging from individual shoulder-fired missiles to crew-served missiles and to those launched from aircraft. Unlike unguided systems, missiles have the great advantage of standoff capability.

First-generation guided missiles were manually directed. Once the missile had been fired, the operator guided it to the target by means of a joystick or a similar device. Second-generation antitank missiles only require that the operator keep the sight on the target. Guidance commands for the missile are transmitted either by radio or by wire. The U.S. TOW (tube-launched, optically tracked, wire-guided) missile is an example of a second-generation antitank missile. Third-generation antitank missiles rely on laser "painting" or marking of the target or a nose-mounted TV camera. They are known as fire-and-forget missiles. The U.S. Javelin is an example of a third-generation antitank missile.

Antitank missiles generally have a hollow-charge or shaped-charge warhead. Double warhead missiles are designed specifically to defeat special or spaced vehicle armor, while top-attack antitank missiles are designed to strike from above against the more lightly armored tops of tanks and armored fighting vehicles (AFVs).

The Soviet Union's AT-3 Sagger is an excellent example of a first-generation ATGM. Entering service in September 1963, it was the first man-portable Soviet antitank missile and was probably the most widely produced ATGM in history. Some 25,000 of these were produced yearly by the Soviet Union alone in the 1960s and 1970s. The Sagger was also manufactured by other Soviet bloc countries as well as by the People's Republic of China and has been widely exported to the Middle East, including Afghanistan, Algeria, Egypt, Iran, Iraq, Libya, and Syria. It was widely used by both Egyptian and

The periscopic sight and joystick control unit for the Soviet Sagger AT-3 antitank guided weapon (ATGW) system, November 14, 1984. (U.S. Department of Defense)

Syrian forces in the 1973 Yom Kippur War. Soviet sources claim that the Sagger accounted for 800–1,000 Israeli tank losses, including those temporarily out of action. The Sagger has also been used by Hezbollah guerrillas.

Guided to its target by means of a joystick and wire, the Sagger has a launch weight of some 24 pounds with a warhead of 5.5 pounds. It has a minimum range of some 500 yards and maximum range of about 1.8 miles. At maximum range, it takes the missile about 30 seconds to reach its target.

The outstanding example of the second-generation ATGM is the U.S.-made TOW. Produced first by Hughes Aircraft Company and now Raytheon Systems Company, the TOW is the world's most widely distributed antitank missile system. More than 500,000 TOWs have been manufactured, and it is employed by more than 45 nations. The TOW is designed to attack tanks, AFVs, bunkers, and fortifications and to defend against amphibious landings. First entering service in 1970, the TOW underwent a number of modifications, the most recent of which is the TOW-2B of 1991. The first use of the TOW in combat came in May 1972 during the Vietnam War. It also saw wartime service with the Israeli Army against Syrian forces and in the Iran-Iraq War (1980–1988). The TOW-2B first saw combat in 2003 in the Iraq War.

The TOW-2B missile weighs 49.8 pounds (64 pounds with carrier) and has an explosive filler of some 6.9 pounds. The missile is 5.8 inches in diameter and is 48 inches in length. It has a maximum range of about 3,750 yards.

TOW missiles may be ground fired from a tripod by a crew of four or, more usually, from AFVs such as the M-1/M-3 Bradley. TOWs may also be fired from helicopters. The missile operates on command line-of-sight guidance. The operator uses a sight to locate the target, and once the missile is fired, he continues to track the target through the sight, with guidance commands transmitted along two wires that spool from the back of the missile. The TOW-2B attacks the target from the top, and its double warheads explode downward when the missile is just above the target. A bunker-buster variant is designed to defeat bunkers, field fortifications, and buildings.

The Soviet Union's second-generation man-portable AT-4 Spigot ATGM entered service in 1972. Designed to replace the Sagger, the Spigot has a minimum range of 70 yards and a maximum range of 2,000 yards in a flight time of 11 seconds. Fired from a folding tripod from a ground mount weighing some 50 pounds, the missile weighs 28.6 pounds. The Soviet counterpart to the TOW is the AT-5 Spandrel. Introduced in 1973, it is intended for vehicle use only and is usually mounted on the BRDM-2 scout vehicle and manned by a crew of three. The missile weighs some 58 pounds and has a minimum range of 75 yards and a maximum range of some 4,000 yards, with a maximum flight time to target of 19 seconds.

The U.S. man-portable Javelin is a third-generation system. A joint venture of Texas Instruments (now Raytheon Missile Systems) of Dallas, Texas, and Lockheed Martin Electronics and Missiles (now Missiles and Fire Control) of Orlando, Florida, the

A soldier aims a Soviet AT-4 Spigot antitank guided missile. (U.S. Department of Defense)

Javelin entered service with the U.S. Army and the U.S. Marine Corps in 1996.

Designed for a two-man crew, the Javelin has a minimum range of 75 yards and a maximum range of some 2,500 yards (more than twice that of its predecessor M-47 Dragon missile) and is used to attack enemy tanks and AFVs. The Javelin system consists of a missile in a disposable launch tube and reusable command launch unit (CLU) with triggering mechanism and an integrated day-night sighting device and target acquisition electronics. The missile weighs 49.5 pounds and is 5.75 feet in length. Fins deploy when the missile is launched. The Javelin employs a small thermal imaging TV camera and sophisticated computer guidance system in its seeker section. To fire the missile, the gunner places a cursor over the selected target. The CLU then sends a lock-on-before-launch signal to the missile. The missile's infrared guidance system and onboard processing guide it after launch. The Javelin is designed for top attack and has a dual 8.5-pound warhead capable of defeating all known armor. The Javelin was successfully employed in 2003 during the Iraq War.

Antitank weapons also include Molotov cocktails and improvised explosive devices (IEDs). These weapons, which were increasingly used by Arab insurgents against Israeli armor and thin-skinned vehicles, were also employed in large numbers during the Iraq War.

SPENCER C. TUCKER

See also

Improvised Explosive Devices; Molotov Cocktail; Tank Warfare; Tanks

References

Gander, Terry J. *Anti-Tank Weapons.* Marlborough, UK: Crowood, 2000.
———. *The Bazooka: Hand-Held Hollow-Charge Anti-Tank Weapons.* London: PRC Publishing, 1998.
Weeks, John S. *Men against Tanks: A History of Anti-Tank Warfare.* New York: Mason/Charter, 1975.

Antonius, George
Born: 1891
Died: May 1942

Lebanese Christian writer who sought to trace the course of and influences on Arab nationalism. Born in Lebanon of Lebanese Egyptian parents, George Antonius was a Greek Orthodox Christian Arab who grew up in Egypt and was educated in Britain. He earned a degree in mechanical engineering at Cambridge University. Following World War I, he secured an administrative position in the Education Department in the British Mandate for Palestine. Although his father-in-law was the publisher of a leading Cairo newspaper, a career in journalism did not appeal to Antonius. In 1930 a wealthy American, Charles Crane, arranged for Antonius to travel to New York City and become a fellow of the Institute for Current World Affairs (ICWA).

Returning to Jerusalem, Antonius worked to complete *The Arab Awakening,* which was published in 1938. The book traced the growth of Arab nationalism, which Antonius identified as having begun with Muhammad Ali Pasha, the reforming khedive of Egypt during 1805–1848, whom many regard as the founder of modern Egypt. Antonius also believed that Protestant missionaries, especially those from Britain and the United States, had been a major influence on the spread of Arab nationalism, as had the American University of Beirut (originally the Syrian Protestant College). Antonius is widely regarded as the first historian of Arab nationalism, although many of his findings were later challenged by others.

In January 1939 Antonius traveled to London, where he served as secretary to the Arab delegates to the Round-Table Conference on the future of Palestine and expressed himself as opposed to British policy in Palestine. Later that year he settled in Beirut. During World War II, he offered in turn but without success his services as an expert on the region to the British, the French, and the Americans. In 1941 he traveled to Baghdad to offer his services as a mediator and there met with exiled mufti of Jerusalem Haj Amin al-Husseini. Pro-Axis Iraqi leader Rashid Ali al-Gaylani was then actively courting the Axis powers and discussing with the German government how the British might be expelled from the Middle East. Suffering from an ulcer, Antonius returned to Beirut only weeks before the British intervened militarily in Iraq and overthrew al-Gaylani in May 1941. Antonius now found himself proscribed by the Vichy French authorities in Lebanon, and he moved on to Jerusalem. Concerned that Antonius's activities might prejudice their own work, the directors of the ICWA decided, meanwhile, to terminate subsidizing his work. Beset by mounting debts and with his health in decline, Antonius died in May 1942.

SPENCER C. TUCKER

See also

Arab Nationalism; Husseini, Haj Amin al-

References

Antonius, George. *The Arab Awakening: The Story of the Arab National Movement.* London: H. Hamilton, 1938.
Dawn, C. Ernest. *From Ottomanism to Arabism: Essays on the Origins of Arab Nationalism.* Champaign: University of Illinois Press, 1973.
Hourani, Albert. *A History of the Arab Peoples.* Cambridge: Harvard University Press, 1991.
Khalidi, Rashid, et al., eds. *The Origins of Arab Nationalism.* New York: Columbia University Press, 1993.
Lukitz, Liora. "The Antonius Papers and *The Arab Awakening:* Over Fifty Years On." *Middle Eastern Studies* 30 (1994): 883–885.
Tibi, Bassam. *Arab Nationalism: A Critical Enquiry.* 2nd ed. New York: St. Martin's, 1991.

Aoun, Michel
Born: February 17, 1935

Lebanese Army general and politician. Born into a poor Christian Maronite family in the Harat Hraik southern suburb of Beirut on February 17, 1935, Michel Aoun ended his secondary education at the Collège des Frères in 1956. In 1958 he graduated from the

Lebanese Military Academy as an artillery lieutenant. He received additional military training in France at Châlons-sur-Marne during 1958–1959 and at the École Supérieure de Guerre in 1978–1980. He also received training at the U.S. Army Artillery School, Fort Sill, Oklahoma, in 1966.

During the Israeli invasion of Lebanon in 1982, Aoun commanded a battalion defending the presidential palace in Baabda. During the Lebanese Civil War, in September 1983 Aoun commanded the 8th Mechanized Infantry Battalion in the Battle of Souq el Gharbo. In June 1984, he was promoted to brigadier general and appointed commander of the Lebanese Army.

In September 1988, outgoing president Amin Jumayyil dismissed the civilian government of Salim al-Huss and appointed a six-man interim military government of three Christians and three Muslims. The Muslims refused to serve, however, and al-Huss, supported by Syria, refused to step aside. There were thus two competing governments in Beirut: one largely Christian and military in East Beirut and the other Muslim-dominated in West Beirut.

From September 1988 to October 1990, Aoun was prime minister and president of the Christian-military government. In 1989, emboldened by support from both France and Iraq, he vowed to remove Syrian influence from Lebanon. Fighting between elements of the Lebanese Army, including Aoun's portion, and the Syrian Army began soon thereafter, leading to an air and ground campaign in which many Lebanese—civilian as well as military—perished. Syrian influence in Lebanon sharply increased upon Iraqi president Saddam Hussein's invasion of Kuwait in August 1990. Finally, in October 1990, Aoun's forces were defeated, and he was driven from office. He sought refuge in the French embassy and was given safe passage abroad and asylum in France in August 1991. Aoun vowed to remain abroad until the last Syrian soldier had departed Lebanon, and he did not return to Lebanon until early May 7, 2005, shortly upon the withdrawal of Syrian troops.

In December 2006 Aoun led his Free Democratic Party in demonstrations in concert with the militant Muslim Hezbollah against the government of Prime Minister Fuad Siniura and President Émile Lahoud, a pro-Syrian figure. Aoun and his supporters strongly believed that a new unity government was required, as the current system, particularly its cabinet structure, does not allow the opposition to block any motion. Critics charged that as part of his quest to become Lebanon's president, Aoun was aiding Hezbollah in its aim to gain veto power in the government. He has not denied his desire to be president, but he has defended his alliance with Hezbollah because he claims that it will help prevent the return of Syria to Lebanon. The alliance is a strange one, for Aoun favors a strong, secular Lebanese state and is an avowed opponent of armed militias.

SPENCER C. TUCKER

See also

Hezbollah; Lebanon; Lebanon, Israeli Invasion of; Siniura, Fuad

References

Fisk, Robert. *Pity the Nation: The Abduction of Lebanon.* 4th ed. New York: Nation Books, 2002.

Rabil, Robert G. *Embattled Neighbors: Syria, Israel and Lebanon.* Boulder, CO: Lynne Rienner, 2003.

Aqaba, Gulf of

The Gulf of Aqaba, also known as the Gulf of Eilat, is a branch of the Dead Sea running east of the Sinai Peninsula and west of the Arabian mainland. It is bordered by Egypt, Israel, Jordan, and Saudi Arabia. The Gulf of Aqaba is roughly 120 miles long, has a maximum width of 15 miles, and passes through the Straits of Tiran at its junction with the Red Sea.

Strategically important, the Gulf of Aqaba has played a major role in the relationships between Israel and the Arab states that border it. The Gulf of Aqaba, with the Israeli port of Eilat at its mouth, was Israel's only accessible waterway to East Africa, Asia, and Australia when Egypt closed the Suez Canal between 1967 and 1975.

Egypt blockaded the Straits of Tiran leading into the gulf from 1949 until 1956 and then again on May 23, 1967, despite the fact that it had been declared an international waterway by the United Nations (UN) in 1958. The 1967 closing of the straits by the Egyptians was one of the key factors precipitating Israel's preemptive attack on Egypt that sparked the Six-Day War.

Following the 1967 war, Israel occupied the Sinai and the strategic points along the Straits of Tiran to ensure access to the Gulf of Aqaba. Israel withdrew from its positions on the Straits of Tiran following the signing of the Camp David Accords of 1978 and the subsequent Israel-Egypt Peace Treaty of 1979.

In the 1980s, the Gulf of Aqaba played a major role in the Iran-Iraq War (1980–1988) when it became a vital supply route for Iraq. During the Persian Gulf War in 1991, the Gulf of Aqaba also served as an important blockade point for coalition forces against goods bound for Iraq.

KEITH A. LEITICH

See also

Camp David Accords; Dead Sea; Eilat, Israel; Iran-Iraq War; Israel-Egypt Peace Treaty; Persian Gulf War; Red Sea; Sinai; Sinai Campaign; Six-Day War; Strait of Tiran Crisis; Straits of Tiran; Suez Canal

References

Bloomfield, Louis M. *Egypt, Israel, and the Gulf of Aqaba in International Law.* Toronto: Carswell, 1957.

Hakim, Ali A. *The Middle Eastern States and the Law of the Sea.* Syracuse, NY: Syracuse University Press, 1979.

Halderman, John W., ed. *The Middle East Crisis: Test of International Law.* Dobbs Ferry, NY: Oceana, 1969.

Porter, Paul A. *The Gulf of Aqaba, an International Waterway: Its Significance to International Trade.* Washington, DC: PublicAffairs, 1957.

Salans, C. F. "The Gulf of Aqaba and the Straits of Tiran." Pp. 807–819 in *The Arab-Israeli Conflict,* edited by John N. Moore. Princeton, NJ: Princeton University Press, 1975.

A windsurfer and tanker in the Gulf of Aqaba, also known as the Gulf of Eilat, near Eilat, Israel. (Steven Allan/iStockphoto.com)

Aqr, Mamudh al-
Born: 1943

Physician and peace and human rights activist who has opposed both Israeli occupation of the West Bank and authoritarian acts by the Palestinian Authority (PA) and served as a member of the Palestinian delegation to the Madrid Peace Conference in 1991 and during the Israeli-Palestinian talks that followed. Mamudh al-Aqr was born in Nablus in the West Bank in 1943. He completed his medical studies at Cairo University in 1969, and between 1970 and 1973 he worked at hospitals in Kuwait.

Al-Aqr spent the next four years providing medical care in the West Bank and then traveled to Great Britain for training in urology. After completing his training at King's College Hospital in London in 1981, he returned to the West Bank. He worked at Maqasid Hospital in Jerusalem and taught at Birzeit University. He also established a clinic in Ramallah in the West Bank.

Al-Aqr has also been quite active in Palestinian political affairs. As a teenager, he was a member of the Movement of Arab Nationalists. From 1967 to 1970, he belonged to the Popular Front for the Liberation of Palestine. When he returned to the West Bank, he founded the Mandela Institute for Palestinian Political Prisoners. His work for peace brought him many friends among the peace movement in Israel.

Al-Aqr's medical and humanitarian accomplishments established him as a popular leader among the Palestinians. During the First Intifada, he covertly wrote and published a pamphlet that was distributed among the Palestinians giving directions on hygiene under adverse conditions and information about simple medical care. Because this act was a violation of Israeli military orders, he was arrested on February 27, 1991, and was placed under administrative detention. He was held without being charged and without communication with the outside world. According to al-Aqr's testimony, Israeli authorities denied him sleep, kept him in a tiny cell, and forced him to sit for hours with his hands tied and a sack over his head. A team of Israeli and Palestinian lawyers worked for his freedom, and he was released after 40 days in custody. The case attracted worldwide attention and caused considerable embarrassment for Israeli authorities.

Al-Aqr was named as one of the Palestinian delegation that met with Israeli negotiators later in 1991 in the Madrid Peace Conference. In these talks, he impressed observers with his dignified insistence on equality for Palestinians and on his determination to negotiate a lasting settlement. After the peace conference, he continued as a Palestinian delegate in bilateral negotiations with the Israelis.

In 1993, al-Aqr was appointed by Palestine Liberation Organization (PLO) chairman Yasser Arafat to the Palestinian Independent Commission for Citizens' Rights (PICCR). The PICCR is one of the first human rights commissions in the Arab world and has the mission of ensuring that human rights are respected in all laws and activities of the PA. Al-Aqr became commissioner general of PICCR in 1995, succeeding Hanan Ashrawi. In that position, al-Aqr has often opposed actions of the PA to silence hard-liners. He joined other secular nationalists in 2001 to write an open letter criticizing PA military courts that tried opponents of Arafat at night in closed sessions. Al-Aqr has taken other stands contrary to certain figures within the PA and their policies in the defense of human rights.

TIM J. WATTS

See also

Administrative Detentions; Arafat, Yasser; Intifada, First; Madrid Conference; Palestinian Authority; Peace Movements; West Bank

References

Hallward, Maia Carter. "Building Space for Peace: Challenging the Boundaries of Israel/Palestine." PhD dissertation, American University, Washington, DC, 2006.

Lonning, Dag Jorund. *Bridge over Troubled Water: Inter-Ethnic Dialogue in Israel-Palestine.* Bergen, Norway: Norse Publications, 1995.

Parsons, Nigel Craig. *The Politics of the Palestinian Authority: From Oslo to Al-Aqsa.* London: Routledge, 2003.

Arab Economic Boycott of Israel

Collective, national, and singular Arab economic boycott of Jewish-owned and Israeli businesses and products. In 1945, the newly formed League of Arab States (Arab League) initiated a formal economic boycott of Jewish goods and services in an attempt to assist the Palestinians in their struggle against Zionism. The Arab League formally declared the economic boycott when it passed Resolution 16 on December 2, 1945, calling on all member states to boycott Jewish goods and services in the British Mandate for Palestine. Following the Arab defeat in the Israeli War of Independence (1948–

A Lebanese student holds up a flyer calling for an economic boycott of Israel during a sit-in at the American University of Beirut, April 9, 2002. (Reuters/Corbis)

1949), the boycott was formalized against Israel. The boycott prohibited direct trade between Arab countries and Israel.

In 1950 a secondary boycott was expanded to include non-Israelis who maintained economic ties with Israel. The secondary boycott was aimed at individuals, businesses, and organizations that conducted trade with Israel. The boycott prohibited public or private Arab entities from engaging in business with any entity that does business in Israel directly or indirectly. Any firms found in violation were put on a blacklist maintained by the Arab League. A prime example of the secondary boycott concerned the U.S.-based Coca-Cola Company, which had operations in Israel. As a consequence of Coca-Cola's commercial activities in Israel, Arab countries refused to import Coca-Cola products and gave their business to rival Pepsi-Cola. A subsequent tertiary boycott prohibited any entity in a member country from doing business with a company or individual that had business dealings with the United States or other firms on the Arab League blacklist.

In 1951 the Arab League created the Central Office for the Boycott of Israel in Damascus, Syria, which operated under the aegis of the league's secretary-general. While the Central Office maintains a register of blacklisted companies with which member states cannot trade, the Arab League does not enforce the boycott itself, and the regulations are not binding on member countries. In fact, several Arab states have chosen not to follow the secondary and tertiary boycotts. International reaction to the boycott ranged from expressions of outrage by the United States to reluctance by Japan to engage in trade with Israel for fear of offending Arab countries.

The boycott was dealt a significant setback on March 26, 1979, when Egypt signed the Israel-Egypt Peace Treaty. The treaty formally ended Egyptian participation in the boycott. The boycott was further eroded when Oman and Qatar established trade relations with Israel following the October 1991 Madrid Conference and the subsequent implementation of the Israeli-Palestinian peace process. In 1993, the Palestinian Authority (PA) gave up the boycott in an attempt to advance the Israeli-Palestinian peace process. On October 26, 1994, Jordan signed the Israeli-Jordan Peace Treaty with the State of Israel that also formally ended Jordanian participation in the economic boycott. In addition, in 1996 member countries of the Gulf Cooperation Council—Bahrain, Kuwait, Oman, Qatar, Saudi Arabia, and the United Arab Emirates—announced that they would only enforce the primary boycott. In 2005 and 2006, Bahrain and Oman agreed to drop the boycott altogether as a provision of their free trade agreements with the United States.

The impact of the boycotts on the Israelis has not been great, although it has most clearly taken a toll. The Israeli Chamber of Commerce has issued estimates suggesting that Israeli exports are about 10 percent lower than they would be without the economic boycott. In addition, foreign investment in Israel is probably 10 percent lower with the boycott in place. Israeli trade relations with South Korea and Japan have especially suffered as a result of the boycott. In spite of the Arab boycott, Israeli products do make their way into the affected nations. In general, these products are shipped

to a third party, which then ships them to the various Arab states. Cyprus has been the leading third-party nation through which boycotted products are sent.

Because the boycott has been sporadically applied and enforced, it has been less than effective in hindering the economic development of Israel and has largely failed to deter companies conducting business with Israel. Despite the failure of the boycott, however, the Arab League has thus far chosen not to repeal the boycott, and the Central Office for the Boycott of Israel still exists. As of 2006, only Syria and Lebanon adhere closely to the boycott.

KEITH A. LEITICH

See also

Arab League; Israel-Egypt Peace Treaty; Israel-Jordan Peace Treaty; Madrid Conference

References

Feiler, Gil. *From Boycott to Economic Cooperation: The Political Economy of the Arab Boycott of Israel.* London: Frank Cass, 1998.

Sarna, Aaron J. *Boycott and Blacklist: A History of Arab Economic Warfare against Israel.* Totowa, NJ: Rowman and Littlefield, 1986.

Sharif, Amer A. *A Statistical Study of the Arab Boycott of Israel.* Beirut, Lebanon: Institute for Palestinian Studies, 1970.

Weiss, Martin A. *Arab Boycott of Israel.* Washington, DC: Congressional Research Service, Library of Congress, 2006.

Arab Higher Committee

Principal political organization of the Arabs of Palestine that took a leading role in the Arab Revolt (1936–1939). Also known as the Fourth Higher Committee of the Arab League, the Arab Higher Committee (AHC) was formed on April 25, 1936. Haj Amin al-Husseini, the mufti of Jerusalem, took the lead in forming the AHC and became its president. The AHC was able to unite Arab religious and political leaders as well as political parties.

Staunchly opposed to Jewish immigration into Palestine, the AHC took the lead in the general strike and rebellions against British Mandate authorities beginning in April 1936 that became the Arab Revolt of 1936–1939. The British banned the AHC outright in 1937 and arrested a number of its leaders, including Dr. Husayn al-Khalidi, the mayor of Jerusalem. All were deported to the Seychelles Islands. The AHC subsequently split into the Arab Higher Committee under al-Husseini and the new Arab Higher Front. The British government ordered the release of AHC leaders from the Seychelles so that they might participate in the London Round Table Conference in Palestine in 1939. The AHC sent a delegation to the United Nations (UN) on the latter's formation, but it rejected the subsequent UN plan for the partition of Palestine.

SPENCER C. TUCKER

See also

Arab Revolt of 1936–1939; Husseini, Haj Amin al-; London Round Table Conference

References

Khalaf, Ossa. *Politics in Palestine: Arab Factionalism and Social Disintegration, 1939–1948.* New York: SUNY Press, 1991.

Levenberg, Haim. *Military Preparations of the Arab Community in Palestine, 1945–1948.* London: Routledge, 1993.

Sayigh, Yezid. *Armed Struggle and the Search for State: The Palestine National Movement, 1949–1993.* New York: Oxford University Press, 2000.

Arab-Israeli War of 1948–1949

See Israeli War of Independence, Israeli-Egyptian Front; Israeli War of Independence, Israeli-Iraqi Front; Israeli War of Independence, Israeli-Jordanian Front; Israeli War of Independence, Israeli-Lebanese Front; Israeli War of Independence, Israeli-Syrian Front; Israeli War of Independence, Overview; Israeli War of Independence, Truce Agreements

---

Arab-Jewish Communal War

Start Date: November 30, 1947
End Date: May 14, 1948

The fighting that erupted on November 30, 1947, between Arabs and Jews in the British Mandate for Palestine is often included as part of the Israeli War of Independence (1948–1949), but this first phase of fighting between Arabs and Jews began well before the Jewish proclamation of independence on May 14, 1948. It erupted on November 30, 1947, immediately following announcement of the United Nations (UN) General Assembly vote approving the partition plan for Palestine. The month before, the Arab League had urged its member states to begin training volunteers for a possible military campaign to prevent the establishment of a Jewish state.

In this first phase of fighting, the Jews were faced with a wave of violence by elements of the Arab Palestinian population, assisted by irregular Arab forces from the neighboring states. The Arab military effort was only loosely coordinated. The Arab Higher Committee announced a general strike, and Arab mobs soon responded by attacking Jewish buses and other vehicles. An Arab mob destroyed the old commercial center of Jerusalem, while Arabs also fired on and broke into Jewish shops in Haifa, Jaffa, and other places. By December, the Arab and Jewish sectors were clearly segregated. Marginal or mixed areas in the cities were quickly evacuated by one side or the other. From the beginning, the fighting to control the lines of communication was especially fierce.

The UN vote on partition was also the signal for violence against Jews within the Arab states. In Aleppo, Syria, Arab demonstrators torched 300 Jewish homes and 11 synagogues. In Aden, Yemen, 76 Jews were slain.

When the fighting began, the principal Jewish military force was the Haganah. Illegally constituted during the British Mandate, this self-defense force consisted of a small fully mobilized nucleus and a larger militia element. The Haganah high command could call on a standing military force of four battalions of the Palmach (commando units) numbering some 2,100 men in all, along with 1,000 reservists who could be called up on short notice, and the Hel Sade (HISH, field army) of about 1,800 men, with another 10,000 reservists. The Haganah could also count on perhaps 32,000 members of the Hel Mishmar (HIM, garrison army), most of whom were older persons assigned to the defense of fixed locations such as towns and cities. Finally, there were Gadna (Youth Battalions) consisting of young people who were receiving some military training with the plan that when they were older they would join the HISH or Palmach. Military equipment was inadequate. The Haganah could count on about 15,000 rifles of a bewildering number of types, some light machine guns, and several dozen medium machine guns and 3-inch mortars. The Haganah's secret arms workshops were also producing the largely stamped Sten submachine gun as well as hand grenades and explosives.

Two other organizations must be mentioned. These were the Irgun Tsvai Leumi (National Military Organization) of about 5,000 members and Lohamei Herut Israel (Fighters for the Freedom of Israel), also known as Lehi or the Stern Gang, with about 1,000 men. These two elements operated very much on their own at the start of the fighting. Indeed, there was no love lost between them and the Haganah, and there had even been armed clashes. During the fighting, however, both organizations disbanded, and their members joined the Haganah to form the new Tz'va Haganah L'Yisrael (Israel Defense Forces, IDF). From the start, David Ben-Gurion, chairman of the Jewish Agency Executive, had charge of both political and defense matters.

The British government manifested a pronounced partiality for the Arab side. This could be seen in its refusal to lift embargoes on Jewish immigration into Palestine and the acquisition of weapons. British authorities refused to recognize the right of the Haganah to exist and disarmed Haganah members when they could be found. At the same time, Britain continued to sell arms to both Iraq and Transjordan with the full knowledge that these might be used against the Jews in Palestine. Also, Arab leaders were occasionally notified in advance of British military evacuations, enabling Arab irregulars to seize control for themselves of such strategically located sites as police stations and military posts.

The early Arab military attacks of the Communal War within Palestine were uncoordinated. They took the form of hit-and-run raids against isolated Jewish settlements with the aim of destroying Jewish property. The attacks were mounted entirely by Palestinian Arabs, although they did receive some financial assistance and arms from the Arab states. Arab efforts early on were, however, handicapped by ongoing tensions between the Nashashibi and Husseini factions.

On September 16, 1947, the Political Committee of the Arab League, meeting in Sofar, Lebanon, had appealed for economic reprisals against both Britain and the United States and for arms and money for the Palestinian Arabs. Following the UN partition vote, Iraqi premier Salih Jabr called for a meeting of Arab leaders in Cairo on December 12. There he called on the Arab states to intervene militarily in Palestine, but Egypt and Saudi Arabia were

Crouched atop the roof of a Jerusalem railroad station, members of the Arab Liberation Army (ALA) guard the main rail corridor to Bethlehem and southern Palestine on May 7, 1948, only seven days before the declaration of the State of Israel. (Bettmann/Corbis)

opposed, and King Abdullah of Jordan disliked even the mention of Arab volunteers. Eventually, the Arab leaders adopted a resolution calling for 10,000 rifles and other light weapons and 3,000 Arab volunteers to be sent into Palestine through Syria with the sum of £1 million to be allocated for the defense of Palestine.

The Cairo decision led to the formation of the Arab Liberation Army (ALA), to be commanded by Iraqi staff officer General Sir Ismail Safwat Pasha. He immediately set up his headquarters outside of Damascus. Field command went to Fawzi al-Qawuqji, guerrilla leader of the Arab Revolt of 1936. Most ALA members were in fact mercenaries. They included a large number of Syrian Arabs along with some Yugoslav Muslims, Circassians from the Caucasus region, Poles, Germans, and Spaniards. In late January 1948, members of the ALA began infiltrating across the Syrian border into Palestine, and al-Qawuqji set up his headquarters in Tiberias in the Galilee region of north-central Palestine. By the end of February 1948, there were perhaps 5,000 members of the ALA in Palestine, and by the end of March their numbers had grown to perhaps 7,000.

In the spring the Arab forces, including the ALA, divided Palestine into three major fronts. The northern sector contained by far the largest Arab force, some 7,000 men under al-Qawuqji and the Syrian Adib al-Shishakli. Another 5,000 were in the central sector, the largest number of whom were under the command of Abd al-Qadr al-Husseini, a nephew of the mufti of Jerusalem. Some 2,000 Arab fighters, most of them Muslim Brotherhood volunteers from Egypt, were located in the southern sector of the Negev Desert.

In the winter and early spring of 1948, the Arab forces launched a series of largely uncoordinated military attacks. These fell on Jewish quarters in the cities, chiefly Jerusalem, as well as the more isolated kibbutzim in the Hebron Hills area. The outnumbered but disinterested British authorities did nothing to inhibit the Arabs, who were soon able to cut key roads, including those between Tel Aviv and Jerusalem, Haifa and western Galilee, Tiberias and eastern Galilee, and Afula and the Beit She'an Valley. The Jewish farms in the Negev were also soon isolated.

Jewish authorities, who had expected to have more time to prepare, were caught off guard by these Arab military moves. Perhaps the most ominous situation was that facing the Jews in Jerusalem, who were now without ammunition and other military supplies and were also cut off from food. The Arabs controlled the low hills

Territory of the State of Israel as proposed by the United Nations (UN) in Nov 1947

Territory beyond the UN line conquered by Israel in 1948–1949.

The frontiers of the State of Israel according to the armistice agreements of 1949

N

LEBANON

Tyre

Kuneitra

SYRIA

Nahariya
Acre
Safed

Sea of Galilee

Haifa
Ein Gev
Nazareth
Tiberias

Beit Shean

Mediterranean

Sea

Netanya
Jenin
Tulkarm

Nablus

Tel Aviv
WEST
Jaffa
Lod
BANK
JORDAN
Ramla
Jericho
Ashdod
Amman
Nitzanim
Jerusalem
Yad Mordechai
Gat
Hebron
Gaza
Ein Gedi

32°N

Khan Yunis
Dead
Rafah
Nirim
Sea
Gevulot
Beersheba

El Arish
Revivim

31°N

NEGEV

EGYPT

30°N

| 0 | 15 | 30 mi |
| 0 | 15 | 30 km |

Eilat

Aqaba

33°E   34°E   36°E

dominating the Tel Aviv–Jerusalem Road into the city and were able to destroy at will the Jewish truck convoys attempting to reach Jerusalem. The difficulty of the military situation facing the Jews was compounded by the decision taken by Ben-Gurion and the Jewish Agency Executive to defend every bit of territory allocated to the future Jewish state under the partition plan as well as Jewish settlements, which in accordance with the plan would be allocated to the Arab state. This decision meant that already meager Haganah resources would have to be dispersed throughout Palestine in a defensive stance, making concentration into larger units for offensive operations impossible. Resupply operations of isolated Jewish settlements through Arab areas such as Galilee and the Negev would be particularly difficult, as would the resupply of Jewish enclaves in the cities, including Jerusalem.

On January 10, 1948, 900 members of the ALA attacked K'far Szold in Upper Galilee but were beaten back. The next day other attacks occurred throughout Palestine against isolated Jewish settlements in the same region but also in the Hebron Hills, the Judean Mountains, and the Negev. The Arabs also managed to get car bombs into the Jewish quarters of Haifa and Jerusalem. Among their successful targets were the offices of the *Jerusalem Post* and the Jewish Agency headquarters in Jerusalem. Jewish road traffic was largely limited to armored cars or armed convoys. Despite efforts to send the convoys at odd times and by circuitous routes, Arab military action soon brought this traffic to a complete halt.

In view of their inability to capture even one Jewish settlement, in March the Arabs decided to concentrate the bulk of their military effort against Jewish road traffic while at the same time not entirely abandoning attacks on the Jewish settlements or enclaves. The Jews did manage to get an armored convoy to isolated Gat and to destroy an Arab armaments convoy near Haifa. At the same time, however, the Arabs registered success in their effort to isolate Jerusalem. From late March they employed land mines for the first time, completely cutting off the coastal road to the Negev. The Arabs also ambushed at Nebi Daniel a large armored Jewish convoy bound for Jerusalem, destroying or capturing all its vehicles. To the north they also destroyed a Jewish convoy bound from Haifa to the isolated Y'hi'am settlement.

By the end of March the situation facing the Jews appeared grim. The Jewish section of Jerusalem was cut off from the coast, and settlements near the city were isolated from Jerusalem. The Negev and settlements of western Galilee were similarly cut off. On the other hand, Jewish forces were now fully mobilized. Some 21,000 men between the ages of 17 and 25 were now under arms. Progress had also been made in the manufacture of light weapons and explosives, and additional weapons were en route to Palestine from Czechoslovakia. Some 50 light liaison aircraft were in service, performing reconnaissance and transport of some light weapons and key personnel to isolated areas. Arab strength was also increasing, however.

Worried about weakening UN and U.S. support for the implementation of partition, the Jewish leadership was determined to take the offensive. This was made possible by the increased strength of the Haganah and the continued evacuation of British military personnel from Palestine. In considering their options, Ben-Gurion and the other Jewish leaders assigned top priority to opening the supply route to Jerusalem.

Code-named Operation NACHSHON, this plan to secure both sides of the Tel Aviv–Jerusalem supply corridor involved the concentration of some 1,500 Jewish troops, armed in large part with weapons that had arrived from Czechoslovakia on April 1, 1948. The operation commenced on April 6. Fighting was intense, especially at Kastel, which changed hands several times before the Arabs finally abandoned it on April 10. Abd el-Kadr al-Husseini, the Arab commander of the Jerusalem area, was killed in fighting on April 9. The operation, which ended on April 15, saw three large Jewish convoys reach the city.

At the same time, the ALA attempted to take the Jewish settlement of Mishmar Ha'Emek. The Arabs opened artillery fire on the settlement on April 4, but the defenders repulsed subsequent ground assaults. On April 12 Haganah forces counterattacked, and the Arab forces retreated. This Arab artillery was then relocated to shell the Jewish sector of Jerusalem in early May. During April 12–14, a Druse mercenary battalion attempted, without success, to take the Ramat Yohanan settlement.

Emboldened by its successes, the Haganah stepped up its offensive, cutting the port of Tiberias in two on April 18 and forcing an Arab evacuation there. On April 21 as British forces were evacuating Haifa, the Haganah began an assault on that city, taking it in two days. Most of the Arab residents left for Lebanon by land and sea, their leaders promising a speedy return. Success here made possible the resupply of Jewish settlements in Upper Galilee, and contact was reestablished with Safed.

On May 1, Arab forces struck back with an assault on the Jewish settlement of Ramot Naftali, previously under siege. Lebanese artillery and tanks took part, but the attack was again defeated. On May 6, Jewish forces opened an assault against the Arab part of Safed but were themselves repulsed. The assault was renewed on the night of May 9–10, and this time Jewish forces were successful. The Arab inhabitants fled the city, and Palmach fighters captured a key mountain citadel there. Many other Arab residents in the general area of Safed now also fled, with the result that by mid-May all the Jewish settlements in Upper Galilee were connected. On April 29, part of the Golani Brigade seized Tzemah as well as a nearby police fort. Other former British police installations were taken, and the city of Akko and villages north to the Lebanese border were also secured by May 17.

In Operation HAMETZ, so named because it began on the eve of Passover (*hametz* means "leaven"), Jewish forces cleared Arab villages around Tel Aviv–Jaffa. On April 29 following Jewish encirclement of Jaffa, which was to be included in the Arab part of Palestine under the partition plan, many of its 70,000 Arab residents fled. The city itself surrendered on May 13 after the final British evacuation.

With the British stepping up their final evacuation, Arab forces again seized control of the Tel Aviv–Jerusalem Road. The Harel Brigade of the Palmach was shifted to Operation JEBUSI to reopen the supply corridor. The Harel Brigade was forced by a British ultimatum, backed by artillery, to withdraw from initial captures, and a Jewish attempt to secure the Jericho Road also failed. On the night of April 28–29, a struggle for control of the Monastery of St. Simon began. Jewish reinforcements from the Jerusalem Brigade tipped the balance. On May 11, in Operation MACCABEE, another effort was made to open the road to Jerusalem, but only one convoy of several dozen vehicles made it through before the Arabs again closed the road on May 17.

With the last British forces quitting Jerusalem on May 14, Jewish forces began Operation KILSHON (PITCHFORK) to prepare for an attack by the Arab Legion. It succeeded to the extent that the Jewish area of the city was made into a continuous whole for the first time, but it also failed to cut a supply corridor to the Jewish quarter of the Old City. Meanwhile, isolated Jewish settlements near Jerusalem were abandoned as indefensible, and the Arab Legion also registered several successes, including the capture of the entire Etzyon Block.

In six weeks of heavy fighting before the proclamation of the State of Israel and the invasion by regular Arab armies, Jewish fighters had secured Haifa, Jaffa, Safed, and Tiberias. They had also captured about 100 Arab villages and had surrounded Akko. Most of the main roads were again open to Jewish traffic. For all practical purposes, the Palestinian Arab military forces had been defeated. The ALA had suffered heavy losses, and Jewish armed strength had now increased to 30,000 men. The arms shipments from Czechoslovakia had filled many deficiencies, including antitank and antiaircraft weapons, but the Jews still lacked fighter aircraft, field artillery, and tanks. On May 15, 1948, moreover, regular Arab armies invaded Israel, beginning the Israeli War of Independence, which continued until July 20, 1949, and the signing of the last armistice agreement with Syria.

SPENCER C. TUCKER

See also

Abdullah I, King of Jordan; Arab Higher Committee; Arab Liberation Army; Arab Revolt of 1936–1939; Ben-Gurion, David; Haganah; Irgun Tsvai Leumi; Israeli War of Independence, Overview; Lohamei Herut Israel; NACHSHON, Operation; Palmach; Qawuqji, Fawzi al-

References

Dupuy, Trevor N. *Elusive Victory: The Arab-Israeli Wars, 1947–1974.* Garden City, NY: Military Book Club, 2002.

Lucas, Noah. *The Modern History of Israel.* New York: Praeger, 1975.

Sachar, Howard M. *A History of Israel: From the Rise of Zionism to Our Time.* 3rd ed. New York: Knopf, 2007.

Smith, Charles D. *Palestine and the Arab-Israeli Conflict: A History with Documents.* 6th ed. New York: Bedford/St. Martin's, 2006.

Arab League

The Arab League, also called the League of Arab States, is a voluntary organization of Arabic-speaking nations. It was founded at the

Delegates to the Arab League meeting in Bloudan, Syria, on July 11, 1946, held to discuss Jewish migration to Palestine. (Corbis)

end of World War II with the stated purposes of improving conditions in Arab countries, liberating Arab states still under foreign domination, and preventing the formation of a Jewish state in Palestine.

In 1943 the Egyptian government proposed an organization of Arab states that would facilitate closer relations between the nations without forcing any of them to lose self-rule. Each member would remain a sovereign state, and the organization would not be a union, a federation, or any other sovereign structure. The British government supported this idea in the hopes of securing the Arab nations as allies in the war against Germany.

In 1944, representatives from Egypt, Iraq, Lebanon, Yemen, and Saudi Arabia met in Alexandria, Egypt, and agreed to form a federation. The Arab League was officially founded on March 22, 1945, in Cairo. The founding states were Egypt, Iraq, Lebanon, Saudi Arabia, Transjordan, and Syria. Subsequent members include Libya (1953), Sudan (1956), Tunisia (1958), Morocco (1958), Kuwait (1961), Algeria (1962), South Yemen (1967, now Yemen), Bahrain (1971), Oman (1971), Qatar (1971), United Arab Emirates (1971), Mauritania (1973), Somalia (1974), Djibouti (1977), and Comoros (1993).

The original goals of the Arab League were to liberate all Arab nations still ruled by foreign countries and to prevent the creation of a Jewish state in Palestine as well as to serve the common good, improve living conditions, and guarantee the hopes of member states. In 1946, Arab League members added to their pact a cultural treaty under which they agreed to exchange professors, teachers, students, and scholars in order to encourage cultural exchange among member nations and to disseminate Arab culture to their citizens.

The Arab League's pact also stated that all members would collectively represent the Palestinians so long as Palestine was not an

Member States of the Arab League

Date	Countries Admitted
March 1945	Egypt; Iraq; Jordan; Lebanon; Saudi Arabia; Syria; Yemen
March 1953	Libya
January 1956	Sudan
October 1958	Morocco; Tunisia
July 1961	Kuwait
August 1962	Algeria
June 1971	United Arab Emirates
September 1971	Bahrain; Qatar; Oman
November 1973	Mauritania
February 1974	Somalia
September 1976	Palestine Liberation Organization
April 1977	Djibouti
November 1993	Union of the Comoros

independent state. With no Palestinian leader in 1945, the Arab states feared that the British would dominate the area and that Jews would colonize part of Palestine. In response to these fears, the Arab League created the Arab Higher Committee (AHC) to govern Palestinian Arabs in 1945. This committee was replaced in 1946 by the Arab Higher Executive, which was again reorganized into a new Arab Higher Executive in 1947.

The State of Israel was declared on May 14, 1948. The next day Egypt, Iraq, Lebanon, Saudi Arabia, Syria, and Transjordan responded with a declaration of war on Israel. Yemen also supported the declaration. Secretary-General Abdul Razek Azzam Pasha declared that the Arab League's goal was to conduct a large-scale massacre and extermination. Although King Abdullah of Jordan (he officially changed the name of Transjordan to Jordan in April 1949) claimed to be the legitimate power in Palestine, the Arab League did not wish to see Jordan in control of the area and thus established its own government on behalf of the Palestinians, the All-Palestine State of October 1, 1948. The mufti of Jerusalem, Haj Amin al-Husseini, was its leader, and Jerusalem was its capital. Although ostensibly the new government ruled Gaza, Egypt was the real authority there. In response, Jordan formed a rival temporary government, the First Palestinian Congress, which condemned the government in Gaza. The Israeli War of Independence ended in 1949, with Jordan occupying the West Bank and East Jerusalem and Egypt controlling Gaza.

In 1950 the Arab League signed the Joint Defense and Economic Cooperation Treaty, which declared that the members of the league considered an attack on one member country to be an attack on all. The treaty created a permanent military commission and a joint defense council.

During the 1950s, Egypt effectively led the Arab League. In 1952 a military coup in Egypt nominally headed by General Muhammad Nagib overthrew King Farouk, but within two years Colonel Gamal Abdel Nasser assumed rule of the nation. A strong proponent of Arab unity, he called for a union of all Arab nations, including Palestine. Nasser ended the All-Palestine government in Palestine, formed the United Arab Republic with Syria, and called for the defeat of Israel.

In 1956 Nasser nationalized the Suez Canal, precipitating the Suez Crisis that brought an Israeli invasion of the Sinai followed by short-lived British and French invasions of Egypt. U.S. economic and political pressures secured the withdrawal of the invaders. Far from toppling Nasser, as the allied British, French, and Israeli governments had hoped, these pressures both strengthened Nasser's prestige in the Arab world and raised the stature of Pan-Arabism and the Arab League.

In the 1960s the Arab League pushed for the liberation of Palestine, and in 1964 it supported creation of the Palestine Liberation Organization (PLO), which was dedicated to attacks on Israel. Following the Six-Day War of 1967, which ended in extensive territory losses for Egypt, Jordan, and Syria, the Arab League met at Khartoum that August and issued a statement in which its members vowed not to recognize, negotiate with, or conclude a peace agreement with Israel. Egypt also agreed to withdraw its troops from Yemen.

The Arab League suspended Egypt's membership in 1979 in the wake of President Anwar Sadat's visit to Jerusalem and agreement to the 1978 Camp David Peace Accords. The league also moved its headquarters from Cairo to Tunis. When the PLO declared an independent State of Palestine on November 15, 1988, the Arab League immediately recognized it. Egypt was readmitted to the league in 1989, and the headquarters returned to Cairo. In the 1990s, the Arab League continued its efforts to resolve the Israeli-Palestine dispute in the Palestinians' favor.

More recently, in 2003 the Arab League voted to demand the unconditional removal of U.S. and British troops from Iraq. The lone dissenting voice was the tiny nation of Kuwait, which had been liberated by a U.S.-led coalition in the 1991 Persian Gulf War.

AMY HACKNEY BLACKWELL

See also

Egypt; Nasser, Gamal Abdel; Pan-Arabism

References

Hourani, Albert. *A History of the Arab Peoples.* Cambridge: Harvard University Press, 1991.
Smith, Charles D. *Palestine and the Arab-Israeli Conflict: A History with Documents.* 6th ed. New York: Bedford/St. Martin's, 2006.

Arab Legion

Police and combat force founded in 1920 and dominated by Arabs in the British Mandate for Palestine. The Arab Legion was originally organized as a 150-man Arab police force under the leadership of British Army lieutenant colonel Frederick Gerard Peake (later Peake Pasha, major general). The unit was increased in size to almost 1,000 men within the year and was renamed the Reserve Mobile Force.

When the British recognized Abdullah as emir of Transjordan, Abdullah's civil police force was combined with the Reserve Mobile

The Camel Corps of the Arab Legion during the coronation of King Abdullah of Transjordan in Amman on May 25, 1946. The event marked the emergence of Transjordan as an independent kingdom. (Library of Congress)

Force as the Arab Legion on October 22, 1923. Peake served as its first commander. For more than 30 years, British officers commanded the legion. It held primary responsibility for policing the capital of Amman and its environs, leaving border security for Transjordan to the newly created Transjordan Frontier Force.

In November 1930, British Army major John Bagot Glubb (later Glubb Pasha, lieutenant general) became Peake's assistant. In March 1931, Glubb created the Arab Legion's Desert Patrol, a motorized unit composed mostly of Bedouin, to end tribal opposition to Abdullah's authority across Transjordan's vast desert regions. Glubb assumed command of the 2,000-man legion upon Peake's retirement in March 1939.

During World War II, Emir Abdullah assumed a pro-Allied stance, allowing the Arab Legion to support the efforts of Britain in the Middle East. The legion participated in the April–May 1941 British offensive against the recently proclaimed pro-Nazi government of Rahid Ali al-Gaylani in Iraq. The legion also played a major role in the relief of the British garrison at the Royal Air Force base at Habbaniya and in the liberation of Baghdad. The legion then joined the Allied operation against Vichy French forces in Syria, playing major roles in the Palmyra and Sukhna offensives in June 1941. So impressed were the British with the legion's performance that it was greatly enlarged, eventually reaching 16,000 men.

The Arab Legion was stationed in the Sinai Desert in 1942 in anticipation of German field marshal Erwin Rommel's advance across Egypt but was not committed after the Afrika Korps was halted at El Alamein. Although several draft plans called for the legion to deploy to the Italian theater of operations, the command was largely used for the remainder of the war to guard vital communications and strategic resources in the Middle East.

On May 25, 1946, Transjordan became an independent kingdom under King Abdullah. The Arab Legion was then reduced in size to 4,500 men. Thirty-seven British officers under Glubb remained with the legion, while a group of Arab junior officers were groomed for the day that the British would leave the mandate.

As tensions grew between Jews and Arabs in the dissolving British Mandate for Palestine, most of the British officers in the Arab Legion temporarily withdrew their services. Although the legion had been designed primarily as a desert force, it saw most of its action around Jerusalem. Glubb opposed this, fearing it would lead to house-to-house fighting. The legion defeated the Jewish Kfar-Etzion bloc settlements south of Jerusalem in May 1948.

When Israel declared its independence on May 14, 1948, King Abdullah ordered Glubb to enter the Old City of Jerusalem, seize the Jewish Quarter, and engage the armed Jewish Haganah in the fight for the New City of Jerusalem. Meanwhile, two regiments of the

Arab Legion bypassed Jerusalem for Latrun to fend off enemy reinforcements and hold the hills of Judea for the Arabs.

Although in sharp contrast with other Arab forces, the Arab Legion fought on a par with the Israelis but nonetheless suffered heavy losses in the fight for the New City of Jerusalem and finally was forced to withdraw. The legion managed to hold the Old City, where supply problems led to a surrender of the Jewish Quarter on May 28.

In June, the fighting shifted to the Latrun area. The Arab Legion successfully fended off heavy attacks by the elite Palmach intending to seize Latrun. By mid-July it was clear that the legion had held.

When the Rhodes negotiations finally established a permanent armistice on April 3, 1949, the Kingdom of Jordan could lay claim to East Jerusalem, Hebron, Nablus, and Judea (commonly referred to as the West Bank) thanks to the efforts of Glubb and the Arab Legion. Of Arab forces, only Glubb's legion turned in an exemplary performance.

After the Israeli War of Independence, the size of the Arab Legion was set at three brigades. Two legion brigades were assigned to the Jordanian-controlled West Bank in an effort to stop Palestinians from crossing over into Israel and to stop Israeli reprisal attacks against fedayeen harbored in the West Bank. The legion also dealt with internal disputes aimed at discrediting the young King Hussein of Jordan, who assumed power a few months after his grandfather, Abdullah, was assassinated on July 20, 1951.

Within the Arab Legion there was a rising tide of anti-British sentiment, known as the Free Officers Movement, led by a clique of young Arab officers assigned to the legion. On March 1, 1956, King Hussein dismissed Glubb from his command along with all British officers in the legion. After more than 25 years of service to Abdullah, Hussein, and the legion, Glubb was evicted from Jordan and subsequently returned to Britain. Brigadier General Rade Einab became the first Arab commander of the legion but was soon replaced by Ali abu Nowar, a friend of the young king and a leader among the Free Officers. Later in 1956, the elite Arab Legion was amalgamated with Jordan's National Guard into the Royal Jordanian Army, an army that still retains many of its British traditions.

THOMAS D. VEVE

See also

Abdullah I, King of Jordan; Fedayeen; Glubb, Sir John Bagot; Haganah; Hussein, King of Jordan; Israeli War of Independence, Israeli-Jordanian Front; Jerusalem; Jerusalem, Old City of; Jordan; Palmach

References

Glubb, John Bagot. *The Story of the Arab Legion.* London: Hodder and Stoughton, 1950.

Lunt, James. *The Arab Legion.* London: Constable, 1999.

Van Dam, Nikolaos. *The Struggle for Power in Syria: Politics and Society under Asad and the Ba'th Party.* London: Croom Helm, 1996.

Vatikiotis, P. J. *Politics and the Military in Jordan: A Study of the Arab Legion, 1921–1957.* New York: Praeger, 1967.

Young, Peter. *The Arab Legion.* London: Osprey, 2002.

Arab Liberation Army

Multinational Arab fighting force created in early 1948 by the Arab League. The Arab Liberation Army (ALA) was an all-volunteer organization dedicated to the destruction of any emerging Jewish state in the Middle East. The ALA was founded as British forces evacuated the area at the end of the British mandate over Palestine. In the months prior to the British withdrawal, the ALA sought to fill the power vacuum created by the departure of British authorities. Initially, the ALA was composed of approximately 5,000 Palestinian and Syrian volunteers. Also among its ranks were Iraqis, Lebanese, Transjordanians, and Egyptians, including some from the Muslim Brotherhood. There were also a few British deserters, Turks, and Germans in the ALA. The organization's only stated political strategy was preventing the creation of Israel, although it also served as a hedge against the desire of Transjordan's King Abdullah to possess parts of Palestine.

At its inception, the ALA was nominally under the command of Iraqi general Taha al-Hashimi, although he proved to be a largely ineffective figurehead given his role to ensure Iraqi support of the organization. The field commander and acknowledged leader of the ALA was Syria's Fawzi al-Qawuqji. Al-Qawuqji had been trained in the army of the Ottoman Empire. He had also led Arab irregulars during the Arab Revolt of 1936–1939, including service as the commander of guerrillas in the Nablus region. He proved incapable of the command of such a large force as the ALA, however.

In the period prior to the end of British occupation, the ALA's primary opponent was the much larger and better-disciplined Haganah, the Jewish self-defense force that included the highly trained Palmach strike force. Haganah had thousands of British Army and Jewish Brigade veterans from World War II. Like the ALA, Haganah sought to fill the void left by the British by driving out the opposition before the British departure. Haganah would go on to be incorporated into the Israel Defense Forces (IDF) after Israeli independence in 1948.

In January 1948, the ALA became the first Arab organization to attempt the capture of a Jewish settlement by attacking Kfar Szold, a small village near the Syrian border. However, British authorities refused to countenance an Arab attack upon British-occupied territory and sent a small armored column to oppose the ALA forces. The ALA, completely unprepared for an encounter with British forces, withdrew from the vicinity of Kfar Szold but soon launched attacks on Yehiam and Kibbutz Tirat Tvzi. All three assaults were in part attempts to arouse Palestinian support for the ALA. At Tirat Tvzi, Jewish militia units from the Haganah routed the ALA forces, killing 60 and capturing a large amount of ALA equipment.

Despite its early humiliations, the ALA launched an ambitious offensive against Mishmar Haemek on April 4, 1948. This assault included more than 1,000 ALA troops supported by seven Syrian-donated artillery pieces. The Israeli defenders of Mishmar Haemek, supplied only with small arms, held off the ALA assault and transformed the surprise attack into a battle of attrition. Even with superior manpower and equipment, the ALA could not break the defensive lines. On April 12, al-Qawuqji increased the pressure on Mishmar Haemek only to discover that a Haganah flanking counterattack had almost completely encircled his troops. Shifting his focus, al-Qawuqji led his troops to break out of the trap but was forced to withdraw to Jenin after the successful escape. Once again, the ALA had suffered a demoralizing defeat.

Following the British withdrawal from Palestine and the proclamation of the State of Israel on May 15, 1948, the ALA joined Egypt, Iraq, Lebanon, Syria, and Transjordan in an attempt to destroy the fledgling nation. In the first attacks of the Israeli War of Independence (1948–1949), the ALA's 10,000 soldiers, backed by 50,000 more volunteers, were given the task of local defense of areas captured by Arab League forces. To assist in their mission, the ALA received armored cars and artillery from their allies. The ALA troops operated in the northern and central sectors of the war, with their largest concentrations in Samaria, Galilee, and Jerusalem. Lebanese elements of the ALA worked in concert with the Lebanese Army, although other members of the ALA failed to coordinate their actions with the invading Arab armies.

On June 11, 1948, after four weeks of bloody combat, the United Nations (UN), with the assistance of mediator Folke Bernadotte, brokered a truce between Israel and the Arab armies. The ALA refused to honor the UN cease-fire and continued attacking Israeli positions for the first two days of the truce. However, because the pressure created by fighting on three fronts was eased, the IDF shifted forces to counter the ALA threat head-on. During an assault on Sejera the ALA absorbed heavy casualties, and its ranks broke and fled the battlefield.

After the truce period, the ALA was in the center of Galilee. This area was perceived by IDF commanders as the weakest part of the Arab lines. In Operation DEKEL, launched on July 8, IDF forces attempted to drive the ALA completely out of Israel. The ALA launched a simultaneous all-out effort against Sejera using armored vehicles, artillery, and close-air support. The assaults were repelled with heavy losses, and the ALA withdrew from Galilee to avoid encirclement by the IDF. The withdrawal continued during the second UN truce (July 18–October 15, 1948).

When the second cease-fire failed, the ALA contained fewer than 4,000 troops in three brigades and required direct support from the Lebanese Army to stay in the field. The IDF decided to completely destroy the ALA while pushing the northern front of the war back into Lebanon. A series of furious Israeli attacks pushed the ALA defenders across the border. In Operation HIRAM (October 29–31, 1948), the IDF annihilated the remnants of the ALA, killing or capturing virtually the entire force. The Lebanese Army was simultaneously driven out of the war entirely, and IDF troops began to occupy parts of Lebanon. The ALA had ceased to exist as an effective combat unit by November 1948.

Most historians argue that the ALA was an ineffective combat unit even when fighting on the tactical defensive against a poorly equipped enemy. The diversity of its ranks made effective command and control difficult, if not impossible, and it proved incapable of any significant offensive attacks. Its primary use to the Arab League was to pin down IDF troops, but even in this endeavor it proved incapable of effective service.

PAUL J. SPRINGER

See also

Arab League; Haganah; Israeli War of Independence, Overview; Qawuqji, Fawzi al-

References

Herzog, Chaim. *The Arab-Israeli Wars: War and Peace in the Middle East from the War of Independence to Lebanon.* Westminster, MD: Random House, 1984.

Levenberg, Haim. *Military Preparations of the Arab Community in Palestine: 1945–1948.* London: Routledge, 1993.

Pollack, Kenneth M. *Arabs at War: Military Effectiveness, 1948–1991.* Lincoln: University of Nebraska Press, 2002.

Sayigh, Yezid. *Armed Struggle and the Search for State: The Palestine National Movement, 1949–1993.* New York: Oxford University Press, 2000.

Arab Nationalism

The concept of an essential unity among Arab nations, especially during the 1950s and 1960s, often combined with socialism and elements of Islam. Arab nationalism arose after World War II as a response to European imperialism and stressed unity of purpose among the newly formed Arab countries of the Middle East. While respectful of Islam, Arab nationalist movements were generally secular in tone and drew heavily on socialist economic principles and anti-imperialist rhetoric. However, while the socialist, anti-Western character of Arab nationalism attracted Soviet political and military support and increased Soviet influence in the Middle East, Arab leaders avoided domination by the Soviet Union and found common cause with the nonaligned nations of the developing world. Political, ideological, and military opposition to the State of Israel served as a focal point of Arab nationalist movements, and repeated Arab military defeats contributed to the decline of such movements. However, Arab nationalist parties, under the banner of Baathism, continue to play a dominant role in the politics of Syria and, until recently, Iraq.

Arab nationalism finds its roots in the late 19th century, as European ideas of nationalism affected the Ottoman Turkish Empire. After World War I, as the British and French acquired mandate authority over the various Arab territories of the Ottoman Empire, Arab nationalist sentiment was divided between unifying notions of Pan-Arabism and individual independence movements in the various Arab regions. Such sentiment contributed to the formation of the Arab League on the one hand and the growth of numerous regional nationalist groups on the other, including the Society of the Muslim Brothers in Egypt and the Étoile Nord Africaine (North African Star) in Algeria. These regional groups combined nationalism with strong Islamic identity in their drive for independence from Britain and France.

In the years following World War II, most of the Arab states gained their independence but were ruled by governments sympathetic to the interests of the European powers. Political crises in the late 1940s and 1950s, including the Arab defeat in the Israeli War of Independence (1948–1949), resulted in the overthrow of many of these regimes and the establishment of new governments. These new regimes were now willing to challenge the Western powers, particularly those in Egypt, Syria, and Iraq.

These countries lay at the heart of the Arab nationalist movements during the Cold War. The ongoing conflict with Israel would play a major role in the growth of Arab unity. The common Israeli enemy provided the Arab states with a greater cause that overshadowed their individual differences. Opposition to Israel and support for Palestinian refugees also served to link the resources of the newly wealthy oil states of the Persian Gulf region to the larger Arab cause. Finally, the conflict with Israel combined with the importance of petroleum resources made the Middle East a region of great interest to the United States and the Soviet Union. Indeed, the two superpowers would play a substantial role in the development and the destiny of Arab nationalist movements.

Arab nationalism during the period of the Cold War stressed Arab unity but not necessarily in the form of a single Arab state. Different states could act in concert to achieve goals that would benefit the entire Arab world. In addition, Arab nationalist movements fit into a broader picture of postcolonial political ideologies in the developing world. Such ideologies stressed national or cultural identity, along with Marxist or socialist ideas, as a counter to Western influence. Encouraged by Soviet influence, socialism served as a widespread reaction of developing nations to their former experiences with European imperialism.

The two most important Arab nationalist movements that took root were Baathism and Nasserism. The Baath, or Resurrection, Party grew to prominence in Syria after World War II. One of its founders, Michel Aflaq, a Syrian Christian, conceived of a single Arab nation embracing all the Arab states and recapturing the glory of the Arab past. While the movement was respectful of Islamic tradition, its rhetoric and agenda were largely secular and increasingly socialist. This socialism grew partly as a response to Western imperialism and partly as a result of increasing Soviet political and military support of Baathist Arab states. The Baath Party increased in influence in Syria and Iraq throughout the late 1950s and early 1960s. In Syria, the party came to dominate the country's turbulent politics after 1963 and continued to do so throughout the regime of President Hafez al-Assad. In Iraq, the party also rose to national control in 1963 and remained dominant until the overthrow of President Saddam Hussein in 2003.

Nasserism, as a movement, reflected the agenda and the political potency of President Gamal Abdel Nasser, leader of Egypt from 1952 until his death in 1970. Raised in an atmosphere of British domination in Egypt, Nasser combined a rejection of imperialist

influence with elements of socialism and progressive Islam. Although he used religious rhetoric to appeal to the Egyptian people, his outlook, like that of the Baathists, was primarily secular. Nasser stressed modernization, state ownership of industry, and Egypt's role as the natural leader of the Arab world. His suspicion of the West, socialist economic policies, and acceptance of Soviet military aid after 1955 drew him toward the Soviet sphere. Nevertheless, he avoided domination by Moscow and gave support to the Non-Aligned Movement of developing nations. Nasser actively sought the leadership of a unified Arab world. Indeed, the temporary union of Egypt and Syria in the United Arab Republic (1958–1961) illustrated his nationalist vision and the overlap of Nasserist and Baathist ideologies.

Israel served as a focal point for Nasser's brand of Arab nationalism. He viewed the defeat of Israel as an expression of Arab unity and a rejection of imperialist interference in the Middle East. In addition, Egyptian leadership in the struggle with Israel contributed to his stature in the Arab world as a whole. His position in Egypt and among Arab nations was greatly enhanced by the Suez Crisis of 1956. However, Egypt's attempted military intervention in Yemen (1962–1967) brought Nasser's vision of Arab nationalism and socialism into conflict with the royalist Islamic views of Saudi Arabia and demonstrated the limits of Nasser's influence. Furthermore, Egypt's disastrous defeat in the June 1967 Six-Day War with Israel dealt a severe blow to his power and prestige. Nasser's authority survived the 1967 war, and the overwhelming rejection of his resignation by the Egyptian people testified to the scope of his popular appeal. However, the defeat signaled the end of the Nasserist vision of Arab unity. By the end of the 1970s, Egypt and Syria had forged a mutual peace, and Egyptian presidents Anwar Sadat and Hosni Mubarak moved Egypt out of the Soviet orbit while forging closer ties to the West, particularly the United States.

ROBERT S. KIELY

See also

Arab Socialism; Assad, Hafez al-; Baathism; Egypt; Hussein, Saddam; Iraq; Mubarak, Hosni; Nasser, Gamal Abdel; Pan-Arabism; Sadat, Anwar

References

Dawisha, Adeed. *Arab Nationalism in the 20th Century: From Triumph to Despair*. Princeton, NJ: Princeton University Press, 2003.
Hourani, Albert. *A History of the Arab Peoples*. Cambridge: Harvard University Press, 1991.
Khalidi, Rashid, et al., eds. *The Origins of Arab Nationalism*. New York: Columbia University Press, 1993.
Tibi, Bassam. *Arab Nationalism: A Critical Enquiry*. 2nd ed. New York: St. Martin's, 1991.

Arab Nationalist Movement

Leftist nationalist movement that began at the American University of Beirut in Lebanon in the 1950s. Among the early leaders were George Habash and Constantin Zureiq. The Arab Nationalist Movement (ANM) was spawned by general discontent with conditions facing much of the Arab people and dissatisfaction with the response by the existing Arab political parties. Initially based on Western ideas and philosophy, the organization had as its goals the establishment of Arab unity and social progress for the Arab peoples. The ANM was socialist but staunchly anticommunist. Strongly influenced by the successes of Egyptian president Gamal Abdel Nasser, the ANM became increasingly anti-Western and anti-Israeli. It was also revolutionary in its orientation.

The organization had numerous branches in the different Arab states, each of which tended to reflect local concerns, but adopted the overall name of the Arab Nationalist Movement in 1958. National tensions and different concerns led in the early 1960s to a split into two main factions: one on the Left led by Muhsin Ibrahim, Mohammad Kishly, and Naef Hawatmeh, and one on the Right led by George Habash, Ahmad al-Khabib, Hani al-Hindi, and Wadi' Haddad. Following the 1967 Six-Day War and the discrediting of Nasserism, both groups then adopted a Marxist approach, but the ANM itself splintered into many different groups and organizations, including the Popular Front for the Liberation of Palestine (PFLP). By 1970, the ANM had largely disappeared. Its legacy remains in a number of left-wing successor organizations in various Arab nations.

SPENCER C. TUCKER

See also

Arab Nationalism; Habash, George; Nasser, Gamal Abdel; Pan-Arabism; Popular Front for the Liberation of Palestine

References

Dawisha, Adeed. *Arab Nationalism in the 20th Century: From Triumph to Despair.* Princeton, NJ: Princeton University Press, 2003.

Khalidi, Rashid, et al., eds. *The Origins of Arab Nationalism.* New York: Columbia University Press, 1993.

Tibi, Bassam. *Arab Nationalism: A Critical Enquiry.* 2nd ed. New York: St. Martin's, 1991.

Arab Oil Embargo
Start Date: October 17, 1973
End Date: March 18, 1974

In October 1973, the Arab members of the Organization of Petroleum Exporting Countries (OPEC) manipulated their vast oil resources to protest U.S. support of Israel during the Yom Kippur War. The Arab oil embargo consisted of three interrelated actions: production curtailments, a total embargo targeted against countries deemed supportive of Israel, and price hikes posted without the consent of the oil companies.

As a result, the price of a barrel of oil nearly quadrupled, from $3.01 in the middle of October 1973 to $11.65 by the end of December. The skyrocketing prices and ensuing chaos created rampant inflation and a global recession that would last throughout the 1970s. Although Arab leaders had attempted to wield the so-called oil weapon in previous Arab-Israeli conflicts, by 1973 a host of polit-

ical, diplomatic, and economic conditions ensured the potency of their oil policies.

When the embargo took effect, worldwide fuel stocks were already strained as demand began to outpace supply. The economic boom of the 1950s and 1960s, created largely by plentiful and cheap oil supplies, vastly increased oil consumption in the industrialized countries. Yet as long as prices were low, conservation efforts remained unpopular, and energy companies had little incentive to invest the huge sums of money required to locate and pump oil from new fields. The liabilities inherent in these trends became obvious by the early 1970s, as U.S. oil production topped out while imports tripled.

Thanks to its enormous oil reserves and geologic qualities that made drilling there economical, the Middle East was quickly becoming the new global center of oil production. Whereas the so-called black gold from Texas and Oklahoma had once supplied the world market, by 1970 industrialized nations looked to the Middle East and North Africa to satisfy upwards of two-thirds of the new demand for oil. Arab leaders approached these changing market conditions in ways consistent with the founding purpose of OPEC in 1960. The Arab oil-producing countries demanded, and received, a larger share of the windfall profits enjoyed by the oil companies along with more control over the production process. They also realized that the staggering amount of money pouring into their treasuries surpassed what their developing economies could spend. The Arabs reasoned that a future embargo would be economically prudent and was sure to have major and prolonged impact because non-Arab oil production was operating at peak capacity. As tensions in the Middle East mounted in the early 1970s, Arab oil producers were well positioned to cut production across the board while retaining the ability to embargo target countries as a tool of diplomatic coercion against Israel and its allies.

Israel's crushing victory in the Six-Day War of June 1967 placed large tracts of Arab land, including the Sinai Peninsula, the Golan Heights, and the West Bank, under the Jewish state's occupation. From Israel's perspective, the occupied territories provided a security barrier against future Arab aggression.

The fact of Israeli military dominance narrowed Arab rhetoric from destroying the Zionist entity to the less ambitious goal of regaining the land lost in the war. The situation was a diplomatic conundrum as represented by United Nations (UN) Resolution 242, which called for secure and recognized boundaries and the withdrawal of Israeli forces from the occupied territories. Israel stipulated that negotiations regarding land transfers must take place directly with the Arabs, as face-to-face diplomacy would signal Israel's legitimacy among its neighbors.

Following the leadership of President Gamal Abdel Nasser of Egypt, Arab leaders refused to engage in direct negotiations while Israel occupied Arab land. Low-level border clashes, which erupted periodically between Israeli and Arab forces, failed to push either side toward a negotiated peace. In the Arab view, a full-scale war launched with weapons shipped from the Soviet Union was the only solution, as Israel remained entrenched and firmly supported by the United States.

When Richard Nixon became president of the United States in 1969, U.S. foreign policy was focused on two basic objectives: creating a viable exit strategy from the war in Vietnam and improving relations with the Soviet Union and China. In the view of Nixon and his national security adviser, Henry Kissinger, maintenance of Israeli hegemony through military support was the best guarantor of regional stability. In this strategy, the Arabs would eventually realize that U.S. diplomacy, not Soviet weapons, would achieve their goals. Until then, Nixon and Kissinger could focus their attention elsewhere.

Anwar Sadat, who succeeded Nasser as president of Egypt in 1970, rejected these assumptions. Sadat believed that Israel could be challenged by a massive surprise attack launched in conjunction with Syrian forces. He also lobbied King Faisal of Saudi Arabia to augment Egypt's war chest with the oil weapon. Recognizing the economic and political benefits of an embargo, Faisal consented, and Sadat began devising his war plans with strong backing from the Arab oil producers. On October 6, 1973—Yom Kippur in the Jewish calendar—Egyptian and Syrian forces launched a two-front attack. Israel was caught unprepared, and in the first week of fighting Israel's war matériel was depleted to dangerously low levels.

Israeli prime minister Golda Meir implored Nixon to commence a military resupply airlift. Although Faisal had repeatedly warned that such blatant support would elicit Arab retaliation in the form of an embargo, Nixon complied with the Israeli request. The Arabs promptly responded with cutbacks in oil production and a complete embargo against the United States and the Netherlands, with Rotterdam the main port of entry for oil into Western Europe. For Nixon, who narrowly defined U.S. interests in Cold War terms, the preeminent objective was to ensure that U.S. arms defeated Soviet arms on the battlefield. He reasoned that an Arab military victory might radicalize the entire region and lead to communist control of Middle Eastern oil, a prospect far more threatening than the temporary disruption in oil supplies instituted by staunchly anticommunist oil sheikdoms.

Although the Arab oil producers lifted the embargo in March 1974 and new Western investment in oil exploration succeeded in limiting OPEC's coercive power, the ripple effects of the energy crisis lingered long thereafter. The oil shortages—represented memorably by long lines of cars waiting at gas stations—effectively highlighted a major fracture within the global anticommunist alliance system. Western Europe and Japan, both far more dependent on Middle Eastern oil than the United States, adopted an explicitly pro-Arab stance following the embargo. Israel became increasingly isolated on the world stage, and the United States has forged much of its subsequent Middle East policy over the objections of its traditional allies.

David Zierler

See also
Arab Nationalism; Brezhnev, Leonid Ilyich; Faisal, King of Saudi Arabia; Golan Heights; Kissinger, Henry Alfred; Meir, Golda; Nasser, Gamal Abdel; Nixon, Richard Milhous; Organization of Petroleum Exporting Countries; Sadat, Anwar; Sinai; Soviet Union and Russia, Middle East Policy; United Nations Security Council Resolution 242; United Nations Security Council Resolution 338; United States, Middle East Policy; Yom Kippur War

References
El-Sadat, Anwar. *In Search of Identity.* New York: Harper and Row, 1978.
Garthoff, Raymond L. *Detente and Confrontation: American-Soviet Relations from Nixon to Reagan.* Washington, DC: Brookings Institution, 1985.
Kissinger, Henry A. *Years of Renewal.* New York: Simon and Schuster, 1999.
Smart, Ian. "Oil, the Superpowers, and the Middle East." *International Affairs* 53 (1977): 17–36.

Arab Population in Israel
See Israel, Arab Population in

Arab Revolt of 1916–1918
Start Date: June 5, 1916
End Date: October 31, 1918

Uprising during World War I by the Arab peoples of north, central, and western Arabia against Ottoman rule. Since the 16th century, the Ottoman government in Constantinople had controlled the area of Syria, Palestine, Iraq, the western provinces of Saudi Arabia, and part of Yemen. Much of the region's population of some 6 million was nomadic. In 1908 the Young Turks came to power in Turkey and promoted Turkish nationalism at the expense of other nationalities of the empire, which the Arabs and other peoples resented. The new government also sent troops into Arab lands and introduced conscription, both of which angered the Arabs.

Under the terms of the Turkish constitution of 1909, the Arab peoples of the empire sent representatives to the Imperial Parliament in Constantinople, where they openly supported Arab rights. At the same time newspapers and political organizations, some secret, sprang up in the Arab lands and promoted Arab nationalism. Damascus and Beirut were centers of this activity but were too close geographically to central Turkey to risk overt action. Arab power was in fact diffuse and largely wielded by local chieftains who had little ability to initiate hostilities against Constantinople on their own.

The center of the Arab nationalist movement was the Hejaz region of central Arabia, which contained the holy cities of Mecca and Medina. The region was connected to Turkey by means of the Damascus-Medina (Hejaz) Railway. Sharif of Mecca Hussein ibn Ali ibn Mohammed was nominal head of the Hejaz. His position was strengthened by his senior position in the Muslim religious hierarchy as a direct descendant of the Prophet Muhammad. Hussein saw the railway as an infringement on his control and had long hoped

Arab guerrillas operating under T. E. Lawrence, July 1917. (Getty Images)

for an independent Arab kingdom under his rule. World War I provided that opportunity.

As early as February 1914, Hussein had been in communication, through his son Abdullah, with British authorities in Cairo. Abdullah met with the British high commissioner in Egypt, Lord Kitchener, and told him that the Arabs were prepared to rebel against Constantinople in return for British support. The British were skeptical, but the entrance of the Ottoman Empire into the war on the side of the Central Powers changed their attitude. Both Sir Harold Wingate, British governor-general of the Sudan, and Sir Henry McMahon, Kitchener's successor as high commissioner in Egypt, kept in touch with Hussein.

In the spring of 1915, Hussein sent his third son, Emir Faisal, to Damascus to reassure Turkish authorities there of his loyalty and to sound out Arab opinion. Faisal had favored the Turks, but the visit to Damascus and the profound discontent of the Arab population he discovered there reversed this view.

Hussein then entered into active negotiations with McMahon in Cairo. Hussein promised to declare war on the Ottoman Empire and raise an Arab army to assist the British in return for British support

for him as king of a postwar Pan-Arab state. The British agreed and soon were providing some rifles and ammunition to the Arabs. Meanwhile, the Turks were endeavoring to stamp out Arab nationalism in Damascus, where they executed a number of Arab nationalist leaders. Many other Arab patriots fled south to Mecca, where they urged Hussein to take up arms. The Turks were well aware of the Arab preparations and from May 1916 blockaded the Hejaz from arms shipments and began a buildup of their forces in Damascus. The actual revolt was initiated by the dispatch of Turkish troops to reinforce their garrison at Medina. Outside Medina on June 5, 1916, Hussein's eldest son Ali and Faisal officially proclaimed the start of the Arab Revolt.

Joined by 30,000 tribesmen, Faisal immediately led an assault on the Turkish garrison at Medina, but the Turks drove off the attackers. The Arabs did succeed, however, in cutting the railway to the north of the city. To the south, Hussein led an attack on the 1,000-man Turkish garrison at Mecca, taking the city after three days of street fighting. Another Arab attack shortly thereafter against the port city of Jiddah was also successful, supported by the British Royal Navy seaplane carrier *Ben-my-Chree* based at Aden. Other cities also fell to the Arabs. In September, the 3,000-man Turkish garrison at Taif, the last city in the southern Hejaz held by the Turks, surrendered to Arab forces supported by British-supplied artillery.

On November 2, Hussein proclaimed himself "King of the Arab Countries." This created some embarrassment for the British government with the French. Finally, the Allies worked out a compromise by which they addressed Hussein as "King of the Hejaz." Hussein largely left leadership of the revolt to his four sons. A number of Arabs in the Turkish Army, including officers, taken prisoner in the fighting helped provide a leadership cadre for the so-called Arab Army. Military strength of its four main forces commanded by Hussein's sons fluctuated wildly, and few of the men involved, who ranged widely in age, were trained.

In October 1916, the Turks managed to drive the Arab Army south of Medina and reopened the railway. The British sent a party of advisers to Hussein, and Arabist captain T. E. Lawrence became Faisal's official adviser, successfully urging Faisal to resume the offensive. Rather than meet Turkish power head-on, the two men initiated a series of hit-and-run raids over northern Arabia that took advantage of the support of the local populations and forced the Turks to divert increasing numbers of troops to the region.

In the spring of 1917, Faisal received pledges of Arab support from Syria once military operations reached there. In July 1917, Lawrence led an attack that captured Aqaba, which then became Faisal's chief base, while forces under Abdullah and Ali contained the Turkish garrison at Medina and protected Mecca. Faisal's northern wing of the Arab Army was the revolt's chief military force and acted on the right flank of Lieutenant General Edmund Allenby's British forces in Palestine. In the autumn of 1917 Lawrence, who understood and effectively practiced guerrilla warfare, led a series of successful attacks on Turkish rail traffic. Allenby's calls for diversionary attacks by the Arab Army produced a series of raids that diverted some 23,000 Turkish troops from participation in the fighting in Palestine. Faisal also cooperated closely with Allenby in the Megiddo Offensive and, with 30,000 men, led the revolt's climactic action, the entrance into Damascus in October 1918.

The Arab Revolt had immense repercussions in the Arab world in fueling Arab nationalism. It helped free the Arab lands from Turkish rule and led to the formation of Arab states. But the victorious Allies thwarted Hussein's ambitions. McMahon's pledge to Hussein preceded by six months the 1916 Sykes-Picot Agreement between the British and French governments, a breach of promises made to the Arabs that in effect set up British and French spheres of influence in the Middle East. Ultimately, much of the territory was awarded as mandates to Great Britain and France under the League of Nations. Faisal received Syria but was deposed and became king of Iraq under British protection. Abdullah became king of the newly created Transjordan. Hussein declared himself caliph of Islam in March 1924 but was forced to abdicate as king of the Hejaz to his son Ali when Abd al-Aziz al-Saud (Ibn Saud) conquered most of the Hejaz.

SPENCER C. TUCKER

See also

Allenby, Sir Edmund Henry Hynman, 1st Viscount; Faisal, King of Saudi Arabia; Hussein ibn Ali, Sharif of Mecca; Ibn Saud, King of Saudi Arabia; League of Nations Covenant, Article 22; Ottoman Empire; Palestine, British Mandate for; Sykes-Picot Agreement; World War I, Impact of

References

Fromkin, David. *A Peace to End All Peace: The Fall of the Ottoman Empire and the Creation of the Modern Middle East.* New York: Avon, 1989.

Glubb, Sir John. *A Short History of the Arab Peoples.* New York: Dorset, 1969.

Hourani, Albert. *A History of the Arab Peoples.* Cambridge: Harvard University Press, 1991.

Lenczowski, George. *The Middle East in World Affairs.* 4th ed. Ithaca, NY: Cornell University Press, 1980.

Tauber, Eliezer. *The Arab Movements in World War I.* London: Frank Cass, 1993.

Thomas, Lowell. *With Lawrence in Arabia.* New York: Garden City Publishing, 1924.

Arab Revolt of 1936–1939
Start Date: April 1936
End Date: 1939

General revolt among Arabs in the British Mandate for Palestine. Although the uprising was aimed primarily at British interests in the area, attacks against Jews were far from uncommon. Although it failed to redress immediate concerns, the revolt had a lasting impact on Britain's policies in the mandate and on the Arab and Jewish communities.

The revolt was the culmination of growing Arab unrest over Jewish immigration and land purchases in Palestine and economic dislocation from increased urbanization and industrialization. It was, in fact, the most severe of a number of communal disturbances between Jews and Arabs dating from the early 1920s. Despite its failure, the Great Revolt (as the Arabs call it) marked the dawn of a distinctive Palestinian Arab nationalism.

The problems that triggered the unrest grew in part from events outside the region. Growing anti-Semitism in Eastern Europe and Nazi control of Germany from 1933 led to an increase in Jewish immigrants entering Palestine. At the same time, growing land purchases by Zionists in Palestine had led to the expulsion of large numbers of Arab peasants from lands on which they had been tenant farmers. These dislocations were also part of a deepening economic crisis that gripped the region as Palestinian agricultural exports to Europe and America declined in the midst of the Great Depression (around 1930–1940).

The many landless Arabs, often forced into slums erected around large cities, formed the rank and file of the revolt. The leadership, however, existed on two levels. The first was a more politically conscious Arab elite dominated by two rival clans: the Husseini family led by Haj Amin al-Husseini, the mufti of Jerusalem, and their rivals, the Nashashibis, represented by Fakhri al-Nashashibi.

British soldiers conduct a weapons search of a truck driver in Palestine, October 12, 1938. (Bettmann/Corbis)

The second element (and the true center of the revolt's leadership) resided among local committees that had emerged in Jerusalem, Nablus, Jaffa, Tulkarm, and elsewhere.

Tensions among Arabs, Jews, and British administrators in Palestine had been building for several months prior to the revolt's outbreak in April 1936. It was clear that a surge of Islamic extremism had accompanied growing economic dislocation among Palestinian Arabs. Sheikh Izz al-Din al-Qassam, a Syrian-born, Egyptian-educated cleric, had been preaching fundamentalist Islam and calling for a jihad (holy war) against both Britons and Jews. At the same time, he was assembling a host of devoted followers, mostly from landless Arabs in the Haifa area. After his followers murdered a Jewish policeman near Gilboa, al-Qassam died in a shootout with British troops on November 20, 1935. His death triggered major nationalist demonstrations among Arabs throughout Palestine. At the same time, discovery by the British of an arms cache in a shipment of cement barrels intended for a Jewish importer fed rumors among Arabs that the Jews were arming for a war against the Arabs. These developments essentially pushed the tension-ridden atmosphere in Palestine into outright rebellion.

The Arab Revolt officially began in April 1936 in the hill country around Tulkarm and spread rapidly. The young nationalists who formed the local committees took the lead. Anxious to gain control of the revolt and to maintain their own credibility, the Hus-

seini and Nashashibi clans formed the Arab Higher Committee to provide rhetorical, financial, and material support for the uprising. During the first six months of the revolt, 200 Arabs, 80 Jews, and 28 British soldiers and policemen died in clashes.

Initially, British reaction was somewhat restrained. Indeed, London hoped that the disturbances would blow over without forcing recourse to measures that might scar Anglo-Arab relations. British authorities imposed no death sentences in response to any of the killings. Only in September 1936 did British authorities impose martial law. Eventually, the government sent 20,000 troops from Britain and Egypt and recruited 2,700 Jewish supernumeraries to contain and quell the disturbances.

The reaction of the Jewish community in Palestine was also restrained. The Jewish Agency for Palestine acted to strengthen its self-defense force (the Haganah) and fortified settlements, leaving suppression of the revolt to the British. As the uprising continued and attacks on Jewish settlements increased, the Palestinian Jews resorted to aggressive self-defense, including ambushes of rebel Arab bands and reprisals against neighboring Arab villages suspected of harboring guerrillas. This doctrine of harsh reprisals developed by the Zionist leadership during the revolt became a permanent fixture of Zionist military policy.

In the first months of the revolt, the British succeeded—through the use of night curfews, patrols, searches, and ambushes—in pushing Arab rebels out of the towns. By mid-May 1936, rural Palestine had become the center of gravity of the revolt and would remain so until the revolt's end in 1939, and leadership remained centered in the local committees. The Arab Higher Committee was increasingly paralyzed by rivalries between the Husseini and Nashashibi clans and never asserted control over the rural bands, although it did provide money, arms, and rhetorical support.

By the autumn of 1937, 9,000–10,000 Palestinian fighters, augmented by non-Palestinians brought in and financed by the Arab Higher Committee, were roaming the countryside. They were often motivated as much by the desire for loot as by nationalist zeal. Internecine violence among rival families resulted in more deaths among the Arabs than action by the British or Zionists. The rebels' practice of extorting food and other valuables from Arab peasants damaged the rural economy and increasingly alienated the rebels from their base of support. To pacify the countryside, the British shrewdly exploited divisions among the Arabs and used combined British-Zionist Special Night Squads (the best known of which was commanded by Captain Orde Wingate) that ambushed rebel bands, launched retaliatory strikes against Arab villages suspected of harboring guerrillas, and carried out targeted assassinations against rebel leaders.

The Arab Revolt collapsed in 1939 in the face of eroding support in the countryside, the arrest or exile of the senior leaders (including Haj Amin al-Husseini, who eventually wound up in Nazi Germany), lack of cohesion in the revolt's organization and leadership, and mounting British pressure. Nevertheless, the revolt had profound consequences for the mandate and the Arab and Zionist camps. The intensity of the uprising stunned British officials in Jerusalem and London and led the government to send a commission chaired by Lord William Robert Peel to Palestine in late 1936. The Peel Commission Report, which appeared in July 1937, proposed the partition of Palestine into a Jewish area and a much larger Arab area. This marked the first time that partition had been proposed as a solution to the Palestine issue. The violence subsided for a time—nearly a year—as the Peel Commission did its work. But both sides essentially rejected the proposal, and fighting ramped up considerably in the fall of 1937. The British eventually backed away from the Peel Commission proposals in the face of opposition from both Arabs and Jews.

More shocking for Palestinian Jews was the implementation of the British government White Paper of May 1939, which restricted Jewish immigration and land purchases over the next 5 years and promised an independent Palestinian Arab state in 10 years if the rights of the Jewish community were protected. From the Jewish perspective, the White Paper represented a surrender to Arab violence and intimidation. It also closed Palestine to European Jews at a time when anti-Jewish violence in Germany and Eastern Europe was intensifying. Indeed, the measure permanently damaged relations between Britain and the Jews in Palestine.

The worst damage, however, was to Palestinian Arabs. Although the Great Revolt gained a permanent place in Arab nationalist mythology, in the short term the Arabs were left with the consequences of a failed revolt. Most of the political leadership was in prison, exiled, or had left politics disgusted and disillusioned. The end of the revolt relieved many Palestinian Arabs who could now resume their normal lives and recoup some of their economic losses. Even so, blood feuds between families that had supported the uprising and those that had opposed it were to disrupt society and paralyze political life for years. The Palestinians had to depend on the Arab states in the region with baneful consequences, leading up to the Israeli War of Independence (1948–1949).

The Arab Revolt spontaneously unraveled throughout 1939 so that by year's end clashes and armed violence had largely ended. Nevertheless, the casualty figures were grim indeed.

It is estimated that some 5,000 Arabs, 400 Jews, and 200 British soldiers and officials died in the uprising. And despite the summoning of 20,000 additional British troops and as many as 15,000 Haganah fighters, it took the better part of three years to conquer the revolt.

The overall legacy of the Arab Revolt, then, was the further poisoning of relations between Arabs and Jews and the further alienation of the British from both communities. The revolt also led to the separation of the Arab and Jewish economies, which had previously been somewhat integrated. This would burden Palestinian Arabs with poverty, high unemployment, and homelessness for the succeeding two generations. The divisions among Arab, Jew, and Briton remained largely dormant during World War II, but they would resurface with even more violence in the postwar years.

WALTER F. BELL

See also

Haganah; Husseini, Haj Amin al-; Land Rights and Disputes; Nashashibi, Fakhri al-; Palestine, British Mandate for; Peel Commission; Qassam, Izz al-Din al-; White Paper (1939); Wingate, Orde Charles; World War I, Impact of; World War II, Impact of

References

Gelvin, James L. *The Israel-Palestine Conflict: One Hundred Years of War.* New York: Cambridge University Press, 2005.

Morris, Benny. *Righteous Victims: A History of the Zionist-Arab Conflict, 1881–2001.* New York: Vintage Books, 2001.

Porath, Yehoshua. *The Palestinian National Movement, 1929–1939: From Riot to Rebellion.* London: Cass, 1974.

Stein, Kenneth W. *The Land Question in Palestine, 1917–1939.* Chapel Hill: University of North Carolina Press, 1984.

Swedenburg, Ted. *Memories of Revolt: The 1936–1939 Rebellion and the Palestinian National Past.* Minneapolis: University of Minnesota Press, 1995.

Arab Riots, Jerusalem
Start Date: April 4, 1920
End Date: April 6, 1920

By early 1920, relations between Arabs and Jews in Palestine had grown extraordinarily tense. In February 1920, Arab raiders attacked the Jewish settlements of Metulla and Tel Hai in the extreme north along the Palestine-Lebanese border. Among those killed at Tel Hai was Joseph Trumpeldor, a Zionist hero who had led the Zion Mule Corps in World War I. His death sent a shock wave through the Jewish community in Palestine. World Zionist Organization (WZO) president Chaim Weizmann warned British Mandate authorities that even worse trouble was brewing. The next month, in March 1920, the Syrian National Congress defied French authorities and offered Prince Faisal the throne of Syria, to include Palestine.

This was also the period of the Arab Festival of Nebi Musa, when devout Arabs traveled on the Jericho Road to make a pilgrimage to the tomb of Moses, a Muslim as well as Jewish patriarch. On April 4, a large number of these pilgrims gathered in Jerusalem to hear speeches by agitators who were promoting Faisal. Their apparent intention was to influence Allied deliberations over the determination of League of Nations mandates.

The crowd soon became unruly and was joined by Arab police. The rioters began attacking Jews, injuring some 160. Synagogues were also burned, and Jewish property was destroyed. Only after some three hours of rioting did the British police arrive and quell the disturbances, arresting some of the instigators. The next morning, however, British authorities released those they had arrested, and the attacks resumed and continued during the next two days until order was finally restored. By then, 6 Arabs and Jews had been killed, and the total of wounded had risen to several hundred.

Although British authorities dismissed the Arab mayor of Jerusalem and handed out stiff prison sentences to several of the instigators, the vast majority of those involved received only light sentences or went unpunished. At the same time, the British sentenced

British soldiers in Jerusalem during the Arab riots of 1920. (Library of Congress)

Vladimir Jabotinsky and several associates, who had organized a Jewish self-defense group during the riots, to 15-year prison terms.

The riots came as a great shock to the Jews, and the event and reaction to the disparity in sentences handed down by the authorities led to an official court of inquiry. The officers of the British military administration insisted that Zionist provocation was responsible for the rioting, while Jews accused the mandatory government of complicity and of doing little to halt the rioting once it had begun. Weizmann sent a telegram to British prime minister David Lloyd George in which he blamed the rioting on "poisonous agitation" and "inflammatory speeches" that the authorities had allowed to continue. Colonel Richard Meinertzhagen, chief British intelligence officer in Cairo, astonished his superiors by fully supporting the Jewish charges. The reaction to this was profound. The British military administration in Palestine was sufficiently compromised so that on April 29, less than a week after the Supreme Allied Council had assigned the Palestine mandate to Britain, the London government announced that the military administration in Palestine would be dissolved in favor of a civilian authority. This event also convinced Jews in Palestine of the necessity of forming a self-defense organization, the Haganah, ready to fight for Jewish Palestine.

SPENCER C. TUCKER

See also

Faisal I, King of Iraq; Haganah; Jabotinsky, Vladimir Yevgenyevich; League of Nations Covenant, Article 22; Palestine, British Mandate for; Weizmann, Chaim

References

Sachar, Howard M. *A History of Israel: From the Rise of Zionism to Our Time.* 3rd ed. New York: Knopf, 2007.

Sanders, Ronald. *The High Walls of Jerusalem: A History of the Balfour Declaration and the Birth of the British Mandate for Palestine.* New York: Holt, Rinehart and Winston, 1983.

Shepherd, Naomi. *Ploughing Sand: British Rule in Palestine, 1917–1948.* New Brunswick, NJ: Rutgers University Press, 1999.

Arab Socialism

A sociopolitical philosophy that swept several Arab nations after World War II. Arab socialism is actually a conglomeration of nationalism, socialism, and Arabism and reached its zenith of influence in the 1950s and 1960s. Socialism, which dates back to the 19th century, adheres to economic collectivism in which the means of production are owned en masse by the population or by the state, which represents the population. There are many permutations of socialism. They range from the rigid command-style socialism of the Soviet Union under Joseph Stalin to the so-called market socialism popular in Western Europe that mixes capitalist market economies with socialist redistributive government policies. Arabism is an outlook that envisions a formal union of Arab nations or greater unity of Arab peoples. The philosophy was secular in the sense that it attracted and invited both Arab Christians and Arab Muslims. Many who supported Pan-Arabism were not anti-Western. Adherents of Arabism believed that all Arabs belonged to a single Arab nation and through unity could reform Arab society. Indeed, the Baath Party used the slogan "one Arab nation with an internal mission."

In the early 1940s Michel Aflaq, the Syrian cofounder of the Baath Party, discussed both socialism and Arabism. His ideas were mirrored and taken in a different direction by Egyptian leader Gamal Abdel Nasser as a component of Nasserism and by others, such as Libyan leader Muammar Qaddafi. Aflaq's ideas were anti-imperialist but not Marxist, as they upheld rights to property and inheritance yet called for a new social order and an end to class conflict.

Several movements in the Arab world after 1945 included elements of Arab socialism within their platforms. The first was the Baath or Renaissance Party founded in 1943. Another important Syrian group under Akram Hawrani formed as a propeasant and proland reform movement. It became the Arab Socialist Party in 1950 and had a following of about 10,000 members. Four political coups occurred during the next few years, and at first Hawrani influenced Adib al-Shishakli, the ruler of Syria, to institute land reform. However, when al-Shishakli banned the Arab Socialist Party, Hawrani left for Lebanon and agreed to a merger with the Baath Party of Aflaq. Baathism had already spread to other nations in the Middle East after the end of World War II. Adherents to the Baath ideology of freedom, Arab unity, and socialism sought Arab solidarity and, ideally, Pan-Arab union. The socialism they proposed was the destruction of feudalism, particularly the domination of large landowners, and state management of the economy and business to promote equity. This was in many ways unlike classical socialist economic principles, which built on the role of the proletariat more than the peasantry. The Baath Party became most prominent in Syria under President Hafez al-Assad, who ruled Syria under its banner from 1970 until 2000, at which time his son Bashar al-Assad assumed control.

Upon al-Assad's 1970 political ascendancy, he immediately engaged his nation in land reform. Baathism was also quite successful

Arab students occupying the Syrian embassy in London in January 1963. Their slogan reads "Our Aims: Unity, Liberty, and Socialism." (Getty Images)

under the regime of Iraqi president Saddam Hussein, who took the reins of power of Iraq in 1979 and held them until the Iraq War of 2003. Even before Hussein seized power, land reform had been carried out by the Baathists in 1970. It is important to point out, however, that Baathism and Arab socialism under al-Assad and Hussein were more about the stability of the state under one-man rule than the realization of the Baath Party's ultimate goals. Indeed, some felt that the application of Arab socialism in their countries was fascistic.

Baathism was also rooted in secularism but not atheism. Aflaq explicitly recognized the Islamic basis of identity in the region, which he felt had created a bond of culture even with non-Muslims. However, the later rise of Islamist, or fundamentalist, doctrines was anathema to the Baath Party in which all Syrians (or all Iraqis) were supposed to be equal, whether Alawis, Sunni Muslims, Ismaili Muslims, or Christians. Indeed, the mutual hatred and political propaganda between Iran and Iraq, which spawned the Iran-Iraq War (1980–1988), came about because of the sharp political and ideological differences in the two countries, with the Iranian leadership insisting that Iraqi Baath leader Hussein was godless and anti-Islamic. Hussein for his part called the Shiites of Iraq and Iran *shu'ubi* (meaning "partisan" or "sectarian"), a historical reference to a literary Persian anti-Arab movement, and said they eroded Arab and Iraqi unity.

The second major movement under the rubric of Arab socialism can be seen in the rule of Egyptian president Nasser (1952–1970). Sometimes known as Nasserism, socialism in Egypt had a distinctive Pan-Arab component to it as well as a healthy disregard for foreign-owned enterprises, which Nasser saw as little more than a continuation of European colonialism. There had been many discussions of land reform even prior to the 1952 revolution. Nasser and the Free Officers had not thoroughly explored the implications of applying socialist policies in Egypt, but in order to assist the common man they did institute a weak land reform program and then later a more aggressive one. These more intrusive measures came after the failure of the United Arab Republic (UAR), the brief union with Syria, and even these were very haphazard. In some cases the old landlords found ways to retain their power, and in other areas newer groups managed to acquire holdings. Nasser began implementing other socialist reforms in 1961: the nationalization of nearly all major industrial and financial concerns and the sequestration of large businesses. Those with foreign passports—Italians, Greeks, Maltese, and Levantine Arabs, many of whom had lived for some time in Egypt and were considered *mutamasirun* (would-be Egyptians)—sold their holdings or saw them seized. On the political side, in 1962 the Arab Socialist Union was declared the sole legitimate party in Egypt. In fact, it was not a true political party in the sense of being independent of the government but was rather a mass party. By the late 1960s, the Arab Nationalist Union, which morphed into the National Democratic Party in the mid-1970s, held a monopoly of power in Egypt that was to long outlast Nasser.

What set Arab socialism apart from earlier European socialism was its rationale that Arab identity was the basis of nationhood. Hence, private property could not be abolished, but exploitation should be. And although vestiges of the old order, such as nomadism and tribalism, were to be abolished, those who adhered to such lifestyles would not be forced into submission if doing so meant the undermining of Arab identity. Indeed, the maintenance of a distinct Arab identity was paramount to all other Arab socialist principles.

Arab socialists eschewed classic Marxian doctrines that called for atheism. Instead, they viewed Islam as an important component of any new society in which an Arab brand of socialism had taken root. Careful to keep religion and government distinct and ever wary of fundamentalism, Arab socialists nevertheless believed that popular support for religion and spiritualism had become a part of the national identity.

Arab socialism has been on the decline since the late 1960s. First, the stinging Arab loss in the 1967 Six-Day War tarnished the reputations of Pan-Arabists and Arab socialists, particularly Nasser. Second, in Syria and Iraq in the 1970s, Baathism had come to stand more for authoritarianism and poorly enacted state management and not the freedom or true socialism that the party had proposed. And the heavy-handed rule of tyrannical leaders such as Hussein and al-Assad did nothing to change this view. Third, since the mid-1970s some of the socialist policies have been undone in Egypt and Iraq, and Syria has tried to embark on more free-market economic policies. Indeed, in Egypt many of the nationalizations of the 1950s and 1960s have been partly reversed through privatization. In Iraq, Baathist economic policies came under severe strain as a result of eight years of war with Iran and the Persian Gulf War (1991) and its aftermath. After the Anglo-American invasion of Iraq in 2003, the Baath Party was banned altogether. While there are still many proponents of Arab socialism, it remains to be seen whether the movement will ever again enjoy the prominence it once had in the Middle East.

PAUL G. PIERPAOLI JR.

See also

Assad, Hafez al-; Baath Party (Syria); Egypt; Hussein, Saddam; Nasser, Gamal Abdel; Iraq; Syria; Zionist/Israeli Socialism

References

Goode, Stephen. *The Prophet and the Revolutionary: Arab Socialism in the Modern Middle East.* New York: Franklin Watts, 1975.

Said, Abdel Moghny. *Arab Socialism.* New York: Barnes and Noble, 1972.

Salem, Paul. *Bitter Legacy: Ideology and Politics in the Arab World.* Syracuse, NY: Syracuse University Press, 1994.

Arabah

Long, narrow plain. Known to the Jews as the Arabah or Arava and to Arabs as the Wadi Araba, the plain forms part of the Negev Desert. It is 103 miles long by about 10 miles wide and runs north to south from the Dead Sea to the Gulf of Aqaba. The border between

Prefabricated concrete houses line a path in Kibbutz Ktura on the Arabah Plain, January 1975. (Sa'ar Ya'acov/Israeli Government Press Office)

Israel to the west and Jordan to the east runs through the middle of the Arabah. The Arabah is arid throughout. It begins at the Dead Sea in salt swamps at 1,373 feet below sea level (the lowest point on Earth), rising sharply for about 9 miles. From this point it gently rises to an elevation of 755 feet above sea level, the watershed between the Dead Sea and the Red Sea. From this point south for about 48 miles, it is essentially slowly descending salt flats.

Much of the Arabah is gravel and sand. The road to Eilat runs along its western border. Some springs provide water for settlements at Eilat. Principal mineral deposits of the Arabah consist of phosphates and copper, the latter once worked by miners under King Solomon.

The Arabah is essentially hot and dry. Temperatures can reach 125 degrees Fahrenheit. Although there is some dewfall at night, generally evaporation exceeds precipitation. Despite its desolate nature, the Arabah has been sparsely inhabited, made possible by winter flooding from the nearby hills.

Archaeological remains of settlements have been discovered that date to the 13th century BC. An important caravan route ran through the Arabah between the Red Sea and the Mediterranean. In biblical times the Arabah was the home of the Edomites.

In 1938, the kibbutz Bet Arava was established near the Dead Sea. Here, successful experiments were carried out in leaching salt from the soil and growing fruit and vegetables. This kibbutz, which grew to 30 acres under cultivation, was destroyed by the Arab Legion in 1947. New settlements were established by the 1960s. These produce fruit and vegetables. While there are a few Jewish settlements on the Israeli side of the Arabah, there are almost none on the Jordanian side. Israel's Timna National Park preserves prehistoric rock carvings and the ancient copper mines. Plans have been discussed for a joint Israeli-Jordanian project to pipe in water from the Red Sea by means of a tunnel. Because much of the Arabah is below sea level, the water could be easily desalinated with energy input.

SPENCER C. TUCKER

See also

Eilat, Israel; Negev Desert; Sinai

References

Evenari, Micchael, et al. *The Negev: The Challenge of a Desert.* 2nd ed. Cambridge: Harvard University Press, 1982.

Israolwitz, Richard, and Jonathan Friedlander, eds. *Transitions: Russians, Ethiopians, and Bedouins in Israel's Negev Desert.* Aldershot, UK: Ashgate, 1999.

Laughlin, John C. H. *Fifty Major Cities of the Bible.* London: Routledge, 2006.

Arafat, Yasser
Born: August 24, 1929
Died: November 11, 2004

Palestinian nationalist and leader of the Palestine Liberation Organization (PLO) for 36 years (1969–2004). Yasser Arafat, officially named Mohammed Abdel Raouf Arafat al-Qudwa al-Husseini, was born on August 24, 1929. Arafat always stated that he was born in Jerusalem, but Israeli officials began to claim in the 1970s that he was born in Cairo to discredit him. There is also some dispute about his date of birth, which is occasionally given as August 4, 1929. He went by the name Yasser as a child.

Arafat's father was a Palestinian Egyptian textile merchant. Neither Arafat nor his siblings were close to their father. His mother, Zahwa, also a Palestinian, was a member of a family that had lived in Jerusalem for generations. She died when Arafat was five years old, and he then lived with his mother's brother in Jerusalem. Arafat vividly remembered British soldiers invading his uncle's house one night, destroying possessions and beating its residents. When Arafat was nine years old his father brought him back to Cairo, where his older sister raised him.

As a teenager in Cairo, Arafat became involved in smuggling arms to Palestine to aid those struggling against both the British authorities and the Jews living there. He attended the University of Fuad I (later Cairo University) in Cairo but left to fight in Gaza against Israel in the Israeli War of Independence of 1948–1949. When the Arabs lost the war and Israel was firmly established, Arafat was inconsolable. He briefly attended the University of Texas but then returned to Cairo University to study engineering. He spent most of his time with fellow Palestinian students spreading his hopes for a free Palestinian state.

Arafat became president of the Union of Palestinian Students, holding that position from 1952 to 1956. He joined the Muslim Brotherhood in 1952. He finally graduated from college in 1956 and spent a short time working in Egypt. During the 1956 Suez Crisis he served as a second lieutenant in the Egyptian Army. In 1957 he moved to Kuwait, where he worked as an engineer and formed his own contracting company.

In 1958 Arafat founded the Fatah organization, an underground guerrilla group dedicated to the liberation of Palestine. In 1964 he quit his job and moved to Jordan to devote all his energies to the promotion of Palestinian nationhood and to organize raids into Israel. The PLO was founded that same year.

In 1968, the Israel Defense Forces (IDF) attacked Fatah at the small Jordanian village of Al Karameh. The Palestinians eventually forced the Israelis back, and Arafat's face appeared on the cover of *Time* magazine as the leader of the Palestinian movement. In consequence, Palestinians embraced Fatah, and Arafat became a national hero. He was appointed chairman of the PLO the next year and within four years controlled both the military (the Palestine Liberation Army, or PLA) and political branches of the organization.

Until his death in November 2004, Yasser Arafat was the leader of the Palestine Liberation Organization (PLO) and the Palestinian Autonomous Region in the Gaza Strip and West Bank city of Jericho. (Bernard Bisson/Corbis Sygma)

By 1970, Palestinians had assembled a well-organized unofficial state within Jordan. However, King Hussein of Jordan deemed them a threat to security and sent his army to evict them. Arafat enlisted the aid of Syria, while Jordan called on the United States for assistance. On September 24, 1970, the PLO agreed to a cease-fire and agreed to leave Jordan. Arafat moved the organization to Lebanon, which had a weak government that was not likely to restrict the PLO's operations. The PLO soon began launching occasional attacks across the Israeli border.

Arafat did not approve of overseas attacks because they gave the PLO a bad image abroad. He publicly dissociated the group from Black September, the organization that killed 11 Israeli athletes at the 1972 Munich Olympics, although there is now evidence of his involvement. In 1974 he limited the PLO's attacks to Israel, the Gaza Strip, and the West Bank. Although Israel claimed that Arafat was responsible for the numerous terrorist attacks that occurred within the country during the 1970s, he denied responsibility. In 1974 he spoke before the United Nations (UN) General Assembly as the representative of the Palestinian people and condemned Zionism but offered peace, which won him praise from the international community.

During the Lebanese Civil War, the PLO initially sided with the Lebanese National Front against the Lebanese forces, who were supported by Israel and backed by Defense Minister Ariel Sharon. As such, when Israeli forces invaded southern Lebanon, the PLO ended up fighting against the Israelis and then the Syrian militia group Amal. Thousands of Palestinians, many of them civilians, were killed during the struggle, and the PLO was forced to leave Lebanon in 1982 and relocate to Tunisia, where it remained until 1993.

During the 1980s, Iraq and Saudi Arabia donated millions of dollars to Arafat to help him rebuild the PLO. Arafat approved the First Intifada (1987) against Israel. In 1988, Palestinians declared Palestinian statehood at a meeting in Algiers. Arafat then announced that the Palestinians would renounce terrorism and recognize the State of Israel. The Palestinian National Council elected Arafat president of this new, unrecognized state in 1989.

Arafat and the Israelis conducted peace negotiations at the Madrid Conference in 1991. Although negotiations were temporarily set back when the PLO supported Iraq in the 1991 Persian

U.S. president Bill Clinton (*center*) leads Israeli prime minister Ehud Barak (*left*) and Palestinian Authority (PA) chairman Yasser Arafat (*right*) through Camp David in 2000. (Avi Ohayon/Israeli Government Press Office)

Gulf War, over the next two years the two parties held a number of secret discussions. These negotiations led to the 1993 Oslo Peace Accords in which Israel agreed to Palestinian self-rule in the Gaza Strip and the West Bank. Arafat also officially recognized the existence of the State of Israel. Despite the condemnation of many Palestinian nationalists who viewed Arafat's moves as a sell-out, the peace process appeared to be moving in a positive direction in the mid-1990s. Israeli troops withdrew from the Gaza Strip and Jericho in May 1994. Arafat was elected leader of the new Palestinian Authority (PA) in January 1996 with 88 percent of the vote in elections that were by all accounts free and fair (but with severely limited competition because Hamas and other opposition groups refused to participate).

Later that same year, Benjamin Netanyahu of the Likud Party became prime minister of Israel, and the peace process began to unravel. Netanyahu, a hard-line conservative, condemned terrorism and blamed Palestinians for numerous suicide bombings against Israeli citizens. He also did not trust Arafat, who he charged was supporting terrorists. Arafat continued negotiations with the Israelis into 2000. That July, with Ehud Barak having replaced Netanyahu as Israeli prime minister, Arafat traveled to the United States to meet with Barak and President Bill Clinton at the Camp David Summit. Despite generous concessions by Barak, Arafat refused to compromise, and a major chance at peace was lost.

On the collapse of the peace process, the Second (al-Aqsa) Intifada began. From the beginning of the Second Intifada in 2000, Arafat was a besieged man who appeared to be losing influence and control within the Palestinian and larger Arab communities. His inability or unwillingness to stop Palestinian terrorist attacks against Israel resulted in his virtual captivity at his Ramallah headquarters from 2002. In declining health by 2004, the PLO leader was beginning to look increasingly like a man past his time.

Flown to France for medical treatment, Arafat died on November 11, 2004, at Percy Military Hospital outside Paris, France. For a time, there were much intrigue and conspiratorial conjecture concerning his mysterious illness and death. Rumors persist that he was assassinated by poisoning, although it is equally likely that he succumbed to unintentional food poisoning. He is buried at his former headquarters in the city of Ramallah.

AMY HACKNEY BLACKWELL

See also

Barak, Ehud; Black September Organization; Clinton, William Jefferson; Gaza Strip; Hamas; Intifada, First; Intifada, Second; Jericho; Lebanon, Civil War in; Madrid Conference; Muslim Brotherhood; Oslo Accords; Palestine Liberation Organization; Palestinian Authority; Pan-Arabism; Ramallah; Terrorism; West Bank

References

Aburish, Said K. *Arafat: From Defender to Dictator*. New York: Bloomsbury, 1998.

Gowers, Andrew. *Arafat: The Biography*. Rev ed. London: Virgin Books, 1990.

Hart, Alan. *Arafat: A Political Biography*. Rev. ed. London: Sidgwick and Jackson, 1994.

Laqueur, Walter, and Barry Rubin, eds. *The Israel-Arab Reader: A Documentary History of the Middle East Conflict.* London: Penguin, 2001.

Said, Edward W. *Peace and Its Discontents: Essays on Palestine in the Middle East Process.* New York: Vintage Books, 1995.

Tessler, Mark. *A History of the Israeli-Palestinian Conflict.* Bloomington: Indiana University Press, 1994.

Wallach, Janet, and John Wallach. *Arafat: In the Eyes of the Beholder.* Rocklin, CA: Prima, 1991.

Archaeological Sites and Projects

The territory that has served as the battleground of the Arab-Israeli conflict is also one of the world's principal venues of archaeological excavation and research. The region formed a pathway for the diffusion of the human race from Africa and has yielded crucial evidence on the evolution of Neanderthals and modern humans and relations between them. As the bridge between North Africa and West Asia, it was also the site of cultural exchange and military struggle between the great ancient civilizations of Egypt and Mesopotamia. Above all, however, its archaeological fame and influence on the evolution of the discipline derive from its connection with the traditions of the three monotheistic peoples: Jews, Muslims, and Christians.

In the archaeological realm as in the political, the region has therefore been the subject of greater international scrutiny, press coverage, and popular interest than any other area of comparable size. Not surprisingly, it has often been hard to disentangle the two. Both Jews and Palestinians have based their claims to sovereignty on their historical presence on the land, the evidence for which has been archaeological as well as textual. As a result, both the findings and the nature of the discipline itself have become a zone of contention in the Arab-Israeli conflict. In recent years, however, archaeology has begun to engender cooperation as well.

The common assertion that Israel is the country with the greatest enthusiasm for archaeology, which forms a central part of its civil religion, contains elements of truth, but this needs to be qualified. Archaeology there came to mean not just excavation of specific artifacts and monuments but the entire culture of the ancient national past and values ascribed to it. To reduce Israeli archaeology to a simple extension of nationalism or to treat even that national dimension monolithically would, however, be to ignore the complexity of its social functions as well as its scientific achievements.

Although the physical remains of ancient civilization in the Holy Land had long attracted the interest of pilgrims and antiquarian scholars, archaeology there arose only in the 19th century in the form of biblical archaeology, the quest for physical and scientific evidence to reinforce a Christian faith under challenge from the new biblical higher criticism, which questioned the unity and historicity of the sacred texts, and from materialistic theories such as Darwinism. At the same time, archaeological exploration provided Western powers with cultural legitimacy and a physical foothold in a volatile region as the grip of the Ottoman Empire weakened in the late 1800s.

Given the rudimentary state of knowledge, much of the early work was topographical. American theologian Edward Robinson attempted to match biblical names with contemporary sites (in 1838 and 1852). Of particular importance were the undertakings sponsored by the British Palestine Exploration Fund (PEF), founded in 1865 and still active today: for example, Charles Warren's pioneering excavations around the Temple Mount (1867–1870) and the great Survey of Western Palestine (1871–1878).

A crucial problem was the inability to date archaeological finds precisely in the absence of corroborating inscriptions. The Egyptologist Flinders Petrie introduced scientific excavation at Tall al-Hasi (1890), identifying ceramic remains—the most common artifacts—according to the strata in which they lay and in relation to finds from other sites. In the generation prior to World War I, Western scholars applied new methods, albeit imperfectly, in major digs at biblical sites such as Gezer, Megiddo (the origin of Armageddon), Jericho, Samaria, and the Galilean synagogues and established archaeological institutions such as the American School of Oriental Research (ASOR), founded in 1900, that continue to shape the field.

During the British Mandate for Palestine archaeology flourished, growing both more ambitious and rigorous under the supervision of a new Department of Antiquities. Greater external support enabled extended undertakings such as the excavation of Megiddo by the Oriental Institute of the University of Chicago (1925–1939). The emphasis on biblical sites was typical of American researchers, whether secular or religious, but other major projects of the era involved prehistoric, Byzantine, and Crusader remains. The imposing Palestine Archaeological Museum (Rockefeller Museum, erected in 1938) in Jerusalem embodied the new importance of the field.

A specifically Jewish and Zionist archaeology arose only gradually, and the first such dig occurred in 1920. It defined itself in contrast to the foreign endeavors, although its focus and its organizations—notably, the Jewish Palestine Exploration Society (founded in 1920) and Hebrew University (founded in 1925)—and accompanying publications, many in Hebrew, were secular and modern, interested in biblical history but not religious truth. Archaeology not only underscored the claim to the land but also forged a common identity, capable of transcending the Diasporic experience by reconnecting Jews to the normality and dignity of past sovereignty. The few Jewish archaeologists generally operated on a modest scale, but excavations such as those at the Bet Alfa synagogue, with its representational Byzantine-era mosaics (begun in 1929), and the catacombs of Bet She'arim (excavated from 1936 to 1939) fired the public imagination, contributing to the centrality of archaeology as an element of national identity during the two decades on either side of independence.

The new Israeli state immediately created its own Department of Antiquities that took over from its predecessor, although the records of the latter remained in the Rockefeller Museum in Jordanian hands. Along with the Hebrew University and other inter-

Young people gaze at a model of Massada in the Israel Museum in Jerusalem, January 12, 1972. The museum is the nation's largest and includes one of the world's largest collections of biblical artifacts and Judaica. (Fritz Cohen/Israeli Government Press Office)

ested entities, the Department of Antiquities oversaw all archaeological endeavors. The department was first part of the Ministry of Labor and Construction and then became part of the Ministry of Education and Culture before acquiring independent status as the Israel Antiquities Authority in 1990.

The national hobby (as commentators invariably characterize it) manifested itself in television quiz shows, hiking and exploration (the Zionist doctrine of knowledge of the land), amateur collecting (often illicit), and volunteerism on digs. The attempt to introduce national epochal designations (e.g., Patriarchal) was short-lived, but archaeology figured prominently on Israeli coins, stamps, and travel posters. Indeed, the symbol of the state itself is not the modern Star of David but rather the menorah from the Temple of Jerusalem, one of the greatest lost archaeological objects.

A few oft-cited discoveries or undertakings captured the headlines and lasting attention. They include Eleazar Sukenik's purchase of portions of the Dead Sea scrolls on the eve of partition in 1947 and the high-profile excavations led by his son, Yigal Yadin, digs at Hazor (said to have been destroyed by Joshua and rebuilt by Solomon) in 1955–1958 and 1968, and the Judean Caves (1960–1961) and Masada (1963–1965), both sites associated with the revolts against Rome. The evolution of Masada as the ultimate symbol of

national and military determination—from Isaac Lamdan's 1920s poem to Yadin's ritual swearing-in of the armored corps on the site—is well known.

The 1967 Six-Day War both simplified and complicated archaeological affairs. The territories and collections of the former British Mandate were reunited. Israeli archaeologists suddenly had access to the scenes of the biblical narrative: Judea and Samaria (the West Bank) and the Sinai. Excavations in East Jerusalem revealed the topography of the ancient city, the architecture of Herod's Temple, and major structures dating from Byzantine, early Muslim Arab, and Crusader rule. The first systematic surveys of the West Bank began revising the picture of early Israelite life.

Paradoxically, at this time of greatest opportunity archaeology began to lose its centrality. It was no longer as compelling a source of legitimacy in a militarily strong state in which new generations could take their identity for granted. Originally a unifying force allowing the secular majority to identify with the Bible as history, archaeology now became a divisive one. Right-wing settlers appropriated it to advance their religious-nationalistic agenda. The ultraorthodox Jews became increasingly obstructionist, protesting supposed disturbance of human remains in order to flex their muscles in the ongoing struggle between religion and secularism. The

Caves near the ancient settlement of Qumran in the West Bank, where the Dead Sea Scrolls were discovered. (iStockPhoto.com)

shift is also reflected in attendance at annual archaeological conventions. In the 1960s, enthusiastic amateurs greatly outnumbered professionals. Today, the proportions are reversed.

Although the early Israeli archaeological profession, like its counterparts elsewhere, quite logically concentrated on the national past (not always subtly), it never did so exclusively, and the variety of projects and discourse has markedly increased. The vast majority of excavation permits do not involve biblical/Jewish sites. Now prehistoric archaeologists outnumber the biblical at Hebrew University.

Even where interest had colored the choice of project or interpretation, it was the robustness of the original data that permitted revision by new generations of more sophisticated and critical researchers. Scholars have questioned not just Josephus's account of mass suicide at Masada but also the circumstances that led their predecessors to accept it despite contradictory archaeological evidence. Even more important has been the thoroughgoing reexamination of biblical history.

Biblical archaeology, which dominated American scholarship during the heyday of the Israeli archaeology cult, was largely the creation of William Foxwell Albright, director of ASOR and professor of Semitic languages at Johns Hopkins University. He combined an exceptional command of Near Eastern cultures with new archae-

ological rigor in his quest to harmonize Scripture and history. The underlying historical truth of the Hebrew Bible was to support the higher truth of Christianity. Although Albright's long-dominant ceramic classification schemas and chronologies have been discarded, the method that he perfected, entailing the thoroughgoing integration of written and material evidence (texts and realia), transcended the limitations of both his findings and his ideology.

By the last third of the 20th century, archaeology had become more professional, technologically advanced, and interdisciplinary. Scholars more scrupulously separated faith and politics from science, even through more neutral or universalizing terminology. Thus, "Syro-Palestinian archeology" replaced "biblical archaeology," while "Middle Bronze Age" replaced "Patriarchal Age."

Until then, the picture of ancient Israel had still seemed fairly clear and familiar. Most mainstream theologians, biblical scholars, and archaeologists alike accepted some form of the German documentary hypothesis. That is, they recognized the Bible as the product of multiple human hands, assembled gradually, well after the events described. They understood it to be a mixture of history, literary adaptation, and myth, but most did not question the essential historicity of the narrative. Thus, we have the Patriarchs (18th century BC), Exodus and the conquest of Canaan (13th century BC), the creation of the monarchy (ca. 1010 BC), and the divided monarchy (Israel, Judah) and its destruction by the Babylonians (ca. 930–586 BC).

Because archaeological findings had confirmed many aspects of the biblical accounts, the assumption was that increased excavation and ever more refined methods of interpretation would close the gaps. When the gaps persisted, archaeology rather than supporting the Bible came to pose the greatest challenge to it. The episodes at the heart of debate are central to Jewish identity and history.

Whereas an absence of archaeological evidence for the lives of the nomadic Patriarchs was understandable, it was more problematic in the case of the public and dramatic events that followed. Although the presence of Semitic migrants or warriors in Egypt is documented, the telltale support for elements of the Exodus story is difficult to reconcile with the traditional dating. The belief in the enslavement and flight of an entire people cannot be sustained. The same holds for the Conquest narrative. Although a few cities mentioned display suggestive signs of violent destruction, others have none, and some—such as Jericho—were not even inhabited at the time.

The Late Bronze Age was, however, a period of upheaval around the Mediterranean, and new settlements sprang up in the Canaanite central hills region (including the West Bank) in the early Iron Age. Archaeologists developed several ultimately unpersuasive alternatives to the theory of wholesale invasion by a foreign people: a limited conquest, gradual settlement by peaceful infiltration, and a rebellion in which a new social group came to power. The consensus arising from the West Bank surveys and comparable data is that the Israelites were in fact Canaanites whose identity coalesced gradually from an amalgam of experiences and backgrounds (so-called indigenous origin and symbiosis models).

Scholars have long recognized that the biblical description of a vast Israelite empire stretching from the Euphrates to Egypt was hyperbole, but they remain sharply divided on the exact nature and extent of the realms of David and Solomon. The only consensus is that the monarchy was undoubtedly far more modest. Many archaeologists describe David and Solomon as regional chieftains rather than grand kings. A few question whether the monarchy was ever united. The 1993 discovery of the ninth-century BC Tel Dan inscription convinced all but the most diehard revisionists that David was a historical figure, but it cannot tell us more. The discovery in 2005 of a massive ancient structure in Jerusalem has not resolved the issue, either. The excavator confidently asserted it to be the long-sought palace of David, whereas other respected archaeologists deemed it more recent.

Ruins of an ancient synagogue at Bar'am in Upper Galilee, Israel. (Corel)

Given the paucity and ambiguity of evidence, researchers have taken up positions along a spectrum of opinions regarding the historicity of the Bible. Diametrically opposed to the beleaguered traditionalists are the increasingly influential revisionists—or, as their detractors have come to call them, biblical minimalists—associated in particular with the Copenhagen and Sheffield Schools (e.g., Thomas Thompson, Niels Peter Lemche, and Philip R. Davies). In their view, the Bible was written no earlier than during the Persian or even Hellenistic periods and is a self-referential fictitious work devoid of historical value. Scholars of biblical texts, they claim support from the new archaeology.

Most archaeologists occupy a broad middle ground. Two contending perspectives have commanded particular attention. Israel Finkelstein of Tel Aviv University, who codirects the new excavations at Megiddo and who conducted pioneering surveys of Iron Age settlements on the West Bank, proposes a provocative low chronology that shifts dates closer to the present. He and Neil Silberman interpret the Torah and Deuteronomistic history as literary creations of the seventh century, which, by depicting a glorious past and common identity, furthered the attempt of King Josiah of Judah to unite the two kingdoms. Perhaps still more representative of the majority of practitioners is William Dever, who directed excavations at the Canaanite city of Gezer during 1966–1971. One of the pioneering critics of Albright's theological and harmonizing approach, Dever contributed greatly to the newer, more skeptical attitude toward early biblical narratives. Nonetheless, he adheres to the more traditional chronology and insists that the Hebrew Bible remains a more concretely historical document. He believed that even the obviously fictionalized accounts draw upon older sources and can, in conjunction with archaeological data, shed light on the events they describe, not merely on the later world of their authors.

The most contentious issue is ultimately ethnicity. The debates turn on the interpretation of ambiguous and technical evidence, ranging from settlement plans and grain storage practices to pottery forms and decoration. The stakes of the debate, however, are high. If the Israelites were originally just Canaanites, then why, when, or to what extent can we speak of a distinct identity? It is here that politics has entered the picture.

The views of the minimalists and the new survey data figure prominently in the leitmotif of a nascent Palestinian archaeological narrative. The essence is reflected in the title of biblical scholar Keith Whitelam's *The Invention of Ancient Israel: The Silencing of Palestinian History* (1996). He argues that biased Western scholarship and Zionist doctrine and archaeology created out of Canaanites a mythical biblical Israel whose history needs to be moved from the center to the margins of a discourse rewritten as the history of ancient Palestinians. More recently, in *Facts on the Ground: Archaeological Practice and Territorial Self-Fashioning in Israeli Society* (2002), anthropologist Nadia Abu El-Haj portrayed Israeli archaeological culture as a colonial form of knowledge in the service of a settler-state bent on shaping public consciousness and the landscape to the needs of Zionism. Her avowedly postmodern and non-

polemical approach helped the book win plaudits for its exploration of the juncture of politics and archaeology.

Because Israel is a new nation, its process of identity construction occurred within recent memory and, like the virtues and injustices that accompanied its birth, remains in plain view rather than concealed by the mists of time. By ascribing to the putative flaws of Israeli archaeology a distinctive character and intentionality, the critique serves to delegitimize the state and its claim to moral authority, drawing a parallel between the purported usurpation of the past and usurpation of the land: suppression of memory and culture on the one hand and suppression of human rights on the other. From the Palestinian perspective, entire eras of history and archaeology are erased from tourism when Israel's history is constructed purely around the biblical period. Giving more attention to the later Muslim eras and the many deserted and unexplored sites that pertain to other figures would also be worthwhile for the sake of history. Abu El-Haj generated particular controversy with Zionists through her empathetic portrayal of Palestinian vandalism and looting of Jewish archaeological remains—including the destruction of the Tomb of Joseph in Nablus in 2000—as a form of resistance.

Archaeological activities in Jerusalem are the most sensitive. For Israelis, it is the site of their historic capital as well as the Temple (hence again the importance of the debates over the united monarchy). Palestinians have tended to view any Israeli undertakings in the city as Judaization and those in the vicinity of the Temple Mount/Haram al-Sharif area as a deliberate threat to the ownership and physical integrity of the complex and its mosques, which remain under the control of the Waqf (Muslim religious trust). Each side has charged the other with causing structural damage to the site through reckless excavation.

The fragility of the situation became all too evident in 1996. After acquiescing to the Waqf's construction of a new worship area in vaults of the Second Temple era under the Mount, the government of Israeli prime minister Benjamin Netanyahu opened an ancient Jewish tunnel running near the Western Wall. The incident provided Palestinian Authority (PA) president Yasser Arafat with an opportunity to remobilize the public, but the popular anger was genuine. Four days of violence resulted in 16 Israelis and 75 Palestinians dead, with 58 Israelis and more than 1,000 more Palestinians wounded. Controversy erupted anew after further construction under the vaults during 1999–2000. Israeli public figures denounced the Waqf for deliberate destruction or disregard of archaeological evidence, exemplified by the precipitous disposal of 13,000 tons of unexamined rubble.

Violence on the scale of the Tunnel Riots threatened to erupt again in early 2007 over access to the Mughrabi Gate, which, under the religious status quo agreements that had prevailed for four decades, was the only point of entry to the Temple Mount under Israeli control. It was used by both non-Muslim visitors and security forces. The Israel Antiquities Authority began legally required salvage excavations prior to erection of a bridge to replace an unsafe ramp damaged by an earthquake in 2004. Whereas some prominent Israeli archaeologists worried that construction jeopardized the Jerusalem Archaeological Park on which the pylons would stand, Arab and Islamic leaders saw a threat to Muslim sites on the Temple Mount itself. Reactions ranged from concern and criticism to charges of a conspiracy to destroy the mosques and resultant threats of a third intifada. (Ironically, the dig almost immediately uncovered major early Islamic structures.) Recognizing the danger of miscommunication and hoping to defuse the controversy, the government took the unusual steps of inviting inspectors from Muslim Turkey and setting up webcams at the construction site to allay any fears.

One corollary of heightened Arab-Muslim concern over Haram al-Sharif has been a tendency in Islamist and popular discourse to deny not just Jewish political claims but also the Jewish historical presence itself. Arafat's insistence that a Jewish temple never existed in Jerusalem was one of the factors that torpedoed the Camp David peace talks in the summer of 2000. The increasingly bitter struggle over archaeology is a logical outgrowth of the two intifadas, which marked the return from state-on-state (Arab-Israeli) warfare to the intercommunal (Palestinian-Jewish) form of the mandate era.

Although controversies such as these garner headlines, a less-told story is that of an emergent Palestinian archaeological profession and tentative cooperation with Israelis. Palestinian archaeological consciousness and institutions developed only recently, in part because ethnic identity tended to be defined by other means. Under the leadership of Albert Glock, the founding figure of Palestinian archaeology, an institute opened at Birzeit University in 1988, and although it faltered after his murder in 1992 and closed in 2003, other programs have arisen in the interim.

The establishment of the PA in the West Bank made fieldwork more feasible. Alongside the governmental antiquities authority, the Palestinian Association for Cultural Exchange (PACE, founded in 1996) and the Center for Architectural Conservation (RIWAQ, founded in 1991) work to preserve sites and inculcate public appreciation of the heritage, particularly Islamic architecture and vernacular village culture. The 1995 Israeli-Palestinian Interim Agreement regulated archaeological cooperation but could not defuse all tensions. Even when Israel relinquished sites, disposition of the artifacts themselves was set aside as a final-status issue, too difficult to resolve. On the other hand, the cooperation between teams of archaeologists from the University of Haifa and PACE, arising from the Wye River Agreement, persisted even during the Second Intifada (2000–2005).

Palestinian archaeology necessarily began by positioning itself in opposition to Israeli and biblical archaeology (at times tendentiously so) and is still in the process of defining its intellectual concerns and public role. Still, professionals on both sides of the Green Line acknowledge that the archaeological heritage of the region necessarily transcends any modern political boundaries and moreover offers mutual opportunities for tourism and economic development.

Archaeology can refine our scientific certainty in dating and classifying artifacts, but assigning meaning to them is ultimately a subjective act of interpretation. That archaeology often serves the ends of heritage as well as history—Israeli or Palestinian—may sometimes be cause for regret but should not occasion surprise. Certainly, the changing perspectives and priorities of the archaeological profession, as much as the finds themselves, are an undeniable part of the stories that it attempts to tell. A political solution to the Arab-Israeli conflict will have to resolve questions such as the ownership of artifacts. It will presumably also open the way to renewed dialogue about the past as well as the future.

JAMES WALD

See also

Al-Aqsa Mosque; Bible; Dome of the Rock; Genesis, Book of; Haram al-Sharif; Intifada, First; Intifada, Second; Jerusalem; Jerusalem, Old City of; Koran; Masada; Palestine, Pre-1918 History of; Religious Sites in the Middle East, Christian; Religious Sites in the Middle East, Jewish; Religious Sites in the Middle East, Muslim; Waqf; West Bank; Western Wall; Wye River Agreement; Zionism

References

Abu El-Haj, Nadia. *Facts on the Ground: Archaeological Practice and Territorial Self-Fashioning in Israeli Society.* Chicago: University of Chicago Press, 2002.
Ben-Yehuda, Nachman. *Sacrificing Truth: Archaeology and the Myth of Masada.* Amherst, NY: Humanity Books, 2002.
Dever, William. *What Did the Biblical Writers Know and When Did They Know It? What Archaeology Can Tell Us about the Reality of Ancient Israel.* Grand Rapids, MI, and Cambridge, UK: Eerdmans, 2001.
Finkelstein, Israel, and Neil Asher Silberman. *The Bible Unearthed: Archaeology's New Vision of Ancient Israel and the Origin of Its Sacred Texts.* New York: Free Press, 2001.
Joffe, Alexander H. "Review of Nadia Abu El-Haj, *Facts on the Ground.*" *Journal of Near Eastern Studies* (2005): 297–304.
Mazar, Amihay. *Archaeology of the Land of the Bible, 10,000–586 B.C.E.* New York: Doubleday, 1990.
Pollock, Susan, and Reinhard Bernbeck, eds. *Archaeologies of the Middle East: Critical Perspectives.* Malden, MA: Blackwell, 2005.
Silberman, Neil Asher. *Digging for God and Country: Exploration, Archeology, and the Secret Struggle for the Holy Land, 1799–1917.* New York: Knopf, 1982.
Silberman, Neil Asher, and David Small, eds. *The Archaeology of Israel: Constructing the Past, Interpreting the Present.* Journal for the Study of the Old Testament Supplement Series 237. Sheffield, UK: Sheffield Academic, 1997.

Arens, Moshe
Born: December 27, 1925

Israeli Likud Party politician and diplomat who served as ambassador to the United States (1981–1983), defense minister (1983–1984, 1990–1992, 1999), foreign minister (1988–1990), and minister without portfolio (1984–1988). Moshe Arens was born on December 27, 1925, in Kovno (Kaunas), Lithuania. He immigrated with his family to the United States in 1939. During World War II he served in the U.S. Army Corps of Engineers and represented Betar,

Israeli defense minister Moshe Arens answers a reporter's question during a press conference, April 27, 1999. (U.S. Department of Defense)

the youth organization of Vladimir Jabotinsky's Revisionist Zionism, in North America. Arens earned a bachelor's degree in mechanical engineering in 1947 from the Massachusetts Institute of Technology and joined Menachem Begin's Irgun Tsvai Leumi (National Military Organization) at the beginning of the Israeli War of Independence (1948–1949). Afterward, Arens settled in the Mevo Betar area southwest of Jerusalem.

Arens returned to the United States in 1951 to complete a master's degree in aeronautical engineering (1953) and then worked in jet engine development in the United States before returning to Israel in 1957 as an associate professor of aeronautical engineering at the Technion-Israel Institute of Technology in Haifa. He joined Israel Aircraft Industries (IAI) in 1962 and as vice president for engineering was in charge of missile development and the Kfir and Lavi fighter jet projects.

Arens was one of the founding members of Begin's Herut (Freedom) Party in 1948. Herut merged into the conservative coalition Likud Party in 1973. In 1974 he was elected as a Likud member to the Knesset (Israeli parliament). Begin became the prime minister

(1977–1983) when Likud won the 1977 elections. Arens voted against the 1978 Camp David Accords but ultimately supported the Israel-Egypt Peace Treaty of 1979 as a fait accompli, notwithstanding his initial opposition to it as giving away too much. Although Arens was denied the position of defense minister in 1980 due in part to his opposition to the Camp David Accords, Begin appointed him Israel's ambassador to the United States, a post Arens held from 1981 to 1983. He served as defense minister from 1983 to 1984 after the Kahan Commission found his predecessor, Ariel Sharon, guilty of negligence in the massacres at Lebanon's Sabra and Shatilla refugee camps in 1982.

Arens served as a minister without portfolio during the national unity coalition under Shimon Peres (1984–1986) and again during the national unity coalition under Yitzhak Shamir (1986–1988). Arens then served as minister of foreign affairs from 1988 to 1990 and as minister of defense from 1990 to 1992.

Although Arens supposedly retired from politics after Likud's 1992 election loss, he wrote *Broken Covenant: American Foreign Policy and the Crisis between the U.S. and Israel* (1994), was one of the chief opponents of the 1998 Wye River Agreement, and unsuccessfully challenged then–Prime Minister Benjamin Netanyahu, his former Washington ambassadorial assistant, for the leadership of Likud in 1999. Netanyahu, whose appointment as Israel's ambassador to the United Nations (UN) (1984–1988) had been arranged by Arens, appointed him defense minister from January to May 1999. Arens again retired from politics following Likud's loss in May 1999 to Ehud Barak's One Israel Party.

Arens serves on the International Advisory Board of the Council on Foreign Relations, on the board of governors of the Technion-Israel Institute of Technology (1999–present), and as chairman of the board of governors at the College of Judea and Samaria (1999–present), located in the West Bank settlement city of Ariel. He remains active in Likud; opposed the Gaza withdrawal of 2005 and Israel's broader disengagement policy with the Palestinian Authority (PA), believing Judea and Samaria (West Bank) to be part of Israel; and supports Likud's Rebels faction led by Technion alumnus and Knesset member Dr. Uzi Landau.

RICHARD M. EDWARDS

See also

Aircraft, Kfir Fighter; Aircraft, Lavi Fighter-Bomber; Begin, Menachem; Camp David Accords; Irgun Tsvai Leumi; Israel-Egypt Peace Treaty; Likud Party; Netanyahu, Benjamin; Peres, Shimon; Shamir, Yitzhak; Wye River Agreement

References

Arens, Moshe. *Broken Covenant: American Foreign Policy and the Crisis between the U.S. and Israel.* New York: Simon and Schuster, 1995.

Arian, Asher. *Politics in Israel: The Second Generation.* Rev. ed. Chatham, NJ: Chatham House, 1989.

Reich, Bernard, and Gershon R. Kieval. *Israel: Land of Tradition and Conflict.* 2nd ed. Boulder, CO: Westview, 1993.

Simon, Merrill. *Moshe Arens: Statesman and Scientist Speaks Out.* Middle Island, NY: Dean Books, 1988.

Arif, Arif al-
Born: 1891
Died: July 30, 1973

Palestinian activist, politician, author, and journalist. Arif al-Arif was born in Jerusalem in 1891 and pursued studies in Istanbul. His academic career was cut short when he was drafted into the Ottoman-Turkish Army during World War I. Captured by Russian forces, he was held in a prison camp in Siberia for three years and finally escaped during the Russian Revolution.

Al-Arif made his way back to Palestine and there began to pursue a writing career. A militant Palestinian nationalist (although he eschewed violence), he was strongly opposed to Zionism and the creation of any type of homeland for Jews in Palestine. In 1919 he began editing Palestine's first official nationalist newspaper, *Southern Syria,* that had been founded and was partly financed by Muhammad Hasan al-Budayri, a Palestinian lawyer.

As editor, al-Arif honed his political views, which were a mixture of Pan-Arabism, Palestinian nationalism, and Pan-Syrianism. In 1920 he was arrested during a series of riots in and around Jerusalem. British authorities sought to convict him of fomenting the revolt, but he escaped to Syria before trial. Haj Amin al-Husseini, the mufti of Jerusalem, had also been charged with inciting the riots and went with al-Arif to Syria. Sometime later, al-Arif was sentenced in absentia to 10 years in prison for his alleged connection to the uprising.

The British shut down al-Arif's newspaper and forbade the publication of any inflammatory newspapers or periodicals. Al-Arif did not return to Palestine until 1929. British authorities did not pursue the earlier charges and sentence against him, so he again began to write while rehabilitating his reputation. He was so successful in this endeavor that he was appointed to a civil service position with the British Mandate authority in 1933 and worked in various capacities for it until 1948.

In 1948, with the commencement of the Israeli War of Independence (1948–1949) and the creation of the State of Israel, al-Arif moved to Transjordan, where he held a ministerial-level post in the Transjordanian government. In 1950 he became the mayor of East Jerusalem. He held this position until 1955. He continued to write, and in 1963 he became the director of Jerusalem's Rockefeller Museum. He wrote many essays, articles, and books during his life, perhaps the most notable of which are *Law and Legend, History of Beersheba and Its Tribes, History of Gaza, Nakba and the Lost Paradise,* and *History of Jerusalem.* Al-Arif died in Ramallah on July 30, 1973.

PAUL G. PIERPAOLI JR.

See also
Husseini, Haj Amin al-; Literature of the Arab-Israeli Wars; Pan-Arabism

References
Hadawi, Sami. *Bitter Harvest: Palestine between 1914–1967.* New York: New World Press, 1967.
Jayyusi, Salma Khadra, ed. *Anthology of Modern Palestinian Literature.* New York: Columbia University Press, 1992.

Arish
See El Arish; El Arish Scheme

Armored Personnel Carriers

Armored personnel carriers (APCs) are wheeled or tracked vehicles designed to transport infantry troops to the battlefield. They are a vital component of modern combined-arms doctrine, which recognizes that armored fighting vehicles, primarily main battle tanks, require infantry and artillery support for maximum battlefield effectiveness. APCs are not nearly as well armored as tanks but typically have enough defensive plating to withstand small arms fire and most shell fragments. Since the 1970s, a general transformation has occurred in the design and use of APCs with the emergence of infantry fighting vehicles (IFVs). IFVs, like APCs, are designed to deliver infantry to the battlefield, but IFVs also carry some degree of offensive firepower, and many include a limited anti-tank capability.

The earliest APCs were modified tanks designed to carry additional personnel. During the first use of tanks in World War I, infantry frequently rode into battle mounted upon the exterior of the tanks. This proved exceptionally dangerous to the exposed troops, who had none of the protection offered by the tank's armor plating. The British soon introduced a new tank design that included a small passenger compartment where troops could wait for the tank to break through enemy lines, then exit the vehicle to exploit any success.

By World War II, Axis and Allied armies had developed vehicles that afforded some protection to troops while also keeping up with armored columns. These vehicles, which typically ran on both tracks and tires (and were thus called half-tracks), facilitated the development of mechanized and motorized infantry units that operated in conjunction with armored forces. The U.S. M-3 half-track had a crew of 3 and was designed to transport 10 fully equipped infantrymen. It saw service during the Arab-Israeli wars with the Israel Defense Forces (IDF) in a variety of configurations.

During the Cold War, the United States and the Soviet Union continued to develop APCs. In 1959 the United States began production of the M-113, the most widely used APC in history. The M-113 is essentially an aluminum box frame on tracks, capable of carrying its 2-man crew and 10 infantry soldiers. Armament varies but usually consists of one .50-caliber and one 7.62-mm machine gun. More than 80,000 M-113s have been built to date, and they are used by more than 50 nations, including Egypt, Iraq, Kuwait, Saudi

Egyptian soldiers man M-2 .50-caliber machine guns atop M-113 armored personnel carriers during a demonstration for visiting dignitaries, December 1, 1990. (U.S. Department of Defense)

Arabia, and Israel. The Soviet Union developed the BTR-40, a wheeled APC, and exported thousands to the Middle East, where they entered service in Iran, Iraq, and Syria. It had a crew of 2 and carried 8 infantrymen. Usual armament was a single 7.62-mm machine gun.

IFVs have also played an extensive role in Arab-Israeli warfare. The Soviet Union in 1967 introduced the first IFV, the BMP-1. It had a crew of 2 and could carry 9 infantrymen. Armament included a 73-mm main gun and a Sagger antitank missile as well as one 7.62-mm gun. Initially hailed as a revolutionary new concept, in practice the BMP-1 proved about equal to its Western equivalents, such as the American-built M-2/M-3 Bradley. The Bradley carries a crew of 3 and 6 infantrymen. It mounts a single 25-mm Bush Master chain gun, one 7.62-mm machine gun, and two TOW missile launchers. Both types of IFVs have been exported to the Middle East, where they have faced each other in combat.

The use of APCs and IFVs in Arab-Israeli combat has grown exponentially. In the Israeli War of Independence (1948–1949), Israel began the war with virtually no armored vehicles. The invading Arab armies included small numbers of tanks but virtually no APCs. By the end of the war, each side employed substantial num-

bers of armored cars, and the IDF had about 280 American-built half-tracks. During the 1956 Suez Crisis, both Egypt and Israel possessed hundreds of foreign-built APCs. Israel used its mechanized forces to transport infantry across the Sinai Peninsula, maintaining a support role for attacking IDF columns. Egyptian APCs and armor units coordinated poorly, often remaining immobile and susceptible to aerial attacks from the Israeli Air Force. The Israeli conquest and occupation of the Sinai clearly demonstrated the utility of APCs when used as part of a larger armored offensive.

In the June 1967 Six-Day War, all of the combatants maintained large numbers of APCs. Egypt's 900 tanks were supported by 1,100 APCs. They were opposed by 700 Israeli tanks and an equal number of Israeli APCs. Once again, the IDF leadership proved more tactically adept than their Egyptian counterparts, particularly in the application of armored warfare. Well-coordinated IDF columns attacked and bypassed Egyptian armored units, outracing the Egyptians to the mountain passes in the western Sinai and preventing an Egyptian retreat across the Suez Canal. Israeli air superiority demonstrated the vulnerability of APCs to aerial attack, and hundreds of Egyptian vehicles were destroyed by relentless air strikes. Ironically, by destroying the majority of Egypt's armored vehicles, Israel forced Egypt to learn the tactical lessons of modern armored warfare and to seek the assistance of the Soviet Union in planning and equipping for the next conflict.

In 1973, war again erupted between Israel and its neighbors. The Yom Kippur War demonstrated that the Arab armies, and Egypt's in particular, had learned the value of combined-arms operations in support of armored units. On the southern front, Egypt created a massive antiair network to neutralize Israel's air superiority, a key factor in the two previous wars. Under the protective umbrella of surface-to-air missiles (SAMs), Egyptian ground forces slowly advanced into the Sinai Peninsula and engaged their Israeli opponents. During this conflict, the Egyptian infantry forces, mounted in APCs, were augmented by easily portable Sagger antitank missiles. In the preceding six years Israel had grown increasingly contemptuous of its enemies, and when the IDF launched an armored counterattack against the advancing Egyptian forces, it did not include sufficient infantry or artillery in support of its tanks. The Israeli tanks were devastated by Egyptian antitank infantry units, which had advanced in APCs along with the Egyptian armored columns. When the Israelis abruptly changed their tactics on October 15, 1973, they managed to counterattack, finally using their mechanized forces to full potential.

In the fighting along the Syrian border on the Golan Heights, both Israel and the Arab belligerents used APCs and tanks in coordinated assaults. That region's uneven terrain was not as ideal for armored warfare as the flat desert of the Sinai, and thus the rapid advances and counterattacks of the southern front were not replicated in the region. Interestingly, by the end of the war Israeli forces had captured hundreds of enemy tanks, primarily of the Soviet-designed T-55 model. The IDF chose to convert many of them into APCs, renaming them Achzarits. The resulting vehicles made excellent APCs out of an obsolete tank design, which, despite its age, had considerably more armor protection than a contemporary APC. The Achzarit remains one of the most effective APCs in the world. In 1984 the IDF also developed the Puma heavy APC. It is based on the British Centurion tank chassis and features exceptional armored protection, always a primary consideration for Israeli tanks and APCs.

PAUL J. SPRINGER

See also

Armored Warfare Doctrine; Israeli War of Independence, Overview; Sinai Campaign; Six-Day War; Suez Crisis; Yom Kippur War

References

Citino, Robert Michael. *Armored Forces: History and Sourcebook.* Westport, CT: Greenwood, 1994.

Foss, Christopher F., ed. *The Encyclopedia of Tanks and Armored Fighting Vehicles.* San Diego: Thunder Bay, 2002.

Hogg, Ian V. *Armour in Conflict: The Design and Tactics of Armored Fighting Vehicles.* London: Jane's, 1980.

Armored Warfare Doctrine

Armored warfare doctrine is the guiding set of principles used by military commanders to deploy mobile ground forces to greatest effect. Modern armored warfare doctrine centers on the concept of combined arms, integrating infantry, artillery, and airpower in support of armored units to multiply the overall effectiveness of the force on the battlefield. It also requires concentration of mass, the placing of an overwhelming number of armored fighting vehicles (AFVs) and tanks at a single decisive point on the battlefield to achieve a breakthrough in the enemy's lines that can then be exploited by follow-on forces.

The superiority of combined-arms operations, rather than armored-pure forces operating independently, has been clearly demonstrated on the battlefield repeatedly in recent history. AFVs are effective offensive systems, combining speed, firepower, and mobility into a single platform. Yet AFVs are vulnerable not only to the firepower of other tanks but also to direct and indirect artillery fire, to man-portable antitank weapons such as missiles and rockets, and to air attack. The requirement to transport infantry forces with the tanks so that the two arms provide mutual support led directly to the development of half-tracks, armored personnel carriers (APCs), and infantry fighting vehicles (IFVs). Self-propelled guns and tank destroyers also developed in response to the challenges of the modern battlefield.

The principle of concentrating at a single decisive point rather than committing combat power piecemeal along the battle line was widely recognized by tacticians long before the advent of armored vehicles. German military theorist Carl von Clausewitz (1780–1831) noted that Napoleon's tactics were based on an assault by superior forces upon the decisive point that would then lead to the collapse of the enemy's center of gravity.

Armored forces give the advantages of speed, shock, and fluidity to the modern commander, allowing him or her to punch holes in the enemy line and move rapidly against vital enemy nodes at operational depth. The first true armored vehicles appeared on the battlefield in 1916 during World War I. The initial British tanks were armored boxes on treads and moved at approximately four miles per hour. They were mechanically unreliable and only thinly armored. British doctrine required tanks to be evenly distributed along the battlefront to facilitate an advance across a broad front.

The early tanks moved slowly, and infantry could easily follow in their wake to exploit breaks in the enemy trench line. The armor plating on the early tanks provided protection from small-arms fire and shell fragments only. They could not withstand a direct hit from even light artillery. Their slow speed made the early tanks easy targets for enemy gunners, and mechanical unreliability sharply reduced the tanks' operational availability.

Initially there was little understanding of the need for tanks to work in close coordination with infantry and artillery. During the period between the world wars military theorists including J. F. C. Fuller and Basil Liddell Hart of Great Britain, Heinz Guderian of Germany, and Adna Chafee of the United States advanced revolutionary but seriously flawed concepts of the potential of armored warfare. Manufacturing processes, meanwhile, became more refined, lowering the weight of the armor while increasing its effectiveness.

The Israel Defense Forces' Armored Corps, including tank and infantry units, in training exercises in the Negev Desert, October 9, 1954. The successful execution of armored warfare doctrine requires that armor, infantry, artillery, and airpower work in tandem. (Israeli Government Press Office)

In the 1920s and 1930s, three major schools of thought emerged about the best way to use tanks on the battlefield. In Britain and France, tank designers split new tanks into two categories: infantry tanks and cavalry tanks. Infantry tanks were designed primarily as support weapons. They carried heavy armor and increasingly powerful main armament. The massive weight of the infantry tanks sacrificed mobility and speed for protection and firepower, but these tanks only needed enough battlefield speed to keep pace with a dismounted infantryman.

Cavalry tanks were designed to replace horse cavalry units. They were fast and mobile but poorly armored and lightly armed. According to the contemporary theorists, they were best used for screening and reconnaissance missions, capable of attacking deep against the enemy's lines of communications.

Pre–World War II American tanks followed the cavalry pattern, and American theorists did not view the tank as an antitank weapon. Instead, they believed that artillery was the main counter to an enemy armored force. Germany, on the other hand, viewed the tank as more of an integrated system. German tank designs increasingly combined the firepower of infantry tanks with the mobility of cavalry tanks to produce a vehicle capable of decisive action on the battlefield. Those tanks were the forerunners of the modern main battle tank (MBT).

The key German advantage of the interwar years was not the design of their tanks or the production of huge numbers. Rather, it was the evolution of an armored warfare doctrine centered on the principle that armored combat vehicles should be concentrated at a decisive point rather than being deployed piecemeal throughout the force.

There were two primary reasons that the Germans looked at tanks differently than other armies in the interwar period. First, the Germans had paid a heavy price for completely misreading the potential of the tank during World War I, and history has shown clearly that defeat in warfare is one of the strongest incentives to military innovation. Second, German artillery in World War I had been so devastating that the Versailles Treaty placed severe restrictions on the amount and size of the artillery allowed to the postwar Reichswehr. Denied adequate artillery firepower, the Germans decided to build it into the tank and also to rely heavily on close air support from the Luftwaffe, especially in the form of the dive-bomber.

A great deal has been written about German armored operations in World War II, the so-called doctrine of Blitzkrieg. Unfortunately, much of what is now widely accepted about Blitzkrieg is little more than myth. Rather than operating from the start with combined-arms teams, the Germans in the early campaigns of the war also led with tanks and followed with infantry. They developed the combined arms Kampfgruppen only after the French campaign in 1940.

The tank and dive-bomber combination worked fairly well in the relatively brief campaigns of 1939 and 1940 but finally showed its weakness when the Germans committed to an extended campaign in the Soviet Union. In the vast expanses of the Steppes, where the Luftwaffe was severely restricted by the weather and could not be everywhere over the battlefield at once, the Germans did not have the conventional tube artillery to fall back on for fire support. By the time the Allies landed in Western Europe in 1944, the Germans had completely lost control of the air, and again the lack of artillery to support their tanks cost them dearly.

Much of the terrain on which the Arab-Israeli wars has been fought is flat and open desert and therefore ideal for armored operations. During the Israeli War of Independence (1948–1949), the Israel Defense Forces (IDF) began the conflict with no tanks. The invading armies of Egypt, Iraq, Lebanon, Syria, and Transjordan all had handfuls of armored vehicles of some form. Egyptian forces included World War II vintage British Valentine and Matilda tanks. The Arab armies committed a total of about 45 tanks to the war. The Arabs, however, failed to coordinate their forces, which allowed the IDF to shift its forces where necessary to parry thrusts. As the war progressed, the IDF was able to import heavy weapons, primarily

from Czechoslovakia. By the end of the war the IDF had some 15 tanks and 280 half-tracks in service.

During the 1956 Suez Crisis and Sinai Campaign, IDF commanders demonstrated a thorough understanding of armored warfare principles. Operations on the Sinai Peninsula followed the classic patterns of bypassing enemy strong points and attacking them from the rear, as at Abu Ageila.

The June 1967 Six-Day War pitted a large Arab coalition against Israel, which by this time had acquired a large number of somewhat obsolescent main battle tanks, primarily from the United States and Great Britain. The Israelis anticipated an Arab attack and launched a preemptive air strike designed to destroy enemy air forces on the ground before following up with an armored attack. Although the Arab belligerents could field 250,000 troops and almost 2,000 tanks, their lack of a unified command structure once again caused them insurmountable difficulties.

The Six-Day War is one of the clearest examples of the vulnerability of armored forces without adequate air defense cover from attack aircraft, particularly in open terrain. Israel once more made a series of armored advances across the Sinai, bypassing Egyptian troop concentrations and striking the rear areas.

The Egyptians belatedly realized that the IDF was attempting to occupy the mountain passes and trap Egyptian armored units

Israeli aircraft provide cover for infantry moving into a forward battle zone in the Golan Heights on August 10, 1973, during the Yom Kippur War. (Israeli Government Press Office)

within reach of IDF aircraft. The blocking action was only partially successful, but Egyptian president Gamal Abdel Nasser later admitted that the Egyptian Army lost 80 percent of its equipment in the Sinai.

Once Egypt was defeated, IDF armored units shifted to deal with Syria and Jordan in turn. At the end of the war, Israeli forces occupied the Sinai Peninsula, the Golan Heights, and the West Bank of the Jordan River, including East Jerusalem. Their success, however, was as much the result of the ineptitude of their opponents as it was IDF tactical skill.

In the October 1973 Yom Kippur War, Egypt and Syria launched a surprise attack, this time catching the Israelis off guard. The Arab nations, particularly Egypt, had learned a great deal about armored warfare in only six years. Drawing upon advice and supplies from the Soviet Union, Egypt established a massive antiaircraft network of guns and missiles along the Suez Canal to neutralize IDF air superiority and protect Egyptian ground forces.

The Egyptian Army also applied combined-arms principles to its planning, sending an unprecedented number of infantry antitank weapons into the field. Contemporary observers noted that one-third of Egyptian infantry troops carried some form of antitank weapon. When Egyptian units crossed the Suez Canal and overran the IDF's Bar-Lev Line, they dug in and prepared for the predictable IDF armored counterattack. The IDF tanks raced ahead of their accompanying infantry and directly into the teeth of the Egyptian antitank defenses.

With no accompanying infantry and little supporting fire to neutralize the Egyptian antitank weapons, the Israelis learned the same bitter combined-arms lesson that the Germans learned in the Soviet Union during World War II. The IDF commanders, expecting a repeat of the 1967 successes, were slow to realize the significance of the mounting casualty reports, and IDF tank losses quickly mounted.

By October 14, however, the Egyptians were under extreme pressure from their Syrian allies to resume offensive operations in the Sinai to ease the desperate Syrian situation on the Golan Heights. Moving out from under their own air defense umbrella, the Egyptians launched a head-on assault against IDF tanks in protected firing positions. The result was the loss of hundreds of Egyptian tanks in a single day. Israeli tanks and infantry then advanced together to the Suez Canal. The infantry neutralized antitank and antiair defenses, while the tanks struck at Egyptian armored forces and prepared positions. On October 15, IDF troops crossed the Suez Canal.

On the Golan Heights, 2,000 Syrian tanks attacked fewer than 200 IDF tanks. The terrain was not conducive to the type of open-maneuver warfare typical of the Sinai. Israeli armored units fought a desperate delaying action until the IDF could mobilize and deploy its reserve forces. Successfully blunting the Syrian offensive, the Israelis then launched a synchronized counteroffensive and pushed into Syria to within artillery range of Damascus.

Ironically, the IDF has always looked to the World War II German Wehrmacht as its role model for tactical and operational doctrine and for battlefield command and control procedures. Indeed, there was much worthy of emulating in terms of pure military effectiveness. The Israelis, however, drew too many false lessons from their apparently easy victory in 1967 and made the same mistake as the Germans in concluding that tanks and tactical airpower almost alone were the keys to success in modern maneuver armored warfare.

Like the Wehrmacht, the IDF came to discount to a degree the value of infantry and to discount almost completely the value of tube artillery. Both armies paid a heavy price for that mistake, but the Israelis survived the 1973 war and afterward modified their doctrine and force structure accordingly. The initial results of the 2006 war in Lebanon, however, seemed to indicate that the Israelis had once again managed to delude themselves into believing the great myth of 20th-century warfare that ground wars can be won from the air.

The single most important lesson of armored warfare is that no single weapons system or arm can do it all. Efficiency and effectiveness are not the same things, especially in military operations. The key to military effectiveness is redundancy and overlapping capabilities. As powerful a weapon as the modern tank is, it can only achieve its full battlefield potential as part of a fully integrated combined-arms team that includes infantry, field and air defense artillery, airpower, communications, and robust logistics.

PAUL J. SPRINGER AND DAVID T. ZABECKI

See also

Armored Personnel Carriers; Israeli War of Independence, Overview; Sinai Campaign; Six-Day War; Suez Crisis; Tank Warfare; Tanks; Yom Kippur War

References

Brown, Jeremy K. *Warfare in the 21st Century*. New York: H. W. Wilson, 2003.

Citino, Robert Michael. *Armored Forces: History and Sourcebook*. Westport, CT: Greenwood, 1994.

Frieser, Karl-Heinz. *The Biltzkrieg Legend*. Annapolis, MD: Naval Institute Press, 2005.

Hogg, Ian V. *Armour in Conflict: The Design and Tactics of Armored Fighting Vehicles*. London: Jane's, 1980.

House, Jonathan M. *Toward Combined Arms Warfare: A Survey of 20th Century Tactics, Doctrine, and Organization*. Fort Leavenworth, KS: U.S. Army Command and General Staff College, 1984.

Kelly, Orr. *King of the Killing Zone*. New York: Norton, 1989.

Macksey, Kenneth, and John H. Batchelor. *Tank: A History of the Armoured Fighting Vehicle*. New York: Scribner, 1974.

Wright, Patrick. *Tank: The Progress of a Monstrous War Machine*. Reprint ed. New York: Viking, 2002.

Arms Sales, International

Throughout the 20th century and into the 21st century, various world powers have used arms sales as a means to gain favor and

Prime Minister Levi Eshkol and Deputy Defense Minister Shimon Peres of Israel inspect a Hawk missile battery at Fort Bliss, El Paso, Texas, June 8, 1964. (Moshe Pridan/Israeli Government Press Office)

influence in the Middle East. The immense wealth generated by oil sales in the aftermath of World War II accelerated this trend as the region became one of the most heavily militarized areas of the world and accounted for the largest share of the world's arms trade. Ultimately, the high concentration of weapons heightened tensions and led to arms races between Israel and the Arab states.

During World War II, both the Axis and Allied powers tried to gain allies in the Middle East through military aid and arms sales. In the immediate aftermath of the war, the increasing importance of oil and the geostrategic importance of the area led the United States to grow increasingly involved in the region's security. The 1947 Truman Doctrine signaled a commitment by the United States to provide military aid to states facing communist insurgencies. By 1947, the United States had formal security commitments with regional states including Saudi Arabia, Iran, and Turkey. As the bipolar Cold War struggle progressed, the United States and the Soviet Union used arms sales as a means to secure allies and gain influence. The military conflict in 1948–1949 that accompanied the creation of Israel led that country and its Arab neighbors to seek ever-larger and more sophisticated weaponry.

Throughout the period of the Cold War, the United States and the Soviet Union were the main arms suppliers to the Middle East.

Great Britain and France were also significant sellers, but after their participation, along with Israel, in the abortive 1956 invasion of the Sinai Peninsula and Suez Canal, Arab states led by Egypt boycotted sales from the former colonial powers. Meanwhile, the United States emerged as the main supplier of weapons to Israel and Iran. However, U.S. manufacturers often faced restrictions on arms sales. These constraints included prohibitions on the sale of the most advanced technology and limitations on sales to states likely to use the weapons against Israel. One result was that the Soviet Union came to be the chief supplier of weapons to such confrontational states as Egypt and Syria.

In the 1970s, European states—mainly France, Italy, West Germany, and Britain—began to regain market share among the Arab states. In 1975, Egypt, Qatar, Saudi Arabia, and the United Arab Emirates each contributed $260 million to create the Arab Organization for Industrialization (AOI). The main goal of the AOI was to create a Pan-Arab body to coordinate weapons development and purchases as well as arms manufacturing. Arab leaders hoped that the AOI would give Arab states military and technological superiority over Israel. The AOI initiated a number of projects with European states, including Anglo-Arab joint manufacturing of Lynx helicopters and Franco-Arab production of parts for the Mirage and Alphajet aircraft. The AOI ceased to function when Egypt's partners withdrew from the organization in protest of the 1978 Camp David Accords and the 1979 Israel-Egypt Peace Treaty. Nevertheless, European states were able to take advantage of their contacts and increase their share of the arms market in the Middle East.

U.S. arms sales were further undercut by the 1979 Iranian Revolution. Iran had been one of the top importers of U.S. arms, but after the overthrow of Mohammad Reza Shah Pahlavi, Iran turned to the Soviet Union to purchase arms and weapons. In the 1980s, Saudi Arabia and Israel remained the main purchasers of U.S. weaponry. However, even the Saudis began to seek other suppliers during the period. In 1985, domestic supporters of Israel were able to block the sale of McDonnell-Douglas F-15 Eagle fighter aircraft and Stinger missiles to Saudi Arabia. In response, the Saudis initiated a series of lucrative arms deals with Britain. The deals began

Arms Imports to Selected Middle Eastern and North African Countries (1970–1974)

Country	Main Supplier(s)	% of Country's Total Imports (1970–1974)
Algeria	France	52%
Egypt	Soviet Union	98%
Iran	United States	60%
Iraq	Soviet Union	94%
Israel	United States	97%
Libya	France	67%
Morocco	United States	69%
Saudi Arabia	United States	51%
Syria	Soviet Union	95%
Tunisia	France	96%

A French-built Egyptian SA-342 Gazelle helicopter lands near a Soviet-built tank during exercises at Cairo West Air Base, al Qahirah, Egypt, in December 1981. (U.S. Department of Defense)

with the 1986 al-Yamamah agreement in which the Saudis purchased $10 billion in arms, including 72 Panavia Tornado aircraft and 60 training aircraft. The al-Yamamah agreement was followed by a Saudi-French deal to purchase helicopters and missiles. The subsequent refusal of the United States to sell the latest version of the M-1 Abrams main battle tank led nations such as the United Arab Emirates to instead purchase French Leclerc main battle tanks.

By 1989, American and Soviet arms sales to the region were roughly equal (at about $2 billion annually), although U.S. sales remained concentrated on Israel, Egypt, and Saudi Arabia. Through the 1980s and 1990s, the United States supplied approximately 60 percent of Saudi arms imports and 90 percent of Israel's imported weapons. Combined West European sales were about two-thirds that of either of the superpowers. Between 1988 and 1991, U.S. sales to the Persian Gulf region alone amounted to $8.1 billion, while Soviet sales were $8.2 billion.

With the end of the Cold War and the collapse of the Soviet Union in 1991, the United States began to dominate arms sales and weapons transfers to the Middle East. Between 1992 and 1995, U.S. sales to the Middle East ballooned to $15.8 billion, while Russian sales were $1.9 billion. Throughout the 1990s, the United States supplied close to 50 percent of the arms and weapons imported into the Middle East.

The expansion of U.S. sales was mainly the result of the demise of the Soviet Union and the inability of the subsequent Russian arms industry to maintain production and develop new weapons and military technology. In addition, during the 1991 Persian Gulf War, there emerged the perception that U.S. weapons were superior to the Soviet-style weapons used by Iraqi forces. Consequently, many countries in the region, especially the Persian Gulf states, sought to replace Soviet-era weaponry with American-made weapons. Following the war, the United States negotiated large contracts to sell main battle tanks, aircraft, helicopters, and Patriot antimissile systems to Bahrain, Israel, Kuwait, Oman, Saudi Arabia, and the United Arab Emirates. However, restrictions on the sale of certain technology continued to constrain U.S. sales. For instance, the United States sold older M-60A3 main battle tanks to Bahrain and Oman instead of the newer M-1A2 Abrams.

Through the 1990s and early 2000s, the Middle East was one of the world's largest arms markets. During the late 1980s and early 1990s, the Middle East accounted for approximately 25 percent of the world's regional arms imports. Saudi Arabia alone purchased more than $68 billion in arms during the 1990s. Nevertheless, there was a significant decline in regional arms imports. Sanctions that prohibited sales to Iraq and Libya, combined with a diminution in oil revenues, contributed to the decline. In 1987, the region spent

$30 billion on imported arms. By 1997, imports to the Middle East had dropped to $19.9 billion. Imports of main battle tanks and artillery pieces declined by half, while orders for aircraft and naval vessels were reduced by about one-third.

A percentage of U.S. arms sales to the Middle East is actually subsidized by the United States. For instance, between 1996 and 2003, Israel was the third-largest importer of American arms, with $9.4 billion in imports. However, a large portion of Israel's arms imports are financed through the U.S. Department of Defense's Foreign Military Financing (FMF) program and the U.S. Department of State's Economic Support Funds (ESF) initiative. These programs provide funds or credit to Israel. On average, the FMF provides $1.8 billion and the ESF $1.2 billion each year to support Israeli purchases of U.S. arms. Israel has received some $46 billion in aid to procure American weapons since the late 1970s. Egypt receives approximately $2 billion each year, $1.2 billion from the FMF and $815 million from the ESF. Since 1978, the United States has granted Egypt $38 billion to buy U.S. arms and weapons.

In contrast, wealthy oil nations such as Saudi Arabia do not receive FMF or other U.S. subsidies. Nevertheless, several states have negotiated a series of concessions from the United States or other suppliers. Saudi Arabia generally requires arms agreements to include clauses stipulating that 30–35 percent of the value of the contract has to be returned to the Saudi economy. This is usually accomplished through licenses that allow local manufacture of parts. Other forms of financial offsets include building production sites in recipient nations or licensing technology to the recipient country. In other cases, offsets involve economic investment in areas unrelated to the actual arms imports.

Israel is the only state in the Middle East with a highly developed domestic arms industry and significant arms exports of its own. Israel was able to develop its internal defense industrial base through support from the United States. As such, Israel is the only state that is allowed to use FMF funding to bolster its own arms industry and can use up to 27 percent of FMF funding for its domestic defense industrial base. By 2000, Israel recorded $2 billion in arms exports, which included 48 different countries ranging from Russia to Colombia to Ethiopia (although none to Arab states). Israeli exports of military technology have often placed the country at odds with the United States, especially over exports of sensitive technology to nations such as the People's Republic of China (PRC). In response, the United States has imposed, or threatened to impose, sanctions on the sale of arms to Israel.

American arms sales to the Middle East remain complicated by Washington's alliances with both Israel and other states in the region, including Egypt and Saudi Arabia. Policymakers in

An Israeli-built Ecuadoran Air Force Kfir aircraft takes off during exercises on August 22, 1986. The Kfir represents the rare case of a Middle Eastern country producing and exporting military aircraft. (U.S. Department of Defense)

Washington often have to balance the sale or transfer of weapons to Arab states with similar sales to Israel and vice versa. For example, in the 1980s the U.S. Congress forbade the export of F-15E fighters to Saudi Arabia after intense lobbying by Israel and pro-Israeli groups. After the 1991 Persian Gulf War the restriction was relaxed, and the United States sold 48 F-15Es to the Saudis. However, in order to maintain Israel's superiority, the Americans sold an even more advanced version of the plane to Israel.

There has also been an expansion of European arms sales in the post–Cold War era. By 1995, the United States was the world's largest arms supplier to the developing world, with $3.8 billion in sales. But collectively, the four major European arms exporters had combined sales of $4 billion. The expansion of Europe's market share occurred as the European states, both individually and collectively, placed fewer restrictions on the sale of new technology. In some cases in which Arab countries were unable to buy the latest U.S. weapons, the same states were able to buy the latest European arms. Several European states have also proved more willing to engage in joint projects and approve offsets whereby some manufacturing or assembly of weapons systems is done in the Arab nations. France and Britain also emerged as leaders in the retrofit market. The two European countries gained highly valuable contracts to modernize aging Soviet equipment or make the weapons compatible with U.S. or Western defense systems. For example, France and Britain both secured contracts to replace the radar systems in Soviet- and Russian-made aircraft.

Iraq was one of the Soviet Union's largest arms importers. However, the end of the Cold War and the subsequent Persian Gulf War led to the cessation of sales to Baghdad. Between 1988 and 1991, Iraq bought $4.1 billion in arms from the Soviet Union. After the Gulf War, United Nations (UN) sanctions meant that Russian sales stopped completely. In addition, Russia had been the main supplier of arms to Yemen. Russia had sold more than $2.1 billion in arms to Yemen in the period from 1988 to 1991, but sales dropped to zero by 1994. Russia did, however, significantly expand arms sales to Iran. However, the more lucrative agreements were oil for arms. In 1991 in an agreement worth $10 billion, Russia transferred MiG-29 aircraft, Su-24 fighter-bombers, and SA-5 surface-to-air missiles (SAMs) to Iran in exchange for Iranian oil exports. Later Russian transfers included T-72 main battle tanks and even three Kilo-class diesel submarines.

During the 1990s, Russia regained market share in the Middle East because of the lower cost of its weaponry and the willingness of Moscow to sell all types of arms to almost any country. In 1994, the United Arab Emirates chose Russian personnel carriers over American and Western models because of the lower costs of the Russian vehicles. Russia was also able to gain new contracts with Kuwait, Oman, and the United Arab Emirates during the mid to late 1990s.

Tom Lansford

See also

Aircraft, Bombers; Aircraft, Fighters; Aircraft, Helicopters; Aircraft, Reconnaissance; Aircraft, Transport; Camp David Accords; Egypt,
Armed Forces; France, Middle East Policy; Germany, Federal Republic of, Middle East Policy; Iran, Armed Forces; Iraq, Armed Forces; Israel, Defense Industry; Israel Defense Forces; Jordan, Armed Forces; Kuwait, Armed Forces; Merkava Tank; Missiles, Air-to-Air; Missiles, Surface-to-Air; Saudi Arabia, Armed Forces; Soviet Union and Russia, Middle East Policy; Submarines; Syria, Armed Forces; Tanks; United Arab Republic; United Kingdom, Middle East Policy; United States, Middle East Policy; Warships, Surface

References

Cornish, Paul. *The Arms Trade and Europe.* London: Pinter, 1995.

Keller, William. *Arm and Arm: The Political Economy of the Global Arms Trade.* New York: Basic Books, 1995.

Krause, Keith. *Arms and the State: Patterns of Military Production and Trade.* New York: Cambridge University Press, 1992.

Laurance, Edward. *The International Arms Trade.* New York: Lexington Books, 1992.

Quandt, William B. *Decade of Decision: American Policy toward the Arab-Israeli Conflict, 1967–1976.* Berkeley: University of California Press, 1977.

Artillery

Artillery used in the Arab-Israeli wars consisted of cannon, rockets, and missiles and generally reflected the equipment and use doctrine of the larger nations that supplied the combatants. Field artillery cannon systems are either towed or self-propelled. A towed gun system consists of a cannon and a vehicle with which to tow it, usually a truck called a prime mover. Self-propelled weapons are cannon or rapid-fire antiaircraft guns integrated into a vehicle, usually tracked, resulting in a self-contained firing platform that is extremely mobile.

Towed guns rely on their prime movers to carry ancillary equipment such as aiming stakes, tools, and the various instruments needed by the gun crew. The prime mover also usually carries a small amount of projectiles and fuses. The majority of the ammunition is carried on separate vehicles and delivered to the gun at its firing position. It is then off-loaded in bulk in anticipation of the specific number of times the unit will fire before changing positions. Self-propelled guns and howitzers also carry all section equipment and a small amount of ammunition. Most self-propelled artillery sections have a second vehicle to transport ammunition and fuses. The two vehicles—the ancillary supply truck and the armed vehicle with the gun itself—constitute one complete weapon system.

Artillery ammunition is classified as fixed, semifixed, or separate-loading. Most direct-fire guns, such as antitank guns, fire fixed ammunition, which comes packaged as a complete unit (projectile, fuse, propellant, and shell casing). Fixed ammunition is something like a huge rifle bullet. Most light field artillery, in the 105-mm to 122-mm range, fires semifixed ammunition in which the projectile and the canister can be separated from each other so the crew can set the precise propellant charge by removing an appropriate number of powder increments. The projectile is also set with a separate fuse of either the point-detonating, time, or variable-time (proximity) variety. The latter two fuses are used for air bursts. Most

The first artillery piece fired during the Israeli War of Independence, at Tiberias, Israel. (Pictorial Library of Bible Lands)

medium and heavy artillery pieces fire separate-loading ammunition, which consists of individual projectile, propellant, and fuse units but no powder canister.

When Israel declared its independence in May 1948 setting off the Israeli War of Independence (1948–1949), it had to use whatever artillery was in place at the time. Because hostilities were imminent and the Jewish state was facing an arms embargo by many Western powers, Israeli agents purchased many tons of arms and ammunition from Czechoslovakia and other nations in Eastern Europe. Ironically, many of those weapons had been manufactured by Nazi Germany during World War II. At the same time, the Arab nations were equipped with British and French equipment, depending upon which country had held the colony or mandate in those particular nations.

During the 1948–1949 war, the most common artillery systems used by the Israelis were World War I–era 65-mm Austrian mountain howitzers, the obsolescent World War I French 75-mm gun, British-made 2- and 3-inch infantry mortars, and the so-called Davidka, an Israeli-improvised heavy mortar. The Israelis also deployed British 25-pounder field guns and British 17-pounder antitank guns that Israeli soldiers captured from opposing armies.

The Arab nations—specifically Transjordan, Egypt, Iraq, and Syria—used mainly British-built artillery pieces, including the

Troops of the Israeli-supported South Lebanon Army (SLA) man a Soviet bloc 130-mm artillery piece near the Israeli border, July 1985. (Time & Life Pictures/Getty Images)

17-pounders and 25-pounders, the latter in both towed and self-propelled versions.

During the 1956 Suez Crisis and the ensuing Sinai Campaign, Israel used the French-made AMX 105-mm self-propelled howitzer and various ad hoc models of Israeli-built self-propelled artillery. The indigenously manufactured guns were mainly hybrids of British and U.S. guns mounted on American-made M-3 half-tracks and M-4 Sherman tank chassis. The Israelis were also particularly successful at mounting American or British 4.2-inch heavy mortars on the M-3 half-track.

The Arab armies in this war relied heavily upon British- and French-manufactured weapons similar to those found in the Israeli arsenal. The Arabs, however, relied far less than the Israelis on local manufacturing and experimentation. The 17- and 25-pounder guns were still the primary Arab systems.

By the 1967 Six-Day War, Israel had U.S.-made 105-mm and 155-mm howitzers, towed and self-propelled in both calibers. The Israel Defense Forces (IDF), however, greatly preferred self-propelled systems, which could keep pace with their highly mobile armored forces. The Israelis also used French-built 155-mm howitzers mounted on Sherman tank chassis in great numbers.

By the mid-1960s many Arab armies were equipped with Soviet-made artillery, the result of Egyptian president Gamal Abdel Nasser's close ties with the Soviet Union, which he established in the mid to late 1950s. Soviet military advisers supplied major weapons systems to Egypt and trained Egyptian forces in their use in the early 1960s. The Soviet artillery included the excellent 122-mm and 130-mm howitzers. These weapons gave the Arab forces a decided advantage in range over the Israeli guns. Both Syria and Iraq also received some Soviet-made guns.

During the October 1973 Yom Kippur War, the Israelis made extensive use of American-made 155-mm M-109 and 8-inch (203-mm) M-110A1 self-propelled howitzers. The Israelis also locally manufactured two versions of a self-propelled 155-mm howitzer with better range than the U.S. models. This allowed the IDF to counter the extended range of Arab artillery. The American-made 175-mm M-107 self-propelled gun also proved invaluable in countering the Arab's range advantage.

Egypt, Syria, and their allies employed Soviet-built 122-mm and 130-mm towed howitzers as well as self-propelled 122-mm and 152-mm howitzers. The self-propelled four-barrel 23-mm ZSU 23/4 air defense system was especially devastating against low-flying Israeli attack aircraft. This Soviet-made gun had already proven itself in the Vietnam War, during which the North Vietnamese used it quite effectively against U.S. aircraft.

In later conflicts, Arab armies began using Soviet rocket and missile systems to achieve extended range and target saturation. The FROG 7, the North Atlantic Treaty Organization (NATO) designation for Free Rocket Over Ground, was the Soviet version of the U.S. Honest John rocket. Soviet fire doctrine stressed the use of rockets to saturate a target area, enhance the psychological effect of fires, and multiply the volume of fire delivered by cannon systems.

The Soviet SS-1 tactical ballistic missile (designated the Scud by NATO) had a mixed record in later Arab-Israeli and Middle East conflicts. Directly derived from the German V-2 of World War II, it is a surface-to-surface weapon with a relatively unsophisticated gyroscope guidance system that only controls the missile during the 80-second phase of powered flight. The resulting inaccuracy produces more of an area weapon than a precision weapon. The greatest potential threat from the Scud is its ability to carry chemical, biological, or nuclear warheads. Fortunately, all Scuds fired in actual war so far have carried only high-explosive warheads.

During the 1948 and 1956 wars the artillery doctrine of most of the Arab armies was patterned after that of the British. After 1956 Soviet artillery doctrine, which stressed area fires by large numbers of artillery pieces, predominated. In the 1973 Yom Kippur War, Egypt was able to commit massive numbers of artillery pieces to the operation to pierce the Bar-Lev Line. Egypt's and Syria's procurement of artillery pieces on a massive scale allowed them to apply fully Soviet artillery doctrine.

Israel continued to rely on American and British artillery procedures that focused on infantry and armor support through the use of direct support, general support, or reinforcing missions. An artillery unit with a direct support mission provides fires to a specific maneuver unit. Normally, one artillery battalion fires in support of one maneuver brigade. Firing units with general support missions answer calls for fire from the entire force and support the overall mission as defined by the maneuver commander, usually the division commander. Units with a reinforcing mission augment the fires of other artillery units, usually those with a direct support mission.

Because the Israelis prefer precision fire to area fire, they generally have eschewed the doctrinal use of rockets, although the U.S. Multiple Launch Rocket System (MLRS) is currently in their arsenal. The doctrinal U.S. and NATO missions for the MLRS includes the suppression of enemy air defense weapons, counterbattery missions, and the attack of fixed targets at extended ranges.

Because of Israel's numerical disadvantage against the Arab states, IDF tactical doctrine focuses on first achieving air superiority and then committing its air force to attack deep targets, destroy enemy artillery, and engage air defense missile launchers as targets of opportunity. This leaves the bulk of the Israeli field artillery committed to providing close support to the armor and infantry units.

JAY MENZOFF

See also

Bar-Lev Line; Israeli War of Independence, Overview; Nasser, Gamal Abdel; Sinai Campaign; Six-Day War; Yom Kippur War

References

Gudmundsson, Bruce. *On Artillery*. Westport, CT: Praeger, 1993.
Hogg, Ian. *Twentieth-Century Artillery*. New York: Barnes and Noble, 2000.
Laffin, John. *The Israeli Army in the Middle East Wars, 1948–1973*. London: Osprey, 1982.
Young, Peter. *The Arab Legion*. London: Osprey, 2002.

Artillery, Antiaircraft

Before guided surface-to-air missiles (SAMs) entered service, antiaircraft artillery (AAA) was the foundation of most national air defenses. Aircraft provided both the primary threat and first line of defense in any air defense system. Antiaircraft artillery did not see widespread deployment until 1916 during World War I. Since then, both antiaircraft artillery and aircraft have improved dramatically in both range and combat capabilities.

In antiaircraft artillery, World War II saw the introduction of radar fire control, which improved engagement accuracy, as well as power-loading and traverse systems that improved the rate of fire and increased the caliber of the weapons that could be employed against aircraft. By war's end, the arrival of jet aircraft transformed the nature, range, height, and pace of aerial warfare and therefore of air defenses.

Most AAA in service since World War II falls into three categories—light, medium and heavy—based on the weapon's caliber or muzzle diameter. Most countries rushed to develop heavy AAA, exceeding 105-mm bore or caliber, at war's end. The Americans

developed a 120-mm heavy AAA weapon to engage high-altitude bombers. The Soviets built a 130-mm weapon. Both entered service in the early 1950s and had a sustained rate of fire (ROF) of 8–12 rounds per minute and a maximum effective range ceiling of about 37,000 feet. But these were largely retired by the late 1970s. Even with power-assisted loading and electrohydraulic traversing systems, their low rate of fire and slow traverse rates made such weapons unsuitable for engaging low-flying, fast-moving jet aircraft, and their lack of range and altitude rendered them ineffective against high-altitude jet bombers. However, medium (55–90-mm) and light (20–40-mm) AAA proved their effectiveness in Korea and Vietnam and during the various Arab-Israeli conflicts.

China, Vietnam, and many Arab countries employed Soviet-designed 23-mm, 55-mm, and 85-mm antiaircraft guns. Their Western equivalents were the American 20-mm, 75-mm, and 90-mm guns; the British 3.7-inch guns; the French 100-mm guns; the Swedish 40-mm guns; and the Swiss 30-mm guns. The four heaviest of these—French 100-mm, American 90-mm, British 3.7-inch (90-mm), and Soviet 85-mm guns—all had a sustained ROF of 12–16 rounds per minute with an operational ceiling exceeding 27,000 feet. The American fully automatic 75-mm gun, known as

An Israeli 3.7-inch radar-equipped antiaircraft gun on parade on May 5, 1957. (Fritz Cohen/Israeli Government Press Office)

the Skysweeper, saw some service in the 1950s. Its sustained ROF was 60 rounds per minute, but it and the 90-mm gun were quickly removed from service as SAMs came on line.

Lighter AAA had a much higher ROF. The Soviet S-60 57-mm gun had a sustained ROF of 120 rounds per minute, while its much smaller 23-mm counterpart fired at 240 rounds per minute. The West's Bofors 30-mm and 40-mm guns fired at 360 and 240 rounds per minute, respectively. The West's early 20-mm cannon fired only 240 rounds per minute and lacked the punch to damage all but the lightest of incoming aircraft or missiles. This led the United States to develop 20-mm Gatling-style cannon that used an electrohydraulic drive to rotate and fire six barrels to provide immense rates of fire (2,000–6,000 rounds a minute). The Dutch employed the system to construct a 30-mm version.

Generally, the lighter the caliber, the higher the rate of fire and the greater its effectiveness. Much of this was because of the nature of their engagements. Even high-speed aircraft have to level off and make a straight run into the target to ensure bombing accuracy. Light and medium AAA simply concentrated their fire along the attacking aircraft's attack axis. This combined with radar-fire control, proximity fuses, and high rate of fire proved deadly against modern jet aircraft flying at low altitude or making an attack run. These guns are especially deadly at close range when linked to a radar fire-control system that tracks both the target and the rounds and works to intersect them.

As with the Western powers, the Soviets shifted to lighter calibers, consolidating four 23-mm cannon into a single mobile weapons system with a highly effective and accurate radar fire-control system (the ZSU-23/4 with Gun Dish Radar). Although these lighter AAA had a range of only 2,000–4,000 yards and could only engage targets operating below 8,000 feet, they proved quite deadly as close-in defensive systems.

Light AAA was particularly effective when integrated with a modern SAM system. This was the case in Vietnam where the North Vietnamese SAMs forced aircraft to drop low to escape engagement, only to encounter dense arrays of light and medium AAA. The result was that AAA was the single greatest cause for aircraft losses and damage during that war. Arab forces never achieved a similar level of integration or effectiveness during their many conflicts with Israel during the Cold War era. Only the advent of precision standoff weapons has diminished AAA's importance in air defense operations by enabling aircraft to attack effectively from outside AAA range. Today, most Western air forces all but ignore the AAA threat in their operational planning.

CARL OTIS SCHUSTER

See also

Missiles, Surface-to-Air

References

Blake, Bernard, ed. *Jane's Weapons Systems, 1987–88*. New York: Random House, 1989.

Dunstan, Simon. *The Yom Kippur War, 1973*. 2 vols. Westport, CT: Praeger, 2005.

Frieden, David R. *Principles of Naval Weapons Systems*. Annapolis, MD: Naval Institute Press, 1985.

Isby, David. *Weapons and Tactics of the Soviet Army*. London: Jane's, 1981.

Ashkenazic Judaism

The larger of the two primary branches of Judaism. During the Middle Ages, Judaism diverged into two cultures differing in laws, customs, liturgy, and language. Ashkenazic Judaism evolved and flourished in Central and Eastern Europe, the environs of the Holy Roman Empire. Sephardic Judaism evolved and took root in the Moorish Iberian Peninsula, primarily Spain, and North Africa. Ashkenazic customs (traditions) and halakic (Jewish law) rulings are based on the Torah understood in the light of the Babylonian Talmudic and ritual tradition. Sephardic customs and halakic rulings are based on the Palestinian Talmudic and ritual traditions. This division of Ashkenazic and Sephardic Judaism can be seen in the structure of the Chief Rabbinate of Israel that represents all of Judaism in Israel and is the final arbiter of halakic and kashruth (Jewish food laws). The Chief Rabbinate has two chief rabbis, one Ashkenazic and one Sephardic. The Jewish community in Rome predates the destruction of the Solomonic Temple and the Diaspora and, along with Yemenite, Ethiopian, and Oriental Jewry, is neither Ashkenazic nor Sephardic.

Ashkenaz was a son of Gomer (Genesis 10:3) and the grandson of Noah's son Japheth. German Jewry of the 10th century traced its lineage to Ashkenaz and applied that name to Germany. The Ashkenazim migrated eastward during the 15th and 16th centuries, shifting the center of Ashkenazic Judaism to Poland and Lithuania. Hasidic Judaism arose in the 17th century and emphasized personal spirituality and piety as opposed to the more academic study of Judaism emphasized by Ashkenazic Judaism.

The Ashkenazic academic approach to Judaism provided the fertile ground from which the Jewish Enlightenment (Haskalah) grew in concert with the Western European Enlightenment of the 17th and 18th centuries. The Jewish Enlightenment fostered a neglect of halakah similar to the West European rejection of the absolutistic truths of supernaturalism in general and Christianity in particular.

The first Jewish immigrants to the Americas were Sephardic. However, by 1750 Ashkenazic Jews dominated the American Jewish community. Ashkenazic Jewish immigration to the United States in the mid-19th through the early 20th centuries was driven by the increase in religious persecution of Jews (pogroms) in Europe and the expanding American economy. Ashkenazic Jews represented a mere 3 percent of world Jewry in the 11th century. Ashkenazic Judaism expanded to comprise 92 percent of world Jewry by 1931 before being decimated by the Nazi-inspired Holocaust. Ashkenazic Jews now comprise approximately 85 percent of world Jewry. Today, the majority of contemporary Jewry in North America is descended from Ashkenazic immigrants from Germany and Eastern Europe.

Many of the Ashkenazic Jews who survived World War II immigrated to Israel, the United States, and France. Mizrahi Jews—Sephardic Jews of North African and the Middle Eastern ancestry—comprise more than half of 21st-century Israel's population. Ashkenazic Jews descended from the World War II Holocaust refugee immigration, and the Zionist immigration of the late 19th and early 20th centuries comprise most of the remaining Israeli citizenry. Ethiopian Jews who came to Israel via Menachem Begin's Operations MOSES (1984) and SOLOMON (1991) constitute approximately 1 percent of the contemporary Israeli population.

In addition to the differences in Talmudic traditions, Ashkenazic and Sephardic Jews differ in their indigenous languages and in some legal and ritual practices. Yiddish (Judeo/Hebrew-German) is the traditional vernacular language of Ashkenazic Jews. Ladino (Judeo/Hebrew-Castilian/Spanish) is the traditional vernacular of Sephardic Jewry. Just as the Gileadites and the Ephramites of biblical times varied in their pronunciation of "Shibboleth," Ashkenazim and Sephardim vary in their pronunciation of one Hebrew consonant and some vowels. Ashkenazim and Sephardim also vary in some halakic and kashruth (kosher) practices. Ashkenazim do not eat rice, corn, peanuts, legumes, and millet during the observance of Passover (Pesach). Sephardic Jews do. Ashkenazim are generally not as strict as Sephardim in their understanding of which meats are kosher, and there are differences in the permissibility of specific slaughter practices as well.

Although they have much in common, Ashkenazic and Sephardic Torah services and worship practices also differ. The terms "Ashkenazic" and "Sephardic" are often used to refer to liturgical traditions (nusakh) that vary in the content of the prayers, the order of the prayers, the text of the prayers, the melodies of the prayers, and the prayer book (Siddur). Ashkenazic brides and grooms refrain from meeting for one week prior to their wedding. Sephardic brides and grooms do not. Ashkenazic Torahs lie flat during a Torah service, while Sephardic Torahs stand. The Ashkenazic understanding of the law is based upon the writings of Rabbi Moses Issreles, and the Sephardic understanding of the law is based upon the writings of Rabbi Joseph Caro.

Zionism and its dreams of the modern State of Israel were based in the European history of intolerance, discrimination, and persecution of the Ashkenazic Jewry. Ashkenazic Jewry founded and fueled the modern Zionist movement and immigration. It also set forth the correlative kibbutz movement in Ottoman Palestine in the late 19th and early 20th centuries. It was the Ashkenazic Zionists who prevailed on the British government to issue the Balfour Declaration (1917), expressing official British support for a Jewish homeland in Palestine. That ultimately led to the formation of the European Ashkenazic–dominated State of Israel by the United Nations (UN) in 1948. This domination of 21st-century Israel by Ashkenazic Jews of European descent now faces a burgeoning Mizrahi post-Zionist backlash. The Mizrahim assert that Mizrahi or Arab Jews (the word is also used for Iranian Jews and those from Kazakhistan, Uzbekistan, Afghanistan, and India) and their ances-

tors are and were discriminated against by Israel's European Ashkenazic Jewish political establishment. These Mizrahim contend that the Zionist immigration policies that promoted Ashkenazic Jewish immigration from the late 19th through the 20th centuries reduced Mizrahi Jews to second-class citizenship. This, they argue, created and promotes social, political, and economic discrimination that separates Ashkenazic Israelis from Sephardic and Mizrahi Israelis.

RICHARD EDWARDS

See also

Balfour Declaration; Holocaust; Kibbutz Movement; MOSES, Operation; Zionism

References

Biale, David. *Cultures of the Jews: A New History*. New York: Schocken, 2002.
Dimont, Max. *Jews, God and History*. New York: Simon and Schuster, 1962.
Gross, N. *Economic History of the Jews*. New York: Schocken, 1975.
Haumann, Heiko. *A History of East European Jews*. Budapest: Central European University Press, 2001.
Seltzer, Robert. *Jewish People, Jewish Thought*. New York: Macmillan, 1980.
Vital, David. *A People Apart: A History of the Jews in Europe*. Oxford: Oxford University Press, 1999.

Ashrawi, Hanan Mikhail
Born: October 8, 1946

Palestinian political leader and founding member of the Palestinian Independent Commission for Citizens' Rights. Hanan Ashrawi was born Hanan Mikhail on October 8, 1946, in Ramallah in what was then the British Mandate for Palestine (now the West Bank). She attended the Quakers' Friends Girls School and then the American University of Beirut in Lebanon, where she received a bachelor's degree in 1968 and a master's degree in English literature in 1970.

In 1969 Ashrawi attended an international conference in Jordan, where she first met Palestine Liberation Organization (PLO) chairman Yasser Arafat. She subsequently formed an outspoken ideological commitment to the PLO. Beginning in 1973, she taught English at Birzeit University in the West Bank and then secured a leave of absence to pursue a doctorate in medieval studies at the University of Virginia, which she earned in 1981. She has been a professor at Birzeit ever since, and from 1986 to 1990 she served as dean of the College of Arts.

Politically active since her student days, Ashrawi joined the General Union of Palestinian Students and the General Union of Palestinian Women. Committed to improving the living conditions of her compatriots, which had deteriorated sharply since the 1967 Six-Day War, she actively entered the political arena following Israel's 1982 invasion of Lebanon in which thousands of Palestinian refugees in Beirut were killed. She emerged as a principal voice

Hanan Ashrawi, spokesperson for the Palestinian delegation to Middle East peace talks, leader of the Palestinian Independent Commission for Citizens' Rights, member of the Palestinian Legislative Council, and media commissioner for the Arab League. (European Community)

of the Palestinian people with the international news circuit during the years of the First Intifada (1987–1990).

Articulate and eloquent, Ashrawi helped to dispel stereotypes about Palestinians. She made frequent appearances on American television during 1988–1991. This came to an end with the Persian Gulf War of 1991 when the PLO supported Iraq against the international coalition. Despite her ties to the PLO, Ashrawi used her strong connections with U.S. secretary of state James Baker III to override Israeli objections to her presence at Middle East peace talks in Madrid that October. There she guided the Palestinian delegation toward accepting an Israeli-proposed period of trial autonomy and relinquishing long-held demands for a Palestinian state.

Despite conflicts with Arafat regarding his autocratic leadership style, Ashrawi remained a committed and active spokesperson for the Palestinian struggle within her roles in several community organizations. She was elected as an independent candidate to the newly established Palestinian Legislative Council on January 20, 1996. She served briefly as higher education minister in President Arafat's government, which she criticized as corrupt. She parted ways with Arafat and left her post in 1998. Because of her role as a

legislator, her many supporters looked to her as the conscience of the Palestinian Legislative Council, hoping that she would help ensure that the Palestinian Authority (PA) and the legislature would be accountable and democratic. She helped found the Jerusalem-based Miftah (The Key), also known as the Palestinian Independent Commission for Citizens' Rights, that worked to promote dialogue, Palestinian nation-building, democratic empowerment, and human rights. In July 2001, the Arab League appointed her as the organization's media commissioner, a newly established post. Ashrawi remains one of the most well-known spokespersons for the Palestinian cause.

SPENCER C. TUCKER

See also

Arafat, Yasser; Baker, James Addison, III; Intifada, First; Lebanon, Israeli Invasion of; Madrid Conference; Palestine Liberation Organization; Six-Day War

References

Ashrawi, Hanan. *This Side of Peace: A Personal Account.* New York: Simon and Schuster, 1996.
Victor, Barbara. *Voice of Reason: Hanan Ashrawi and Peace in the Middle East.* New York: Harcourt Brace, 1994.

Assad, Bashar al-
Born: September 11, 1965

President of the Syrian Arab Republic (2000–present) and head of the Baath Party. Bashar al-Assad was born in Damascus, Syria, on September 11, 1965. His father was Hafez al-Assad, strongman and president of Syria from 1971 to 2000. The Alawi sect to which al-Assad belongs encompasses approximately 12 percent of the Syrian population. Bashar was not as well known to the Syrian public as his popular elder brother, Basil, who died in an automobile accident in 1994.

Beginning in the mid-1980s, the younger al-Assad studied medicine at the University of Damascus, training in ophthalmology at the Tishrin Military Hospital and then the Western Eye Hospital in London. After Basil's death, Bashar enrolled in the military academy at Homs. He became a colonel in the Syrian Army in 1999.

Although Syria is technically a republic, President Hafez al-Assad first groomed his son Basil, then Bashar, as his successor although never openly declaring this intent. Bashar's acquisition of both military and Baath Party credentials was imperative to his legitimacy, but most observers believed that the senior power brokers in the Syrian government assented to his succession as a matter of convenience. In 2000, he was elected secretary-general of the Baath Party and stood as a presidential candidate. The People's Assembly amended the constitution to lower the minimum presidential age to 35, and al-Assad was duly elected president for a seven-year term. A general referendum soon ratified the decision.

A reform movement, dubbed the Damascus Spring, emerged during the first year of al-Assad's rule. Some Syrians hoped that their young president, who had announced governmental reforms, an end to corruption, and economic liberalization, would open Syria to a greater degree. Indeed, reformers hoped to end the State of Emergency Law, which allows for the abuse of legal and human rights, and issued public statements in 2000 and 2001. Political prisoners were released from the notorious Mezze Prison, and certain intellectual forums were permitted. However, by mid-2001, the president reined in the reformists, some of whom were imprisoned and accused of being Western agents.

Under al-Assad, Syria has opened somewhat in terms of allowing more media coverage than in the past, although censorship remains. Cellular phones are now prevalent, and Syria finally allowed the Internet, whereas under Hafez al-Assad even facsimile machines were prohibited. Economic reform and modernization received top priority. Job creation, the lessening of Syria's dependence on oil revenue, the encouragement of private capital investments, and the mitigation of poverty are the key goals in the economic sphere. The government created foreign investment zones, and private universities as well as private banks were legally permitted. Employment centers were established after 2000, and al-Assad announced his support of an association with the European Union (EU). However,

Bashar al-Assad, who became president of Syria in June 2000 following the death of his father Hafez al-Assad. (AFP/Getty Images)

these changes were too gradual to instill much confidence in Syrian modernization.

Under al-Assad, Syria's relations with Iraq had improved prior to the change of regime in the latter country in April 2003, and Syrian-Turkish relations are also less tense than in the past. However, the United States has shown great irritation with evidence that foreign fighters were crossing into Iraq from Syria and that former Iraqi Baathists were using Syria for funding purposes. The ensuing 2004 sanctions against Syria under the Syria Accountability Act, first enacted by the U.S. Congress in 2003, have discouraged investors and the modernization of Syrian banking systems.

Syria adamantly and consistently opposed the American presence in Iraq after the Anglo-American invasion there in March 2003, and the country's own Islamist movement reemerged. President al-Assad also had to deal with an influx to Syria of Iraqi refugees, who posed an additional burden on the economy. Furthermore, al-Assad did not wish to encourage radical Islamists on Syrian territory and made efforts to contain them.

In terms of the Arab-Israeli situation, al-Assad inherited a hard-line position toward Tel Aviv along with sympathies toward the Palestinian cause during the Second (al-Aqsa) Intifada and its aftermath. Yet internally, the public saw the president as promoting an honorable peace for Syria, deemed necessary for further economic development. While Syria has continued to express hopes for a peace agreement, it insists on Israeli withdrawal from the Golan Heights. Syria demonstrated its lack of desire for war during the Israeli invasion of southern Lebanon in 2006, despite public statements that seemed bellicose.

Other important changes came with the shift in Syria's position in Lebanon. When former Lebanese prime minister Rafik Hariri was assassinated in a bombing in February 2005, suspicions fell on Syria. Anti-Syrian Lebanese demonstrated, as did pro-Syrian groups such as Hezbollah. The United Nations (UN) inquiry into Hariri's death as well as comments by former Syrian vice president Abd al-Halim Khaddam implicated Syrians at the highest level and pro-Syrian elements in Lebanon intelligence services in the assassination. A tribunal was scheduled, although the Syrian government sought to postpone its formation and caused a political crisis in Lebanon. Syrian troops withdrew from Lebanon in April 2005, however, thereby ending a long period of direct and indirect influence over the country. Lebanon has also been a good economic partner for Syria through trade and the absorption of large numbers of Syrian laborers. The U.S. government continued to charge al-Assad with aiding and bolstering Hezbollah in Lebanon, but the Syrian view was that the organization was a wholly Lebanese entity. It could, however, encourage its quiescence along the Israeli border.

SHERIFA ZUHUR

See also

Assad, Hafez al-; Baathism; Golan Heights; Hezbollah; Lebanon; Syria

References

Darraj, Susan Muaddi. *Bashar al-Assad*. New York: Chelsea House, 2005.
George, Alan. *Syria: Neither Bread nor Freedom*. London: Zed, 2003.
Leverett, Flynt. *Inheriting Syria: Bashar's Trial by Fire*. Washington, DC: Brookings Institution Press, 2005.

Assad, Hafez al-
Born: October 6, 1930
Died: June 10, 2000

Syrian political leader and president of Syria (1971–2000). Hafez al-Assad was born in modest circumstance at Qardaha in western Syria on October 6, 1930. A member of the minority Alawi sect of Shia Islam, he was the first member of his family to attend secondary school. At age 16 he began his political career by joining the Baath Party in Latakia (Ladhakiyya). As a secular organization, the Baath Party actively recruited members from all sects and branches of Islam as well as from Christian groups. Baathism opposed imperialism and colonialism and espoused nonalignment except with other Arab countries. As a youth, al-Assad participated in Baathist demonstrations against the French occupation of Syria and for Syrian independence.

With no money to attend college, al-Assad secured a free education at the Syrian Military Academy. Graduating in 1955, he was commissioned an air force lieutenant. After initial training as a pilot, he received advanced fighter training and advanced to squadron leader in 1959.

Al-Assad opposed the 1958 union of Syria with Egypt in the United Arab Republic (UAR), for which he was assigned to duty in Egypt during 1959–1961. In Cairo, he worked with other Syrian military officers committed to the Syrian Baath Party. He favored Pan-Arabism but was opposed to the union with Egypt because it had resulted in a concentration of power in Egyptian hands, most notably those of Gamal Abdel Nasser. Al-Assad's outspoken opposition to the UAR led to his brief imprisonment in Egypt at the breakup of the UAR in 1961.

On March 27, 1962, the army seized power in Syria and abolished the parliament. Army leaders promised to introduce so-called just socialism. Then on March 8, 1963, the Baath Party, supported by allies from within the military, toppled the previous regime. In 1964 al-Assad become commander of the Syrian Air Force. Although Amin al-Hafiz, a Sunni Muslim, was the nominal leader of Syria, in effect a group of young Alawites, including al-Assad, came to control affairs of state.

Rivalries within the leadership of the state led to yet another coup on February 23, 1966. The coup was led by General Salah al-Jadid and entailed considerable bloodshed. Al-Assad, as minister of defense (1966–1970), became one of the key members of the new government. His political position was considerably weakened by the disastrous Six-Day War of June 1967 that saw Syria lose the Golan Heights to Israel. A protracted power struggle then ensued between al-Assad and his mentor al-Jadid, then chief of staff of the Syrian armed forces.

By the autumn of 1970 al-Jadid and al-Assad were locked in a struggle for control of power. Al-Jadid then decided to intervene against King Hussein's government in Jordan, which had moved against the militant Palestinians there. Jordanian aircraft savaged the invading Syrian tanks, which then withdrew. This cleared the way for al-Jadid and his allies to be removed from power, attacked by al-Assad for the Jordanian fiasco. In the so-called corrective revolution, al-Assad forced Syrian president Nur al-Din al-Atasi to resign on October 17. This was followed by the arrest of Premier Yusuf Zuayyin and Foreign Minister Ibrahim Makhus. On November 21 al-Assad became prime minister.

Al-Assad and his nationalist faction were more committed to Arab unity and the destruction of Israel than to socialism, while his rivals had concentrated on Arab socialist economic reform. In 1971 al-Assad was elected president for the first of five terms. The previous regime had been a military dictatorship, but upon coming to power al-Assad increased its repressive nature. Political dissenters were subject to arrest, torture, and execution, although usually the regime got its way through bribes and intimidation. The government became strongly totalitarian with a cult of personality but-

Hafez al-Assad, president of Syria from 1971 until his death in June 2000. (Embassy of the Syrian Arab Republic)

tressing the one all-powerful leader, in part an effort to end the sharp fractures in Syrian society.

The only major threat to al-Assad's rule came in the late 1970s and early 1980s. It was centered on the opposition of conservative Muslims and Sunni Muslims to the basically secular and reformist Alawite regime. Various opposition groups joined the Islamic Front coalition with the aim of overthrowing the regime and establishing an Islamic state. Other Syrians supported the movement because of discontent with the regime's authoritarianism, cronyism, and widespread corruption. The discontent was centered in the cities of Damascus, Homs, and Hama. In 1980 the Islamic Front destroyed a number of government installations in Damascus, but in 1982 it seized control of part of Hama and called on the population to join in a jihad against the government. Al-Assad's military, under the overall direction of his brother Rifat al-Assad, struck back hard. In two weeks of fierce fighting and artillery fire, large parts of Hama were destroyed. Some 10,000 to 38,000 people died.

With Soviet support, al-Assad dramatically increased Syrian military strength. Syrian educational curriculums were revised to stress al-Assad's position that Syria was the champion of the Arab cause against Israel and Western imperialism. In his foreign policy, al-Assad employed a mix of diplomacy, war, and state-sponsored terrorism.

In foreign affairs, al-Assad's chief immediate aim was to regain the Golan Heights from Israel. Six years after the 1967 war, with no progress toward that return of territory captured by the Jewish state, al-Assad and Egyptian president Anwar Sadat carefully planned and then initiated a surprise attack on Israel that would force it to fight simultaneously on two fronts. The conflict began on October 6, 1973. Known as the Yom Kippur War or Ramadan War, it caught Israel completely by surprise. Despite initial Egyptian and Syrian military successes, which included a Syrian drive into the Golan Heights and Egyptian crossing of the Suez Canal, Israel secured the initiative and was on the brink of a crushing victory over its two opponents when a cease-fire brokered by the United Nations (UN) took effect on October 22. Al-Assad then falsely sought to shift the blame for the defeat on Sadat and Egypt, resulting in lasting enmity between the two men. Al-Assad's continued intransigence in determining terms for the return of the Golan Heights to Syria prevented any fruitful peace negotiations with Israel. Indeed, al-Assad opposed all peace accords between the Palestinians and the Israelis as well as Jordan's decision in 1994 to end the state of war between itself and Israel.

In 1976 al-Assad sent troops into Lebanon, ostensibly on a peace-keeping mission to end the civil war raging there but in reality to secure Syrian control. Israel's invasion and occupation of southern Lebanon (1982–1985) led him to support changes in the Lebanese constitution while securing Syria's virtual control of Lebanon. Although Syrian forces in Lebanon were reduced after 1999, they remained in the country until 2005, and Syria's political influence in the Lebanese government and the activities of Syrian-sponsored Lebanese operatives remained a cause of great concern.

Al-Assad regularly supported radical Palestinian and Muslim terrorist groups based in Lebanon and allowed them to establish bases and administrative centers in Syria. The United States routinely accused Syria of state-sponsored terrorism. Al-Assad supported Iran in the Iran-Iraq War (1980–1990) and participated in the coalition formed to force Iraq from Kuwait in the Persian Gulf War (1991), but the relationship between al-Assad and Iraqi dictator Saddam Hussein improved in 1998 when Israel began to develop a strategic partnership with Turkey.

Al-Assad died in Damascus of a heart attack on June 10, 2000. He was succeeded in power by his son, Bashar.

RICHARD EDWARDS AND SPENCER C. TUCKER

See also

Assad, Bashar al-; Baathism; Egypt; Hussein, Saddam; Iran; Iran-Iraq War; Iraq; Jadid, Salah al-; Lebanon; Sadat, Anwar; Six-Day War; Syria; Terrorism; United Arab Republic; Yom Kippur War

References

Friedman, Thomas. *From Beirut to Jerusalem.* New York: Anchor Books, 1995.

Patterson, Charles. *Hafiz Al-Asad of Syria.* Englewood Cliffs, NJ: Prentice Hall, 1991.

Seale, Patrick. *Assad of Syria: The Struggle for the Middle East.* Berkeley: University of California Press, 1988.

Assimilation

Process by which a minority group within a larger society adopts the cultural mores and societal, political, and economic policies of the larger group. Within the Middle East and specifically in relation to the nation of Israel, there are two major uses of the term "assimilation." While both of these uses are related through the general definition of the term, each poses a particular issue. The first concept of assimilation deals with Jewish immigration to Palestine and Israel. The second concerns Palestinian Muslims living and/or working in Israel.

Between 1875 and 2006, more than 4 million individuals immigrated to Israel from around the world. Those who moved first to the region set the parameters for the later immigrants. The rules established were intended to create a sense of nationalism, born from the principles of the Zionist movement. Because the immigrants were originally citizens of many different nations, the need to create a central Jewish/Israeli culture was paramount. Over the last 50 years, the process of assimilation of these disparate immigrants has led to the development of a more homogenous Israel. As Israel was initially a nation of immigrants, the government had to develop a process by which immigrants from various nations would come together as citizens of one nation, Israel.

Originally, the only connection among the varying immigrant groups was a spiritual belief in the Jewish faith. These people came from many different nations, although the earliest immigrants came mostly from Europe. While many also had some knowledge of Hebrew with which to read the Torah, their daily languages ranged from German to French to Spanish to Italian. To create a true Jewish homeland in Israel, government officials determined that citizens of Israel had to commit to renouncing the citizenship of their previous country, learning Hebrew and using it as their national language, and serving for a term in the Israeli military.

Currently, the Ministry of Immigrant Absorption handles aliya, or the return of the Jewish people to their homeland. According to the 1950 Law of Return, Jews from anywhere in the world have the right to move to Israel, and Israel must be able to accommodate them, grant them automatic citizenship, and provide benefits for relocation. But to accommodate all of these immigrants, Israel also requires that these individuals assimilate into Israeli society. If these individuals had not assimilated as part of a unified culture, the cohesion of Israel would have been lost.

The first step in the assimilation process is for the immigrant to enter an Absorption Center. Absorption Centers are apartment buildings with intensive language centers, known as *ulpans,* attached to them where the immigrant is taught Hebrew, the official language of Israel. Residence in the Absorption Center is not required by the government, but an understanding of the Hebrew language is paramount for success in Israel. Residence in the Absorption Center can last up to six months. While in residence, the immigrant is exposed to all parts of Israeli culture and society, from social interactions to daily tasks. The immigrant, called an *oleh* (the plural of which is *olim*), is expected to interact with others in their Absorption Center, learning not only Hebrew but Jewish culture and traditions. This type of intensive assimilation aids in the breaking down of previous cultural ties.

All Israeli citizens and permanent residents are obligated to complete national military service. The length of service depends on the age at which the *oleh* came to Israel. Compulsory military service is another important part of the assimilation process. This ties the individual to Israel not only through her or his social circles and new cultural identity but also through the shared experience of military service.

The second use of the word "assimilation" in the context of Israel is the question of the future of the relationship between Israel and Palestine or, more accurately, the relationship between the Israeli government and those Palestinians who wish to live within the national borders of Israel or the settlements. Israeli officials believe that to best serve the needs of society, all permanent residents have to conform to the assimilation process. At the same time, Israeli officials impose ambiguous policies on Palestinians in Israel. On the one hand, they expect Palestinians to retain their own cultural identity and attempt to make it impossible for them to do otherwise. On the other, as most Israelis speak very poor or little Arabic, although they claim it is their second language, they require Palestinians to function linguistically and politically as Israelis. There was, until the Second (al-Aqsa) Intifada, a refusal to allow Palestinians to call themselves Israelis, and this attitude still exists. Israeli exclusionary policies have led to the increasing rejection of assimilation by Palestinians. Policies have been debated for years on the proper way to resolve the Palestinian question. Obviously, the early years of the Arab-Israeli conflict used warfare and bloodshed to determine who should control the region. In the nearly three decades since the 1979 Camp David Accords, political possibilities have been presented, although violence is still used by both sides.

The policy of assimilation is not applied in the same way to Palestinians as it is to Jewish immigrants to Israel. Instead, the idea is that cultural values should be held separately. For that reason, there is little integration in the Arab versus Israeli educational system, and consequently Arab students are at a disadvantage when they enter Israeli universities. The idea of assimilation does not apply to living areas, and Arabs are expected to reside in their own villages and neighborhoods. Many Israelis have never socialized with their Arab fellow citizens or visited their homes. This lack of contact is thought to provide safety, but it also engenders fear and suspicion. The success of the assimilation or integration of Palestinians within the dominant Jewish culture in Israel depends largely on the ability of Israeli leaders to recognize in their Palestinian neighbors the refugees whom their ancestors once were.

PAUL G. PIERPAOLI JR.

See also

Aliya Bet; Anti-Arab Attitudes and Discrimination; Diaspora; Expellees and Refugees, Palestinian; Immigration to Palestine/Israel; Law of Return; Right of Return, Palestinian; Zionism

References

Barnett, Michael. *Israel in Comparative Perspective.* New York: SUNY Press, 1996.

Ganim, Asad. *The Palestinian-Arab Minority in Israel, 1948–2000: A Political Study.* Albany, NY: SUNY Press, 2001.

Herzog, Hanna. "Political Ethnicity as a Socially Constructed Reality: The Case of the Jews in Israel." Pp. 140–150 in *Ethnicity, Pluralism, and the State in the Middle East,* edited by Milton J. Esman and Itamar Rabinovich. Ithaca, NY: Cornell University Press, 1988.

Schar, Howard. *The Course of Modern Jewish History.* New York: Vintage Press, 1990.

Smith, Charles D. *Palestine and the Arab-Israeli Conflict: A History with Documents.* 6th ed. New York: Bedford/St. Martin's, 2006.

Vago, Bela, ed. *Jewish Assimilation in Modern Times.* Boulder, CO: Westview, 1981.

Aswan High Dam Project

The Aswan High Dam (al-Sadd al Ali) was a major Egyptian development project and one of the largest engineering undertakings of the second half of the 20th century. Egyptian president Gamal Abdel Nasser, convinced that the dam would solve many Egyptian social and economic problems, made its construction a high priority. The plan involved building a new dam on the Nile River south of Aswan, the first cataract in southern Egypt.

The Nile River has rightly been called the lifeblood of Egypt. Each year the river flooded, depositing rich nutrients and aiding farmers, but this flooding was uneven. In some years it nearly wiped out entire crops, while in drought years it often did not provide sufficient water. Heavy floods also brought misery for an expanding Egyptian population along the river. Construction of a new high dam on the Nile, it was believed, would provide a regular, consistent flow of water and prevent damaging floods.

Not only would such a dam end the regular flooding by the Nile, but it would also allow for the irrigation of 1.4 million acres of new land in the largely desert country and provide hydroelectric power to expand Egypt's industrial capacity, bringing jobs and increasing national prosperity. Nasser also saw the project as a hallmark of his regime and a model for economic development in the developing world.

This was not the first effort to dam the Nile. The British had taken control of Egypt in 1882, and during 1899–1902 they built a dam at Aswan. Later known as the Aswan Low Dam, it was nearly 2,000 yards long and some 75 feet high. Because its height was determined to be inadequate, the Low Dam was raised in 1907–1912 and again in 1939–1943.

The Low Dam nearly overflowed in 1946, and rather than raise it a third time the Egyptian government decided to build a new dam about four miles upriver. Planning for the new dam began in earnest in 1952 following the Egyptian Revolution of that year. Financing remained a problem, however, so Nasser approached the United States. President Dwight D. Eisenhower's administration was initially interested in the project, hoping to link financial support for the project to Western foreign policy initiatives. Eisenhower also hoped that the course of construction, predicted to take as long as 18 years, would see Egypt aligned with the United States and perhaps even provide sufficient leverage for Washington to prod the Egyptian government into making a peace agreement with Israel. Furthermore, funding through the U.S.-dominated World Bank might allow Washington to block Egyptian arms deals with the Soviet Union and economic policies deemed contrary to Western interests.

Nasser was reluctant to make any arrangement that would limit his freedom of action in foreign policy. Still, the Egyptians clearly preferred U.S. assistance to that of the Soviets. At the same time as he was pursuing the dam project, however, Nasser was seeking to build up and modernize the Egyptian military. Toward that end he sought to acquire modern weapons from the United States and other Western nations. When the U.S. and British governments refused to supply the advanced arms, which they believed might be used against Israel, in 1955 Nasser turned to the Soviet bloc. In September 1955, encouraged by Moscow, he reached a barter arrangement with Czechoslovakia for substantial quantities of modern weapons, including jet aircraft and tanks, in return for Egyptian cotton.

This arms deal impacted the Aswan High Dam project. In December 1955 the Eisenhower administration announced that it was willing to lend $56 million for the dam construction, while Great Britain pledged $14 million and the World Bank $200 million. There were strings attached, however. Egypt had to provide matching funds and must not accept Soviet assistance.

Nasser was unhappy with the conditions and delayed accepting them. With the Egyptian president expecting a Soviet offer, the controlled Egyptian press launched a major propaganda campaign against the West, especially the United States. But when no Soviet offer was forthcoming, Nasser accepted the Western aid package on July 17, 1956. But only two days later, U.S. secretary of state John Foster Dulles announced that the offer had been withdrawn. The British government immediately followed suit. The official U.S. reasons were that Egypt had failed to reach agreement with the Sudan over the dam (much of the vast lake created by the dam would be in Sudanese territory) and that the Egyptian part of the financing for the project had become "uncertain." The real reasons for the rejection were quite different. In the U.S. Congress, strong opposition came from a number of powerful interests including fiscal conservatives skeptical about foreign aid, supporters of Israel concerned about Egyptian hostility toward the Jewish state, and Southerners who believed that expanded Egyptian cotton

Egypt's Aswan High Dam nears completion of its first stage, April 4, 1964. (Bettmann/Corbis)

production resulting from new irrigated lands would undercut U.S. cotton growers. But Dulles was also determined to teach Nasser and other neutralist leaders a lesson. Dulles was angry over Nasser's demarche to the communist bloc and arms purchases but particularly was upset over Egypt's recent recognition of the People's Republic of China (PRC).

Nasser was furious and, a week later, took action. On July 26, he nationalized the Suez Canal Company, claiming that this revenue would pay for the construction of the cherished dam project. He had contemplated this step for some time, but the U.S. rejection of the funding for the dam prompted its timing. In 1955 the canal produced net revenues of nearly $100 million, of which Egypt received only $2 million. Seizure of the canal would not only provide fund-

ing for the Aswan High Dam project but would also raise Nasser's stature in the eyes of Arab nationalists.

Nasser's decision prompted what became known as the Suez Crisis and eventually led to collusion among the governments of Israel, Britain, and France. These three states then secretly planned military intervention against Egypt with the aim of driving Nasser from power and returning the canal to control by the Suez Canal Company. Supposedly to protect the canal, Israel invaded Egypt at the end of October, and Britain and France followed suit in early November. This military intervention caught the United States by surprise, but within days heavy financial pressure from Washington, along with Soviet threats, brought about a withdrawal. The canal remained in Egyptian control.

Plans for the dam went forward, and in 1958 the Soviet Union agreed to assist with the project. Moscow provided technical and engineering assistance, including heavy equipment. The Soviet Zuk Hydroproject Institute designed the enormous rock and clay dam. Moscow, which saw this as an opportunity to gain a foothold in the Middle East, ultimately may have paid up to one-third of the cost of the project. Construction of the dam began in 1960. The first stage was completed in 1964 when the reservoir began filling. The dam was completed on July 21, 1970, and the reservoir reached capacity in 1976.

The United Nations Education, Scientific and Cultural Organization (UNESCO) raised concerns about the loss of historic sites from the rising waters, and an international effort was undertaken beginning in 1960 to move 24 major monuments, some of which were given to nations that had helped fund the relocation effort. One such example is the Nubian Temple of Dandur, given by Egypt to the United States and now located at the Metropolitan Museum of Art in New York City.

The Aswan High Dam is some 11,800 feet in length and 364 feet high. It is 3,200 feet wide at the base and 130 feet wide at its top. The reservoir behind the dam, Lake Nasser, is some 300 miles long and 10 miles across at its widest point. The dam's 12 generators are capable of producing 2.1 gigawatts of electricity. At first producing half of Egypt's power, the dam now produces perhaps 15 percent of the total.

The dam brought electricity to some Egyptian villages for the first time. It also mitigated damage from floods in 1964 and 1973 and from droughts during 1972–1973 and 1983–1984. It also led to the development of a new fishing industry on Lake Nasser. Unfortunately, much of the economic benefit promised by the dam has also been outstripped by the rapidly expanding Egyptian population.

The dam has also had negative impacts. More than 90,000 people had to be relocated because of the rising waters of Lake Nasser, and the fishing industry on Lake Nasser is remote from markets. Tremendous silting behind the dam lowers the water capacity of Lake Nasser and threatens the dam's generators, and restricting the flow of water on the Nile and its nutrients has adversely affected farming along the river and the fishing industry in the eastern Mediterranean. The dam has also led to erosion along the Nile Delta and the intrusion of salt water into areas used for the production of rice.

STEPHEN ZUNES AND SPENCER C. TUCKER

See also

Dulles, John Foster; Eden, Robert Anthony; Egypt; Eisenhower, Dwight David; Nasser, Gamal Abdel; Suez Crisis

References

Lytle, Elizabeth Edith. *The Aswan High Dam*. Monticello, IL: Council of Planning Librarians, 1977.

Parks, Peggy J. *Aswan High Dam*. San Diego: Blackbirch, 2003.

Shibl, Yusuf A. *The Aswan High Dam Project*. Beirut, Lebanon: Arab Institute for Research and Publishing, 1971.

Attlee, Clement Richard
Born: January 3, 1883
Died: October 8, 1967

British Labour Party leader, deputy prime minister (1942–1945), and prime minister (1945–1951). Clement Attlee was born into a middle-class family on January 3, 1883, in Putney, London. He was privately educated at Haileybury before attending University College, Oxford, from which he graduated in 1904 with a degree in history. In 1906 he was called to the bar, and he spent several unhappy years as a solicitor before the death of his father gave him the financial independence to follow a new career as a lecturer and social activist in the poor areas of London's East End. By then a committed Christian socialist, Attlee became an influential figure in the London branch of the Labour Party, which he had joined in 1908.

At the outbreak of World War I in August 1914, Attlee immediately enlisted in the army and served as a junior officer in the Gallipoli Campaign and in Mesopotamia (present-day Iraq), where he was badly wounded. Following recuperation in England, he served on the western front, where he was again wounded in fighting near Lille in the summer of 1918.

In November 1922, Attlee entered Parliament as the Labour Party member for Limehouse, a seat he was to hold for nearly three decades. Throughout the 1920s he consolidated his role in the national party and held posts in the two brief Labour governments of the period. In October 1935 he became party leader, shepherding Labour through the difficult years of the worldwide depression and the growing diplomatic confrontation with Nazi Germany.

Attlee had little initial role in World War II because Neville Chamberlain's Conservative-dominated government chose not to invite the other parties to join it in coalition. But in May 1940 the Chamberlain government fell, and the new prime minister, Winston Churchill, asked Attlee to join the new war cabinet. Attlee was initially appointed lord privy seal, and in February 1942 he became deputy prime minister. His administrative reforms improved the efficiency of the British war effort. Although Attlee himself opposed such a step because of the continuing war with Japan, the other leaders of the Labour Party insisted on an end to participation in the Churchill coalition on May 28, 1945, three weeks after victory in Europe. A general election was immediately announced.

Labour won the ensuing election, and on July 26, 1945, Attlee became prime minister with a landslide House of Commons majority of 147 seats. He immediately took Churchill's place in the ongoing Potsdam Conference.

Attlee's government inherited huge problems both at home and overseas. Reconstruction of the country's shattered economy after a hugely expensive war required the continuation of wartime austerity controls for some years. Indeed, Britain did not abandon food rationing until the early 1950s. Moreover, the Labour government was committed to a comprehensive reorganization of Britain's social services to create a cradle-to-grave welfare state system and

Clement Attlee, British Labour Party leader, deputy prime minister (1942–1945), and prime minister (1945–1951). (Library of Congress)

the bringing into public ownership of large transport and manufacturing sectors such as the railways and the coal industry. All these radical domestic reforms had to take place in the context of sweeping global change in which Britain faced major security commitments in Europe as well as nationalist agitation in its empire in the Middle East and Southeast Asia.

In foreign affairs, Attlee presided over the end of British rule in the Indian subcontinent in 1947, but the partition of the old Raj into Muslim and Hindu states led to great loss of life in sectarian fighting. Palestine was perhaps the most vexing of Attlee's imperial problems. When Labour came to power, British policy in that strife-torn territory was still based on the 1939 White Paper, which heavily restricted Jewish immigration and placed legal blocks on the sale of Arab land to Jewish settlers. The White Paper had been originally introduced to quell a three-year insurrection of Palestinian Arabs and had been largely successful in that regard. But World War II had profoundly changed the character of the Palestine problem, in particular because of the need to find a home for hundreds of thousands of Jewish survivors of the Nazi death camps who were scattered across continental Europe, many of whom were clamoring to immigrate to Israel. Frustrated by Britain's apparent intransigence, some members of the Jewish community in Palestine were by the end of the war involved in an armed insurgency against the colonial security forces. Thus, Attlee's government faced both the immedi-

ate problem of restoring order as well as the longer-term question of how to accommodate rival Arab and Jewish aspirations for the troubled mandate.

Labour had traditionally been supportive of Zionism, and in the spring of 1944 the party had advocated, as part of its National Executive Committee's annual report, unrestricted Jewish immigration into Palestine and the creation of a Jewish-majority state within the British Commonwealth. But Attlee, like Churchill and many other British politicians, had been shocked when the Jewish terrorist group Lohamei Herut Israel (also known as Lehi or the Stern Gang) had assassinated British minister of state Lord Moyne in Cairo in November 1944, and Attlee's sympathy for the Zionist cause had correspondingly withered. Also, upon his arrival at Downing Street, Attlee chose to place his powerful deputy Ernest Bevin at the Foreign Office. Bevin took a pugnaciously imperialist attitude toward foreign policy in general, and it was not difficult for his pro-Arab advisers in Whitehall to convince him that the solution to Palestine lay in resisting further Jewish immigration and in bolstering the British position there. As with most diplomatic questions, Attlee was content to defer to his foreign secretary on this point. Attlee was in any case temperamentally inclined toward retaining a strong British presence in the Middle East as a block to the Soviet Union.

British policy was complicated, however, by the pro-Jewish attitude of President Harry S. Truman's administration in the United States. It was no secret that because of Britain's parlous postwar financial situation the country was highly dependent on the continued goodwill of Washington, so Attlee had little choice but to involve the Americans in the deliberative process. The result was the 1946 Anglo-American Committee of Inquiry, which recommended allowing 100,000 new Jewish immigrants into Palestine but also proposed binational self-government for the mandate, under overall British auspices, in which neither Arabs nor Jews would predominate. Attlee cautiously welcomed the report pending further discussion. But he was angered when Truman appeared to undermine both him and the committee by publicly demanding that Britain immediately grant the immigrants entry into Palestine (while ignoring the power-sharing recommendations). Truman's clumsy partisanship, Attlee believed, had alienated the Arabs and encouraged the Jews to seek still more advantageous terms. By the end of the year, Britain's enthusiasm for its Palestine leasehold was also greatly diminishing because of the spike in political violence, illustrated most spectacularly by the bombing of the King David Hotel by the terrorist group the Irgun Tsvai Leumi (National Military Organization) in July 1946. The deaths of British servicemen across Palestine shook support at home for Bevin's policy of retrenchment. Increasingly he and Attlee sought a quick and cheap way out of the Palestine cauldron.

By 1947, with attempts to find a plan of self-government acceptable to all parties having apparently failed, Attlee announced that Britain would abandon the mandate the following year and handed the problem of its political future over to the United Nations (UN). His administration was unhappy with the General Assembly's subsequent partition proposal, believing, rightly as it turned out, that it would be unworkable, and Britain abstained in the final vote. The mandate was formally terminated on May 15, 1948. This was immediately followed by the declaration of the State of Israel and the 1948–1949 Israeli War of Independence.

In other foreign affairs, Attlee preserved the Anglo-American alliance and committed Britain to Cold War partnership with the United States through the 1949 North Atlantic Treaty Organization (NATO) pact. He also funded the creation of an independent British nuclear deterrent, and in 1950 he authorized British military intervention in the Korean War, a controversial decision that split his Labour Party.

In the autumn of 1951, with its postwar reform government running out of steam, Labour was narrowly defeated in a general election. Attlee stepped down on October 26, to be replaced by Churchill. Attlee remained party leader until a second electoral defeat in May 1955, shortly after which he resigned and was appointed to the House of Lords as Earl Attlee of Walthamstow. He maintained an active retirement, writing and campaigning on behalf of the party. Attlee died in London of complications arising from pneumonia on October 8, 1967.

ALAN ALLPORT

See also

Anglo-American Committee of Inquiry; Arab-Jewish Communal War; Arab Revolt of 1936–1939; Bevin, Ernest; Churchill, Sir Winston; Irgun Tsvai Leumi; Lohamei Herut Israel; Truman, Harry S.; United Kingdom, Middle East Policy; White Paper (1939)

References

Attlee, Clement. *As It Happened*. New York: Viking, 1954.
Beckett, Francis. *Clem Attlee*. London: Richard Cohen, 1997.
Burridge, Trevor. *Clement Attlee: A Political Biography*. New York: Random House, 1986.
Harris, Kenneth. *Attlee*. London: Weidenfeld and Nicolson, 1995.
Williams, Francis. *A Prime Minister Remembers: The War and Post-War Memoirs of the Rt. Hon. Earl Attlee, Based on His Private Papers and on a Series of Recorded Conversations*. London: Heinemann, 1961.

Attrition, War of
Start Date: July 1967
End Date: August 1970

The War of Attrition was a long series of low-level, protracted clashes between the Israelis and the Arabs from July 1967 to August 1970. Israel had emerged victorious from the Six-Day War of June 1967, more than doubling the territory under its control. On the Golan Heights, Israeli forces had penetrated into Syria a distance of 20 miles, which now placed most Jewish towns and farms in northern Israel beyond the reach of Syrian artillery. On the eastern border, Israeli troops now stood on the defensive on the banks of the Jordan River. Israel also controlled the Sinai Peninsula together with the strategic Straits of Tiran. The most important function of the Sinai for the Israelis, however, was as a buffer against any Egyptian attack.

Within three weeks of the end of the Six-Day War, a large-scale clash between the Israelis and Egyptians became the first major incident of the War of Attrition. As the conflict played out, both sides deployed new equipment provided by the superpowers and developed new tactics. The Suez Canal Zone and the Jordanian border were the two principal areas of the fighting, with additional clashes taking place on the Golan Heights.

The Soviets put pressure on the Egyptians to maintain an aggressive posture against the Israelis along the Suez Canal. On July 1, 1967, Egyptian troops crossed the Suez Canal and attempted to ambush Israeli forces on the eastern bank. The main engagement took place 10 miles south of Port Said. The Israelis responded by committing a mechanized infantry company to counterattack the Egyptians. Despite supporting artillery fire from the Egyptian side of the canal, the attacking forces were driven back. Major Uriel Menuhuin, the commanding officer of the Israeli infantry company, was killed, and 13 other Israeli soldiers were wounded in the battle.

The next major incident occurred on July 11. The Israeli government maintained that the 1967 cease-fire line ran down the middle of the Suez Canal and resolved to test its position by launching a number of small boats into the canal. The Israeli force drew fire from the Egyptians, and both sides opened fire from tanks that were dug into defensive positions on either side of the canal. Both sides also launched air sorties in support of the ground action. The Israeli Air Force (IAF) downed seven Egyptian aircraft during the fight. Israeli ground force casualties were 9 killed and 55 wounded.

On the night of July 11 the Israeli destroyer *Eilat*, accompanied by two torpedo boats, encountered and sank two Egyptian torpedo boats off the Rumani coast. Following that incident, the conflict temporarily settled down into a routine of running low-level clashes.

Egyptian president Gamal Abdel Nasser made it clear that it would only be a matter of time before Egypt attempted to recapture the Sinai. He also made no secret of his cold-blooded strategy of attrition. With Egypt's huge population advantage over Israel, Egypt could afford to absorb lopsided casualty ratios almost indefinitely.

A second major round of fighting began in September 1967 when Egyptian forces operating from fortified positions on Green Island engaged Israeli shipping in the Gulf of Suez. This action led to widespread artillery exchanges along the Suez Canal during which the cities of Kantara, Ismailia, and Suez were hit. Many Egyptians fled to escape the danger, with an estimated 700,000 becoming internal refugees.

The naval war escalated on October 21, 1967, when the *Eilat* approached Egyptian territorial waters near Port Said and came under attack from two Egyptian missile boats firing Soviet-supplied Styx missiles. The first missile hit the *Eilat* near the boiler room, cutting off the electrical supply. In all, the Egyptians fired four missiles at the *Eilat*, sinking it. Of the destroyer's 190-man crew, 47 were killed or missing, and another 90 were wounded. It was the first time in history that a warship had been sunk by guided missiles.

Burning oil installations and refineries at Suez damaged by Israeli artillery fire during the War of Attrition, photographed on October 24, 1967. (Israeli Government Press Office)

The Israelis responded to the Egyptian attack on October 25 with an artillery barrage against Egyptian oil refineries in Suez. The shelling claimed more than $100 million worth of oil and petrochemical products and killed or wounded 103 people.

There were no major incidents during the next 11 months, but in the intervening period the Egyptian armed forces received a wide array of new equipment from Soviet bloc sources, including large numbers of modern artillery pieces. Even more significantly, the Soviets sent 1,500 military advisers.

In June 1968 the Egyptians started sporadic artillery bombardments against the leading Israeli positions on the eastern bank of the Suez Canal. On September 8, 1968, the Egyptians resumed large-scale hostilities with a coordinated artillery barrage along a 65-mile front of the canal. The artillery bombardment lasted three weeks, with Israeli losses totaling 28 killed and wounded.

The Israelis retaliated on the night of October 30 with a heliborne commando raid against two Egyptian bridges and an electricity substation on the Nile just north of Aswan. That attack exposed the inability of Egyptian forces to protect their own territory from Israeli attack. Egyptian attacks along the Suez Canal then declined for a period.

In the meantime, the Israel Defense Forces (IDF) General Staff decided to strengthen defenses along the Suez Canal. The resulting

Bar-Lev Line of fortifications, named for chief of staff Lieutenant General Chaim Bar-Lev, was based on 35 small strong points located every seven miles between which IDF patrols maintained constant observation of Egyptian forces on the other side. Strong armored formations in assembly areas some distance from the canal were positioned to counterattack any Egyptian attempt to cross.

The Bar-Lev fortifications were completed in March 1969. On March 8 the Egyptians commenced a massive artillery barrage against the Bar-Lev positions. During the IDF's counterbarrage on March 20 the Egyptian chief of staff, General Abd al Muneim Riadh, and several other senior Egyptian officers were killed at an Egyptian observation post close to Ismailia.

Another short lull followed, but the conflict resumed with a vengeance on April 10, 1969. The fighting escalated significantly on May 1 when Nasser declared the termination of the cease-fire that officially had been in existence since 1967. The Egyptian high command hoped that their continuous artillery exchanges across the Suez Canal would eventually wear down the Israelis and give Egyptian forces an opening to cross the canal to the eastern bank.

The investment made by the Israelis in the Bar-Lev Line proved its worth, as the Egyptian artillery inflicted only moderate damage. The Israelis strengthened their canal defenses by constructing an earthen berm close to the bank. Its chief purpose was to prevent

Egyptian artillery from having direct line-of-sight observation of Israeli forces moving along the Suez Canal. The Israelis also continued to launch commando raids across the canal. The targets of many of these raids were electrical installations, which were relatively easy to damage. The electricity disruptions had a direct and negative impact on the Egyptian civilian population.

The Israelis conducted one of their most successful commando operations against Green Island on July 19, 1969. Green Island was a man-made island fortress in the northern section of the Gulf of Suez. The position was heavily fortified, and the Egyptian garrison there numbered about 200 troops. The Israeli commandos took the island at a cost of only 16 casualties (killed or wounded). They then blew up most of the installation and withdrew.

During that same month the IAF increased the number of offensive missions it flew, resulting in the downing of five Egyptian aircraft. The main target of the Israeli air strikes was the new Egyptian surface-to-air missiles (SAMs), acquired from the Soviet Union. During the next two months, Israeli aircraft flew more than 1,000 combat sorties.

On September 8, 1969, the Israelis launched a large-scale offensive. Israeli divers sank two Egyptian torpedo boats in the port of Ras-a-Sadat in the northern part of the Gulf of Suez, 16 miles to the north of the planned Israeli landing site. Their objective was to reduce the risk of Egyptian interception of the Israeli landing craft. The following day, an Israeli task force, including armor, landed at A-Dir at dawn and struck southward down the Gulf of Suez toward the intended objective, the Egyptian army base at Ras Abu-Daraj. The attack was supported by Israeli helicopters and aircraft.

The Egyptians were slow to respond to the assault on Ras Abu Daraj, and the Israelis were thus able to destroy 12 enemy positions, including 2 radar stations, and inflict more than 100 casualties before disengaging with only minimal losses of their own. The most vexing thing for the Egyptian high command was the fact that the IDF had operated for more than 10 hours on Egyptian soil without being significantly challenged by Egyptian forces. The poor response was mainly the result of inadequate communications and the rigid Egyptian command structure based on the Soviet model, which allowed little room for individual initiative. Many Egyptian commanders were afraid to move their forces unless they received explicit orders from their superiors, something hard to achieve in any fluid engagement. Nasser reacted by dismissing the senior commanders responsible for the defense of that area.

Three days later, on September 11, 1969, the Egyptians suffered another reverse when they lost 11 aircraft while shooting down only a single Israeli plane. On October 25, the Israelis scored another significant victory when they successfully attacked a radar station

Palestinian commando leaders planning an operation into Israel, photographed in Jordan in December 1968. (Time & Life Pictures/Getty Images)

Two United Nations (UN) observers in front of their badly damaged headquarters in Kantara, the result of Egyptian shelling from across the Suez Canal, photographed on April 29, 1969, during the War of Attrition. (Israeli Government Press Office)

at Ras-Arab on the Gulf of Suez. The Egyptians had newly installed Soviet P-12 radar equipment at the site. The attack force flew to the objective in 2 U.S.-built Sikorsky CH-53 Sea Stallion helicopters. The Egyptian garrison was quickly overcome, and then the Israeli forces worked diligently to remove the P-12 equipment, which was housed in two trailers partially dug into the ground. The Israelis dug out the trailers and then sling-loaded them beneath the 2 helicopters. Despite the helicopters being dangerously overloaded, the pilots were able to coax the helicopters back to the Israeli side of the Gulf. The Israelis subsequently made the information exploited from the equipment available to other Western intelligence agencies.

The Israelis launched 23 raids across the Suez Canal and the Gulf of Suez from October 1969 to July 1970. What concerned the Egyptian high command most during this period was the considerable investment they had made in Soviet SAM systems, which seemed to produce little results in degrading the effectiveness of the IAF. The poor results also concerned the Soviets, as they had the same systems deployed in Eastern Europe and the Soviet Union. In December 1969 several Soviet generals arrived in Cairo to evaluate the overall situation. The next month, Nasser traveled to Moscow. As the result of these meetings, the Soviets deployed more of their own personnel to Egypt to man new SAM-3 Goa systems.

The SAM-3, designed specifically to engage low-flying aircraft, was more effective than the longer-range and larger SAM-2. The SAM-3 system also could be deployed on a three-missile mobile-launch platform, increasing the flexibility of the Egyptian coverage. Many of the SAM-3s were manned almost exclusively by Soviet personnel. The Soviets at that point had committed almost 4,000

military advisers to Egypt, including pilots who flew frontline aircraft. This, of course, increased the chances of a direct confrontation between Soviet and Israeli forces.

Nevertheless, the strengthening of the Egyptian air defense umbrella had relatively little impact on the effectiveness of the IAF. The IAF did, however, make significant changes to its mission-attack profiles. Instead of attacking facilities close to the Suez Canal and the Gulf of Suez, the Israelis now flew missions to strike positions as close as 25 miles from Cairo. Many of these attacks were carried out against Egyptian Army reserve units, further degrading the overall morale of the Egyptian armed forces. The attacks also made clear to the capital's population the relative impotence of the Egyptian Air Force.

Between February and March 1970, the Egyptian Air Force lost 20 aircraft to the Israelis. On April 8, 1970, an IAF air strike killed 47 Egyptian children at a school inside a military compound, which brought the Israeli air offensive to a halt. That same month the Soviet air elements in Egypt assumed a much more aggressive posture, taking over direct responsibility for the defense of Egyptian air space. This freed the Egyptian Air Force to focus its operations in the Sinai in support of army operations along the Suez Canal, which included reconstructing SAM batteries in more forward positions. The renewed Egyptian offensive resulted in relatively high Israeli casualties between April and May 1969, with 64 Israeli soldiers killed and 149 wounded.

By June 1969 the number of Soviet advisers had grown to almost 12,000, including more than 100 pilots. That same month the Soviets again intervened to reorganize the Egyptian air defenses. Instead of defending the entire, approximately 100-mile, length of the Suez Canal, the Soviets decided that the vast majority of the SAMs should be located in a box, 25 miles wide and 45 miles long, covering the central and southern sectors of the canal. The SAM systems were positioned in packs whereby a small number of launchers could be protected by conventional short-range antiaircraft guns. Such a configuration allowed the defenders to engage an enemy aircraft with multiple missiles, increasing the kill probability. Nevertheless, the Israelis managed to destroy five SAM sites in July.

Since April, Soviet-piloted MiGs had been approaching IAF aircraft, but the Israeli pilots had standing orders to break off all such contacts. It was only a matter of time, however, before the Soviets and Israelis would clash head-on. On June 25, two Soviet-piloted MiG-21s fired on and hit an Israeli A-4 Skyhawk, which made a forced landing at a base in the Sinai. A series of running dogfights over the next few days resulted in no losses for either side. On July 30, a patrol of Israeli aircraft engaged eight Soviet-piloted aircraft, with the Israelis downing four and losing none. A fifth MiG was hit and later crashed on its way back to its base. Three of the Soviet pilots were killed, and another two were wounded. Neither side issued a communiqué about the engagement, but the Soviets were greatly shaken by the results. That same day, Moscow dispatched senior air force commanders to Egypt to investigate.

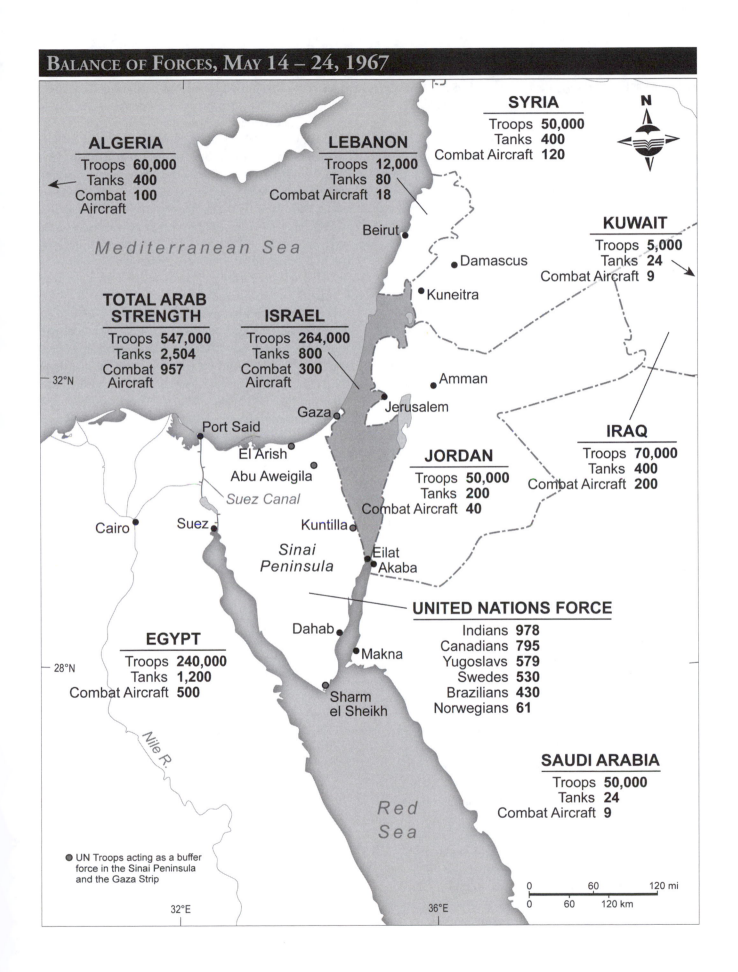

BALANCE OF FORCES, MAY 14 – 24, 1967

ALGERIA
Troops **60,000**
Tanks **400**
Combat **100**
Aircraft

LEBANON
Troops **12,000**
Tanks **80**
Combat Aircraft **18**

SYRIA
Troops **50,000**
Tanks **400**
Combat Aircraft **120**

KUWAIT
Troops **5,000**
Tanks **24**
Combat Aircraft **9**

Mediterranean Sea

Beirut

Damascus

Kuneitra

TOTAL ARAB STRENGTH
Troops **547,000**
Tanks **2,504**
Combat **957**
Aircraft

ISRAEL
Troops **264,000**
Tanks **800**
Combat **300**
Aircraft

Amman

Gaza

Jerusalem

IRAQ
Troops **70,000**
Tanks **400**
Combat Aircraft **200**

Port Said

El Arish

Abu Aweigila

Suez Canal

JORDAN
Troops **50,000**
Tanks **200**
Combat Aircraft **40**

Cairo

Suez

Kuntilla

Sinai Peninsula

Eilat
Akaba

Dahab

Makna

UNITED NATIONS FORCE
Indians **978**
Canadians **795**
Yugoslavs **579**
Swedes **530**
Brazilians **430**
Norwegians **61**

EGYPT
Troops **240,000**
Tanks **1,200**
Combat Aircraft **500**

Sharm
el Sheikh

Nile R.

SAUDI ARABIA
Troops **50,000**
Tanks **24**
Combat Aircraft **9**

Red Sea

● UN Troops acting as a buffer
force in the Sinai Peninsula
and the Gaza Strip

32°N

28°N

32°E

36°E

0   60   120 mi
0   60   120 km

Although the major area of conflict in the War of Attrition was along the Suez Canal, clashes also occurred in other areas, principally along the border with Jordan. Between 1968 and 1969, the majority of the fighting took place in the Beyt Shean Valley.

Following the Six-Day War, the Palestine Liberation Organization (PLO) had tried to retain a foothold in the West Bank. Because of the IDF's very effective system of patrolling and the relatively poor local support, the PLO was forced to withdraw entirely to the East Bank of the Jordan. From there, the PLO launched a series of attacks, and the Jordanian Army and units of the Iraqi Army stationed in Jordan often fired artillery on Israeli positions across the border.

Many of the PLO attacks were aimed at civilian targets. Following an attack on an Israeli school bus on March 18, 1968, in which a doctor and teacher were killed, the IDF launched a major attack on the PLO base at Karameh, located just south of the Dead Sea within eight miles of Jericho. The PLO previously had moved the original population away, and many of its fighting elements were located there. The PLO established three defensive positions to the north and east of the settlement and also fortified Karameh itself. The defenses had at least 11 firing positions for artillery, some of which had been prepared to accommodate self-propelled guns.

The Israeli attack began at dawn on March 21, 1968. The Israelis planned to launch three armored thrusts across the Jordan River to seal off Karameh. The village itself would be assaulted by paratroopers. The Israeli armored elements came under fire from the Jordanian Army but succeeded in crossing the Jordan at the Damya Bridge in the north and the Allenby Bridge in the south. The IDF paratroopers came under heavy fire from PLO fighters hiding in caves to the west of the village. The assault faltered, and the paratroopers became bogged down in house-to-house combat. After a few hours of fighting, the Israelis had managed to kill approximately 120 PLO fighters and took a large number of prisoners.

That same day the Israelis also mounted an attack against the village of Safi, held by the Jordanian Army, south of the Dead Sea. Israeli losses during that operation were 28 killed and 69 wounded, with a half-dozen armored vehicles destroyed. The Jordanian Army lost 40 soldiers killed, while the PLO lost more than 200. Both sides claimed the engagement as a victory. For the Israelis, the action at Karameh forced the Jordanian Army and the PLO to pull back farther to the east, thus making it harder for them to hit Israeli positions with artillery fire. The PLO, however, tried to turn the fighting at Karameh into a propaganda victory, claiming that it had fought bravely despite being outnumbered and that it had inflicted serious damage on the Israelis.

The engagement at Karameh was the last major encounter of the War of Attrition along the Jordanian border. From that point on, the fighting largely took the form of terrorist actions by the PLO and intermittent artillery fire from Jordanian positions.

The War of Attrition came to an official end on July 31, 1970, when the Israeli government accepted the terms of a cease-fire that went into effect on August 8. The cease-fire was the result of nego-tiations that began in October 1969 that eventually produced a plan put forth by U.S. secretary of state William P. Rogers requiring a preliminary cease-fire of three months' duration. Both sides initially rejected the proposal, but negotiations resumed in April 1970.

The agreement required a three-month freeze on military activity during which neither side was allowed to make any military changes or improvements in the zone that ran 31 miles on either side of the Suez Canal. Almost the same day the cease-fire went into effect, however, the Egyptians started moving new SAM batteries into the Canal Zone. By October they had some 100 SAM sites in place, and those batteries would prove to be a critical factor at the start of the Yom Kippur War in October 1973. Nasser still intended to pursue a war of liberation to regain control of both banks of the canal and the entire Sinai, but on September 28, 1970, he died of a heart attack and was replaced by Anwar Sadat.

During the War of Attrition, Israeli casualties were 367 soldiers killed and more than 3,000 soldiers and civilians wounded. Egypt sustained losses of 8,000–10,000 men and several thousand civilians. The IAF lost 14 aircraft to enemy action while shooting down 98 Egyptian planes. Jordan lost approximately 130 soldiers. The PLO suffered at least 250 fighters killed. The Soviets lost 3 pilots and perhaps another 50 or more advisers on the ground.

RALPH BAKER AND DAVID T. ZABECKI

See also

Artillery; Artillery, Antiaircraft; Bar-Lev, Chaim; Bar-Lev Line; Egypt; Egypt, Armed Forces; *Eilat* Sinking; Israel; Israel Defense Forces; Jordan; Jordan, Armed Forces; Karameh, Battle of; Missiles, Surface-to-Air; Nasser, Gamal Abdel; Palestine Liberation Organization; Rogers, William Pierce; Rogers Plan; Sadat, Anwar; Sinai; Six-Day War; Soviet Union and Russia, Middle East Policy; Suez Canal; Yom Kippur War

References

Bar-Siman-Tov, Yaacov. *The Israel-Egyptian War of Attrition, 1969–1970: A Case-Study of Limited Local War.* New York: Columbia University Press, 1980.

Heikal, Mohamad. *Autumn of Fury.* New York: Random House, 1983.

Herzog, Chaim. *The Arab-Israeli Wars: War and Peace in the Middle East from the War of Independence to Lebanon.* Westminster, MD: Random House, 1984.

———. *The War of Atonement: The Inside Story of the Yom Kippur War.* London: Greenhill, 2003.

Korn, David A. *Stalemate: The War of Attrition and Great Power Diplomacy in the Middle East, 1967–1970.* Boulder CO: Westview, 1992.

Nordeen, Lon. *Fighters over Israel.* London: Greenhill, 1991.

Roth, Stephen J. *The Impact of the Six-Day War: A Twenty-Year Assessment.* London: Palgrave Macmillan, 1988.

Avukah

A radical association of American college students founded in 1925. Avukah, or American Student Zionist Federation, worked to establish a strong identity among Jews and to defend the Jewish cultural heritage. Avukah was also known for its strong support for a Jewish homeland in Palestine.

Avukah (Hebrew for "torch") was founded at Harvard University by a Jewish student named Joseph S. Shubow. Shubow was disconcerted that his fellow Jewish students were more interested in fitting in with the Gentile majority and considered their self-effacing attitude to be cowardly. With fellow members of the Harvard Zionist Society, he invited interesting speakers to meetings, wrote editorials that appeared in the *Harvard Crimson,* and generally made attendance at Zionist meetings a fashionable thing to do. The national Jewish student organization, the Intercollegiate Zionist Organization, had become nearly inactive. Shubow sent invitations to Jewish organizations at other colleges and universities, inviting representatives to attend a conference in Washington, D.C., preceding the National Zionist Convention. Fewer than 100 students from 22 institutions were at the first meeting on June 27, 1925, at the Mayflower Hotel. After discussions, they agreed to form a new group to spark the flame of Zionism among their fellows.

The new group was loosely organized at first and concentrated on activities designed to promote Jewish culture. In 1928, for example, Avukah called upon the New York City Board of Education to protect Jewish rights and culture by authorizing classes to teach Hebrew in the public schools. The request alienated many working-class Jews who preferred Yiddish, a language that upper-class and Zionist Jews saw as crude. Few Jewish students took the Hebrew class before it was dropped by the schools. Other activities had better results. In 1932 and 1936, Avukah issued the *Brandeis Avukah Annual,* a Zionist anthology paying homage to Zionist and U.S. Supreme Court justice Louis Brandeis. The organization also started the Avukah Summer School to indoctrinate young people with the principles of Zionism. The summer school camps were popular, and by 1940 three camps were organized, serving New York, New England, and the Midwest. The curriculum of the camps included lectures and discussions.

Avukah established fellowships for travel to Palestine to demonstrate to American Jews what had been and could be done. The leadership created a system of regional organizations to address local concerns more efficiently. As a part of the educational mission of Avukah, a number of books were published by the organization, including *A Short History of Zionism* by S. H. Sankowsky and *Analysis of Zionism* by Meir Yaari.

At the 1937 annual convention, Avukah's membership discussed how to counter fascism and promote Zionism. A program was agreed upon to address the needs of Jews in the United States and other countries, and Zionism as a world movement to combat fascism was promoted. The membership also discussed how to support a homeland in Palestine for Jews and for other oppressed people where they could live in peace and without fear. Avukah issued a number of books later in 1937 that included *My Impressions of Palestine* by John McGovern and *Diagram of Zionism,* an outline of the theory of Zionism.

Avukah's idealism and program of Zionism attracted many talented young Jewish people. Members included Arthur Goldberg, future U.S. Supreme Court justice; Zellig Harris, founder of mod-

ern linguistics; and Shimon Agranat, future chief justice of Israel. By 1941, Avukah had several thousand members in 65 chapters. Many members entered military or government service during the war, causing Avukah to decline. In 1943, its New York headquarters was permanently closed, marking the end of the organization.

TIM J. WATTS

See also

Brandeis, Louis Dembitz; Youth Aliya; Zionism

References

Shubow, Joseph Shalom, and Louis Dembitz Brandeis. *A Collection of Essays on Contemporary Zionist Thought, Dedicated to Justice Louis D. Brandeis.* New York: Avukah, American Student Zionist Federation, 1932.

Urofsky, Melvin I. *American Zionism from Herzl to the Holocaust.* Lincoln: University of Nebraska Press, 1995.

Azzam Pasha, Abdel Rahman
Born: March 8, 1893
Died: June 1976

Egyptian-born soldier, politician, diplomat, and first leader of the Arab League. Abdel Rahman Azzam Pasha was born on March 8, 1893, in Shubak al-Gharbi in the province of Giza, Egypt. His family, having resided in Egypt for centuries, had produced numerous tribal and national political leaders. Azzam's high school education was at the Saidiyya Secondary School in Cairo. He then moved to London, where he studied medicine for three years. In the summer of 1913 he fought in the Second Balkan War, first with the Albanians and then with the Turkish Army as a volunteer.

At the outbreak of World War I in 1914, Azzam returned to Egypt. There he joined the revolutionary forces in Egypt's Western Desert. In 1915 and 1916 he fought with the Sufi Sannusi forces against the Italians and British. In 1917 he was selected to go to Austria-Hungary and Germany for formal military studies. He was also sent to Constantinople to seek help for the fighting in North Africa.

When World War I ended in November 1918, Azzam refused to obey the Turkish order to surrender. Instead, he joined with other Arabs who had declared Tripoli independent and there fought against the Italians until 1923, when the Sannusi movement collapsed.

Azzam subsequently returned to Egypt, where he was elected to the Egyptian Parliament as a member of the Nationalist Party. He was reelected for two additional terms as a Wafdist, during which he gained a reputation as an ardent advocate of Arabism.

In 1945 when the Arab League was founded, Azzam was unanimously elected its first secretary-general. In his new role, he announced the Arab League's opposition to the Balfour Declaration. He asserted that British promises to Sharif Hussein ibn Ali had inspired the Arab Revolt of 1936–1939 and that these had nullified any promises to Zionists.

During the 1948–1949 Israeli War of Independence, Azzam attempted to secure cooperation among the Arab states but achieved only imperfect success. He later served as the Egyptian ambassador to Iraq, Saudi Arabia, Afghanistan, and Turkey.

Azzam wrote many articles to promote Arab nationalism. He died in early June 1976 in Cannes, France.

ANDREW J. WASKEY

See also

Arab League; Balfour Declaration; Egypt; Pan-Arabism; Zionism

References

Coury, Ralph M. *The Making of an Egyptian Arab Nationalist: The Early Years of Assam Pasha, 1893–1936.* London: Ithaca, 1998.

Nafi, Bashir M. *Arabism, Islamism, and the Palestine Question, 1908–1941: A Political History.* London: Ithaca, 1998.

B

Baath Party (Syria)

Ruling Syrian political party. The Baath Party, or Regional Command of the Arab Socialist Renaissance Party, has long been the dominant political party of Syria. It is part of a larger movement for Arab unification and is socialist in orientation. As part of the only legal political coalition, the National Progressive Front (which includes several other legal parties), the Baath Party currently holds 135 seats in the 250-member People's Assembly.

The Arab Baath movement was founded in 1944 by Michel Aflaq (a Syrian Christian) and Salah al-Din al-Bitar (a Syrian Sunni Muslim) in the Syrian capital of Damascus. The third founder, or founder of the first Baath movement, was Zaki al-Arsuzi. His bookstore al-Baath al-Arabi, established in 1938, provided the actual name of the group he later founded. In 1944, however, his followers went over to the Aflaq–al-Bitar faction.

The Baath Party eventually established itself as a secular Pan-Arabist party in most Arab countries. Baath eventually became the ruling party in Iraq and began its dominance of Syrian politics following a military coup in 1963. The Baath Party became the only legal party in Syria, but with the emergence of different factions, both Aflaq and al-Bitar were forced out of the party. Aflaq went to Iraq, where he became a leader in the Arab Baath Socialist Party.

Inter-Baath splits occurred in Syria in 1963 and in 1966. Another in 1970 brought Hafez al-Assad to the fore. One faction stressed economic reform along socialist lines, and the other placed more emphasis on nationalism. Al-Assad led the latter. He became Syrian president in 1971 after the opposing Baath faction was forced out of the governing coalition.

Theoretically, the Baath Party is first and foremost a party of Arab unity, with the goal of achieving a single Arab state. This goal was dealt a severe blow, however, when the United Arab Republic (UAR), the union between Syria and Egypt, ended in 1961, and since then the party has been preoccupied with the more immediate concerns of the nation. Still, Baath's Arab nationalist tendencies have continued in its hard-line policy toward Israel.

The Baath Party is also a socialist, though not a Marxist, party, emphasizing collective ownership of the means of production and land redistribution. In more recent years, critics have claimed that the party has abandoned socialism and is only used as a justification for dictatorship. Although some claim that Aflaq's original intention was Arab democracy with an emphasis on human rights, others say that he stressed individual loyalty to the Baath ideology.

As the Baath Party developed, it was intended to be a mass party but with a hierarchical structure. Factional rivalry has not allowed the party to achieve this goal, however. The smallest unit in the party is the cell, which may be associated with a school, village, factory, or other local entity. Above the cell is the division, and above the division is the branch. At the highest level of administration is the Regional Command. Local units elect delegates to the central congresses, and these congresses elect representatives to the Regional Command and other top party organs. The highest central authority in the party is the Regional Congress, which is held roughly every four years. Leadership of the party passed to al-Assad's son, Bashar, following the elder al-Assad's death in 2000.

Article 8 of the Syrian Constitution stipulates: "The leading party in the society and the state is the . . . Baath Party. It leads a patriotic and progressive front seeking to unify the resources of the people's masses and place them at the service of the Arab nation's goals." The party has won more seats than any other group in all legislative elections since its establishment as the ruling party in 1963. In the 2003 elections, it secured 135 seats in the People's Assembly.

A Syrian man reads a Baath newspaper in a shop in Damascus on June 11, 2000. Syrian president Hafez al-Assad, who died the day before, is featured on the front page. (Reuters/Corbis)

The Baath Party in Syria has an estimated 800,000 members. The central party reaches its membership through a party newspaper, *al-Baath,* and a government newspaper, *al-Thawra.* The Baath Party recruits members among the nation's youths through the Revolutionary Youth Federation.

SPENCER C. TUCKER

See also

Assad, Bashar al-; Assad, Hafez al-; Baathism; Syria

References

Marr, Phebe. *The Modern History of Iraq.* 2nd ed. Boulder, CO: Westview, 2003.

Price, Daniel E. *Islamic Political Culture, Democracy, and Human Rights.* New York: Praeger, 1999.

Seale, Patrick. *Assad of Syria: The Struggle for the Middle East.* Berkeley: University of California Press, 1988.

Van Dam, Nikolaos. *The Struggle for Power in Syria: Politics and Society under Asad and the Ba'th Party.* London: Croom Helm, 1996.

Baathism

Arab political philosophy. Baathism (also spelled Ba'thism) means "resurrection," "rebirth," or "renaissance" and is the core doctrine of the Baath Party (also formerly known as the al-Baath Arab Socialist Party, or al-Baath). The basic Baathist beliefs are revealed in the Baathist motto and economic dogma *wahdah, hurriyah, ishtirrakiyah,* meaning "unity, freedom, socialism," with "unity" referring to Pan-Arab unity, "freedom" referring to freedom from non-Arab countries and in particular Western interests, and "socialism" referring to Arab socialism. Baathism is thus a combination of Pan-Arabism, Arab socialism, nationalism, and militarism. The Baath Party has as its goal the formation of a single secular and socialist Arab state.

The secular socialist emphasis of Baathism is attractive to marginalized and disadvantaged peoples in the Middle East. Hafez al-

Assad rose to the presidency of Syria (1971–2000) after joining the Baath Party in Latakia (Ladhakiyya), Syria, at age 16. He came from an impoverished community where his father had been a political leader and was an Alawite, a small sect of Shia Islam, but the party found many active adherents from other sects and branches of Islam as well as from Christian groups.

Baathism opposes imperialism and colonialism. It embraces only alliances with Arab countries. Baathists saw foreign domination, especially European and particularly French colonialism, as responsible for the cultural and moral deterioration that had weakened the Arab world and dampened the positive values of Islam while giving rise to class divisions. This belief was particularly true among older generations of Syrian Arab nationalists. Baathism was founded on the conviction that Arabs needed a secular revival of the unity that had once transcended their differences through shared Islamic values and beliefs.

Baathism did not espouse an Arab nationalism rooted in the personal charisma of any one individual. Baathism's earliest proponents were three middle-class educators: Zaki al-Arsuzi, Salah al-Din al-Bitar, and Arab Christian Michel Aflaq. The movement spread slowly throughout Syria in the 1940s. As the Baath Party began to emerge in Damascus, Syria, in the early 1940s, a few Syrian teachers promoted the party in Iraq, and then Fuad al-Rikabi, an Iraqi Shia, headed a group of about 50 Baathists by 1951.

The Baath Party traces its initial founding to 1944, but the official founding of the party is best dated from its first party congress in Damascus on April 7, 1947. This congress established an executive committee and approved a constitution. Creation of the State of Israel in 1948 and the ensuing Israeli War of Independence (1948–1949) greatly aided the growth of Baathism, as many in the Arab world saw their disunity as the key factor in their military defeat. In 1953 the Baath Party merged with the Syrian Socialist Party to form the Arab Socialist Baath Party. Baath Party branches were soon founded in Iraq, Jordan, and Lebanon.

In 1963 the Baathists seized power in Syria in a military coup, popularly known as the 8th of March Revolution, that made the Baath Party the only legal Syrian political party. The ruling military junta removed Aflaq and al-Bitar from the party in 1966, but the party remained divided into nationalist and progressive wings until the nationalist wing, led by General al-Assad, seized control in November 1970 by arresting Prime Minister Nur al-Din Atasi; Salah al-Jadid, chief of staff of the Syrian armed forces and the effective leader of Syria; and other members of the government. Al-Assad and the nationalists were more committed to Arab unity and the destruction of Israel than to socialism, while Atasi's progressive wing had been more committed to neo-Marxist economic reform.

Iraqi Baathists, Arab nationalists, and some others overthrew Abdul Karim Qassem and briefly seized control of the government in February 1963, making Abd al-Salem Arif the president. He then used the Republican Guard to rid himself of the right-wing Baath faction. It was not until 1968 that the Iraqi Baath Party took complete control. This control lasted until 2003 when, in the Iraq War, a coalition led by the United States removed Baathist leader and Iraqi dictator Saddam Hussein from the presidency and banned the Iraqi Baath Party in June 2003.

The Syrian Baath Party is no longer guided by its founding ideology. Having abandoned its commitment to socialism and having failed to foster Arab unity, the party is more committed to the orderly management of the country under a military dictatorship. Although Baathism in Syria remains somewhat splintered into smaller factions, the major internal threat to the party is from the Muslim Brotherhood.

The Syrian Baath Party remains active in Lebanon, Yemen, Jordan, Sudan, Bahrain, and Iraq. The Syrian Baath Party in Palestine is known as al-Saiqa (the Thunderbolt), and the Iraqi Baath Party in Palestine is known as Jabhat al-Tahrir al-Arabiyah (the Arab Liberation Front, or ALF).

RICHARD EDWARDS

See also

Assad, Hafez al-; Hussein, Saddam; Iraq; Syria; United Arab Republic

References

Alahmar, Abdullah. *The Baath and the Regenerating Revolution: A Search in the Aspects of the Baathist Arab Socialist Party and Its National Guiding Experience.* Damascus, Syria: Dar Albaath, 1991.

Chand, Attar. *The Revolutionary Arabs: A Study of the Arab Baath Socialist Movement.* Delhi, India: Homeland Publications, 1981.

Kienle, Eberhard. *Ba'th Versus Ba'th: The Syro-Iraqi Conflict, 1968–1989.* New York: Tauris, 1990.

Babylon, Project

See Project Babylon

Baghdad Pact
Start Date: February 4, 1955
End Date: March 12, 1979

Treaty of mutual cooperation and mutual defense among the nations of Turkey, Iraq, Pakistan, Iran, and Great Britain agreed to in principle on February 4, 1955. The Baghdad Pact, also known as the Central Treaty Organization (CENTO) or the Middle East Treaty Organization (METO), was part of an effort by the United States and the West in general to establish regional alliances to contain the spread of Soviet influence.

The United States and Great Britain were the pact's chief sponsors. Each had different reasons for trying to lure Arab countries to join a defensive alliance. In the end, the Baghdad Pact failed because Arab leaders saw it as an attempt by the West to continue its colonial domination over the region. The Baghdad Pact in its different forms was the least effective of the anticommunist regional alliances sponsored by the United States.

As the Cold War developed in the late 1940s and early 1950s, the U.S. government adopted a policy of communist containment.

Representatives of the five nations of the Baghdad Pact, as well as a delegation from the United States, meet in Ankara, Turkey, in January 1958. (Bettmann/Corbis)

In Europe, the North Atlantic Treaty Organization (NATO) was formed in 1949 to prevent the expansion of Soviet control on that continent. President Dwight D. Eisenhower's administration continued this process along other borders of the Soviet Union. The Middle East was viewed as a key area, in large part because it was the main source of oil for the West. The British government was expected to be the key to the formation of an alliance here since it already had extensive relations with the Arab states. As such, British diplomats laid the groundwork for regional defense agreements. The first attempts included Egypt, but the government of President Gamal Abdel Nasser was more interested in Pan-Arab agreements that excluded Britain. Indeed, Egypt refused to join a proposed Middle East Defense Organization in 1953, causing that initiative to collapse.

The United States and Britain therefore tried to create an alliance among the northern tier of Arab states. Turkey was already bound in an alliance to the West, thanks to NATO. Its status as a Muslim nation helped to encourage other Muslim countries to consider defensive alliances with the Western powers. In February 1954, Turkey and Pakistan signed a pact of mutual cooperation, one of the first in the region. Following much diplomatic activity, Iraqi prime minister Nuri al-Said announced that Iraq would sign a mutual defense pact with Turkey.

On February 24, 1955, Turkey and Iraq signed the Pact of Mutual Cooperation, which became better known as the Baghdad Pact, aimed at preventing Soviet aggression. The treaty included language inviting members of the Arab League as well as other interested nations to join. Britain signed the alliance on April 5, 1955. As a result, the Royal Air Force received the right to base units in Iraq and to train the Iraqi Air Force. Pakistan joined on September 23, 1955, and Iran joined on October 12, 1955. The United States remained a shadow member of the group but did not officially join. American relations with Israel were an obstacle that might have prevented Arab members from joining. A permanent secretariat and permanent council for the alliance was created and headquartered in Baghdad.

Nasser viewed the Baghdad Pact as an attack on his own vision of Pan-Arabism, to be achieved under his leadership. He therefore immediately attacked the pact as Britain's way of continuing its colonial presence in the Middle East. He called it a hindrance to real Pan-Arab movements. At the time, Nasser had great prestige in the Arab world as a nationalist and opponent of Israel, and his condemnation of the treaty caused opposition to it among ordinary Arab peoples. Jordan had been expected to join the Baghdad Pact, but riots there convinced King Hussein I to withdraw his support for it. Syria refused to sign the treaty, instead forming a union with

Egypt known as the United Arab Republic (UAR), to take effect on February 1, 1958. Even Lebanon, which requested Western assistance to help settle a civil war in 1958, refused to join the pact, despite pressure from the United States and Britain to do so. Saudi Arabia also opposed the pact because it feared that Iraq would become the dominant regional power.

The Baghdad Pact received a serious blow in October 1956 when Britain joined France and Israel in an invasion of Egypt in reaction to the Suez Crisis. The U.S. government opposed the attack and helped force its allies to withdraw. The action discredited Britain across the Middle East. To try to prop up the Western orientation of the pact, the United States joined the Military Committee of the organization in 1958 and funneled military assistance and other funds through the pact's organizations.

The gravest threat to the Baghdad Pact occurred on July 14, 1958, when Iraqi officers overthrew King Faisal II and the Iraqi monarchy. Popular sentiment in Iraq held that the pact simply modified Britain's colonial dominance of Iraq. Indeed, the alliance had weakened support for the government and the royal family. When Iraqi Army officers overthrew the government, few Iraqis were willing to defend the old order. The royal family was slaughtered, as was Nuri al-Said. The ruling officers, sympathetic to Nasser, withdrew Iraq from the Baghdad Pact on March 24, 1959. That same year, the United States officially joined the alliance, which changed its name to the Central Treaty Organization.

The alliance proved to be weak, however. When Pakistan and Iran were involved in conflicts with India and then Iraq during the 1960s, they tried to invoke the alliance to involve Britain and the United States. Britain and the United States refused to be drawn into the regional conflicts, however, because they saw the alliance as one limited to stopping aggression on the part of the Soviet Union. As a result, Pakistan and Iran came to regard the alliance with considerable cynicism.

CENTO declined in importance as the British Empire continued to contract. In 1968, Britain decided to withdraw its forces from the Persian Gulf, making British bases on Cyprus the closest ones to the Middle East. In 1974, budget cutbacks forced Britain to withdraw specific troop commitments to CENTO. After that, CENTO became a chiefly symbolic structure rather than an effective defensive mechanism. In 1979, Iran withdrew from CENTO following the overthrow of Shah Reza Pahlavi. On March 12, 1979, Pakistan withdrew as well. CENTO and the vestiges of the Baghdad Pact had now collapsed entirely.

TIM WATTS

See also

Arab League; Arab Nationalism; Egypt; Hussein, King of Jordan; Iran; Iraq; Nasser, Gamal Abdel; Pan-Arabism; Said, Nuri al-; Turkey, Middle East Policy; United Arab Republic; United Kingdom, Middle East Policy; United States, Middle East Policy

References

CENTO Public Relations Division. *The Story of the Central Treaty Organization.* Washington, DC: CENTO, 1959.

Dann, Uriel. *Iraq under Qassem: A Political History, 1958–1963.* New York: Praeger, 1969.

Kuniholm, Bruce. *The Origins of the Cold War in the Near East.* Princeton, NJ: Princeton University Press, 1980.

Podeh, Elie. *The Quest for Hegemony in the Arab World: The Struggle over the Baghdad Pact.* New York: Brill, 2003.

Baker, James Addison, III
Born: April 28, 1930

U.S. politician, influential Republican adviser, secretary of the treasury, and secretary of state. Born on April 28, 1930, in Houston, Texas, to a wealthy local family, James Baker III studied classics at Princeton University, graduating in 1952. After two years in the U.S. Marine Corps, he earned a law degree from the University of Texas at Austin in 1957. That same year he joined a law firm in Houston, where he practiced until 1975.

Baker first entered politics in 1970, working for George H. W. Bush's U.S. senatorial campaign, a contest that Bush lost. Beginning in 1975, Baker spent a year as undersecretary of commerce in President Gerald Ford's administration. Baker then managed Ford's unsuccessful 1976 presidential campaign. After managing Bush's unsuccessful bid for the Republican presidential nomination in 1980, Baker became a senior adviser to President Ronald Reagan's 1980 campaign when Bush withdrew from the race.

James A. Baker III served as chief of staff and treasury secretary for President Ronald Reagan and as secretary of state for President George H. W. Bush. (U.S. Department of State)

From 1981 until 1985, Baker served as White House chief of staff. In 1984 he successfully engineered Reagan's reelection campaign. Reagan subsequently appointed him secretary of the treasury in 1985. In 1988 Baker managed Vice President Bush's presidential campaign and was rewarded by being appointed secretary of state in 1989. In that role, Baker helped reorient U.S. foreign policy at the end of the Cold War. He was involved in negotiations that led to the reunification of Germany and the dismantling of the Soviet Union. He also presided over pre–Persian Gulf War negotiations and helped to construct the 34-nation alliance that fought with the United States in the war. Baker initially opposed sending Pershing antimissile batteries to Israel to protect that nation against Iraqi Scud missile attack but gave way when he was reminded by Defense Secretary Dick Cheney of the possible political cost to the administration of a failure to aid Israel. In 1992 Bush named Baker White House chief of staff and campaign manager in his bid for reelection, which Bush lost.

After leaving government service in 1993, Baker joined the Houston-based law firm of Baker Botts and become senior counselor to The Carlyle Group, a corporate banking firm in Washington, D.C. In 1995 he published his memoirs, *The Politics of Diplomacy: Revolution, War and Peace, 1989–1992,* about his years at the State Department. In 2000 Baker served as President-elect George W. Bush's transition adviser. In 2004 Baker served as the personal envoy of United Nations (UN) secretary-general Kofi Annan in seeking to reach a peaceful solution to the conflict over the Western Sahara. In 2003 Baker was a special presidential envoy for President George W. Bush on Iraqi debt relief.

JOHN DAVID RAUSCH JR.

See also

Bush, George Herbert Walker; Bush, George Walker; Persian Gulf War; Reagan, Ronald Wilson

References

Baker, James A., III, with Thomas M. DeFrank. *The Politics of Diplomacy: Revolution, War, and Peace, 1989–1992.* New York: Putnam, 1995.

Hurst, Steven. *Foreign Policy of the Bush Administration: In Search of a New World Order.* New York: Continuum International Publishing Group, 1999.

Baker Plan
Start Date: November 1, 1989
End Date: June 1990

A five-point plan put forth by U.S. secretary of state James A. Baker III on November 1, 1989, to establish guidelines for the election of a Palestinian governing council and to jump-start flagging peace efforts between Israel and the Palestinians. Baker's initiative was based largely on a four-point plan previously proposed by the Israelis earlier in the year. In a nutshell, the Israelis called for strengthening relations with Egypt, the promotion of peaceful relations with other Arab nations, the amelioration of the Palestinian refugee

dilemma, and the holding of Palestinian elections and temporary Palestinian self-rule. Despite ongoing dialogue between Israel and Egypt, however, there was little forward momentum in the peace process. The chief stumbling block was the Israelis' refusal to enter into direct talks with the Palestine Liberation Organization (PLO), despite its 1988 renunciation of violence against Israel and its acceptance of Israel as a legitimate entity.

By the spring of 1989, President George H. W. Bush's administration had grown frustrated with the stalemated peace process and vowed to take a more active role in it. In a move that surprised many and angered Jews in Israel as well as in the United States, Secretary of State Baker pointedly blamed Israel for the impasse during a speech to the American Israel Public Affairs Committee (AIPAC) and seemingly embraced many of the positions taken by the Palestinians and the PLO. Nevertheless, throughout the summer and early fall, American officials worked with both the Israelis and the Egyptians to arrive at a compromise. The ultimate goal was to empower Egypt to bring Palestinians (but not the PLO) into discussions with the Israelis that would lead to elections and eventual autonomy and statehood.

On November 1, 1989, Baker formally presented his plan to the Israelis and Egyptians. The five-point plan involved the following steps and conditions. First, the Israelis had to meet with a Palestinian delegation in Cairo. Second, the Egyptians were required to act as facilitators (but could not speak for the Palestinians). Third, a mutually approved list of Palestinian attendees acceptable to Israel had to be drawn up before the meeting. Fourth, Palestinians were obliged to show a willingness to discuss elections and other negotiable issues, and the Israelis had to accept such dialogue per their May 1989 four-point proposal. Fifth, the foreign ministers of Egypt, Israel, and the United States were to meet in Washington, D.C., within two weeks' time.

Later in November, the Israelis agreed to move forward with the Baker Plan but with two preconditions. First, the PLO could not be involved in the selection of the Palestinian delegates at the proposed conference. Second, Israel insisted that the discussion be limited to preparations for Palestinian elections. The Baker Plan precipitated a political donnybrook in Israel, and in March 1990 the Unity government fell. When Prime Minister Yitzhak Shamir formed a new government that June, one of his first moves was to reject in toto the Baker Plan. The Israeli rejection angered the Bush administration and famously prompted a perturbed Baker to publicly give Shamir the telephone number of the White House with the exhortation to "call when you're serious about peace."

PAUL G. PIERPAOLI JR.

See also

American Israel Public Affairs Committee; Baker, James Addison, III; Bush, George Herbert Walker; Palestine Liberation Organization; Shamir, Yitzhak

References

Baker, James A., III, with Thomas M. DeFrank. *The Politics of Diplomacy: Revolution, War, and Peace, 1989–1992.* New York: Putnam, 1995.

Hurst, Steven. *Foreign Policy of the Bush Administration: In Search of a New World Order.* New York: Continuum International Publishing Group, 1999.

Segev, Tom. *One Palestine, Complete: Jews and Arabs under the British Mandate.* New York: Owl Books, 2001.

Baldat al-Shaykh Massacre
Start Date: January 30, 1947
End Date: January 31, 1947

Mass killing of Palestinian civilians carried out by the Palmach, Haganah, and allied Jewish paramilitary members in the Palestinian town of Baldat al-Shaykh in the British Mandate for Palestine during January 30–31, 1947. The massacre at Baldat al-Shaykh was in retaliation for the killing and wounding of some 60 Jews at the Haifa Petroleum Refinery. Although the details of the melee at the refinery remain very sketchy, the end result was approximately 60 Jews dead or injured and an unknown number of Palestinian casualties.

Late in the evening of January 30, 1947, a band of 150–200 well-armed Jews decided to mount a retaliatory raid against two Palestinian towns: Baldat al-Shaykh and Hawasa. The men were mostly Palmach commandos from the 1st Battalion, although there was also a detachment of men from the so-called Carmelie Brigade (Haganah). As the hour of the planned assault approached, the decision was made to concentrate on Baldat al-Shaykh. Furthermore, the attackers would not attempt to infiltrate into the center of the towns. Rather, they would direct their power on outlying areas.

The assault began a bit after midnight on January 31 and lasted for just one hour. The attackers caught most of the town's residents asleep as they burst into homes indiscriminately, firing machine guns and lobbing grenades into Palestinian homes. When the mayhem ended at about 1:30 a.m., approximately 60 Palestinians—many of them women, children, and elderly—lay dead. The attack outraged the Palestinians and brought international condemnation upon the Palmach. A later report by those Palmach members involved in the attack stated that "due to the fact that gunfire was directed inside rooms, it was not possible to avoid injuring women and children."

The Baldat al-Shaykh Massacre was part of the opening salvo in a series of mass killings involving both Jews and Palestinians that precipitated the Arab-Jewish Communal War (November 1947–May 1948) and was a precursor to the forthcoming Israeli War of Independence (May 1948–March 1949).

PAUL G. PIERPAOLI JR.

See also
Arab-Jewish Communal War; Haganah; Israeli War of Independence, Overview; Palmach

References
Hadawi, Sami. *Bitter Harvest: Palestine between 1914–1967.* New York: New World Press, 1967.

Rosenfield, Daniel. *Code Name: Amnon: The Life and Times of a Haganah Fighter, 1943–1949.* New York: Rosenfield, 2003.

Balfour, Arthur James
Born: July 25, 1848
Died: March 19, 1930

British political leader, prime minister (1902–1905), and foreign minister (1916–1919). Arthur James Balfour was born on July 25, 1848, in Whittinghame, East Lothian, Scotland. He was educated at Eton and Trinity College, Cambridge. He began his political career in 1878 as the private secretary to his uncle, the Marquess of Salisbury, who was then foreign secretary for Prime Minister Benjamin Disraeli. Balfour was a Unionist (Conservative) who served in the British House of Commons from 1874 to 1905. He first rose to prominence in 1897 as the first lord of the treasury. He became leader of the House of Commons in 1892 and then prime minister in July 1902, a post he held until December 1905.

Arthur James Balfour, prime minister of Great Britain during 1902–1905 and British foreign secretary during World War I. He is known for the Balfour Declaration of November 1917, a proclamation that was designed to win Jewish support for the war effort and proposed creation of a Jewish homeland in Palestine. (Library of Congress)

The major events of Balfour's prime ministership were the Education Act (also known as the Balfour Act), which in 1902 reorganized the local administration of elementary and secondary schools; the Wyndham Land Purchase Act that in 1903 encouraged the sale of lands owned by absentee British landlords to their Irish tenant farmers; and the formation of the Committee of Imperial Defense in 1904 to coordinate Britain's global military strategy. Balfour was nicknamed "Bloody Balfour" for his unyielding opposition to Irish home rule and his harsh response to threats to British authority there from the Catholic Irish.

Balfour led the Conservative Party until November 1911. He returned to government at the beginning of World War I, in 1915 succeeding Winston Churchill as first lord of the Admiralty in the first World War I coalition cabinet led by Herbert Henry Asquith. Balfour became the foreign secretary in December 1916 in the second wartime coalition cabinet, led by David Lloyd George. Balfour's primary responsibility in this post was securing the support of the United States for the Allied war effort.

In April 1917, Balfour traveled to the United States to secure additional U.S. antisubmarine warfare vessels and merchant shipping. He understood neither the sincerity of the Austro-Hungarian peace overtures nor the threat posed by the Bolsheviks in Russia.

Balfour is perhaps best remembered for the so-called Balfour Declaration. Zionist leaders Chaim Weizmann and Nahum Sokolow met with Balfour and convinced him of the need to rally world Jewish opinion, especially in Britain and the United States, behind the Allied war effort. Balfour then wrote a letter, approved by the British government, to the English Jewish banker Baron Rothschild that committed Britain to support creation of a Jewish homeland in Palestine. This letter was published on November 2, 1917, and became known as the Balfour Declaration. Although it came to be regarded as the cornerstone for the later formation of the State of Israel, it greatly angered the Arabs.

Balfour attended the Paris Peace Conference in 1919, but he resigned as foreign secretary for health reasons in October 1919. He remained in the cabinet, however, as lord president of the council until 1922. He led the British delegations to the first meeting of the League of Nations in 1920 and the Washington Naval Conference (1921–1922).

In 1922 Balfour was created Earl Balfour, Viscount Traprain. He was also a highly regarded author of books that explored issues of modern religion such as *The Foundations of Belief* (1900), *Theism and Humanism* (1915), *Theism and Thought* (1923), and *Opinions and Arguments* (1927).

Balfour returned to government service during 1925–1929 as the lord president of the council in Stanley Baldwin's Conservative government. In this position, in a document known as the Balfour Report (1926), Balfour helped define the relationship between Great Britain and the Dominion countries. This was explicitly stated in the 1931 Statute of Westminster, issued a year after Balfour's death, which occurred on March 19, 1930, in Woking, Surrey, England.

RICHARD EDWARDS

See also

Balfour Declaration; League of Nations Covenant, Article 22; Sokolow, Nahum; Weizmann, Chaim; Zionism

References

Egremont, Max. *Balfour: A Life of Arthur James Balfour.* London: Collins, 1980.

MacKay, Ruddock F. *Balfour: Intellectual Statesman.* New York: Oxford University Press, 1985.

Sanders, Ronald. *The High Walls of Jerusalem: A History of the Balfour Declaration and the Birth of the British Mandate for Palestine.* New York: Holt, Rinehart and Winston, 1983.

Stein, Leonard. *The Balfour Declaration.* New York: Simon and Schuster, 1961.

Zebel, Sydney Henry. *Balfour: A Political Biography.* Cambridge: Cambridge University Press, 1973.

Balfour Declaration
Event Date: November 2, 1917

The Balfour Declaration of November 2, 1917, was a promise by the British government to support the creation of a national homeland for the Jewish people. The British government issued the declaration in an effort to gain the support of Jews around the world for the Allied war effort. The promise apparently contradicted an earlier pledge by London to the Arabs to support the establishment of an independent Arab state after World War I. The Balfour Declaration helped encourage Jewish immigration to Palestine during the 1920s and 1930s, but it alienated Arabs from the British Mandate government. Indirectly, the Balfour Declaration led to the creation of the State of Israel and to ongoing conflict between Arabs and Jews in the Middle East.

Before World War I, Palestine was a part of the Ottoman Empire and included the Sinai Peninsula and parts of present-day Lebanon and Syria. A small number of Jewish settlements were located in Palestine, with a total population of approximately 50,000 people. The Zionist movement, developed in the 19th century, taught that Judaism was not only a religion but also a national group. Zionists called for Jewish immigration to traditional Jewish lands to establish a Jewish state for Jews from around the world. Zionism was formally organized in 1897 when smaller groups came together to create the World Zionist Organization (WZO) at Basel, Switzerland. Theodor Herzl became the group's first president. Supporters of Zionism included influential Jews and non-Jews throughout Europe and the United States.

When World War I began, Zionists urged the various governments to support their movement. The most fertile ground was in Great Britain. Although the total number of Jews in Britain was small, they included influential individuals such as Sir Herbert Samuel and the Rothschild banking family. The leader of the Zionists in Britain was Dr. Chaim Weizmann, chemistry professor at Manchester University. Weizmann had discovered a revolutionary method of producing acetone, important to the munitions indus-

Foreign Office,
November 2nd, 1917.

Dear Lord Rothschild,

I have much pleasure in conveying to you, on behalf of His Majesty's Government, the following declaration of sympathy with Jewish Zionist aspirations which has been submitted to, and approved by, the Cabinet.

"His Majesty's Government view with favour the establishment in Palestine of a national home for the Jewish people, and will use their best endeavours to facilitate the achievement of this object, it being clearly understood that nothing shall be done which may prejudice the civil and religious rights of existing non-Jewish communities in Palestine or the rights and political status enjoyed by Jews in any other country"

I should be grateful if you would bring this declaration to the knowledge of the Zionist Federation.

Arthur Balfour's letter to Lord Rothschild declaring British support for a Jewish homeland in Palestine, dated November 2, 1917. (Israeli Government Press Office)

try. Members of the British government understandably held Weizmann in high esteem. Others believed that the West had a moral duty to Jews because of past injustices.

Events during the spring of 1917 aided Weizmann's campaign for British support for a Jewish homeland in Palestine. The first was the March Revolution in Russia. Some of the more prominent leaders of the revolution were Jews, and Weizmann argued that they were more likely to keep Russia in the war if an Allied goal was a Jewish homeland. Another important event was the entry of the United States into the war in April 1917. The large Jewish population in the United States could campaign for greater and more immediate U.S. contributions to the war effort. Jewish financial contributions toward the war effort might be increased with support for a homeland as well. Weizmann also told his friends in the British government that support for a Jewish homeland might prevent German Jews from giving their full support to Kaiser Wilhelm II's war effort.

Arthur James Balfour was foreign secretary and supported a promise of a Jewish homeland after the war. On a trip to the United States, he conferred with Supreme Court justice Louis Brandeis, a Zionist. Brandeis was an adviser to President Woodrow Wilson and told Balfour that the president supported a homeland for the Jews. At the time, however, Wilson was reluctant to give it open support since the United States was not formally at war with the Ottoman Empire. Other prominent Americans, such as former presidential candidate William Jennings Bryan, supported a Jewish homeland, many because they believed it would fulfill biblical prophecies.

Members of the Zionist movement in Britain helped draft a declaration that was approved by the British cabinet and released by Balfour on November 2, 1917. The key sentence in the document was "His Majesty's Government view with favour the establishment in Palestine of a national home for the Jewish people." The declaration went on to state that the civil and religious rights of the existing non-Jewish peoples in Palestine were not to be prejudiced. In response to fears by some Jews that a homeland in Palestine would harm their efforts to assimilate into other societies, the declaration also called for nothing that would harm those efforts. The French government pledged its support for the declaration on February 11, 1918. Wilson finally gave open approval in a letter to Rabbi Stephen Wise on October 29, 1918.

The declaration did indeed win Jewish support for the Allied war effort, but it had unintended effects as well. Correspondence between British high commissioner in Egypt Henry McMahon and Sharif Hussein of Mecca in 1915 had promised the establishment of an independent Arab state upon the defeat of the Ottomans. It was understood that this state would include Palestine. The declaration was also a violation of the Sykes-Picot Agreement between Great Britain and France that provided for joint rule over the area directly after the war. The apparent double-dealing by the British government alienated many Arabs and caused them to doubt whether they could trust British promises.

At the end of World War I, the League of Nations granted a mandate over Palestine to Great Britain. Language from the Balfour Declaration was incorporated into the mandate's wording. During the next 30 years, the Jewish population of Palestine increased from 50,000 to 600,000 people. This dramatic increase in immigration of Jews to Palestine led to numerous clashes with Palestinians already living there. Ultimately the task of trying to keep conflicting promises to Arabs and Jews proved too much for the British. They gave up their mandate in 1948, and the State of Israel was created. The result has been hostility and sporadic wars between Jews and Arabs ever since.

TIM WATTS

See also

Arab Revolt of 1916–1918; Balfour, Arthur James; Herzl, Theodor; Sykes-Picot Agreement; Weizmann, Chaim

References

Lenczowski, George. *The Middle East in World Affairs.* 4th ed. Ithaca, NY: Cornell University Press, 1980.

Sanders, Ronald. *The High Walls of Jerusalem: A History of the Balfour Declaration and the Birth of the British Mandate for Palestine.* New York: Holt, Rinehart and Winston, 1983.

Stein, Leonard. *The Balfour Declaration.* New York: Simon and Schuster, 1961.

Baltim, Battle of

Start Date: October 12, 1973
End Date: October 13, 1973

The Battle of Baltim during the 1973 Yom Kippur War took place off the Egyptian port of Baltim on the night of October 12–13 and was fought between Egyptian and Israeli missile boats.

The Israeli Navy had been seeking an opportunity to replicate with the Egyptian Navy its victory over the Syrians in the October 6 Battle of Latakia (Ladhakiyya). That chance presented itself on October 12 when four Egyptian missile boats, all Osa-class, sortied from Port Said, Egypt. This move was anticipated. The Israeli Army had launched a ground counterattack in the area that day against Egyptian forces in the hope of regaining the Suez Canal. The Israeli Navy command believed that the missile boats at Port Said would then attempt to flee to the naval base at Alexandria, 110 miles to the west. The Israeli ground attack stalled, however, and Israeli Navy leaders decided to try to draw out the boats by shelling land targets in the Nile Delta area.

Commander Michael Barkai had charge of the flotilla of 10 Israeli missile boats dispatched from Haifa. At 9:00 p.m. local time the missile boats picked up radar contacts and charged in line abreast at 40 knots toward the Egyptian coast, only to discover that they had been chasing a phantom, no doubt the result of freak atmospheric conditions. The Israeli missile boats had been dispatched in a hurry, and 2 had been on station for some time, so 4 of them had fuel barely sufficient to return to Haifa.

Barkai informed Israeli Navy commander Rear Admiral Binyamin Telem of the situation, and Telem suggested that Barkai send to Haifa only the four boats that were low on fuel and remain on station with the six remaining. Barkai agreed and shifted his flag from the *Miznak* to the *Herev*. As Barkai was transferring to the *Herev*, the Israelis learned that four Egyptian boats had sortied from Alexandria and were headed east.

At 11:00 p.m. Barkai immediately ordered his six remaining missile boats to intercept the Egyptians. The Israeli boats moved in pairs on parallel tracks. To the north were the two large Israeli-manufactured Reshef-class boats: the *Reshef* and the *Keshet*. In the center were the *Eliat* (named for the Israeli destroyer sunk by an Egyptian Styx missile in 1967) and the missileless *Misgav*. On the south were the *Herev* and the *Soufa*. The Israelis did not know if the Egyptian boats were aware of their presence.

Just before midnight, Barkai took the *Herev* and the *Soufa* in close to shore to shell Damietta in the Nile Delta. As they were preparing to open fire, the *Herev* picked up readings off Baltim to the west. In order to determine if it was another false reading, Barkai ordered his northern boats to send up chaff rockets and see if these would draw missile fire. The chaff cloud immediately drew two pairs of Styx rockets, and Barkai responded by ordering his own boats, which were within the 27-mile range of the Egyptian Styx missiles but well beyond the 12 miles of the Israeli Gabriel missiles, to charge what were soon

identified as four Egyptian Osa-class missile boats. At 12:15 a.m. the Egyptians began launching their Styx missiles. The situation was tense, for while electronic countermeasures (ECM) on the Israeli boats would help, the boats themselves would remain one of many targets identified by Styx radar. The Egyptian boats then fired their last barrage of missiles at a range of 18 miles, still well beyond effective Gabriel range, then turned to run back into Alexandria.

The chase was on, with the Israelis endeavoring to close to within their own firing range. Barkai divided up the targets and ordered none of his boats to fire until they had closed to within 10.5 miles. After a 25-minute chase, the *Keshet* closed to within Barkai's imposed range and fired a Gabriel missile that hit one of the Egyptian missile boats, setting it alight. With the *Keshet* taking on water from a burst pipe, the *Misgav* dashed in to finish off the Egyptian missile boat with cannon fire. Meanwhile, the *Reshef* had also fired at and hit another Egyptian missile boat. The *Reshef* then closed with the *Eilat*, which had also fired a missile at the same Egyptian boat, and they sank the Egyptian boat with cannon fire. A third Egyptian missile boat was also destroyed by the *Herev* and the *Soufa*. The last Egyptian Osa-class boat managed to escape to the protection of the guns and missile defenses of Alexandria. At 1:30 a.m. on October 13, the Israeli boats began turning northeast and ran for Haifa. The Battle of Latakia and the Battle of Baltim were the two major naval engagements of the war.

SPENCER C. TUCKER

See also
Latakia, Battle of; Yom Kippur War

References
Erell, Shlomo. "Israeli Saar FPBs Pass Combat Test in the Yom Kippur War." *U.S. Naval Institute Proceedings* (September 1974): 115–18.
Rabinovich, Abraham. *The Boats of Cherbourg: The Secret Israeli Operation That Revolutionized Naval Warfare.* New York: Seaver, 1988.

Bangalore Torpedo

Explosive device employed on land and designed to destroy small strongholds, booby traps, mines, tunnels, etc. The Bangalore Torpedo was developed in 1912 in Bangalore, India, and was based on the design of a British Army captain. The torpedo was originally intended to destroy booby traps and barricades left over from the South African War (Boer War, 1899–1902) and Russo-Japanese Wars (1904–1905).

The Bangalore Torpedo employed a series of attachable extensions to deliver a small explosive charge approximately 3 feet to 6.5 feet from the operator. Initially, the explosive charge weighed approximately 2–4 pounds and was attached at the tip. In 1915, however, engineers began to include explosives in some of the extension tubes to improve its capability against extensive battlefield obstacles.

During World War I, the Bangalore Torpedo was most commonly employed against thick barbed-wire entanglements. The torpedo would be placed under the barbed wire and then detonated, scattering the wire. The Bangalore Torpedo remained a popular weapon during World War II, the Korean War, and the Vietnam War and was used to remove beach obstacles, clear paths through minefields, and remove other impediments to troop movements. In Vietnam, the torpedoes were used to destroy tunnels and booby traps. However, the communist Viet Cong often disarmed the torpedoes when U.S. troops withdrew to a safe distance and later used the explosives recovered from them against the Americans.

In the Arab-Israeli conflicts, both Arab and Israeli forces made extensive use of the Bangalore Torpedo. The Israelis were reportedly using the torpedo with deadly accuracy against insurgent pockets as early as 1950. Arab militaries followed through with their own version of the torpedo. Because they were lightweight, inexpensive, and easy to operate, Bangalore Torpedoes also found their way into the hands of terrorists and other radicalized insurgents.

In the 1980s, Western militaries began to replace the Bangalore Torpedo with remotely fired explosive cords that allowed engineers to destroy the obstacles or mines from ever greater standoff distances. Although they remain in the inventories of many militaries, the last Bangalore Torpedoes reportedly were employed to destroy obstacles in Angola and Bosnia in the mid-1990s.

CARL OTIS SCHUSTER

See also

Arms Sales, International; Terrorism

References

Bishop, Chris. *Encyclopedia of Weapons of World War II.* New York: Metrobooks, 2002.

Dowswell, Paul. *20th Century Perspectives: Weapons & Technology of WWI.* New York: Heinemann, 2003.

Laffin, John. *A Western Front Companion 1914–1918.* London: Sutton Publishers, 1995.

Banna, Sabri Khalil, al

See Abu Nidal

Bar-Ilan, Meir

Born: 1880
Died: April 17, 1949

The principal leader of religious Zionism in the years before the founding of Israel. Meir Bar-Ilan was born Meir Berlin in 1880 in Volozhin, Lithuania, then part of the Russian Empire. His father was Rabbi Naphtali Zevi Judah Berlin, known as the Netziv. The elder Berlin was head of the Volozhin Yeshiva, one of the most respected rabbinical academies in Russia. Bar-Ilan studied at Volozhin before continuing his studies at traditional yeshivas in Telshe, Brisk, and Novardok following his father's death in 1894. He was deeply influ-

enced by his father's Zionism and commitment to settlement in Eretz Israel and Hebraized his name to Bar-Ilan as a symbol of his commitment to religious Zionism.

In 1902 Bar-Ilan moved to Germany, where he studied a more modern form of Orthodox Judaism. He attended the University of Berlin and joined the Mizrahi movement. In 1905 he served as a delegate to the Seventh Zionist Congress, representing the Mizrahi. At the congress, the British government offered a plan to settle Jewish immigrants in Uganda as a temporary homeland. Bar-Ilan broke with most of his Mizrahi comrades to vote against the plan. He had come to the conclusion that only Palestine would be acceptable as a Jewish homeland. He coined the phrase that was later adopted by Mizrahi as its slogan: "The land of Israel for the people of Israel according to the Torah of Israel."

In 1911 Bar-Ilan was appointed secretary for the world Mizrahi movement and worked with groups around the world to achieve Zionism's goals. That same year, he founded the first Hebrew-language weekly newspaper, *Ha'Ivri.* The paper was intended to be an open forum for Zionist issues. Over the next 10 years, articles as well as literary works on the problems facing Zionism appeared regularly in its pages. In 1913 Bar-Ilan traveled to the United States to organize local Mizrahi organizations into a national group. He presided over the first national convention in Cincinnati in 1914. He returned to Germany before World War I broke out but immigrated to the United States in 1915.

While in the United States, Bar-Ilan worked with Jewish organizations to advance the Zionist cause and to promote Jewish education. He established the Mizrahi Teachers Institute in New York in 1917. The institute later became part of Yeshiva University. Bar-Ilan himself served temporarily as president of Yeshiva University in 1923 when its president, Bernard Revel, was absent. Bar-Ilan also served on the Board of Directors for the Jewish National Fund, which raised money for the creation of a Jewish homeland in Palestine and the settlement of Jews there.

Bar-Ilan was elected president of Mizrahi at the First Mizrahi Congress in 1920 and was recognized as the leader of religious Zionism for the remainder of his life. In 1926 he settled in Jerusalem. He opposed the partition of Palestine and urged noncooperation with British authorities. He convinced local Jewish officials to establish an educational system that included traditional religious values. Bar-Ilan believed that education was the only way in which Orthodox Judaism could influence the society being created in Palestine. Between 1938 and 1949, he edited the Tel Aviv daily newspaper *Ha tsofeh,* which represented Orthodox opinions.

Bar-Ilan was also recognized as a biblical scholar and wrote many works on Hebrew history. After Israel achieved independence in 1948, he assembled a council of experts to review legal issues in light of traditional religious law. In elections for the first Knesset (Israeli parliament), he organized the various religious parties into the National Religious Front.

After Bar-Ilan's death in Jerusalem on April 17, 1949, his dedication to education was recognized by the founding of Bar-Ilan

University. This institution has the goal of combining traditional Jewish learning with modern academic scholarship.

TIM J. WATTS

See also

Jewish National Fund; Mizrahic Judaism; Zionism

References

Elon, Amos. *The Israelis: Founders and Sons.* New York: Holt, Rinehart and Winston, 1971.

O'Brien, Conor Cruise. *The Siege: The Saga of Israel and Zionism.* New York: Simon and Schuster, 1986.

Urofsky, Melvin I. *American Zionism from Herzl to the Holocaust.* Lincoln: University of Nebraska Press, 1995.

Vital, David. *Zionism, the Formative Years.* New York: Oxford University Press, 1982.

Bar Kokhba

Zionist organization in Prague. Bar Kokhba (Bar Kochba), which was established in Maccabia in 1893, was first called Verein der Jüdischen Hochschüler in Prag (Association of Jewish College Students in Prague). The organization was typical of many such groups established by Jewish students encountering problems in secular education in German universities. These included difficulties associated with assimilation, the desire to preserve Jewish identity, and an effort to aid fellow Jews then experiencing persecution.

At first not Zionist, in 1899 the organization changed its name to Bar Kokhba, for the leader of the second-century Jewish revolt in Palestine against Rome, and joined the World Zionist Organization (WZO). Nonetheless, the organization emphasized educational and cultural work. It was during Bar Kokhba meetings that Martin Buber delivered his "Three Lectures on Judaism" in which he traced the rise of Zionism to Jews in the West who found themselves torn between the circumstances of their environment and their Jewish heritage. The organization disappeared during World War I.

SPENCER C. TUCKER

See also

World Zionist Organization; Zionism

References

Hertzberg, Arthur, ed. *The Zionist Idea: A Historical Analysis and Reader.* Philadelphia: Jewish Publication Society, 1997.

Laqueur, Walter. *A History of Zionism: From the French Revolution to the Establishment of the State of Israel.* Reprint ed. New York: Schocken, 2003.

Bar-Lev, Chaim

Born: November 16, 1924
Died: May 7, 1994

Israeli Army officer and politician. Chaim Bar-Lev was born Haim Brotzlewsky in Vienna, Austria, on November 16, 1924. When he was four years old, his family moved from Vienna to Zagreb, Yugo-

Chaim Bar-Lev, Israeli army general and politician, shown in 1973 while serving as minister of trade and industry. (Israeli Government Press Office)

slavia, where his father was the manager of a textile-processing plant. Bar-Lev immigrated with his family to Palestine in 1939. He studied at the Mikve Yisrael agricultural college with plans to become a veterinary surgeon. While at the college, he joined the Haganah. After leaving school, he enlisted in the Palmach, where he trained as both a pilot and a paratrooper.

Bar-Lev commanded a company of commandos during the years before Israel's independence. In 1946 he led a force that blew up the Allenby Bridge across the Jordan River near the town of Jericho. The action was an attempt to prevent Arab militiamen stationed in Transjordan from entering Jewish towns west of the Jordan.

During the Israeli War of Independence (1948–1949), Bar-Lev was a colonel in command of the 8th Palmach Battalion responsible for defending Jewish settlements in the Negev Desert. He commanded the 27th Armored Brigade during the 1956 Sinai Campaign and Suez Crisis. His brigade captured the Gaza Strip before reaching the Suez Canal. In 1962 he was the commanding officer of the Northern Command. During the Six-Day War in June 1967, he served as the deputy chief of staff of the Israel Defense Forces (IDF).

In 1968 Bar-Lev was promoted to lieutenant general and appointed chief of the General Staff, the nation's highest-ranking military officer. During his tenure, he approved a proposal to build a high sand dune wall dotted with fortifications along the east bank of the Suez Canal. The wall, later dubbed the Bar-Lev Line, was designed to be a protective barrier. Bar-Lev served as chief of staff until 1972, when he retired from the army. He then joined the Labor Party and was appointed minister of commerce and industry that same year.

During the 1973 Yom Kippur War, Bar-Lev was recalled to active duty. The Egyptians had overrun the Bar-Lev Line. Even though he was out of the army before the fortified wall was completed and was not serving when the line was overrun, Bar-Lev was blamed for the collapse of the line. During the war, he became the unofficial commander in the south, reorganizing the front and guiding the Israeli forces to an eventual victory. He subsequently returned to his position in the government, serving until the Labor Party was defeated in 1977.

Bar-Lev became secretary-general of the Labor Party in 1978. From 1984 until 1988, he served as minister of police and was a member of the Knesset (Israeli parliament). In 1992 he was appointed Israel's ambassador to Russia. Bar-Lev died in a Tel Aviv hospital on May 7, 1994.

DAVE RAUSCH

See also

Bar-Lev Line; Haganah; Israel Defense Forces; Israeli War of Independence, Overview; Labor Party; Palmach; Sinai Campaign; Yom Kippur War

References

Dunstan, Simon. *The Yom Kippur War, 1973.* 2 vols. Westport, CT: Praeger, 2005.

Herzog, Chaim. *The Arab-Israeli Wars: War and Peace in the Middle East from the War of Independence to Lebanon.* Westminster, MD: Random House, 1984.

Williams, Louis. *The Israel Defense Forces: A People's Army.* Lincoln, NE: Authors Choice, 2000.

Bar-Lev Line

Early warning line constructed by the Israelis to stop or blunt a sudden Egyptian offensive. The line was located on the Sinai Peninsula, running north to south along the eastern shore line of the Suez Canal from the Mediterranean Sea to the Red Sea. In the aftermath of the 1967 Six-Day War, it became apparent to Israeli leaders that no long-term peace settlement with Egypt was imminent.

Devastating Egyptian artillery and commando attacks in 1968 led Israel Defense Forces (IDF) chief of staff Lieutenant General Chaim Bar-Lev to seek a means of protecting IDF observation points that would provide immediate warning of any Egyptian Army attack across the Suez Canal while at the same time preventing Egyptian observation of Israeli defenses. After much internal discussion, the IDF sanctioned the construction of an early warning line, which was then named after the chief of staff.

Built at a cost of some $500 million and largely completed by March 1969, the line consisted of some 20 concrete observation posts running north and south along the east bank of the Suez Canal for nearly 100 miles. Approximately 500 IDF military personnel manned the line.

The line was not designed as a static defense. Rather, the IDF remained committed to a flexible mobile counterattack for its primary response to a cross-canal attack. Occasionally, the strong points were abandoned and later reopened. The IDF normally stationed garrisons of 15–20 men at the strong points.

A sand embankment of 20–25 yards high built at water's edge at an angle of 45 degrees ran the length of the line. A secondary sand embankment was constructed about 1.5 miles behind the main defense line. Dedicated artillery fire and armored patrols using embankment access roads provided additional security to the strong points. Mobile armored units situated behind the front lines were responsible for repelling any canal crossing. Prepositioned equipment behind the line provided support to units arriving to defend the line. Pipes were installed to carry oil to the canal, to be ignited upon attack. All plans operated on the presupposition that the IDF would have sufficient early warning to allow the shifting of units forward.

During the 1969–1970 War of Attrition, the Bar-Lev Line came under constant artillery barrage and regular commando attacks. Although these attacks exposed the weakness of the line, the IDF remained committed to the ability of the Bar-Lev Line to provide sufficient early notification of an impending attack.

In January 1973, Egyptian president Anwar Sadat ordered his military leadership to begin secret planning for a cross-canal attack. The Egyptian Army conducted detailed planning and training to penetrate the Bar-Lev Line and move quickly into the Sinai Desert. Repeated Egyptian training for the upcoming attack was soon interpreted by routine military maneuvers by IDF intelligence. Thus, the IDF failed to detect the warning signs of an impending attack. Only in the final hours immediately prior to the Egyptian assault did IDF intelligence finally recognize an abnormal situation. This led to a limited call-up of reserves. The Egyptian deception plan and IDF overconfidence in the Bar-Lev Line had set the stage for a successful Egyptian crossing of the canal.

A massive artillery barrage signaled the start of the Egyptian attack launched on October 6, 1973, with much of the IDF on leave for Yom Kippur. Egyptian surface-to-air missiles (SAMs) protected the bridging operations. Water cannon mounted on Egyptian pontoons blasted openings in the sand berms of the Bar-Lev Line, allowing for the passage of armored vehicles and troops. The Israeli plan to burn oil on the canal failed because sand weight had collapsed the oil pipes, rendering them useless. Under cover of Soviet-supplied air defenses and new antiarmor weaponry, the Egyptians passed 80,000 men across the canal.

With the exception of only Strong Point Budapest, located at the northern end of the Bar-Lev Line, Egyptian forces overran all IDF strong points. The surrounded garrisons either managed spectacular

An Israeli soldier observes the Suez Canal through binoculars from his sandbagged outpost along the Bar-Lev Line during the War of Attrition in 1970. (Moshe Milner/Israeli Government Press Office)

escapes or suffered heavy casualties and were captured. On October 9, the IDF admitted that the Bar-Lev Line had been completely breached.

Although the IDF later brought about a stunning reversal of fortune, the successful Egyptian crossing of the canal demonstrated a complete breakdown of the Israeli early warning system. The Bar-Lev Line placed too much reliance on signals intelligence and technology. The IDF had become overconfident and failed to identify the emerging capabilities of the Egyptian Army. Ironically, the IDF, which had long achieved success from its rapid mobile units backed by local initiative and boldness, in the end believed that it had gained military security in the Bar-Lev Line. Although the Bar-Lev Line was not originally designed as a static defensive line, the failure of the line to provide sufficient early warning of the Egyptian attack relegated it to membership in military history's long list of failed defensive lines.

THOMAS VEVE

See also

Attrition, War of; Bar-Lev, Chaim; Egypt, Armed Forces; Israel Defense Forces; Sadat, Anwar; Six-Day War; Suez Canal; Yom Kippur War

References

Dunstan, Simon. *The Yom Kippur War, 1973.* 2 vols. Westport, CT: Praeger, 2005.

Herzog, Chaim. *The Arab-Israeli Wars: War and Peace in the Middle East from the War of Independence to Lebanon.* Westminster, MD: Random House, 1984.

Rabinovich, Abraham. *The Yom Kippur War: The Epic Encounter That Transformed the Middle East.* New York: Schocken, 2005.

Sunday Times, The. *The Yom Kippur War.* Garden City, NY: Doubleday, 1974.

Barak, Ehud
Born: February 12, 1942

Israeli Army officer, chief of the General Staff, and prime minister (1999–2001). Ehud Barak (Borg) was born February 12, 1942, in Kibbutz Mishmar Ha-Sharon, Palestine (now northern Israel). The kibbutz had been founded in 1932 by his Lithuanian immigrant father. Barak earned a degree in physics and mathematics at Hebrew University in 1976 and a master's degree in economic engineering systems at Stanford University in 1978. His studies were persistently interrupted by the demands of military service.

In 1959 Barak joined the Israel Defense Forces (IDF), serving first as a soldier and then rising to become chief of the General Staff (1991). He served in and commanded elite special forces units and

General Ehud Barak, former chief of staff of the Israel Defense Forces (IDF), headed the Labor Party in 1997 and was prime minister of Israel during 1999–2001. (Israeli Government Press Office)

was a reconnaissance group commander in the 1967 Six-Day War. In 1972 he led the successful rescue of hijacked Sabena Airlines hostages at Ben-Gurion Airport in Tel Aviv during which future prime minister Benjamin Netanyahu was wounded. In 1973 in a raid against the organization that murdered Israeli athletes at the 1972 Munich Olympics, Barak disguised himself as a woman in order to gain access to Palestine Liberation Organization (PLO) terrorists in two seven-story buildings in Muslim West Beirut in the covert Operation SPRING OF YOUTH. He served as a tank battalion commander in the Sinai during the 1973 Yom Kippur War. He next commanded a tank brigade and then an armored division.

Barak was a principal planner for the Entebbe raid (1976) in which Jonathan Netanyahu, a member of his Operation SPRING OF YOUTH team, died rescuing Israeli hostages and an Air France aircrew. In 1982 Barak was appointed as head of the IDF Planning Branch and promoted to major general. He served as deputy commander of Israeli forces in Lebanon during Operation PEACE FOR GALILEE. He was appointed head of the Intelligence Branch (April 1983) at IDF General Headquarters, commander of the IDF Central Command (January 1986), and deputy chief of staff (May 1987). He

assumed the position of chief of the General Staff in April 1991, being promoted to lieutenant general, the highest rank in the IDF.

During 1994, Barak participated in the signing of the Gaza-Jericho Agreement (also known as the Cairo Accord) with the Palestinians and negotiations that led to the Treaty of Peace with Jordan as well as Syrian-Israeli negotiations. In 1995 he resigned as the chief of staff and began his political career as Prime Minister Yitzhak Rabin's interior minister (July–November 1995). Barak replaced Shimon Peres as minister of foreign affairs (November 1995–June 1996) after Peres became prime minister following the assassination of Rabin on November 4, 1995. Barak assumed the leadership of the Labor Party after Peres was defeated by Likud's Benjamin Netanyahu in the May 1996 elections following a series of Palestinian suicide bombings that killed 32 Israeli citizens.

Barak served on the foreign affairs and defense committees after being elected to the Knesset in 1996. In 1999 he meshed factions of the Labor, Gesher, and Meimad parties into the One Israel Party. It was under this banner of a softer approach to the Palestinians that he was elected prime minister (May 17, 1999) and assumed the office of minister of defense (July 6, 1999).

As prime minister, Barak renewed peace talks with the PLO's Yasser Arafat in September 1999 and agreed to finalize peace accords by September 2000 that would transfer more Israeli-occupied territory in the West Bank to Palestinian control. Barak withdrew all Israeli forces from a narrow security zone established by Peres and thereby ended Israel's 17-year occupation of southern Lebanon. Additionally, Barak renewed peace talks with Syria that had been stalemated for 3 years.

All of these efforts to establish peace between Israel and its Arab neighbors began to unravel in the summer of 2000. Barak's frustration over the lack of progress in confirming a framework for peace with the Palestinian side led him to call on the aid of U.S. president Bill Clinton. This resulted in the Camp David Summit of July 2000. The summit was a failure, and even though Clinton and Prince Bandar of Saudi Arabia openly blamed Arafat for the failure to reach an agreement, Barak came under heavy criticism from Israeli right-wing politicians as having offered Arafat too much and by Israeli left-wing politicians as having offered too little.

Three parties resigned from Barak's coalition government, leaving him with a minority government that barely survived a confidence vote in the Knesset. The death knell of his peace process and premiership was sounded when violence erupted in September 2000 in the West Bank and in Gaza and when Arafat openly disregarded the cease-fire agreement he made with Barak. In December, Barak called for special elections for February 2001. Following his defeat in this election, he resigned the prime ministership on May 7, 2001. The Likud Party's Ariel Sharon succeeded him.

Barak then worked as senior adviser with the U.S. firm Electronic Data Systems and also helped found a private firm emphasizing security work. In 2005 he announced his intention to reenter Israeli politics. He made a bid for the leadership of the Labor Party late that same year, but his poor standing in the polls caused him to drop out of the race early and throw his support to Peres, who failed to win the post. Barak remains the most decorated soldier in Israeli history, having been awarded the Distinguished Service Medal and four citations for courage and operational excellence.

RICHARD EDWARDS

See also

Arafat, Yasser; Entebbe Hostage Rescue; Intifada, Second; Israel Defense Forces; Lebanon, Israeli Invasion of; Netanyahu, Benjamin; Netanyahu, Jonathan; Peres, Shimon; Rabin, Yitzhak; Sharon, Ariel; Six-Day War; Yom Kippur War

References

Gelvin, James L. *The Israel-Palestine Conflict: One Hundred Years of War*. New York: Cambridge University Press, 2005.

Lévy, Paule-Henriette. *Ehud Barak: Le Faucon de la Paix*. Paris: Plon, 1999.

Maddy-Weitzman, Bruce, and Shimon Shamir. *The Camp David Summit—What Went Wrong? Americans, Israelis, and Palestinians Analyze the Failure of the Boldest Attempt Ever to Resolve the Palestinian-Israeli Conflict*. Sussex, UK: Sussex Academic, 2005.

Swisher, Clayton E. *The Truth about Camp David: The Untold Story about the Collapse of the Middle East Peace Process*. New York: Thunder's Mouth, Nation Books, 2004.

Barghuti, Marwan
Born: June 6, 1959

Palestinian leader, politician, and prominent member of Fatah. Marwan Barghuti was born on June 6, 1959, in Ramallah. He earned a bachelor's degree in history and political science and a master's degree in international relations from Birzeit University, where he was president of the student body. He was arrested numerous times, beginning in 1976, by Israeli authorities and spent six years in an Israeli prison for his political organizing. During the First Intifada (1987–1993), he was exiled to Jordan.

Barghuti returned to the West Bank in 1994 as part of the exchanges negotiated at the 1993 Oslo Accords. He became the general secretary of Fatah in 1996 and supported the peace process with the Israelis. However, he was opposed to Israeli prime minister Ehud Barak's efforts to put aside interim agreements and move to final status negotiations at the 2000 Camp David meetings. Barghuti opposed Barak because of Israel's stated intent to main-

Fatah's West Bank leader Marwan Barghuti shown during a press conference at the European Parliament in Strasbourg, France, February 19, 1997. (Philippe Huguen/AFP/Getty Images)

tain most of the settlements, control Jerusalem, and not recognize the right of return for Palestinian refugees.

During the Second (al-Aqsa) Intifada, which began in September 2000, Barghuti was a member of the coordinating committee for the West Bank. He was also accused of being a leader in Fatah's Tanzim, or military organization. Soon after the uprising began, Israeli authorities accused him of forming the al-Aqsa Martyrs Brigades, which carried out activities in the Palestinian-controlled territories and also suicide attacks in Israel. He was again arrested in 2002 and tried in a civilian court for 26 deaths allegedly carried out under his supervision. Twenty-one of these charges were dropped, but he was nevertheless sentenced to five life sentences for the deaths of 4 Israelis and a Greek Orthodox monk. He also received an additional 40-year sentence for attempted murder. Barghuti denied establishing the al-Aqsa Martyrs Brigades and claimed that he had opposed attacks on civilians and attacks within Israeli territory. Throughout his trial, he refused to provide a defense, asserting that the proceedings were illegal because Israel lacked jurisdiction and was overriding the designated responsibilities of the Palestinian Authority (PA). He also argued that he should have had diplomatic immunity as an elected member of the Palestinian Legislative Council.

Despite his legal woes and eventual imprisonment, Barghuti enjoyed popularity among many Palestinians when he criticized corruption in the PA and called for a more democratic leadership. From prison, he helped to negotiate a unilateral truce in the intifada in June 2003. His popularity remained high even after his June 2004 sentencing, and he remained politically active. He became a candidate for president in the PA's presidential election of 2005. At the time, the media suggested that he would have defeated Mahmoud Abbas in the presidential elections. Fatah apparently convinced him to withdraw his candidacy, but then his wife, Fadwa Barghuti, registered him as an independent.

In December 2005, Barghuti established a new Palestinian political party called al-Mustaqbal (the Future), which claims to represent the younger generation within Fatah. Al-Mustaqbal includes other prominent figures such as Muhammad Dahlan, Kadura Faris, Samir Mashharawi, and Jibril Rajub. Barghuti was also influential in issuing the Document of National Reconciliation of Palestinian Prisoners issued on May 11, 2006, and revised on June 28, 2006. This was designed principally to heal the division between Hamas and Fatah.

Defenders argue for Barghuti's release from prison, speculating that it might be negotiable in time. Some defenders reason that Barghuti, along with al-Mustaqbal, could strengthen Fatah in its struggle for primacy over the Hamas Party. Barghuti remains a key political player, as signaled by Hamas and Fatah's acceptance of the so-called prisoner's document in 2006.

Sherifa Zuhur

See also

Abbas, Mahmoud; Al-Aqsa Martyrs Brigades; Fatah; Hamas; Intifada, First; Intifada, Second; Palestine Liberation Organization; Palestinian Authority

References

Barghuti, Marwan, with Lisa Hajjar. "Competing Political Cultures: An Interview with Marwan Barghuti and Introduction by Lisa Hajjar." Pp. 105–111 in *The Struggle for Sovereignty: Palestine and Israel, 1993–2005*, edited by Joel Beinin and Rebecca Stein. Stanford, CA: Stanford University Press, 2006.

Usher, Graham. *Dispatches from Palestine: The Rise and Fall of the Oslo Peace Process.* London: Pluto, 1999.

———. *Palestine in Crisis: The Struggle for Peace and Political Independence after Oslo.* London: Pluto, 1995.

Bashar, Abu

See Abed Rabbo, Yasser

Basle Program

Start Date: August 29, 1897
End Date: 1951

Program of action devised by the World Zionist Organization (WZO) and articulated and formally adopted at the First Zionist Congress in Basel (Basle), Switzerland, that convened on August 29, 1897. The primary goal of the First Zionist Congress was to outline and adopt a plan of action aimed at securing a Jewish homeland in Palestine. The congress, which was attended by some 200 Jews from 17 nations and was called and chaired by Zionist pioneer Theodor Herzl, adopted a revised version of the original program on August 30.

The Basle Program encompassed four points. First, it sought to promote Jewish settlement in Palestine among agricultural workers, artisans, and tradesmen. Second, it hoped to bring together Jews from every nation of the world. Third, it sought to enhance Jewish identity and Jewish nationalism. Fourth, the program sought to pave the way for dialogue with sovereign states in order to gather support for the Zionist cause. Above all, of course, the congress embraced the concept of a Jewish state in Palestine "secured by public law."

This last and key point caused some friction during the congress. Although all in attendance essentially embraced the Zionist ideal, there was some disagreement over the precise wording of the Basle Program. Some delegates wanted the program to read "to create a home for the Jewish people in Palestine *legally*," which some found too ambiguous and subject to multiple interpretations. Others preferred the wording "to create a home for the Jewish people in Palestine by international law." This was closest to Herzl's desires, but the congress could not agree on which wording would work best. A commission was henceforth charged with hammering out a compromise position and came up with the wording "secured by public law," which covered the local, regional, national, and international contexts.

The Basle Program remained virtually unchanged until the formation of the State of Israel in May 1948. Indeed, the program provided most of the foundation for the 1917 Balfour Declaration.

Not until 1951, at the Twenty-Third Zionist Congress, was a new program adopted. Known as the Jerusalem Program, the new goals updated the Basle Program of 1897 in light of the new developments since the foundation of Israel.

PAUL G. PIERPAOLI JR.

See also

Balfour Declaration; Herzl, Theodor; Zionism; Zionist Conference

References

Bein, Alex. *Theodor Herzl: A Biography*. London: Jewish Publication Society of America, 1943.

Brenner, Michael. *Zionism: A Brief History*. Translated by Shelley Frisch. Princeton, NJ: Markus Wiener, 2003.

Laqueur, Walter. *A History of Zionism: From the French Revolution to the Establishment of the State of Israel*. Reprint ed. New York: Schocken, 2003.

Pappe, Ilan. *A History of Modern Palestine: One Land, Two Peoples*. Cambridge: Cambridge University Press, 2003.

Bedouin

Nomadic and seminomadic desert-dwelling peoples generally located in the Arabia peninsula, North Africa, the Levant, Iraq, the Negev Desert, and the Sinai Peninsula. Bedouin territories include present-day Jordan, Saudi Arabia, Kuwait, Yemen, Oman, the Arab Emirates, Israel, Egypt, Sudan, Syria, Iraq, Lebanon, Algeria, and Libya. Bedouin are of Arab origin and practice Islam. The Bedouin are organized by clans into tribes. Individual households, or bayts (tents), are comprised of three or more adults: a man and his wife or wives and his parents or siblings plus their children. A tribe, or hamula, is presided over by a sheikh, which is a patrilinear position usually handed down from elder brother to younger brother and sometimes from father to son. While the sheikh has status and commands great respect, he is not a ruler in the ordinary sense of the word.

For centuries, the Bedouin have been nomads who engage in light agriculture, usually animal husbandry, and live off of the land. As they have been forcibly settled by governments since the 19th century, those retaining their traditional ways are mostly seminomadic. They move throughout their prescribed lands seasonally, following freshwater sources or moving to take advantage of various plant supplies. Many have herded sheep, goats, and camels. Traditionally, Bedouin move in groups containing several families and live in tents, which aid in their ability to pick up stakes and move when the situation warrants. However, beginning in the 1950s, more and more Bedouin have given up their lifestyle to work and live in cities and towns throughout much of the region. Indeed, expanding population, urban sprawl, government policies, and the shrinking of suitable grazing lands have pushed many Bedouin into sedentary, urban lifestyles. It is difficult to determine the precise number of Bedouin in the Middle East, although estimates vary from as little as 750,000 to well over a million. While Bedouin are noted for their generous hospitality, they are also fiercely territorial and do not take violations of their land rights lightly.

A Bedouin woman leads a camel while carrying a baby in a back sling, Sinai, Egypt. (Corel)

Bedouin culture is a complex and fascinating one and has been many centuries in the making. Bedouin tents are functional and well designed. Most are divided in two by a cloth curtain (*ma'nad*), which separates the tent into a seating/living area for men and a place to entertain guests, and another area (the *maharama*) in which women cook, socialize, and receive female guests. Bedouin have their own unique poetry, storytelling, music, and dance, much of which is reserved for the reception of guests, special occasions, and the like. Both Bedouin men and women wear traditional and prescribed clothing that can often indicate the status or age of the wearer, especially in the case of their head wear. Clothing also varies depending upon the area or nation the Bedouin inhabit. The Bedouin have their own tribal, or customary, law, and thus disputes may be solved and punishment meted out according to those laws rather than resorting to civil courts of a state or locality.

Currently, Bedouin make up about 12 percent of the total Arab population in Israel. As part of the Arab minority, they face many of the same hurdles as their Arab brethren, including institutional and societal discrimination, reduced socioeconomic opportunities, substandard education, and poor health care. However, they have come under additional pressure as the Israeli government has tried to impose settlement policies on them and reduce or eliminate their traditional land areas. A fair number of Bedouin (5–10 percent of Bedouin males) serve in the Israeli military. Their intricate knowledge of the local terrain makes them valuable rangers and trackers.

Bedouin have faced similar pressures even in Arab states, however, as governments have purposely adopted land-use and settlement policies that are at odds with traditional Bedouin culture and lifestyle. Nevertheless, Bedouin have held fast to their tribal and cultural identities, even after they have settled and adopted modern, urbanized lifestyles. For others, the restrictions and pressures on them have meant an abandonment of a truly nomadic way of life. Now they are at best seminomadic and have adopted some of the trappings of urbanization. Agricultural pursuits, including animal husbandry, are the main livelihoods for these Bedouin in transition.

PAUL G. PIERPAOLI JR.

See also

Israel, Arab Population in

References

Alotaibi, Muhammad. *Bedouin: The Nomads of the Desert.* Vero Beach, FL: Rourke, 1989.

Ingham, Bruce. *The Bedouin of Northern Arabia.* London: Kegan Paul International, 1986.

Losleben, Elizabeth. *The Bedouin of the Middle East.* Minneapolis, MN: Lerner, 2002.

Nevins, Edward, and Theon Wright. *World without Time: The Bedouin.* New York: John Day, 1969.

Beersheba

City located in the Negev Desert region of southern Israel. An ancient place that has seen numerous cultures rise and fall, Beersheba (Ber Sheva, Bir Saba) has a current population of some 190,000 people, making it the fifth-largest Israeli city. It is also the biggest city in the Negev. Archaeological digs indicate evidence of human habitation in the area dating back some 4,000 years. Since then, the area has been continually inhabited, with settlements having been razed and rebuilt many times.

Beersheba figures prominently in the Old Testament (Torah). Indeed, it is mentioned at three separate points in the book of Genesis and was the location where the Israelites entered into a pact with the Philistines. Both Abraham and Isaac swore oaths in Beersheba. The locale is also mentioned in the book of Joshua.

After the Jewish Diaspora, Beersheba was controlled by the Byzantine Empire. From the 16th century until 1917, Beersheba was under the control of the Ottoman Empire. The Ottoman Turks built a city center, a railway, a police station, and a fort under an officer by the name of Arnaout. During World War I, Beersheba became momentarily famous for a battle there between British Empire forces and the Ottoman Turks. Beginning in 1917, the Turks began digging an elaborate set of trench works to impede enemy progress. Just outside Beersheba ran a trench line almost four miles long. On October 31, 1917, following a surprise long march, the Australian 4th Light Horse Brigade successfully charged the trench lines and captured the Beersheba wells. The area would remain under British control until 1948.

During the British Mandate for Palestine (1920–1948), Beersheba acted as a regional center of administration. Although the area was destined to become an Arab possession per the 1947 United Nations (UN) partition plan, Beersheba and its surrounding area were taken by Israeli forces in October 1948. Immediately prior to that, Egyptian troops had held the town. Since then, no rebuilding of the original mosque or the mandate- and Ottoman-era official buildings was permitted, despite the historical significance of these buildings in the old city of Beersheba.

Beginning in the 1950s, Beersheba underwent a building boom during which an entirely new commercial district was constructed just north of the existing city center. As commerce, industry, and universities moved into the city, the population grew rapidly. Located in the city is the Ben-Gurion University of the Negev as well as the well-respected Soroka Hospital. Beersheba's population includes Bedouin, Russian and Ethiopian immigrants, and longtime settlers or more recent transplants to the Negev. The city consists of a series of individual neighborhoods and districts.

Beersheba's population nearly doubled during the late 1980s and throughout the 1990s. This was not the result of Israeli migration but rather was due to the huge influx of Russian Jews to Israel (many of whom settled here) as the Soviet Union first eased its emigration restrictions in the late 1980s. The collapse of the Soviet Union in 1991 only hastened the Russian-Jewish exodus to Israel and Beersheba. Because of its more isolated location, Beersheba was spared from the high number of terrorist attacks experienced, for example, in Jerusalem. This changed, however, after 2001 with a violent shooting spree and bombing attempts, and, in 2004, when two August suicide bombings of buses killed 16 people. A year later, another suicide bomber gravely injured 2 Israeli security guards at a bus depot.

PAUL G. PIERPAOLI JR.

See also

Negev Desert; Suicide Bombings

References

Evenari, Micchael, et al. *The Negev: The Challenge of a Desert.* 2nd ed. Cambridge: Harvard University Press, 1982.

Israolwitz, Richard, and Jonathan Friedlander, eds. *Transitions: Russians, Ethiopians, and Bedouins in Israel's Negev Desert.* Aldershot, UK: Ashgate, 1999.

Laughlin, John C. H. *Fifty Major Cities of the Bible.* London: Routledge, 2006.

Begin, Menachem
Born: August 16, 1913
Died: March 9, 1992

Prime minister of Israel (1977–1983) and recipient (with Egyptian president Anwar Sadat) of the 1978 Nobel Peace Prize, awarded for

Menachem Begin was a militant Zionist who became prime minister of Israel during 1977–1988. He is perhaps best remembered for his part in the Camp David Accords (1978), which established the basis for peace between Egypt and Israel. (Israeli Government Press Office)

the Camp David Accords that resulted in the 1979 Israel-Egypt Peace Treaty. Menachem Wolfovitch Begin was born to an Ashkenazic Jewish family in Brest-Litovsk (Brisk), Russia (now Belarus), on August 16, 1913. He fled with his family to Vilnius, Poland, to escape the battling German and Russian armies in World War I. Begin's father was an ardent Zionist, and Begin was a member of the Hashomer Hatzair scout movement until age 13 and joined Vladimir Jabotinsky's Betar youth movement at age 16. Betar was a subset of the Zionist Revisionist movement committed to the creation of a Jewish state on both sides of the Jordan River. Begin took up the leadership of the Organization Department of Betar for Poland in 1932.

Begin graduated from the University of Warsaw with a law degree in 1935 and assumed the leadership of Betar Czechoslovakia in 1936. He returned to Warsaw in 1937 and was imprisoned for a short time because of his Zionist activities. He became head of Betar in Poland in 1938. Under his overall leadership, some 100,000 members engaged in self-defense, weapons, agricultural, and communications training. Members of Betar also transported to Pales-

tine immigrants declared illegal by the British government. Begin advocated the establishment of a Jewish national homeland in Palestine by conquest and pushed this position at the 1938 Betar convention.

In 1939 Begin fled Warsaw when the Germans invaded Poland. He managed to cross into eastern Poland, which the Soviets invaded two weeks later, and thus avoided the roundup of Jews by the Nazis. Both his parents and a brother died in Nazi concentration camps during the war. In 1940 he was arrested by the Soviets and sent to a concentration camp in Siberia. He was released following the agreement establishing a Polish army to fight the Germans that followed the German invasion of the Soviet Union in June 1941.

Begin duly enlisted in the Free Polish Army in exile and was sent for training in 1942 to the British Mandate for Palestine. He left the army there in 1943 and joined the Jewish national movement in Palestine. He openly criticized the Jewish Agency for Palestine and worldwide Zionism as too timid in their approach to a Jewish state. In 1942 he had joined Irgun Tsvai Leumi (National Military Organization) and commanded the movement from 1943 to 1948. Under Begin's leadership, Irgun declared war on the British and resumed attacks on Palestinian Arab villages and British interests. The declaration came in February 1944.

The British had already classified Irgun as a terrorist organization. The Jewish Agency for Palestine, Haganah, and Histadrut had all declared its operations as terrorist acts. Nevertheless, Irgun's operations were so successful under Begin that the British launched an extensive manhunt for him. He avoided capture by disguising himself as an Orthodox rabbi. Meanwhile, he directed the Irgun bombing of the British military, police, and civil headquarters at Jerusalem's King David Hotel on July 22, 1946, that killed 91 people. Begin and Irgun claimed to have issued three warnings in an attempt to limit casualties.

In anticipation of and following the partitioning of Palestine in 1947, Irgun and Haganah increasingly coordinated. Israel declared its independence on May 15, 1948, and announced the absorption of Haganah into its national military, the Israel Defense Forces (IDF), effective May 18, 1948. All other armed forces were banned. Irgun signed an agreement to be absorbed by the IDF on June 1, 1948, which formally occurred in September 1948. Begin also played a key role in the *Altalena* Incident of June 23, 1948.

After Israel's independence, Begin led Israel's political opposition from 1948 to 1977, reforming what remained of Irgun into the rightist Herut (Freedom) Party with himself as its head. In 1965, Herut merged with the Liberal Party, creating the Gahal Party, which formed the understructure of the future Likud (Unity) Party. Just prior to the June 1967 Six-Day War, he joined the National Unity Government's cabinet as a minister without portfolio. The government was dissolved on August 1, 1970.

The Likud Party's May 17, 1977, victory in the national elections for the ninth Knesset allowed Begin, the chairman of Likud since 1970, to form the new government. On June 21 he became Israel's sixth (and first non-Labor) prime minister. Domestically, Begin moved to turn the Israeli economy away from the centralized, highly planned enterprise that characterized it under Labor. The prime minister also actively promoted immigration to Israel, especially from Ethiopia and the Soviet Union. Finally, he sought infrastructure improvements, advances in education, and the renewal of Israel's poorest neighborhoods.

It was in the realm of foreign policy, however, that Begin most asserted himself. One of his first acts as prime minister was to challenge King Hussein of Jordan, President Hafez al-Assad of Syria, and President Sadat of Egypt to meet with him to discuss peace. Sadat, but not the others, accepted the challenge and arrived in Israel on November 19, 1977. Following intermittent negotiations, Begin and Sadat met with U.S. president Jimmy Carter at Camp David, Maryland, and signed the Camp David Accords after nearly two weeks of negotiations (September 5–17, 1978).

The accords included two framework agreements that established guidelines for both the Israel-Egypt Peace Treaty and a potentially wider Middle East peace agreement. The bilateral treaty was signed in Washington, D.C., on March 26, 1979. Begin attended and participated in Sadat's funeral in Cairo after the Egyptian leader was assassinated by Muslim fundamentalists in October 1981.

Despite Begin's willingness to seek peace with Egypt, the other Arab states, including Syria and Jordan, remained hostile toward Israel. And Begin was uncompromising on the place of the West Bank and the Gaza Strip, seized by Israel during the Six-Day War, in the modern State of Israel. He considered them part of the historical lands given to Israel by God. Indeed, he promoted and oversaw the expansion of Jewish settlements in the West Bank and the Gaza Strip that continue to be an impediment to Palestinian-Israeli peace accords to the present day.

From May 28, 1980, to August 6, 1981, Begin served concurrently as Israel's prime minister and defense minister. When Israeli intelligence notified Begin that Iraq was close to producing weapons-grade nuclear fuel at its Osiraq/Tammuz nuclear reactor, he ordered the Israeli Air Force's successful destruction of the facility on June 7, 1981. Shortly thereafter he enunciated the Begin Doctrine, which held that Israel would act preemptively to counter any perceived threat from weapons of mass destruction (WMDs).

On June 30, 1981, Begin was reelected prime minister. It was soon apparent to the second Begin government that the Lebanese government was unable or unwilling to stop terrorist attacks launched from its soil. As such, in June 1982 Begin authorized Operation PEACE FOR GALILEE, the Israeli invasion of southern Lebanon. The operation was designed to drive Palestine Liberation Organization (PLO) Katyusha rockets out of the range of Israel's northern border and to destroy the terrorist infrastructure that had developed in southern Lebanon.

Although the PLO was driven from Lebanon, the Israeli presence in the country lasted three years. (A limited Israeli force remained until 2000.) The Israeli operation resulted in such a high number of Palestinian civilian deaths that worldwide public opinion turned against Israel. The failure of Operation PEACE FOR GALILEE to progress

in the intended time frame and the large number of casualties on both sides weighed heavily on Begin. Tired and still mourning the recent death of his wife, he resigned as prime minister on September 15, 1983. Over the next nine years he lived quietly, if not reclusively, in Tel Aviv. Begin died of heart failure on March 9, 1992, in Tel Aviv.

RICHARD EDWARDS

See also

Altalena Incident; Camp David Accords; Carter, James Earl, Jr.; Gaza Strip; Haganah; Irgun Tsvai Leumi; Jewish Agency for Israel; Lebanon, Israeli Invasion of; Likud Party; Osiraq Raid; Sadat, Anwar; Sinai; West Bank; Zionism; Zionist Conference

References

Begin, Menachem. *The Revolt*. Los Angeles: Nash Publishing, 1972.
———. *White Nights: The Story of a Prisoner in Russia*. New York: Harper and Row, 1979.
Perlmutter, Amos. *The Life and Times of Menachem Begin*. Garden City, NY: Doubleday, 1987.
Seidman, Hillel. *Menachem Begin: His Life and Legacy*. New York: Shengold, 1990.
Sofer, Sasson. *Begin: An Anatomy of Leadership*. New York: Blackwell, 1988.
Temko, Ned. *To Win or to Die: A Personal Portrait of Menachem Begin*. New York: Morrow, 1987.

Beilin, Yossi
Born: June 12, 1948

Leftist Israeli politician and ardent proponent of a comprehensive peace settlement between Israel and its Arab neighbors, particularly the Palestinians. Yossi Beilin was born on June 12, 1948, in Petach Tikva, Israel, and was educated in Israeli schools. He worked for a number of years as a journalist before earning his PhD in political science from Tel Aviv University, where he also taught. From 1977 to 1984 he was the official spokesman of the Labor Party. From 1984 to 1986 he served as the Israeli government secretary, and from 1986 to 1988 he was director general for political affairs for the Israeli Foreign Ministry.

Beilin decided to enter electoral politics and was elected to the Knesset (Israeli parliament) in 1988 as a Labor Party candidate. After that, he served in several government posts, including deputy minister of finance (1988–1990), deputy minister of foreign affairs (1992–1995), minister of economy and planning (1995), and minister without portfolio (November 1995–July 1996). From 1996 to 2001, he was minister of justice.

Beilin's greatest contributions have come in the area of peace negotiations and foreign policy. In 1992, as deputy foreign minister and with the blessing of Foreign Minister Shimon Peres, Beilin opened a secret dialogue with the Palestinians in an attempt to hammer out a comprehensive peace settlement. The end result was the historic 1993 Oslo Accords, signed with much fanfare on the White House lawn in September 1993. Both Israeli prime minister Yitzhak Rabin and Palestine Liberation Organization (PLO) chairman Yasser

Israeli Labor Party politician Yossi Beilin in August 1992. (Israeli Government Press Office)

to abstain from launching—or encouraging—any violence against the Israeli people. The accord also called for Jerusalem to be divided, with much of East Jerusalem going to the Palestinians.

Although the accord received much play in the Israeli press, it proved to be unpopular in Israel. The governing Likud Party dismissed it out of hand, and the Labor Party remained silent on the issue, which was hardly a ringing endorsement. Public support was never much higher than 30 percent. Even among many Palestinians, the Geneva Accord was tepidly received.

Realizing that his support from Labor was weakening, Beilin left the party to join Meretz in 2003, a dovish social democratic party. Still unable to garner the support he needed to hold office again, he founded a splinter Meretz group, which was eventually reunited with Meretz under the new umbrella Meretz-Yachad Party. Beilin has led Meretz-Yachad since 2004. In 2006 he was again elected to the Knesset and remains a vocal proponent of a long-lasting peace in the Middle East.

PAUL G. PIERPAOLI JR.

See also

Abbas, Mahmoud; Arafat, Yasser; Geneva Accord; Israel; Labor Party; Likud Party; Oslo Accords; Rabin, Yitzhak; Peres, Shimon

References

Beilin, Yossi. *Touching Peace: From the Oslo Accord to a Final Agreement.* Translated by Philip Simpson. London: Weidenfeld and Nicolson, 1999.

Lerner, Michael. *The Geneva Accord and Other Strategies for Healing the Israeli-Palestinian Conflict.* Berkeley, CA: North Atlantic Books, 2004.

Watson, Geoffrey R. *The Oslo Accords: International Law and the Israeli-Palestinian Peace Agreements.* New York: Oxford University Press, 2000.

Arafat signed the agreements. As a follow-up, Beilin and Mahmoud Abbas, a moderate Palestinian leader, negotiated the 1995 Beilin–Abu Mazen Agreement, which produced an informal working paper that sought to end for good the Israeli-Palestinian conflict. During 1992–1995, Beilin also headed the Israeli delegation to the multilateral peace process. In January 1991 he attended the Taba Talks with Palestinian representatives.

When Ehud Barak's government fell in March 2001, Beilin found himself without a government position for the first time in many years. Nevertheless, he pushed forward with plans to solidify a lasting peace with the Palestinians while also lobbying hard for a unilateral withdrawal of Israeli troops from Lebanon. In July 2001 he embarked on an unofficial ad hoc diplomatic mission with Palestinian leaders to draw up a concrete plan of action to bring the Palestinian-Israeli conflict to a close. The delegation included Israeli and Palestinian intellectuals, former government officials, academics, journalists, and opinion makers from within the civilian sector. The result was the Geneva Accord, signed on December 1, 2003.

Among other things, the 2003 Geneva Accord called for the creation of an autonomous Palestinian territory located mainly in the West Bank and the Gaza Strip. The Palestinians were to officially recognize Israel and respect its current land rights. They were also

Beirut

Capital of Lebanon and Lebanon's principal city. Beirut is a coastal city, located about midway along Lebanon's Mediterranean coastline. Parallel to the city and to its east are scenic mountains that provide a dramatic canvas to this cosmopolitan locale. The population of Beirut is difficult to ascertain. First, for political reasons, the Lebanese have not conducted a thorough census since 1932. Second, the many wars and conflicts that have plagued Beirut since the end of World War II have lent a very transient nature to Beirut's citizenry. Currently, estimates of Beirut's population range from a low of about 940,000 to just over 2 million. The true figure probably lies between these two, and several sources have estimated the city's population at approximately 1.3 million.

Prior to the highly destructive Lebanese Civil War (1975–1990), Beirut was known as the Paris of the Middle East. (Lebanon was part of a French mandate from 1920 to 1943 and had strong connections with the French.) Besides its physical beauty and general prosperity, the city has historically been home to a diverse and cosmopolitan population. It is the home of a number of colleges and universities, various multinational organizations, and a checkerboard of diverse neighborhoods and sections.

Nejmeh Square in downtown Beirut, Lebanon. (Marc Helfter/Fotolia)

Beirut's residents include all 18 recognized Lebanese religious groups: Alawite, Armenian Catholic, Armenian Orthodox (Gregorian), Assyrian Church of the East, Chaldean Catholic, Copts, Druze, Evangelical Christian (including Protestant groups such as Baptists and Seventh-day Adventists), Greek Catholic (Melkite), Greek Orthodox, Ismaili (Sevener Shia), Jewish, Maronite (Maronite Catholic), Roman Catholic (Latins), Sunni Muslim, Twelver Shia, Syriac Catholic, and Syriac Orthodox. Also represented in Beirut are Buddhists and Hindus who are migrant workers from South Asia. Most of Beirut's Lebanese Jews fled the country with the beginning of the civil war. It is perhaps a bitter irony that the civil war was so damaging and so enduring because of the interference of outside powers, including Israel, Syria, and the Palestine Liberation Organization (PLO).

Beirut slowly began to rebuild and reestablish itself as a world-class city after 1994, but these efforts were sometimes hampered by political and sectarian infighting and even interference from Syria, which did not vacate Lebanon until April 2005. Unfortunately, the Israeli-Hezbollah War (Lebanese-Israeli War according to the Lebanese, or the Fifth Arab-Israeli War) that raged during July and August 2006 wrought more damage to Beirut. As the Israelis retaliated against Hezbollah guerrilla attacks and rocket assaults emanating from southern Lebanon, they hit key infrastructures in Beirut, including water and sewage-treatment facilities, power plants, the airport, roads, and bridges and destroyed much of southern Beirut. While the mandate-era downtown district newly restored since the civil war was largely spared during this latest conflict, it will take months—perhaps years—to replace outlying districts and infrastructure. The damage to tourism and foreign investment is likely to be considerable as well.

In the civil war of 1975–1990, Beirut was bifurcated along religious lines, with the eastern sectors of the city dominated by Christians and the western zones controlled mostly by Muslims. Many districts of Beirut became a virtual ghost town of abandoned and bombed-out buildings. The war also forced many of Beirut's elite to seek shelter in other nations, causing a massive exodus of academics, writers, and intellectuals. By the early 1980s, Beirut's once-proud reputation as the cultural and intellectual center of the Middle East had all but evaporated. Although the city has been unified—at least tentatively—since the early 1990s, sectarian tensions still lurk just below the surface. In addition to Christian-Muslim friction, enmity between Shiites and Druze and, more recently, Sunnis and Shiites is problematic.

During the Lebanese Civil War, Beirut became infamous in the international media for the many abductions that occurred there. Tens of thousands of Lebanese were kidnapped or disappeared during the war. Some of those kidnapped and held hostage were Westerners, and a large number of them were foreign journalists or academics.

In 1982 David Dodge, the president of the American University of Beirut, was kidnapped, probably by one of the three groups that eventually formed Hezbollah. Two years later, Malcolm Kerr, of the same university, was gunned down inside the university itself. For the next 10 years or so, some 30 other Westerners would be abducted. In perhaps the most notorious abduction, Terry Waite, an emissary of the Archbishop of Canterbury, disappeared in Beirut on January 20, 1987. He had been sent to negotiate the release of 4 Britons and would not see freedom again until November 1991. It is probably no exaggeration to conclude that Beirut has suffered more than any other city by far as a result of the ongoing Arab-Israeli conflict.

PAUL G. PIERPAOLI JR.

See also

Hezbollah; Lebanon; Lebanon, Civil War in; Lebanon, Israeli Invasion of; Lebanon, Israeli Operations against

References

Makdisis, Jean Said. *Beirut Fragments: A War Memoir.* New York: Persea Books, 1990.

McCullin, Don. *Beirut: A City in Crisis.* London: New English Library, 1983.

Beit She'an Valley

Hebrew name of the eastern portion of the great transverse valley that connects the Jordan Valley with Haifa Bay to the west and divides Galilee from Samaria. The Beit She'an (Bet Sh'an) Valley is the lowest point of this geographical feature. It goes from 330 feet below sea level in the west to 985 feet below sea level in the east. The valley is approximately 10 miles on a side. Much of the soil of the valley is poor. Temperatures range from very hot in the summer to occasional freezes in winter, rendering the area unsuitable for the production of subtropical fruit. The valley's chief asset is an abundance of springs, although much of the water is saline.

The Beit She'an Valley was quite swampy and malarial when the first Jewish community was established there in 1936. Only after the creation of the State of Israel was land reclamation undertaken. Swamps were then drained and irrigation canals constructed. Today the valley is a major agricultural center, producing fruits, dates, and cotton.

The chief town of the valley is Beit She'an, located some 18 miles south of Lake Kinneret (Sea of Galilee). Formerly an Arab town, it was captured by Israeli forces in May 1948 and then resettled by Jews. In 2001 it had a population of nearly 16,000 people, more than 99 percent of whom were Jews. One of the major cities of ancient Israel because of its location at the junction of the Jordan River Valley and Jezreel Valley, Beit She'an controlled access from the interior to the coast and lay astride a major road north from Jerusalem to the Sea of Galilee. Beit She'an is today a prominent archeological

An ancient Roman theater from the second century AD below the city of Beit She'an, Israel. Archaeological findings have revealed 18 occupation levels in Beit She'an, dating back to the fourth millennium BC. (Richard T. Nowitz/Corbis)

---

site. Among the finds have been Canaanite temples and a fortress as well as a Hellenistic-Roman temple, a bust of Alexander the Great, and a large Roman amphitheater.

SPENCER C. TUCKER

See also

Geography of the Middle East; Jordan River; Lake Kinneret; Water Rights and Resources

References

Beck, John A. *The Land of Milk and Honey: An Introduction to the Geography of Israel.* St. Louis: Concordia, 2006.

Orni, Ephraim. *Geography of Israel.* Philadelphia: Jewish Publication Society of America, 1977.

Tal, Y. *Pollution in a Promised Land: An Environmental History of Israel.* Berkeley: University of California Press, 2002.

Bekáa Valley

Valley located in Lebanon extending from the center of the country to the Syrian border and at the very northern extreme of the much larger Great Rift Valley, which runs south into northern Africa. The Bekáa (Biqa) Valley holds great significance because of its agricultural output, archaeological sites dating to antiquity, and role in the Arab-Israeli conflict. Located some 19 miles east of Beirut, the valley runs north to south for about 75 miles. It is on average approximately 10 miles wide. Two rivers—the Litani and the Orontes—begin in the valley.

Since ancient times, the fertile soil and moderate climate of the Bekáa Valley have made it a favored agricultural site. The valley's

Syrian rocket batteries following a strike by Israeli Air Force aircraft in the Bekáa Valley in Lebanon on June 9, 1982, as part of Israel's Operation PEACE FOR GALILEE. (Ya'acov Sa'ar/Israeli Government Press Office)

climate is essentially Mediterranean, meaning that it has temperate and somewhat wet winters and warm and dry summers. In the northern valley, which is reserved chiefly for grazing animals, precipitation is low—just 9 inches per year on average—because the mountain range to the west inhibits moisture from the Mediterranean Sea, and the water table is far beneath the surface. Peasants here are among the poorest in Lebanon and receive little to no assistance from the central government. In the southern half of the valley rainfall is more plentiful, about 25 inches per year. At the southern end, farmers cultivate cotton, vegetables, sugar beets, tobacco, and wheat. Fruit farms, olive orchards, and vineyards are also found in the southern part of the area. After the Litani hydroelectric complex came on line in 1957, farmers benefited from increased water supplies from the complex's reservoir and interconnected canals. Hashish and opium were cultivated in the water-poor areas of the valley, and after an interdiction program the farmers reverted to vegetables but could not market them due to cheaper Syrian produce.

The Bekáa Valley has always attracted a sizable number of migrant farmworkers from Syria. In the small nation of Lebanon, the valley plays a central role in the lives of most Lebanese. Indeed, it comprises about 40 percent of all the arable land in Lebanon.

The vast majority of Bekáa Valley inhabitants are Shia Muslims, and their numbers have been rising steadily. At the same time, the area's Christian population has been falling during the past 40 or so years, mostly because of the various wars that have afflicted the area. There are three primary towns in the valley: Zahlah (or Zahlem), Baalbek, and Hirmil. Zahlah is the largest of the three, with some 100,000 people. Most of the inhabitants are Christians. Baalbek once had a minority population of Greek Catholics and is now predominantly Shia, as is Hirmil. Baalbek is home to the impressive array of ancient ruins known as Heliopolis to the Romans and Nabateans. Roman temples dedicated to Bacchus, Venus, and Jupiter, all Roman gods of antiquity, and an ancient theater lie in the archaeological site. At Anjar, not too far from these ruins, are the remains of an Umayyad city that prospered under the earliest Muslim caliphs from about AD 660 to AD 750. A Palestinian refugee camp, an Armenian community, and a Syrian prison facility were located at or near Anjar.

In more recent times, the Bekáa Valley served as the training grounds for the Palestinian Resistance Movement and Hezbollah and as a depot for stolen cars and smuggled goods during the Lebanese Civil War. The Palestinian Resistance Movement (PRM), the arm of the Palestine Liberation Organization (PLO) that used Lebanon as its base of operations from 1970 to 1982, maintained some training facilities for militants in the valley. During the Israeli invasion of Lebanon in 1982, the valley was the scene of a fierce but unsuccessful Israeli air campaign that sought to eradicate Syrian antiaircraft missile sites from the area.

The radical Shia group known as Hezbollah based some of its operations and community services in the Bekáa. In the 1980s, an estimated 1,000–1,200 Iranian Revolutionary Guards (*pasdarans*) were housed in the valley and trained as Islamic militants. The empty barracks that housed them remain. Israel alleges that Hezbollah still maintains training facilities and funnels arms, money, and war

Important Geographical Features of the Middle East

Place	Location	Significance
Bekáa Valley	near Lebanon-Syria border	basing site for many radical organizations
Giddi Pass	Sinai Peninsula	strategic passage across the Sinai
Golan Heights	border between Israel, Lebanon, and Syria	strategic plateau near Syrian capital
Gulf of Aqaba	between Sinai and Arabian mainland	provides strategic access to non–Middle Eastern countries
Jordan River	Great Rift Valley	important source of water
Mitla Pass	Sinai Peninsula	strategic passage across the Sinai
Sea of Galilee	northeastern Israel	important source of water
Sinai Peninsula	between Egypt and Middle East	linkage between North Africa and the Middle East
Straits of Tiran	between Sinai and Arabian Peninsulas	important shipping lane
Suez Canal	between Mediterranean and Red Seas	important shipping lane

matériel into Lebanon from Syria through the valley. A fierce split within Hezbollah factions during 1996–1997 actually diminished the party's activities and support in some villages in the valley. Hezbollah receives political support from Baalbek to Hirmil, and its other primary bases are in southern Lebanon and Beirut. Since around the mid-1990s, Hezbollah has increased its military and political strength, winning seats in the Lebanese legislature and engaging in a short war with Israel in July and August 2006.

PAUL G. PIERPAOLI JR. AND SHERIFA ZUHUR

See also

Hezbollah; Lebanon; Lebanon, Israeli Invasion of; Palestine Liberation Organization; Syria

References

Norton, Richard Augustus. *Hezbollah: A Short History.* Princeton, NJ: Princeton University Press, 2006.

Salibi, Kamal. *A House of Many Mansions: The History of Lebanon Reconsidered.* Berkeley: University of California Press, 1990.

Sayegh, Phillip. *Baalbeck: God's Paradise: History of Baalbeck.* Baalbeck, Lebanon: Moustapha Ibrahim El Jamaal and Sons, 1964.

Bel-Gal, Avigdor
Born: 1938

Israeli general. Avigdor Bel-Gal was born in 1938 and joined the Israel Defense Forces (IDF) in 1958 at the age of 20. He gained the nickname "Yanush" and was rapidly promoted. On the eve of the Yom Kippur War in October 1973, he was a colonel and commanded the 7th Armored Brigade. His troops were deployed on the Golan Heights. In the initial Syrian attacks, Bel-Gal's men faced two Syrian divisions. During the next four days, his brigade was subjected to almost constant attack. The Syrians eventually broke through the Israeli lines, and Bel-Gal was forced to withdraw with only seven tanks still operational. Within two days, with the arrival of reserves, the brigade had been rebuilt and was ordered to counterattack. Bel-Gal then faced not only Syrian forces but also a brigade of Moroccan troops, but the assault was successful.

In 1974 Bel-Gal was promoted to brigadier general. He took part in the decision for the Entebbe Raid in 1976. He then was sent to the United States, where he served in several military liaison positions. On his return to Israel in 1982, he was advanced to major general and received command of two divisions that took part in the Israeli invasion of Lebanon to destroy the Palestine Liberation Organization (PLO) there. Bel-Gal's divisions were charged with outflanking Syrian troops in the Bekáa Valley and were also assigned the task of helping to secure the Beirut-Damascus Road.

Syrian resistance in the Bekáa Valley proved stronger than had been anticipated, but Bel-Gal employed helicopters armed with air-to-surface missiles to good effect. Within three days, a cease-fire was arranged with the Syrians. However, Bel-Gal's troops then became embroiled in the siege of Beirut.

Passed over for appointment to the position of chief of staff of the IDF, Bel-Gal retired from the army in 1983. He subsequently pursued a career in business. In 1996 he became chairman of Israel Aircraft Industries, a post he continues to hold. In 1997 he testified in a libel trial that concerned Ariel Sharon's role in the 1982 Israeli invasion of Lebanon. Sharon had been accused of having withheld information from the Israeli government about the operation. That same year, Bel-Gal traveled to Russia to broker a deal for natural gas but was unsuccessful.

RALPH MARTIN BAKER

See also

Entebbe Hostage Rescue; Lebanon, Israeli Invasion of; Yom Kippur War

References

Asher, Jerry, and Eric Hammel. *Duel for the Golan: The 100-Hour Battle That Saved Israel.* Pacifica, CA: Pacifica Press, 1987.

Gabriel, Richard. *Operation Peace for Galilee: The Israeli-PLO War in Lebanon.* New York: Farrar, Straus and Giroux, 1985.

Rabinovich, Abraham. *The Yom Kippur War: The Epic Encounter That Transformed the Middle East.* New York: Schocken, 2005.

Belkovsky, Zvi
Born: 1865
Died: 1948

Russian Jew and Zionist leader. Born in Odessa in 1865, Zvi Belkovsky (Belkovski) studied law in that city. While a student, he actively participated in early Zionist organizations. Offered a professorship at a Russian university if he would convert to Christianity, he refused and during 1893–1897 taught at Sofia University in Bulgaria, where he continued his Zionist activities.

In 1898 Belkovsky returned to Russia and took up residence in St. Petersburg, where he both wrote for scholarly publications and practiced law. Interested in establishing an international Zionist organization, he was an early follower of Theodor Herzl. Belkovsky participated in the first Zionist conference in Basel, Switzerland, in 1897 and in others that followed. He also helped write the statutes of both the Jewish Colonial Trust and the Jewish National Fund. As head of the St. Petersburg branch of the Russian Zionist Organization, he suffered arrest by the authorities.

Following the Russian Revolution of 1917, Belkovsky chaired the Executive Committee of the Russian Jewish Communities and then headed the illegal Russian Zionist Central Committee. Again arrested in 1924 for participating in illegal activities, he was tried and sentenced to internal exile in Siberia, but the sentence was then converted to deportation.

Making his way to Palestine, Belkovsky again practiced law and served on the Jewish Arbitration Court in Tel Aviv. He also published the first bibliography of works on Zionism. Belkovsky died in Tel Aviv in 1948.

SPENCER C. TUCKER

See also

Herzl, Theodor; World Zionist Organization; Zionism

References

Hertzberg, Arthur, ed. *The Zionist Idea: A Historical Analysis and Reader.* Philadelphia: Jewish Publication Society, 1997.

Laqueur, Walter. *A History of Zionism: From the French Revolution to the Establishment of the State of Israel.* Reprint ed. New York: Schocken, 2003.

Ben-Ari, Uri
Born: 1925

Israeli Army officer. Uri Ben-Ari was born in 1925 in Berlin, Germany. He escaped the Holocaust when his parents sent him to Palestine as a youth. He received much of his education in a kibbutz, joined the Palmach, and in 1946 was a company commander. In the Israeli War of Independence (1948–1949), he distinguished himself in fighting in the Jerusalem sector and in the Negev Desert. In 1952, as a lieutenant colonel, he executed a brilliant maneuver during military exercises by employing the speed of his armored forces to surround the opposing side.

As the 1956 Suez Crisis came to a head, Ben-Ari, having been promoted to the rank of colonel, took command of the 7th Armored Brigade just as planning for the Sinai Campaign began. There was still doubt in the minds of some in the Israeli high command that

armored formations could hold their own in the forthcoming campaign. They had originally been given the task of screening Jordanian forces, but Ben-Ari pushed hard and received approval for his forces to be included in the initial assault.

Ben-Ari launched his unit forward in the first hours of the conflict and, having captured Kusseima, carried out a flanking move through the Daika Pass. This success made possible the second major battle of the campaign and possibly its most important, the capture of the Egyptian stronghold at Abu Ageila.

The success of the 1956 Sinai Campaign provided a major boost to Ben-Ari's career, and he was promoted to brigadier general and assigned command of the Armored Corps. However, he resigned from active service after he had allegedly protected a subordinate accused of criminal misconduct. Ben-Ari then took up several positions in private enterprise. For several years he served as the general manager of the Lewin-Epstein Company in Tel Aviv.

Ben-Ari returned to active service during the June 1967 Six-Day War, when he commanded the 10th Mechanized Brigade on the Jerusalem front, helping to destroy Jordanian resistance to the north of the city by securing the road from Jerusalem to Ramallah. Upon the outbreak of the 1973 Yom Kippur War, he was serving as chief of staff to the commander of the southern front, Major General Shmuel Gonen. Ben-Ari later held the post of Israeli consul

Israeli general Uri Ben-Ari (*center*) next to Prime Minister Menachem Begin (*speaking*) during a press conference at John F. Kennedy International Airport, New York City, on March 20, 1978. (Israeli Government Press Office)

general in Washington, D.C. He permanently retired from the army in 1974.

RALPH MARTIN BAKER

See also

Armored Warfare Doctrine; Gonen, Shmuel; Israeli War of Independence, Israeli-Jordanian Front; Israeli War of Independence, Overview; Palmach; Sinai Campaign; Six-Day War; Tank Warfare; Yom Kippur War

References

Golani, Moti. *Israel in Search of a War: The Sinai Campaign, 1955–1956.* East Sussex, UK: Sussex Academic, 1997.

Hammel, Eric. *Six Days in June: How Israel Won the 1967 Arab-Israeli War.* New York: Scribner, 1992.

Herzog, Chaim. *The Arab-Israeli Wars: War and Peace in the Middle East from the War of Independence to Lebanon.* Westminster, MD: Random House, 1984.

Kurzman, Dan. *Genesis 1948: The First Arab-Israeli War.* New York: Da Capo, 1992.

Ben-Gurion, David
Born: October 16, 1886
Died: December 1, 1973

Zionist leader, defense minister (1948–1954 and 1955–1963), and prime minister of Israel (1948–1953, 1955–1963). Celebrated as Israel's "Father of the Nation," David Ben-Gurion was born David Grün in Plonsk, Poland, on October 16, 1886. Educated in his Zionist father's Hebrew school, as a teenager he joined the Zionist youth group Erza. He then taught at a Hebrew school in Warsaw and joined the Poalei Zion (Workers of Zion). Ben-Gurion believed that Zionism would be achieved by Jewish settlement in Palestine and by collective farming and industrialization of the land.

Putting his beliefs into action, Ben-Gurion moved to Jaffa, Palestine, in 1906 and established the first Jewish workers' commune there. He then began organizing other workers into unions. In Jerusalem in 1910 he began writing for the newspaper *Ahdut,* publishing his first article on Zionism under the name Ben-Gurion ("son of the lion" in Hebrew).

Ben-Gurion then moved to Jerusalem and joined the editorial staff of a Hebrew-language newspaper. He left Palestine in 1912 to earn a law degree from the University of Constantinople during 1912–1914. Returning to Palestine to take up his union work, he was expelled by the Ottomans—who still controlled Palestine—in March 1915.

Settling in New York City, Ben-Gurion met Russian-born Paula Munweis, whom he married in 1917. Buoyed by the 1917 British Balfour Declaration that proposed a Jewish homeland in Palestine, Ben-Gurion joined the Jewish Legion, a volunteer British military unit formed to help defeat the Turks. In 1920 he returned to union organizing. Indeed, he helped found the Histadrut, a powerful federation of Jewish labor unions. During 1921–1935 he served as its general secretary. The Histadrut became in effect a state within

A devout Zionist while still in his teens and a guerrilla fighter in his adult years, David Ben-Gurion later delivered Israel's Declaration of Independence and served as his nation's first prime minister (1948–1953 and 1955–1963). (United States Holocaust Memorial Museum)

British-controlled Palestine. Ben-Gurion was also a driving force behind the establishment of the Haganah, the paramilitary force of the Zionist movement that helped facilitate illegal Jewish immigration to Palestine and protect the Jewish settlements there. Within the Zionist movement in Palestine, however, he was known as a moderate who opposed the radical approach advocated by Ze'ev Jabotinsky and Menachem Begin. Briefly Ben-Gurion cooperated with Begin's Irgun Tsvai Leumi (National Military Organization) but only rarely supported violence, and then only against military targets. While Ben-Gurion agreed to Begin's plan to bomb the King David Hotel, it was only with the aim of humiliating the British. When it became apparent that the effort would result in loss of life, Ben-Gurion ordered Begin to call off the bombing, which Begin refused to do.

When it became clear after World War II that Britain was not sympathetic to the establishment of a Jewish state in Palestine, Ben-Gurion pursued other avenues to achieve Jewish statehood. He supported the United Nations' (UN) 1947 partition plan that called for separate Jewish and Arab states in Palestine. In May 1948 the UN formally partitioned Palestine, and the State of Israel was born.

Prime Ministers of Israel (1948–Present)

Name	Political Party	Term Years
David Ben-Gurion	Mapai	1948–1954
Moshe Sharett	Mapai	1954–1955
David Ben-Gurion	Mapai	1955–1963
Levi Eshkol	Mapai/Labor	1963–1969
Yigal Allon (interim)	Labor	1969
Golda Meir	Labor	1969–1974
Yitzhak Rabin	Labor	1974–1977
Menachem Begin	Likud	1977–1983
Yitzhak Shamir	Likud	1983–1984
Shimon Peres	Labor	1984–1986
Yitzhak Shamir	Likud	1986–1992
Yitzhak Rabin	Labor	1992–1995
Shimon Peres	Labor	1995–1996
Benjamin Netanyahu	Likud	1996–1999
Ehud Barak	Labor	1999–2001
Ariel Sharon	Likud/Kadima	2001–2006
Ehud Olmert	Kadima	2006–Present

Ben-Gurion was concurrently prime minister and defense minister of the new nation. Austere and ascetic, he insisted that the new state be marked by full social and political equality without regard to race, religion, or sex. As its defense minister, he immediately consolidated all the Jewish paramilitary organizations into the Israel Defense Forces (IDF), enabling them to effectively fight both the Arab Palestinians and the surrounding Arab nations.

As Israel's prime minister, Ben-Gurion promoted Jewish immigration from the Arab states (Operation MAGIC CARPET). He also oversaw establishment of the Jewish state's governmental institutions, advocated compulsory primary education, and urged the creation of new towns and cities. Deeply involved in rural development projects, he urged the establishment of new settlements, especially in the Negev. He was also one of the founders of Mapai, the political party that held power in the first three decades of the Jewish state.

Ben-Gurion retired from politics in 1953 only to return as prime minister and defense minister in 1955. His second period as prime minister coincided with the 1956 Suez Crisis in which the Israeli government worked secretly with the French and British governments to seize control of the Suez Canal and topple Egyptian president Gamal Abdel Nasser from power. Although the IDF performed admirably, heavy pressure from the U.S. government brought the withdrawal of the British, which in turn forced the French and Israelis to remove their own forces.

The last years of Ben-Gurion's premiership were marked by general Israeli prosperity and stalled secret peace talks with the Arabs. He resigned his posts in June 1963 but retained his seat in the Knesset (Israeli parliament). In 1965 he broke with the Mapai Party over Prime Minister Levi Eshkol's handling of the Lavon Affair. Ben-Gurion then formed a new party, Rafi. When it voted to merge with Mapai to form the Labor Alignment in 1968, he formed another new party, the State List. He resigned from the Knesset and left politics altogether in 1970. Among his books are *Israel: An Achieved Personal History* (1970) and *The Jews in Their Land* (1974). He spent his last years on his kibbutz. Ben-Gurion died in Tel Aviv–Jaffa on December 1, 1973.

RICHARD EDWARDS

See also

Balfour Declaration; Begin, Menachem; Eshkol, Levi; Lavon Affair; MAGIC CARPET, Operation; Suez Crisis; Zionism

References

Bar-Zohar, Michel. *Ben-Gurion: The Armed Prophet.* Translated by Len Ortzen. London: Barker, 1967.

Kurzman, Dan. *Ben-Gurion: Prophet of Fire.* New York: Simon and Schuster, 1983.

Zweig, Ronald W., ed. *David Ben-Gurion: Politics and Leadership in Israel.* Jerusalem: Y. I. Ben-Zvi, 1991.

Ben-Zvi, Yitzhak
Born: November 14, 1884
Died: April 23, 1963

Historian, Labor Zionist leader, Israeli politician, and second president of the State of Israel (1952–1963). Yitzhak Ben-Zvi was born Yitzhak Shimshelevits on November 14, 1884, in Poltava, Ukraine, in the Russian Empire. His father was an ardent Zionist and visited Palestine in 1901 to see about planning a settlement there. Because of educational quotas placed on Jews by the Russian government,

Yitzhak Ben-Zvi, Israeli historian, Zionist leader, and second president of the State of Israel (1952–1963). (Library of Congress)

Ben-Zvi was not admitted to high school until 1901 when he was 17. He visited Palestine for two months in 1904. Determined to immigrate to Palestine, on his return to Russia he joined the Pa'ole Zion (Workers of Zion) party. He became active in the Jewish self-defense groups formed in Ukraine to defend Jews during the pogroms in 1905. The next year, the Russian police searched the family home and discovered weapons there. His father was then arrested, tried, and sentenced to live in exile in Siberia but was able to get to Palestine in 1922. Ben-Zvi escaped to Vilna, where he continued clandestine Workers of Zion work and organized a conference in Minsk in 1906 before traveling to Germany, Austria, and Switzerland to recruit new members. He then returned to Minsk and was arrested and imprisoned several times before he was able to immigrate to Palestine in 1907.

Settling in Jaffa (Yafo, Yaffa), Ben-Zvi helped organize the Hashomer Jewish self-defense group of the Second Aliya. In 1909 he was a cofounder of the Gymnasia High School in Jerusalem and was among its first teachers. In 1910 he helped found the first Palestinian Hebrew-language Socialist journal, *Ahdut*.

During 1912–1914 Ben-Zvi pursued legal studies in Constantinople (Istanbul) along with David Ben-Gurion. Both returned to Palestine in August 1914 at the outbreak of World War I. Turkish administrator Ahmad Jamal Pasha's policies led to their imprisonment and expulsion in 1915 when they refused to accept Turkish citizenship. Ben-Zvi and Ben-Gurion then went to Egypt and, with some difficulty, on to New York City, where they raised money for Zionist causes, founded the Hehalutz (Pioneer) movement, and coauthored *The Land of Israel, Past and Present*.

Active in recruiting for the Jewish Legion, Ben-Zvi and Ben-Gurion returned to Palestine in late 1918. British high commissioner for Palestine Sir Herbert Samuel appointed Ben-Zvi to the Government Advisory Council, but Ben-Zvi resigned to protest British restrictions on Jewish immigration that followed the Arab riots in the spring of 1921. Ben-Zvi was active in the secret Jewish self-defense group the Haganah and was also a major figure in the Jewish labor movement in Palestine, serving as a member of the secretariat of the Histadrut. He also helped found the Ahdut Ha'avodah (Labor Union) party.

Elected to the first Knesset (Israeli parliament) in January 1949 as a representative of the Mapai Party, Ben-Zvi was elected by the Knesset as the second president of Israel on December 1952 following the death of Chaim Weizmann. During Ben-Zvi's decade in that largely ceremonial office, he was much admired for his inclusiveness and personal modesty. He moved the president's residence to Jerusalem but, seeking to set an example, lived there in a small prefabricated dwelling. Well known as an expert on Jewish history and ethnology, in 1948 Ben-Zvi, with the support of the Jewish Agency, the Ministry of Education and Culture, and the Histadrut, established an institute to study Jewish Oriental communities and their history. It was subsequently named for him and affiliated with the Hebrew University of Jerusalem. Ben-Zvi was also the longest-serving Israeli president, having been elected to a third term in December 1962 (before the presidency was limited to two terms). Ben-Zvi died in office while in Jerusalem on April 23, 1963.

SPENCER C. TUCKER

See also

Aliya, Second; Ben-Gurion, David; Haganah; Hashomer; Hehalutz Movement; Histadrut; Israel; Jamal Pasha, Ahmad; Jewish Agency for Israel; Labor Zionism; Pogroms; Samuel, Sir Herbert Louis; Weizmann, Chaim

References

Sachar, Howard M. *A History of Israel: From the Rise of Zionism to Our Time*. 3rd ed. New York: Knopf, 2007.

Shepherd, Naomi. *Ploughing Sand: British Rule in Palestine, 1917–1948*. New Brunswick, NJ: Rutgers University Press, 1999.

Bernadotte, Folke
Born: January 2, 1895
Died: September 17, 1948

United Nations (UN) mediator in 1948 in the Israeli War of Independence. Born in Stockholm, Sweden, on January 2, 1895, Folke Bernadotte, Count of Wisborg, was the son of Prince Oscar of Sweden who, by marrying without the consent of his father King Oscar II, left the royal family. Following military training, Bernadotte became a cavalry officer in the Royal Horse Guards. During 1930–1931 he studied banking in New York and Paris, but given his deep religious faith, humanitarian work was a more natural pursuit.

Bernadotte represented Sweden in 1933 at the Chicago Century of Progress Exposition, and in 1939 he was Swedish commissioner-general at the New York World's Fair. As vice chairman of the Swedish Red Cross during World War II, Bernadotte, who spoke six languages, facilitated the exchange of British and German prisoners of war and the release of many concentration camp internees.

On November 29, 1947, the Arab states rejected the UN General Assembly vote to partition Palestine into Arab and Jewish states. Five Arab armies moved into Palestine the day after Israel unilaterally proclaimed its establishment as a state on May 14, 1948. Six days later, on May 20, the UN Security Council agreed to the appointment of Bernadotte, a proven diplomat, as mediator to seek a peaceful solution to the conflict. Ten days later Bernadotte initiated discussions with Arab and Jewish leaders, and he succeeded in securing agreement to a 30-day truce commencing on June 11, 1948. Drawing upon his experience in Red Cross work, Bernadotte also initiated the humanitarian relief program for Palestinian refugees.

Bernadotte presented two consecutive plans to restore peace. The first (on June 27, 1948) suggested that Palestine (defined as the British Mandate of 1922 and thus including Transjordan) would comprise a union of the two peoples. Bernadotte considered the original UN partition plan untenable. Instead of establishing individual states, he proposed that Arabs and Jews form a union con-

Swedish diplomat Count Folke Bernadotte, appointed by the United Nations Security Council to seek a peaceful end to the Israeli War of Independence, was assassinated in Jerusalem on September 17, 1948, by a Zionist underground group. (United States Holocaust Memorial Museum)

sisting of a small Jewish entity and an enlarged Transjordan. There would also be a free port at Haifa and a free airport at Lydda (Lod). Israel would receive western Galilee and unlimited immigration for two years, after which the UN would assume control. Between 250,000 and 300,000 Arab refugees would be permitted to return to Arab lands with compensation, and Transjordan would control the Negev and Jerusalem, despite Israeli claims to exclusivity in the latter. Bernadotte also proposed a reconciliation committee as the first step toward achieving a lasting peace.

Both sides rejected the plan. The Arabs opposed a Zionist entity in Palestine, while Jews opposed the reduction in the size of their state and circumscription of its sovereignty in several important aspects. The Israelis found especially objectionable the handing over of Jerusalem to the Arabs, and it was perhaps this that sealed Bernadotte's fate. Fighting resumed on July 8 until a second UN cease-fire was declared on July 18.

Bernadotte's second plan, of September 16, formally recognized the Jewish state. He proposed that the whole of Galilee be defined as Jewish territory. Arab Palestine was still to be merged with Transjordan, and the whole of the Negev was to be given to the Arab state. Jerusalem now would be placed under UN control. Major changes had been made to reconcile the Israelis, but the principal winner was still King Abdullah of Transjordan. The Jewish state still would have covered only some 20 percent of Palestine.

One organization that saw Bernadotte's efforts as a threat was the Fighters for the Freedom of Israel (Lohamei Herut Israel, or Lehi), a Jewish underground group that had waged a campaign of personal terror to drive the British out of Palestine. Lehi considered Bernadotte a British agent and saw his plan as a threat to its goal of Israeli control of both banks of the Jordan River. It is now generally accepted that the Central Committee of Lehi took the decision to assassinate Bernadotte. On September 17, 1948, Bernadotte and Colonel André Serot of the French Air Force were assassinated in Jerusalem by a group of armed men led by Avraham Stern. Three days after Bernadotte's death, his final report on his peace efforts was published in Paris. While it gave the UN General Assembly a formula for peace, the plan was never implemented.

PETER OVERLACK

See also

Israeli War of Independence, Overview; Lohamei Herut Israel; United Nations General Assembly Resolution 194

References

Bernadotte, Count Folke. *Instead of Arms: Autobiographical Notes.* Stockholm: Bonniers, 1948.

Marton, Kati. *A Death in Jerusalem.* New York: Arcade, 1996.

Persson, Sune O. *Mediation & Assassination: Count Bernadotte's Mission to Palestine in 1948.* London: Ithaca, 1979.

Bethlehem

Historic West Bank town important to Judaism, Christianity, and Islam. Bethlehem (Bayt Lahm) has a present population of about 38,000 people, of whom approximately 50 percent are Muslim and 50 percent are Christian (Palestinian). Bethlehem boasts one of the largest Palestinian Christian communities in the Middle East. For Jews, Bethlehem is known as the birthplace of King David, the second king of the Israelites, as told in the Old Testament (Torah). David was crowned king in Bethlehem by Samuel, who was the first major Jewish prophet. Known as Ephrath in the Old Testament (in the books of Genesis and Ruth), Bethlehem is the locale where Rachel is believed to have been buried (actually on the outskirts). Rachel, mentioned in Genesis, was the second and most-favored wife of Jacob.

It would be difficult to overemphasize the centrality of Bethlehem to Christianity, for it is believed to be the birthplace of Jesus Christ. The birth of Jesus was prophesied in the Old Testament, and it was expected that his birth would occur in Bethlehem, the birthplace of his forebear King David. In the New Testament, the gospels of Matthew and Luke both name Bethlehem as the birthplace of Jesus. The Church of the Nativity, perhaps the most revered church in all of Christendom, is located in Bethlehem over a small cave where Jesus is said to have been born. Built by the Roman Emperor Constantine beginning in AD 330, the Church of the Nativity may be the oldest Christian Church in the world. Nearby is another grotto

The skyline of Bethlehem, located about six miles south of Jerusalem in Israel. (Corel)

where St. Jerome is said to have translated the Bible into Latin. For many years, and since the early 1500s, the Roman Catholic Church and the Greek Orthodox Church fought for control over the Church of the Nativity.

Yet Bethlehem has significance for Muslims as well. The Prophet Muhammad, it is believed, stopped in Bethlehem and prayed en route to Jerusalem upon the instructions of the archangel Gabriel, who informed Muhammad that the latter's "brother" and fellow prophet Jesus had been born there. Throughout the first 500 years or so after the birth of Christ, Bethlehem saw a number of invasions, violent occupations, and other calamities. In AD 614, the Persians took control of Bethlehem, an occupation that lasted only until 637, when Muslim armies seized control. Throughout these invasions, the Church of the Nativity was spared major damage or destruction. In 1099 the Christian Crusaders won control of the town, and in the 1100s the Christians commissioned major artwork—including mosaics—within the church. In 1187, however, Bethlehem fell to Saladin. In the 1300s, Christians returned to Bethlehem to administer the church. From 1517 until 1917 (except for a brief period from 1831–1841), the Ottoman Empire ruled Bethlehem and its surrounding areas.

With the end of World War II, Bethlehem passed into the hands of the British, who maintained a League of Nations mandate over all of Palestine until 1948. Beginning in 1947, Bethlehem witnessed a major influx of Palestinian refugees who were fleeing advancing Jewish forces first during the Arab-Jewish Communal War and then during the Israeli War of Independence (1948–1949). When the fighting finally stopped, Bethlehem and the West Bank remained in Arab (Jordanian) control, but the makeup of Bethlehem's population had changed dramatically. In June 1967 as a result of the Six-Day War, Israel occupied the West Bank, including Bethlehem.

The Israelis administered the city until December 1995, when the newly created Palestinian Authority (PA) took control. This had been part of the agreements associated with the 1993 Oslo Accords. The PA has designated Bethlehem as the seat of the Bethlehem Governorate. After the outbreak of the Second (al-Aqsa) Intifada in 2000, the town was the scene of several showdowns between Palestinians and Israelis. In 2002, Palestinian militants holed themselves up in the Church of the Nativity for five weeks after Israeli troops invaded the town. The crisis was diffused only after international intervention. Most recently, the construction of the Israeli Security Fence has caused major problems for Bethlehem because the route of the fence has cut off from their homes scores of Palestinians who work in the town.

PAUL G. PIERPAOLI JR.

See also

Bible; Church of the Nativity; Israeli Security Fence; Koran; Oslo Accords; Palestinian Authority; West Bank

References

Mansour, Atallah. *Narrow Gate Churches: The Christian Presence in the Holy Land under Muslim and Jewish Rule.* Carol Stream, IL: Hope Publishing House, 2004.

Raheb, Mitri. *Bethlehem Besieged: Stories of Hope in Times of Trouble.* Minneapolis, MN: Augsburg Fortress, 2004.

Bevin, Ernest
Born: March 9, 1881
Died: April 14, 1951

British trade union leader, Labour Party politician, minister of labor, and foreign secretary from 1945 to 1950. Born in Winsford, Somerset, on March 9, 1881, and orphaned at the age of 8, Ernest Bevin left school at age 11 and worked a series of odd jobs to support himself. He eventually worked his way up from dockworker to secretary of the dockworkers union by age 20. He continued to rise through union ranks and became general secretary of the Transport and General Workers Union in 1931. Influential in Labour Party politics throughout the 1930s, he became minister of labor in Winston Churchill's wartime coalition government in 1940 and was responsible for mobilizing manpower for the war effort. After Labour's 1945 electoral victory, Bevin became foreign secretary to Prime Minister Clement Attlee, accompanying him to the last Allied conference at Potsdam in the summer of 1945.

tion (NATO), founded on April 4, 1949. He preserved Britain's freedom of action in international affairs, however, by eschewing Anglo-European integration.

Throughout his time at the Foreign Office, the future of Western colonialism in the post–World War II Middle East was a major preoccupation for Bevin. He helped to negotiate the December 1945 Bevin-Bidault Plan to evacuate British and French troops from Lebanon and Syria, the abortive Anglo-Egyptian Bevin-Sidqi Agreement of October 1946 on Egypt, and the 1949 Bevin-Sforza Plan for Libya. Bevin took an uncompromising position on the Anglo-Iranian oil dispute, which some American officials believed helped propel Iranian leaders toward the Soviet Union.

The most contentious Middle Eastern issue confronting Bevin, however, was the future of the British Mandate for Palestine, which the British government's 1917 Balfour Declaration had pledged would become a Jewish homeland but which also had a sizable indigenous Palestinian population. Zionists, many of them American and politically influential, sought to create a Jewish state there, and the Truman administration annoyed Bevin by demanding that an additional 100,000 Jews be permitted to move to Palestine. Bevin, by contrast, followed the policy set out in the 1939 British White Paper and sought to restrict Jewish migration to the mandate, a policy that Marshall and the State Department but not the White House found congenial.

Assassinations of British individuals by Jewish terrorist organizations, the need to ensure British access to Middle Eastern oil reserves, and genuine sympathy for dispossessed Palestinians all made Bevin unsympathetic to Jewish demands. Ideally, he hoped to promote economic development throughout the Middle East, with Jewish expertise helping to encourage growth and peaceful progress around the region.

Faced with a near irresolvable dilemma and caught between conflicting Arab and Jewish demands, in April 1947 Bevin handed the problem of Palestine's future off to the United Nations (UN). When the UN recommended its partition into Jewish and non-Jewish states by April 1948, Bevin refused to permit British military and civilian authorities to implement this settlement and withdrew the British administration before the partition date. Documents in Israeli archives, however, suggest that Bevin quietly promoted partition, meeting secretly with Zionist leader Golda Meir and King Abdullah of Transjordan and acquiescing in a scheme devised by them whereby Abdullah obtained the West Bank of the Jordan River in exchange for accepting Jewish control of the remainder of Palestine. Bevin sought to keep Britain aloof from the internal Arab-Jewish Communal War that began in November 1947 and the full-scale Israeli War of Independence that broke out in May 1948 immediately after establishment of the State of Israel.

In January 1950 Bevin angered the United States by officially recognizing the People's Republic of China (PRC), but the following June his fundamental belief in Anglo-American partnership against communism impelled him to firmly support American intervention in Korea. Anxious to maintain both close relations with the

Ernest Bevin, British trade union leader, Labour Party politician, minister of labor, and foreign secretary (1945–1950). (Library of Congress)

Bevin's years as a trade unionist ingrained in him a deep distrust of Soviet-style communism. After 1945 he was convinced that the Soviet Union was bent on expanding its influence over the whole of Europe and the Middle East. But a Britain badly weakened by six years of war had to look elsewhere for help in reestablishing world order and stanching Soviet expansionism. Bevin therefore turned over British commitments in the Mediterranean, particularly in Greece and Turkey, to the United States on February 21, 1947. This decision ultimately led to the March 1947 Truman Doctrine, which pledged American responsibility for anticommunist and anti-Soviet policies in the region.

Having cast Britain's lot with the United States, Bevin worked tirelessly to convince President Harry S. Truman's administration of the need for financial and military support for European reconstruction and the unification of Western Europe as a bulwark against Soviet expansionism in what soon became known as the containment policy. A similar consensus was emerging within the Truman administration, and on June 5, 1947, U.S. secretary of state George Marshall announced that the United States would establish an aid package for both Western and Eastern Europe, the so-called Marshall Plan or European Recovery Program. Bevin then turned to military concerns and negotiated the 1948 Brussels Treaty, which was ultimately expanded into the North Atlantic Treaty Organiza-

United States and prestige in his own country, in July 1950 he supported the decision to commit British troops to the UN forces in Korea. He also endorsed the October 1950 decision to cross the 38th Parallel. Health problems forced him to resign on March 10, 1951. Bevin died in London on April 14, 1951.

CHRIS TUDDA AND PRISCILLA ROBERTS

See also

Abdullah I, King of Jordan; Acheson, Dean; Arab-Jewish Communal War; Attlee, Clement Richard; Churchill, Sir Winston; Israel; Israeli War of Independence, Overview; Marshall, George Catlett; Meir, Golda; Palestine, British Mandate for; Truman, Harry S.; West Bank

References

Barclay, Sir Roderick. *Ernest Bevin and the Foreign Office.* London: Latimer, 1975.

Bullock, Alan. *Ernest Bevin: Foreign Secretary, 1945–1951.* New York: Norton, 1983.

Chaitani, Youssef. *Dissension among Allies: Ernest Bevin Palestine Policy between Whitehall and the White House, 1945–47.* London: Saqi, 2002.

Cohen, Michael J. *Palestine and the Great Powers, 1945–1948.* Princeton, NJ: Princeton University Press, 1982.

Kent, John. *British Imperial Strategy and the Origins of the Cold War 1944–49.* Leicester, UK: Leicester University Press, 1993.

Louis, William Roger. *The British Empire in the Middle East, 1945–1951: Arab Nationalism, the United States, and Postwar Imperialism.* New York: Oxford University Press, 1984.

Stephens, Mark. *Ernest Bevin: Unskilled Labourer and World Statesman.* London: Stevenage, 1981.

Weiler, Peter. *Ernest Bevin.* Manchester, UK: Manchester University Press, 1993.

Bezalel Academy of Arts and Design

Influential college located in Israel. Since 1968, the Bezalel Academy of Arts and Design has been controlled and funded by the Israeli government. Despite early difficulties and closure from 1929 to 1935, the school, founded by Boris Schatz in 1906, is regarded as the pioneering Zionist aesthetic enterprise in Israel and an important incubator of new artists.

Reconstituted under modernist leadership, Bezalel became the premier artistic educational institution in the State of Israel. Its artistic collections formed the nucleus of the Israel Museum, which absorbed them in 1965.

Named after the creator of the Tabernacle of the Covenant (Exodus 35), Bezalel was part of the Zionist effort to forge a new national culture. Paradoxically, the quest for authenticity and return to origins entailed viewing the national past through an orientalizing lens. The decorative objects and works of art, widely exported and sold to tourists, depict Jewish symbols, biblical subjects, folkloric

A life-drawing class in progress at the Bezalel Academy of Arts and Design in Jerusalem in May 1950. (Teddy Brauner/Israeli Government Press Office)

themes, and landscapes. In fact, both the school and its critics shared the orientalist aesthetic and subject matter: an idealized historical past or timeless landscape rather than contemporary struggles and the building up of the Yishuv, or the Jewish community in Palestine prior to 1948.

The State of Israel began to support Bezalel in 1952, assumed control in 1968, and transformed it from a crafts school into an accredited institution of higher learning in 1975. In 1990 the school moved to the Mount Scopus campus of Hebrew University. However, in the spring of 2005 Bezalel officials concluded that a location in the core of western Jerusalem would be more advantageous. Some 1,800 students currently pursue bachelor's degrees in art, design, and architecture there. The centennial celebrations in 2006 included an exhibition on Schatz at the Israel Museum. Bezalel served an important role in the Zionist movement, particularly prior to 1948.

JIM WALD

See also

Herzl, Theodor; Jerusalem; Zionism

References

Manor, Dalia. *Art in Zion: The Genesis of Modern National Art in Jewish Palestine.* London: RoutledgeCurzon, 2005.

Museumsberg Flensburg. *Design and Fashion: Junges Design aus Israel/Young Design from Israel.* Flensburg, Germany: Museumsberg and Kulturbüro Flensburg, 2002.

Shilo-Cohen, Nurit, ed. *Bezalel, 1906–1929.* Jerusalem: Israel Museum, 1983.

Bialik, Haim Nachman
Born: January 11, 1873
Died: July 4, 1934

Russian-born Hebrew writer and poet, considered by many to be the greatest modern Hebrew poet. Haim Nachman Bialik was born on January 11, 1873, in Radi (Radomyshl), Volhynia, in the Pale of Settlement, the area of western Russia to which most Russian Jews were legally confined. From age seven, following his father's death and mother's departure, Bialik grew up in the house of his severe, pious paternal grandfather in Zhitomir.

Bialik hoped that study for the rabbinate, first in the Talmudic Academy of Volozhin in Lithuania (1890) and then in cosmopolitan Odessa (1891), would enable him to reconcile the traditional and the modern. Instead, it propelled him toward the latter, represented by the Haskalah (Jewish Enlightenment) and Zionism.

In Odessa, Bialik became a disciple of Ahad Ha'Am, whose spiritual Zionism, in contrast to the later political Zionism of Theodor Herzl, proposed to achieve national redemption by making Palestine the site of a secular Jewish cultural renewal rather than mass settlement and statehood. In the 1890s, Bialik married and pursued various occupations in several locales, but in the two decades following his return to Odessa in 1900 as a teacher, he established himself as the leading Hebrew writer.

Russian-born Haim Nachman Bialik, an important poet and translator of the Hebrew language. Bialik, part of the Jewish Diaspora, settled in Palestine in 1924. (Library of Congress)

The year 1901 witnessed two milestones for Bialik: the publication of his first book of poetry in Warsaw and the cofounding (with Yehoshua Hana Ravnitzky and others) of the Hebrew educational publishing house Moriah. He is best known for the "Poems of Wrath" (1903–1906), written in response to intensified social unrest and anti-Semitic violence. "Be-Ir ha-Haregah" (In the City of Slaughter) created a sensation by virtue of its unsparing portrait of victims as well as perpetrators of the Kishinev Pogrom of 1903. Although the charge of passivity was not entirely accurate (Kishinev witnessed nascent Jewish resistance), the poem catalyzed a growing Jewish national consciousness and militant spirit of self-defense in Eastern Europe and Palestine.

Even more innovative was the prose poem "Megillat ha-Esh" (Scroll of Fire), published in 1905, in which legends of the destruction of the Temple in Jerusalem are the vehicle for reflections on national destiny, love, and the poetic mission. Bialik increasingly turned from poetry to other forms of writing and activity, but the consistent underlying concept that he articulated was kinnus, or ingathering. This was the equivalent of cultural immigration to Palestine, comprising both authorship and publication of texts by others.

During World War I (1914–1918), Bialik's age consigned him to noncombatant service. Although the new Bolshevik regime that came to the fore in 1917 officially condemned anti-Semitism, it also rejected Jewish nationalism and shut down Moriah in 1921. The intervention of famed author Maxim Gorky nonetheless enabled Bialik and other Hebrew writers to leave Russia. In Berlin, they resurrected the press as Dvir. In 1924 they relocated it to Palestine. Bialik and Ravnitzky's pioneering critical editions of medieval Hebrew poets, such as their *Sefer Ha-Aggadah* (Book of Legends), a magisterial compilation of ancient rabbinic lore published during 1908–1911, made the cultural legacy accessible to a modern audience.

After immigrating, Bialik also produced highly accomplished juvenile literature and the autobiographical poem "Yatmut" (Orphanhood), which he wrote shortly before his death, but was increasingly occupied with public affairs. He traveled to the United States and Europe on behalf of the World Zionist Organization, served on the board of the Hebrew University of Jerusalem, and led the Hebrew Writers' Union (1927–1934). His sixtieth birthday in 1933 was an occasion for national celebration within the Yishuv (Jewish community of Palestine). Bialik died of a heart attack on July 4, 1934, in Vienna.

Ironically, some factors that initially made his work so successful subsequently limited its reception. His pathos now seems antiquated. Many translations poorly captured his stylistic complexity, and none could convey his masterful allusions to classical texts. In Israel, Bialik's role as canonical political author tended to obscure the range of his literary achievement. He ambivalently cast himself in a prophetic role, but rather than artificially separating his work into the public and private, critics today view it as an integral whole whose tensions enhance rather than diminish its appeal. Bialik played a signal part in the revival of Hebrew, which, though preceding the creation of the Jewish state, connected Diaspora culture with ancient and modern nationhood. Bialik's true accomplishment as national poet rests on his creation of a national literary sensibility rather than subject matter alone.

James Wald

See also

Anti-Semitism; Herzl, Theodor; Literature of the Arab-Israeli Wars; Pale of Settlement; Pogroms; Zionism

References

Bialik, Hayim Nahman. *Songs from Bialik: Selected Poems of Hayim Nahman Bialik.* Edited and translated by Atar Hadari. Syracuse, NY: Syracuse University Press, 2000.

Bialik, Hayim Nahman, and Yehoshua Hana Ravnitzky, eds. *The Book of Legends, Sefer Ha-Aggadah: Legends from the Talmud and Midrash.* Translated by William G. Braude. New York: Schocken, 1992.

Feinstein, Sara. *Sunshine, Blossoms and Blood: H. N. Bialik in His Time; A Literary Biography.* Lanham, MD: University Press of America, 2005.

Hirschfeld, Ariel. "Locus and Language: Hebrew Culture in Israel, 1880–1990." Pp. 1011–1060 in *Cultures of the Jews: A New History,* edited by David Biale. New York: Schocken, 2002.

Penkower, Monty Noam. "The Kishinev Pogrom of 1903: A Turning Point in Jewish History." *Modern Judaism* 24(3) (2004): 187–225.

Bible

The Bible is a compilation of ancient documents now accepted as the sacred canon for, among others, Christianity and Judaism. It has served as the seed text for several other religions. The Bible (from the Latin *biblia sacra,* or "holy books") is commonly divided into two sections, the 33 canonical works of the Hebrew Bible (Tanakh) and the 27 books of the New Testament.

The Tanakh, or what Christians refer to as the Old Testament, is the primary Jewish canonical scripture consisting of three main sections. The Torah (teaching or law) is the most important document of Judaism and is comprised of five books: Genesis, Exodus, Leviticus, Numbers, and Deuteronomy. These are often referred to as the Pentateuch (Greek for "five containers"). The Nevi'im (Prophets), encompasses 17 books that tell of the rise of the Jewish monarchy and the empowerment of the children of Israel. The Ketuvim (writings) are made up of 11 books containing material ranging from the poetry of the Psalms to the Five Scrolls, which include the prophecies of the book of Daniel.

The books of the Torah were fixed about 400 BC, and the remainder of the Jewish canon was fixed over a period of time between 200 BC and AD 100. Around 250 BC Greek-speaking Jews, most probably in Alexandria, produced the Septuagint, a Greek translation of Jewish sacred writings. Not all of the books of the Septuagint were accepted into the Jewish canon, however, because some were never written in Hebrew originally or because the Hebrew original versions were lost. Those excluded books now comprise the Jewish Apocrypha and include the First and Second Maccabees, which tell the Hanukkah story.

The books of the Jewish Apocrypha are included in the Old Testament canon of the Greek Orthodox version of the Bible. In many other Christian denominations the books of the Jewish Apocrypha have a semicanonical status and are often included in a separate section between the Old Testament and the New Testament. The writings that now make up the Pseudepigrapha, on the other hand, consist of early Hebrew religious texts not recognized as part of either the Jewish or the Christian canons or the Jewish Apocrypha.

The term "New Testament" was likely coined by Tertullian from the Latin phrase "Novum Testamentum" and implies "the new covenant." This refers to the belief that in the Tanakh, the first covenant was made between God and man through Moses. Jesus Christ established a new covenant, which was documented in a new set of scriptures that became the New Testament.

The New Testament is a collection of works by Christ's apostles. Many texts from various sources were used during the early stages of the developing Christian Church. In AD 367, St. Athanasius, the bishop of Alexandria, drew up the list of the 27 books of the New Testament canonical works that was confirmed by the Third Council of Carthage in AD 397. The debate over the canon continued, however, until the New Testament canon was confirmed once and for all by the Roman Catholic Church at the Council of Trent (1545–1563).

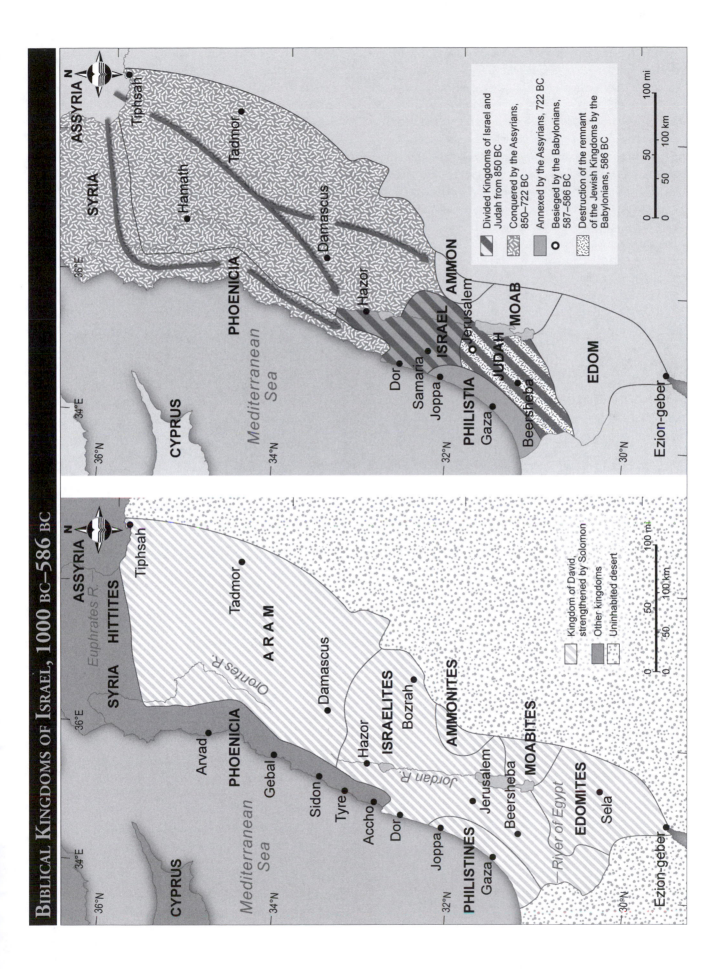

BIBLICAL KINGDOMS OF ISRAEL, 1000 BC–586 BC

Left map (1000 BC)

ASSYRIA
HITTITES
SYRIA
Tiphsah
Euphrates R.
ARAM
Tadmor
Damascus
Orontes R.
PHOENICIA
Arvad
Gebal
Sidon
Tyre
Accho
Dor
Hazor
Jordan R.
ISRAELITES
Bozrah
AMMONITES
Joppa
PHILISTINES
Gaza
Jerusalem
Beersheba
MOABITES
River of Egypt
EDOMITES
Sela
Ezion-geber
Mediterranean Sea
CYPRUS

36°E
36°N
34°E
34°N
32°N
30°N

Kingdom of David, strengthened by Solomon
Other kingdoms
Uninhabited desert

N

0   50   100 mi
0   50   100 km

Right map (850 BC–586 BC)

ASSYRIA
Tiphsah
SYRIA
Hamath
Tadmor
Damascus
Hazor
PHOENICIA
Dor
Samaria
Joppa
ISRAEL
AMMON
Jerusalem
JUDAH
MOAB
PHILISTIA
Gaza
Beersheba
EDOM
Ezion-geber
Mediterranean Sea
CYPRUS

36°E
36°N
34°E
34°N
32°N
30°N

N

Divided Kingdoms of Israel and Judah from 850 BC
Conquered by the Assyrians, 850–722 BC
Annexed by the Assyrians, 722 BC
Besieged by the Babylonians, 587–586 BC
Destruction of the remnant of the Jewish Kingdoms by the Babylonians, 586 BC

0   50   100 mi
0   50   100 km

The early Christian texts that did not make it into the canon comprise the Christian Apocrypha. Although the mainstream Church considered such writings heretical, they nonetheless remained popular and influential for many years after their exclusion from the canon and were widely represented in literature and art. Ironically, the books of the Jewish Apocrypha have greater theological status among Christians than do those of the Christian Apocrypha, which have a status similar to the books of the Pseudepigrapha.

The King James Version of the Bible recognizes five divisions of New Testament works. The first section is made up of the Gospels (Good News), and in each of the four gospels (Matthew, Mark, Luke, and John) one of Christ's apostles tells the life story and details the ministry of Christ. Next is the Acts of the Apostles, where the narrative continues and details how each Apostle continued to spread Christ's ministry. The Pauline Epistles are 14 epistolary writings generally attributed to Paul. These letters provide instruction in moral guidance, Church doctrine, and the nature of the Church itself. The General Epistles, 7 epistolary books written by apostles other than Paul, targeted a more universal audience of churches.

Revelation (also known as the Apocalypse of John) refers to its author as John "of the Island which is called Patmos" (1:9), who early theologians believed was the Apostle John. Revelation's importance lies in the fact that the text has been interpreted by most Christians as prophesying a terrifying apocalyptic scenario known to them as Armageddon, or the end of days.

The Bible remains relevant to ongoing Arab-Israeli conflicts for many reasons. One is ethnic monotheism, which holds that there is only one God who belongs only to His chosen people. This concept creates a cultural dichotomy in that the world is automatically divided into the One God's chosen people in the Promised Land and those on the outside, who are to be converted, saved, or destroyed. Islam recognizes the sacred message of Judaism but rejects the notion that the Jews are God's chosen people.

KEITH MURPHY

See also

Genesis, Book of

References

Asimov, Isaac. *Asimov's Guide to the Bible.* 2 vols. New York: Avenel, 1981.

Lamsa, George M. *Holy Bible: From the Ancient Eastern Text.* San Francisco: Harper and Row, 1957.

Nicholson, Adam. *God's Secretaries: The Making of the King James Bible.* New York: Perennial, 2004.

Panati, Charles. *Sacred Origins of Profound Things: The Stories behind the Rites and Rituals of the World's Religions.* New York: Arkana Penguin, 1996.

Biltmore Program
Start Date: May 6, 1942

Series of Zionist resolutions advocating unfettered Jewish immigration to Palestine and the creation of a Jewish state passed during the Biltmore Conference held in New York City during May 6–11, 1942. The Biltmore Program took its name from the Biltmore Hotel, where the conference convened. The Biltmore Conference encompassed both Zionist and non-Zionist Jewish organizations and was intended to take the place of the international World Zionist Congress, which had been postponed because of World War II. The meeting, billed as the "Extraordinary Zionist Conference," marked the first time in which Zionist and non-Zionists came together to formulate a common resolution on immigration to Palestine.

The Biltmore Program, consisting of eight resolutions, called upon the Jewish Agency for Israel to control and monitor future Jewish immigration to Palestine. Indeed, the resolution went even further by advocating the establishment of a Jewish Commonwealth in Palestine. As such, the Biltmore Program rejected any binational or biethnic solution to the disposition of Palestine. The seriousness of the Biltmore Conference was emphasized by the attendance of several internationally renowned Zionists, including Chaim Weizmann, David Ben-Gurion, and Nahum Goldmann. The Biltmore Program came to serve as the platform of the World Zionist Organization.

The Biltmore Program came during the Nazi-inspired Holocaust, whose horrors were just becoming known to the outside world. Surely the Jews assembled at the Biltmore Hotel were under no illusions about the fate of hundreds of thousands of Jews throughout Eastern and Central Europe. The resolution that passed in 1942 was thus a clear effort to speed up Jewish immigration to Palestine, which many Jews hoped would alleviate the suffering of several million European Jews and prevent further deaths during the Holocaust. At the same time, however, those in attendance in the Biltmore Hotel also knew full well that their declaration flew in the face of British policy in Palestine, which was most recently summed up by the 1939 White Paper. That position paper had severely restricted Jewish immigration in the British Mandate. The Biltmore Program effectively denounced British policy but was not universally accepted by Jews. Some rejected the formation of a single Jewish state in Palestine, while others believed that it placed undue pressure on the British. Nevertheless, most Jewish groups in the United States supported the Biltmore Program.

PAUL G. PIERPAOLI JR.

See also

Holocaust; Jewish Agency for Israel; Palestine, British Mandate for; White Paper (1939); World Zionist Organization; Zionism; Zionist Conference

References

Gelvin, James L. *The Israel-Palestine Conflict: One Hundred Years of War.* New York: Cambridge University Press, 2005.

Sachar, Howard M. *A History of Israel: From the Rise of Zionism to Our Time.* 3rd ed. New York: Knopf, 2007.

Bilu
Start Date: 1882
End Date: 1904

Movement of Jewish pioneers who began the First Aliya (1882–1904) to settle in Palestine and there establish a Jewish state. The

The only remaining survivors of the Bilu settlers of Rishon Le Zion attending a garden party at Rehovot, Israel, on May 13, 1951. (Fritz Cohen/Israeli Government Press Office)

term "Bilu" is an acronym derived from a verse in the book of Isaiah (2:5): "Bet Ya'akov L'khu V'Nelkha" ("House of Jacob, let us go [up]").

Bilu was established in 1882 in Kharkov by Jewish university students who were reacting to a series of pogroms (persecutions) of Jews in Russia during the period 1881–1882 as well as the anti-Semitic May Laws of Czar Alexander III. The movement developed other branches and members beyond students. Bilu prompted settlement in Palestine and the development of agricultural pursuits there. The leaders of the organization sent representatives to Constantinople and met there with British writer and adventurer Laurence Oliphant, who was advocating Jewish settlement in Palestine and endeavoring to secure from the Ottoman government a land cession for this in northern Palestine.

In July 1882 the first group of 14 members of Bilu (13 men and 1 woman) arrived in Palestine with the plan to establish a communal settlement there. After an initial training period working as farm laborers at Mikveh Israel, they pooled their resources to establish the Rishon L'Zion (First to Zion) agricultural cooperative on lands purchased in the Arab village of Eyun Kara. The settlement lacked water, and after a few months the starving Bilu members departed, a half dozen leaving Palestine to return to Russia and the remainder returning to Mikveh Israel. An appeal to Baron Edmond de

Rothschild for financial assistance was not immediately successful, although later he made support of Zionist colonies in Palestine his principal philanthropic endeavor and assisted Bilu groups. Some Bilu members went on to found Zikhron Ya'akov. Although the first Bilu members experienced little success, their example served as an inspiration for others to follow.

SPENCER C. TUCKER

See also

Aliya, First; Oliphant, Laurence; Rothschild, Edmond de

References

Pappe, Ilan. *A History of Modern Palestine: One Land, Two Peoples.* Cambridge: Cambridge University Press, 2003.

Sachar, Howard M. *A History of Israel: From the Rise of Zionism to Our Time.* 3rd ed. New York: Knopf, 2007.

Biological Weapons and Warfare

Biological weapons are forms of natural organisms that are used as weapons or modified versions of germs or toxins to kill or harm people or animals. The first type of biological weapon includes diseases such as anthrax or smallpox, while the second category includes toxins or poisons such as ricin or aflatoxin. Along with

A female Israeli soldier with gas mask shown on November 13, 2002. She was participating in a Home Command drill simulating an attack with unconventional weapons. (Moshe Milner/Israeli Government Press Office)

nuclear and chemical arms, biological weapons are considered to be weapons of mass destruction (WMDs).

Israel's advanced nuclear program prompted several Arab states to initiate biological weapons programs as a means to counter the Israeli nuclear arsenal. The proliferation of WMDs, including biological weapons, is one of the most serious security issues in the Middle East.

By the early 1970s, several Arab states had established biological weapons programs as a means to balance Israel's nuclear arsenal as they concurrently sought to develop their own nuclear and chemical weapons programs. Biological weapons were attractive to many states because they were perceived as being less expensive and easier to manufacture. Biological agents could also be developed far more quickly than nuclear or chemical programs.

The Middle Eastern country with the oldest biological weapons program is Israel. During the Israeli War of Independence (1948–1949), there were charges that Israeli units infected Arab wells with malaria and typhoid. Following independence, a biological weapons unit was created. Israel's program was designed to develop both

offensive and defensive capabilities, and its successful nuclear program overshadowed its chemical and biological efforts. In the 2000s, Israel's biological and chemical weapons programs were increasingly focused on counterproliferation in the region and efforts to prevent bioterrorism.

Egypt began a wide-scale biological program in the 1960s and recruited European scientists to advance the program. By 1972, Egypt had an offensive biological weapons capability, a fact later confirmed by President Anwar Sadat in public addresses. In 1972, Egypt signed the Biological Weapons Convention (which bans the use of these arms) but did not ratify the convention. Among the Arab states, Egypt went on to develop one of the most comprehensive biological weapons programs, including anthrax, cholera, plague, botulism, and possibly smallpox. These agents were weaponized in such a fashion that they could be delivered in missile warheads. Beginning in the late 1990s, Egypt began working with the United States to develop more effective biological weapons defenses, ranging from decontamination plants to national contingency planning to stockpiles of personal gas masks.

Following the Yom Kippur War of 1973, evidence emerged from captured documents and equipment that Syria had a highly developed WMD program that included biological weapons such as anthrax, botulinum, and ricin. Syria's program proceeded with aid and products from Chinese and European firms. In the 1990s, Western intelligence agencies identified the town of Cerin as the center of Syria's biological weapons program. Toward the end of the decade, Syria also launched an effort to acquire missiles capable of delivering biological warheads into Israeli territory. Syria also developed a robust chemical weapons program. Syria's military planners hoped that their biological and chemical arsenals would deter Israel from using its nuclear weapons in the event of a conflict. For Israel and the United States, Syria's biological weapons program is especially troublesome because of the country's sponsorship of anti-Israeli groups such as Hezbollah and the fear that these weapons might be shared with terrorists.

Libya attempted to develop a broad WMD program in the 1970s that included biological weapons. However, international sanctions prevented that nation from acquiring significant biological arms. Instead, its program remained mainly at the research level. In 2003, Libyan leader Muammar Qaddafi renounced WMDs and pledged that his country would dismantle its WMD programs as part of a larger strategy to improve relations with the United States and Europe.

In 1974 the Iraqi government officially launched a biological weapons program, and within a year the country established facilities for research and development of biological agents. Through the 1970s and 1980s, Iraq obtained cultures and biological agents from Western governments and firms through both legitimate and illicit means. Among the biological weapons Iraq obtained were anthrax, salmonella, and botulinum. By 1983, Iraq began stockpiling biological warheads and accelerated its program, including efforts to develop new types of weapons.

During 1987–1988, Saddam Hussein's regime employed chemical weapons against Iraq's Kurdish minority. There have been charges that this activity included rotavirus, a major killer of the young in developing countries. Iraq reportedly invested heavily in a rotavirus biological warfare program. Used either by itself or employed with other biological agents, rotavirus would produce major deaths and illness among children and infants.

Large-scale Iraqi production of anthrax and aflatoxin began in 1989, and that same year Iraqi scientists initiated field tests of biological weapons. In 1990, Iraq stockpiled some 200 bombs and 100 missiles capable of delivering biological agents.

Under the terms of the cease-fire that ended the 1991 Persian Gulf War, Iraq began destroying its biological weapons capability. Also in 1991, Iraq ratified the Biological Weapons Convention. United Nations (UN) weapons inspectors were granted limited access to biological weapons facilities and were able to verify the extent of the program and confirm that some materials had been destroyed. The belief by President George W. Bush's administration that Hussein's regime had not complied with UN resolutions to destroy its WMD programs was a major justification for the U.S.-led invasion in 2003. Following the occupation of Iraq, U.S. and international inspectors were unable to find any hidden WMDs.

The Iranian military worked with the United States during the 1960s and 1970s to develop defensive strategies against biological weapons. Iran signed the Biological Weapons Convention in 1972 and ratified it a year later. Following the Iranian Revolution in 1979, however, the country began a secret biological weapons program. The Iraqi use of chemical weapons in the war between the two countries during 1980–1988 accelerated the Iranian program. Through the 1980s and 1990s, Iranian agents and representatives attempted to acquire biological agents, both legally and illicitly. The country also hired large numbers of scientists and experts on WMDs from the former Soviet Union. As a result, Iran has been able to develop small amounts of biological weapons. Iran has also developed the missile capabilities to deliver WMDs to Israeli territory.

TOM LANSFORD

See also

Arms Sales, International; Chemical Weapons and Warfare; Iran-Iraq War; Iraq War; Missiles, Intermediate-Range Ballistic; Nuclear Weapons; Persian Gulf War; Qaddafi, Muammar; Terrorism

References

Cordesman, Anthony. *Iran's Developing Military Capabilities.* Washington, DC: CSIS, 2005.
Guillemin, Jeanne. *Biological Weapons: From the Invention of State-Sponsored Programs to Contemporary Bioterrorism.* New York: Columbia University Press, 2005.
Walker, William. *Weapons of Mass Destruction and International Order.* New York: Oxford University Press, 2004.
Zubay, Geoffrey, et al. *Agents of Bioterrorism: Pathogens and Their Weaponization.* New York: Columbia University Press, 2005.

Biqa' Valley
See Bekáa Valley

Black September
Start Date: September 6, 1970
End Date: July 1971

Armed conflict between the Jordanian Army and various factions of the Palestine Liberation Organization (PLO) that began in September 1970. The confrontation also led to fighting between Jordan and Syria. The struggle did not end until July 1971, when the PLO was permanently expelled from Jordan and relocated to Lebanon.

Relations between Jordan and the PLO had steadily deteriorated during the late 1960s for two primary reasons. First, PLO attacks on Israel launched from Jordanian territory frequently resulted in Israeli retaliation against Jordan. Second, the PLO sought to create a state within a state in northern Jordan. For obvious reasons, Jordan's King Hussein did not look favorably on such a scheme and came to believe that the PLO threatened his hold on the country and, as a result, directly threatened the monarchy. Hussein and PLO chairman Yasser Arafat were unable to resolve the dilemma as fighting escalated during the spring and summer of 1970.

Tensions increased when the Popular Front for the Liberation of Palestine (PFLP) hijacked four Western airliners on September 6, 1970, and a fifth airliner three days later. One plane was forced to land in Cairo and another hijacking failed, but the three other planes were taken to Dawson Field, an abandoned air base in northern Jordan. The passengers survived the ordeal, but the aircraft did not. They were deliberately destroyed on September 12, 1970, in a theatrical event staged for the media. The hijackings and their aftermath, which seemed to prove that King Hussein did not have control over his own country, deeply embarrassed him.

Sensing that he now had to take strong and decisive action, Hussein ordered the army to launch an offensive against PLO guerrilla organizations. The operation began on September 17, 1970. The ensuing conflict pitted the Jordanian Army of 70,000 troops with heavy weapons against the PLO, which had approximately 12,000 regulars and 30,000 militiamen armed with light weapons. The offensive was supposed to take two days but quickly bogged down into a war of attrition because of stiff Palestinian resistance and Jordanian tactical errors. Fighting was concentrated in northern Jordan, especially around Amman and Irbid.

On September 19, 1970, Syria sent a task force with 300 tanks and 16,000 troops, but no air cover, to assist the PLO. The Syrians won the initial engagement against the Jordanians. However, that prompted the Jordanian Air Force to attack Syrian forces on September 22, 1970. Syria suffered 600 casualties and lost 120 armored vehicles, prompting its subsequent withdrawal within a few days. Fighting between Jordan and the PLO subsided after Arab leaders compelled Hussein and Arafat to reach a cease-fire agreement during a meeting in Cairo on September 27, 1970. Hostilities resumed in November 1970, however, and continued until the final PLO defeat in July 1971, at which point the PLO withdrew and reestablished itself in Lebanon. Approximately 600 Jordanians died in the

Jordanian gunners load an American 155-mm howitzer at their position near Amman on September 17, 1970, during the Black September coup attempt in Jordan. (Genevieve Chauvel/Sygma/Corbis)

fighting, while more than 1,200 were wounded. Palestinian casualties ran into the thousands, but the exact figures are unknown.

Black September produced numerous aftershocks. The stressful negotiations undertaken by Egypt may well have precipitated President Gamal Abdel Nasser's fatal heart attack on September 28, 1970. Afterward Anwar Sadat took power, eventually reversed many of Nasser's policies, and made peace with Israel. In Syria, Minister of Defense Hafez al-Assad used the events of Black September to seize power in a bloodless coup d'état on November 13, 1970. In so doing, he swept aside the civilian leadership in what has been termed the Corrective Revolution and established an authoritarian regime. PLO forces relocated to Lebanon, where they contributed to the Lebanese Civil War (1975–1990) and the 1982 Israeli invasion of Lebanon. Those events led to U.S. involvement in Lebanon and the beginning of an anti-Western terrorism campaign. Black September also spawned a terrorist group of the same name whose attacks included the 1972 Munich Olympics massacre of Israeli athletes. Lastly, Black September further discredited the idea of Arab and Palestinian nationalism, thus encouraging the rise of militant Islamist organizations.

CHUCK FAHRER

See also

Arab Nationalism; Arafat, Yasser; Assad, Hafez al-; Hussein, King of Jordan; Jordan; Jordan, Armed Forces; Lebanon, Civil War in; Munich Olympic Games; Nasser, Gamal Abdel; Palestine Liberation Organization; Popular Front for the Liberation of Palestine; Syria; Syria, Armed Forces

References

Cooley, John K. *Green March, Black September: The Story of the Palestinian Arabs.* London: Frank Cass, 1973.

Dobson, Christopher. *Black September: Its Short, Violent History.* New York: Macmillan, 1974.

Mishal, Shaul. *The PLO under Arafat: Between Gun and Olive Branch.* New Haven, CT: Yale University Press, 1986.

Pollack, Kenneth M. *Arabs at War: Military Effectiveness, 1948–1991.* Lincoln: University of Nebraska Press, 2002.

Black September Organization

Palestinian terrorist group founded in the autumn of 1971, so-named for the conflict between Palestinians and Jordanian armed forces that began in September 1970 (Black September) and saw the forced expulsion of Palestinians from Jordan. The Black September

Two masked Black September guerrillas on a terrace of the Saudi Arabian embassy in Khartoum, Sudan, where they were holding Arab diplomats hostage and executed two Americans and one Belgian, March 3, 1973. (Bettmann/Corbis)

organization was said to be an offshoot of Fatah, the wing of the Palestine Liberation Organization (PLO) controlled by Yasser Arafat, because some Palestinians identified with Fatah joined Black September. Soon, other Palestinian militants began to join Black September, including certain members of the Popular Front for the Liberation of Palestine (PFLP).

The extent to which the Black September organization was tied to Fatah, or even to Arafat, remains somewhat murky. Nevertheless, it is more than probable that Black September received monetary aid and intelligence information via the PLO. If Arafat did indeed acquiesce to the formation of the Black September organization and if indeed he did funnel resources to the group, he took considerable pains to disguise such activity.

The first significant act taken by Black September occurred in November 1971 when several members attacked and killed Jordanian prime minister Wasfi Tal in Cairo, Egypt. The assassination was said to be retribution for Tal's hard-line policies toward the Palestinians and the PLO's subsequent eviction from Jordan. A month later the group struck again when it unsuccessfully tried to assassinate a Jordanian ambassador. Black September was also likely responsible for two acts of sabotage on foreign soil: one in West Ger-

many and the other in the Netherlands. Three months later, members of Black September hijacked Sabena Airlines flight 572, a Belgian jetliner that had just left Vienna en route to Tel Aviv. A daring commando raid by Israel's Sayeret Maktal managed to defuse the crisis, and just one passenger died in the event. Two of the Black September hijackers were killed, and two more were taken prisoner by the Israelis.

Without a doubt, Black September's most spectacular terrorist scheme unfolded during the 1972 Olympic Games in Munich. There, in front of worldwide media assembled for the Olympics, Black September members murdered 11 Israeli athletes, 9 of whom they had previously kidnapped. The terrorists also shot and killed a West German police officer during an abortive rescue attempt of the hostages. The murders shocked the world, but the Black September organization undoubtedly achieved its aim of international exposure and notoriety thanks to the venue in which the killings occurred and the concentration of print and broadcast journalists in Munich at the time. The Munich massacre saw the Israelis take immediate and bold steps to crush the Black September organization and apprehend or kill those responsible for the attacks.

Despite Israeli reprisals and an international hunt for Black September members, the organization pulled off another terrorist attack, this time on the Saudi embassy in Khartoum, Sudan, in March 1973. In the course of the assault, two American diplomats and the Belgian chargé d'affaires were killed. In the autumn of that year, around the time of the Yom Kippur War, Arafat allegedly pressured the Black September organization to disband. The following year, Arafat would only sanction terrorist attacks in Israel proper, in the West Bank and the Gaza Strip. It is likely that the Black September organization persisted for a time thereafter.

PAUL G. PIERPAOLI JR.

See also

Arafat, Yasser; Black September; Fatah; Munich Olympic Games; Palestine Liberation Organization; Popular Front for the Liberation of Palestine; Sayeret Matkal; Terrorism

References

Dobson, Christopher. *Black September: Its Short, Violent History.* New York: Macmillan, 1974.

Livingstone, Neil C., and David Haley. *Inside the PLO.* New York: William Morrow, 1990.

Yodfat, Aryeh Y., and Yuval Arnon-OHannah. *PLO Strategy and Tactics.* New York: St. Martin's, 1981.

B'nai B'rith

Jewish civic and community service group founded in New York City in 1843. B'nai B'rith (meaning sons of the covenant) is the oldest continuously existing Jewish service group in the world. Founded by 11 German Jews as a male-only fraternal order, B'nai B'rith was designed to serve Jews who were prohibited from joining fraternal organizations such as the Odd Fellows and the Masons.

A membership certificate for B'nai B'rith, circa 1876. B'nai B'rith was founded in New York City in 1843. (Library of Congress)

The charter members of the organization also hoped that it would serve as a way for American Jews to maintain their Jewish identity while at the same time integrating newly arrived immigrants to American society and instructing members on how to become responsible civic-minded citizens. Indeed, B'nai B'rith was rather unique in that it did not cling to Old World beliefs and traditions but rather hoped to foster a form of civic Judaism adapted to American values and communities. This was in contrast to many other similar organizations that involved immigrants and tended to keep members immersed in the ways of the Old World instead of adapting to the New World.

Initially, B'nai B'rith was a highly secretive organization (like many other fraternal groups), but it sought secrecy not to exclude but rather to keep its financial affairs from prying eyes. Not wanting the nature or particulars of its charitable support made public, the founders thus settled on secrecy. Also kept secret were the particulars of the fraternal ceremonies and rituals.

B'nai B'rith grew rapidly in the years after its creation and thus had a profound impact on Jewish life, Jewish identity, and Jewish communities. By the 1860s B'nai B'rith had become a national organization, with chapters in almost every corner of the United States. Before long, the organization had become renowned for its charitable causes and the construction of hospitals, orphanages, and schools for the mentally challenged.

In 1895 the organization began offering Jewish women the opportunity to join the cause by creating women's auxiliary associations. B'nai B'rith continued to grow, and by the early part of the 20th century it had become an international as well as a national organization. As Zionism gained momentum in the early decades of the 20th century, the organization added Zionist goals to its wide-ranging platform. It also spun off or created a number of important allied organizations. These include the Anti-Defamation League of B'nai B'rith (1913), the Jewish college-student group Hillel (1923), and several Jewish youth organizations. B'nai B'rith Women, an auxiliary group created in 1909, retained auxiliary status until 1947, at which time it was recognized as equal to the male fraternal order.

In more recent times, B'nai B'rith has championed Israel and has paired up with other organizations (such as the American Israel Public Affairs Committee) to urge U.S. policymakers to take certain stances vis-à-vis Israel and the Middle East. Programs to combat anti-Semitism are also an important part of the organization's platform. Its welfare and public service programs take up the lion's share of its activities and budget and include the funding of health services, education, scholastic scholarships, the arts, music, museums, and the like. Headquartered in Washington, D.C., B'nai B'rith now has active chapters in more than 50 nations and has some 180,000 paid members.

PAUL G. PIERPAOLI JR.

See also

American Israel Public Affairs Committee; Anti-Semitism; Lobbies, Jewish

References

Dershowitz, Alan M. *The Case for Israel.* New York: Wiley, 2004.

Grusd, Edward E. *B'nai B'rith: The Story of a Covenant.* New York: Appleton-Century-Crofts, 1966.

Terry, Janice. *U.S. Foreign Policy in the Middle East: The Role of Lobbies and Special Interest Groups.* London: Pluto, 2005.

Bombs, Gravity

Gravity bombs, sometimes called dumb bombs or iron bombs in the popular press, are bombs and other explosive ordnance that do not contain internal guidance systems. Before the days of cruise missiles, gravity bombs were the primary aircraft-delivered weapons for attacking targets on the surface below, whether on water or land. Today, bombs lacking a guidance system are called dumb bombs because they fall dumbly to the target by the force of gravity along a ballistic path, unable to adjust for poor aiming, weather, wind, or visibility conditions. Dumb bombs are simple, consisting of an aerodynamically streamlined shape filled with high explosives. Up until Operation ENDURING FREEDOM in Afghanistan in 2001, dumb bombs constituted the vast majority of such weapons used in war and still remain the dominant bomb type in the arsenals of most Middle Eastern nations, including Israel.

On dumb bombs, stabilizing fins are attached at the back, and a detonating fuse is installed just before the bombs are loaded onto a

An Israeli Air Force Skyhawk dropping bombs during an Israel Defense Forces (IDF) exercise in the Negev Desert, October 28, 1976. (Moshe Milner/Israeli Government Press Office)

plane. The bombs come in four types: high explosive or general purpose, cluster bombs, daisy cutter, and fuel air explosives (FAE). Of these bombs, the first is the most commonly used and comes in varying sizes, based on weight, ranging from 220 to 2,200 pounds. American and British bombs are designated by weight in pounds (250, 500, 1,000, 2,000), while most other countries use kilograms. For example, the former Soviet Union's bombs came in 100-, 200-, 500-, and 1,000-kilogram sizes. Fusing was determined by the mission. Proximity or variable-timed fuses, which detonate at various heights above the ground, were used against dug-in infantry. Quick fuses that detonated very quickly after impact were also used against surface targets to maximize blast effect. Delayed fuses were placed in the bomb's tail to hold up the detonation until the bomb had penetrated a predictable depth into the target to ensure destruction of armored targets such as bunkers.

Cluster bomb units carried up to 100 smaller (50-kilogram) bombs that were released at a predetermined altitude above a target area about the size of a football field. They were used against moving targets such as tanks, armored personnel vehicles, and naval missile boats. Daisy cutters refer to the 15,000-pound bombs dropped from Lockheed MC-130 Hercules aircraft to clear out a landing area for helicopters, collapse tunnels, or destroy troop concentrations. Finally, FAEs differ from other bombs in that they employ an aerosol spray to create a mist of fuel that, when ignited,

creates an overpressure followed immediately by a series of alternating underpressures and overpressures to flatten objects in an area (vehicles, aircraft) and inflict maximum personnel casualties.

Dumb bombs were employed in all of the various bombing missions executed during the Arab-Israeli wars, and more than 80 percent of all bombs dropped during Operation DESERT STORM (1991) were dumb bombs. Ten years later, that percentage had dropped to just 20 percent during Operation ENDURING FREEDOM (2001) and Operation IRAQI FREEDOM (2003). Nevertheless, dumb bombs still dominate the arsenals of the world's air forces. But the United States and most Western countries have developed guidance kits to retrofit onto gravity bombs to convert them into smart bombs. Increasingly, dumb bombs are used only on battlefields located some distance from civilian populations. This trend will likely continue in the years ahead as bombs become more deadly and the international community places increasingly stringent standards against inflicting innocent civilian casualties.

CARL OTIS SCHUSTER

See also

Bombs, Precision-Guided; Iraq War; Persian Gulf War

References

Frieden, David R. *Principles of Naval Weapons Systems.* Annapolis, MD: Naval Institute Press, 1985.

Werrell, Kenneth. *Chasing the Silver Bullet.* Washington, DC: Smithsonian Scholarly Press, 2003.

Yenne, Bill. *Secret Weapons of the Cold War.* New York: Berkley Publishing, 2005.

Bombs, Precision-Guided

Precision-guided munitions, commonly called smart bombs, refer to bombs that have integral guidance systems that compensate for environmental interference and poor aim and that ensure the bomb's accurate emplacement against the target. They differ from dumb or iron bombs in that they have a guidance system and related power source. Typically, a modern smart bomb has a circular probable error of 20–94 feet. But even a highly trained pilot operating in an optimal environment can, at best, reliably place a dumb bomb within 300 feet of the aim point. Most modern smart bomb systems rely on a computer-based guidance system that accepts a target designated by the aircraft's pilot or weapons officer or a forward air or ground controller and guides the bomb onto it. The target's identification and designation are derived from electro-optical, infrared, or radar imaging. However, a growing number of guidance systems guide the bomb onto the target's geographic location using the target's and bomb's Global Positioning System (GPS) respective location. The bomb reverts to inertial guidance if the GPS link is lost. GPS-guided bombs are employed against fixed targets, while the others can be used against moving targets or those in which a specific entry point (e.g., ventilation shaft) is required.

The Germans employed the first guided bombs during World War II. The German Fritz bombs were radio-controlled bombs that the plane's bombardier guided into the target using a joystick. He tracked the bomb's path via a flare in the bomb's rear. The Americans also employed a television-based guided bomb called the Azon bomb in 1945 and continued to pursue bomb guidance systems after the war. The resulting AGM-62 Walleye relied on a TV camera installed in the bomb's nose that transmitted the target's image back to the aircraft's weapons officer. He steered the bomb to the target by keeping the aim in the TV crosshairs. The early Walleyes required so much operator attention, however, that they were primarily employed from crewed aircraft such as the navy's A-6 Intruder.

In 1968 during the Vietnam War, the U.S. Air Force introduced the Bolt-117, the first laser-guided bomb. These early bombs guided onto the reflected beam of a laser designator that illuminated the target. The early versions had to be illuminated by a second aircraft in the target area. By 1972, this system had given way to an automatic laser-tracking illuminator that enabled the bombing aircraft to illuminate the target as it withdrew. However, these early laser-based systems were vulnerable to smoke and poor visibility, which interfered with the laser beam.

By the late 1970s, the United States introduced improved laser, infrared, and electro-optical target designation systems. Israel acquired some of these weapons and used them in strike missions over Lebanon in the mid-1980s, but the first significant, large-scale use of smart bombs came in 1991, when the United States led a United Nations (UN) coalition to drive Iraqi troops out of Kuwait (Operation DESERT STORM). In that war, U.S. aircraft used precision weapons in approximately 20 percent of their strike missions over Iraq. They were employed primarily against high-priority targets located within population areas or in circumstances where the target's first strike destruction had to be guaranteed (Scud surface-to-surface missile launchers, for example).

The lessons learned from that war drove U.S. development of the Joint Direct Attack Munition (JDAM), Joint Standoff Weapon (JSOW), and GPS-based bomb guidance systems. During Operation ENDURING FREEDOM (2001), more than 80 percent of the bombs dropped were smart bombs, and a similar percentage marked the air missions over Iraq in Operation IRAQI FREEDOM.

Precision weapons will continue to gain ground in the years ahead as the world takes an increasingly harsh view of collateral damage and casualties inflicted on civilians. The introduction of cost-effective retrofit guidance kits has enabled many countries to convert their dumb bombs into smart bombs at little expense. Israel and most of the Arab frontline states are now acquiring guidance kits for their bomb arsenals. However, blast effects remain a problem regardless of the weapon's precision. For example, the Palestinian terrorists' strategic placement of their facilities within apartment blocks and housing areas has driven Israel away from the use of bombs. Israel increasingly employs short-range tactical missiles with small warheads (less than 30 kilograms) against terrorist targets in the occupied territories and southern Lebanon. Still, smart bombs will figure prominently in any future Middle Eastern conflict.

CARL OTIS SCHUSTER

See also

Aircraft, Bombers; Bombs, Gravity; Iraq War; Persian Gulf War

References

Allen, Charles. *Thunder and Lightning: The RAF in the Gulf; Personal Experiences of War.* London: Her Majesty's Stationery Office, 1991.

Drendei, Lou. *Air War Desert Storm.* London: Squadron Signal Publications, 1994.

Frieden, David R. *Principles of Naval Weapons Systems.* Annapolis, MD: Naval Institute Press, 1985.

Pollack, Kenneth M. *Arabs at War: Military Effectiveness, 1948–1991.* Lincoln: University of Nebraska Press, 2002.

Werrell, Kenneth. *Chasing the Silver Bullet.* Washington, DC: Smithsonian Scholarly Press, 2003.

Winnefield, James, et al. *A League of Airmen: U.S. Air Power in the Gulf War.* Santa Monica, CA: RAND, 1994.

Yenne, Bill. *Secret Weapons of the Cold War.* New York: Berkley Publishing, 2005.

Border War
Start Date: 1949
End Date: 1956

Persistent series of clashes between Israel and bordering Arab states that involved civilians as well as organized armed forces. The struggle of the State of Israel over the determination of its borders following the Israeli War of Independence (1948–1949) constituted the basis for its rationale of retaliation. This ongoing struggle was shaped by the continuation of the Arab states' hostility toward Israel.

Following the Israeli War of Independence, many difficult and controversial problems remained to be resolved between Israel and its neighbors. Neither the Arab States nor the United Nations (UN) recognized as permanent borders the cease-fire lines that had been drawn. Hundreds of thousands of Arab refugees, most of them Palestinians, were living in temporary crowded camps along Israel's borders, often in full view of their former homes and fields. But they were unable to return to their lands and possessions.

For the Arab states, the border issue was not of paramount importance. In 1947 they had not accepted the UN partition plan of Palestine and thus did not recognize Israel's right to exist. They were waiting for an opportune moment to commence a second round of fighting, which, they hoped, would reverse the previous military failure and restore the alleged stolen lands to their owners.

Israeli leaders, for their part, sought to preserve the relative tranquility attained by the Jewish state's successful completion of the 1948–1949 war and to establish the cease-fire lines as the state's permanent borders. During the first few years following the war, the Israeli government stuck to the territorial status quo, demarcated by the demilitarized zones adjoining the cease-fire lines, and their status as delineated in Israel's interpretation of the truce agreements. The Israelis were initially prepared to overlook the many border incursions affecting daily life along its borders with Egypt and Jordan as long as they did not see in these violations a threat to the state's survival.

Nevertheless, the persistent problem of infiltrations into Israeli territory was quite bothersome to the security and military establishments during these years. The war along the borders took place between Arab refugees and newly settled Israelis in these frontier areas. The Arabs freely crossed the cease-fire lines in order to return to their homes, cultivate their fields, or reap their crops. In the initial phase, these infiltrations were carried on quite innocently and were largely motivated by a desire on the part of the Arabs to return to their homes. However, as the border crossings became increasingly accompanied by theft, smuggling, and the like, they quickly degenerated into armed and violent incursions.

Over time, infiltrators became more adept at executing these forays. Soon, border violations became economically profitable. In the refugee camps and Arab villages stretched along the Israeli border, bands of robbers organized and operated nightly within Israeli territory. In the earliest stages, at least, these infiltration activities did not receive support from the Arab host nations. They were essentially regarded as a localized affair, a conflict between frontier settlers and refugee infiltrators intent upon smuggling and theft.

In the first phase of the Border War (1950–1953), the retaliatory actions of the Israel Defense Forces (IDF) targeted civilians with the objective of harming those Arab villages from which the infiltrators set out. These reactive operations, which were justified as an eye for an eye, sought to inflict property damage in the appropriate villages and pressure the Arab governments to stop the raids. Despite widespread actions by the IDF, infiltration activity continued, unaffected by the large number of trespassers who were killed and wounded in clashes. Penalizing actions by the IDF against the Arab villages did not bring about the hoped-for results, and it appeared that Israel had no adequate response to the problem of border incursions.

Israel now came to regard infiltration as a threat to its sovereignty. The government feared a situation in which an increasing stream of returning refugees would endanger the demographic balance of the new Jewish state. In addition, the return of refugees and their control over grazing lands and cultivable fields raised the specter of a loss of Israeli territory along the unrecognized borders. This would also blur potential demarcation lines for state borders. However, the greatest peril was the serious threat to which residents in the frontier settlements, mostly new immigrants, were subjected. Many residents abandoned the settlements for safer havens in the central part of Israel, thereby weakening the settlements' social infrastructure. At the same time, this population loss would make the settlements even more vulnerable to murderous attacks and robbery.

In August 1953 the IDF created Unit 101 to deal with the incursions. This occurred against the background of military failure during 1951–1953. The inability of the IDF to cope with infiltration activities and the terror of the fedayeen led to the decision for a nonconventional solution. Unit 101, commanded by Ariel Sharon and numbering about 40 men, carried out the vast majority of reprisal operations, more than 70 in all, from the end of 1953 until the Sinai Campaign in 1956. In January 1954, Unit 101 was merged into the Israeli Paratroop Battalion.

The Qibya Raid in October 1953 was a turning point and marked a change in IDF policy with regard to the Border War. On the evening of October 12–13, 1953, Arab infiltrators tossed a hand grenade into a house in the Israeli village of Yahud. Susan Kanias and two of her children were killed, while a third child was slightly injured. The footprints of the perpetrators led directly to the Jordanian border.

On October 15, men of Unit 101 entered the Jordanian village of Qibya, occupied it, and blew up 45 buildings. An inquiry into the operation revealed that Unit 101 had killed 69 civilians, half of them women and children. The Israeli government then ordered the IDF to refrain from attacking civilian targets and to concentrate on military objectives in retaliatory cross-border operations.

It should be noted that among the consequences of the Qibya operation was a significant reduction in infiltration into Israel along the Jordanian border. Establishment of an Israeli border guard unit within the Israeli police also made a notable contribution to pacifying Israel's eastern border. In addition, Jordanian forces assumed responsibility for closing that long border to infiltrators and restoring calm along it.

A derailed train of tanker cars north of Kibbutz Eyal, victim of a mine laid by Arab infiltrators, shown on October 22, 1953. (Fritz Cohen/Israeli Government Press Office)

Until 1954 Jordan was the center of infiltration activities against Israel, but in that year leadership passed to Egypt. In May and June 1954 alone, the Israeli government made some 400 complaints of infiltration activities to the Israel-Egypt Mixed Armistice Commission. Egyptian groups of infiltrators backed by Haj Amin al-Husseini, the former grand mufti of Jerusalem, and the Muslim Brotherhood operated from the Gaza Strip to mine roads, bridges, and water pipelines and steal equipment and livestock. The infiltrators were soon organized into a fedayeen battalion, and their activities came to be a direct threat to the Israeli settlement program in south Israel.

Following some 45 incidents in February 1955, Israel responded with an operation in the Gaza Strip on February 28, only six days after David Ben-Gurion returned as Israeli prime minister. A turning point in Israeli-Egyptian relations, this devastating IDF military strike involved a reprisal raid of brigade strength against the Egyptian military headquarters in Gaza. It saw IDF units blowing up a number of buildings. In the raid, 38 Egyptian soldiers were killed and another 24 were wounded, which was a humiliation for the Egyptians and a blow to President Gamal Abdel Nasser. The Israeli raid served as the justification for Nasser's arms deal with Czechoslovakia. In response to the raid, the fedayeen mounted dozens of terrorist attacks, and by midyear the Egyptian-directed guerrilla campaign was in high gear. Receiving reinforcements from the regular Egyptian Army, the fedayeen grew into a select military unit. Egyptian intelligence operatives went on to establish similar units in Jordan, Syria, and Lebanon.

Growing Pan-Arab sentiment stoked by Nasser led to the expulsion of British officers from Jordan in early March 1956. They were replaced by radical anti-Israeli officers, again opening the way to infiltration activities from Jordan into Israel and raising the level of violence and interstate tensions.

Israel now adopted a policy of restraint. From September 1954 until September 1956, the IDF did not carry out any military operations against Jordan. Despite the Jordanian government's stated intention to halt terrorist activities originating from its territory, hostile acts continued to increase during July and August 1956. The situation along the borders continued to deteriorate, and it was clear to all that the Jordanian Legion was responsible for these provocations. In September 1956 Jordan joined the Syrian-Egyptian Defense pact, placing its armed forces under Egyptian command. An escalation in shooting incidents along the Jordanian border followed.

On September 10, 1956, the Jordanian National Guard attacked a group of IDF cadets undergoing orientation training some 300 feet

Two Egyptian soldiers guarding an outpost on the frontier with Israel at El Sabha, Egypt, where Israeli and Egyptian troops had recently clashed, shown on November 8, 1955. (Bettmann/Corbis)

from the Jordanian border. Six of the cadets were killed and their bodies dragged across the border and mutilated. In reprisal, on the night of September 11–12 the IDF Paratroop Battalion launched operation JONATHAN, a raid on the al-Rahwa Police Station in Jordan. More than 29 Jordanian soldiers died in the attack, and the police compound was blown up. The paratroopers suffered 1 killed and 3 wounded.

That same evening, 3 Druze guards were killed inside Israel at an oil rig site at Ein Ofarim in the Arabah bordering Jordan. Israel took revenge for these murders in Operation GARANDAL. On the night of September 13–14, Israeli paratroopers raided the police station at Garandal, Jordan, blowing up the stronghold and those inside as well as an empty school nearby. Jordanian casualties were 16 killed and 6 wounded. The raiders sustained losses of 1 killed and 12 wounded.

On September 22, 1956, machine-gun fire from Jordanian Legion positions opposite Kibbutz Ramat Rahel was directed at a crowd of archaeological conference attendees. Four were killed and 20 others injured. A day later, shots were fired by a Jordanian soldier at a woman and her daughter as they were gathering firewood beside their house at Aminadav inside Israel. The daughter died, and her hand was cut off. Another incident occurred on the same day at Kibbutz Maoz Haim in the Beit She'an Valley. A member of the kibbutz working in the fields was killed and his body dragged over the border.

On the night of September 25–26, Israeli paratroopers attacked a Jordanian police station in the sector and outposts of the National Guard located in this sector. The paratroopers occupied and demolished the police station as well as three military positions close by. The Jordanians sustained 39 killed and 12 wounded.

On October 9, 1956, 2 Israelis died while working in an orchard near the village of Even Yehuda. This time, the victims' ears were cut off. On October 10, Israeli paratroopers demolished the Qalqilya police station. Casualties among the IDF forces were 8 killed and 29 wounded. Overall, the frenzy of violence that began on September 10 claimed 18 IDF soldiers dead and 68 injured. Israeli reprisals claimed the lives of 100 Jordanian policemen, National Guard soldiers, and civilians.

Meanwhile, another border war emerged in northern Israel. In May 1951 a border incident took place on the crest of the heights dominating an area in northern Israel where the Jordan River enters the Sea of Galilee. This small-scale clash quickly grew into a five-day battle.

Initial tensions started in March 1951 when Israel began to drain the swamps of the Chula Lake. The Syrians fired on the tractors that entered the demilitarized zone. Israel had persisted in the swamp-draining project in order to assert sovereignty over its sector of the zone. The demilitarized areas had been delineated in the cease-fire agreement between Syria and Israel at the end of the war in 1949. They straddled both sides of the border at a breadth of between 15 and 30 miles. Israel regarded the zone as its sovereign territory, with the attendant obligation to keep it free of military personnel but legitimately open to development for civilian purposes. The Syrians, on the other hand, maintained that the zone was a no-man's-land with no entry rights to either side and that it was certainly not for development or agricultural cultivation.

At the beginning of April, Israel sought to assert its sovereignty over the demilitarized zone at al-Hama, where the Jordanian, Syrian, and Israeli borders met. On April 4, an IDF patrol set out for the zone and encountered a Syrian ambush. Seven Israeli soldiers were killed in the incident, and the IDF responded with an air strike against the Syrian police station close to where the hostilities took place. Two women were killed and six additional civilians were wounded in the attack.

The Battle of Tel Mutila occurred against this backdrop of rising tensions and the shooting incident with the Syrians. The battle began when a number of IDF soldiers from the Golani Brigade ascended the Tel to capture a herd of cattle grazing on the heights. The force was caught in a Syrian crossfire, and four soldiers were killed. Tel Mutila had strategic military importance because it dominated the area where the Jordan River enters the Sea of Galilee. The peak of the Tel was 1,200 feet above ground level and gave the IDF a position of dominance over the entire demilitarized zone in an area controlled by Syrian military positions situated above on the Golan Heights.

On May 2, a reserve force from the 3rd Brigade, augmented by two squads from the Golani's 13th Battalion, attacked and secured Tel Mutila. The Syrians were concentrated in nearby military posts on the ridge overlooking the Tel. On May 3, the 13th Battalion was reinforced by a company of officer trainees and succeeded in occupying the post where the Jordan enters the Sea of Galilee. The Syrians continued to harass IDF forces in the area with intermittent gunfire. Golani Brigade units continued in their efforts to occupy the entire area that had been penetrated by Syrian forces. However, repeated attacks during May 4–6 failed to dislodge the Syrians. In the end, Israeli Air Force planes fired a few rounds at the Syrian command post. This brought the withdrawal of Syrian forces from the positions. Five days of fighting resulted in the deaths of 40 IDF soldiers. It was the first major military encounter with the Syrians since the 1948–1949 war.

In 1955, Israel dominated most of the demilitarized zone in the area of the Sea of Galilee, but the Syrians more than once directed gunfire on Israeli fishing vessels from the fortified heights overlooking the water basin. Despite the arrangement by which the international border passed inland from the east bank of the Sea of Galilee, there was no way of preventing Syrian farmers and fishermen from using the waters for irrigation and fishing. Syrian emplacements were located at the water's edge and provided protection for them. For years, the Syrians demanded a change in the border westward to the middle of the Sea of Galilee or at least an arrangement that would permit joint use of the lake. The Israeli government, however, was not prepared to compromise regarding control of water sources that it deemed vital for Israel's economic development and agriculture.

From the end of 1953 to the beginning of 1954, firefights periodically occurred between Syrian posts and Israeli patrol vessels on the Sea of Galilee. The Syrians wanted to fish in the northwestern sector of the sea. When they were chased away by Israeli police patrols, the Syrian military responded with gunfire, often directed at the Israeli fishermen in the area. Israeli police patrols were then replaced by armored patrol vessels outfitted with antitank weapons and machine guns.

The Israelis executed a reprisal operation on the Sea of Galilee, code-named ALEI ZAYIT (Olive Leaves), on the night of December 11–12, 1955. During the fight, 6 IDF soldiers were killed and 5 were seriously wounded, while the Syrians lost 54 killed and 30 taken prisoner. The Israelis demolished most of the Syrian positions and fortifications in the sector and razed a number of structures. In spite of the heavy blow sustained by the Syrian military, it resumed operations the next day. Within a short time, the destroyed emplacements were reconstructed, and shooting at Israeli fishermen and farmers resumed.

Following the 1956 Sinai Campaign, the Israeli borders were largely quiet. The Israelis undertook a policy of restraint, even in those cases in which infiltrators and terrorists penetrated the borders during the 1960s. For all intents and purposes, the Suez Crisis and the resultant Sinai Campaign brought the Border War to an end.

MOSHE TERDIMAN

See also
Arab Legion; Ben-Gurion, David; Expellees and Refugees, Palestinian; Fedayeen; Gaza Strip; Golan Heights; Husseini, Haj Amin al-; Israel Defense Forces; Israeli War of Independence, Overview; Israeli War of Independence, Truce Agreements; Jordan River; Lake Kinneret; Muslim Brotherhood; Nasser, Gamal Abdel; Sinai Campaign; Suez Crisis; Terrorism

References
Drori, Ze'ev. *Israel's Reprisal Policy, 1953–1956: The Dynamics of Military Retaliation.* London: Frank Cass, 2005.
Morris, Benny. *Israel's Border Wars, 1949–1956: Arab Infiltration, Israeli Retaliation, and the Countdown to the Suez War.* Oxford, UK: Clarendon, 1993.
Shalev, Aryeh. *The Israel-Syria Armistice Regime, 1949–1955.* Tel Aviv: Tel Aviv University, 1993.

Boutros-Ghali, Boutros
Born: November 14, 1922

Egyptian diplomat and the sixth secretary-general of the United Nations (UN) (1992–1997). The UN's first Arab leader, Boutros Boutros-Ghali was born on November 14, 1922, in Cairo to a well-regarded Coptic Christian family. One of his ancestors, Boutros-Ghali (1846–1910), had served as Egypt's prime minister. Boutros Boutros-Ghali was educated at Cairo University and received a degree in law in 1946. He also holds degrees in political science, economics, and public law from the University of Paris. In 1949 he earned his doctorate in international law, also from the University of Paris. He also holds a diploma in international relations from the Institute d'Études Politiques de Paris.

From 1949 to 1977 Boutros-Ghali was a professor of international law and international relations at Cairo University. During that time he was a Fulbright research scholar at Columbia University in New York (1954–1955), director of the Center of Research of The Hague Academy of International Law (1963–1964), and visiting professor of law at Sorbonne University (1967–1968). In 1977 he was appointed Egypt's minister of state for foreign affairs and served in that post until 1991. That same year, he became deputy prime minister for foreign affairs under President Hosni Mubarak.

Boutros-Ghali attended the historic September 1978 Camp David Summit Conference along with Egyptian president Anwar Sadat. During the negotiations Boutros-Ghali played a not insignificant role, and by 1979 Israel and Egypt had signed a peace accord. As a Christian in an overwhelmingly Muslim nation, Boutros-Ghali brought a unique vision to his role in Egyptian foreign policy. Nevertheless, he was a strong and loyal supporter of Egyptian sovereignty and frequently decried the heavy-handed approach to foreign affairs that Western nations, particularly the United States, often practiced. He was active in the Non-Aligned Movement as well as the Organization of African Unity (OAU).

In addition to his role in the Israeli-Egyptian peace process, Boutros-Ghali helped win the release in 1990 of South African anti-apartheid leader Nelson Mandela from many years in jail as a political prisoner. That momentous occasion ultimately brought about the demise of South Africa's apartheid regime. Boutros-Ghali is an

Boutros Boutros-Ghali of Egypt was the sixth secretary-general of the United Nations (UN), serving during 1992–1997. (Corel)

expert on development in the Third World and believes that water conservation is a key to African and Middle Eastern political stability. He became the sixth secretary-general of the UN on January 1, 1992, commencing a five-year term.

Boutros-Ghali assumed his UN post at a time of tremendous crisis within the organization. It was also a period of considerable international tension, particularly in the Middle East. Enormous budgetary difficulties and greatly increased demands on the UN to increase international peacekeeping efforts combined with growing expectations and harsh criticism to create a nearly impossible leadership situation. When Boutros-Ghali became secretary-general, the UN had become highly in demand to help deal with myriad crises. These included extensive African drought and starvation, global warming and pollution, Serbian ethnic-cleansing campaigns in Bosnia and Herzegovina, human rights abuses, terrorism and militant fundamentalism, violations of the Nuclear Non-Proliferation Treaty, various civil wars, and peace negotiations in Cambodia, Afghanistan, and Somalia.

During his term in office, Boutros-Ghali witnessed a potentially momentous peace-making effort between Israel and the Palestinians in the 1993 Oslo Accords. As a result, the Palestinian Authority (PA) was created, and Israel and the Palestinians formally recognized each other for the first time. In 1994 Israel and Jordan concluded a peace treaty. The 1995 assassination of Israeli prime

minister Yitzhak Rabin seemingly derailed Arab-Israeli peace-making efforts, however.

Another Middle East conundrum haunted Boutros-Ghali's term as secretary-general: the aftermath of the 1991 Persian Gulf War. When that conflict ended in 1991, the UN came under considerable pressure—particularly by the Americans—to enforce the disarmament of Iraq by means of economic pressure and by UN-sponsored weapons inspections. Several times during Boutros-Ghali's tenure, the United States launched unilateral air attacks against Iraqi weapons and air facilities in retaliation for alleged violations of the terms of the cease-fire. By 1996, the United States had all but accused the UN's chief of abdicating his responsibility to monitor and enforce sanctions and inspections of Iraq.

Boutros-Ghali's time at the helm of the UN was not an altogether happy one. He was controversial, and his perceived failures only added to his burden. Indeed, he came under fire for the UN's inability to deal with Rwanda's murderous genocide in 1994 and his inability to rally support for UN involvement in the ongoing Angolan Civil War. Meanwhile, the deepening enmity between American leaders and Boutros-Ghali left him open to criticism that he had allowed too much U.S. influence in the UN and that the very role of the UN had now been clouded in the post–Cold War world.

In 1996 Boutros-Ghali sought a second term in office. While 10 UN Security Council nations (including Egypt) backed his continuation as secretary-general, the United States adamantly objected. He eventually capitulated to U.S. pressure to step down but not before engineering a replacement from Africa, Ghana's Kofi Annan. When Boutros-Ghali stepped down in 1996, he became the first secretary-general not to be reelected. In 1997 he became secretary-general of La Francophonie, an organization of French-speaking nations. He stayed on the job until 2002. Since then, he has served as the president of the Curatorium Administrative Council at The Hague Academy of International Law.

PAUL G. PIERPAOLI JR.

See also
Camp David Accords; Egypt; Iraq; Israel; Mubarak, Hosni; Oslo Accords; Palestinian Authority; Persian Gulf War; Rabin, Yitzhak; United Nations Peacekeeping Missions

References
Benton, Barbara, ed. *Soldiers for Peace: Fifty Years of United Nations Peacekeeping.* New York: Facts on File, 1996.
Boutros-Ghali, Boutros. *Egypt's Road to Jerusalem: A Diplomat's Story of the Struggle for Peace in the Middle East.* New York: Random House, 1997.
———. *Unvanquished: A U.S.-U.N. Saga.* New York: Random House, 1999.

Brandeis, Louis Dembitz
Born: November 13, 1856
Died: October 5, 1941

American jurist, Zionist leader, and associate justice of the U.S. Supreme Court (1916–1939). The first Jew to sit on the high court,

Louis Dembitz Brandeis, distinguished American jurist, Zionist leader, and associate justice of the U.S. Supreme Court (1916–1939). (Library of Congress)

Louis Brandeis was born in Louisville, Kentucky, on November 13, 1856, the son of Jewish Czech immigrant parents. In 1877 he graduated from Harvard University Law School at the head of his class and reportedly with the highest grades ever granted at the school until that time. This was no small feat in an age when Jewish enrollment at Harvard was very restricted.

Brandeis began practicing law in Boston and soon earned a reputation as a brilliant attorney who tended to take cases advocating for the working class and consumers. His championing of such causes and progressive outlook earned him the sobriquet "the people's advocate." Deeply distrustful of corporate America, in 1908 Brandeis presented a legal brief to the U.S. Supreme Court that virtually revolutionized the way in which lawyers presented cases to the Court. The case revolved around working conditions for American women in factories. Brandeis's brief, which married social science with the law and used an impressive array of statistics and other empirical information, soon became the model for all similar Supreme Court briefs.

Impressed with his facile mind, his progressive stances on social and economic issues, and his sterling educational credentials, President Woodrow Wilson nominated Brandeis to the Supreme Court in 1916. The nomination was highly controversial owing to Brandeis's Jewish background, and it was staunchly opposed by former president William Howard Taft (who would later become the Court's chief justice) and the president of Brandeis's alma mater. Nevertheless, Brandeis's appointment was approved by the U.S. Senate on a party-line vote.

Brandeis went on to become one of the best justices to serve on the Court, taking progressive liberal positions that were often in stark contrast to the Court's majority, which would remain staunchly conservative until the late 1930s. Many times, Brandeis paired with Justice Oliver Wendell Holmes in writing masterful dissenting opinions, particularly in cases involving business regulation, consumer protection, labor unions, and other socioeconomic issues. A life-long Democrat, Brandeis championed the New Deal of President Franklin D. Roosevelt, with whom he enjoyed a long friendship, and nearly always sided with the minority liberals on the Court when it came to New Deal legislation. But in 1937 when Roosevelt unveiled his so-called court-packing scheme to overcome the conservative anti–New Deal bias of the Supreme Court, Brandeis refused to support any part of it.

Not a practicing Jew, Brandeis became active in the Zionist movement only later in life. Indeed, it was not until 1912 that he became interested in Zionism after he had met Jacob de Haas, a former associate of Zionist leader Theodor Herzl. In 1914, upon de Haas's urging, Brandeis agreed to chair the executive committee of the U.S. General Zionist Affairs group. Brandeis now threw himself into the Zionist cause and helped build a major following of American Zionists. From just 12,000 supporters in 1914, the movement mushroomed to 175,000 supporters in 1919. In just a few years, Brandeis became the undisputed head of the American Zionist endeavor.

In 1917 during World War I, Brandeis used his clout and relationship with President Wilson to help shape the 1917 Balfour Declaration. Before the declaration was made public, Brandeis met with British foreign secretary Arthur Balfour to guide its language. In 1918 Brandeis single-handedly drafted the agenda of the Zionist Organization of America (ZOA). In 1920, just prior to the San Remo Conference that granted the Palestine Mandate to Britain, Brandeis again prevailed upon Wilson, who insisted on an adjustment to the northern border of Palestine. In 1921 after disagreement with Chaim Weizmann and his supporters, Brandeis withdrew from the ZOA and took a lower-profile position within the American Zionist movement. When the Peel Commission recommended the division of Palestine in 1937, Brandeis lobbied hard for a unitary Palestine. In 1939 at the age of 83, Brandeis retired from the Supreme Court. He died on October 5, 1941, in Washington, D.C.

PAUL G. PIERPAOLI JR.

See also

Balfour Declaration; Herzl, Theodor; Peel Commission; San Remo Conference; Weizmann, Chaim; Zionism

References

Rabinowitz, Ezekiel. *Justice Louis D. Brandeis: The Zionist Chapter in His Life.* New York: Philosophical Library, 1968.
Strum, Philippa. *Louis D. Brandeis: Justice for the People.* Cambridge: Harvard University Press, 1984.

Urofsky, Melvin I. *Louis D. Brandeis and the Progressive Tradition.* Boston: Little, Brown, 1981.

Brandt, Willy
Born: December 18, 1913
Died: October 8, 1992

Chancellor of West Germany during 1969–1974. Herbert Frahm, born in Lübeck on December 18, 1913, was an active member of the youth organization of the Social Democratic Party of Germany (SPD). He strongly opposed the rising tide of National Socialism. When Adolf Hitler gained power in 1933, Frahm changed his name to Willy Brandt and, under some risk to his life, left Germany for Norway. He returned secretly to Berlin in 1936 to reorganize resistance to Hitler and in 1937 went to Spain to work in humanitarian relief and as a journalist. After 1940, Brandt lived in Stockholm. Returning to Germany after the war, he worked as a journalist and covered the Nuremberg War Crimes Trials for the Scandinavian press. He also became active in the SPD.

In 1948, his German citizenship restored, Brandt was elected a member of West Germany's first parliament. A fierce anticommunist and pragmatic socialist, in 1957 he became the mayor of West Berlin and was thrust into international prominence in the crisis that resulted in the erection of the Berlin Wall.

In 1966 Brandt became foreign minister and vice-chancellor in the SPD–Christian Democratic Union (CDU) Grand Coalition government. The 1969 federal elections led to a new coalition govern-

Willy Brandt, mayor of West Berlin, boarding his plane to return to Germany following a trip to the United States in 1958. (Library of Congress)

ment with the Free Democratic Party. Brandt became chancellor, and Walter Scheel served as foreign secretary. Brandt's Ostpolitik (Eastern Policy) of improving ties with Soviet bloc nations led to treaties with Poland, the Soviet Union, and East Germany. For this work, Brandt was awarded the 1971 Nobel Peace Prize.

Along with Social Democrat leaders, Brandt invested his international prestige in attempts to settle the Israeli-Palestinian conflict. In 1972 he faced an immediate crisis when terrorists from Black September, a Palestinian guerrilla group, entered the competitors' village at the Munich Olympic Games. Two Israelis were killed, and 9 hostages were taken. The terrorists demanded the release of 200 Arab guerrillas jailed in Israel and safe passage for themselves and the hostages. The rescue attempt failed, and all the hostages, 5 of their captors, and 1 West German police officer were killed.

In mid-October 1973, Brandt informed the United States that West Germany would remain neutral in the Middle East conflict and would not permit the United States to resupply Israel from German military bases. On October 30, 1973, President Richard M. Nixon sent Brandt a sharply worded protest note. Following the Yom Kippur War in November 1973, Brandt met with French president Georges Pompidou, and the two drafted an official European declaration for a unified foreign policy. The document aligned the European Community (EC) with the Arab League, expressed support for an Israeli withdrawal from the occupied territories, and stated the intention to pressure the United States to end its support for Israel. Yet when Brandt visited Israel in June 1973 as chancellor, he had pursued constructive talks with Prime Minister Golda Meir. He continued his mediation efforts and met with President Anwar Sadat in Egypt in April 1974. Later that same year, scandal within Brandt's cabinet led him to resign as chancellor.

In their capacity as representatives of the Socialist International, in Vienna in July 1978 Brandt and Austrian chancellor Bruno Kreisky met Yasser Arafat, leader of the Palestine Liberation Organization (PLO), who was accorded the honors of a head of state. In protest, Israel recalled its ambassador from Vienna for consultations. The meeting with Arafat marked a decisive turn in efforts to enable democratic socialism to influence anti-Western revolutionary movements in the Third World. In January 1979, Brandt and Kreisky formulated the Vienna Document, recommending ongoing dialogue to improve relations between Israel and Egypt. Sadat, Israeli prime minister Shimon Peres, and PLO representatives agreed on it. West German chancellor Helmut Schmidt confirmed his country's support of self-determination for the Palestinians in 1981. In November 1990 Brandt met with Iraqi president Saddam Hussein at Hussein's request. Hussein asked the Socialist International to mediate in the deepening Gulf crisis. Brandt died on October 8, 1992, at Unkel, near Bonn.

PETER OVERLACK

See also

Arab Oil Embargo; Black September Organization; Germany, Federal Republic of, Middle East Policy; Munich Olympic Games; Yom Kippur War

References

Brandt, Willy. *My Life in Politics.* New York: Viking Penguin, 1992.

Marshall, Barbara. *Willy Brandt: A Political Biography.* London: Palgrave Macmillan, 1997.

Pulzer, Peter G. J. *German Politics, 1945–1995.* Oxford: Oxford University Press, 1995.

Brenner, Joseph Hayyim
Born: 1881
Died: May 1921

Jewish intellectual and vocal Zionist. Joseph Brenner was born in Novy Mlini, Ukraine, in 1881. He received a traditional Jewish schooling and studied for a time in a yeshiva (a school that emphasizes studies of the Jewish Torah). As a young man he made his way to Gomel, a large industrial city in Belorussia. There he became an activist in the Jewish labor movement.

By 1900 or so, Brenner had moved to Bialystock (then in northeastern Poland) and then to Warsaw trying to make a name for himself as a writer. He also taught Hebrew to make ends meet. In 1901 his writing career, which had resulted in only a few short stories written but not published, was cut short, and he was drafted into the Russian Army. When the Russo-Japanese War (1904–1905) broke out he deserted, making his way to and settling in London.

Once in London, Brenner became far more of an activist in the budding Zionist movement while working for a printing company during the day. He soon became involved in the incipient Po'alei Zion movement. Meanwhile, he continued with his writing career, which came to focus on the Jewish condition during the Diaspora and the creation of a Jewish homeland in Palestine. His work came to include novels, plays, and articles that cogently and eloquently articulated his viewpoints. In 1909 he went to Palestine, where he lived for the remainder of his life. Once there, he became well known for his articles on Zionist issues that were published in a variety of periodicals in Palestine and elsewhere.

It did not take long for Brenner to become one of the great intellectuals of the so-called Second Aliya (or wave of Jewish immigration to Palestine). Several themes pervaded his writing, which was suffused with an abiding despair and angst over the Jewish condition. First and foremost, Brenner believed that for the Jewish condition to improve, the Jewish identity must be freed from the slavishness of religion and the influence of rabbinic thought. Second, he advocated a secular Jewish identity, which would take hold in a new Jewish state in Palestine. Never afraid of hard work and cognizant of his working-class background, he joined the Gedud Ha'avodah (Labor Battalions) during the Third Aliya (ca. 1919–1923). For a time he worked on a road crew near Galilee. At about the same time, he was also instrumental in the founding of the Histadrut (Labor Federation). Brenner died at age 40 in May 1921 during the Arab riots in Jaffa. His voice and writings survived him and became a major corpus of thinking in the evolving Zionist movement.

PAUL G. PIERPAOLI JR.

See also

Zionism; Zionist Conference

References

Laqueur, Walter. *A History of Zionism: From the French Revolution to the Establishment of the State of Israel.* Reprint ed. New York: Schocken, 2003.

Sachar, Howard M. *A History of Israel: From the Rise of Zionism to Our Time.* 3rd ed. New York: Knopf, 2007.

Joseph Hayyim Brenner, prominent Zionist intellectual of the early 20th century. Born in Ukraine, Brenner immigrated to Palestine in 1909. (Library of Congress)

Brezhnev, Leonid Ilyich
Born: December 19, 1906
Died: November 10, 1982

Leader of the Soviet Union from 1964 to 1982. Born on December 19, 1906, in Kamenskoje (present-day Dniprodzerzhynsk) in the Ukraine, Leonid Ilyich Brezhnev was trained in metallurgy and graduated from the Dniprodzerzhynsk Metallurgical Institute (DMT) as a technical engineer in 1935. He continued to live and work in

Leonid Brezhnev was the dominant leader of the Soviet Union from 1966, when he became general secretary of the Communist Party, until his death in 1982. (AFP/Getty Images)

Ukraine, joining the Communist Party of the Soviet Union (CPSU) in 1931.

Between 1935 and 1936, Brezhnev was political commissar in a Soviet Army tank company. In 1936 he took over the directorate of DMT, and he became Communist Party secretary in Dnepropetrovsk in 1939. He served as a political commissar in the Soviet Army during World War II, ending the war in charge of the Political Administration of the 4th Ukrainian Front.

After the war, Brezhnev helped oversee the rebuilding of industry in Ukraine and again became first secretary in Dnepropetrovsk. In 1950 he was admitted to the ranks of the Supreme Soviet. Later that year he became first secretary of the CPSU in Moldavia. In 1952 he became a member of the CPSU's Central Committee and was admitted as a candidate member of the Politburo. In 1955 Brezhnev became first secretary of the party in Kazakhstan. In February 1956 he was appointed as a candidate member of the Politburo.

In 1959 Brezhnev, now a full Politburo member, became second secretary of the Central Committee, and the next year he was promoted to president of the Presidium of the Supreme Soviet, nominally head of state of the Soviet Union. Although he owed much to

Nikita Khrushchev for his rise in the party, Brezhnev joined with Alexei Kosygin in 1964 to help overthrow the Soviet leader.

In the power sharing following Khrushchev's ouster, Brezhnev became first secretary of the CPSU on October 15 and Kosygin became prime minister. In 1966 Brezhnev named himself general secretary of the CPSU and began to dominate the collective Soviet leadership. In 1975 he became an army general, and in 1976 he was named marshal of the Soviet Union (the highest military rank). In 1977 he replaced Nikolai Podgorny as head of state.

Brezhnev's domestic policies tended toward conservatism in the cultural and social spheres. He reversed the cultural liberalization process begun under Khrushchev, while his economic policies ultimately brought about stagnation. By the late 1970s, the Soviet Union was reeling from sinking standards of living, declining output, corruption, and stagnating technologies. In foreign policy, Brezhnev engaged in détente with the West beginning in the late 1960s, oversaw the Warsaw Pact invasion of Czechoslovakia in 1968, aided North Vietnam in its war with the United States, and bolstered Arab regimes in the Middle East. He was also forced to deal with tense relations with the People's Republic of China (PRC) that nearly resulted in full-blown war between the two communist giants. Détente was dealt a crippling blow when Brezhnev authorized the invasion and occupation of Afghanistan in December 1979.

Under Brezhnev, the Soviet Union remained fully engaged in the Middle East and influenced the situation not only at the Israeli-Syrian border but beyond it as well. With Soviet help, Syria supported the Palestinian guerrillas in their fights against Israel. Moscow further contributed to an escalation of the conflict when it released false intelligence information indicating that Israel was building up troops at the Syrian border.

Prior to the 1967 Six-Day War, the Kremlin had supported Egypt both financially and with military equipment. However, most of the weaponry that was delivered to Egypt was defensive in nature. Only after Egyptian president Gamal Abdel Nasser threatened to tell the Egyptian population that Moscow had abandoned them did the Soviets supply the country with antiaircraft missiles.

During the Six-Day War, Brezhnev, together with President Lyndon Johnson's administration in the United States, sought a diplomatic solution to the conflict. Also after 1967, the Soviet Union tried to push Egypt into seeking a peaceful solution to the conflict with Israel because Brezhnev did not want to be drawn into a conflict with the United States.

Soviet influence in the Middle East became more pronounced after the Six-Day War. The danger of a Soviet-U.S. confrontation in the area also increased, especially during President Richard Nixon's administration. When the October 1973 Yom Kippur War began, Brezhnev sent a message to Washington threatening that he would intervene on Egypt's behalf if the Americans did not cooperate with Moscow in ending the war.

The Americans, however, were upset that Brezhnev had not warned them about the planned attacks. Had Brezhnev known about such plans but not disclosed them, that would have been contrary to U.S.-Soviet agreements dating from 1972 and 1973. Most likely, however, Moscow was just as surprised as Washington at the turn of events. Washington convinced the Egyptian leadership to drop its request for assistance from Moscow, and the crisis was brought to an end. After the war, Egypt withdrew from its alliance with the Soviet Union and turned toward the United States.

As the tumultuous 1970s gave way to the 1980s, the Soviet Union was in considerable trouble. Its economy was at best stagnant, and it soon became clear that Afghanistan was becoming a military and diplomatic quagmire. Perhaps one of Brezhnev's last significant acts abroad was the pressure his government put on communist leaders in Poland to suppress the Solidarity movement there in December 1981, resulting in the imposition of martial law in Poland. His health was in serious decline in the early 1980s, and by 1982 he was leader in name only. Brezhnev died of coronary complications on November 10, 1982, in Moscow.

THOMAS J. WEILER

See also

Johnson, Lyndon Baines; Khrushchev, Nikita; Nasser, Gamal Abdel; Nixon, Richard Milhous; Six-Day War; Soviet Union and Russia, Middle East Policy; Yom Kippur War

References

Bacon, Edwin, and Mark Sandle, eds. *Brezhnev Reconsidered.* Basingstoke, UK: Palgrave MacMillan, 2002.

Edmonds, Robin. *Soviet Foreign Policy: The Brezhnev Years.* Oxford: Oxford University Press, 1983.

Kelley, Donald R., ed. *Soviet Politics in the Brezhnev Era.* New York: Praeger, 1980.

Steele, Jonathan. *Soviet Power: The Kremlin's Foreign Policy from Brezhnev to Andropov.* New York: Simon and Schuster, 1983.

B'riha
Start Date: 1944
End Date: May 1948

The mass migration of Jews from Europe to Palestine that occurred between 1944 and 1948. B'riha is Hebrew for "flight" and is also the name of the organization that facilitated the movement of the Jews to Palestine. Under the terrible impetus of the Holocaust, the Nazi plan to kill all the Jews of Europe, many Jews tried to escape to Palestine. Then, with the end of the war, many Jewish survivors had no desire to return to their homelands, where, especially in Central and Eastern Europe, they had often been subject to persecution.

Late in 1944, Jewish partisans and members of Zionist youth movements operating in the areas of Vilna and Rovino began efforts to remove surviving Jews from the Soviet Union to Romania. In January 1945 members of the Jewish resistance and survivors of the fighting in the Warsaw Ghetto set up at Lublin, Poland, a coordinating committee to facilitate this movement. Between February and May 1945, B'riha arranged for the illegal movement of some 1,500 Jews to Romania. Passing through Hungary, Yugoslavia, and southern Austria, they reached B'riha collection points in Italy. After May 1945, B'riha moved some 15,000 additional Jews through Bratislava and Budapest to Italy. Another 12,000 Jews collected in the Graz area of Austria were passed over the border into Italy in late 1945. The return to Poland from the Soviet Union of some 175,000 Polish Jews created a large population pool from which B'riha could draw. In September 1945 the Mosad L'Aliya Bet (illegal immigration center) took charge of the collection of the B'riha Jews.

Following the pogrom in Kielce, Poland, in July 1946, a large increase occurred in the number of Jews attempting to leave Poland. The American Jewish Joint Distribution Committee provided funds and worked with the Czechoslovak government to establish transit facilities for them in Bratislava, while an agreement with the Polish government allowed unofficial but legal exit for many. Between July 1 and September 30, 1946, some 73,000 Polish Jews left their homeland with B'riha. Then in the spring of 1947, 17,000 Jews left Romania in an unorganized exodus.

In all, perhaps 250,000 Jews left Eastern Europe under B'riha. This was the largest organized mass exodus of Jews in modern history. Of these, by far the largest number (170,000) came from Poland, while 35,000 came from Romania and the rest came chiefly from Hungary and Czechoslovakia. Ultimately, the vast majority of these Jews settled in Palestine. With the establishment of the State of Israel in May 1948, B'riha was no longer necessary, and it was dissolved early in 1950.

SPENCER C. TUCKER

See also

Aliya Bet; American Jewish Joint Distribution Committee; Holocaust; Immigration to Palestine/Israel

References

Dekel, Efrayim. *B'riha: Flight to the Homeland.* New York: Herzl, 1973.

Hadari, Ze'ev V. *Second Exodus: The Full Story of Jewish Illegal Immigration to Palestine, 1945–1948.* London: Valentine Mitchell, 1991.

Britain, Middle East Policy

See United Kingdom, Middle East Policy

Brodetsky, Selig
Born: February 10, 1888
Died: May 18, 1954

British mathematician and Zionist leader. Born in Olviopol, Ukraine, in imperial Russia on February 10, 1888, Selig Brodetsky left Russia and settled in England with his family in 1893. Raised in London in modest financial circumstances, he went on to a distinguished academic career. In 1911 he graduated with honors from Cambridge University, where he helped found its Zionist society. He then studied at the University of Leipzig, earning his doctorate in mathematics there in 1913.

Returning to Britain, Brodetsky became lecturer of applied mathematics at the University of Bristol during 1914–1919. He continued his active involvement in Zionist activities and supported plans to establish a Hebrew University in Jerusalem. In 1920 he accepted a position at the University of Leeds, where he was lecturer (1920–1924) and then professor of mathematics (1924–1948). He became a leader of British Zionists and regularly attended international Zionist conferences. During 1928–1951 he was a member of the Zionist Executive.

Brodetsky first visited Palestine in 1925 when he attended the opening of the Hebrew University. He then traveled in the United States on behalf of the university. He held a number of positions in the Zionist movement and for many years was president of the Zionist Federation of Great Britain and Ireland. During 1939–1949 he was president of the Board of Deputies of British Jews and in this capacity often spoke out against the British government's Palestine policies. In 1946 he was one of the witnesses heard by the Anglo-American Committee of Inquiry.

Brodetsky moved to Israel in 1949 to become president of the Hebrew University but resigned two years later because of health issues and disagreements with the university's Board of Governors. He published extensively in his field of mathematics. Brodetsky

died in London on May 18, 1954. His memoirs were published posthumously in 1960.

SPENCER C. TUCKER

See also

Anglo-American Committee of Inquiry; World Zionist Organization Executive; Zionism

References

Brodetsky, Selig. *Memoirs: From Ghetto to Israel.* London: Weidenfeld and Nicolson, 1960.

Halpern, Ben, and Jehuda Reinharz. *Zionism and the Creation of a New Society.* Waltham, MA: Brandeis University Press, 2000.

Brzezinski, Zbigniew
Born: March 28, 1928

International relations scholar, diplomat, and U.S. national security adviser during 1977–1981. Born the son of a Polish diplomat in Warsaw, Poland, on March 28, 1928, Zbigniew Brzezinski received his PhD from Harvard University in 1953 and became a U.S. citizen in 1958. Following his graduation, he joined the faculty of Harvard

Foreign policy specialist Zbigniew Brzezinski served as an adviser to Democratic presidents John F. Kennedy, Lyndon B. Johnson, and Jimmy Carter. (Jimmy Carter Library)

and then moved on to Columbia University in 1960, where he stayed until 1977.

Brzezinski served as a foreign policy adviser to U.S. president John F. Kennedy and as a member of the State Department's influential policy planning staff during the Lyndon Johnson administration. In 1968 Brzezinski resigned his State Department post in protest over U.S. Vietnam War policies. He subsequently returned to academia and directed the Trilateral Commission from 1973 to 1976. After serving as foreign policy adviser to Jimmy Carter in the latter's successful 1976 presidential campaign, Brzezinski was named Carter's national security adviser in 1977.

As national security adviser, Brzezinski played a critical role in the normalization of relations with the People's Republic of China (PRC) as well as in the 1978 Camp David Accords. Most significant perhaps to both Carter and Brzezinski was the 1978 Iranian Revolution and the resultant hostage crisis that dominated their last year in office.

Following Carter's defeat in the 1980 election, Brzezinski returned to Columbia University. In 1989 he joined the faculty of Johns Hopkins University. He has written and edited numerous books on international relations.

BRENT M. GEARY

See also

Camp David Accords; Carter, James Earl, Jr.

References

Andrianopoulos, Gerry Argyris. *Kissinger and Brzezinski: The NSC and the Struggle for Control of US National Security Policy.* New York: St. Martin's, 1991.

Brzezinski, Zbigniew. *Power and Principle: Memoirs of the National Security Adviser, 1977–1981.* New York: Farrar, Straus and Giroux, 1985.

Bull, Gerald Vincent
Born: March 1928
Died: March 22, 1990

Aerophysicist engineer and arguably the 20th century's top artillery designer. Born in North Bay, Ontario, Canada, in March 1928, Gerald Vincent Bull was raised by an aunt after his mother died. An outstanding student, Bull was the youngest person ever to earn a doctorate from the University of Toronto. A superb engineer, in 1951 he went to work for the Canadian Armament and Research Development Establishment (CARDE). There he developed an innovative alternative to expensive wind tunnels, firing the model down a barrel and using high-speed cameras to record its behavior during flight. His engineering prowess brought rapid promotions, and in 1959 he became the chief of CARDE's Aerophysics Department.

Bull, who had little patience for bureaucracy, left CARDE in 1961. The brilliant engineer had a stubborn personality and a deep commitment to developing the best artillery. These would drive him to accept employment with any agency willing to fund his dreams, and ultimately this cost him his life.

Shortly after leaving CARDE, Bull convinced the U.S. government that large guns were potentially more cost-effective platforms

Artillery designer Vincent Gerald Bull (*left*) shown in 1965 with premier of Quebec Jean Lesage and one of Bull's giant guns. (AP/Wide World Photos/Montreal Star)

than rockets for launching small satellites testing nose cones for orbital reentry. The resulting U.S.-Canadian High Altitude Program (HARP) enabled him to study and demonstrate his ideas. He built a small test center along the Vermont-Quebec border to conduct model testing and a launch range in Barbados for flight tests. There, he modified an old U.S. Navy 16-inch gun, extended its barrel to 36 meters, and developed special propellants to launch projectiles weighing nearly 400 pounds to altitudes of some 110 miles. The project's entire cost was $10 million, or about twice that of a single Atlas missile launch.

Despite the demonstrated economy of his project, his enemies at CARDE convinced the Canadian government to withdraw funding. However, Bull was able to transfer all the assets to the corporation he had founded to manage the project. He now became a consultant to any military willing to fund his research.

Using the knowledge he gained from HARP, Bull became the world's foremost expert at extending the range of artillery shells. His use of base bleed technology to reduce the drag of the projectiles enabled him to extend the range by as much as 50 percent without reducing the projectile's throw weight. Bull was first hired by South Africa to develop artillery that could outrange the Soviet M-46 field guns being supplied to the Cuban forces the South Africans were fighting in Angola. The resulting 155-mm gun was the world's longest-ranged field gun until the late 20th century. However, a change in American administration made Bull's once-legal work for South Africa a criminal activity. He was convicted of illegal arms trafficking for selling the guns and ammunition to South Africa.

Imprisoned for six months and bankrupt, on his release Bull moved to Brussels, Belgium, and began to work for the People's Republic of China (PRC) and Iraq.

Iraq was then locked in a long war with Iran (1980–1988). Impressed with Bull's guns, which Baghdad had acquired from South Africa, Iraqi dictator Saddam Hussein hired Bull in 1981 to develop a supergun that Iraq could use for artillery purposes and to launch satellites into orbit. Bull designated the program Project Babylon. Although the international media and the Iraqi government reported that the gun was to be used to attack Israel, there was little to suggest that it might be a practical military weapon. The prototype model had a barrel 45 meters long fixed along an embankment and a bore of 350-mm (14 inches). The gun also weighed more than 2,100 tons. Reportedly, the gun was to be ready for test firing in 1991. Later media reporting indicates that Bull briefed both Israeli and British intelligence agencies on the project.

The supergun was not the only project Bull worked on for Iraq. He also agreed to assist Iraq in developing a multistage missile based on the Soviet-supplied Scud. Ostensibly designed to strike targets deep inside Iran, the missile also had the capacity to strike Israel. Given Iraq's possession and use of chemical agents in its war with Iran, the Israeli government viewed the missile project as a major strategic threat. Bull reportedly received warnings from the Israelis to abandon the project. If he did receive such warnings, he ignored them. On March 22, 1990, he was found in his Brussels apartment, dead from five bullet wounds to the head. None of his neighbors heard the shots, and the assassin has never been identified. Although United Nations (UN) inspectors destroyed Bull's Iraqi supergun and its supporting equipment after the first Persian Gulf War, the South African G-5 155-mm served the Iraqi Army through three wars, and derivative variants remain in service today with the armies of Germany, Italy, Greece, and the Netherlands. In fact, virtually all long-range artillery pieces and extended-range ammunition rounds introduced into service since 2000 are based on Bull's design principles.

CARL OTIS SCHUSTER

See also

Artillery; Mossad; Project Babylon

References

Adams, James. *Bull's Eye: The Assassination and Life of Supergun Inventor Gerald Bull.* New York: Times Books, 1992.

Bull, Gerald V., and Charles H. Murphy. *Paris Kanonen: The Paris Guns (Wilhelmgeschütze) and Project HARP.* Bonn, Germany: Verlag E. S. Mittlre and Sohn, 1988.

Lowther, William. *Arms and the Man: Dr. Gerald Bull, Iraq and the Supergun.* Novato, CA: Presidio, 1991.

Bunche, Ralph Johnson

Born: August 7, 1904
Died: December 9, 1971

American political scientist and United Nations (UN) diplomat. Ralph Bunche was the first African American and the first person

As a high official of the United Nations (UN) for 25 years, American Ralph Bunche led peacekeeping efforts in troubled areas of the world, including the Middle East. (Carl Van Vechten Collection/Library of Congress)

of non-European ancestry to win the Nobel Peace Prize (1950) for his work in mediating an end to the war between Arabs and Jews in 1949. Bunche was born in Detroit on August 7, 1904, and studied international relations at the University of Southern California–Los Angeles (UCLA), graduating summa cum laude in 1927. He received his doctorate in government and international relations from Harvard University in 1934. From 1928 until 1950 he served as chairman of the political science department at Howard University in Washington, D.C. He also wrote and lectured extensively.

During the early years of World War II, Bunche served in the Office of Strategic Services (OSS). Moving to the State Department in 1943, he served as acting chair of the Division of Dependent Area Affairs. He also became involved in the Institute of Pacific Relations and the International Labor Organization. He was a member of the American delegation to Dumbarton Oaks and San Francisco, which paved the way for the organization of the UN. There Bunche drafted the trusteeship system for the UN Charter. The trusteeship system concerned the UN role in supervising the Trust Territories assigned to the organization (to include the World War I mandate territories). His experience with trusteeships led UN secretary-general

Trygve Lie to name Bunche the first director of the UN Trusteeship Department in April 1946. This experience began his affiliation with the UN.

In June 1947 Bunche was assigned to assist with the UN takeover of the British Mandate for Palestine, and he became assistant to the UN Special Commission on Palestine. He subsequently became secretary to the UN Palestine Commission, tasked with carrying out the UN's Palestine partition plan.

When full-scale fighting broke out between Arabs and Jews in 1948, Bunche was named Count Folke Bernadotte's chief assistant mediator. When Bernadotte was assassinated in September 1948, Bunche became chief UN mediator. Thanks to his tireless diplomacy held on the island of Rhodes, Bunche managed to broker an end to the Israeli War of Independence in 1949. This took the form of a series of armistice agreements between Israel and the states of Egypt, Lebanon, Jordan, and Syria. Bunche's success in this regard also provided a well-needed boost to the UN's reputation. For his efforts, Bunche received the 1950 Nobel Peace Prize.

From 1955 to 1967, Bunche served the UN as undersecretary for special political affairs. Following the eruption of renewed fighting between Israel and Egypt in the Suez Crisis of 1956, Bunche established standards for future UN peacekeeping activities when he supervised the postwar deployment of UN troops to Egypt. As the primary mediator for the UN secretary-general, Bunche secured at least temporary halts to regional conflicts in the Congo (1960), Cyprus (1962), and Kashmir (1965). In 1963 he was awarded the Presidential Medal of Freedom by the U.S. government. In 1968 he became the UN's undersecretary-general. Bunche retired from the UN for reasons of health shortly before his death in New York City on December 9, 1971.

THOMAS VEVE

See also

Bernadotte, Folke; Israeli War of Independence, Overview; Israeli War of Independence, Truce Agreements; Suez Crisis; United Nations, Role of; United Nations General Assembly Resolution 194; United Nations Peacekeeping Missions; United Nations Special Commission on Palestine

References

Mann, Peggy. *Ralph Bunche: UN Peacemaker.* New York: Coward, McCann and Geoghegan, 1975.

Rivlin, Benjamin, ed. *Ralph Bunche: The Man and His Times.* New York: Holmes and Meier, 1990.

Urquhart, Brian. *Ralph Bunche: An American Life.* New York: Norton, 1993.

Burma Road
Event Date: 1948

Name given to a supply road constructed by the Haganah that linked Tel Aviv with Jerusalem during the Arab-Jewish fighting that immediately preceded the Israeli War of Independence (1948–1949). The purpose of this road, approximately 16 miles long, was to secure a supply line to the Jewish quarter of the city of Jerusalem. The route was wryly named after the famous World War II supply route that linked India to China through Burma, used to transport supplies to Chinese troops fighting the Japanese.

During the Arab-Jewish Communal War (November 1947–May 1948) the Jordanians surrounded Jerusalem, besieging the Jewish quarter of roughly 100,000 people and cutting them off from outside sources of military supplies as well as food. At the same time, the Jordanian Arab Legion cut the main road from Tel Aviv to Jerusalem by occupying the former British strong point at Latrun. Keeping Jerusalem's Jewish population supplied with basic necessities and the war materials to continue its defense became the principal military objective of Jewish leaders.

Jewish Agency head David Ben-Gurion played an important role in the establishment of the supply route, imposing his belief that Jerusalem was simply too important to be abandoned. As a consequence, Jewish forces concentrated on the relief effort. The only Israeli forces not involved were those already fully committed in Galilee. The operation to open a supply corridor to Jerusalem was known as Operation NACHSHON.

Credit for the success of the Burma Road is due, in large part, to General David "Mickey" Marcus, under whose guidance the construction was accomplished. Marcus, who served in Israel under the cover name of Michael Stone, was an American-born U.S. Army colonel who had come to Palestine to serve as military adviser to Ben-Gurion. During the ensuing fighting, Marcus was charged with organizing the supply and transport sections of the Haganah and the nascent Israeli government. While Marcus's efforts met with success, he did not live to witness their full fruition, as he was shot and killed by one of his own sentries on June 10, 1948, shortly after the Burma Road was completed.

Work on the Burma Road began on March 31, 1948, with crews working both outward from Jerusalem and inward from Tel Aviv. The construction, although heavily opposed by forces of the Arab Legion, was completed in roughly 10 weeks, and the road was opened to traffic on June 10. The term "road" is somewhat of a misnomer in that the supply line was essentially makeshift and was constructed mainly at night to reduce the vulnerability of construction crews to Jordanian interdiction efforts.

The first major supply convoys reached Jerusalem on June 10, with much of their cargo consisting of arms shipments from Czechoslovakia. While the road did not remain open constantly and numerous vehicles were lost on it to enemy fire as they attempted to negotiate the route, enough material entered Jerusalem to allow the Jews there to continue its resistance.

The Burma Road was a success on two counts. First, the shipments into the city allowed the Jews there to withstand attacks by the Arab Legion. Second, the population managed to hold out until the end of hostilities, ensuring that part of the city would remain in Jewish control. Thus, the road played a significant role in the logistics of the Israeli effort toward independence and ultimate sovereignty. Today the remnants of the Burma Road run parallel and a few miles to the south of the main highway linking Jerusalem and Tel Aviv.

JAMES R. MCINTYRE

See also

Arab-Jewish Communal War; Arab Legion; Ben-Gurion, David; Haganah; Israeli War of Independence, Overview; Jerusalem; Latrun, Battles of; Marcus, David; NACHSHON, Operation

References

Maan, Abu Nowar. *The Jordanian-Israeli War, 1948–1951: A History of the Hashemite Kingdom of Jordan.* Reading, UK: Ithaca Press, 2002.

Milstein, Uri. *History of Israel's War of Independence.* 4 vols. Lanham, MD: University Press of America, 1996–1999.

Tal, David. *War in Palestine, 1948: Strategy and Diplomacy.* New York: Routledge, 2004.

Bush, George Herbert Walker
Born: June 12, 1924

U.S. congressman, ambassador, director of the Central Intelligence Agency (CIA) during 1975–1976, vice president during 1981–1989, and president of the United States during 1989–1993. George Herbert Walker Bush was born on June 12, 1924, in Milton, Massachusetts, to a wealthy and patrician family. His father, Prescott Bush, was a prominent U.S. senator from Connecticut. Educated at the elite Phillips Andover Academy, on his 18th birthday the younger Bush enlisted in the U.S. Navy, becoming its youngest pilot and seeing service in the Pacific flying a torpedo bomber. He was shot down by Japanese aircraft and later rescued from the sea by an American submarine. After his World War II service, he married Barbara Pierce, graduated from Yale University with an economics degree, moved to western Texas, and embarked upon a career in the oil business. Opening his own oil enterprise in 1950, by 1954 he was the president of Zapata Offshore Company. His oil dealings paid handsome dividends, and he had become wealthy in his own right in the span of a few years.

Bush entered electoral politics as a Republican in 1964, the year in which he lost a bid for the U.S. Senate. Undeterred, he won a seat in the U.S. House of Representatives in 1966. In 1970 he again ran unsuccessfully for the U.S. Senate. President Richard M. Nixon appointed Bush ambassador to the United Nations (UN) in 1971. In this post for two years, Bush fought to preserve Nationalist China's (Taiwan) seat in that organization, an effort that was ultimately unsuccessful.

During 1973–1974, Bush served as the chairman of the Republican National Committee (RNC) at the direct request of President Nixon. Bush's tenure with the RNC took place during the Watergate Scandal that ultimately forced Nixon to resign in August 1974. Bush steadfastly defended Nixon, to little avail.

President George H. W. Bush talks with troops in Saudi Arabia on November 23, 1990, during Operation DESERT SHIELD. (U.S. Department of Defense)

Bush then served during 1974–1975 in President Gerald R. Ford's administration as chief of the U.S. liaison office to the People's Republic of China (PRC). Although the United States and the PRC had not yet established full and normal diplomatic relations, Bush nonetheless acted as the de facto ambassador to the PRC. In 1975 he took over the CIA. The agency was then reeling from a series of shocking and embarrassing revelations about its role in assassination plots, coups, and other covert operations conducted in the name of the Cold War. Bush tried to rehabilitate the CIA during his tenure, and his efforts met with some success. He left the agency in 1977 after Jimmy Carter defeated Ford in the presidential election. Bush then became chairman of the First International Bank of Houston.

In 1980 Bush sought the Republican presidential nomination but lost to former California governor Ronald Reagan. During the primaries, Bush assailed Reagan's political agenda, referring to his economic prescriptions as "voodoo economics." Despite such rhetoric, Reagan named Bush his running mate in an attempt to balance the ticket and provide a moderating force to his conservative platform. The pair went on to win an overwhelming victory in the 1980 elections. As vice president Bush loyally backed Reagan's hard-line Cold War policies. Bush did not wield much power in the administration, however, and what effects he did have on policy were well disguised. During Reagan's first term, military spending increased dramatically, and the administration provided considerable aid to foreign governments and insurgents to combat communism.

Bush bolstered these measures by traveling around the globe soliciting support for Reagan's policies, particularly in Central America. Bush met with Panamanian strongman Manuel Noriega, who had allied himself with the anticommunist Nicaraguan Contras. The Contras were fighting the Sandinista government and receiving U.S. military and financial aid. After Congress voted to cut off assistance to the Contras in 1983, the Reagan administration began covertly aiding them. Members of the National Security Agency concocted a plan by which proceeds from the sale of weapons to Iran were diverted to the Contra rebels. When the Iran-Contra story broke in 1986, Bush denied any knowledge of the illegal operation. Questions remained about Bush's role in the Iran-Contra Affair when he ran for the presidency in 1988, but he nonetheless secured a sound victory that November over Massachusetts governor Michael Dukakis.

When Bush took office in January 1989, the Cold War was winding down. During Ronald Reagan's second term, relations between the United States and the Soviet Union had improved remarkably, and in Bush's first year as president he continued to negotiate with Soviet premier Mikhail Gorbachev. In November 1989, the momentous fall of the Berlin Wall ushered in the end of the Cold War. Bush's reactions to the changes in Eastern Europe were calculatingly restrained. He and his foreign policy advisers were wary of antagonizing the Soviet leadership and were fearful that the Soviet military might be employed to stanch the prodemocracy movements. But Soviet weakness and Gorbachev's promises not to inter-

vene led to a peaceful revolution. By January 1992 the Soviet Union had been officially dissolved, and later that year President Bush and the new Russian leader Boris Yeltsin declared an end to the Cold War.

Bush dealt with a series of foreign policy crises, including China's brutal crackdown against protesters in Tiananmen Square during May–June 1990. This event severely strained Sino-U.S. relations, although Bush's experience as liaison to China in the 1970s may have been a moderating factor in that impasse. In December 1989, Bush launched Operation JUST CAUSE, which saw a U.S. invasion of Panama that resulted in the capture and extradition of Panamanian president Noriega. Noriega, formally an ally of the United States and someone with whom Bush had once conducted diplomatic business, was taken to the United States and tried on a variety of drug and drug trafficking charges.

After Iraq invaded and occupied Kuwait in August 1990, Bush successfully mounted an international coalition force that liberated Kuwait and dealt a crippling blow to Iraqi dictator Saddam Hussein's military. Almost immediately, the Bush administration made it clear that the Iraqi takeover of Kuwait would not be permitted to stand. To pressure Hussein to withdraw and to protect Saudi Arabia, the United States embarked on Operation DESERT SHIELD. This operation saw the eventual positioning of nearly 500,000 U.S. troops in the region, mostly in Saudi Arabia. Meanwhile, Bush was carefully building an international coalition—which would include many Arab nations—that would ultimately expel Iraqi forces from Kuwait. The Bush administration was also building support in the UN, which on November 29, 1990, passed a resolution authorizing military action against Iraq if it did not withdraw by January 15, 1991. Bush's job in assembling such impressive international cooperation was undoubtedly made easier by the end of the Cold War. The Soviet Union did not interfere in the crisis and indeed gave its tacit support to the international coalition.

When the UN deadline passed and Hussein defiantly remained in Kuwait, the Persian Gulf War began, code-named Operation DESERT STORM. The conflict, which now had a 34-nation coalition arrayed against Iraq, began on January 17, 1991, with massive bombing raids against Iraqi targets by U.S. and coalition air assets. The next day, Hussein ordered Scud surface-to-surface missiles fired into Israel in an obvious attempt to draw the Israelis into the war and thereby break apart the unlikely multinational coalition that included Arab states. The Bush administration implored Israel not to react to the attacks, which caused only light damage. It also sent Patriot air defense missile batteries to Israel that were intended to intercept and shoot down incoming Scuds. Although these had less success than was claimed at the time, the Patriots were a factor in Bush's success in keeping Israel out of the war. The Iraqis also fired Scuds into Saudi Arabia, but Hussein's ploy to split the coalition did not work.

On February 24, 1991, after sustaining a withering aerial bombardment campaign that destroyed much of Iraq's important infrastructure, the United States commenced the ground war to liberate

Kuwait. It lasted less than 100 hours. On February 26, Iraqi troops were beating a hasty retreat from Kuwait. By February 27, with Iraqi forces badly beaten and with many surrendering, Bush, supported by Chairman of the Joint Chiefs of Staff Colin Powell, brought the war to a close. A cease-fire was declared, and the Persian Gulf War was over. The conflict liberated Kuwait, protected Saudi Arabian and Middle Eastern oil supplies, and had not turned into a larger conflagration, despite Iraqi missile attacks against Israel. However, Hussein's repressive regime was left firmly in place. Presciently, Secretary of Defense Dick Cheney defended the decision not to oust Hussein and invade Iraq because such a move would have "bogged [the United States] down in the quagmire inside Iraq."

Following the war, Bush enjoyed meteoric approval ratings. However, a deep economic recession combined with his inability to offer solutions to the downturn resulted in a near free fall in his popularity. In November 1992 he lost a close election to Democrat Bill Clinton. One of Bush's last significant accomplishments as president was the brokering of the North American Free Trade Agreement (NAFTA), which his successor Clinton signed in 1993. Since leaving office, Bush has assembled his presidential library in Texas, has coauthored a book on foreign affairs, and has been involved in various humanitarian missions.

JUSTIN P. COFFEY AND PAUL G. PIERPAOLI JR.

See also

Baker, James Addison, III; Iraq; Iraq, Armed Forces; Kuwait; Nixon, Richard Milhous; Persian Gulf War; Reagan, Ronald Wilson

References

Bush, George. *All the Best, George Bush: My Life in Letters and Other Writings.* New York: Scribner, 1999.

Bush, George H. W., and Brent Scowcroft. *A World Transformed.* New York: Knopf, 1998.

Green, John Robert. *The Presidency of George Bush.* Lawrence: University of Kansas Press, 2000.

Parmet, Herbert S. *George Bush: The Life of a Lone Star Yankee.* New York: Scribner, 1997.

Bush, George Walker
Born: July 6, 1946

Republican politician, governor of Texas (1995–2001), and president of the United States (2001–). George Walker Bush was born in New Haven, Connecticut, on July 6, 1946, and grew up in Midland and Houston, Texas. He is the son of George H. W. Bush, president of the United States during 1989–1993. The younger Bush graduated from the exclusive Phillips Academy in Andover, Massachusetts, and from Yale University in 1968. He volunteered for the Texas Air National Guard after graduation and became a pilot, although questions later surfaced about his actual service. He earned an MBA from Harvard University in 1975 and returned to Texas, founding Arbusto Energy Company in 1977. He then served as a key staffer during his father's 1988 presidential campaign

President George W. Bush during a one-day emergency summit meeting to discuss the war in Iraq. The summit was held at Lajes Field in the Azores on March 17, 2003. (U.S. Department of Defense)

and later became one of the owners of the Texas Rangers baseball team.

In 1994 Bush was elected governor of Texas. As governor, he worked with the Democratic-dominated legislature to reduce state control and taxes. In 1996 he won reelection.

In 2000, having set records for fund-raising and having campaigned as a compassionate conservative, Bush easily won the 2000 Republican nomination for the presidency of the United States. His platform included tax cuts, improved schools, Social Security reform, and increased military spending. On foreign policy issues, he downplayed his obvious lack of experience but eschewed foreign intervention and nation-building.

The U.S. presidential election of November 2000 was probably the most contentious in American history. The Democratic candidate, Vice President Al Gore, won a slim majority of the popular vote, but the electoral vote was in doubt. Confusion centered on Florida. Eventually, the issue reached the U.S. Supreme Court. On December 12, 2000, a deeply divided Court halted the recount in

Florida, virtually declaring Bush the winner. For many Americans, Bush was an illegitimate and unelected president.

As president, Bush secured a large tax cut in hopes that this would spur the economy, and he pushed forward Social Security reform. The course of his presidency was forever changed on September 11, 2001, when 19 hijackers associated with the Al Qaeda terrorist organization seized commercial airliners and crashed them into the World Trade Center and the Pentagon. The attacks killed 2,657 Americans and 316 foreign nationals. Over the next few days, Bush visited the scenes of the attacks, reassuring the public and promising to bring those responsible to justice. The catastrophe of September 11 seemed to bring legitimacy and purpose to Bush's presidency.

On September 20, Bush appeared before Congress and accused Al Qaeda of carrying out the attacks. He warned the American people that they faced a lengthy war against terrorism. He demanded that the Taliban government of Afghanistan surrender members of Al Qaeda in their country or face retribution. When the Taliban failed to comply, U.S. and British forces began a bombing campaign on October 7. Indigenous forces, with heavy American support, defeated the Taliban and by November 2001 had captured the capital of Kabul. Taliban resistance continued, but the multinational coalition was nevertheless able to establish a new government in Afghanistan.

The Bush administration also sought to improve national security. A new Department of Homeland Security was created to coordinate all agencies that could track and defeat terrorists. In October 2001, Congress passed the so-called Patriot Act, giving the federal government sweeping powers to fight the war on terror. Many Americans were uncomfortable with this legislation and feared that it might undermine American freedom.

In 2002 the Bush administration turned its attentions toward Iraq. Intelligence reports suggested that Iraqi dictator Saddam Hussein was continuing to pursue weapons of mass destruction (WMDs). When Bush demanded that he comply with United Nations (UN) resolutions demanding inspection of certain facilities, Hussein refused. By the end of 2002, the Bush administration had formulated a new policy of preemptive warfare to destroy regimes that intended to harm the United States before they were able to do so.

By the beginning of 2003 a military buildup against Iraq was taking place. However, Bush's efforts to create a multinational coalition failed to achieve the success of the Gulf War coalition against Iraq in 1991. Nearly all of the forces were American or British.

Military operations commenced on March 19, 2001, and Baghdad fell on April 9. At that point organized resistance was minimal, but manpower resources, while sufficient to topple Hussein, were clearly insufficient to maintain the peace. Rioting and looting broke out, and weapons stockpiles were pillaged by insurgents. Religious and ethnic tensions came to the fore between Sunnis, Shias, and Kurds. Far more American troops were killed trying to keep order in Iraq than had died in the overthrow of the regime. Although Bush

won reelection in November 2004 in large part because of his tough stance on the so-called war on terror, support for the war gradually waned, the consequences of American military and Iraqi civilian dead, reports of American atrocities committed in Iraq, and the war's vast expense. Meanwhile, large budget deficits and trade imbalances piled up. Clearly, the failure to find WMDs in Iraq undercut the stated reason for the attack, although Bush then claimed that the war was about overthrowing an evil dictatorship and bringing democracy to Iraq.

The Bush administration was at first ambivalent toward the Arab-Israeli conflict, but with violence escalating, in August 2001 at the urging of Crown Prince Abdullah of Saudi Arabia, Bush issued a letter supporting the concept of a Palestinian state. September 11 and ensuing events in Iraq soon took precedence, however. Bush and his advisers realized that Arab support, or at least acquiescence, in his Iraq policies would be more likely if a peace process were under way.

On June 24, 2002, Bush publicly called for a two-state solution. He failed to outline specific steps but supported a process in which each side would meet certain criteria before moving to the next step. The result was called the Road Map to Peace. Bush agreed to work with the European Union (EU), the UN, and Russia in developing it. This so-called Quartet developed a series of steps intended to provide assurances for each side but without involving the Israelis or Palestinians in its development.

The Road Map to Peace was unveiled in March 2003 just before the invasion of Iraq, but no details were announced. In June of that year, Bush arranged a summit conference at Aqaba, Jordan, involving Prime Minister Ariel Sharon of Israel and Prime Minister Mahmoud Abbas of the Palestinian Authority (PA). Progress on the plan stalled. The Bush administration's push for elections in the Palestinian-controlled West Bank backfired when these were won by the radical Hamas organization, which has called for the destruction of Israel. The peace process then ground to a halt. The Bush administration, faced with mounting American public dissatisfaction over the continuing American troop presence in Iraq, concentrated on that issue to the exclusion of virtually all others, foreign and domestic.

TIM J. WATTS

See also

Abbas, Mahmoud; Bush, George Herbert Walker; Hamas; Hussein, Saddam; Iraq; Israel; Palestinian Authority; Terrorism

References

Bruni, Frank. *Ambling into History: The Unlikely Odyssey of George W. Bush.* New York: HarperCollins, 2002.

Daalder, Ivo H., and James M. Lindsay. *America Unbound: The Bush Revolution in Foreign Policy.* Washington, DC: Brookings Institution, 2003.

Schweizer, Peter. *The Bushes: Portrait of a Dynasty.* New York: Doubleday, 2004.

Singer, Peter. *The President of Good & Evil: The Ethics of George W. Bush.* New York: Dutton, 2004.

Woodward, Bob. *Bush at War.* New York: Simon and Schuster, 2002.

C

Cadogan, Alexander George Montagu
Born: November 25, 1884
Died: July 9, 1968

British civil servant, diplomat, and permanent representative to the United Nations (UN) during 1946–1950. Alexander George Montagu Cadogan was born on November 25, 1884, in Great Britain. He was the son of George Henry Cadogan, Fifth Earl Cadogan, and Lady Beatrix Jane Craven. After graduating from Eton College, the younger Cadogan joined the civil service in 1908. He was working in the British embassy in Vienna, Austria, when World War I began in 1914. From 1934 to 1936, he served as British ambassador to China.

Beginning in 1938 and during all of World War II, Cadogan was the senior civil servant (permanent secretary) in the Foreign Office. As such, he presided over all diplomatic initiatives and oversaw the day-to-day running of the Foreign Office. He was the United Kingdom's representative to the Dumbarton Oaks Conference in 1944 and was permanent secretary in the Foreign Office until 1946, at which time he became the British ambassador to the UN.

As the United Kingdom's first permanent representative to the UN, Cadogan, who was pessimistic about the potential success of the UN and concerned about the threat of international communism, presided over the dissolution of the British Mandate for Palestine in 1948. Although Arthur Creech Jones had made the announcement, it was Cadogan who orchestrated the end of the mandate. Cadogan left his post at the UN in 1950.

In 1952 Cadogan became chairman of the board of governors for the British Broadcasting Company (BBC), a position he would hold until 1957. In 1956, in addition to his BBC responsibilities, he was also a government director of the Suez Canal Company. As the 1956

Sir Alexander Cadogan, British civil servant, diplomat, and permanent representative to the United Nations (UN) during 1946–1950. (Harry S. Truman Library)

Suez Crisis escalated and Prime Minister Anthony Eden made preparations for military action, the Labour Party became increasingly critical of the government's actions. After the British bombed Egyptian airfields on October 31, 1956, following the Israeli ground invasion, Eden went on television to justify the action. Hugh Gaitskell, Labour's leader, demanded equal broadcast time to present his party's views. Over Eden's objections, Cadogan allowed Gaitskell broadcast time. Gaitskell's condemnation of the war was heard throughout the Middle East on the BBC's Arabic Service by British troops, allies, and enemies alike. Gaitskell's broadcast no doubt put even more pressure on Eden to withdraw from the Sinai and certainly boosted the efforts of foreign leaders who opposed the operation to call Eden to task for it. Neither Eden nor the Conservatives ever forgave Cadogan for his decision. Cadogan died on July 9, 1968, in London.

MICHAEL R. HALL

See also

Creech Jones, Arthur; Eden, Robert Anthony; Palestine, British Mandate for; Sinai Campaign; Suez Crisis

References

Dilks, David, ed. *The Diaries of Sir Alexander Cadogan.* New York: Putnam, 1971.

Hull, Cordell. *International Organization for the Maintenance of Peace and Security: Remarks of the Honorable Cordell Hull and Remarks of Sir Alexander Cadogan.* Washington, DC: U.S. Government Printing Office, 1944.

Residents of Jericho celebrate the signing of the Gaza-Jericho Agreement, also known as the Second Cairo Agreement, on May 4, 1994. (Avi Ohayon/Israeli Government Press Office)

Cairo Accord
Start Date: May 4, 1994

Accord signed by Israeli officials and representatives of the Palestine Liberation Organization (PLO) on May 4, 1994, in Cairo, Egypt, that led to the creation of the Palestinian Authority (PA) and to promises of land transfers by Israel. In the main public ceremony on May 4, Israeli prime minister Yitzhak Rabin and PLO chairman Yasser Arafat together signed the agreement to much fanfare. Sometimes called the Gaza-Jericho Agreement, the Cairo Accord was a direct result of the 1993 Oslo Accords and showcased the concept of land for peace whereby the Israelis agreed to turn over land to the Palestinians in return for certain guarantees. These guarantees usually took the form of security for Israel.

The accord was actually a follow-up to the Cairo Agreement of 1969. The Cairo Agreement had been designed to regulate Palestinian activity and more clearly determine the status of the refugees in Lebanon. The agreement allowed the Palestine Liberation Organization (PLO), or the Palestinian Resistance Movement as it was known at the time, the freedom to organize resistance within the camps as long as Lebanese sovereignty was maintained. In 1987 during one of the lulls during the Lebanese Civil War, a new Lebanese government abrogated the agreement, as the Palestinian leadership had been exiled to Tunis.

Terrorism against Israel continued to persist in southern Lebanon and the occupied territory of Gaza and in certain attacks planned in the West Bank. Meanwhile, Palestinian resentment toward Israel was especially strong in both the West Bank and the Gaza Strip. Displaced Palestinians all over the world had always argued for a return (al-awda) to their homes, whether in Israel or the West Bank and Gaza. With the possibility of a two-state solution, many hoped that refugees could negotiate a return to their original homes in Jericho and the Gaza Strip. Palestinians knew that many Israelis did not recognize their right of return, in contrast with the rights of world Jewry, or they hoped that a set number of refugees could be resettled or compensated. However, the Oslo Accords put off the refugee issue until a later stage of negotiation.

The Cairo Accord laid the groundwork for the PA, which would become the governing body of the Palestinians in the occupied territories. It also stipulated that the Israelis turn land over to the Palestinians. In this case, they were bound to withdraw from most of the Gaza Strip and all of Jericho. Per the agreement, Israeli forces left Gaza by the end of May 1994. Subsequent withdrawals would eventually give 95 percent of the Palestinians living in Samaria and

Judea (West Bank) control over their own affairs. In return, the Palestinians were to end any support for terrorism against Israel or Israeli citizens and actively participate in an antiterror campaign designed to deter rogue elements from engaging in acts of violence. Other particulars of the agreement included joint Palestinian-Israeli civic and security arrangements and economic protocols.

Immediately after the signing of the Cairo Accord, the Palestinians made preparations for the PA's first elections, which were a prerequisite to Palestinian self-government. Those elections were held in January 1996, and a legislative assembly was elected and seated. In those same elections, Arafat became the PA's first president.

Since May 1994 the peace process has remained volatile, disappointing, and unpredictable. In many ways, the Cairo Accord marked the high point of Israeli-Palestinian cooperation. In November 1995, Rabin was assassinated by an Israeli right-winger. The Palestinians have been unable to stem the tide of attacks on Israel, so Israel has not moved forward with its withdrawals according to the agreed-upon timetables. Subsequent agreements have also been abrogated by both sides. By the late 1990s, Israel's hard-line Likud Party, generally disdainful of the land-for-peace formula, had placed any further movement toward accommodation with the Palestinians on hold. For their part, the Palestinians have not done enough to curb violence, which accelerated dramatically after the start of the Second (al-Aqsa) Intifada in September 2000, provoked in part by Likud leader Ariel Sharon's visit to the Temple Mount. The Cairo Accord remains only partly realized, and only time will tell if the peace process regains the momentum it had in the early 1990s.

CHARLES F. HOWLETT AND PAUL G. PIERPAOLI JR.

See also

Arafat, Yasser; Gaza Strip; Intifada, Second; Israel; Likud Party; Oslo Accords; Palestine Liberation Organization; Palestinian Authority; Rabin, Yitzhak; West Bank

References

Brown, Nathan J. *Palestinian Politics after the Oslo Accords: Resuming Arab Palestine.* Berkeley: University of California Press, 2003.

Freedman, Robert Owen, ed. *The Middle East and the Peace Process: The Impact of the Oslo Accords.* Gainesville: University Press of Florida, 1998.

Weinberger, Peter. *Co-opting the PLO: A Critical Reconstruction of the Oslo Accords, 1993–1995.* New York: Rowman and Littlefield, 2006.

Cairo Agreement
Start Date: November 3, 1969
End Date: June 1982

Agreement brokered by Egyptian president Gamal Abdel Nasser regarding Lebanon and signed in Cairo on November 3, 1969, by Yasser Arafat, chairman of the Palestine Liberation Organization (PLO), and Lebanese Army commander general Emile al-Bustani. Al-Bustani was acting under the authority of then–Lebanese pres-

Egyptian president Gamal Abdel Nasser (*right*) meets with Yasser Arafat, chairman of the Palestine Liberation Organization (PLO), on November 2, 1969, at Cairo, Egypt, in an effort to end fighting between Lebanese troops and guerrilla forces. (Bettmann/Corbis)

ident Charles (Sharl) Hilu. The negotiations took place in Cairo in the presence of Egypt's Minister of Foreign Affairs Mahmud Riyadh and Minister of War Muhammad Fawzi. The agreement allowed the PLO to operate in refugee camps in southern Lebanon and to recruit, arm, train, and employ fighters against Israel while using Lebanon as its primary base of military operations. The Cairo Agreement was an attempt to regulate Palestinian political and military activity in Lebanon while respecting Lebanese sovereignty.

Following the end of the June 1967 Six-Day War, more than 400,000 Palestinian refugees had settled in refugee camps in southern Lebanon as well as in the coastal cities of Tyre and Sidon. Within the refugee population, various Palestinian political factions were eager to establish a new front for attacks against Israel particularly after the revolution of 1969. The Lebanese government and its army sought to restrain the Palestinians from such activities. Palestinians in Lebanon, whether arriving before or after 1967, had no rights. They were not allowed to join the army or government service, as were Palestinians in Jordan. Instead, Palestinians in Lebanon were attacked by the Lebanese Army, repressed by the Deuxieme Bureau government agents, and typically denied work or travel permits. Most lived in extreme poverty, existing on day labor if available. Those who could obtain education tried to emigrate or began political

Israeli foreign minister Shimon Peres, Israeli prime minister Yitzhak Rabin, Egyptian president Hosni Mubarek, and U.S. secretary of state Warren Christopher shown here during an effort to convince Yasser Arafat (*center right*), chairman of the Palestine Liberation Organization (PLO), to sign the Cairo Agreement in 1994. (Tsvika Israeli/Israeli Government Press Office)

information work, while camp Palestinians supported the armed struggle. Some Lebanese factions feared that the presence of the Palestinians would endanger the fragile communal and political balance in Lebanon and that raids into Israel would prompt retaliatory Israeli raids into Lebanon. Other groups saw the Palestinians as an ally in the process of political transformation. Non-Palestinians in southern Lebanon joined the fedayeen, or freedom fighters. As such, relations between Lebanon and the PLO deteriorated when Palestinian fedayeen, supported by the Muslim and Druze communities, openly clashed with the Maronite-dominated government forces throughout southern Lebanon in October 1969. In an effort to mediate the conflict between PLO forces and the Lebanese Army, Nasser brokered the Cairo Agreement, which defined the extent to which Palestinian commando, military, and political activities could be carried out in Lebanon.

The Cairo Agreement granted the PLO virtual autonomy in southern Lebanon. While the PLO was allowed to carry out attacks against Israel from Lebanese soil, the PLO agreed to fire on Israel from within the Jewish state. The accord also stipulated that the various Palestinian factions were free to train and carry arms within the confines of their refugee camps. The Palestinians were also granted unimpeded transit to Lebanon's border with Israel. In addition, PLO camps were required to be located away from Lebanese towns. The Cairo Agreement ultimately resulted in the establishment of an autonomous area within Lebanon under PLO control. Arafat and the PLO were successful in gaining diplomatic recognition from a number of states while establishing diplomatic missions in more than 100 countries.

Even though the aim of the Cairo Agreement was to control Palestinian military and political activity in Lebanon, it failed to do so. PLO guerrillas enjoyed free rein in southern Lebanon, which lay beyond Beirut's control. Many of the most infamous Palestinian terrorist attacks of the 1970s were planned or originated in Lebanon. The border area soon became a launching site for Palestinian attacks against Israel and Israeli reprisals. Some Lebanese were unhappy with the terms of the accord because repeated PLO guerrilla attacks from Lebanon against Israel caused the Israelis to retaliate. The Israelis argued that it was Beirut's responsibility to secure its own borders, yet the Lebanese had virtually no control over PLO actions in southern Lebanon. Thus, the Cairo Agreement proved a bane to the Lebanese, who were constantly caught between the Palestinians and Israelis, but its advocates believed that it prevented a Black September–type organization from emerging in Lebanon.

In the long term, the Cairo Agreement was significant in that it legitimized an armed Palestinian presence in Lebanon and established the PLO as a state within a state. The agreement also prevented the Palestinians from assimilating into Lebanese society, and they were both discriminated against and suffered economically. Both sides broke the terms of the agreement when it suited their own interests. Following the June 1982 Israeli invasion of southern Lebanon, which resulted in the PLO expulsion from Beirut, the Cairo Agreement became virtually meaningless. Another effect of the accord was increased tensions within Lebanon between Christians and Muslims as well as between Lebanese and Palestinian Arabs. This would eventually lead to civil war.

KEITH A. LEITICH

See also

Arafat, Yasser; Fedayeen; Lebanon; Lebanon, Civil War in; Lebanon, Israeli Invasion of; Nasser, Gamal Abdel; Palestine Liberation Organization; Six-Day War

References

El-Khazen, Farid. *The Breakdown of the State in Lebanon, 1967–1976.* Cambridge: Harvard University Press, 2000.

Gresh, Alain, and Dominique Vidal. *The New A–Z of the Middle East.* New York: Tauris, 2004.

Khalaf, Samir. *Civil and Uncivil Violence in Lebanon: A History of the Internationalization of Communal Conflict.* New York: Columbia University Press, 2004.

Sayigh, Rosemary. *Palestinians from Peasants to Revolutionaries.* London: Zed, 1979.

Cairo Declaration, Palestine Liberation Organization
Event Date: November 7, 1985

Official declaration by Palestine Liberation Organization (PLO) chairman Yasser Arafat on November 7, 1985, denouncing terrorism. As the late 1970s and early 1980s progressed, the PLO found itself in a rather isolated position in world affairs. While it certainly enjoyed the support of many non-Palestinian Arabs and more than a few Arab governments, it was having a difficult time currying favor among Western nations. Also, the PLO's forced move to Tunis in 1982 diminished the organization's effectiveness, and the 1979 Egyptian-Israeli peace agreement made Arab rapprochement with Israel an attainable goal. Thus, by 1985 Arafat and much of the PLO leadership decided that a fresh approach to the Palestinian dilemma was needed. The organization also knew that it would have to soften its rhetoric considerably in order to engage in discussions with U.S. policymakers.

Arafat was a keen politician, so he knew that gaining entrance to Western diplomatic circles would provide an enormous boost to the PLO's standing and would build legitimacy for the Palestinian cause. However, the United States had made it an official policy not to engage in any discussions with the PLO unless it abandoned terror tactics, recognized Israel's right to exist, and accepted United Nations (UN) Resolution 242, passed in 1967. Thus, Arafat and the Palestinian Legislative Council decided to alter their tactics.

Critics charged that Arafat's declaration was a rhetorical sleight of hand. Affirming an earlier pledge to eschew terrorism outside Israel and Palestine, Arafat now went further and vowed that henceforth the PLO would take "deterrent" steps against individuals or groups who violated this pledge. However, in the very same declaration, the PLO affirmed that the struggle against the "Israeli occupation" would continue "by all means possible," to include "armed struggle." While "terrorism" was now off limits, the continuing armed struggle against Israel would not end. Without such a declaration, the PLO would have lost its popular support. Many in the West, not necessarily understanding Palestinian fatigue with victimhood, believed that "armed struggle" was merely a euphemism for "terrorism" in the occupied territories or elsewhere. As such, the Cairo Declaration brought the PLO no new diplomatic openings with the West. Yet it did seem to signal the beginning of a change in the PLO's modus operandi.

Arafat had to move slowly and incrementally. Indeed, there was a hard-line constituency within the PLO that would not have been satisfied with sudden compromise and grand diplomatic overtures. Many on the Arab Left would likewise not have taken in good stride a great tactical turn on the part of the PLO. Three years later, the PLO would meet the West halfway by officially recognizing the State of Israel in the Algiers Declaration (1988). Yet rhetorical window dressing aside, there is ample evidence to suggest that some individuals within the PLO had not abandoned terrorism and clandestinely supported such activity during and after the Oslo Accords of 1993.

PAUL G. PIERPAOLI JR.

See also

Algiers Declaration; Arafat, Yasser; Palestine Liberation Organization; Palestinian Legislative Council; United Nations Security Council Resolution 242

References

Abbas, Mahmoud. *Through Secret Channels: The Road to Oslo; Senior PLO Leader Abu Mazen's Revealing Story of the Negotiations with Israel.* Reading, UK: Garnet, 1997.

Aburish, Said K. *Arafat: From Defender to Dictator.* New York: Bloomsbury, 1998.

Livingstone, Neil C., and David Haley. *Inside the PLO.* New York: William Morrow, 1990.

Rubin, Barry. *Revolution until Victory? The Politics and History of the PLO.* Reprint ed. Cambridge: Harvard University Press, 2003.

Camp David Accords
Start Date: September 5, 1978
End Date: September 17, 1978

Peace agreement reached between Egypt and Israel in September 1978 at Camp David, the U.S. presidential retreat in rural Maryland.

U.S. president Jimmy Carter locks hands with Egyptian president Anwar Sadat (*left*) and Israeli prime minister Menachem Begin (*right*) after the signing of the Camp David Accords on September 17, 1978. (Jimmy Carter Library)

During 1977 and 1978, several remarkable events took place that set the stage for the Camp David negotiations. In autumn 1977, Egyptian president Anwar Sadat indicated his willingness to go to Israel in the cause of peace, something that no Arab leader had done since the creation of the Jewish state in 1948. On November 19, 1977, Sadat followed through on his promise, addressing the Knesset (Israeli parliament) and calling for peace between the two nations. The Israelis welcomed Sadat's bold initiative but took no immediate steps to end the state of belligerency, instead agreeing to ministerial-level meetings in preparation for final negotiations.

In February 1978, the United States entered into the equation by hosting Sadat in Washington, with both President Jimmy Carter and Congress hailing the Egyptian president as a statesman and a courageous leader. American adulation for Sadat led to greater cooperation by the Israelis, and they thus agreed to a summit meeting in September at Camp David.

During September 5–17, 1978, Carter hosted a conference that brought together Sadat and Israeli prime minister Menachem Begin

and their respective staffs at Camp David. Carter participated as an active player in the resultant talks. As was expected, the discussions proved difficult. Begin insisted that Sadat separate the Palestinian issue from the peace talks, something that no Arab leader had been willing to do before. Israel also demanded that Egypt negate any former agreements with other Arab nations that called for war against Israel.

Sadat bristled at Begin's demands, which led to such acrimony between the two men that they met in person only once during the entire negotiation process. Instead, Carter shuttled between the two leaders in an effort to moderate their positions. After several days of little movement and accusations of bad faith directed mostly at Begin, however, Carter threatened to break off the talks. Faced with the possibility of being blamed for a failed peace plan, Begin finally came to the table ready to deal. He agreed to dismantle all Jewish settlements in the Sinai Peninsula and return it in its entirety to Egypt. For his part, given Begin's absolute intransigence on it, Sadat agreed to put the Palestinian issue aside and sign an agreement

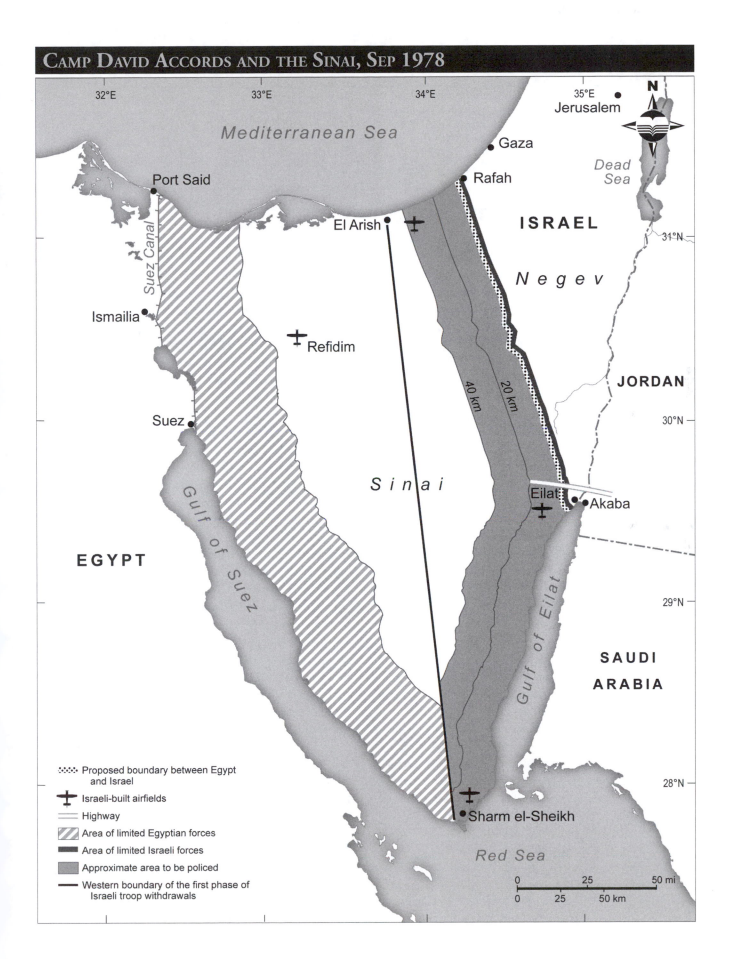

CAMP DAVID ACCORDS AND THE SINAI, SEP 1978

Mediterranean Sea

Port Said

El Arish

Gaza

Rafah

Jerusalem

Dead Sea

ISRAEL

Negev

Ismailia

Refidim

40 km

20 km

JORDAN

Suez

Sinai

Eilat

Akaba

EGYPT

Gulf of Suez

Gulf of Eilat

SAUDI

ARABIA

Sharm el-Sheikh

Red Sea

Proposed boundary between Egypt and Israel

Israeli-built airfields

Highway

Area of limited Egyptian forces

Area of limited Israeli forces

Approximate area to be policed

Western boundary of the first phase of Israeli troop withdrawals

0   25   50 mi

0   25   50 km

Important Peace Treaties and Conferences

Date	Name	Parties
September 1978	Camp David Accords	Egypt; Israel
March 26, 1979	Israel-Egypt Treaty	Egypt; Israel
October–November 1991	Madrid Conference	Israel; Jordan; Lebanon; Palestinians; Syria
September 13, 1993	Oslo Accords	Israel; PLO
October 26, 1994	Israel-Jordan Peace Treaty	Israel; Jordan
October 23, 1998	Wye River Memorandum	Israel; PA
July 2000	Camp David Summit	Israel; PLO
January 2001	Taba Summit	Israel; PA
December 1, 2003	Geneva Convention	Israel; PLO

separate from the other Arab nations. On September 15, 1978, Carter, Sadat, and Begin announced that an agreement had been reached on two frameworks, the first for a peace treaty between Egypt and Israel and the second for a multilateral treaty dealing with the West Bank and the Gaza Strip.

The framework regarding Egypt and Israel had 11 major provisions: (1) the two nations would sign a peace treaty within three months; (2) this treaty would be implemented within two to three years after it was signed; (3) Egypt would regain full sovereignty of the Sinai to its pre–Six-Day War (1967) borders; (4) Israel would withdraw its forces from the Sinai, with the first such withdrawal to occur nine months after signature of the treaty; (5) Israel was to have freedom of navigation through the Suez Canal and the Strait of Tiran; (6) a highway would be built between the Sinai and Jordan to pass near Eilat with the guarantee of free passage through Israeli territory for both nations; (7) Egyptian forces in the Sinai would be limited to one division in the area 30 miles (50 km) east of the Gulf of Suez and the Suez Canal; (8) there would be no other Egyptian forces in the Sinai; (9) Israeli forces would be restricted to four infantry battalions in the area 1.8 miles (3 km) east of the international border with Egypt; (10) United Nations (UN) forces would be positioned in certain areas; and (11) the peace between the two nations would be complete, including full diplomatic recognition and an end to any economic restrictions on the other nation's goods, with free movement of goods and people.

The second framework, officially known as the "Framework of Peace in the Middle East," was far more general and skirted major issues. It contained seven major provisions: (1) UN Security Council Resolutions 242 and 338 were recognized as holding "in all their parts" the basis for a peace settlement; (2) the peace settlement would be negotiated by Egypt, Israel, Jordan, and "the representatives of the Palestinian people"; (3) residents of the West Bank and Gaza would secure "full autonomy"; (4) Egypt, Israel, and Jordan were to agree on "modalities for establishing the elected self-governing authority" in these areas, and the Egyptian and Jordanian delegations "may include Palestinians from the West Bank and Gaza or other Palestinians as mutually agreed"; (5) a withdrawal of Israeli forces would occur, with remaining forces grouped in certain agreed-upon locations; (6) as soon as the self-governing authority ("admin-

istrative council") had been established, a five-year transitional period would begin, by the end of which the final status of the West Bank and Gaza would have been agreed to, understanding that there would be recognition of "the legitimate rights of the Palestinian people and their just requirements"; and (7) in the transitional period, representatives of Egypt, Israel, and Jordan as well as those of the self-governing authority "will constitute a continuing committee" to agree on "the modalities of admission of peoples displaced from the West Bank and Gaza in 1967."

Despite a feeling of euphoria in the United States and an upward spike in Carter's approval ratings, the agreement in fact was a retreat from the president's own program in 1977 that called for Israeli withdrawal from the occupied lands with only minor territorial adjustments and a homeland for the Palestinian people based on self-determination rather than on autonomy under Israeli administrative control. Much was also simply left out. There was no mention in the framework of the future of Jerusalem and the Golan Heights or about Israeli settlements in the West Bank and the future of the Palestine Liberation Organization (PLO), which the United States steadfastly refused to recognize.

Over the next several months, Secretary of State Cyrus Vance made numerous trips to the Middle East to finalize the agreement. The United States promised that it would help organize an international peacekeeping force to occupy the Sinai following the Israeli withdrawal. Washington also agreed to provide $2 billion to pay for the relocation of an airfield from the Sinai to Israel and promised economic assistance to Egypt in exchange for Sadat's signature on a peace treaty.

Finally, on March 26, 1979, in a White House ceremony, Sadat and Begin shook hands again and signed a permanent peace treaty, normalizing relations between their two nations. Hopes that other Arab nations, particularly the pro-Western regimes in Jordan and Saudi Arabia, would soon follow Egypt's lead and sign similar agreements with Israel were quickly dashed. Indeed, the Camp David Accords produced a strong negative reaction in the Arab world, where other states and the PLO denounced the agreement and condemned Sadat for having "sold out" the Arab cause. Egypt was expelled from the Arab League, and several Middle Eastern nations broke off diplomatic relations with Cairo. Not until the mid-1990s would another Arab nation, Jordan, join Egypt in normalizing relations with Israel. Nonetheless, the Camp David Accords were, without doubt, President Carter's greatest foreign policy success.

BRENT GEARY AND SPENCER C. TUCKER

See also

Begin, Menachem; Brzezinski, Zbigniew; Carter, James Earl, Jr.; Egypt; Israel; Palestine Liberation Organization; Sadat, Anwar

References

Brzezinski, Zbigniew. *Power and Principle: Memoirs of the National Security Adviser, 1977–1981.* New York: Farrar, Straus and Giroux, 1985.

Carter, James E. *Keeping Faith: Memoirs of the President.* New York: Bantam, 1982.

Lenczowski, George. *The Middle East in World Affairs.* 4th ed. Ithaca, NY: Cornell University Press, 1980.

Quandt, William. *Camp David: Peacemaking and Politics.* Washington, DC: Brookings Institution, 1986.

Telhami, Shibley. *Power and Leadership in International Bargaining: The Path to the Camp David Accords.* New York: Columbia University Press, 1990.

Cantonization Plan

See Morrison-Grady Plan

Carmel, Moshe

Born: January 17, 1911
Died: August 14, 2003

Israeli Army officer and politician. Moshe Carmel was born in Minsk (Mazowiecki), then part of Russia and now belonging to Belarus, on January 17, 1911.

Carmel immigrated to Palestine in 1924. In the 1930s he joined the Haganah underground Jewish militia organized to protect Jewish settlements from Arab attacks and became one of its leaders. He was arrested for this activity and imprisoned by the British Mandate authorities during 1939–1941.

Following his release from prison, Carmel resumed his military career. He became the military commander of the Haifa district in 1947. During the Israeli War of Independence (1948–1949), the Haifa district was the northern front.

In April 1948, Carmel's brigade attacked the port city of Haifa. After the city fell on April 22, all but 4,000 of its 70,000 Arab residents fled the city. In May 1948, when the Arab armies invaded Israel, Carmel's brigade was the only one to hold its part of the front. On May 18, the brigade captured Acre, a city in the Arab section of Palestine.

Carmel led Operation HIRAM in late October 1948 that resulted in the Israeli military capturing large areas in Galilee, including the city of Nazareth, which the United Nations (UN) partition plan had allocated to the Arabs.

Moshe Carmel, Israeli army officer and politician, shown in December 1969. (Israeli Government Press Office)

During Operation HIRAM, Carmel instructed his commanders to purge the conquered territories of all enemy elements. For this reason, some historians identify Carmel as a cause of the Palestinian refugee crisis.

Carmel retired from the Israel Defense Forces (IDF) as a major general in 1958. From 1955 until 1977, he served in the Knesset (Israeli parliament). He was the parliamentary leader of the Unity of Labor Party until it merged with Mapai to form the Labor Party in 1969. Carmel served several terms as minister of transport. He also served as director of El Al, Israel's national airline. Carmel died in Tel Aviv on August 14, 2003.

DAVE RAUSCH

See also

Haganah; Israel, Arab Population in; Israeli War of Independence, Overview

References

Herzog, Chaim. *The Arab-Israeli Wars: War and Peace in the Middle East from the War of Independence to Lebanon.* Westminster, MD: Random House, 1984.

Morris, Benny. *The Birth of the Palestinian Refugee Problem Revisited.* 2nd ed. Cambridge: Cambridge University Press, 2004.

Carter, James Earl, Jr.
Born: October 1, 1924

U.S. Navy officer, Democratic Party politician, governor of Georgia (1971–1975), president of the United States (1977–1981), and Nobel laureate (2002). Born on October 1, 1924, in Plains, Georgia, James "Jimmy" Carter was raised on his family's farm close to the town of Archery, Georgia. After having attended Georgia Southwestern College and the Georgia Institute of Technology, he graduated from the U.S. Naval Academy in 1946. He then pursued graduate work in physics at Union College and spent seven years as a naval officer working under Admiral Hyman Rickover in the nuclear submarine program. Carter eventually served on the nuclear submarine *Seawolf.*

Carter left the navy and returned to Georgia upon his father's death in 1953 to run the family farm, eventually building it into a large and prosperous enterprise. He became actively involved in a number of local boards dealing with education and health care. Carter entered state politics in 1962, serving two terms in the Georgia Senate. He also became a born-again Christian with a profound commitment to his Baptist faith. In 1966 he ran unsuccessfully for governor of Georgia. He spent the next several years tending to his booming agricultural concerns and methodically laying the groundwork for his planned 1970 gubernatorial campaign. Having given some 1,800 speeches across the state, he was elected governor of Georgia in 1970. As governor, he pursued a moderate approach. He also sought to bridge the racial divide by appointing African Americans to state offices, and he was the first governor from the Deep South to publicly denounce racial discrimination and segregation.

In December 1974 amid the fallout of the Watergate Scandal and an economy mired in a deep recession and plagued by high inflation, Carter decided to run for the presidency. Running as a Washington outsider who promised to restore honesty and integrity to government, he secured the Democratic Party nomination. Attracted by his modesty, integrity, and moderate positions, many voters threw their support behind him. He went on to win the presidential election of November 1976 by a narrow margin.

Carter's first major act as president in January 1977 was to extend a pardon to draft evaders, military deserters, and others who had violated the Selective Service Act from 1964 to 1973 during the controversial Vietnam War. The psychic and political wounds from Vietnam had yet to heal, and the nation still remained deeply divided over its involvement in the war. Carter's move generated controversy among the public and elicited criticism from Congress, which contributed to a rift between it and the administration that only widened during the Carter presidency.

Carter was unable to inspire public confidence or to fulfill his election promise to end stagflation (rampant inflation coupled with economic recession). To solve the ongoing energy crisis, a contributory factor to economic stagnation, he proposed energy taxes, limits on imported oil, and greater reliance on domestic sources of energy. Congress largely stymied these plans. The Carter administration also deregulated the nation's airline industry, passed major environmental legislation to encourage cleanup of hazardous waste sites, revamped the civil service, and created the Departments of Energy and Education.

Carter frequently criticized other nations for human rights abuses, often linking economic and military cooperation to a country's commitment to the American ideals of freedom and equality. Such disapproval of the Soviets' treatment of political dissidents undermined détente and delayed SALT II (Strategic Arms Limitation Treaty) negotiations, which finally resulted in a 1979 treaty never ratified by Congress because of the Soviet invasion of Afghanistan that same year. In response to the Afghan situation, the administration enunciated the Carter Doctrine, which committed the United States to protecting oil interests in the Persian Gulf. Carter also imposed a controversial and ineffective American grain embargo on the Soviet Union and ordered a U.S. boycott of the 1980 Olympic Games in Moscow. In January 1979 he also extended full diplomatic recognition to the People's Republic of China (PRC), effectively cutting most American ties with Taiwan.

Perhaps Carter's singular achievement as president came in his brokering of a peace between Israel and Egypt. He invited Egyptian president Anwar Sadat and Israeli prime minister Menachem Begin to the presidential retreat at Camp David, Maryland, in September 1978. The meetings between the heretofore implacable enemies were tense and nearly broke down numerous times. When Sadat threatened to quit the talks, Carter personally implored him to stay, and Sadat agreed. Begin also wanted to end the talks at one point, and Carter prevailed upon him to see the negotiations through.

Following two weeks of intense negotiations, a deal was reached for a peace treaty between Israel and Egypt, known as the Camp David Accords. The treaty was signed on March 26, 1979. The accords represented a true diplomatic breakthrough, provided a framework for future Middle East peace initiatives, and helped temporarily bolster Carter's sagging popularity.

In September 1977 Carter signed the controversial Panama Canal Treaties, ceding the canal to Panama and ensuring the neutrality of the waterway. Congress narrowly ratified the treaties in March 1978, but Carter nevertheless came under additional fire for having ceded an important U.S. strategic interest.

If the Camp David Accords and the prospects of a wider peace in the Middle East were the most important of Carter's legacies, another conflict in the Middle East ultimately brought about his downfall. Indeed, the 1979–1980 Iranian hostage crisis doomed Carter's presidency. The genesis of the crisis was the steadfast and long-standing U.S. support of Mohammad Reza Shah Pahlavi of Iran. Since 1953 when the U.S. Central Intelligence Agency (CIA) helped engineer the overthrow of Mohammad Mosaddeq that paved the way for the shah's autocratic rule, the United States had supported the shah and sold him billions of dollars of weaponry. Despite the shah's blatant human rights abuses and increasingly dictatorial rule, the United States saw him as a key ally and an

Jimmy Carter, president of the United States during 1977–1981. Carter signed the Camp David Accords with Egyptian president Anwar Sadat and Israeli prime minister Menachem Begin on September 17, 1978. (Library of Congress)

important stabilizing force in the volatile Middle East. The presidential administrations of Richard M. Nixon and Gerald R. Ford particularly sought to use the shah as a way to keep Soviet influence in the region to a minimum and to counteract Pan-Arabism. As protests and violence against the shah's rule increased in 1978 and early 1979, the Carter administration attempted to remain above the fray. Carter himself publicly praised the shah.

On January 16, 1979, however, a popular revolution forced the shah to flee Iran with his family. At first, Carter sought to recognize the new and interim revolutionary regime, but these efforts proved in vain. There was little chance that Carter's initiative would have lasted, however. In February, Ayatollah Ruhollah Khomeini arrived in Iran after years of exile. This fundamentalist cleric, who was rabidly anti-Western and anti-American, sought to establish an Islamic republic in Iran. A plebiscite in the spring of 1979 overwhelmingly endorsed such a step, and Khomeini now became the leader of Iran.

In October 1979 the Carter administration decided to admit the shah to the United States for badly needed cancer treatment. Although he remained in the country for only a few weeks, the move enraged radical Iranian militants, egged on by Khomeini. In November 1979 a group of radical Iranian students seized the U.S. embassy in Tehran, taking the Americans there hostage. Carter struggled tirelessly to defuse the crisis through diplomacy, but the Iran hostage

crisis dragged on for 444 days and ruined his presidency. In the meantime the price of oil rose dramatically, adversely affecting the U.S. economy. Interestingly, Carter never invoked the Carter Doctrine to protect Middle East oil. Such a move probably would have invited disaster, given the Soviet Union's December 1979 invasion of Afghanistan and the resultant tense relations between Moscow and Washington. In April 1980 a U.S. hostage rescue attempt failed, and Secretary of State Cyrus R. Vance resigned in protest against the operation. The crisis and failure of the rescue attempt contributed greatly to Carter's defeat in the November 1980 presidential election. The hostages were released on January 20, 1981, only moments after Ronald Reagan was sworn in as president.

Carter has continued leading a vigorous public life following his presidency, acting as a mediator in international conflicts, working on the eradication of poverty, supervising elections in the developing world, promoting human rights, and writing books and memoirs. In 2002 he was awarded the Nobel Peace Prize for his accomplishments.

One of Carter's books, *Palestine: Peace Not Apartheid*, published in 2006, created considerable controversy. In it, Carter holds that Israel's "continued control and colonization" of Palestinian territory remain "the primary obstacles" to a peace settlement. He also declares that Israeli policies in the occupied territories constitute "a system of apartheid" in which the two peoples are completely separate, "with Israelis totally dominant and suppressing violence by depriving Palestinians of their basic human rights." Many praised Carter for his candor, while others condemned the book as one-sided and filled with misconceptions.

JOSIP MOCNIK AND PAUL G. PIERPAOLI JR.

See also

Begin, Menachem; Camp David Accords; Iran; Khomeini, Ruhollah; Reza Pahlavi, Mohammad, Shah of Iran; Sadat, Anwar

References

Brinkley, Douglas. *The Unfinished Presidency: Jimmy Carter's Journey beyond the White House.* New York: Viking, 1998.

Carter, James E. *Keeping Faith: Memoirs of the President.* New York: Bantam, 1982.

Kaufman, Burton I. *The Presidency of James Earl Carter, Jr.* Lawrence: University Press of Kansas, 1993.

Maga, Timothy P. *The World of Jimmy Carter: Foreign Policy, 1977–1981.* New Haven, CT: University of New Haven Press, 1994.

Strong, Robert A. *Working in the World: Jimmy Carter and the Making of American Foreign Policy.* Baton Rouge: Louisiana State University Press, 2000.

Central Treaty Organization

See Baghdad Pact

Chakkour, Youssef

See Shakur, Yusuf bin Raghib

Chamberlain, Joseph
Born: July 8, 1836
Died: July 2, 1914

British politician and secretary of state for the colonies (1895–1903). Joseph Chamberlain was born in London on July 8, 1836. His father owned a wholesale boot and shoe business. Despite being a good student, Chamberlain did not attend college but joined his father in the family business for two years, learning the craft of cordwaining. He also taught Sunday school in the slums of south London, where he saw firsthand the effects of urban poverty and became interested in social reform. Chamberlain was also a religious dissenter. He and his family were Unitarians.

In 1854 Chamberlain moved to Birmingham to join his uncle's wood screw business. His uncle purchased a patent that allowed him to manufacture a revolutionary wood screw with a pointed end. This business eventually made Chamberlain quite wealthy. He sold it in 1874.

In 1869 Chamberlain became a Birmingham town councilor. An advocate of free, secular, and compulsory elementary education, he was mayor of Birmingham during 1873–1876. An advocate of social reform, he began a program of slum clearance that endeared him to the working-class population of Birmingham.

In 1876 Chamberlain won election to Parliament as a Liberal from Birmingham. Throughout his parliamentary career, he supported such liberal policies as the expansion and improvement of free public schools and better conditions for the working class. In 1880 he became president of the Board of Trade in Prime Minister William Gladstone's cabinet and carried out numerous reforms. Chamberlain and a number of other Liberals split with Gladstone on the issue of home rule for Ireland, however. Their opposition led to the formation of the Liberal Unionist Party.

In 1895 Chamberlain became colonial secretary in the cabinet of Conservative prime minister Lord Salisbury, a position that Chamberlain also held in Arthur James Balfour's cabinet until 1903. In his new post, Chamberlain lobbied for an increase in British military forces around the world and became a staunch supporter of the South African War (Boer War) of 1899–1902. While in office, he developed plans to foster imperial trade that would provide preferential treatment to colonial imports and protection for English manufacturers.

Chamberlain met Zionist leader Theodor Herzl in October 1902, during which time Herzl asked for British government support for the establishment of an autonomous Jewish settlement in the Sinai Peninsula (the El Arish Scheme). According to Herzl's diaries, Chamberlain supported the plan and referred the Zionist leader to Foreign Secretary Lord Lansdowne but also told Herzl that the plan would have to be proposed by Lord Cromer, British consul general in Egypt, who was then running Egyptian affairs. The plan ultimately collapsed under Egyptian government opposition.

Joseph Chamberlain, British politician and secretary of state for the colonies during 1895–1903. (Library of Congress)

In April 1903 Chamberlain again met with Herzl and suggested instead a self-governing Jewish settlement for immigrants in Uganda. This plan became known as the East Africa Scheme. Although Herzl presented the East Africa Scheme to the Sixth Zionist Congress at Basel, Switzerland, that October, it too was never realized. In any case, Chamberlain left office in September 1903. He continued to voice support for a Jewish settlement within the British Empire and expressed great admiration for Herzl.

Chamberlain suffered a paralytic stroke in July 1906, although he made a partial recovery. He died in London of a heart attack on July 2, 1914. Despite never becoming prime minister, he was one of the most important British politicians of the era. He was also the father of British statesmen Sir Austen Chamberlain (1863–1937) and Neville Chamberlain (1869–1940).

Spencer C. Tucker

See also

Balfour, Arthur James; East Africa Scheme; El Arish Scheme; Herzl, Theodor; United Kingdom, Middle East Policy; Zionism

References

Browne, Harry. *Joseph Chamberlain: Radical and Imperialist.* London: Longman, 1983.

Fraser, Peter. *Joseph Chamberlain: Radicalism and Empire, 1868–1914.* New York: A. S. Barnes, 1967.

Marsh, Peter T. *Joseph Chamberlain: Entrepreneur in Politics.* New Haven, CT: Yale University Press, 1994.

Chamoun, Camille
Born: April 3, 1900
Died: August 7, 1987

Prominent Lebanese politician and premier. Camille Chamoun (Kamil Shamun) was born on April 3, 1900, into a prominent Maronite Christian family at Deir al-Qamar in Lebanon. Although a Maronite Christian, he came from the Shuf district where many Muslin Druze lived, and he thus understood the principle of local support. The Druze, largely concentrated in Lebanon's Shuf Mountains and western Beirut, had once dominated Mount Lebanon and the Maronites. The latter gained social ascendancy. The Maronites, originally followers of St. Maroun, are Eastern-rite Catholics recognized by Rome in the sixth century and were largely concentrated in the Mount Lebanon district, eastern Beirut, and some areas of southern Lebanon. Muslims and Christians first experienced a serious violent conflict in 1860 in present-day Syria and Lebanon. Lebanese political tensions between religious groups also had roots in economics, as some Maronites became wealthy through commerce. They opposed the unification with Syria preferred by some Muslims and other Christian groups. Each sect possessed feudal lords who commanded the political loyalties of peasants or residents of urban areas.

Chamoun received his elementary education at a Catholic school in Deir al-Qamar and graduated from high school in Beirut in a Francophone educational system. During World War I, the Chamoun family was exiled for anti-Turkish and Lebanese nationalist activities on the part of Chamoun's father. Following the war Lebanon became a French mandate, and French colonialism thus became a target of Lebanese nationalists. Chamoun, meanwhile, immersed himself in his studies. Upon graduation from the Faculty of Law at the University of Saint Joseph in Beirut and obtaining his law license in 1923, he became a successful lawyer, businessman, and property holder. He also began expressing his political views in articles for the newspaper *Le Réveil.*

Although the economy had expanded during the French mandate, there was much about the system of French-dominated governance that the Lebanese disliked, including press censorship and preference for French investors. Chamoun wanted this situation changed. In 1929 he won his first election campaign and became an elector, whose duty it was to help choose delegates to Lebanon's National Assembly. That year, he also married Zalfa Thabit, whose family had important connections in British social circles. Chamoun subsequently learned English and developed contacts with British politicians.

Lebanese politician and premier Camille Chamoun. (UPI-Bettmann/Corbis)

Chamoun's nationalism subsequently intensified, and upon winning election to the Chamber of Deputies in 1934 he sided with the Constitutional Bloc led by Sheikh Bishara al-Khuri that sought an end to French domination. Chamoun won reelection in 1937 and was appointed minister of finance (although the Constitutional Bloc was a minority party). During World War II, he emerged as one of the crucial architects of Lebanese independence. In 1941, Free French and British forces invaded Lebanon and ousted the colonial government controlled by Vichy, which had collaborated with Nazi Germany. Britain supported Lebanese independence, a move that France opposed. Chamoun lobbied the British to ensure their continued support for nationhood. Such activities earned him the label from the French of "agent of British intelligence" and led to his arrest and imprisonment in November 1943, along with al-Khuri, and Riyadh al-Sulh. Massive public demonstrations, however, led to their release after only 11 days, on November 22, a day that has since been celebrated as Lebanon's Independence Day. The French government-in-exile agreed to allow Lebanon's independence.

Elections that year made the Constitutional Bloc the majority party in the National Assembly, and al-Khuri became president and es-Sulh prime minister. Chamoun became minister of finance. Then, because of his close ties to the British, Chamoun was made ambassador to Great Britain. He held this post during 1944–1946.

Chamoun's demonstrated political acumen helped bring British support for the withdrawal of French troops at a time when the French government had developed second thoughts about relinquishing total control of Lebanon. Chamoun also secured Lebanese membership in the United Nations (UN). Now enormously popular, he planned to become president, but al-Khuri moved to amend the Lebanese Constitution to allow himself another term. Chamoun subsequently resigned his ministerial post and cooperated with the opposition National Socialist Front Party led by Kamal Jumblat (Junblat), a Druze leader. Al-Khuri remained president, but by 1951 his opponents gained a larger following, and widespread discontent over charges of corruption led to his resignation in 1952.

With Jumblat's support, Chamoun won election by the National Assembly as president. Chamoun now ran into a formidable problem. He had antagonized his Constitutional Bloc followers and many Maronites by having cooperated with Jumblat, and when he tried to win back these people, he antagonized Jumblat and many Druze, who opposed his pro-Western, conservative politics and alleged corruption. Nevertheless, Chamoun initiated several reforms: a change in the election system that weakened the domination of public office by landholding aristocrats and urban elites, suffrage for women, and an independent judiciary. The economy expanded under Chamoun, and he promoted a free exchange of ideas, including relative freedom of the press.

Yet many members of the politically disadvantaged Muslim communities objected to Chamoun's refusal to let Lebanon join the United Arab Republic (UAR) in 1958, and Pan-Arabists who favored Egyptian president Gamal Abdel Nasser held demonstrations that threatened to overthrow the government in June 1958. Chamoun believed that both his own power and Lebanese unity were imperiled. He then called on the United States for assistance, and President Dwight D. Eisenhower dispatched U.S. marines to Beirut. This action brought charges that Chamoun was a tool of Western imperialism and was too close to the pro-Israeli United States. U.S. diplomat Robert Murphy helped persuade Chamoun to resign in 1958. He was succeeded by General Fuad Shihab, a Christian who nonetheless was popular with Lebanese Muslims.

Chamoun remained politically active. In 1959 he formed a new opposition organization in 1959, the National Liberal Party (al-Ahrar), and he won election to the National Assembly in 1960 but was defeated in 1964 amid charges of gerrymandering. He again won election to the National Assembly in 1968 and 1972. He successfully maneuvered Suleiman Franjieh into the presidency in 1970. Chamoun held a succession of ministerial posts in the 1970s and 1980s.

In 1975, however, Lebanon's long-standing political and sectarian tensions erupted in civil war, and Chamoun obtained Israeli support for the Maronite forces. He helped found the Lebanese Front, heading it during 1976–1978. It was a mostly Christian grouping of different parties. Its united militia was known as the Lebanese Forces (LF). Chamoun was initially inclined toward Syria but then opposed the growing Syrian presence in Lebanon. In 1980 the LF was largely destroyed in a surprise attack by the Phalangists, the militia headed by Christian rival Bashir Gemayel.

The bloodshed in Lebanon continued. Following the Israeli invasion of Lebanon in 1982, Chamoun entered into tacit cooperation with Israel against Syria, which was then occupying much of Lebanon and controlling its affairs. In 1984 Chamoun entered the National Unity Government as deputy prime minister, but the civil war, which by the end of the decade had claimed some 130,000 lives, overwhelmed this effort. Chamoun died in office in Beirut on August 7, 1987. Four years later a peace accord was signed, although it took several more years for peace to return to most of Lebanon. Chamoun was one of the most significant figures of Lebanese politics.

SPENCER C. TUCKER

See also

Eisenhower, Dwight David; Lebanon; Lebanon, U.S. Interventions in; Murphy, Robert Daniel; Nasser, Gamal Abdel; United Arab Republic

References

Cobban, Helena. *The Making of Modern Lebanon*. London: Hutchinson, 1985.

El-Khazen, Farid. *The Breakdown of the State in Lebanon, 1967–1976*. Cambridge: Harvard University Press, 2000.

Laffin, John. *The War of Desperation: Lebanon, 1982–1985*. London: Osprey, 1985.

Chancellor, Sir John Robert
Born: October 20, 1870
Died: July 31, 1952

British Army officer, colonial administrator, and high commissioner for Palestine (1928–1931). John Robert Chancellor was born in Edinburgh, Scotland, on October 20, 1870. At age 20 he joined the British Army's Royal Engineers and rapidly advanced in rank. He served in the Dongola Expedition in 1896 and the 1897–1898 Tirah Expedition. In 1902 he graduated from the Army Staff College, served with the Intelligence Department of the War Office, and then held successive appointments in the upper echelons of the military and served as a military liaison to civilian authorities.

Chancellor began his long career as a colonial administrator in 1911 when he was named governor of Mauritius, a post he held until 1916. In 1913 he received a knighthood. From 1916 to 1921 he was governor of Trinidad and Tobago, and from 1923 to 1928 he served as the governor of Southern Rhodesia. He arrived in Palestine to serve as high commissioner of the British mandate there in 1928, just prior to the Arab Uprising of 1929–1930.

Chancellor began his tenure in Palestine with no publicly stated position on the Arab-Jewish conflict. In private, however, he seemed to favor the Arab position and was no great proponent of a Jewish state in Palestine. Furthermore, he suspected the loyalty of the Palestinian Jews to Great Britain. When Arab Palestinians pushed for more democratic representation, Chancellor appeared eager to take the issue up with London. Among other things, he hoped that the formation of an indigenous legislative council would empower Palestinian Arabs, who would curtail further Jewish immigration to Palestine.

In 1929 Chancellor traveled to London to discuss Palestinian self-government issues but was called back when Arab rioting broke out over Jewish immigration and land purchases. Upon his return, he publicly and sharply denounced the rioting but in a later proclamation took a much softer stance against the Arab violence.

In 1930 Chancellor played a significant role in the crafting of the White Paper prepared by Colonial Secretary Sidney Webb, Lord Passfield. The Passfield White Paper was designed to discourage Zionist aspirations, revoke the 1917 Balfour Declaration's support for a Jewish homeland in Palestine, and curtail future Jewish immigration to the region. The White Paper caused a storm of protest among Zionists worldwide, and in February 1931 British prime minister Ramsay MacDonald was compelled to issue a letter of conciliation to Zionists. That same year, Chancellor was recalled from Palestine.

While Chancellor was high commissioner he was never popular with Jews, including Jews already living in Palestine and those among the larger Diaspora. While it is undeniable that he was never a proponent of the Zionist vision in Palestine and favored tough restrictions on Jewish immigration, he was also acting in the larger interests of Great Britain. Indeed, as a mandatory power Britain was duty bound to treat both the Arabs and Jews in Palestine equally.

Chancellor largely left public life after 1931, but in 1945 he penned a letter to the London *Times* in which he embraced the partitioning of Palestine to stem the animosity and bloodshed that had plagued the area for years. He believed that an independent Jewish state would be virtually self-sufficient thanks in large part to donations and subsidies from wealthy Jews in Western Europe and the United States. An Arab-Palestinian state, however, would likely require monetary assistance initially, he concluded. Chancellor died on July 31, 1952, in Lanark, Scotland.

PAUL G. PIERPAOLI JR.

See also

Balfour Declaration; Palestine, British Mandate for; White Paper (1930)

References

Sachar, Howard M. *A History of Israel: From the Rise of Zionism to Our Time*. 3rd ed. New York: Knopf, 2007.
Shepherd, Naomi. *Ploughing Sand: British Rule in Palestine, 1917–1948*. New Brunswick, NJ: Rutgers University Press, 1999.

Chemical Weapons and Warfare

Chemical weapons use the toxic effects from man-made substances to kill or incapacitate enemy forces. Chemical weapons range from riot control agents such as tear gas and pepper spray, which cause short-term incapacitation, to lethal nerve agents such as tabun and sarin, which can kill humans with only a miniscule exposure. The use of living organisms, such as bacteria, viruses, or spores, is not classified as chemical warfare but rather is considered biological warfare. However, certain chemical weapons such as ricin and botulinum toxins use products created by living organisms.

Chemical weapons are typically described by the effects they have on victims. The major classes of chemical weapons are nerve agents, blood agents, vesicants, pulmonary agents, cytotoxic proteins, lachrymatory agents, and incapacitating agents. Nerve agents quickly break down neuron-transmitting synapses, resulting in the paralysis of major organs and quick death. Blood agents cause massive internal bleeding or prevent cells from using oxygen, leading to anaerobic respiration, seizures, and death. Vesicants, also known as blistering agents, burn skin and respiratory systems, either of which can be fatal. Pulmonary agents suffocate victims by flooding the respiratory system. Cytotoxic agents prevent protein synthesis, leading to the failure of one or more organs. Lachrymatory agents cause immediate eye irritation or blindness, although the effects are deliberately temporary. Incapacitating agents, also temporary, cause effects similar to drug intoxication.

The most important characteristics of an effective chemical weapon are its ability to be delivered accurately and its ability to persist as a danger to enemy troops. Throughout history, delivery methods for chemical weapons have evolved from simple dispersion, often by releasing a gas into the wind, to artillery shells or missile warheads containing chemical agents and to aerodynamic dispersal from aircraft. Since World War II, binary chemical weapons have been developed that contain two substances that are harmless by themselves but when combined form a weapons grade chemical agent.

Primitive chemical weapons were used as early as the Stone Age, when hunter-gatherer societies used poison-tipped weapons for hunting. Sources of poisons included animal venoms and vegetable toxins. Undoubtedly, poison-tipped weapons were also used in intertribal warfare. Ancient writings describe efforts to poison water systems to halt invading armies. Chinese texts from approximately 1000 BC describe methods to create and disperse poisonous smoke in war. Ancient Spartan and Athenian armies both used chemical weapons by the fifth century BC. The Roman Army, however, considered the use of poisons abhorrent, and Roman jurists condemned enemies for poisoning water supplies. With the dawn of the gunpowder era, besieging armies launched incendiary devices and poisonous projectiles into enemy fortifications. By the 19th century, inventors in Britain and the United States proposed the development of artillery shells containing toxic gasses.

During World War I (1914–1918), more chemical weapons were used than during any other war in history. At the Second Battle of Ypres (April 22, 1915), German troops opened canisters of chlorine gas and waited for the wind to push the gas into Allied trenches. Soon both sides were using artillery shells to deliver chemical attacks, incorporating a wide variety of chemical agents.

Aisha Aminpour on November 22, 2006, shows the effects of the chemical bombing of her village of Bolhassan, Kurdestan, Iran, in 1987. Aminpour, then only two years old, ran from the site of the bombing in bare feet. The chemicals progressively disfigured her feet. Unable to walk, she suffers from deep blisters that never heal. (Carlos Cazalis/Corbis)

Although they caused a great deal of panic and disruption on the battlefield and caused more than 1 million mostly nonlethal casualties in World War I, chemical weapons were never decisive by themselves. The chemical weapons of the period were relatively weak by modern standards, and no army of the time had developed nerve agents. Although early gas masks and other countermeasures were relatively primitive, they did neutralize the chemical effects to some degree. The Germans, under their artillery genius Colonel Georg Bruchmüller, came the closest to achieving decisive breakthroughs with chemical weapons during the 1918 offensives, but the German Army didn't have the operational mobility to exploit the tactical advantage.

During World War II (1939–1945), chemical weapons were used in a few isolated instances, although both the Axis and the Allies had developed large arsenals of extremely toxic agents. Both sides feared retaliation by the enemy, and neither chose to use its massive stockpiles of chemical weapons.

In the Middle East, the first modern large-scale use of lethal chemical agents occurred during the Iran-Iraq War (1980–1988). Early in the war, Iraq dropped bombs containing mustard agent and tabun on Iranian troops, causing 100,000 casualties including 20,000 deaths. Iraq accused Iran of having used chemical weapons first, but the allegations were never confirmed by United Nations (UN) investigators. Near the end of the war, the Iraqi government used chemical weapons against rebellious Kurdish Iraqi citizens.

During the Persian Gulf War (1991), Iraq was accused of launching Scud missiles with chemical warheads against Israel, although no traces of chemical weapons were found. Iraq did not strike the attacking coalition forces with chemical weapons. One possibility is that the Iraqis feared that the coalition would retaliate with its own chemical weapons or perhaps even tactical nuclear weapons. A more likely possibility, however, is that the Iraqis never had the planning and coordination time necessary to employ chemical weapons. Virtually every successful use of chemical weapons in the 20th century was in an offensive operation, where the attacker had the initiative and necessary time to plan and tightly control the use of such weapons and their effects. Being on the defensive from the start, the Iraqis never had that flexibility.

Chemical weapons in the hands of terrorist groups pose a significant potential threat. On March 20, 1995, Aum Shinrikyo, a Japanese apocalyptic cult, released sarin gas on a Tokyo subway, killing 12 commuters and injuring more than 5,000. In 2002 the

Major Classes of Chemical Weapons

Class	Effects	Severity	Examples
blistering agents	burn skin and respiratory system	mild to severe	Lewisite; mustard gas
blood agents	cause internal bleeding, prevent oxygen uptake	moderate to severe	cyanogen chloride; hydrogen cyanide
cytotoxic agents	prevent protein synthesis	moderate to severe	ricin
incapacitating agents	produce effects similar to intoxication	mild to moderate	Agent 15; KOLOKOL-1; LSD
lachrymatory agents	cause eye irritation or temporary blindness	mild to moderate	bromine; thiophene; xylyl bromide
nerve agents	break down neural synapses causing paralysis	moderate to severe	sarin; soman; tabun
pulmonary agents	cause suffocation	mild to severe	chlorine; diphosgene; phosgene

terrorist organization Al Qaeda released a videotape purportedly showing the deaths of dogs from a nerve agent. Al Qaeda has repeatedly announced its intention to obtain chemical, biological, and nuclear weapons.

There have been many attempts to prohibit the development and use of chemical weapons. In 1874 the Brussels Declaration outlawed the use of poison in warfare. The 1900 Hague Conference banned projectiles carrying poisonous gasses, as did the Washington Arms Conference Treaty of 1922 and the Geneva Protocol of 1929. None of the prohibitions proved sufficient to eradicate chemical warfare, however. The most recent effort to eliminate chemical weapons was the multilateral Chemical Weapons Convention (CWC) of 1993. The CWC came into effect in 1997 and prohibited the production and use of chemical weapons. Numerous nations known to maintain or suspected of maintaining chemical weapons stockpiles refused to sign or abide by the treaty, including several in the Middle East. Egypt, Libya, and Syria, all known to possess chemical weapons, each refused to sign the CWC, although Libya acceded to the treaty in early 2004 and has vowed to dismantle its chemical weapons program.

Israel, long suspected of having a sophisticated chemical weapons capability, signed the CWC but never ratified the agreement. Iran signed and ratified the CWC but refused to prove that it had destroyed known stockpiles of chemical weapons and does not allow international inspectors to examine its facilities.

In future Middle Eastern conflicts, chemical weapons are far more likely to be used in terrorist attacks than in large-scale military operations. Chemical weapons are not easy to use. They are difficult and awkward to store, transport, and handle; their use requires detailed and expensive planning and lead times; once released their effects are difficult to predict and control; and one's own troops require specialized equipment and extensive training to operate in a chemical environment.

PAUL J. SPRINGER

See also

Biological Weapons and Warfare; Iran, Armed Forces; Iran-Iraq War; Iraq, Armed Forces; Nuclear Weapons; Persian Gulf War

References

Butler, Richard. *The Greatest Threat: Iraq, Weapons of Mass Destruction, and the Crisis of Global Security.* New York: PublicAffairs, 2000.

Morel, Benoit, and Kyle Olson. *Shadows and Substance: The Chemical Weapons Convention.* Boulder, CO: Westview, 1993.

Solomon, Brian. *Chemical and Biological Warfare.* New York: H. W. Wilson, 1999.

Torr, James D. *Weapons of Mass Destruction: Opposing Viewpoints.* San Diego: Greenhaven, 2005.

Tucker, Jonathan B. *War of Nerves: Chemical Warfare from World War I to Al-Qaeda.* New York: Pantheon, 2006.

China, People's Republic of, Middle East Policy

The policy of the People's Republic of China's (PRC) toward the Middle East has gradually evolved from passivity to activism. This evolution can be divided into three phases. The PRC's birth in October 1949 marked the beginning of the first phase. Chinese general policy toward the Middle East was one of preliminary exploration. Because the majority of Middle Eastern nations still recognized the Nationalist regime on Taiwan (the Republic of China) and were under American influence, the PRC resorted to people-to-people contact in socioeconomic areas with a view toward enhancing Middle Eastern understanding of the PRC. This, Chinese leaders hoped, would facilitate the establishment of formal diplomatic relationships in the future.

The Afro-Asian Conference held in Bandung, Indonesia, in April 1955 began the second phase of the PRC's relations with the Middle East. Through participation in the Bandung Conference, the PRC showed its determination to establish leadership in the developing world, independent of the Soviet Union. At the conference, PRC premier Zhou Enlai presented the "Five Principles of Peaceful Coexistence" on which future Sino–Middle Eastern relationships would be based. Zhou advocated mutual respect of sovereignty and territorial integrity, mutual nonaggression and noninterference, mutual beneficial cooperation on an equal basis, and peaceful coexistence. Moreover, he endorsed the ideas of nonalignment and persistent resistance to Western imperialism and colonialism. These principles impressed the leaders of nations in the developing world, which began to look upon the PRC as the champion of sovereignty and independence against increasing U.S.-Soviet influence in the world.

In May 1956 Egypt became the first Arab nation to accord diplomatic recognition to the PRC by rejecting Taiwan. (This action led the United States to remove its financial support for the Aswan High Dam project, which in turn triggered the Suez Crisis of 1956.) The Egyptian initiative was followed by others throughout the 1950s, a trend intensified by the PRC's moral support to Arab resistance against Western imperialists, exemplified by the 1956 Suez Canal Crisis and the Anglo-American interventions in Lebanon and Jordan.

The PRC's ideological interest in the Middle East became increasingly important throughout the 1960s and the 1970s, when the Sino-Soviet split became an established fact and the PRC was preoccupied with its highly ideological and dogmatic decade-long Cultural Revolution (1966–1976) at home. By strictly adhering to the Bandung spirit, the PRC's diplomatic role was confined to frequent high-level official exchanges of visits and opinions and also to public support and endorsement of such Arab causes as the first Non-Alignment Movement summits and the Baghdad Pact, also known as the Central Treaty Organization (CENTO). In both these instances, the PRC refrained from participation and left its policy trajectory to Middle Easterners.

On the Israeli question the PRC took a cautious stance. While the PRC explicitly stated that it would adopt a pro-Palestinian stance in the recovery of lost territory, it refused to guarantee the Arab world that it would not maintain relations with Israel. What the PRC could offer were mere proposals for a peaceful solution to the Palestinian-Israeli conflict. Yet this position was clarified in the early 1970s when Sino-Soviet relations reached their nadir and the PRC was admitted to the United Nations. During the oil crisis of 1973–1974 in the aftermath of the Yom Kippur War, the PRC openly condemned Israeli expansionism, thereby boosting its image in the Arab world and foreshadowing growing ties to the region in the coming decades.

Having recovered from the disastrous Cultural Revolution and beginning diplomatic normalization with the West by 1979, the PRC embarked on economic modernization, which accompanied a certain degree of ideological and political liberalization in the name of socialism with Chinese characteristics. Chinese interests in the Middle East became more diverse, marking the third phase of relations that were characterized by activism and pluralism.

In the third phase, economic interests took top priority. The period from 1979 to 1992 began a second wave of Chinese diplomatic efforts in establishing formal relationships with Middle Eastern countries (the first having occurred in 1956). In 1990 a formal relationship was created with Saudi Arabia, and in 1992 a formal relationship was created with Israel. Chinese economic interests were twofold: the extraction of oil and natural gas from the Middle East, which had become far more important to Chinese economic prosperity, and arms sales, namely the importation of U.S.-made weapons and technology from Israel and arms exports to Iran.

Given the growing economic ties with the Middle East, the ideological appeal of the PRC's diplomacy gave way to a highly pragmatic and cautious policy. On Arab-Israeli issues throughout the 1990s, the PRC gradually retreated from its previous overt support of Palestine. Instead, it positioned itself as an ardent supporter of a peaceful, enduring settlement and a promoter of stability in the Middle East. It has become clear in recent years that economic considerations have become paramount, while ideology has only a

small role in shaping Chinese policy toward the Middle East. Proof of this may be seen in the Chinese importation of oil from Sudan and the export of Chinese weapons to that nation.

LAW YUK-FUN

See also
Arms Sales, International; Baghdad Pact; Suez Crisis; Yom Kippur War

References
Harris, Lillian Craig. *China Considers the Middle East.* London: Tauris, 1993.
Kumaraswamy, P. R., ed. *China and the Middle East: The Quest for Influence.* New Delhi, India: Sage, 1999.
Shichor, Yitzhak. *The Middle East in China's Foreign Policy, 1949–1977.* Cambridge: Cambridge University Press, 1979.

Chinese Farm, Battle of the
Start Date: October 14, 1973
End Date: October 18, 1973

Pivotal battle on the Egyptian Front during the Arab-Israeli Yom Kippur War of 1973. The battle was fought to secure the gap between the Egyptian Second and Third Armies and the crossing site over the Suez Canal used by the Israel Defense Forces (IDF) during Operation GAZELLE (October 18–23). The incorrectly named Chinese Farm was a failed experimental station that had been run by a Japanese agricultural assistance mission to Egypt. Israeli soldiers mistook the Japanese lettering on signs and building walls for Chinese. The farm dominated the intersection of two critical roads through the Sinai. The Lexicon Road was the main route parallel to the canal, running roughly north and south from the Great Bitter Lake to Lake Timsah. The Tirtur Road ran roughly east and west, from the canal back into the interior of the Sinai, and was a main axis of advance for the IDF. The two roads crossed just north of the Great Bitter Lake and just south of Chinese Farm.

Following the surprise Egyptian crossing of the Suez Canal on October 6, the IDF committed two hastily mobilized reserve divisions: the 162nd Reserve Armored Division under Major General Avraham Adan and the 143rd Reserve Armored Division under Major General Ariel Sharon, recently retired from the IDF and called back for the mobilization. Sharon from the start pushed his forces toward the enemy, and he had to be restrained constantly by the commander of the IDF Southern Command, Major General Shmuel Gonen. Sharon's last assignment before retiring only months earlier had been commanding general of Southern Command, and there was constant friction between the two generals.

As early as October 9, reconnaissance elements from Sharon's 14th Armored Brigade, commanded by Colonel Amnon Reshef, penetrated to the Chinese Farm sector and discovered a gap between the two Egyptian armies. Sharon continued to push for permission to cross the canal and exploit the gap. On October 10, former IDF chief of staff Lieutenant General Chaim Bar-Lev was brought out of retirement and made an adviser to Gonen, effectively superseding

Former Israel Defense Forces (IDF) chief of staff General Chaim Bar-Lev (*center left*) confers with General Ariel Sharon (*with bandage*) on October 17, 1973, during the Battle of Chinese Farm in the Sinai during the Yom Kippur War. (Yossi Greenberg/Israeli Government Press Office)

the latter in command. Apparently the real reason for the change in command was to keep Sharon under control. Although many in the IDF and the Israeli government considered Sharon to be a loose cannon, all recognized that they desperately needed his fighting abilities at this point in the war.

On October 14, Egyptian forces on the east bank of the canal launched a major offensive along a 100-mile front. More than 1,000 Egyptian tanks faced 750 Israeli tanks. But the Egyptians committed the fatal mistake of moving out beyond the protective umbrella of their relatively immobile surface-to-air missile (SAM) batteries, becoming easy prey for the Israeli Air Force. In the ensuing combat, the Egyptians lost more than 250 tanks and hundreds of men. The IDF lost only 25 tanks.

Driving along the Tirtur Road and just south of Chinese Farm, Sharon reached the canal on the night of October 15. He established a bridgehead with his 247th Reserve Paratroop Brigade, under Colonel Dani Matt. Meanwhile, major elements of the Egyptian 16th Mechanized Division under Brigadier General Fuad Aziz Ghali and the 21st Armored Division under Brigadier General Ibrahim Urabi reached Chinese Farm and dug in. Both divisions had been badly mauled in the fighting on October 14 but still had significant remaining combat power. Initially unaware of the size of the Egyptian force

at Chinese Farm, Sharon sent a company of the 14th Armored Brigade's 40th Armored Battalion to secure the crossroads and clear the area. The IDF company was decimated, and the Egyptians closed the corridor behind Sharon.

On the night of October 15, the remainder of the 40th Armored Battalion and a paratroop unit designated Force Shmulik resumed the attack on Chinese Farm, where they encountered withering interlocking fire from Egyptian armored vehicles dug into the farm's old irrigation ditches. By morning the Israelis held the crossroads but still had not taken Chinese Farm. The 14th Armored Brigade lost 60 tanks and more than 120 men in the fighting up to this point.

Although cut off, Sharon continued to push to be allowed to exploit his crossing, while the IDF high command insisted that Chinese Farm first be cleared. Leaving one battalion to hold the line west of Chinese Farm, Sharon nonetheless disengaged the remainder of the 14th Armored Brigade and started to cross the canal in force. By early on October 16 Sharon had managed to get 27 tanks and 7 armored personnel carriers (APCs) across the waterway on improvised rafts. Adan, meanwhile, pushed forward with his division to break through the corridor and move up a pontoon bridge. He also committed one battalion from the 35th Paratroop Brigade to clear Chinese Farm. This battalion, under Lieutenant Colonel Amir Jaffe, battled for more than 14 hours, suffering 40 dead and 80 wounded, but the Egyptians still held the farm.

Ignoring IDF high command orders, Sharon continued to focus on exploiting his crossing, moving his headquarters to the west bank of the canal. Adan managed to reach the canal with the bridge on October 17. Finally, after Sharon and Adan clashed sharply over who had the responsibility to take Chinese Farm, Sharon redirected the 14th Armored Brigade to clear out the Egyptians once and for all. At the same time, the Egyptians made one final effort to close the corridor again, pushing from the north with the 16th and 21st Divisions and from the south with the Third Army's 25th Independent Armored Brigade. Sharon and Adan concentrated three armored brigades against the Egyptians. After a day and a half of savage fighting, the Egyptians had lost another 250 tanks.

Chinese Farm finally fell on October 18. By that time, Adan's division had two brigades on the west side of the canal. The Israelis expanded the bridgehead as the 146th Reserved Armored Division under Brigadier General Kalman Magen started to cross behind Adan. By October 19 the Israelis had about 350 tanks across. They broke out the next day, with Adan's division heading south toward the port of Suez, Magen's division following behind that of Adan, and Sharon's division heading north toward Ismailia. Within days the 63,000 soldiers of the Egyptian Third Army, commanded by Major General Muhammad Abd al-Munim Wasil, were completely cut off.

DAVID T. ZABECKI

See also

Adan, Avraham; Bar-Lev, Chaim; Gonen, Shmuel; Sharon, Ariel

References

Dunstan, Simon. *The Yom Kippur War, 1973*. 2 vols. Westport, CT: Praeger, 2005.

Herzog, Chaim. *The War of Atonement: The Inside Story of the Yom Kippur War*. London: Greenhill, 2003.

Church of the Holy Sepulcher

Significant Christian holy site in Jerusalem. The Church of the Holy Sepulcher (or Sepulchre), also known as the Church of the Resurrection, is located in the northwest quarter of the Old City of Jerusalem. The church sits atop the site believed since the third century AD to be that of Jesus Christ's crucifixion, Golgotha (the place of the skull) also known as the Hill of Calvary, and the tomb out of which Jesus arose. There is no record of veneration of this site during the first three centuries of the early Christian church. Nineteenth-century British general Charles George Gordon argued for a different site near the Nablus Gate, a site known today as Gordon's Golgotha and the Garden Tomb.

The Via Dolorosa (Italian for "Trail of Tears") is a street in the Old City of Jerusalem that is the alleged path trod by Jesus. On this route he carried his cross to Golgotha. It is divided by the Roman Catholic and Lutheran Churches into the 14 Stations of the Cross that pilgrims follow to remember Jesus's steps toward his death. The final five stations, the last being the placing of Jesus's body in the tomb, are contained within the walls of the Church.

Constantine I (the Great), the first Christian Roman emperor, had the church site excavated in 325–326 following the First Council of Nicaea (325) and directed Bishop (Saint) Makarios (Macarius) of Jerusalem, also the builder of the Church of the Nativity in Bethlehem, to construct a church there. The church was completed in 335 CE and blended three churches encompassing three different holy sites. These were the basilica (Martyrium), an enclosed colonnaded atrium (Triportico) built around an excavated Golgotha, and a rotunda called the Anastasis (Resurrection) covering a cave identified by St. Helena (248–328), the mother of Constantine I, and Bishop Makarios as the site of Jesus's burial and resurrection. The original church building was burned by the Persians under Khosrau II in 614 and was rebuilt by Modestus, abbot of the monastery of Theodosius, during 616–626. Emperor Heraclius restored the True Cross to the Church in 630. On October 18, 1009, the rebuilt church was leveled to the ground by the Fatimid caliph al-Hakim. Although some in Christendom (Raoul Glaber, for example) blamed the Jews in part for the actions of the caliph, the destruction of the Church helped spur the First Crusade (1095–1099).

In 1048 the Fatimid caliph allowed Byzantine emperor Constantine IX Monomachos to construct a series of small chapels on the site. The site was subsequently captured on July 15, 1099, during the First Crusade. The importance of the Church of the Holy Sepulcher to Christendom is clearly seen in the choice of Godfrey of Bouillon, the first Crusader monarch of Jerusalem, as protector and defender of the Holy Sepulcher, a position above that of king. The Crusaders added a bell tower when they reunified the three holy sites under one building in the mid-12th century. This new church housed the Crusader kingdom's scriptorium and served as the seat of the first Latin Patriarchs.

The church came under the control of the Muslim general Saladin (Salah al-Din al-Ayyubi) when he captured Jerusalem in 1187. The treaty ending the Third Crusade (1189–1192) permitted Christian pilgrimages to visit the site, and it again came under Christian control as the consequence of a treaty negotiated by Holy Roman emperor Frederick II on March 18, 1229. Khwarezmian Turk forces took the city back from the Ayyubids in 1244, and it eventually came under the authority of the Ottoman Empire until its collapse at the end of World War I. The church was then placed under British authority with the League of Nations' Mandate of Palestine that ended in 1948 with the declaration of the State of Israel. The Church of the Holy Sepulcher remained under Jordanian authority until the Israelis captured the Old City of Jerusalem in the June 1967 Six-Day War.

The church building has undergone periodic restorations and improvements over the centuries. It was renovated by Franciscan friars in 1555, and the sections damaged by a 1808 fire were rebuilt during 1809–1810 as the Ottoman Baroque style structure that

The Church of the Holy Sepulcher in Jerusalem. It sits atop the site believed since the third century AD to be that of Jesus Christ's crucifixion. (Corel)

remains into the 21st century. The current dome was added in 1870 and was restored during 1994–1997. Although some restorations began in 1959, others such as portions of the exterior held in place by iron scaffolding installed by the British in 1947 remain undone. This is a reflection of centuries-old disagreements on the administration of the building by its primary custodians, the Greek Orthodox, the Armenian Apostolic, and Roman Catholic Churches. The building was first divided among the various churches in 1767 with a status quo document signed in 1852 making the divisions permanent and assigning lesser custodial responsibilities to the Coptic Orthodox, the Ethiopian Orthodox, and the Syriac Orthodox Churches that also share the building. Disagreements among all of the custodians continue into the 21st century despite this status quo document.

The main entrance to the church is a single door in the south transept controlled by the Nuseibeh and Joudeh families, two neutral neighboring Muslim families given this responsibility by Saladin in 1192. The door is unlocked on a rotating schedule agreed upon by the various religious communities. Common areas of worship within the building are used on an agreed-upon schedule. The building also serves as the headquarters of the Orthodox patriarch of Jerusalem and the Catholic archpriest of the Basilica of the Holy Sepulcher.

RICHARD EDWARDS

See also

Church of the Nativity; Jerusalem; Jerusalem, Old City of; Religious Sites in the Middle East, Christian; Religious Sites in the Middle East, Jewish; Religious Sites in the Middle East, Muslim

References

Biddle, Martin, et al. *The Church of the Holy Sepulchre.* New York: Rizzoli, 2000.

———. *The Tomb of Christ.* Phoenix, AZ: Sutton, 2000.

Clark, Victoria. *Holy Fire: The Battle for Christ's Tomb.* New York: Macmillan, 2005.

Crown-Tamir, Hela. *How to Walk in the Footsteps of Jesus and the Prophets: A Scripture Reference Guide for Biblical Sites in Israel and Jordan.* Jerusalem: Gefen, 2000.

Mansour, Atallah. *Narrow Gate Churches: The Christian Presence in the Holy Land under Muslim and Jewish Rule.* Carol Stream, IL: Hope Publishing House, 2004.

Poole, Karen, ed. *Jerusalem & the Holy Land.* New York: Dorling Kindersley, 2007.

Willis, Robert. *The Architectural History of the Church of the Holy Sepulchre at Jerusalem.* Elibron Classics Replica Edition. Boston: Adamant Media Corporation, 2005.

Church of the Nativity

Sacred Christian and Muslim shrine located near Bethlehem. The Church of the Nativity in Bethlehem (the House of Bread) is located

Main altar of the Church of the Nativity in Bethlehem, Israel. (Corel)

in Manger Square six miles from Jerusalem. It is the traditional site of the birthplace of Jesus and is sacred to Christians, who revere Jesus as the son of God, and Muslims, who revere Jesus as a prophet. It is the second major holy site for Christendom in the Middle East and was built by St. Helena (AD 248–328), the mother of Constantine I (the Great), on the site identified by St. Justin Martyr (a second-century Christian apologist). The church is administered by the Greek, Roman, and Armenian Churches, although Bethlehem has been under control of the Palestinian Authority (PA) since 1995, at which time Israeli troops were withdrawn from the area.

The original building was constructed by Bishop (Saint) Makarios (Macarius) of Jerusalem, also the builder of the Church of the Holy Sepulcher in Jerusalem, following the First Council of Nicaea in 325. This structure was destroyed in the Samaritan Revolt of 529. The primary access to the current structure, little changed from when it was built during the reign of Emperor Justinian (527–565), is through the Door of Humility, a low door that requires that one bend in order to enter. The door itself may be a later addition installed by the Ottomans to prevent horses from entering the basilica. The Church of the Nativity is the only significant church in the Holy Land that has survived intact from the early Christian era.

The church compound of approximately 13,000 square feet houses two churches, a crypt, and the Grotto of the Nativity. The High Altar stands above the Grotto (an underground cave) and is largely Armenian in design. The Grotto contains what is claimed to be the original manger in which Jesus lay after his birth. The believed site of the birth is marked by a hole in the center of a 14-point silver star on a marble stone surrounded by silver lamps. This star was stolen in 1847, and its theft played a key role in the crisis over which government or governments had authority of the Holy Places that led to the Crimean War (1854–1856).

On April 2, 2002, some 200 Palestinians (including 50 militants) fleeing the Israel Defense Forces' (IDF) Operation DEFENSIVE SHIELD (March–April 2002) in the West Bank seized the church and took 150 civilian and clerical hostages after the IDF surrounded Bethlehem on April 1. The IDF laid siege to the compound, and during this siege a fire erupted on the top floor on May 1 but did little permanent damage. The cause of the fire remains in dispute. The Palestinians claim that an IDF flare caused the blaze, but the Israelis assert that the Palestinians set the fire on purpose. Israeli snipers killed 7 of the armed militants. Another 40 people were wounded during the siege, and 95 people were released one by one during the crisis. No Israelis died in the engagement, and the IDF claimed that more than 40 explosive devices were found once the church compound had been vacated. The siege ended on May 10 with a settled negotiated by the European Union (EU) whereby 13 militants were deported to Cyprus and 26 were transferred to the Gaza Strip.

The present-day condition of the church is far from ideal. The main roof, last replaced in the 19th century, is in a poor state of repair, allowing moisture and rainwater to seep into the sanctuary. This problem not only endangers the paintings and mosaics in the church but also poses a fire hazard should water come into contact with electrical wiring. The small size of the doorways and limited access to them create a constant concern that a fire or other catastrophe could trap churchgoers and pilgrims in the building.

There are also several important chapels surrounding the Church of the Nativity and its immediate environs. They include the Chapel of the Innocents, which memorializes the deaths of the children ordered by Herod, and the Chapel of St. Jerome, where St. Jerome, the bishop of Bethlehem, first translated the Old Testament into Latin. Another significant chapel is that of St. Joseph, where an angel appeared to Joseph, the husband of the Virgin Mary and the earthly father of Jesus, and told him to flee to Egypt for safety.

RICHARD EDWARDS

See also

Church of the Holy Sepulcher; DEFENSIVE SHIELD, Operation; Religious Sites in the Middle East, Christian; Religious Sites in the Middle East, Muslim; West Bank

References

Crown-Tamir, Hela. *How to Walk in the Footsteps of Jesus and the Prophets: A Scripture Reference Guide for Biblical Sites in Israel and Jordan.* Jerusalem: Gefen, 2000.

Mansour, Atallah. *Narrow Gate Churches: The Christian Presence in the Holy Land under Muslim and Jewish Rule.* Carol Stream, IL: Hope Publishing House, 2004.

Poole, Karen, ed. *Jerusalem & the Holy Land.* New York: Dorling Kindersley, 2007.

Raheb, Mitri. *Bethlehem Besieged: Stories of Hope in Times of Trouble.* Minneapolis, MN: Augsburg Fortress, 2004.

Churchill, Sir Winston
Born: November 30, 1874
Died: January 24, 1965

British soldier, author, statesman, and prime minister (1940–1945 and 1951–1955). Winston Leonard Spencer Churchill was born on November 30, 1874, at Blenheim Palace, Oxfordshire, England. He was the grandson of the seventh duke of Marlborough and grew up with all the privileges of a scion of the Victorian elite. In 1893 Churchill entered the Royal Military College at Sandhurst. After graduation he spent several years traveling to the imperial periphery, such as Afghanistan and the Sudan, acting in the capacity of war correspondent as well as soldier. In 1899 he was taken prisoner by the Boers during the war in South Africa but made a daring and much-publicized escape. This notoriety allowed him to secure a seat as a Conservative member of Parliament in 1900.

Winston Churchill, British politician, author, and prime minister (1940–1945 and 1951–1955). (Library of Congress)

In 1904 Churchill abandoned the Tory Party because of a row over tariff reform. Two years later, when the Liberals entered power, he joined their government as undersecretary of state for the colonies. He was subsequently promoted to a series of more senior offices, including in 1910 home secretary and the following year first lord of the Admiralty.

As first lord of the Admiralty, Churchill helped prepare the Royal Navy for the test of war in August 1914. He became enticed by the prospect of forcing the Dardanelles and sending a fleet to Constantinople to drive the Ottoman Empire from the war. This was the genesis of the ill-fated 1915 Gallipoli Campaign that led to his downfall. Churchill became the scapegoat for its failure and resigned his post to take up command of a western front infantry battalion. In May 1916 he returned to London as a civilian to begin an impassioned series of speeches and newspaper articles criticizing the government's conduct of the war. The following July, Prime Minister David Lloyd George offered him the post of minister of munitions. It was not a cabinet position, but Churchill made the most of his opportunity by dramatically reorganizing Britain's industrial war effort. By the time of the armistice, Churchill's successful tenure had largely rehabilitated his reputation.

In 1919 Lloyd George appointed Churchill joint minister of war and air. But in 1922 the wartime coalition fell, and Churchill lost his seat in Parliament. Seeing that the Liberal Party was in decline, in

1924 he again allied with the Conservatives. In November 1924 he became Tory prime minister Stanley Baldwin's chancellor of the exchequer and held that post for five years.

By the early 1930s Churchill's career was at its nadir, and he might easily have retired from politics had it not been for the rise to power in Germany of Adolf Hitler. Churchill became the spokesman of those Parliament members who opposed the diplomatic efforts of Prime Minister Neville Chamberlain, who pursued an appeasement policy toward Hitler.

When war began, within hours Churchill was back in charge of the Royal Navy. Just as in 1914, however, he was soon frustrated by inactivity. As a way of breaking the deadlock he promoted the idea of mining Norwegian coastal waters, through which Swedish ore was shipped to Germany during the winter months. This legally dubious proposal was preempted by Hitler on April 9, 1940, when German forces marched into Denmark and Norway. The Franco-British reaction was a clumsy expedition that resulted in a series of humiliating defeats.

The Norwegian fiasco led to Chamberlain's departure, and on May 10, 1940, the same day that German forces began their offensive against France and the Low Countries, King George VI offered Churchill the opportunity to form a government. Throughout the summer of 1940, Prime Minister Churchill oversaw the successful defense of the United Kingdom's airspace against the attacks of the German Luftwaffe. It was during these critical months that he made his most famous wartime speeches. Once the United States entered the war in December 1941, much of Churchill's time was spent in transatlantic diplomacy, during which time he established a close relationship with U.S. president Franklin Roosevelt. During the first two years of the Anglo-American alliance, Churchill was able to engineer many of its key decisions. But after the November 1943 Tehran Conference among Churchill, Roosevelt, and Soviet leader Joseph Stalin, Churchill found himself more and more sidelined.

Toward other areas of the world, Churchill held beliefs that sometimes ran contrary to popular opinion or Conservative dogma. Such was certainly the case in his approach to the Middle East. He was a self-proclaimed, lifelong Zionist and seemed to have a quasi-mystical belief in the destiny of the Jewish people.

As a backbencher in 1939, Churchill had sharply condemned the government White Paper that placed a fixed ceiling on the number of Jewish immigrants allowed into Palestine. In 1944, at a meeting with Zionist leader Dr. Chaim Weizmann, Churchill expressed his long-term desire that the territory should become a Jewish homeland, although he also held vague hopes that a lasting settlement might be reached between Jews and Arabs through some kind of regional federation with the Saudi princes. However, with the Labor Party's victory at the polls in the July 1945 elections and his departure as prime minister, Churchill lost the opportunity to shape the postwar settlement in the Middle East, and he was a spectator throughout the dramatic events that witnessed the creation of Israel three years later.

Many expected Churchill to retire gracefully from politics. But a man of such restless energy found it impossible to willingly withdraw from the public scene, and he remained in the Commons as leader of the Opposition. Churchill did not figure prominently in the Clement Attlee administration, however, deferring many of his leadership duties to younger men as he instead spent his time writing and traveling. The blockbuster success of his six-volume history *The Second World War,* published between 1948 and 1954, brought him financial security and, in 1953, the Nobel Prize for Literature.

While in Opposition, Churchill did attack Attlee's policies in Palestine, although not always with a clear statement of what he would have done himself given the opportunity. While condemning terrorist activity against British security forces in the region, Churchill never disguised where his sympathies lay. Thus, when Israeli statehood was proclaimed in May 1948, the Conservative leader urged the Labour government to immediately recognize the new nation, which put him at odds with many members of his own party.

In October 1951 the Attlee government was defeated, and Churchill returned to 10 Downing Street. His second tenure as British prime minister was a pale imitation of his earlier triumphs. Now almost deaf and with a failing memory, he was often incapable of performing the duties of office. By the time he had returned to power, the focus of British attention in the Middle East had shifted to Egypt and the troubled Suez Canal Zone. Churchill's essentially Victorian and condescending attitude toward Egypt and its people did not help his understanding of the rapidly changing situation there. Indeed, Foreign Secretary Anthony Eden had great difficulty in persuading the prime minister that the lifetime of the British military presence in the Middle East was coming to a close.

Churchill grudgingly accepted the eventual withdrawal of the Canal Zone garrison in 1954, but he was angered by President Gamal Abdel Nasser's continued refusal to allow Israel-bound vessels to use the waterway and quietly hoped for some kind of Anglo-American initiative to depose the Soviet-backed leader.

Churchill's interest in Israel continued throughout his second premiership. At one point he even seriously proposed inviting that country to join the British Commonwealth. The climactic events of the 1956 Anglo-Egyptian standoff over Suez did not take place until Churchill had resigned, although he expressed public and private support for the government's actions and was disappointed by President Dwight D. Eisenhower's demands that the British and French withdraw.

Meanwhile, Churchill continued to maintain quixotic notions that he would be able to end or at least mitigate the ongoing Cold War, particularly after Stalin's death in 1953. The prime minister's visions were, for the most part, politely ignored. Finally, on April 5, 1955, Churchill bowed to the inevitable and tendered his resignation. He retained his seat in the Commons for another nine years, however. Churchill died in London on January 24, 1965.

ALAN ALLPORT

See also

Attlee, Clement Richard; Eden, Robert Anthony; Eisenhower, Dwight David; Nasser, Gamal Abdel; Roosevelt, Franklin Delano; Stalin, Joseph; Suez Crisis; United Kingdom, Middle East Policy; Weizmann, Chaim

References

Cannadine, David, and Roland Quinault, eds. *Winston Churchill in the Twenty-First Century.* Cambridge: Cambridge University Press, 2004.

Charmley, John. *Churchill: The End of Glory.* London: Hodder and Stoughton, 1993.

Churchill, Winston. *Blood, Toil, Tears, and Sweat: The Speeches of Winston Churchill.* Boston: Houghton Mifflin, 1989.

Gilbert, Martin. *Churchill: A Life.* New York: Holt, 1991.

———. *In Search of Churchill: A Historian's Journey.* New York: Wiley 1994.

Climate of the Middle East

The climate of the Middle East is surprisingly variable. This runs contrary to the popular perception abroad that the region is a uniformly hot and dry desert environment. The Middle East is a region of great temperature extremes and considerable variances in precipitation. Nevertheless, a good deal of the Middle East is known for its blazing hot summers and great dust storms that can reduce visibility to less than one-quarter of a mile, making land travel difficult at best and air travel impossible. Except in mountainous regions and on high plains, the region's winters range from cool and rainy to mild and relatively dry.

Syria's climate is mostly characterized as that of a desert. There are three principal climate zones in Syria, however. They include a somewhat humid Mediterranean-style climate in the west, a semi-arid central steppe, and a torrid desert environment in the east and southeast. The coastal climate experiences mild, rainy winters from December to February and hot, relatively dry summers. Because of the elevation, the highlands experience cold winters punctuated by occasional snow. Sometimes this weather affects areas as far south and west as Damascus. The eastern deserts receive 10 inches or less of rainfall a year and are characterized by hot summers with temperatures as high as 120 degrees. High winds blowing from the south (from Arabia) can create dust storms, particularly in the desert.

The climate of Jordan, like that of Syria, is largely desert. In the west, a rainy season from November to April brings most of an entire year's rainfall. Aside from that the area is very dry. Jordan's summers are quite hot, with average high temperatures over 100 degrees, higher still in the desert. The winters are moderately cool with snow occasionally at higher elevations. In the late spring and early fall, the country is subject to periodic hot, dry winds from the south-southeast, which can drive relative humidity to 10 percent or less. These winds sometimes produce dust and sand storms that can greatly impede transportation, pose health dangers, and force vehicles to halt.

Border region between Lebanon and Israel, including farmlands and snow-topped Mt. Hermon. (iStockPhoto.com)

The Egyptian climate is characteristic of a true desert environment. There are two seasons: a hot, dry summer from May to October and a moderate, slightly wet winter from December to March. Most of the country's rain falls along and close to the northern coast, and owing to the moderating influence of the Mediterranean Sea, the northern part of Egypt is slightly cooler. For this reason, Alexandria on the Mediterranean coast is a popular tourist destination, particularly in the summer months. There are, however, some variations. In the Delta and North Nile Valley, occasional winter cold snaps can bring light frosts and even small amounts of snowfall. In the south, near Aswan, there are great temperature fluctuations in the summer. High temperatures can be as high as 126 degrees or better during the day and then dip as low as 48–50 degrees at night. Sometimes between mid-March through May howling dust storms occur, precipitated by southerly winds that can reach 90 miles per hour and wreak havoc. These dust storms are known as the *sirocco* by Europeans and the *khamsin* by the Egyptians.

Saudi Arabia has a dry, hot, harsh climate characterized by great temperature extremes. Except for the Asir Province, which is subject to monsoons from the Indian Ocean region and is more temperate, and the sometimes humid conditions of the coast of the Hejaz, the nation's climate is all desert. The desert areas experience dry, cloudless summers with high temperatures of 120 degrees and higher. Temperatures of 125–130 degrees are not uncommon. During times of drought, which are not that infrequent, the southern two-thirds of Saudi Arabia can go for two years or more without measurable rainfall. In the late spring and summer, strong winds often create choking sand and dust storms.

The climate of Iraq is similar to that of the southwestern United States. It is mostly a semiarid desert that experiences hot, dry summers and mild to cool winters with periodic rainfall. The mountainous regions along the Iranian and Turkish borders have cold winters with periodic heavy snowfalls. The great majority of Iraq's precipitation comes in the winter (December to April), while the northern areas receive more rainfall over a slightly longer time span. From June to September, winds from the north and northwest can whip up heavy dust storms (called *shamal* by Iraqis) that cause plummeting humidity and decreased visibilities. As in the American Southwest, the southern two-thirds of Iraq is prone to flash flooding.

Iran's climate may be the most varied of all the major nations in the Middle East. It has arid and semiarid climate zones and even a subtropical climate along the Caspian Sea coast. In the northwest, summers are hot and dry, the autumn and spring are mild, and the winters are cold and frequently snowy. Most of the country's rainfall occurs from October to April, with the most falling near the coast. In the south, particularly near the Persian Gulf, average summer high temperatures are 112 degrees. Tehran, shielded by the Alborz Mountains, is more temperate, with average summer high temperatures of 96 degrees.

Lebanon enjoys a fairly typical Mediterranean climate, with hot, sunny summers and mild, wet winters. Along the coast, which is warm and humid, there is rain but not snow. Heavy snow falls in Lebanon's mountain areas in the winter. Lebanon's climate may be the most moderate of the Middle East countries owing to its small size and proximity to the coast. Rainfall is greatest from December to April.

The climate of Israel is moderately temperate. It features very hot and dry summers in the southern and western deserts. Elsewhere, the climate is similar to that of Lebanon, with long, dry, hot summers and short, rainy, cool winters. Seventy percent of the nation's rain occurs from November to April, with rainfall slackening the farther south one goes. Only about one-third of the small country is capable of agricultural pursuits that do not require heavy irrigation. In the winter, light snow is not uncommon at higher elevations.

Despite the many variations in the region's climate, almost all of the Middle East nations feature extremely hot summers and dust and sand storms. From a military perspective, the region can be daunting for troops as well as equipment. The searing heat of the summers is dangerous for troops, who can quickly succumb to heat exhaustion, heat stroke, and dehydration. For this reason, military

action in the dead of summer is avoided, particularly on the Arabian Peninsula. The heat can also take a heavy toll on equipment, especially trucks, armored personnel carriers, and tanks.

Another perilous weather phenomenon is the region's frequent dust and sand storms. Greatly reduced visibilities can ground aircraft and reduce visibilities to a quarter of a mile or less. Moving a large number of troops in the midst of one of these storms is ill-advised. Airborne sand and dust can also foul the engines of ground vehicles as well as aircraft. The perils of operating in such conditions were graphically illustrated in April 1980 when President Jimmy Carter's administration attempted to mount a clandestine rescue of American embassy workers being held in Tehran, Iran. On their way toward Tehran, two of eight RH-53 U.S. helicopters broke down in a sand storm. A third was damaged on landing, but when it attempted to take off after surveying the damage to the downed choppers, it clipped a U.S. Air Force C-130 transport airplane. The helicopter went down, resulting in the deaths of eight U.S. servicemen. The debacle was a major embarrassment for Carter.

The failed hostage mission serves as a stark example of the inherent dangers of military operations in the often inhospitable climate of the Middle East. And the lack of rainfall throughout much of the region may well serve as the flashpoint for a future Middle East conflict as nations there scramble for precious water supplies.

PAUL G. PIERPAOLI JR.

See also
Geography of the Middle East

References
Gleick, P. H. "Water, War and Peace in the Middle East." *Environment* 36(3) (1994): 6–11.
Gribbin, John. *Weather Force: Climate and Its Impact on Our World.* New York: Putnam, 1979.
Riley, Dennis, and Lewis Spolton. *World Weather and Climate.* New York: Cambridge University Press, 1982.

Clinton, William Jefferson
Born: August 19, 1946

American politician and president of the United States (1993–2001). William "Bill" Jefferson Clinton was born William Blythe in Hope, Arkansas, on August 19, 1946. His early life was characterized by hardships and struggles that formed his character and attitudes throughout his public life. His biological father, William Blythe III, was killed in an automobile accident prior to his son's birth, and young Blythe was raised by his mother, Virginia Kelley. His mother's marriage to Roger Clinton prompted William's adoption and changing of his name to William Clinton just prior to starting secondary school.

Clinton was a bright and astute student who hoped to pursue a medical career until he met President John F. Kennedy on a Boys' Nation trip to Washington, D.C. This experience led Clinton to focus his future career aspirations on public service and politics. Ken-

Bill Clinton, American politician and president of the United States (1993–2001), shown in 1992. (Library of Congress)

nedy's charisma and his liberal outlook on the place of the national government in the lives of the American people molded Clinton's own political outlook.

Clinton received an academic scholarship to attend Georgetown University in Washington, D.C., where he earned a bachelor of science degree in international affairs. During his time at Georgetown he spent a year assisting Arkansas senator J. William Fulbright. Clinton's credentials as a progressive Democrat and social liberal were further developed under the tutelage of this prominent senator. In 1968 as the United States was being transformed by social changes and wracked by protests against the Vietnam War, Clinton was selected as a Rhodes Scholar. He spent 1968 to 1970 studying at Oxford University. On his return to the United States, he enrolled in the Yale University School of Law.

While studying at Yale, Clinton met his future wife Hillary Rodham, who shared many of the liberal and progressive ideas that would become the hallmark of Clinton's political career. They were married in 1975.

Clinton's initial foray into national politics occurred shortly after receiving his law degree. In 1974 he was defeated in a congressional race for Arkansas's Third District. After a brief career as a professor at the University of Arkansas (1974–1976), he was named state attorney general and was elected governor in 1978, at age 32 the youngest governor in the nation. In 1980 he suffered a

humiliating reelection defeat, caused by widespread opposition to an automobile licensing tax. Clinton's resiliency and commitment were apparent when he successfully regained the Arkansas governorship in 1982, a post he held until his election as president in 1992.

In the summer of 1992, Clinton secured the Democratic Party nomination to run against incumbent President George Herbert Walker Bush, a Republican. Clinton was bedeviled, however, by questions regarding his marital fidelity and the emerging Whitewater real estate scandal in Arkansas. He benefited from an economic downturn and businessman H. Ross Perot's Independent Party candidacy.

Clinton won the November 1992 election with a minority of the popular vote. During his first term, he balanced domestic issues and foreign policy in a highly effective manner. At home, he lobbied unsuccessfully for major health care reform, including coverage for those without health insurance. He also demanded that the Department of Defense remove all restrictions pertaining to homosexuals serving in the military. The ensuing firestorm forced Clinton to institute the "Don't Ask, Don't Tell" policy, which failed to satisfy either side. Clinton was successful, however, in raising taxes and reducing expenditures to reduce—and then eliminate—the federal deficit and in pushing through major welfare reforms. In foreign affairs, he promoted free trade agreements, brokered peace efforts in the Middle East, removed U.S. military personnel from Somalia, and restored diplomatic relations with the Socialist Republic of Vietnam.

The congressional elections of 1994, however, brought Republican majorities in both the House and Senate. The Republicans' "Contract with America," crafted chiefly by Republican congressman Newt Gingrich, called for reducing the role of government and continuing the conservative policies of Ronald Reagan and was a thorough repudiation of Clinton's presidency. A standoff between Clinton and congressional leaders led to a federal government shutdown in November and December 1995.

In the 1996 presidential campaign, Clinton promised a tough approach to crime, supported welfare reform, called for reducing the federal deficit, and insisted on the need to continue affirmative action programs. Robert Dole, a respected senator and World War II veteran, was the Republican candidate. The booming U.S. economy and suspicions regarding the Republicans' agenda ensured a respectable Clinton victory. He was the first Democrat to secure a second presidential term since Franklin D. Roosevelt.

In 1997 Clinton submitted to Congress the first balanced budget in nearly three decades. The cooperation of congressional Republicans and significant compromises by Clinton generated significant budget surpluses during the remainder of his presidency. By decade's end, the American economy was more robust than at any time since the mid-1960s, unemployment stood at a historic low, and the stock market had reached new highs.

In addition to significant domestic accomplishments, Clinton responded effectively to a series of international crises. In 1998 he authorized air strikes in Iraq, and in 1999 he prodded a North Atlantic Treaty Organization (NATO) response to genocide conducted by Serbs against Albanians in Kosovo. He also worked mightily to secure a resolution to the Israeli-Palestinian conflict, a major Clinton administration goal.

Clinton constantly prodded all sides to negotiate and come to an agreement, but his efforts were stymied by uncooperative leaders and events. The assassination of Israeli prime minister Yitzhak Rabin in November 1995 and continued terrorist attacks by Islamic groups had brought the election of hard-line prime minister Benjamin Netanyahu, who promised to bring peace and security but also not to return any of the occupied territories. He now delayed in carrying out troop withdrawals in accordance with the 1993 Oslo Accords, in which Israel had agreed to give up land for peace, while the Palestinian side failed to crack down on terrorism. He demanded that Yasser Arafat and the Palestinian Authority (PA) move directly against the Hamas terrorist organization.

With tensions dramatically increasing, Clinton intervened directly and applied pressure on both sides. In October of 1998 he succeeded in bringing together Netanyahu and Arafat at the Wye River estate in Maryland. Following days of difficult negotiations and sometimes bitter wrangling, Clinton secured agreement on what became known as the Wye River Agreement. Israel agreed to withdraw from some additional 13 percent of West Bank territory, and the PA renounced the use of terrorism and agreed both to suppress it and to eliminate the weapons that the PA had stockpiled. The PA also agreed to halt the most virulent anti-Israeli propaganda.

Netanyahu returned to Israel, however, to find strong opposition from within his ruling Likud coalition to the additional territorial concession. He nonetheless carried out a partial withdrawal. Meanwhile, although the PA did crack down on militants, it failed to implement most of the provisions in the Wye River Agreement, whereupon a month later Netanyahu suspended withdrawals.

Forced to call new elections, Netanyahu curried favor with the Israeli religious right, alienating many secular Israelis. In the ensuing May 1999 elections, Netanyahu was defeated by the Labor coalition known as One Israel headed by former Israeli Army chief of staff Ehud Barak.

Clinton reached out to Barak, whose premiership began with much promise but ended after only 17 months. Barak removed Israeli troops from southern Lebanon in May 2000, but negotiations with Arafat and the PA ran afoul of right-wing charges that he was making too many concessions. Clinton again set up a meeting in the United States. During July 11–24, 2000, Clinton hosted a summit at the presidential retreat of Camp David, Maryland. Despite generous concessions by Barak, the parties were unable to secure agreement, and a new wave of violence, the Second (al-Aqsa) Intifada, erupted. Clinton made one last try, at the White House during December 19–23, 2000. Both his and Barak's terms were nearing their ends. The U.S. plan, apparently endorsed by Barak, would have ceded to the Palestinians some 97 percent of the West Bank and full Palestinian control of the Gaza Strip, with a land link

between the two. Barak also agreed that Arab neighborhoods of East Jerusalem might become the capital of the new Palestinian state. Palestinian refugees would also have the right of return to the Palestinian state and compensation from a fund raised by international donors. These concessions were anathema to the Likud and other Israeli rightists, but in the end, despite heavy pressure from Clinton, Arafat rejected the agreement. Barak, who came under a storm of criticism for this process, was forced to step aside.

Clinton's second term was also marked by personal scandal and legal problems. Kenneth Starr, the independent counsel investigating Whitewater, leveled against the president charges of sexual misconduct and lying to a federal grand jury. He did not, however, ever find evidence of wrongdoing in the Whitewater deal. In September 1998, the U.S. House of Representatives passed two articles of impeachment against the president, but in early 1999 the Senate acquitted Clinton on both counts. In order to end the Whitewater investigation, Clinton agreed to a five-year suspension of his law license and a $25,000 fine.

After leaving the presidency, Clinton assisted his wife in her successful senatorial campaign in New York, opened his own office in Harlem in New York City, and established a presidential library in Little Rock, Arkansas. He has also traveled extensively abroad and raised significant sums of money for charitable causes, including AIDS and, with former President Bush, tsunami relief.

JAMES F. CARROLL AND SPENCER C. TUCKER

See also
Arafat, Yasser; Netanyahu, Benjamin; Oslo Accords

References
Clinton, William Jefferson. *My Life*. New York: Knopf, 2004.
Maraniss, D. *First in His Class*. New York: Simon and Schuster, 1995.
Posner, R. A. *An Affair of State: The Investigation, Impeachment, and Trial of President Clinton*. Cambridge: Harvard University Press, 1999.

Committee of Jewish Delegations at the Peace Conference
Start Date: March 25, 1919
End Date: 1933

Established at the Paris Peace Conference on March 25, 1919, following World War I, the Committee of Jewish Delegations at the Peace Conference (Comité des délégations Juives auprès de la Conférence de la Paix) was an organization claiming to represent the interests of some 10 million Jews worldwide. Seeking to lobby the conferees on behalf of the interests of Jews everywhere, the committee included representatives of Jewish organizations from Palestine, the United States, Canada, Russia, Ukraine, Austria, Hungary, Poland, Romania, Czechoslovakia, Italy, Yugoslavia, and Greece. A number of the delegates had been elected as the result of Jewish congresses or assemblies, while others were the appointed representatives of Jewish national congresses or communities. In addition, the committee included representatives of B'nai B'rith and the

World Zionist Organization. The committee took a definite Zionist approach to Jewish issues.

Julian W. Mack, president of the American Jewish Congress, was elected as the committee's first head. The committee presented two formal memorandums to the peace conference. The first concerned civil and cultural rights for Jews in all countries, and the second was a statement of the historic right of the Jewish people to Palestine. The committee did help secure the minority rights treaties that were imposed by the Paris Peace Conference on the defeated states and those newly created by the peace conference. States such as Poland and Germany later violated the minorities provisions, however.

The committee did not disband with the end of the peace conference but continued in existence in Paris under Dr. Leo Motzkin, who remained its chairman until his death in 1933. During this period, the committee lobbied such organizations as the Inter-parliamentary Union and the League of Nations regarding Jewish rights. In the 1930s, the committee merged with the World Jewish Congress.

Spencer C. Tucker

See also

B'nai B'rith; World Jewish Congress; World Zionist Organization; Zionism

References

Hertzberg, Arthur, ed. *The Zionist Idea: A Historical Analysis and Reader.* Philadelphia: Jewish Publication Society, 1997.

Herzl, Theodor. *The Jewish State.* Mineola, NY: Dover, 1989.

Laqueur, Walter. *A History of Zionism: From the French Revolution to the Establishment of the State of Israel.* Reprint ed. New York: Schocken, 2003.

Unity in Dispersion: A History of the World Jewish Congress. New York: World Jewish Congress, 1948.

Communist Party of Israel

Israeli political party. The Israeli Communist Party, also known as HaMiflagah HaQomonistit HaYisra'elit, or Maki, is a Jewish-Arab, anti-Zionist political party that traces its roots to 1919 and the founding of the Palestine Communist Party. The earliest members of the party came from Eastern Europe and Russia and had embraced Marxist socialism. The communist movement in Palestine was born within the confines of the Zionist movement, which supported the idea of a homeland for the Jewish people in Palestine, and was isolated from the Arab inhabitants in Palestine. The failure of the 1905 Russian Revolution and the anti-Jewish attacks that sprang from it had led many Jews to migrate to Palestine.

By 1919, when the Palestine Party was formed, Jews in Palestine numbered just 56,000. During the early 1920s, the party split over the issue of Zionism. In 1923, the Party's Second Congress adopted a measure supporting the Arab national movement as "opposed to British imperialism," a move that won it membership in the Communist International (Comintern). A year later, the party became the official Comintern section in Palestine.

A workers' demonstration in the streets of Tel Aviv organized by the Communist Party of Israel and the Mapam Party demanding a raise in salaries, October 26, 1949. (Pinn Hans/Israeli Government Press Office)

From the earliest days of the British Mandate for Palestine, the communists maintained that it was possible to unite the Jews and Arabs in Palestine. They argued that the Jewish workers and farmers and the Arabs who supported nationalism had a common enemy in Zionist British imperialists. The British generally favored Zionist claims in Palestine until the White Paper of 1939, which intended to limit Jewish immigration into Palestine. Partly because of its opposition to those who denounced Zionism, the British banned the Communist Party in Palestine until 1942, when the Soviet Union joined the Allies during World War II.

During their occupation of Palestine, the British repressed the communists there at every possible turn. A few years into World War II, Soviet leader Joseph Stalin officially dissolved the Comintern, which all but ended the Palestine Communist Party. But those who believed in the communist cause remained.

In 1948 following the formation of the new Israeli state, the Israeli Communist Party was founded. While not Zionist, the party nevertheless recognized Israel. A split in the party in 1965 divided the group among those who were pro-Palestinian and those who were pro-Israeli. The Israeli faction, led by Moshe Sneh, was never able to gain much support in Israel, despite taking popular stances such as supporting the 1967 Six-Day War, and eventually disappeared. The pro-Palestinian group, known as the New Communist List, or Rakah, maintained a continual presence in the Knesset (Israeli parliament) and came to be made up chiefly of Arabs, although it was led by a Jew, Meir Vilner, until 1990. By 1990 and the end of Vilner's term, Rakah had officially changed its name to Maki, as the Maki of old was long defunct.

The Communist Party in Israel holds that Israel is unfairly occupying the land it captured during the 1967 Six-Day War. The party views Israel's rule of Palestinian territory as an act of state terrorism and also supports the establishment of a separate, independent Palestinian state. According to the party platform, Israel unfairly controls East Jerusalem, which the party believes should be given to the Palestinians as the capital of a new Palestinian state (with West Jerusalem as the capital of Israel). Maki holds that there should be free access to the holy sites and free, safe movement between the two cities. The party disagreed with Israeli prime minister Ariel Sharon's 2005 Gaza disengagement plan because it was not an attempt at a mutual understanding between the Palestinians and the Israelis. The party also supports the right of Palestinian refugees to move back into the areas taken by Israel in the 1948–1949 Israeli War of Independence or to be justly compensated for the loss of their land.

Under Vilner, the party often ignored Soviet missteps while scrutinizing in detail the Israeli leadership. In the Knesset elections held on March 28, 2006, Hadash, a far left-wing coalition made up of the Israeli Communist Party and other leftist groups, garnered three Knesset seats (out of 120). Today, the Israeli Communist Party remains highly critical of Israeli's actions in the ongoing conflict between Israel and Arabs in the Middle East.

GREGORY MOORE

See also

Gaza Strip Disengagement; Israel; Labor Party; Likud Party; Sharon, Ariel; White Paper (1939); Zionism; Zionist Conference

References

Budeiri, Musa. *The Palestine Communist Party, 1919–1948: Arab & Jew in the Struggle for Internationalism.* London: Ithaca Press, 1979.
Nahas, Dunia. *The Israeli Communist Party.* London: Portico, 1976.
Rubenstein, Sondra. *The Communist Movement in Palestine and Israel, 1919–1984.* Boulder, CO, and London: Westview, 1985.

Conscription Policies

The major armies involved in the Arab-Israeli wars were manpower-intensive and remain so to this day. Egypt, Israel, Jordan, and Syria all have obligatory military service.

The Egyptian constitution requires universal male conscription for three years. Exemptions are given to permanent government employees, brothers of those who have died in service, and sole male children, or breadwinners. Conscripts may serve in the military, prison guard service, police force, or military economic service units. Conscripts who have obtained a degree from colleges or universities need serve only 18 months. Since conscription age begins at 18, however, conscripts may defer their service until age 28. Thereafter, they stay on in the reserves for the remaining 18 months. Since 1946, universal compulsory conscription has been employed in Syria. Males must register at age 18 and begin military service at age 19. They must serve for 30 months. After conscript duty, discharged

Israel Defense Forces (IDF) inductees bidding goodbye to family and friends, November 28, 1995. (Sa'ar Ya'acov/Israeli Government Press Office)

conscripts may enlist for 5 further years in the regular service or as a reservist for 18 years. Those enlisted for regular service can become professional, noncommissioned officers and serve until the age of 45 or retire after 20 years of service.

Jordan has had a very stringent recruitment policy based on careful screening for potential subversives against the Hashemite monarchy. However, in 1966 the government passed an urgent act calling for mandatory two-year military service for all physically fit males. This act did not have much success given the continued political screening of recruits. In 1976 the new National Service Law did come into effect. It called again for the two-year conscription of all physically fit males at age 18. The need to use well-educated personnel in the increasingly modern armed forces led to the encouragement of service deferments for those in higher education. In any case, by the age of 28 every male is expected to fulfill his conscription commitments. Elite units are made up solely of volunteers, which are rigorously selected from the conscription cohorts.

Given the resource and population asymmetry between Israel and the Arab states surrounding it, Israel has required since its

Conscription Policies of Selected Middle Eastern and North African Countries

Country	Military Obligation
Algeria	Males: 18 months
Bahrain	None
Egypt	Males: 18–30 months
Iran	Males: 18 months
Iraq	None
Israel	Males: 36 months Females: 24 months
Jordan	None
Lebanon	Males: 12 months
Morocco	Males: 18 months
Oman	None
Saudi Arabia	None
Syria	Males: 18–30 months
Tunisia	Males: 12 months
United Arab Emirates	None

inception in 1948 universal male and female conscription. This applies to Jewish citizens and Druze and Circassian (Muslims resettled by the Ottomans in Palestine) men as well as resident aliens. Other Arab-Israelis including Bedouin may volunteer for service, although Muslim non-Bedouin Arabs are often discouraged from doing so. Arabs may not serve in the air force. Ultraorthodox Jews who study in religious schools (Yeshivots) are excused from conscription. Males currently serve for three years, while females serve —almost entirely in noncombat positions—for two years. Exemptions are given to those whose fathers or brothers have died in service unless a parental waiver is granted.

New immigrants to Israel are required to serve the full conscript term if under the age of 18 upon arrival. Male immigrants between the ages of 19 and 23 serve for increasingly reduced terms. Those over age 24 are required to serve for only 120 days. Female immigrants over the age of 19 are exempt from conscription. Incentives to volunteer exist. In addition to salaries, certain benefits accrue only to those who have served the military or their family members. After being discharged, men are required to serve on a yearly basis for 30 or more days in the reserves until the age of 40 if in a combat unit or until the age of 54 if in a noncombat unit. Women, although subject to reserve duty call-up until the age of 34, have rarely been required to do reserve duty.

SERGIO CATIGNANI

See also
Egypt, Armed Forces; Israel Defense Forces; Jordan, Armed Forces; Syria, Armed Forces

References
Cordesman, Anthony. *Peace and War: The Arab-Israeli Military Balance Enters the 21st Century.* Westport, CT: Praeger, 2001.
Feldman, Shai, and Yiftah S. Shapir. *Middle East Strategic Balance, 2003–2004.* Brighton, UK: Sussex Academic, 2004.
Luttwak, Edward, and Don Horowitz. *The Israeli Army.* London: Allen Lane, 1975.

Copenhagen Bureau
Start Date: January 1915
End Date: 1918

Center for Zionist activities during World War I. On the outbreak of World War I in the summer of 1914, the World Zionist Organization (WZO) found itself on the horns of a dilemma. Representing Jews on both sides of the conflict, it could not afford to be seen as favoring one side over the other for fear of retribution. At the time, WZO headquarters was situated in Berlin. At first, there was discussion of transferring WZO headquarters to New York or to The Hague in the Netherlands, but the entry of the Ottoman Empire into the war on the side of the Central Powers that fall and concerns felt for the Yishuv (Jewish population) of Palestine, which was under Ottoman rule, led to the decision to remain in Berlin, where the WZO could lobby the German government on behalf of Jews within the Ottoman Empire.

In December 1914 the General Council of the WZO met for the first time since the start of the war. The meeting occurred in neutral Copenhagen. The General Council decided to maintain the Berlin headquarters but also to open an office in Copenhagen to serve as a clearinghouse for Zionist affairs and a link between Berlin and Zionist organizations in states on both sides of the war as well as in neutral nations. Dr. Leo Motzkin was the first head of the Copenhagen Bureau but was succeeded in July 1916 by Victor Jacobson. Throughout the war the bureau lobbied the German Legation in Copenhagen regarding Turkish policy toward the Jews in Palestine and sought to secure a pledge from the German government to press the Turks for Jewish immigration to Palestine. The Copenhagen Bureau ceased to function at the end of the war.

The Copenhagen Bureau is perhaps best known for its October 28, 1918, appeal to Zionist organizations worldwide to press their national governments for the realization of Jewish demands at the peace conference following the war. This so-called Copenhagen Manifesto asked that the conferees meet the just demands of all nations, both large and small; that they confirm the historical boundaries of Palestine as the national homeland of the Jewish people; that full equality for Jews in all countries be secured; and that cultural, social, and political autonomy be granted to Jews of all nations where they were in large numbers and their mass demanded it. The manifesto expressed the hope that on the day the peace treaty was signed the 2,000-year-long suffering of the Jewish people would come to an end and that the Jewish people would then "become an equal member of the covenant of free nations."

SPENCER C. TUCKER

See also

Balfour Declaration; Committee of Jewish Delegations at the Peace Conference; World War I, Impact of; World Zionist Organization; Zionism

References

Brenner, Michael. *Zionism: A Brief History.* Translated by Shelley Frisch. Princeton, NJ: Markus Wiener, 2003.

Laqueur, Walter. *A History of Zionism: From the French Revolution to the Establishment of the State of Israel.* Reprint ed. New York: Schocken, 2003.

Creech Jones, Arthur

Born: May 15, 1891
Died: October 23, 1964

British politician. Born on May 15, 1891, in Bristol, England, Arthur Creech Jones was a Labour Party member of Parliament from 1935 to 1950 and again from 1954 to 1964. At an early age, he developed an interest in the Fabian Society, an organization dedicated to the establishment of a democratic socialist state in the United Kingdom. He and the Fabians sought to advance the socialist cause by reformist rather than revolutionary means. He was a leading figure in the Fabian Colonial Bureau, established in 1940 to defend the views and aspirations of Britain's colonial subjects.

In October 1946 Creech Jones became secretary of state for the colonies in Prime Minister Clement Attlee's Labour government. Creech Jones held this post until February 1950. Attlee believed that the surge in independence struggles in British colonies after World War II required a colonial secretary who could be sympathetic to colonial viewpoints and simultaneously defend British national interests. For his part, Creech Jones believed that British colonialism conferred lasting benefits on colonial subjects. Nevertheless, he also held that colonialism was not to be an indefinite situation.

Creech Jones was sympathetic to Zionism. Basing his ideas on the Balfour Declaration during World War I, he supported the Zionist case for the partition of Palestine. Unlike most members of the cabinet, he held that partition was the only practicable solution, even if Britain had to impose it by force. Foreign Secretary Ernest Bevin, however, intended to surrender the British Mandate for Palestine to the United Nations (UN). Creech Jones disagreed with this decision but had little choice but to accede.

On September 26, 1947, Creech Jones announced to a stunned UN General Assembly that the British government, after 25 years in Palestine, was prepared to end its mandate there. During his announcement he expressed his hope that the UN would be more successful than the British had been in ameliorating the differences between Arabs and Jews in Palestine. He informed the General Assembly that the British government had been unable to convince the Arabs and Jews to reach a peaceful agreement for the division of land in Palestine and had decided to withdraw from Palestine rather than continue to attempt to impose a territorial distribution policy unilaterally.

Creech Jones lost his seat in Parliament in 1950 and was replaced by James Griffiths as colonial secretary. Creech Jones returned to Parliament in 1954, but because the Conservatives had returned to power in 1953, he had only minimal influence. He retained his seat in Parliament until his death in London on October 23, 1964.

MICHAEL R. HALL

See also

Attlee, Clement Richard; Balfour Declaration; Palestine, British Mandate for; United Kingdom, Middle East Policy; United Nations, Role of

References

Attlee, C. R. *Twilight of Empire: Memoirs of Prime Minister Clement Attlee.* London: A. S. Barnes, 1962.

Ovendale, Ritchie. "The Palestinian Policy of the British Labour Government 1947: The Decision to Withdraw." *International Affairs* 56(1) (January 1980): 73–93.

Cruise Missiles

See Missiles, Cruise

Cunningham, Sir Alan Gordon

Born: May 1, 1887
Died: January 30, 1983

British Army general and last British high commissioner in Palestine (1945–1948). Born in Dublin, Ireland, on May 1, 1887, Alan Cunningham was the younger brother of future British admiral of the fleet Andrew Browne Cunningham. The younger Cunningham graduated from the Royal Military College, Sandhurst, in 1906 and was commissioned in the army. He served with distinction in the artillery in France during World War I and then was a staff officer at the Straits Settlements during 1919–1921. Promoted to brigadier general, he commanded the 1st Division of the Royal Artillery from December 1937 until September 1938, when he assumed command of the 5th Antiaircraft Division.

During 1940, Cunningham commanded three infantry divisions in succession in Britain. In October 1940 he assumed command of British forces in Kenya, and in January and February 1941 he led three divisions in the conquest of Italian Somalia (Somaliland). He then rapidly advanced into Ethiopia and, in cooperation with General William Platt's forces from the Sudan, forced the surrender of the remaining Italian forces in Italian East Africa. Cunningham then took command of the British Eighth Army in Egypt in September 1941.

Two months later, in November 1941, the Eighth Army began Operation CRUSADER, which was designed to relieve the siege of Tobruk. Having had little time to prepare, Cunningham was out-

General Sir Alan Gordon Cunningham, last British high commissioner in Palestine (1945–1948). (Bettmann/Corbis)

maneuvered by Afrika Korps commander General Erwin Rommel at Sidi Razagh, near Tobruk. In the resulting Battle of Totensonntag, the Eighth Army sustained heavy losses, and General Sir Claude J. A. Auchinleck relieved Cunningham of his command at the end of the month. Cunningham then commanded the Staff College, Camberley (1942–1943); was general officer commanding Northern Ireland (1943–1944); and headed the Eastern Command (1944–1945).

In the fall of 1945, Cunningham was promoted to full general and appointed the British high commissioner for Palestine. While he himself was not hostile to the Jews there, British Palestinian policy was decided in London rather than in Jerusalem. Cunningham's principal task was to keep order in the mandate during the sessions there of the Anglo-American Committee of Inquiry and the United Nations Special Commission on Palestine (UNSCOP). Cunningham had his hands full in the face of Jewish opposition to British policy, illegal immigration by Jews into Palestine, and various acts of terror and sabotage by Arabs against Jews and by Jewish militant organizations against the Arabs and British.

Cunningham endeavored to enforce British immigration policy and to oust the Jewish Agency from control. His policy included mass arrests of Jewish leaders in June 1946. In January 1947 London granted Cunningham authority to proclaim martial law in any part of the mandate that he saw fit, but British military resources were not sufficient to halt the growing violence between Arabs and Jews, and Cunningham was able to maintain security only in British enclaves and main lines of communication. On May 8, 1948, he was able to secure a truce between the two sides in Jerusalem. A week later, on May 14, the State of Israel was proclaimed, and the same day Cunningham departed the country from Haifa. Knighted on his return to Britain, he died on January 30, 1983.

SPENCER C. TUCKER

See also
Anglo-American Committee of Inquiry; Jewish Agency for Israel; United Nations Special Commission on Palestine

References
Barnett, Correlli. *The Desert Generals.* New York: Viking, 1961.
Sachar, Howard M. *A History of Israel: From the Rise of Zionism to Our Time.* 3rd ed. New York: Knopf, 2007.
Sherman, A. J. *Mandate Days: British Lives in Palestine, 1918–1948.* Baltimore: Johns Hopkins University Press, 2001.

Cyprus

The third-largest island in the Mediterranean Sea and an important staging, transit, and evacuation area for refugees, internees, the United Nations (UN), and international relief agencies transiting to and from Israel, Palestine, and Lebanon. Cyprus, with a current population of about 700,000 people, encompasses roughly 3,500 square miles. It is strategically located in the easternmost part of the Mediterranean and is 60 miles west of Syria, 67 miles west of Lebanon, 124 miles northwest of Israel, 236 miles north of Egypt, and just 47 miles south of Turkey. Cyprus was a British Crown colony when the island was used to intern more than 50,000 illegal Jewish immigrants seeking entry into the Jewish communities of Palestine following World War II and the Nazi Holocaust.

Members of the tribes of Israel first came to Cyprus when the Northern Kingdom of Israel was conquered by the Assyrian Empire in 722 BC and were followed by several hundred Jews, called such because they were members of the tribes of Israel that resided in the Southern Kingdom of Judah when Judah was conquered by Babylon in 587 BC. The Apostle Paul and Barnabas, a Cypriot, preached Christianity among the Jews of Cyprus in the first century AD. Cyprian Jews participated in the Second Jewish-Roman War, also known as the Kitos War (AD 115–117), and for this the Emperor Trajan destroyed Salamis and forbade any Jew to land in Cyprus. Yet the Cyprian Jewish community began to grow and prosper as the fortunes of Rome waned.

Cyprus was invaded by Arabs and Muslims on numerous occasions before being annexed by the Ottoman Empire in 1571. Perhaps the most important of these raids occurred during a series of invasions in the seventh and eighth centuries BC. Umm Haram, the foster mother and alleged aunt of the Prophet Muhammad, fell from her mule and died in the 647–649 BC invasion of Cyprus. A mosque known as Hala Sultan Tekkesi was erected in her honor and is considered, following Mecca, Medina, and Jerusalem, to be the fourth holiest place in Islam.

The Ottoman Turks ceded Cyprus to Britain in June 1878. Russian and Romanian Jewish refugees fleeing the late-19th-century persecutions in Europe that gave rise to the World Zionist Organization (WZO) in 1897 unsuccessfully attempted to settle in Cyprus in 1883, 1885, and 1891. Davis Trietsch tried but failed to gain the endorsement of the Third Zionist Congress (1899) for a Zionist settlement in Cyprus. Theodor Herzl then used the pamphlet *The Problem of Jewish Immigration to England and the United States Solved by Furthering the Jewish Colonization of Cyprus* to make a similar proposal to the British Parliament House Select Committee on Alien Immigration in 1902, and this was rejected as well.

The 1919 Treaty of Versailles that ended World War I granted Great Britain control of Palestine, and the League of Nations officially established the British Mandate for Palestine in June 1922. Cyprus was made a British Crown colony in 1925.

Although the British limited legal Jewish immigration into Palestine to 18,000 a year from 1945 to 1948, some 80,000 illegal Jewish immigrants entered the British Mandate for Palestine during that period. The British attempted to enforce the quota by blockading Palestine and in August 1946 began sending the intercepted illegal Jewish immigrants to British detention camps built at Karaolos and Xylotymbou on Cyprus. The only exceptions to the policy were the 4,515 displaced persons (all Jewish, some orphaned children) onboard the *Exodus* in 1947 who were eventually returned to Germany. Most of the 66 ships that attempted to run the blockade were intercepted. Americans and Canadians who helped crew some of these ships were also interned on Cyprus. The British interned 53,510 illegal Jewish immigrants in detention camps on Cyprus during 1946–1949.

Great Britain informed the United Nations (UN) on February 14, 1947, that it would no longer administer the Mandate for Palestine. This prompted the UN General Assembly to partition Palestine into independent Jewish and Arab states on November 29, 1947. Some 28,000 Jews were still interned in the Cyprus camps when the Mandate was dissolved, partition was enacted, and the independent Jewish State of Israel was created at midnight Palestinian time on May 14, 1948. About 11,000 internees remained in the camps as of August 1948, with the British releasing and transporting the internees to Haifa at the rate of 1,500 a month. Israel began the final evacuation of the Cyprus camps in December 1948 with the last 10,200 Jewish internees, mainly men of military age, evacuated to Israel during January 24–February 11, 1949.

From 1950 to 1952 approximately 130,000 Iraqi Jews were permitted to immigrate to Israel. The first flight left Baghdad on May 19, 1950, and flew 86 Jewish immigrants to Israel via Nicosia, Cyprus. Iraqi Jews numbering 38,000 eventually used this route through Cyprus to a new home in Israel.

British and French forces employed Cyprus as a major staging area for their military operations against Egypt during the Suez Crisis of 1956. Cyprus became independent on August 16, 1960, and remained neutral in the disputes between Israel and the Arab States, often serving as a place of refuge and transit for those escaping the various conflicts. The unwritten truce between the Palestinians and the Israelis was briefly broken following the massacre of Israeli athletes during the 1972 Munich Olympics. As part of Operation WRATH OF GOD, Mossad agents assassinated Palestine Liberation Organization (PLO) member Hussein Al Bashir with a bomb in a hotel room in Nicosia, Cyprus, on January 24, 1973. Bashir was the Fatah representative in Cyprus, and Mossad also believed him to be the head of the Black September organization in Cyprus and to have participated in some capacity in the Munich attack.

On April 1, 2002, units of the Israel Defense Forces (IDF) surrounded Bethlehem as part of Operation DEFENSIVE SHIELD (March–April 2002), and the following day some 200 Palestinians including 50 militants seized the Church of the Nativity in Bethlehem and took 150 civilian and clerical hostages. The IDF then laid siege to the compound. The siege ended on May 10 when the European Union (EU) negotiated a settlement that deported 13 militants to Cyprus and transferred 26 militants to the Gaza Strip. Cyprus served as a transit point for 12 of the Palestinians, who were eventually given refuge in six EU states. One of the Palestinians was allowed to remain in Cyprus.

RICHARD EDWARDS

See also

Black September Organization; Church of the Nativity; *Exodus* Incident; Hezbollah; Lebanon, Israeli Operations against; Mossad; Suez Crisis; United Kingdom, Middle East Policy; World War I, Impact of; World War II, Impact of; World Zionist Organization

References

Mallinson, William. *Cyprus: A Modern History*. London: Tauris, 2005.
Panteli, Stavros. *The History of Modern Cyprus*. Herts, UK: Topline, 2005.
———. *Place of Refuge: The History of the Jews in Cyprus*. London: Elliot and Thompson, 2004.

Czechoslovakia, Middle East Policy

Consistent with Czechoslovakia's traditional role as a purveyor of weaponry to militarily weaker states, the agreement of September 1955 whereby the Czechoslovak government would provide arms to Egypt in exchange for cotton became an important part of the Soviet bloc's bid to gain a strategic hold in the Middle East. The 1952 Egyptian Revolution that ultimately brought Colonel Gamal Abdel Nasser to power led the Soviet Union to view Egypt as a key force in African and Third World independence movements. Meanwhile, the United States and Great Britain continued to view Egypt in strictly strategic terms, namely its role in controlling the Suez Canal. As a result, the Soviet Union used Nasser's Egypt as a base from which to influence the entire region. Although many of the Soviet satellite states figured in the Kremlin's larger Middle East policy, Czechoslovakia certainly played the most significant role thanks to its large arms industry and exportable technical knowledge. During the Cold War, Czechoslovakia became a crucial provider of arms and industrial technology to the Middle East. It was also involved in various cultural exchanges with Arab states and thereby expanded Czechoslovak penetration in the region.

The September 1955 Czechoslovak-Egyptian arms deal was actually just part of a much larger framework of Soviet bloc military and economic penetration into the Arab world. In March 1955 the Czechoslovak government opened an expansive industrial exhibition in Cairo. This was followed by a July 1955 Czechoslovak delegation to Cairo that secured a long-term trade, payment, and barter agreement between the two nations. Between 1955 and 1959 Czechoslovakia's share of Egypt's foreign trade nearly doubled, and by 1960 Czechoslovakia had granted Egypt a total of $80.5 million worth of loans, not including any of the arms credits. Czechoslovakia pursued similar policies with Syria prior to Syria's inclusion in the United Arab Republic (1958). Eventually, during the 1970s, Iraq too became an outlet for Czechoslovak arms. Indeed, the Soviet Union and Czechoslovakia became Iraq's primary supplier of arms as a result of the 1972 Soviet-Iraqi Treaty of Friendship and Cooperation. This relationship temporarily ended when Iraq invaded Iran in 1980, thus beginning the Iran-Iraq War (1980–1988). That conflagration forced the Iraqi government to secure arms elsewhere, including from the United States.

Besides the sale of arms, the high level of industrial and technical knowledge exported from Czechoslovakia to Egypt was equally significant. Between 1956 and 1961, Czechoslovakia built 35 industrial installations in Egypt. These projects included power plants, sugar mills, water-treatment facilities, toy and bicycle factories, and shoe manufacturing. In order to successfully staff these new industries, Egyptian engineers and technical workers often traveled to Czechoslovakia to receive advanced training. Such exchanges were not limited to Egyptians traveling to Czechoslovakia. In 1961 the Czechoslovak government began the construction of a polytechnic institute in Cairo to train designers, technicians, and foremen. It was staffed largely by Czechoslovak instructors who had relocated to Egypt. Meanwhile, there was a steady increase in the number of Egyptian university students enrolling in Czechoslovak universities. In fact, Egyptian students represented one of the largest contingents of foreign students in Prague.

Although Czechoslovakia attained impressive levels of economic penetration into Egypt, Czechoslovak investment in Egyptian cultural affairs allowed the Soviet bloc to expand its reach throughout the remainder of the region. By 1960 the Czechoslovak government had opened an Egyptian cultural center in Egypt, signed a scientific and cultural cooperation agreement with Cairo, and assisted in the preservation of several monuments in the Aswan Dam region. The intention of the Czechoslovak government was not just to promote Czechoslovak and Soviet interests in Egypt but also to supply Egypt with the necessary tools to promote its interests throughout the Arab world and, in turn, Soviet interests as well. Nasser's acquisition of several Czechoslovak-made medium-wave transmitters to broadcast Egypt's Voice of the Arabs Radio was critical in the diffusion of Soviet penetration in the Arab world.

The policies pursued by the Czechoslovak government with the explicit backing of the Soviet Union ultimately led to an increase in tensions among the United States, Great Britain, and the Soviet Union. The 1955 arms agreement represented the first time that the Soviet bloc had infiltrated the predominantly Western-controlled Arab world. As a result an impasse between the United States and Egypt emerged, leading to the retraction of Western funding for the construction of the Aswan Dam. In an attempt to raise funds for the dam construction and assert Egyptian sovereignty, Nasser announced the nationalization of the Suez Canal, which ultimately led to the 1956 Suez Crisis.

By the mid-1970s, however, Egypt had begun to reorient its foreign policy away from the Soviet bloc and toward the West. By the end of the decade, Egypt was purchasing most of its military hardware from the United States. Only Syria continued buying arms in large quantities from the Soviet bloc. Nevertheless, by relying on satellite states such as Czechoslovakia, the Soviet Union was able to attain considerable leverage in the Arab world.

JONATHAN H. L'HOMMEDIEU

See also

Egypt; Iraq; Nasser, Gamal Abdel; Soviet Union and Russia, Middle East Policy; Suez Crisis; Syria; United Kingdom, Middle East Policy; United States, Middle East Policy

References

Hopwood, Derek. *Egypt*. New York: Routledge, 1993.

Szulc, Tad. *Czechoslovakia since World War II*. New York: Viking, 1971.

Troen, Selwyn. *The Suez-Sinai Crisis, 1956: Retrospective and Reappraisal*. Edited by Moshe Shemesh. New York: Columbia University Press, 1990.

Wolchik, Sharon. *Czechoslovakia in Transition: Politics, Economics, and Society*. London: Pinter, 1993.

D

Dahlan, Muhammad Yusuf
Born: September 29, 1961

Palestinian politician and important figure in both Fatah and the Palestinian Authority (PA). Muhammad Dahlan was born on September 29, 1961, in the Khan Yunis Refugee Camp in the Gaza Strip. His family had fled from Hammama, Palestine (now Nitzanim, Israel). Dahlan became politically active as a teenager in Khan Yunis, recruiting other youngsters for civic projects. He earned a degree in business administration from the Islamic University of Gaza, where he was also a student leader and expanded his earlier activities to include charitable work such as the delivery of food and medicine but also the spreading of Palestinian nationalist propaganda. The organization he founded became the Fatah Youth Movement (Fatah Shabiba) in 1981.

By the time he was 25 years old, Dahlan had been arrested by the Israeli authorities on 11 separate occasions. Altogether he spent six years in Israeli prisons, becoming fluent in Hebrew in the process. One of the leaders of the First Intifada (1987–1994) in which the Fatah Youth Movement was very much involved, he was again arrested by the Israeli authorities in 1988 and deported to Jordan. He then went to Tunis, where he worked with the leaders of the Palestine Liberation Organization (PLO).

A protégé of PLO chairman Yasser Arafat, Dahlan returned to Gaza with Arafat in July 1994. Arafat appointed him to head the Preventive Security Service (PSS) for the Gaza Strip, a PLO security force, as well as to head Fatah in Gaza. The two posts made Dahlan one of the most powerful figures in the new Palestinian Authority. With a police force of 20,000 men, Dahlan also became the most powerful figure in Gaza, which some came to refer to as Dahlanistan. To enforce his authority, Dahlan's associates reportedly used strong-arm methods, including torture. As with many other Fatah leaders, he became wealthy through PLO monopolies such as oil and cement and kickbacks on building contracts. The fact that he had been born in a refugee camp and been imprisoned by the Israelis and had the loyalty of other such prisoners helped shield him from some Palestinian criticism, however.

As head of the PSS in Gaza, Dahlan was responsible for ensuring support from all members of Hamas for the 1993 Oslo Accords. Reportedly, he met regularly with Israeli security officials and U.S. Central Intelligence Agency (CIA) representatives to coordinate security issues. In 1995 following a number of Hamas suicide attacks, Dahlan, reportedly on the orders of Arafat, ordered the PSS to crack down on Hamas militants, arresting some 2,000 of them. The PSS also raided Islamic charities, schools, and mosques. Dahlan was able to succeed in such activities in large part because of the initial Palestinian support for the Oslo Accords and his tough methods. Because the Likud government of Prime Minister Benjamin Netanyahu in Israel was obstructionist toward the peace process, however, the PA crackdown on militants soon lost support, and Dahlan himself backed off from it.

Dahlan was a regular member of negotiations with Israeli government officials on a variety of issues. He was also a participant in the Wye River negotiations (1998), and he took part in the Camp David Summit (2000) and the Taba negotiations (2001). Reportedly, he tried hard to reach an agreement at Camp David.

Dahlan's relationship with Israeli authorities cooled considerably with the beginning of the Second (al-Aqsa) Intifada in September 2000. Although he claimed that he remained committed to the peace process, Israeli officials blamed him for some of the violence in the Gaza Strip, and he was suspected of being involved in a November 2000 attack on an Israeli school bus. In May 2001 his

Muhammad Yusuf Dahlan, prominent Palestinian politician and Fatah figure, during an interview in Ramallah on June 7, 2003. (Reuters/Corbis)

motorcade came under attack from the Israel Defense Forces (IDF) in Gaza, and four of his bodyguards were wounded. Israeli prime minister Ariel Sharon denied that Dahlan was deliberately targeted and expressed regret for what the Israeli government later called an unfortunate mistake.

Dahlan reportedly offered to resign from the PSS in November 2001 in protest of the PA's policy of arresting Popular Front for the Liberation of Palestine (PFLP) and Islamic Jihad members. Arafat supposedly refused the resignation. Anticipating that Arafat would be forced to unify his security forces, Dahlan began to expand his authority among low-level commanders in the West Bank PSS, seeking to undermine the authority of its commander Jibril Rajob. Reportedly enjoying the support of U.S. president George W. Bush's administration, Dahlan also began to see himself as the possible successor to Arafat. Expecting to be named to head the security service, Dahlan resigned as head of the PSS. Arafat, however, resisted U.S. pressure to unify the security services. Although in July 2002 Arafat appointed Dahlan his national security adviser, the position was devoid of any real power, let alone control of security services.

When Arafat was pressured into naming Mahmoud Abbas as the PA's first prime minister in February 2003, Abbas sought to name Dahlan the minister of interior. Arafat opposed this, and after considerable turmoil within the PA leadership Arafat agreed in April that Abbas would retain that post as well as the prime ministership, while Dahlan would become minister of state for security affairs. Abbas then authorized Dahlan to restructure the PA's Ministry of the Interior with a view toward cracking down on militants opposed to the peace process. In effect, Dahlan controlled some 20,000 security personnel but without having the title of interior minister. It proved an impossible situation, with a Likud government in Israel and Hamas militants both opposing the U.S.-sponsored Road Map to Peace. Dahlan instead proposed negotiations with Hamas to achieve a cease-fire, which was reached in July 2004. The cease-fire collapsed soon thereafter following the Israeli assassinations of Hamas and Islamic Jihad leaders.

Abbas resigned on September 6, 2003. The new prime minister, Ahmed Qurei, dropped Dahlan from his cabinet. This decision led to protest demonstrations, especially in Khan Yunis, supporting Dahlan in Gaza and to Dahlan's posturing as a reformer when he called for elections in Fatah organizations that would bring in new leadership, although Dahlan was careful not to attack Arafat personally. Dahlan was seen as a prime mover in a wave of intra-Palestinian violence between his supporters and those favoring the Fatah old guard in the summer of 2004 in the Gaza Strip.

Appointed Palestinian minister for civil affairs, Dahlan had charge of coordinating with Israeli minister of defense Shaul Mofaz the Israeli pullout from Gaza. In January 2006 Dahlan narrowly won election to the Palestinian Legislative Council in the general elections as a representative of Khan Yunis.

In March 2007, over Hamas objections, Palestinian president Mahmoud Abbas named Dahlan to head the newly reestablished Palestinian National Security Council, which had control of all security services in the Palestinian territories. Dahlan resigned from this post in July 2007, but the National Security Council had already been dissolved following the Hamas takeover of Gaza in mid-June. Many in Fatah held Dahlan responsible for that easy Hamas victory, during which time he and key lieutenants were absent from Gaza. In the course of the fighting, Dahlan's Gaza residence—which many Palestinians had come to view as a symbol of Fatah corruption—was seized by Hamas militants and then demolished.

SPENCER C. TUCKER

See also

Arafat, Yasser; Fatah; Intifada, First; Intifada, Second; Islamic Jihad, Palestinian; Netanyahu, Benjamin; Oslo Accords; Palestine Liberation Organization; Palestinian Authority; Popular Front for the Liberation of Palestine; Qurei, Ahmed Ali Mohammed; Sharon, Ariel; Wye River Agreement

References

Pappe, Ilan. *A History of Modern Palestine: One Land, Two Peoples.* Cambridge: Cambridge University Press, 2003.

Parsons, Nigel Craig. *The Politics of the Palestinian Authority: From Oslo to Al-Aqsa.* London: Routledge, 2003.

Rubin, Barry. *Revolution until Victory? The Politics and History of the PLO.* Reprint ed. Cambridge: Harvard University Press, 2003.

Sayigh, Yezid. *Armed Struggle and the Search for State: The Palestine National Movement, 1949–1993.* New York: Oxford University Press, 2000.

Daoud, Muhammad
Born: May 16, 1937

Palestinian militant and mastermind of the Black September organization terrorist attack on Israeli athletes at the 1972 Munich Summer Olympics. Muhammad Daoud, more commonly known as Abu Daoud, was born in the Jerusalem community of Silwan on May 16, 1937. Little is known of his early life, but from the time he was a youth he demonstrated a penchant for militancy.

Black September refers to a violent struggle in September 1970 when Jordan's King Hussein expelled the Palestinians and the Palestine Liberation Organization (PLO) from the country. In the process, many Palestinians were killed or imprisoned before the conflict ended in July 1971. The PLO was then forced out of Jordan to Lebanon. Daoud was first an operative and then a leader of the Black September organization, named in commemoration of this event. The organization's original goal was to avenge the events of Black September and to gain the release of Palestinians imprisoned in Jordan.

The alleged purpose of the Munich attack was to protest the exclusion of the Palestinians from the 1972 Summer Olympic Games. Daoud planned the attack and led it during its initial phases. In response to the attacks, Israeli prime minister Golda Meir authorized, in Operation WRATH OF GOD, the assassination of those known to be responsible for the Munich massacre, and the 1973 Operation SPRING OF YOUTH, led by Ehud Barak, carried out an attack on Popular Front for the Liberation of Palestine (PFLP) headquarters in Beirut. Daoud's role in the event was well known to the Mossad Israeli intelligence agency, and he contends that it was Mossad that inflicted 13 wounds to his left wrist, chest, stomach, and jaw when he was shot at close range in a Warsaw, Poland, hotel on July 27, 1981.

Immediately following the 1972 Munich attack, Daoud went to Eastern Europe. He was arrested late that same year while leading a team into Jordan with the goal of taking hostage the Jordanian prime minister and other members of the cabinet. They were to be exchanged for Palestinians imprisoned for actions committed during Black September. Daoud was convicted and sentenced to death in March 1973. King Hussein commuted the sentence to life in prison and later released him along with 1,000 other prisoners in a September 1973 general amnesty. Daoud then moved to Lebanon and remained there until the onset of the civil war in 1975, at which time he returned to Amman.

In January 1977 Daoud was arrested in Paris. Although the Jerusalem Magistrates Court issued a warrant on January 10 seeking his extradition on charges stemming from the Munich attack, a French court released him when the government of West Germany failed to expeditiously request his extradition. Daoud then returned to Jordan again. He was allowed to move from Jordan to the West Bank city of Ramallah in 1993 following the Oslo Accords. He became a member of the Palestinian National Council (PNC) in 1996, and in 1999 he publicly and unrepentantly admitted his role in the Munich attack in his book *Palestine: From Jerusalem to Munich*. In addition to admitting his role in the Munich massacre and in the ensuing Lufthansa hijacking, Daoud also asserted that PLO chairman Yasser Arafat had granted prior approval for the Munich attack, which Arafat and others denied.

Daoud's admission led to the issuance of a German arrest warrant that resulted in the revocation of his Israeli VIP travel card. He was denied reentry into the Palestinian Authority (PA) territories on June 13, 1999. He protested the revocation of his VIP card and asserted that the warrant was null and void because so many years had passed since Munich. Nevertheless, he moved to Syria, the only country that would allow him residence.

RICHARD M. EDWARDS

See also

Arafat, Yasser; Black September; Black September Organization; Mossad; Munich Olympic Games; Oslo Accords; Palestine Liberation Organization; Palestinian Authority; Ramallah; Terrorism

References

Abu Daoud. *Memoirs of a Palestinian Terrorist*. New York: Arcade, 2002.
Abu Douad [Muhammad Daoud Audeh], with Giles du Jonchay. *Palestine: De Jerusalem à Munich*. Paris: Éditions Anne Carriere, 1999.
Jonas, George. *Vengeance: The True Story of an Israeli Counter-Terrorist Team*. New York: Simon and Schuster, 2005.
Klein, Aaron. *Striking Back: The 1972 Munich Olympics Massacre and Israel's Deadly Response*. New York: Random House, 2005.
Roman, Michael. *Black September*. Orlando: Northwest Publishing, 1995.

Darwish, Mahmoud
Born: March 13, 1941

Palestinian Arab poet and writer and former member of the Palestine Liberation Organization (PLO) Executive Committee. Born on March 13, 1941, into a Sunni Muslim landowning family in the village of al-Barwi near Akko (Acre) in the British Mandate for Palestine, Mahmoud Darwish was forced at age seven to flee with his family to Lebanon before advancing Israeli forces during the Israeli War of Independence (1948–1949). He and his family returned to Israel as illegal immigrants in 1949 only to find that his village had been destroyed. Following graduation from secondary school Darwish moved to Haifa, where he worked in journalism. He had written his first poetry while in school but published his first collection in 1960. His reputation as the leading Palestinian resistance poet was established in his second collection of poems, *Awraq al-Zaytun*, in 1964. He joined the Israeli Communist Party in 1961 and edited the communist newspaper *Al-Ittihad*. He was arrested several times, imprisoned, and placed under house arrest.

In 1970 Darwish went to Moscow to study. Not wishing to return to Israel he settled in Egypt, where he worked for the newspaper *Al-Ahram*. He then moved to Beirut, where he worked for the PLO and edited its journal *Shu'un Filistiniyya*. Later he became editor-in-chief of the Palestinian literary and cultural periodical *Al-Karmil, Studies in Arabic Language and Literature*. Following the Israeli invasion 1982, Darwish moved to Cyprus.

Mahmoud Darwish, Palestinian poet, writer, and former member of the Palestine Liberation Organization's Executive Committee. (Reuters/Corbis)

Elected to the Executive Committee of the PLO in 1987, Darwish headed the Supreme Council for Education, Propaganda, and Heritage. He wrote the Palestinian Declaration of Independence, which was formally presented by the PLO in Algiers on November 15, 1988. He resigned from the PLO Executive Committee in 1993 to protest the Oslo Accords, demanding a tougher stance in negotiations with Israel. Darwish believed that the Oslo Accords would only lead to greater violence. He has also been attacked for defending Palestinian Arab mainstream politics.

After living in Tunisia, France, and Jordan, in 1996 Darwish settled in the West Bank city of Ramallah, where the PLO headquarters was located. In 2000 the government of Israeli prime minister Ehud Barak narrowly escaped a vote of no confidence over a decision by the minister of education to include Darwish's poetry in the school curriculum.

Darwish seeks in his poetry to interpret the experience of Palestinian Arab exile and give voice to the hopes of the Palestinian people. His poetry readings in the Arab world are widely attended. Sometimes called "the Poet of Palestine" or the "Poet of Palestine Resistance," Darwish has published more than 20 books. His awards include the Lotus Prize by the Union of Afro-Asian Writers (1969), the Lenin Prize (1983), the Dutch Prince Claus Foundation prize, and the French knighthood of Arts and Belles Letters (1997). He has also been mentioned as a contender for the Nobel Prize for Literature.

SPENCER C. TUCKER

See also
Barak, Ehud; Oslo Accords; Palestine Liberation Organization

References
Darwish, Mahmoud. *Memory for Forgetfulness: August, Beirut, 1982.* Berkeley: University of California Press, 1995.
Nassar, Hala Kh., and Najat Rahman. *Mahmoud Darwish, Exile's Poet: Critical Essays.* Northampton, MA: Interlink, 2006.

Dayan, Moshe
Born: May 20, 1915
Died: October 16, 1981

Israeli general and political leader during the formative years of the State of Israel. Moshe Dayan was born on May 20, 1915, in Degania Kibbutz near the Sea of Galilee. His parents had immigrated to Palestine from Russia. At age 14 Dayan joined the Haganah, the Jewish self-defense militia in the British protectorate of Palestine. Initially Haganah was suppressed by British authorities, but during the 1936–1939 Arab Revolt its members were encouraged to help quell the rebellion. At the beginning of the revolt Dayan was in England studying at the London School of Economics, but he returned to Palestine in 1936 and rejoined Haganah. He served in ambush and patrol units and trained under British Army captain Orde Wingate. In 1939, because of his membership in the banned organization, he was sentenced to five years in prison and was imprisoned at Akko (Acre).

Released in February 1941, Dayan led reconnaissance forces into Vichy France–controlled Syria to support the subsequent British invasion there. During one mission in Syria, on June 8, 1941, Dayan was shot by a sniper and lost his left eye. From then on, he became well known for his trademark black eye patch.

Dayan was then posted to the Haganah General Staff, where he worked to gather intelligence on Arab military capabilities. In May 1948, Israel proclaimed its independence and was immediately attacked by the neighboring Arab nations of Egypt, Iraq, Lebanon, Syria, and Transjordan. In the ensuing Israeli War of Independence (1948–1949), Dayan led the defense of the Deganya settlements during May 19–21, 1948. He then raised the 89th Commando Battalion, a mobile unit in jeeps and half-tracks, leading it in capturing Lod and Ramallah (July 9–19) on the central front. Named commander in the Jerusalem vicinity on July 23, he proved both an exceptional strategist and tactician. As such, he rose rapidly through the ranks of the Israel Defense Forces (IDF). In 1950 he became head of the Southern Command, and two years later he assumed control of the Northern Command. In 1953, General Dayan was named chief of army operations and then chief of staff of the IDF.

Dayan remained chief of staff from 1953 until 1958. In this post he reinvigorated the IDF. He ordered the very best officers into the fighting units and also toughened training, leading the way by completing a parachute and commando course himself. At 50 percent, the IDF's proportion of combat to noncombat forces was probably the conflict, but his presence contributed to military morale and confidence in the Eshkol government. The quick war included conquest of the Golan Heights, the West Bank, and the Sinai Peninsula. Dayan's prominent public role in the conflict inflated his popularity within Israel. He pushed for open annexation of the occupied territories and used his position to create Jewish settlements in the West Bank and on the Golan Heights. He remained minister of defense under Golda Meir, who became prime minister after Eshkol's death on February 26, 1969.

Dayan's image was tarnished by the Yom Kippur War (1973), which began with heavy losses in troops, equipment, and territory by the IDF. Although later exonerated by an official inquiry, Dayan's ministry clearly ignored the signs of heightened tensions and troubling troop movements. Despite Israel's eventual victory, the toll of the war led Meir to resign along with her entire cabinet in May 1974.

The war had deeply depressed Dayan, who went into a political eclipse for a time. Despite his ties to the Labor Party, he joined Prime Minister Menachem Begin's Likud Party government in 1977, serving as foreign minister. In this capacity Dayan assisted in negotiating the 1978 Camp David Accords and the 1979 Israel-Egypt Peace Treaty, the latter of which established a lasting peace with Egypt. Soon after the treaty was signed, however, Dayan disagreed with Begin over the status of Palestinian territories occupied by Israel and the construction of Jewish settlements there. Dayan believed that Israel should disengage entirely from the territories seized in the 1967 war. In 1981 he formally left the Labor Party to form a new party, Telem, which won only two seats in the 1981 parliamentary elections. One of Telem's positions was that Israel should withdraw from the occupied territories.

Dayan was an amateur archeologist, and he also wrote four books. He died on October 16, 1981, of colon cancer in Tel Aviv. An able and resourceful military commander, Dayan led by example. He was, however, somewhat less successful as a politician.

PAUL SPRINGER

See also

Begin, Menachem; Camp David Accords; Eshkol, Levi; Haganah; Israel Defense Forces; Israel-Egypt Peace Treaty; Israeli War of Independence, Overview; Labor Party; Likud Party; Meir, Golda; Sinai Campaign; Six-Day War; Suez Crisis; Wingate, Orde Charles; Yom Kippur War

References

Dayan, Moshe. *Moshe Dayan: The Story of My Life*. New York: Morrow, 1976.

Slater, Robert. *Warrior Statesman: The Life of Moshe Dayan*. New York: St. Martin's, 1991.

Teveth, Shabtai. *Moshe Dayan: The Soldier, the Man, the Legend*. Boston: Houghton Mifflin, 1973.

Dayr Yasin Massacre

See Deir Yassin Massacre

Moshe Dayan, Israeli general and prominent political figure during the State of Israel's formative years. (Israeli Government Press Office)

the world's highest. Dayan insisted that henceforward officers were to lead from the front. During the 1956 Suez Crisis, he planned and oversaw the so-called Lightning Campaign of late October that saw Israeli forces advance quickly through the Sinai toward the Suez Canal. In March 1957 a cease-fire was declared, and the IDF withdrew from the Sinai, replaced by the United Nations Emergency Force (UNEF).

In 1958 Dayan retired from the IDF and joined the Mapai Party led by David Ben-Gurion, Israel's first prime minister. Dayan was elected to the Knesset (Israeli parliament) in 1959 and served in the cabinet as minister of agriculture during December 1959–November 1964. In 1964 he left Mapai and helped form Rafi, Ben-Gurion's separatist party. Dayan was reelected to parliament, and in June 1967 Prime Minister Levi Eshkol named him minister of defense as part of the prime minister's unity government, created to counter a growing threat of war. The members of Rafi rejoined Mapai to form the Labor Party in 1968.

While serving as defense minister, Dayan presided over the June 1967 Six-Day War. He was not an integral part of IDF planning for

Dead Sea

Landlocked inland sea located between Israel (to the west) and Jordan (to the east). The lowest land point on earth at 1,373 feet below sea level, the Dead Sea is also among the world's saltiest bodies of water, with a salinity approximately nine times greater than that found in average ocean water. The Dead Sea is approximately 42 miles long (north to south) and 11 miles wide. At its greatest depth, the water is about 1,075 feet deep, making the Dead Sea the deepest hypersaline body of water in the world. The sea is fed by the Jordan River to the north and is part of the larger Jordan Rift (or Great Rift Valley). No rivers or streams drain into or run out of the sea, which explains in part its hypersaline waters. The water derives its name from the fact that the high salt concentrations prevent the growth of aquatic plants of any kind and will not sustain fish or other maritime life. While Dead Sea waters contain certain microscopic organisms, they are free of normal aquatic species and thus appear dead.

The Dead Sea figures in both Islamic and Jewish history. It is thought that the biblical (Old Testament) cities of Sodom and Gomorrah, destroyed by God's wrath, were located along its southern shores. On the west side of the Dead Sea was the sprawling complex known as Masada where, during AD 66–70, the Jews held off Roman armies. And located a bit north of the sea is Jericho, thought to be the world's oldest continually inhabited settlement.

As more and more of the Jordan River's waters have been diverted for agricultural and industrial purposes, the salinity of the Dead Sea has increased while its surface area has decreased. While the sea may never disappear altogether, it is quite likely that its size

will continue to shrink. Since the early years of the 20th century, the Dead Sea has been used to produce potash and bromine as well as magnesium. These minerals have wide applications for both industry and agriculture. (Potash is an essential ingredient in many fertilizers.) Both Jordan and Israel operate extensive facilities to extract these resources. The process involves the use of massive evaporation pans so large that they can be seen from space. The Israelis also operate a large power plant along the shores of the Dead Sea.

In an effort to save the Dead Sea from eventual extinction, Israel, Jordan, and the Palestinian Authority (PA) have adopted a joint plan to construct a canal between the Red Sea and the Dead Sea that would bring more water into the Dead Sea. The resulting flow of water would not only bring much-needed water into the sea but would also allow for the construction of a desalination plant—probably in Jordan—and a massive hydroelectric plant.

PAUL G. PIERPAOLI JR.

See also

Desalination; Israel; Jordan; Jordan River

References

Kreiger, Barbara. *The Dead Sea: Myth, Politics, and History.* Boston: Brandeis University Press, 1997.

Niemi, Tina M., et al., eds. *The Dead Sea: The Lake and Its Setting.* New York: Oxford University Press, 1997.

Stevens, Serita, and Rayanne Moore. *Red Sea, Dead Sea.* New York: St. Martin's, 1991.

Dead Sea Scrolls

See Qumran and the Dead Sea Scrolls

Decolonization

Decolonization was the process by which European nations granted independence to their colonial overseas possessions. In 1945 following World War II when the United Nations (UN) came into being, roughly one-third of the world's population—750 million people—resided in non-self-governing colonial dependencies. By the end of the 20th century, fewer than 2 million of the world's 6.1 billion people remained in colonial territories. The former colonies varied greatly in their ability to overcome entrenched social and political problems.

During the era of mercantilism in the 16th, 17th, and early 18th centuries, empire-building appeared desirable as a means of building up a nation's wealth. In addition to economic motives, colonies were held to be useful for naval bases and as a sign of national prestige. The colonization impulse peaked in the 18th century and waned on the impact of free enterprise economics. Colonies were found to be an economic burden and of scant benefit to the mother country. Late in the 19th century, a new age of imperialism began. Much of the impulse this time was geopolitical, based on the desire to control key resources, geographical locations, and populations and to deny these to a rival.

The Dead Sea as seen from a satellite in space on August 7, 1999. (NASA)

Arab protesters gather in the Rawdat el Maaref Hall in Jerusalem to voice their opposition to British policy in Palestine, 1929. (Library of Congress)

The first colonial era had generated extensive migrations of Europeans. The second wave, however, was more along the lines of a commercial and political arrangement. Europeans exploited their colonies as they were and usually did not seek to make them over in the image of the homeland. This was particularly true of the British, but the French did at least profess to believe in their civilizing mission, and Germans spoke about exporting their *Kultur* (culture).

Investments in colonial infrastructure and social programs were limited, and the co-option of elites was a preferable means of gaining local cooperation in exploiting a colony's natural resources. When the Europeans, Japanese, and Americans largely concluded the race for empire by 1914 or so, almost all of Africa and much of Asia were under the control of colonial powers. European states had approximately 80 colonies, with the British Empire far and away the largest and the only one that really formed anything approaching a cohesive, economic unit.

World War I encouraged nationalist forces in colonies around the world. Nationalist leaders took inspiration from U.S. president Woodrow Wilson's "Fourteen Points" speech on war aims that stressed self-determination. Nonetheless, as far as the Middle East was concerned, Britain secured control over Palestine and Iraq, while France obtained Syria and Lebanon.

World War II finally broke the existing system apart. Colonial powers such as France and Britain emerged from World War II in a greatly weakened state and with their prestige in tatters. The war, which had severed or severely weakened ties with the mother countries, also heightened nationalism in the colonies. The defeat of France by Germany in 1940 sent shock waves through the French Empire, and Free French leader General Charles de Gaulle acknowledged that there would have to be a new relationship after the war between Metropolitan France and its overseas colonies, which had helped keep the struggle against Germany alive in the name of France. The Japanese, who brought their own form of colonial domination, nonetheless skillfully exploited resentment of European control in such places as Malaya, Indochina, and the Dutch East Indies. Nor did it help the colonial powers that U.S. president Franklin D. Roosevelt and Soviet leader Joseph Stalin, for very different reasons, emerged as staunch opponents of colonialism.

In many colonies by the 1940s and 1950s, elites seized the opportunity to play the nationalist card. Often the colonizing power simply granted independence and the transition was peaceful, as in the case of the United States and the Philippines. The 1960 UN Declaration on the Granting of Independence to Colonial Countries and Peoples stated that all people have the right to self-determination.

Decolonization of the Middle East and North Africa

Country	Received Independence on	Received Independence from
Algeria	July 5, 1962	France
Bahrain	August 15, 1971	Britain
Egypt	February 28, 1922	Britain
Iraq	October 3, 1932	Britain (League of Nations mandate)
Israel	May 14, 1948	Britain (League of Nations mandate)
Jordan	May 25, 1946	Britain (League of Nations mandate)
Kuwait	June 19, 1961	Britain
Lebanon	November 22, 1943	France (League of Nations mandate)
Libya	December 24, 1951	United Nations Trusteeship
Morocco	March 2, 1956	France
Qatar	September 3, 1971	Britain
Syria	April 17, 1946	France (League of Nations mandate)
Tunisia	March 20, 1956	France
United Arab Emirates	December 2, 1971	Britain

A Special Committee on Decolonization came into existence in 1962 to recommend ways to apply the declaration and observe its implementation.

The British had already begun decolonization well before the UN declaration. In the 1931 Statute of Westminster, Britain had granted virtual full independence to the self-governing dominions of Canada, Australia, New Zealand, and South Africa. Egypt received nominal independence in 1922, although the British continued to dominate Egyptian affairs until after World War II, and the last British hold on that country did not end until after the 1956 Suez Crisis. Indian independence came in 1947 but only amid sectarian Muslim-Hindu religious bloodshed and considerable chaos that produced India and Pakistan, states that remained bitter rivals thereafter. Burma and Sri Lanka became independent in 1948. Ghana and Malaya followed in 1957.

British decolonization accelerated after 1960, with the focus switching primarily to Africa as the following nations became independent: Nigeria (1960); Sierra Leone and Tanzania (1961); Jamaica, Trinidad, Uganda, and Western Samoa (1962); Kenya and Zanzibar (1963); Malawi and Zambia (1964); and Gambia, Lesotho, and the Cook Islands (1965). Guyana, Barbados, Lesotho, and Botswana were decolonized in 1966, and Mauritius and Swaziland were decolonized in 1968. Next came Fiji in 1970, followed by Tuvalu in 1978, Kiribati in 1979, Zimbabwe and Vanuatu in 1980, and finally Hong Kong in 1997.

In the Middle East, the British government decision to terminate its mandate over Palestine brought about the State of Israel in 1948. Israel's declaration that it was a sovereign nation triggered an invasion by the armies of its neighboring Arab states. Conflict in the region, ranging from low-intensity struggles to full-scale wars, has continued ever since.

Because Britain had prior experience with the process and less at stake in its overseas possessions, decolonization was for Britain, with the notable exceptions of Palestine and India, most usually a matter of negotiation, transfer of sovereignty, and little resistance. Most of the time, the Europeans recognized that negotiation was more palatable than forced decolonization through internal resistance. Generally, the transfer was gentle enough in the British Empire that a representative of the royal family could attend the ceremonies.

Indicative of this process was the new appellation that the British had for their holdings. Previously the British Empire, during World War II it became the British Commonwealth of Nations, and in 1945 it became simply the Commonwealth of Nations. This implied that Britain was merely an equal member.

Similarly, the French Empire became the French Union in 1945. Under President de Gaulle in 1958, it became The Community. But French decolonization was far more turbulent than its British counterpart. The French controlled their possessions tightly from Paris, whereas the British tended to grant considerable self-government and autonomy. The French attitude toward decolonization was colored in part by France's defeat by Germany in 1940 and the belief among many French leaders that only with its empire intact could France continue to be counted as a major power. Thus, Paris declined to recognize the inevitable in Indochina. The French refused meaningful concessions to the new government of North Vietnam led by veteran communist Ho Chi Minh. Mistrust and miscalculation led in November 1946 to the eight-year Indochina War. The 1954 Geneva Conference called for independence for Cambodia, Laos, and Vietnam, with elections set to occur in a divided Vietnam two years later.

In 1956 France gave independence to Morocco and Tunisia, but no peaceful transition occurred in the case of Algeria. The French had acquired Algeria in 1830, and the modern Algerian political entity was largely their creation. Algeria was technically an integral part of France, formed into three French departments, but the Muslim Algerians did not have full rights, and Algeria was in effect controlled by the European minority. The French had crushed an Algerian nationalist outbreak at Sétif in 1945, but in November 1954 the National Liberation Front (FLN) began a guerrilla war against the French to bring about Algerian independence.

The ensuing Algerian War was long and bloody. A succession of French leaders were determined to retain control of this possession,

Soldiers man barricades during an antigovernment uprising in Algiers during the Algerian War on January 20, 1960. (Manuel Litran/Corbis)

seeing it, as French Premier Guy Mollet put it, as "France's California." The French Army was also determined that it would not again be betrayed by the politicians, and when it appeared as if Paris might open negotiations with the FLN, army generals in Algeria teamed up with Europeans there to overthrow the French Fourth Republic and bring de Gaulle back to power. De Gaulle announced an ambitious developmental program for Algeria, but this so-called Constantine Plan came too late in the day to succeed. In the end, de Gaulle entered into negotiations with the FLN that brought Algeria independence in 1962.

Portugal also fought long, costly colonial wars in Africa, for Portuguese dictator António Salazar was determined to maintain control of his nation's considerable overseas possessions. Fighting began in Angola in 1961, in Guinea in 1963, and in Mozambique in 1964. Ultimately, Portugal committed a sizable force of manpower and routinely spent half of its national budget on the fighting. In consequence, pressing problems in Portugal itself went unaddressed. A revolution in Portugal in 1974, brought about by younger army officers who were convinced that the colonial struggles could not be won, brought independence to its two giant African colonies of Angola and Mozambique as well as Portuguese Timor in southeast Asia by the end of 1975.

Italy lost its African possessions of Italian East Africa and Libya during the course of World War II. Ethiopia was restored to independence by British Empire troops in 1941. In 1949 the UN voted in favor of granting Libya independence. Full independence came in 1951.

Spain lost most of its overseas colonies after the war. Spanish Morocco was joined to the Kingdom of Morocco, but the almost

purely Spanish cities of Cueta and Melilla across the Straits of Gibraltar in North Africa remained Spanish. Moroccan nationalists demanded the return of these as well as Ifni and the phosphate-rich Spanish Sahara. Spain indeed gave up the latter in 1975. Spanish Equatorial Africa also received independence in 1968.

In 1945 Belgium still retained control of the mineral-rich Belgian Congo in Central Africa. The colony was among the worst-administered of any in Africa, and virtually nothing had been done to prepare it for independence, with few university-educated locals present. In December 1959, riots broke out in the capital of Leopoldville (Kinshasa), sparked by the French grant of independence for the neighboring French Congo (Congo-Brazzaville). In January 1960, King Baudouin of Belgium announced his intention to end colonial rule, leading to independence for the Congo in June 1960. Soon the Congo lapsed into a bloody civil war.

The UN played an important role in the decolonization process. Articles 73–74 of Chapter XI of the UN Charter called for self-determination and set guidelines for decolonization. The UN set up a new program of trust territories to replace the mandate system set up after World War I. These included territories taken from the Axis powers or placed into the trusteeship system voluntarily. The term "trust" implied that these territories would work their way toward self-rule.

Nations administering trusteeships had an obligation to help the territories develop self-government and educational institutions as well as to foster social and economic development. Periodically, the UN received and reviewed reports on the trust territories and their progress toward self-rule. Trusteeships that became independent included British-administered Togoland, which joined the Gold Coast in 1957 to form Ghana; Somaliland, which joined British Somalia in 1960 to create Somalia; French-administered Togoland, which became Togo in 1960; French-administered Cameroon, which became independent under the same name in 1960; and the British-administered Cameroons, which split in 1961 with the north combining with Nigeria and the south joining Cameroon.

Tanganyika won independence in 1961, and in 1964 it combined with Zanzibar, independent in 1963, to create the United Republic of Tanzania. Belgian-administered Ruanda-Urundi split into the independent Rwanda and Burundi in 1962. In the Pacific, Western Samoa became Samoa in 1962. Nauru became independent in 1968, and New Guinea joined with Papua to become Papua New Guinea in 1975. Micronesia (1990), the Marshall Islands (1990), and Palau (1994), three states of the Trust Territory of the Pacific Islands, became self-governing in free association with the United States in the 1990s. The Northern Mariana Islands became self-governing in commonwealth with the United States in 1990.

Decolonization left a mixed legacy. During the Cold War years in Asian nations such as Vietnam, the Philippines, and China and also throughout much of Latin America and the Middle East, the United States was often perceived as seeking to substitute its own brand of anticommunist imperialism in place of Western colonialism. The Soviet Union, on the other hand, sought to encourage and align itself with nationalist movements in the developing world and to win the loyalties of such nations once they gained independence. This was certainly the case in the Middle East.

Some of the new states prospered, while others remained poor and underdeveloped. India and some Pacific Rim states such as Hong Kong, Singapore, and Malaysia adjusted well and played important economic roles in the 1980s and 1990s. Poverty continues to plague the nations of sub-Saharan Africa, however, where the states are often artificial constructs carved out by the European imperialist powers with no regard for tribal or cultural boundaries and with few or no economic resources. Often the leaders of such states were able to work the Cold War to their advantage, playing off the superpowers against one another. After the end of the Cold War, the Americans and Soviets lost interest in the developing world, and longstanding rivalries reemerged as foreign aid was sharply reduced. Often civil war and famine were the result.

The postcolonial era saw the developing world's debts grow at a rate that made them impossible to repay. Much of the debt was owed to the most powerful states economically, the so-called G-8 countries. Nations in the developing world faced soaring oil prices in the 1970s, and they were forced to borrow heavily to stay afloat. Debt during 1973–1993 grew at more than 20 percent a year. With compound interest, the area's total debt by 1993 was $1.5 trillion. After renegotiation in 2000, the debt was still $350 billion. Only in the first decade of the 21st century did the G-8 states begin to take steps toward cancelling that debt and developing coherent aid programs that had the potential to lift much of Africa from poverty and end the negative legacy there of decolonization.

JOHN H. BARNHILL AND SPENCER C. TUCKER

See also

Israeli War of Independence, Overview; Palestine, British Mandate for; United Nations, Role of

References

Birmingham, David. *The Decolonization of Africa.* Athens: Ohio University Press, 1996.

Christie, Clive J. *A Modern History of Southeast Asia: Decolonization, Nationalism and Separatism.* London: Tauris, 1996.

Gifford, Prosser, and William Roger Louis. *Decolonization and African Independence.* New Haven, CT: Yale University Press, 1988.

Holland, R. F. *European Decolonization, 1918–1981.* New York: Palgrave Macmillan, 1985.

Naylor, Phillip C. *France and Algeria: A History of Decolonization and Transformation.* Gainesville: University Press of Florida, 2000.

Deedes, Sir Wyndham

Born: 1883
Died: 1956

British Army general and ardent Zionist. Wyndham Deedes was born in East Kent, England, in 1883. A career British Army officer, in 1915 he was a brigadier general stationed in Cairo, where he was assigned to intelligence duties and worked to secure Arab support against the Turks. He entered Jerusalem with Lieutenant General Sir Edmund H. H. Allenby in December 1917. A deeply religious Christian, Deedes believed that the only way that Christians could atone for previous injuries committed against the Jews was by working to establish a Jewish state in Palestine. In 1918 he met and became close friends with Zionist leader Chaim Weizmann.

As part of the British administration in Palestine after World War I, Deedes assisted the Zionist Commission in its interaction with British authorities. In 1920 he became chief secretary of the Palestine administration under High Commissioner for Palestine Sir Herbert Samuel, who later attributed the relative calm of the period 1920–1929 in the mandate to Deedes's ability to deal effectively with both Jews and Arabs. During the Arab riots of 1921, Deedes took strong steps to halt the Arab attacks and authorized the enlistment of Jewish volunteers to help defend Jaffa (Yafo) and Tel Aviv.

Deedes retired from the British military in 1923 to spend the rest of his life working among the poor in the London slums. He kept in contact with Zionist leaders, however, and both wrote and spoke on behalf of their cause. After the Nazis moved against the Jews in Germany, Deedes supported the Youth Aliya, and in 1943 he founded the British Association for the Jewish National Home in Palestine in order to build support for what would become the State of Israel. Deedes died in London in 1956.

SPENCER C. TUCKER

See also

Allenby, Sir Edmund Henry Hynman, 1st Viscount; Palestine, British Mandate for; Samuel, Sir Herbert Louis; Weizmann, Chaim; Youth Aliya; Zionism

References

Deedes, Sir Wyndham, et al. *Palestine, 1917–1944.* London: British Association for the Jewish National Home in Palestine, 1944.

Presland, John. *Deedes's Bey: A Study of Sit Wyndham Deedes.* London: Macmillan, 1942.

Shepherd, Naomi. *Ploughing Sand: British Rule in Palestine, 1917–1948.* New Brunswick, NJ: Rutgers University Press, 1999.

DEFENSIVE SHIELD, Operation

Start Date: April 3, 2002
End Date: May 10, 2002

Israeli military operation launched against Palestinian militant groups in the West Bank between April 3, 2002, and May 10, 2002. Numerous suicide bombings and Israeli reprisal attacks had taken place since the late summer of 2001. A particularly horrifying suicide bombing occurred at a hotel where a group had gathered to celebrate the religious holiday of Passover.

In response to the bombings, Israeli prime minister Ariel Sharon directed the Israel Defense Forces (IDF) to launch Operation DEFENSIVE SHIELD. The goals of the operation were to enter the West Bank, locate villages and towns harboring or aiding terrorists, arrest the terrorists and their supporters, seize weapons, destroy secret bases

Israeli tank near the Mukata'a, Yasser Arafat's West Bank headquarters in Ramallah, during Operation DEFENSIVE SHIELD, on April 3, 2002. (Dov Randel/Israeli Government Press Office)

and camps (as well as any matériel of use to the terrorists), and minimize civilian casualties.

IDF forces began the operation on April 3, rolling into the West Bank towns of Nablus, Ramallah, Jenin, and Bethlehem, all identified as terrorist centers. Hebron and Jericho were not targeted. The IDF imposed strict curfews on the civilian population, which according to Palestinian sources resulted in numerous civilian deaths, as did the denial of emergency medical services during the curfew hours. IDF troops encountered mixed opposition, with action taking place in Jenin, in Bethlehem, and at the Palestinian Authority (PA) compound in Ramallah.

In Bethlehem, 26 Palestinian gunmen seized the Church of the Nativity, holding the clergy there hostage. The IDF finally negotiated their release by allowing the gunmen safe passage to Cyprus or the Gaza Strip and releasing 24 terror suspects from a hospital where they were being detained. In Ramallah, the IDF engaged in a siege of the PA compound, trapping Arafat and others, that lasted nearly a month and involved additional attacks all through Ramallah. The siege was lifted when U.S. negotiators arranged for 6 men wanted by the IDF in the compound to be placed in a PA jail in Jericho. The Israelis captured numerous documents at the PA compound, which purportedly demonstrated the PA knowledge of, and collusion with, many of the terrorist organizations attacking Israel.

Significant fighting occurred in Jenin and the refugee camp in its environs. In order to minimize civilian deaths, the Israelis decided to forgo air strikes in favor of a ground attack. Thousands of booby traps had been set, and the IDF employed heavily armored bulldozers to demolish houses suspected of harboring terrorists and any places that might have been rigged with explosives. The Israelis claim that fair warning was given before the bulldozing, but

Casualties of Operation DEFENSIVE SHIELD (April–May 2002)

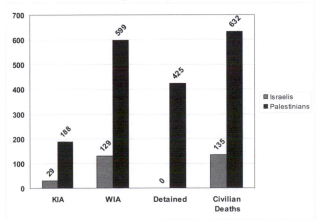

Palestinian sources refute this and claim that no warning was given. The fighting in Jenin was heavy at times, and running gun battles with armed militants were common. The IDF claims that it destroyed 10 percent of the houses in the Jenin refugee camp through offensive action. IDF sources claim 52 Palestinian dead including 22 civilians. The Palestinians accused the IDF of perpetrating a massacre in Jenin, but investigation by both the United Nations (UN) and independent human rights organizations could find no evidence of a mass killing.

The operation officially ended on May 10, 2002. The IDF claimed more than 5,000 small arms and explosives captured along with computers, chemicals, cell phones, and weapon-making components. The IDF also claimed that intelligence documents captured at Arafat's compound vindicated the operation. These documents provided ample evidence of PLO collusion with the radicals and identified key figures of interest to the Israelis. Palestinian casualties during the operation included 188 dead, 599 wounded, and 425 others detained. Israeli casualties included 29 dead and 129 wounded. Total civilian casualties were 632 for the Palestinians and 135 for the Israelis.

Officially, the Israeli government viewed the operation as a success. Most Israelis believed that it had been necessary. However, at least 54 percent believed that it damaged Israel in the realm of world opinion.

Rod Vosburgh

See also

Al-Aqsa Martyrs Brigades; Arafat, Yasser; Fatah; Hamas; Islamic Jihad, Palestinian; Palestinian Authority; Ramallah; Sharon, Ariel; Suicide Bombings; Terrorism

References

Dor, Daniel. *The Suppression of Guilt: The Israeli Media and the Reoccupation of the West Bank.* London: Pluto, 2005.

Finkelstein, Norman G. *Image and Reality of the Israel-Palestine Conflict.* New York: Norton, 2003.

Reinhart, Tanya. *Israel/Palestine: How to End the War of 1948.* New York: Seven Stories Press, 2004.

Degania, Battle for the
Event Date: May 20, 1948

A hard-fought battle on May 20, 1948, between Israeli and Syrian forces for control of the Jordan River Valley during the Israeli War of Independence (1948–1949). Degania was Palestine's first collective settlement, or kvutzah, located in the Jordan Plain west of the Sea of Galilee (Lake Kinneret). Degania means "cornflower" and comes from the Arab designation of the land, Umm Juni.

Arthur Ruppin purchased uncultivated land here in 1909 for the Jewish National Fund, and that same year a group of Jewish immigrants attempted to farm the land along conventional lines but failed. The next year, 36 others asked to farm the area on a collectivist basis, and Ruppin agreed. He also provided the settlers with two mud-brick dormitories, basic farm equipment, and a half

dozen mules. Although conditions were difficult and malaria took a heavy toll, the effort succeeded and in 1911 brought in a successful harvest.

Degania was organized along strict collectivist lines with full equality among the sexes. Degania Alif (A) became the designation for this first settlement and was known as the "Mother of the Kvutzah." Its members wanted to keep the same arrangement rather than be organized along the lines of the larger collective settlement, or kibbutz. Thus in 1920 with the arrival of another group of settlers, Degania Bet (B) was organized just to the south. In 1932 a portion of the land was given to a third collective settlement, Kibbutz Afikim.

The two Deganias were the scene of heavy fighting during the Israeli War for Independence. On May 18, 1948, the Syrian Army's 1st Brigade, commanded by Brigadier General Husni al-Zaim, attacked Zemach, about a mile due east of Degania A on the Sea of Galilee. Al-Zaim had at his disposal some 30 armored vehicles including Renault tanks. The Jewish Haganah defenders had only small arms and two 20-mm antitank guns. Part of the Syrian brigade swept around to the south of Zemach, outflanking the defenders who also lost one of their antitank guns to Syrian fire. Most of the defenders were killed, and the remainder withdrew.

It now looked as if the way was open for the Syrians to overrun the entire Jordan Valley. The two villages of Degania A and B became the new front line. That night, the Israelis rushed up reinforcements but also evacuated the villages of Shaar HaGolan and Masada to the east. At the same time, the Syrians beat back an attempt by Palmach forces to retake the police post in Zemach.

The Syrian attack on the two Deganias opened at dawn on May 20 with an artillery bombardment. The thrust of the Syrian attack was against Degania A, which was defended by only 70 men and the one remaining 20-mm gun. The attacking Syrian infantrymen were preceded by five tanks and some armored cars. The Syrian tanks easily overcame the defensive fire and broke through the Israeli outer perimeter. The one Israeli antitank gun crew knocked out one Syrian armored car. Israeli fire also damaged one of the Renault tanks, which then withdrew. Still, the remainder of the Syrian tanks proceeded and came up against the Israelis' last trenches. There the defenders, who were fighting for their homes, attacked the tanks and armored cars with both Molotov cocktails and British World War II PIAT (Projector Infantry Anti-Tank) hollow-charge explosives. The leading Syrian tank was disabled by a Molotov cocktail but continued to fire until it was destroyed by other gasoline bombs. (This tank has never been removed but is kept in situ as a permanent memorial to the defenders.) The bulk of the Syrian infantry had not kept up with the tanks, and they thus fell prey to Israeli small arms fire. At midday, having lost two more armored cars, the Syrians withdrew from Degania A and concentrated on Degania B to the south.

Here the Syrians committed eight tanks and armored cars and two infantry companies. All were driven back. At the same time, and for the first time in the war, Israeli artillery came into battle.

The guns had been received only a few days before at Tel Aviv and were immediately sent north. Positioned in the hills overlooking the Sea of Galilee, their shells caused the Syrians to withdraw from Remesh, Shaar HaGolan, and Masada, which were then reoccupied by the Israelis. By May 23, the Israelis had won the battle for control of the Jordan Valley.

Today the two Deganias have a population of some 1,000 people. In addition to farming, there is also a metal factory there.

SPENCER C. TUCKER

See also

Antitank Weapons; Israeli War of Independence, Israeli-Syrian Front; Kibbutz Movement; Zaim, Husni al-

References

Herzog, Chaim. *The Arab-Israeli Wars: War and Peace in the Middle East from the War of Independence to Lebanon.* Westminster, MD: Random House, 1984.

Lustick, Ian. *From War to War: Israel vs. the Arabs, 1948–1967.* New York: Garland, 1994.

Pollack, Kenneth M. *Arabs at War: Military Effectiveness, 1948–1991.* Lincoln: University of Nebraska Press, 2002.

De Gaulle, Charles
Born: November 22, 1890
Died: November 9, 1970

French Army general, head of the provisional French government (1944–1946), and first president of the Fifth French Republic (1959–1969). Charles André Marie Joseph de Gaulle, arguably the greatest French statesman of the 20th century, was born on November 22, 1890, in Lille, France, into a conservative Catholic but socially progressive family. De Gaulle graduated from the French Military Academy of Saint-Cyr in 1912 after joining the 33rd Infantry Regiment in 1909. He fought in World War I and was twice wounded. Wounded a third time in March 1916 at Verdun, he was taken prisoner by the Germans. He passed the remainder of the conflict as a prisoner of war in Germany.

Following the war, de Gaulle returned to Saint-Cyr to teach history, and during 1919–1920 he served in the French military mission to Poland as an infantry instructor. For services rendered to the Poles in their war with Russia, he was awarded the highest Polish decoration and received promotion to major. Returning to France, he taught and studied at the École de Guerre (War College). He then served as aide to the commander of the French Army, Marshal Henri Phillipe Pétain.

De Gaulle became a proponent of new military tactics centered on the use of tanks for high-speed warfare. These concepts were based on his personal experience in Poland. In 1934 he published a book describing his ideas for a mechanized and highly mobile force of tanks, infantry, and artillery with its own organic air support. In another book, he described his concept of leadership. Unfortunately for France, his reformist ideas had little impact in his own country, although they were influential in Germany.

Charles de Gaulle, French Army general, leader of the Free French in World War II, head of the provisional French government (1944–1946), and first president of the Fifth French Republic (1959–1969). (Library of Congress)

De Gaulle served in the occupied Rhineland, in the Middle East, and on the National Defense Council as major and then lieutenant colonel. He was promoted to colonel in 1937. In May 1940 when the Germans invaded France, de Gaulle assumed command of the 4th Tank Division. Achieving one of the few successes scored by the French Army in the campaign, he was advanced to brigadier general on June 1. A week later Premier Paul Reynaud made de Gaulle undersecretary of state for national defense.

De Gaulle urged the government to fight on in North Africa. His advice rejected, on June 17 he flew to London and, a day later, spoke over the BBC to urge his countrymen to continue the fight. The new Vichy government headed by Pétain declared de Gaulle a traitor and sentenced him to death in absentia. De Gaulle headed the Free French during the war, but his relations with Britain and the United States were often difficult and almost always strained. De Gaulle acted as if he were a true head of state, while the British and U.S. governments persisted in treating him as an auxiliary. De Gaulle was embittered by blatant British efforts to dislodge the French from prewar positions of influence in Syria and Lebanon and by the failure of the Anglo-Saxon powers to consult him in matters regarding French national interests.

From August 1944 de Gaulle served as the interim president of the French government in Paris until he resigned in January 1946 after his proposals for a new constitutional arrangement were rejected. He retired to write his memoirs, but in April 1947 he reentered the political lists with the newly formed Rassemblement du Peuple Francais (RDF, Rally of the French People).

The RDF had only limited success, and de Gaulle withdrew from politics again in May 1953. Finishing his wartime memoirs, he remained in contact with political and military circles. Meanwhile, the Fourth Republic was stumbling from one crisis to another. No sooner was the Indochina War ended in 1954 than fighting broke out with nationalists in Algeria. In May 1958 the Fourth Republic finally collapsed under the weight of the Algerian War. De Gaulle then returned to power on June 1, 1958, technically as the last premier of the Fourth Republic.

De Gaulle received emergency powers for six months. In September the French electorate approved a new constitution that tilted power toward the executive as de Gaulle sought, thereby establishing the Fifth Republic. General elections in November strongly supported de Gaulle coming back, and in January 1959 he was inaugurated president.

At first de Gaulle sought to achieve victory in Algeria and announced the Constantine Plan, a major economic initiative to win the support of Muslim Algerians. However, the plan came too late to succeed. De Gaulle ultimately decided that there was no other option than to grant Algeria its independence. Meanwhile, those who sought to keep Algeria French mounted several assassination attempts on the president. A military coup seemed possible. Indeed, de Gaulle had to put down several such attempts, supported by European settlers in Algeria. He managed to achieve a cease-fire in Algeria in March 1962. Backed by a referendum, the country became independent in July 1962. In 1965 de Gaulle won a second seven-year term as president, this time by popular vote.

Internationally, de Gaulle sought to carve out a role as leader of a Europe that would serve as a third force between the Soviet Union and the United States. His anger over what he regarded as U.S.-British domination of the North Atlantic Treaty Organization (NATO) led him to remove France from the military structure of the alliance. In a most controversial decision, France exploded an atomic bomb and developed its own independent nuclear strike force. De Gaulle also lectured, and sometimes berated, the United States on a wide variety of issues including its Vietnam policy, which he opposed.

Regarding the Middle East, de Gaulle, as with his predecessors, viewed Israel as a natural ally. France had gone to war with Britain on the side of Israel against Egypt in 1956, and France under de Gaulle remained Israel's main arms supplier and also assisted Israel in the field of nuclear research. Already in 1957 the two countries had signed an agreement for a research reactor. This reactor was later upgraded with French assistance, and another was secretly built with French support at Dimona, near Beersheba, in the Negev Desert. This cooperation, however, also benefited the French, who sought a nuclear force of their own. Thus, both parties to the agreement assisted one another. France shipped plutonium to Israel while getting heavy water from the United States via Israel. Some experts believe that the cooperation was so close that France's first successful nuclear test in 1960 made Israel a nuclear power at the same time.

In return, Israel supplied France with intelligence data about North Africa and the Near East. De Gaulle saw Israel as a natural ally in the fight against Algerian rebels, who were aided by Egypt. However, this did not prevent him from pressuring Israeli prime minister David Ben-Gurion to make Israeli nuclear research public and allow inspections in early 1960. De Gaulle later offered fighter planes in exchange for halting work at Dimona. Israel refused and continued work there with French assistance until the reactor came on line in 1964.

Following Algerian independence and with Ben-Gurion's departure from power in 1963, de Gaulle adopted a more pro-Arab stance. France sought better relations with the Arabs, which it hoped would improve relations with the communist bloc and the developing world. Although France delivered 72 French Mirage II jets to Israel in 1961, additional arms were not forthcoming. In 1965, a high-ranking Egyptian general was welcomed in Paris. An urgent Israeli appeal to France for help just prior to the 1967 Yom Kippur War went unanswered. In a meeting on May 24, 1967, de Gaulle warned Israeli special envoy Abba Eban that Israel must refrain from war. De Gaulle went on to explain that the situation was much different than it had been in 1956. He now saw himself as a mediator between East and West and did not wish to jeopardize improved French relations with Arab states. He assured Israel that France would stand by its side if Israel were attacked but not if Israel were to initiate the fight. True to his word, he was sharply critical of Israel's 1967 preemptive campaign, and relations between the two states went into a deep freeze thereafter.

Domestically, the de Gaulle government introduced the concept of dirigisme, a mixture of free market economy and state-directed interventionist policies. The franc was devalued, and many high-profile projects were undertaken, some in collaboration with Great Britain such as the supersonic passenger plane Concord.

In May 1968, massive demonstrations erupted in Paris and other major cities. They were sparked by students, but workers and others soon joined. Demonstrations and strikes were commonplace, and the nation was brought to a virtual standstill. Although de Gaulle considered using the army to crush the protests, Premier Georges Pompidou convinced him to dissolve the National Assembly and hold general elections.

Forced to decide between de Gaulle and the demands of the street, voters decided in June to back de Gaulle with 358 of 487 seats in the French National Assembly. Perhaps because of his success, Pompidou found himself replaced as premier by Maurice Couve de Murville in July. In 1969 de Gaulle proposed a constitutional change to convert the upper house (Senate) into an advisory body. He had made the issue a personal referendum on his leadership, and when it was defeated in a national vote in April 1969 he stepped aside on April 28.

De Gaulle retired to his home at Colombey-les-Deux-Églises to write his final set of memoirs. He died there on November 9, 1970. His concepts, vision, and charisma endured and still influence French politics to his day. Perhaps his greatest legacy to France was the constitutional structure of the Fifth Republic.

THOMAS J. WEILER

See also
Ben-Gurion, David; Eban, Abba Solomon; France, Middle East Policy; Nuclear Weapons; Suez Crisis; Yom Kippur War

References
Cook, Don. *Charles de Gaulle: A Biography*. New York: Putnam, 1983.
De Gaulle, Charles. *Memoirs of Hope: Renewal and Endeavor*. Translated by Terence Kilmartin. New York: Simon and Schuster, 1971.
Lacouture, Jean. *De Gaulle*. 2 vols. Translated by Patrick O'Brian and Alan Sheridan. New York: Norton, 1990, 1992.
Ledwidge, Bernard. *De Gaulle*. New York: St. Martin's, 1982.

Deir Yassin Massacre
Start Date: April 9, 1948
End Date: April 11, 1948

A massacre of Arab civilians by Jewish forces during April 9–11, 1948, in the British Mandate for Palestine. The incident occurred just one month prior to the declaration of the State of Israel and the beginning of the Israeli War of Independence (1948–1949). Since the 1930s, Palestine had seen increasing violence between Arabs and Jews for control of Palestine. In one sense, Deir Yassin (Dayr Yasin) was a continuation of that struggle.

Beginning on April 9, 1948, Jewish forces attacked the Arab village of Deir Yassin near Jerusalem. The village of about 750 persons overlooked the important Tel Aviv–Jerusalem Road and was slated for occupation under Plan Dalet. The forces involved included members of the paramilitary Palmach organization, which was part of the Jewish self-defense organization Haganah, and members of the Jewish terrorist organizations Irgun Tsvai Leumi (National Military Organization) and Lohamei Herut Israel (Lehi or Stern Gang). The raiders killed somewhere between 96 and 254 Arab villagers, mostly elderly, women, and children. Their bodies were then dumped into the village well or left in the streets. In addition, some survivors were paraded naked in West Jerusalem and then were returned to Deir Yassin and murdered. About 100 orphaned village children were left outside the wall of the Old City in Jerusalem.

The massacre, which was widely publicized in official Israeli radio broadcasts intended to terrify Arabs, was the major impetus in the flight of hundreds of thousands of Arabs from Palestine.

Arabs claim that what happened at Deir Yassin was a premeditated and deliberate act of terrorism by Jews. The flight of terrified villagers from their homes served to facilitate Jewish efforts to secure Arab lands and create a Jewish state in Palestine. Israelis defended the attack on Deir Yassin as part of Operation NACHSHON, meant to break the Arab siege of Jerusalem, but according to Arabs, Deir Yassin had remained neutral in the growing violence between armed Arab and Jewish groups. Villagers had even made a pact with the Haganah that they would not aid armed Arab groups on the understanding that they would not then be targets of Jewish attacks. Some Israeli officials dispute these claims, contending that armed Arabs along with Iraqi volunteers from the Arab Liberation Army (ALA) were given sanctuary and stationed in the village, thus violating any pact that may have existed.

Also in dispute is whether villagers fought the attackers and whether a truck equipped with a loudspeaker warned the villagers of the impending attack in Arabic before it began. Most accounts, even from Israelis, claim that the truck either never arrived or arrived after the fighting had already begun. Irgun leader Menachem Begin, who was not a combatant in the massacre but shared in the responsibility for it, disputed both of these claims. In his book *The Revolt* (1951), he insisted that the Deir Yassin massacre was a fabrication by anti-Semites.

The number of villagers killed is also in dispute. The initial death toll was said to be 254, publicized by an Irgun commander who later admitted that he exaggerated to force the Arabs to panic and flee their homes. One subsequent and disputed study concluded that no more than 120 Arabs died in the attack. Yet International Red Cross representative Jacques Reynier counted 150 maimed bodies (including disembowelments and decapitations) in the cistern, while others were scattered through the streets of the village. That testimony and survivors' reports supported the higher figure of dead originally given. Arab League president Azzam Pasha pointed to the massacre at Deir Yassin as the principal reason for the Arab states' invasion of Palestine following the proclamation of the State of Israel in May 1948.

STEFAN BROOKS

See also
Arab League; Azzam Pasha, Abdel Rahman; Begin, Menachem; Haganah; Irgun Tsvai Leumi; Israeli War of Independence, Overview; Lohamei Herut Israel; NACHSHON, Operation; Palmach

References
Begin, Menachem. *The Revolt*. Los Angeles: Nash Publishing, 1972.
Collins, Larry, and Dominique Lapierre. *O Jerusalem!* New York: Simon and Schuster, 1972.
Kanaana, Sharif, and Nihad Zeitawi. *The Village of Deir Yassin*. Monograph No. 4, Destroyed Palestinian Villages Documentation Project. Birzeit, Palestine: Documentation Center of Birzeit University Press, 1988.
Khalidi, Walid, ed. *All That Remains: Palestinian Villages Occupied and Depopulated by Israel in 1948*. Washington, DC: Institute for Palestine Studies, 1992.
McGowan, Daniel, and Marc Ellis. *Remembering Deir Yassin: The Future of Israel and Palestine*. Brooklyn, NY: Olive Branch, 1998.
Morris, Benny. *The Birth of the Palestinian Refugee Problem Revisited*. 2nd ed. Cambridge: Cambridge University Press, 2004.

Democratic Front for the Liberation of Palestine

Leftist group within the Palestine Liberation Organization (PLO). In 1969, Nayef Hawatmeh and Yasser Abed Rabbo broke off from the Popular Front for the Liberation of Palestine (PFLP), headed by George Habash. They believed that the PFLP focused too narrowly on military concerns. Their new organization was known as the Popular Democratic Front for the Liberation of Palestine (PDFLP), but in 1974 it changed its name to the Democratic Front for the Liberation of Palestine (DFLP).

Hawatmeh headed the organization as its secretary-general and its chief representative to the PLO. Arab nationalist and Marxist in orientation, the DFLP was known as the most intellectually oriented of the Palestinian resistance groups. Publicly, the DFLP called for a democratic, unified, and unitary Palestinian state that would allow "both Arabs and Jews to develop their national culture." Originally, the DFLP believed that this state could only be achieved through the political activation of the masses and a "people's war." Gradually, however, the organization shifted to a slightly more moderate stance. Although it condemned attacks carried out outside of Israel, such as airline hijackings by the PFLP, at the same time the DFLP refused to give up armed struggle, and it mounted a number of small-scale raids against Israeli targets. Its largest and most notorious operation was the so-called Ma'alot Massacre of May 17, 1974, in which 26 Israelis were killed and another 60 wounded.

In 1974 the DFLP was struggling with factionalism from within its ranks and the PLO in general. Four years later, it joined the Rejectionist Front. Beginning in the early 1980s, the DFLP was known as the leading pro-Soviet and pro–People's Republic of China (PRC) organization within the PLO. The collapse of the Soviet Union and a subsequent reduction in Chinese aid cost the DFLP some of its popular support. Although the DFLP leadership supported PLO chairman Yasser Arafat's efforts to begin peace negotiations with Israel, many of the organization's rank and file did not. The party also suffered with the rise of Hamas in the 1980s.

In 1991 the DFLP split when cofounder Abed Rabbo supported the negotiations in Madrid that led to the formation of the Palestinian Authority (PA). The faction led by Abed Rabbo constituted itself as the Palestine Democratic Union (FIDA). It rejected terrorist activities in favor of negotiations and also turned its back on Marxism in favor of the democratization of Palestinian society. There were reports of armed clashes between the two factions during this split. The DFLP tended to retain control of the foreign branches, while the FIDA secured most of the membership within the Left Bank.

Palestinian youths hold pictures of Nayef Hawatmeh aloft during a march on the anniversary of the founding of the Democratic Front for the Liberation of Palestine (DFLP), Ramallah, West Bank, February 22, 1989. (Ricki Rosen/Corbis)

The other faction of the DFLP opposed the Declaration of Principles signed in 1993, claiming that the Oslo negotiations had led to an agreement that denied the Palestinians their legitimate rights. The DFLP had little influence in the Second (al-Aqsa) Intifada, which broke out in 2000.

The DFLP continues to support military activities but insists that these be confined to targets only in the so-called occupied territories and not within the Green Line. It argues that Palestinians should fight only against the occupation rather than against Israeli citizens. Although the DFLP retains considerable influence within the PLO, it did not do well in either the PA presidential election in 2005 or the Palestinian Legislative Council elections of 2006. In the former, its candidate, Taysir Khalid, won only 3.5 percent of the vote. In the latter election, the DFLP won only 2.8 percent of the popular vote and two seats on the 132-person council. Active among Palestinians primarily in Syria and Lebanon and with only a limited presence in the West Bank and the Gaza Strip, the DFLP is believed to receive some financial and military support from Syria.

SPENCER C. TUCKER

See also

Abed Rabbo, Yasser; Arafat, Yasser; Habash, George; Hamas; Hawatmeh, Nayef; Madrid Conference; Oslo Accords; Palestine Liberation Organization; Palestinian Authority

References

Gresh, Alain. *The PLO: The Struggle Within.* London: Zed, 1988.

Nassar, Jamal R. *The Palestine Liberation Organization: From Armed Struggle to the Declaration of Independence.* New York: Praeger, 1991.

Rubin, Barry, and Judith Colp Rubin. *Yasir Arafat: A Political Biography.* New York: Oxford University Press, 2003.

Said, Edward W. *The Question of Palestine.* New York: Vintage Books, 1992.

Der Judenstaat

The most influential publication advocating the reestablishment of a Jewish state. In February 1896, Jewish journalist and Zionist Theodor Herzl published in Vienna what is easily regarded as the most important Zionist publication. This short book of some 23,000 words, *Der Judenstaat* (*The Jewish State*) was subtitled *Versuch einer modernen Lösung der Judenfrage* (*An Attempt at a Modern Solution of the Jewish Question*). It dispassionately examined the situation facing Jews around the world and called for the establishment of a state in which the Jewish people would be masters of their own fate.

Herzl acknowledged that Jews were divided and scattered across the world in many different states in which they were always a minority. Jews spoke different languages, followed different cultural traditions, and were even splintered religiously. Herzl said that Jews had always been marked by a sense of homelessness, and wherever they lived in large numbers they had been subjected to anti-Semitism, which inevitably resulted in the destruction of Jewish property and bloodshed.

Herzl attributed anti-Semitism to religious differences and economic and political factors. Despite the emancipation that had come with the French Revolution, he pointed out that restrictive laws could easily be restored, as indeed had been the case in Russia. This oppression, he claimed, had one positive effect in that it brought the Jews together as one people. Jews, whether they wished it or not, he wrote, were "a group of unmistakable cohesiveness. We are a people."

Herzl saw the so-called Jewish question not as a social or even religious problem but rather as a nationalist issue. Only an idea could provide the necessary impetus to unite the Jews: the concept of a Jewish state. After all, he wrote, "'Next year in Jerusalem' is our ancient watchword." Herzl acknowledged that there was danger in advancing the idea of a Jewish state, for it was then a turbulent time of nationalism and international rivalries, but he argued for a peaceful process, one based on diplomatic efforts, discussion, and creative political activity.

Herzl believed that the creation of a Jewish state would end anti-Semitism because with the immigration of most European Jews to the new state, the economic basis of anti-Semitism would disappear. Those few Jews who remained behind would easily assimilate, as there would be no more competition from a Jewish middle class.

Herzl believed that the first step in creating the Jewish state was that of convincing Jews of its necessity. Anti-Semitism would provide the motive. To achieve the state, he called for the creation of two organizations: the Society of Jews and the Jewish Company. The former would educate public opinion, prepare for the Jewish state, and negotiate with the Great Powers to facilitate the acquisition of territory and a political arrangement. The latter, which Herzl thought should be organized as a joint-stock company, would raise the funds necessary to purchase land and equipment as well as to construct housing and provide financial support for the immigrants.

Herzl also advanced many specific ideas as to how the state should be organized including its economy, agriculture, education, and civil service. He strongly favored the right of individuals to own private property, which he believed promoted liberty, but he also advocated some type of state socialism. He believed strongly that the state should protect the worker and called for the workday to be limited to seven hours and the exclusion of women and children from the labor force. He also favored a military force, but only to defend the state and never to be employed in its aggrandizement. Herzl suggested that such a Jewish state would be a "rampart of Europe against Asia, an outpost of civilization as opposed to barbarism."

Palestine, as the original home of the Jews, should become the focal point of this effort, which became known as Zionism for Mount Zion. As Herzl put it, "Palestine is our unforgettable historic homeland."

The first reaction to *Der Judenstaat* was largely negative among Jews and non-Jews alike. Indeed, the publisher of the book was forced to bring out a countering work, *National Judaism*, by Chief Rabbi Moritz Güdemann. Assimilationist Jews rejected the notion of Jews as a separate people, while members of Hoveve Zion (Lovers of Zion) feared that expression of Jewish nationalism might have a negative impact on Turkish policies toward Jewish immigration to Palestine. Russian Jews knew little of the book or its author, as government censorship prevented its publication there. On the other hand, Jewish youth groups throughout Europe and especially those of university students enthusiastically embraced the book and rallied to Herzl, who now became the leader of a Jewish nationalist movement, a position he held until his death in 1904.

SPENCER C. TUCKER

See also
Assimilation; Herzl, Theodor; Hoveve Zion; Zionism

References
Elon, Amos. *Herzl.* New York: Holt, Rinehart and Winston, 1975.
Herzl, Theodor. *The Jewish State.* Mineola, NY: Dover, 1989.
Laqueur, Walter. *A History of Zionism: From the French Revolution to the Establishment of the State of Israel.* Reprint ed. New York: Schocken, 2003.
Pawel, Ernst. *The Labyrinth of Exile: A Life of Theodor Herzl.* New York: Farrar, Straus and Giroux, 1989.
Robertson, Ritchie, and Edward Timms, eds. *Theodor Herzl and the Origins of Zionism.* Edinburgh, UK: Edinburgh University Press, 1997.

Desalination

The process by which seawater is converted to freshwater that is fit for human and animal consumption as well as for agricultural irrigation. Currently, there are some 7,500 desalination facilities located throughout the world, 60 percent of which are located in the Middle East. Because of the hot and dry climate of that region and its growing population, freshwater supplies are a precious commodity. Indeed, very high evaporation rates and low rainfall render all but the most robust water sources unreliable for a good part of the year. Perhaps the most abundant (and most used) freshwater resource in the region is the Jordan River, whose waters are partly claimed by several countries.

One of the largest desalination facilities in the word is located in Saudi Arabia, which produces about 25 percent of all the desalinated water in the world. Desalination can also be applied to brackish water and effluent and is routinely carried out on ships, submarines, and islands that lack adequate freshwater supplies.

There are two primary methods of desalinating water. The first is by reverse osmosis. In this manner, untreated water is forced through a series of permeable membranes (or filters) under high pressure. The result is water free from high levels of salt and other minerals. This process can be repeated several times to ensure that the water is completely potable. The second method of converting seawater to freshwater is by distillation. While there are several different methods of this, the basic process of distillation heats untreated water to a high temperature at a lower atmospheric pressure, which causes the salt and other deposits to leach out, thus leaving clean, treated water. It is akin to evaporation, which witnesses the removal of water but not the minerals and deposits. The water is recovered and used as freshwater.

Reverse osmosis has become the preferred method of desalination because it does not require heat (and thus energy) to convert the water. It is also gentler to the environment than distillation. In August 2005, a reverse osmosis desalination plant located in Ashkelon, Israel, became fully operational and is now the world's largest desalination plant. In the Middle East and North Africa, distillation plants frequently serve as electric plants as well.

There are drawbacks to desalination. Besides the large initial startup costs involved in building a desalination plant, the facilities can also produce by-products that are harmful to the environment. The key by-product of desalination is brine, a slurry of highly concentrated salt and mineral deposits, which must be disposed. Oftentimes, brine is pumped back into the ocean. This is problematic in the Middle East, however, because much of the saltwater there is already high in salt concentrations. The Dead Sea, for example, is nine times as salty as the average ocean. The dumping of brine into the area's seawater can seriously harm the environment, killing fish, birds, and other species.

Because of the high geopolitical tensions and low supplies of water that are part and parcel of the Middle East, the role of desalination plants is crucial. They not only provide badly needed freshwater but also lower the likelihood of conflict over the control and consumption of natural water resources. And as the population of the region continues to increase, water supplies will play an even larger role in the comfort and prosperity of Middle Easterners.

PAUL G. PIERPAOLI JR.

See also
Climate of the Middle East; Dead Sea; Jordan River; Water Rights and Resources

References
Amery, Hussein A., and Aaron T. Wolf, eds. *Water in the Middle East: A Geography of Peace.* Austin: University of Texas Press, 2000.
Dolatyar, Mustafa, and Tim S. Gray. *Water Politics in the Middle East: A Context for Conflict or Cooperation?* New York: Palgrave Macmillan, 1999.
Gleick, P. H. "Water, War and Peace in the Middle East." *Environment* 36(3) (1994): 6–11.
United States Army. *Water Desalination.* Honolulu: University Press of the Pacific, 2005.

Detentions, Administrative
See Administrative Detentions

Diaspora

Greek term for the dispersion of the Jews. It is generally dated from the Babylonian exile of 586 BC. The term "diaspora" also describes all Jews residing outside of Israel. Diaspora today means the dispersion of any people, including the Palestinians, but for a long time it was applied only to the Jews.

The Jews who were deported to Mesopotamia originally thought of this as exile (*Galut* in Hebrew). When it became possible for the

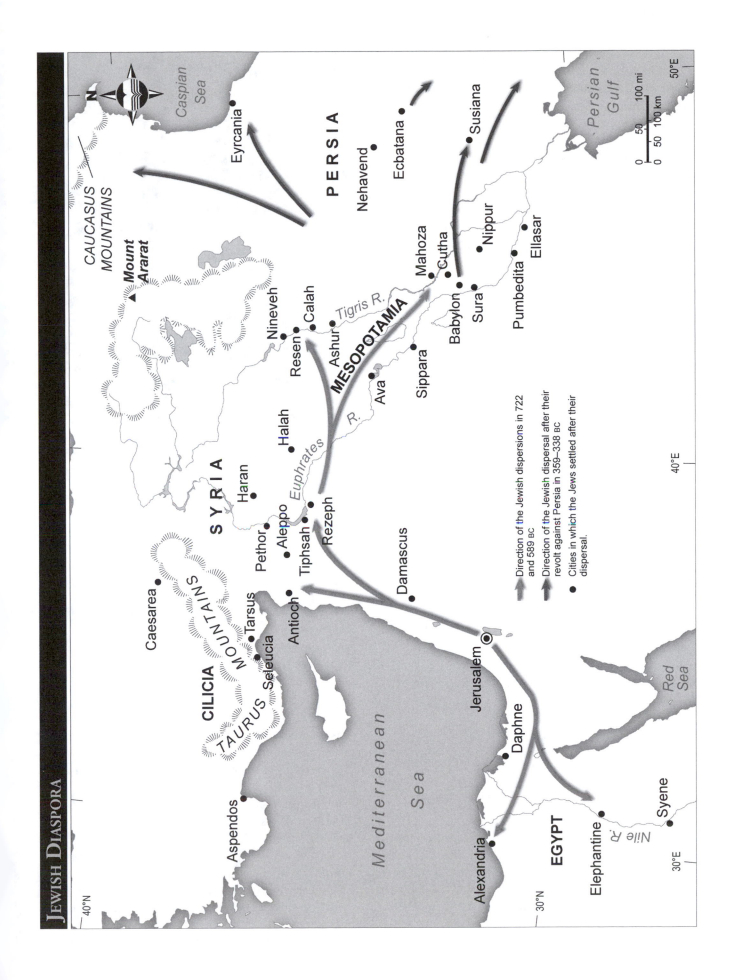

JEWISH DIASPORA

PERSIA

Caspian Sea

Eyrcania

Nehavend

Ecbatana

Susiana

Mahoza
Cutha
Babylon
Sura
Nippur
Pumbedita
Ellasar

Persian Gulf

100 mi
50   100 km
0   50   100

CAUCASUS MOUNTAINS

Mount Ararat

Nineveh
Resen
Calah
Ashur
Tigris R.

MESOPOTAMIA

Ava
Sippara

Euphrates R.

Halah

SYRIA

Haran
Pethor
Aleppo
Tiphsah
Rezeph

Damascus

CILICIA
TAURUS MOUNTAINS
Caesarea
Tarsus
Seleucia
Antioch
Aspendos

Mediterranean Sea

Jerusalem

Daphne

EGYPT

Alexandria
Elephantine
Syene
Nile R.

Red Sea

40°N
30°N
30°E
40°E
50°E

N

Direction of the Jewish dispersions in 722 and 589 BC

Direction of the Jewish dispersal after their revolt against Persia in 359–338 BC

● Cities in which the Jews settled after their dispersal.

Jews to return to Palestine, however, only a few thousand of the Babylonian Jews took advantage of the opportunity to do so. By the time the Romans crushed the Great Jewish Revolt of AD 66–70, captured Jerusalem, and destroyed its Temple, there were already thriving Jewish communities in Babylonia, Syria, Egypt, Asia Minor, Greece, and Rome. Nonetheless, the end of the Great Jewish Revolt and Bar Kokhba's Revolt of AD 135 greatly increased the numbers of Diaspora Jews. Many Jews fled, while others were sold into slavery and dispersed throughout the empire.

When the Romans expanded their empire north in Europe, Jews established new communities in those lands, and the spread of the Byzantine Empire also saw some limited Jewish communities established as well. Jews settled as far as India, Central Asia, and even China. Persecutions in one place brought new Jewish diasporas in other areas. Jews also found their way to North and South America and Australia. Indeed, as a result of the persecutions (pogroms) in Russia and Poland, the United States came to have the world's largest Jewish population.

The two key elements of Jewish consciousness came to be the Diaspora and a longing for Israel, but only rarely until after the proclamation of the State of Israel in 1948 were most Jews able to return. Even then many Jews living in the Soviet Union found it impossible to move to Israel because of Soviet restrictions on emigration. The awareness of Jews that they lived in the Diaspora was certainly the prime motivator in the birth of Zionism at the end of the 19th century.

Spencer C. Tucker

See also

Pogroms; Zionism

References

Barclay, John M. G. *Jews in the Mediterranean Diaspora: From Alexander to Trajan (323 BCE–117 CE)*. Berkeley: University of California Press, 1999.

Comay, Joan. *The Diaspora Story: The Epic of the Jewish People among the Nations*. New York: Random House, 1980.

Gold, Steven J. *The Israeli Diaspora*. Seattle: University of Washington Press, 2002.

Grant, Michael. *The Jews in the Roman World*. New York: Scribner, 1973.

Diaspora Nationalism

See Galut Nationalism

Dimona, Israel

Established in 1955 by 30 families, most of whom were Jewish immigrants from North Africa, Dimona is an Israeli city in the Negev Desert located 22 miles south of Beersheba and 21 miles west of the Dead Sea. One of several development towns established by Israeli prime minister David Ben-Gurion during the 1950s, Dimona, which means "south" in Hebrew, was named after a town in the Bible (Joshua 15:21–22).

Black Hebrew children play together with other children at Dimona on December 16, 1980. The Black Hebrews of Dimona claim descent from Jews expelled from Jerusalem in AD 70. (Sa'ar Ya'acov/Israeli Government Press Office)

Ben-Gurion repeatedly called for pioneering settlements in outlying areas, especially in the Negev Desert. In 2005, Dimona had a population of 40,000 people. Although the population declined during the 1980s, an influx of Russian immigrants during the 1990s and smaller numbers of Ethiopian Jews has made Dimona the third-largest city in the Negev Desert.

Israel's Negev Nuclear Research Center, known in Hebrew as the Hakirya Lemchkar Garini Ba-Negev (KAMAG), is located about nine miles south of the city. KAMAG is commonly referred to as the Dimona reactor or simply Dimona. It is Israel's largest and most significant nuclear facility. Construction of the facility, which is an efficient producer of plutonium, began in 1958. The Israeli government selected the site because of its relative isolation in the desert and the availability of housing in the city of Dimona.

KAMAG, which employs about 3,000 people, is Israel's most guarded facility. Although the Israeli government has never officially admitted to possessing nuclear weapons and has repeatedly claimed that the Dimona reactor is solely for peaceful purposes, most scholars agree that Israel has the largest and most sophisticated nuclear arsenal outside the United States, Russia, China, France, and the United Kingdom. In 1986 Mordechai Vanunu, a former nuclear technician at the facility, was sentenced to 18 years in prison for revealing Israeli nuclear secrets to the world.

The close proximity of KAMAG to Iraq made Dimona a target of Iraqi missiles during the 1991 Persian Gulf War. Patriot missiles provided by the United States were located in the area, and little damage was inflicted on the facility. Recently, safety concerns surrounding the nuclear reactor have prompted the Israeli government to distribute antiradiation tablets to Dimona's residents.

Dimona is also the home to the Black Hebrews, a small religious community that claims to be descended from Jews who were expelled from Jerusalem by the Romans in AD 70. According to their leader, Ben Ammi Ben Israel, after wandering for more than 1,000 years, the Black Hebrews eventually migrated to West Africa, only to be sent to the United States of America during the 18th century as slaves. Ben Israel, also known as Ben Carter, a native of Chicago, claims that the angel Gabriel revealed this information to him in 1966. In 1969 the Israeli government granted Ben Israel and his followers temporary residency and settled them in Dimona until their claims to Jewish heritage could be evaluated. In 2003 the Israeli government granted permanent resident status to Ben Israel and 2,500 of his followers. The Black Hebrews, however, are not recognized as Jews or citizens by the Israeli government.

MICHAEL R. HALL

See also
Nuclear Weapons

References
Beres, Louis Rene. *Security or Armageddon: Israel's Nuclear Strategy.* Lexington, MA: D. C. Heath, 1986.

Evron, Yuri. *Israel's Nuclear Dilemma.* Ithaca, NY: Cornell University Press, 1994.

Gilling, Tom, and John McKnight. *Trial and Error: Mordechai Vanunu and Israel's Nuclear Bomb.* New York: HarperCollins, 1995.

Hersh, Seymour M. *The Sampson Option: Israel's Nuclear Arsenal and American Foreign Policy.* New York: Random House, 1991.

Pry, Peter Vincent. *Israel's Nuclear Arsenal.* Boulder, CO: Westview, 1984.

Dome of the Rock

Islamic shrine and holy site located in Jerusalem in the State of Israel. The al-Aqsa Mosque (Masjid al-Aqsa, literally the "farthest mosque") is both a building and a complex of religious buildings in Jerusalem known to Muslims as the al-Haram al-Sharif (the Noble Sanctuary). The land is known to Jews as the Har Ha-Bayit (Temple Mount). It is regarded as the historic site of the Jewish temples.

When viewed as a complex of buildings, the al-Aqsa Mosque is dominated and bounded by two major structures, the al-Aqsa Mosque building on the east and the Dome of the Rock (Qubbat

The Dome of the Rock was built on Jerusalem's Temple Mount during AD 685–691. (Corel)

as-Sakhrah, or the Mosque of Omar) on the west. The Dome of the Rock is a shrine for pilgrims and not a mosque used for daily public worship, although it was formerly used for worship. The al-Aqsa Mosque and the Dome of the Rock are, as a complex, the third-holiest Islamic pilgrimage site after Mecca and Medina. The entire precinct is inviolable according to Islamic law.

The Dome of the Rock surrounds and covers a large rock (the Noble Rock). Islamic tradition holds that from that site the Prophet Muhammad during his Night Journey from Mecca to Jerusalem ascended in 621 in the company of the angel Gabriel through the heavens to Allah. Before returning to Earth, Muhammad received the Commandments, met with Moses, and was ordered to oblige Muslims to pray 50 times a day, a commandment that was reduced to 5. Some Jewish traditions assert that the rock was the platform upon which Abraham intended to fulfill God's divine command to sacrifice Isaac. Some extrabiblical Jewish traditions believe it to be the foundation stone used by God to create the world.

The Dome of the Rock, constructed during 685–691, is the oldest holy structure in Islam. It was built under the orders of the ninth caliph, Abd al-Malik ibn Marwan, and was designed by architects Raja Ibn Haywah al-Kindi and Yazid Ibn Sallam. The structure is more than a simple dome and has an apex of approximately 115 feet. The dome rests on a drum (circle) formed by 16 piers and columns surrounded by an octagonal arcade framed by 24 piers and columns. Although the basic design of the arcade and elevated center dome remains unchanged after more than 14 centuries, there have been numerous restorations. The wooden dome is approximately 60 feet in diameter and was originally covered with gold leaf. In 1961 this leaf was replaced with gold-colored anodized aluminum covering that soon was so visibly worn and rusted that King Hussein of Jordan paid for a replacement covering in 1993. Each outer wall is 60 feet wide by 36 feet high and is covered with Turkish tiles commissioned by the Ottoman ruler Suleiman the Magnificent in the 16th century to replace the original mosaics and marble. The mosaic tiles on the inside of the walls date from the Omayyad era. The Koranic verses, or suras, "Ya Sin" (known as the Heart of the Koran) and "al-Isra'" (meaning "Night Journey") are inscribed in tile on the inside in the top of the dome.

The site of al-Aqsa complex is holy to both Islam and Judaism and thus remains a source of conflict. The complex has seen numerous confrontations between Muslims and Jews since the capture of the Western Wall and the Temple Mount by the Israelis in the 1967 Six-Day War. The entire area (including the Western Wall) was once included within a waqf, or Islamic endowment of property, that, under Islamic law, cannot be seized by any government. The first confrontation particular to the Dome of the Rock was an attempt by the Israeli Gush Emunim (Bloc of the Faith) right-wing messianic Zionist movement to dig a tunnel leading to the dome. It was, however, discovered and closed. Yoel Lerner, a member of Meir Kahane's Kach movement, attempted to dynamite the dome in 1982. Two extreme messianic Jewish groups were arrested for planning to facilitate the coming of the messiah by blowing up the dome and

allowing the rebuilding of the Jewish Temple that they assert must be built where the Dome of the Rock now stands. The first was the TNT gang in 1983, and the second was the Lifta gang in 1984.

On September 28, 2000, Israeli retired general and politician Ariel Sharon visited the Temple Mount. The resulting civil violence marked the beginning of the continuing Second (al-Aqsa) Intifada. The Jewish Temple Mount Faithful movement seeks to have the Dome of the Rock removed to Mecca in order that it might construct a Third Temple where the dome now stands.

RICHARD EDWARDS

See also

Al-Aqsa Mosque; Intifada, Second; Jerusalem; Sharon, Ariel

References

Creswell, K. A. C. *Early Muslim Architecture: With a Contribution on the Mosaics of the Dome of the Rock in Jerusalem and the Great Mosque in Damascus.* 2nd ed. Oxford, UK: Clarendon, 1969.

Nuseibeh, Said. *The Dome of the Rock.* New York: Rizzoli, 1996.

Dreyfus Affair
Start Date: 1894
End Date: July 12, 1906

The Dreyfus Affair was one of the most important events in France in the decades preceding World War I. This manifestation of anti-Semitism, known in French history simply as l'Affaire, bitterly divided France, rocked the army, and impeded military preparedness. Internationally, it had a profound impact on the growth of Zionism.

The Dreyfus Affair is extraordinarily complex, and certain aspects of the case remain in dispute even today. The basic facts of the case are easily established. A maid in the German embassy, Marie Bastian, worked for the Deuxième Bureau (French military intelligence) and periodically passed along messages purloined from the embassy wastebaskets. It soon became apparent that key defense secrets, including master plans of French fortresses, were finding their way to German military attaché Maximilien von Schwarzkoppen. The culprit had to be someone with access to the highest levels of the French Army, probably a General Staff officer. In December 1894, on the flimsiest of evidence, the army arrested and sentenced a brilliant young officer of the General Staff, Captain Alfred Dreyfus, to military degradation and perpetual imprisonment on the so-called dry guillotine of Devil's Island. French nationalists applauded this action, as did influential anti-Semitic publicists in France, for Captain Dreyfus was a Jew, one of some 300 Jewish officers in the army.

Dreyfus protested his innocence, which was to be expected. But the army high command was surprised to learn that secrets continued to flow to the Germans. The traitor was in fact another officer, Commandant Ferdinand Walsin-Esterhazy. Some believed that Dreyfus was still guilty in league with Esterhazy, but those in charge knew the truth. With the honor of the army at stake, however, the minister of war, General Auguste Mercier, and chief of the General

Wrongly accused as a German spy, French Army captain Alfred Dreyfus was condemned to life in prison during a secret military trial in 1894. (Library of Congress)

Staff General Raoul de Boisdeffre ordered a cover-up. Major Hubert Henry, an officer of the Deuxième Bureau, undertook to strengthen the case against Dreyfus by forging new documents. Army honor seemed secure.

Despite this, Dreyfus gradually won more supporters. All France took sides, and government stability was threatened. In 1896 the army returned Dreyfus to France and retried him by court-martial, but again he was found guilty (although with attenuating circumstances). Finally in 1906 the civilian High Court of Appeal ruled in his favor. Ultimately Dreyfus was reinstated to his rank and awarded the Legion of Honor. However, his military career was ruined and his health shattered by the horrible conditions of his confinement. Most of those who were really guilty in the incident escaped any punishment including Esterhazy, who fled to Britain and put out conflicting versions of his role.

Throughout the incident, Dreyfus remained steadfast in his patriotism and the belief that right would prevail. He was, however, a reluctant hero. Dreyfus never sought notoriety, nor did he wish to be a vehicle against the anti-Semites. (He never once even wrote the word "Jew" in the journal he kept on Devil's Island or in moving letters to his wife.) Alfred Dreyfus owed his vindication to his brother Mathieu Dreyfus, who dedicated 12 years of his life to Alfred's cause, as well as to the courage of a growing number of Dreyfusards, as

Dreyfus's supporters were called, including celebrated novelist Émile Zola, who risked much to publish a ringing newspaper accusation of the authorities (the famous "J'Accuse" article). But Dreyfus also owed a special debt to army lieutenant colonel Georges Picquart, who as a subsequent chief of the Deuxième Bureau discovered the forgeries and insisted on pursuing the case, even though it led to his forced retirement and a year in military prison. Ultimately, Picquart too was vindicated. He fared better than Dreyfus, however, being made a general and later becoming minister of war.

The Dreyfus Affair must be understood in the circumstances of 1890s' French nationalism against Germany and anti-Semitism. Both of these were exploited by army leaders. Blinded by reason of state, they were fully prepared to sacrifice a man they knew to be innocent.

More important was the impact of the Dreyfus Affair on French political life. Its immediate effect was to bring the political Left into power and to keep it there for most of the time until World War I. The moderates had been badly split over the issue and were chiefly concerned about keeping things quiet. Leftist leaders convinced many French voters that they had saved the French Republic from a clerical-monarchist plot.

The Dreyfus Affair sharpened suspicions of the political Left toward both the army and the church. A new wave of antimilitarism and anticlericalism followed, with steps to republicanize the army and to weaken church influence. Army prestige and morale plummeted as a great many career officers resigned their commissions or retired. Fortunately for France, a nationalist revival occurred by 1911, stimulated by what Frenchmen perceived as aggressive German government policies.

The Dreyfus Affair also had profound repercussions abroad. Theodor Herzl, a Jew and the Paris correspondent for Austria's leading newspaper the *Neue Freie Presse,* was deeply shaken by the incident. He recalled that the shouts in Paris of "Death to the Jews" marked a turning point in his thinking and led to his decision to found the international Zionist movement with its goal of establishing a Jewish state in Palestine. Herzl's *Der Judenstaat* (*The Jewish State*) was published in February 1896.

SPENCER C. TUCKER

See also
Anti-Semitism; Herzl, Theodor; Zionism

References
Bredin, Jean-Denis. *The Affair: The Case of Alfred Dreyfus.* Translated by Jeffrey Mehlman. New York: George Braziller, 1986.
Chapman, Guy. *The Dreyfus Trials.* New York: Stein and Day, 1972.

Druze

A people who adhere to a Muslim sect, derived from Ismaili Shia Islam. The name "Druze" is a misnomer, probably derived from the 11th-century figure Nashtakin al-Darazi, regarded as the first Druze, or heretic. The Druze call themselves *muwahhidun,* or believers in

Druze political refugees who revolted against French rule in Syria, photographed in Jordan circa 1926. (Library of Congress)

monotheism (*tawhid*), a central principle of Islam, meaning unicity or strict monotheism. They are also known as Ahl al-Tawhid and Bana Maruf. Historically, some other Muslims treated the Druze as an extremist sect or disclaimed their Islamic beliefs, as today some discredit all of Shia Islam. The Druze number about 1 million people and are most numerous in Syria (400,000–500,000) and Lebanon (300,000–400,000). Smaller communities exist in Israel (60,000), the Golan Heights (15,000), Jordan (10,000–20,000), and elsewhere in the world (90,000).

The Druze are Arabs and tribal in origin. They are divided between the Qays and Yaman, or northern and southern traditional family rivalries. Their esoteric teachings were not revealed to all Druze, meaning that the common folk (*juhhal*) were excluded from some of the secrets of the faith possessed by the *uqqal*, or wise elders, although commoners may seek initiation into the sect's esoteric teachings. The Druze are an endogamous group, marrying within the faith, and no longer accept converts. The earliest *muwahhidun* were followers of the Fatimid caliph al-Hakim (966–1021) who developed into a reform movement under Hamza ibn Ali and others. The group proselytized and established a community in the Levant among 12 Arab Tanukhi tribes.

An intra-Druze war in 1711 spelled defeat for one faction, some of whom moved to the Hawran and Suwaida districts of Syria. Maronite Christians moved from northern Lebanon into some formerly Druze areas in Lebanon at this time.

The Druze religion is an offshoot of Ismaili Islam that developed in the 10th century. The Druze adhere to five articles of faith and seven acts of worship that correspond to the so-called Five Pillars of Islam (actually seven pillars including jihad [striving] and walaya [allegiance]). However, the esoteric interpretation of the acts of worship differs, or goes beyond the exoteric (outward) practice in Sunni Islam. The articles of faith include (1) *tawhid,* or unicity of God, and the idea that He has no opponents (Satan is not a separate force); (2) veneration (*taqdis*) of seven who preached a Message (including Abraham, Muhammad, and Muhammad ibn Ismail) and their divine Helpers as well as five luminaries, or key principles; (3) metempsychosis (*taqamus*), the rebirth of souls in a new body; (4) the need for initiation (*ta'aqul*), as faith should be pursued through reason; and (5) erudition or esoteric knowledge, known as *ma'rifa.*

In addition, the required acts of worship must include key principles that correspond to pillars of the Druze. These are speaking truth to attain unicity; supporting fellow believers with pure hearts; abandonment of old (polytheistic) ways and of sin; self-purification, or fleeing from evil nature and oppression; declaring the unity of God (true declaration of the *shahada* following esoteric understanding); being content and patient (*ridha*) with God's will as the expression of jihad; and submission to God's will.

For purposes of self-protection, the Druze, like other Shia Muslims, may practice *taqiyya* (dissimulation, or not admitting that one is a Druze). However, in their home areas, Druze are identified by their family names and their more classical pronunciation of Arabic.

The Druze belief in *taqamus,* a doctrine meaning transmigration of the soul after death, and tolerance of other faiths, or races. Their esoteric teachings sparked other sects' suspicion of their beliefs. These suspicions were politically promoted at times, for example in Ibn Taymiyya's fatwa against them when the Mamluk forces aimed to reconquer local dynasties cooperating with the Mongols.

The Druze abstain from alcohol, tobacco, and pork. The five-pointed, multicolor star of the Druze represents the five Luminaries referred to above, or five seminal principles: reason and intelligence; the universal soul; the word; historical precedence; and immanence (*al-tali',* or the following).

The Druze in Lebanon—mainly found in Mount Lebanon, the Wadi Taym area, and Beirut—became involved in the Lebanese Civil War (1975–1991). Under the leadership of Kamal Jumblat, their participation in the Lebanese National Movement pitted them against establishment Christian forces. The Druze fought effectively against the Christian Maronite Phalangist militia. Since the end of the war, certain Druze and Maronites have reconciled. In Lebanon, Israel, and Syria, the Druze are officially recognized by the respective governments and maintain their own religiously based court system.

In Syria, the Druze were leaders in the nationalist resistance to the French. Later, some were involved in a coup attempt against the Hafez al-Assad government and were subsequently treated poorly by the central government. Their region remains underdeveloped and poorly funded to this day. Nonetheless, some key Druze politicians were supporters of the Baath Party.

In Israel, the Druze live mainly in the Galilee and Carmel regions. The Druze of the Golan Heights suffered from expulsion from their villages or actual separation of territory. In all, the Druze have had about 80 percent of their former lands confiscated by Israel. The Israeli government treated the Druze more favorably than other Arabs as part of a policy aimed at dividing Arabs and creating loyalty to the state. The Druze routinely serve in the Israel Defense Forces (IDF) but nevertheless experience discrimination as non-Jews.

Sometimes the Israeli, Syrian, and Lebanese Druze communities have tried to support one another. When the IDF attempted to establish Christian domination in Lebanon over the Shuf area, Palestinian Druze vocally opposed this policy, which may have partially prompted Israeli withdrawal from the area. Some Druze officers have, in recent years, risen to general officer rank in the IDF.

PAUL G. PIERPAOLI JR. AND SHERIFA ZUHUR

See also

Lebanon; Lebanon, Civil War in

References

Abu Izzeddin, Nejla M. *The Druzes: A New Study of Their History, Faith, and Society.* Leiden: Brill, 1984 and 1993.

Betts, Robert Brenton. *The Druze.* New Haven: Yale University Press, 1990.

Dana, Nissim. *The Druze in the Middle East.* Eastbourne, East Sussex, UK: Sussex Academic, 2003.

Swayd, Samy S. *The Druzes: An Annotated Bibliography.* Kirkland, WA: ISES Publications, 1998.

Dubnow, Simon Meyervich
Born: September 10, 1860
Died: December 8, 1941

Distinguished Russian Jewish historian and advocate of Jewish autonomy. Born on September 10, 1860, to a poor family in the town of Mstislavl in Belarus in the Russian Empire, Simon Dubnow received a traditional Jewish education and then entered into a state Jewish school, where he learned Russian and Hebrew in addition to his native Yiddish. He was unable to graduate, however, because these schools were closed under czarist decree. He then continued his education on his own through extensive reading.

In 1880 Dubnow acquired forged documents that enabled him to move from the Pale of Settlement to the capital of St. Petersburg. There he wrote articles on both contemporary issues and, increasingly, Jewish history for the press, especially the Russian-Jewish magazine *Voskhod.* Forced to leave the capital during an expulsion of Jews from that city in 1890, he settled in Odessa, living there until 1903 and then in Vilna from 1903 to 1907. He now published books and articles on the life of Jews in Russia and Poland, on which he became the authority.

Dubnow was concerned with more than the mere history of the Jews, however. Actively involved in contemporary issues involving the Jews of Russia, he called for full civil rights for Jews, the modernization and expansion of their educational opportunities, and, following pogroms in Russia, the organization of Jewish self-defense groups. In 1906 he founded the Jewish People's Party, also known as Folkspartei.

Allowed to return to St. Petersburg in 1907, Dubnow founded and directed the Jewish Literature and Historical-Ethnographic Society. He also edited the *Jewish Encyclopedia.* After the 1917 Russian Revolution, he became professor of Jewish history at Petrograd University. In 1922 he immigrated to Kaunas (Kovno) and later moved to Berlin. There he published in German his monumental 10-volume history of the Jewish people, later published in Russian, Hebrew, and in English. It is still considered the standard work on the subject.

Dubnow pursued a sociological approach in his study and was fascinated with how the Jews had managed to survive as a separate people without their own nation. He attributed this to their spirit, to following their own laws and customs while remaining faithful to their own religion. Repeatedly, they had created new centers when others were destroyed.

Dubnow completely rejected assimilation. He believed that the Jews would continue to survive if they developed spiritual centers. He was initially ambivalent toward Zionism, disagreeing with the

Zionist contention that Jews, without their own state, would disappear as a separate people. In the mid-1930s he referred to the progress made by the Yishuv (Jews in Palestine) as the greatest miracle in contemporary Jewish history, and in his last years he moved toward acceptance of the Zionist ideal.

Dubnow moved to Riga, Latvia, in October 1933, following the Nazi assumption of power in Germany the previous January. When the Germans invaded Latvia and occupied Riga in July 1941, he was removed with other Jews to the Riga ghetto. He was among the thousands of Jews shot to death by German soldiers in the Rumbula Forest near Riga on December 8, 1941.

SPENCER C. TUCKER

See also

Assimilation; Pale of Settlement; Pogroms; Zionism

References

Dubnow, Simon. *History of the Jews in Russia and Poland: From the Earliest Times until the Present Day (1915)*. 10 vols. Philadelphia: Jewish Publication Society of America, 1916–1929.

Steinberg, Aaron, ed. *Simon Dubnow: The Man and His Work; A Memorial Volume on the Occasion of the Centenary of His Birth (1860–1960)*. Paris: World Jewish Congress, 1963.

Dulles, John Foster
Born: February 25, 1888
Died: May 24, 1959

U.S. secretary of state (1953–1959). Born in Washington, D.C., on February 25, 1888, John Foster Dulles graduated in 1908 from Princeton University, where he studied under Woodrow Wilson. In 1911 Dulles earned a law degree from George Washington University, and joined the prestigious Wall Street law firm of Sullivan and Cromwell. Appointed to the U.S. delegation at the 1919 Paris Peace Conference, Dulles unsuccessfully sought to restrain Allied reparations demands on Germany.

Active between the wars in internationalist organizations, Dulles initially opposed American intervention in World War II. Once American belligerency seemed probable, however, he focused intensely on postwar planning. He also became prominent in Republican politics, advising 1944 presidential candidate Gov. Thomas E. Dewey on international affairs. President Harry S. Truman, seeking to secure bipartisan political support for his foreign policy, included Dulles in virtually all major international meetings beginning with the 1945 San Francisco Conference that drafted the final United Nations (UN) Charter. Briefly appointed Republican senator for New York in 1948–1949, Dulles strongly supported creation of the North Atlantic Treaty Organization (NATO). He also supported European integration as a means of strengthening the continent's economies and militaries.

By the late 1940s Dulles had become a dedicated anticommunist. When the Chinese communists won control of the mainland in 1949, he advocated American backing for Chiang Kai-shek's Guo-

John Foster Dulles, U.S. secretary of state (1953–1959). (Library of Congress)

mindang (Kuomintang, Nationalist) regime on Taiwan. In June 1950 when North Korea invaded the South, Dulles urged U.S. intervention and the extension of protection to Taiwan. As a foreign affairs adviser to Dwight D. Eisenhower's Republican presidential campaign in 1952, Dulles argued that the Truman administration had been timorous in merely containing Soviet communism when it should have moved to roll back Soviet influence.

Named secretary of state by Eisenhower in 1953, Dulles deferred to the president's leadership. A supporter of Eisenhower's New Look defense policy of heavy reliance on nuclear weapons, Dulles rhetorically threatened to wreak massive retaliation against American enemies, tactics nicknamed "brinkmanship." In practice, however, he was often far more cautious. Although Dulles's bellicose anticommunist rhetoric alarmed many European leaders, his policies proved pragmatic.

Dulles and Eisenhower ended the Korean War in July 1953, pressuring both sides to accept an armistice, and established a series of military alliances in Asia. When possible, Eisenhower avoided direct major military interventions, preferring to rely on covert operations orchestrated by the Central Intelligence Agency (CIA), headed by Dulles's younger brother Allen. The CIA played key roles in coups that overthrew Left-leaning governments in Iran in 1953 and Guatemala in 1954.

Indeed, the U.S.-sponsored coup in Iran that ousted Mohammad Mosaddeq and strengthened Mohammad Reza Shah Pahlavi's hand showcased Dulles's approach to Middle East politics. Dulles believed that to advance American interests in Iran, the region had to remain free of major Soviet influences, free of leftist or communist regimes, and free of Pan-Arabism. Mosaddeq's socialist policies and references to imperialism and Western exploitation did not sit well with Dulles or Eisenhower. In the Middle East, Dulles's ardent anticommunism was mixed with considerable concerns that the region's oil supplies would be compromised by instability or Soviet advances. The 1953 coup in Iran, while accomplishing its goals in the short term, served only to create significant long-term problems. As the shah of Iran became more autocratic throughout the 1960s and 1970s, many Iranians would hold the United States responsible for the excesses of his regime. When he was ousted by an Islamic fundamentalist revolution in 1979, U.S.-Iranian relations were severed.

In Indochina in 1954, Dulles and Eisenhower withstood pressure from U.S. military leaders and—after Britain had declined to assist—refused to authorize air strikes to rescue French troops surrounded by Viet Minh forces at Dien Bien Phu. Nevertheless, Dulles and Eisenhower ended up backing noncommunist South Vietnam by 1956.

Dulles and Eisenhower considered the strengthening of West European allies their first priority. Thus, seeking to reinforce NATO, Dulles also backed proposals for a multinational European Defense Community (EDC), a plan that France vetoed in 1954. While Dulles sought to help U.S. allies in Europe, however, he nevertheless deplored British and French imperialism.

Dulles's relations with Britain and France reached their nadir in 1956. Following the 1952 revolution, Gamal Abdel Nasser became Egypt's leader in 1954. Initially, Nasser sought military aid from the United States. The powerful Israeli lobby, however, prevented such assistance. Nasser then obtained arms from the Soviet bloc. This, in turn, led Dulles in 1956 to rescind an earlier American pledge to provide Nasser with funding for his project to build a dam on the Nile south of Aswan.

Believing he had been betrayed, Nasser nationalized the Suez Canal, which was co-owned by the British and French governments. While openly joining Dulles in negotiations with Egypt, British and French leaders covertly intrigued with Israeli leaders for an Israeli attack against Egypt that would enable Britain and France to intervene militarily in Egypt and regain the canal. The invasion began in early November 1956, just before the U.S. presidential election. Dulles and Eisenhower strenuously pressured all three powers to withdraw, which occurred in a matter of weeks. Nevertheless, the episode soured Anglo-American relations.

Although Dulles hoped to align the United States with nationalist forces around the world, the open growth of Soviet interest in the Middle East brought the January 1957 announcement of the Eisenhower Doctrine. Authored chiefly by Dulles, the doctrine conferred upon the United States the right to intervene militarily (if requested) against indigenous or external communist threats in the region. This provoked significant anti-Americanism throughout the world. Just four months after Eisenhower had enunciated the Eisenhower Doctrine, Jordan's King Hussein faced a significant threat from indigenous Pan-Arab and communist forces. Dulles and Eisenhower responded by offering Hussein $10 million in economic aid. And to project American power, they dispatched the Sixth Fleet to the eastern Mediterranean.

As if to make good on the Eisenhower Doctrine, when Lebanese president Camille Chamoun argued that he faced a Muslim, Pan-Arab threat, the Eisenhower administration decided to intervene. Kamal Jumblat's followers had attacked the Lebanese president's palace in May. Dulles and Eisenhower intervened in the crisis, as a regional threat seemed more credible when the coup in Iraq in July of 1958 brought down the monarchy and a second coup had been attempted in Jordan, although it failed. On July 15, 1958, the first wave of nearly 15,000 U.S. troops landed in Lebanon to restore order. Many arrived without orders, and as they met no opposition and could not identify the rebels, they acted as a peacekeeping force and deterrent to other Middle Eastern countries. The crisis in Lebanon was soon over, and American troops departed Lebanon in early fall.

The emergence of Nikita Khrushchev as top Soviet leader in the mid-1950s seemed to promise a relaxation of Soviet-American tensions. As such, the Eisenhower administration hoped to conclude substantive disarmament agreements with Khrushchev. In practice, however, Khrushchev was often far from accommodating. The Soviets' success in launching the first space satellite (Sputnik) in 1957, Soviet possession of nuclear and thermonuclear weapons, and Khrushchev's seeming readiness from late 1958 onward to provoke an international crisis over Berlin all alarmed American leaders, including the ailing Dulles, diagnosed in 1957 with cancer.

Although American nation-building efforts in both Taiwan and South Vietnam enjoyed apparent success, during the Second Taiwan Straits Crisis in 1958 Dulles was notably more cautious about gratuitously challenging either communist China or possibly, by extension, the Soviets. When his cancer worsened, he resigned as secretary on April 15, 1959. Dulles died in Washington, D.C., on May 24, 1959.

PRISCILLA ROBERTS

See also

Eden, Robert Anthony; Egypt; Eisenhower, Dwight David; France, Middle East Policy; Iran; Israel; Khrushchev, Nikita; Macmillan, Maurice Harold; Nasser, Gamal Abdel; Reza Pahlavi, Mohammad, Shah of Iran; Soviet Union and Russia, Middle East Policy; Suez Crisis; United Kingdom, Middle East Policy

References

Guhin, Michael A. *John Foster Dulles: A Statesman and His Times*. New York: Columbia University Press, 1972.

Hoopes, Townsend. *The Devil and John Foster Dulles*. Boston: Little, Brown, 1973.

Immerman, Richard H. *John Foster Dulles: Piety, Pragmatism, and Power in U.S. Foreign Policy*. Wilmington, DE: Scholarly Resources, 1999.

Marks, Frederick W., III. *Power and Peace: The Diplomacy of John Foster Dulles*. Westport, CT: Praeger, 1993.

Toulouse, Mark G. *The Transformation of John Foster Dulles: From Prophet of Realism to Priest of Nationalism*. Macon, GA: Mercer University Press, 1985.

E

East Africa Scheme
Start Date: April 2, 1903
End Date: July 1905

Popularly known as the Uganda Scheme, the East Africa Scheme was a plan to resettle Jews in British East Africa. On April 2, 1903, British colonial secretary Joseph Chamberlain suggested to Zionist leader Theodor Herzl that Uganda in British East Africa might be an ideal place to settle Jewish immigrants. Herzl at first chose to ignore the proposal because of his concerns that it might jeopardize his own plan for an autonomous Jewish settlement in the Sinai.

When it was apparent that there was no chance of the Sinai plan succeeding and Chamberlain again mentioned the Uganda idea to Leopold J. Greenberg, Herzl's representative, Herzl instructed Greenberg to pursue negotiations. Sir Clement Hill, superintendent of African protectorates, suggested that the Jewish settlement could be politically independent with its own administration.

Lacking authority to act on his own concerning the proposal, Herzl first conferred with a number of Zionist leaders and then brought the matter before the Sixth Zionist Congress in Basle, Switzerland, held during August 23–28, 1903. In his opening address to the congress, Herzl outlined the Sinai Plan and explained why it had to be abandoned. He then presented the Uganda proposal. He did not recommend either acceptance or rejection, but he did stress that no other location could take the place of Palestine as the Jewish homeland. He also noted the importance of an offer from the British government and the advantage that this scheme might have for Jewish victims of persecution in Russia. (At the time there was great outrage over pogroms in Russia, most notably in Kishinev in April 1903.)

Austrian newspaper *Die Welt* of August 14, 1903, reporting a proposal for the creation of a Jewish settlement in East Africa. (Getty Images)

Herzl recommended that an investigative committee of experts be formed to visit Uganda and then report its findings at the next Zionist congress. Following debate, this proposal was adopted. The commission that chose the experts who would visit Uganda consisted of Joseph Cowen, Leopold J. Greenberg, Leopold Kessler, and Chaim Weizmann.

Some representatives, most notably from Russia, strongly objected to the East Africa plan, however, and a number walked out of the congress hall. The final vote on the proposal was 295 in favor to 178 opposed. A total of 98 delegates abstained. Herzl then met with those opposed and told them that he had not abandoned Palestine as the ultimate goal of the Zionist movement. Only then did the dissidents agree to return.

British support for the plan soon faltered, however. This was largely as a consequence of opposition to it from prominent Britons who claimed that it was unfair and would be a burden on the British taxpayers. In April 1904 in Vienna, Herzl met with leaders of the Zionist anti-Uganda faction and healed the rift. Herzl died only two months later.

When the Seventh Zionist Congress met in Basle in July 1905, the East Africa proposal was the most important agenda item. There was little chance of it being favorably received, as the experts who had visited Uganda found it to be unsuitable for Jewish settlement. By an overwhelming majority, the congress voted to reject all colonization schemes except those in Palestine and adjacent countries.

SPENCER C. TUCKER

See also

Chamberlain, Joseph; Herzl, Theodor; Kishinev Pogrom; Weizmann, Chaim; Zionism

References

Bein, Alex. *Theodor Herzl: A Biography.* London: Jewish Publication Society of America, 1943.

Brenner, Michael. *Zionism: A Brief History.* Translated by Shelley Frisch. Princeton, NJ: Markus Wiener, 2003.

Laqueur, Walter. *A History of Zionism: From the French Revolution to the Establishment of the State of Israel.* Reprint ed. New York: Schocken, 2003.

Eban, Abba Solomon
Born: February 2, 1915
Died: November 17, 2002

Israeli diplomat, cabinet minister, and foreign minister of Israel (1966–1974). Born Aubrey Solomon Eban in Cape Town, South Africa, on February 2, 1915, to Lithuanian immigrant parents, he moved to England at a young age and was educated at St. Olave's Grammar School, where he read the classics. His grandfather had a profound influence on him and saw to it that his education also included a thorough background in Hebrew studies and the language. Eban went on to study at Queen's College, Cambridge. An excellent student, he excelled in foreign languages and was ultimately fluent in 10, including Arabic.

Abba Eban, Israeli diplomat, cabinet minister, and foreign minister of Israel (1966–1974), photographed in December 1965. (Israeli Government Press Office)

Upon graduation, Eban became a lecturer in Middle Eastern languages and literature at Pembroke College, Cambridge, in 1938. Already an active Zionist from his student days, he divided his time between the university and working for Zionist causes.

Eban enlisted in the British Army in 1940 and, following a very brief assignment censoring letters written by Arabic-speaking British soldiers, of whom there were but few, was sent to Cairo and then on to Jerusalem, where he served as a liaison officer with the Jewish Yishuv of Palestine. Rising to the rank of major, he worked closely with Jewish leaders.

Leaving the British Army at the end of the war, Eban decided to dedicate himself to the formation of a Jewish state. He also changed his first name from Aubrey to the more Hebrew-sounding Abba. An articulate spokesman for the Jewish cause, in 1947 he began his diplomatic career as a liaison officer to the United Nations (UN) Special Commission on Palestine and as a member of the Jewish Agency delegation to the UN General Assembly. On the formation of the Jewish state in 1948, Eban became Israel's first representative to the UN. In 1949 he became its permanent UN representative.

Eban gave his first speech in a public forum at the UN on May 1, 1948, and his eloquent delivery marked a turning point in his career. In a time when UN debates were regularly televised, Eban proved to be an elegant, erudite, and urbane speaker and a witty debater who won much support for his nation in the United States and around the world. In 1952 he was vice president of the UN General Assembly.

Eban also served concurrently as Israeli ambassador to the United States from 1950 until his election to the Knesset (Israeli parliament) as a member of the Mapai Party in 1959. During 1959–1960 he was minister without portfolio, and in 1960 he became minister of education and culture. In this post he revamped the Israeli educational system and helped establish that nation's educational TV network. During 1963–1966 he was deputy prime minister to Levi Eshkol. During 1958–1966 Eban was also president of the Weizmann Institute at Rehovot.

In 1966 Eban became foreign minister of Israel. His eight-year tenure in that post included some of the most difficult episodes in Israeli history: the Six-Day War of 1967 and the Yom Kippur War of 1973. During his years as foreign minister, Eban successfully worked to strengthen Israel's ties with the United States and Western Europe. Although he strongly supported his nation in its wars, he was also an advocate of returning territories captured by Israel from its neighbors in return for peace, and he played an important role in shaping UN Security Council Resolution 242 in 1967.

Eban stepped down as foreign minister in 1974 but continued as a member of the Israeli Knesset until 1988, serving on its Committee on Foreign Affairs and Security and chairing it during 1984–1988. Retiring from politics when he failed to win reelection due to a split in the Labor Party, he was a visiting professor at Princeton University and Columbia University. He also wrote nearly a dozen books including his memoirs, and he hosted a number of television documentaries that focused on Jewish history and the Middle East. In 2001 he received the Israel Prize, the most prestigious award given by his country. Eban died in Israel on November 17, 2002.

MICHAEL POLLEY AND SPENCER C. TUCKER

See also

Six-Day War; United Nations Security Council Resolution 242; Yom Kippur War; Zionism

References

Eban, Abba. *Abba Eban: An Autobiography.* New York: Random House, 1977.
———. *My People: The Story of the Jews.* New York: Random House, 1984.
———. *Personal Witness.* New York: Putnam, 1992.

Eden, Robert Anthony
Born: June 12, 1897
Died: January 14, 1977

British prime minister from 1955 to 1957. Robert Anthony Eden was born on June 12, 1897, into a prosperous landed family at Windlestone Hall near Bishop Auckland, Durham, England. Educated

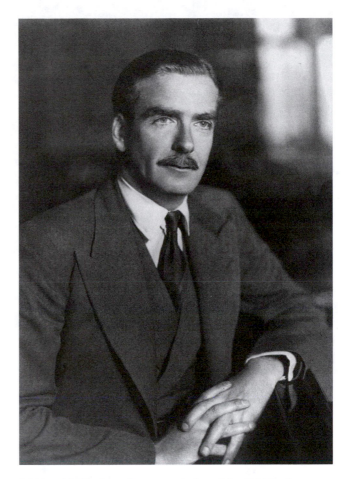

British political leader and statesman Anthony Eden, British prime minister during 1955–1957. (Library of Congress)

---

at Eton, he fought in France in World War I and won the Military Cross. By 1918 he was a brigade major.

After the war Eden attended Christ Church College, Oxford, gaining first-class honors in the Persian and Arabic languages in 1922. In 1923 he was elected a Conservative representative to the House of Commons. In Parliament he specialized in defense and foreign affairs, rising to become parliamentary private secretary at the Foreign Office in 1926 and later undersecretary in Ramsay MacDonald's government. In 1935 Eden became the minister for League of Nations affairs in Stanley Baldwin's third government. A convinced advocate of League of Nations principles, Eden proved an excellent diplomat and negotiator.

From the mid to late 1930s, Eden attempted to counter aggressive fascist policies in Europe by negotiation. He privately opposed the policy of Foreign Secretary Sir Samuel Hoare, who tried to appease Italy during its invasion of Abyssinia (Ethiopia) in 1935. When Hoare resigned after the failure of the public disclosure of the Hoare-Laval Pact, Eden succeeded him as foreign minister in December. While he did not protest when Britain failed to support France in action to oppose the German remilitarization of the Rhineland in 1936, in February 1938 he resigned over Prime Minister Neville Chamberlain's appeasement policy.

Eden now found himself closely allied with Winston Churchill, then a rebel backbench Conservative member of Parliament and a leading critic of appeasement. In May 1940 Churchill became prime minister and appointed Eden secretary of state for war. Appointed foreign secretary that December, he was one of Churchill's closest confidants. Eden's wartime role was limited, however, simply because Churchill personally conducted the most important negotiations with U.S. president Franklin Roosevelt and Soviet leader Joseph Stalin.

Following the war and the Labour Party victory of July 1945, Eden became shadow prime minister in the House of Commons. When the Conservatives returned to power in October 1951, he again became foreign secretary. When in April 1955 Churchill finally retired, Eden succeeded him as prime minister.

Eden's international reputation and his political viability were soon entangled in the 1956 Suez Crisis. The Free Officers who enacted the 1952 Egyptian Revolution then moved to end British influence in the country. However, the British opposed the prospect of nationalization of the Suez Canal, and some leaders in Great Britain as well as Israel hoped that the outspoken nationalist Gamal Abdel Nasser, who had become the leader of Egypt, could be overthrown. In September of 1955, Nasser spoke on behalf of the Non-Aligned Movement at the Bandung Conference. Then, he announced that he would purchase military equipment from the Soviet bloc. In July 1956, President Dwight Eisenhower cancelled a promised grant to the Egyptians of $56 million that was to go toward the building of the Aswan High Dam. That same month, Nasser announced that he intended to nationalize the Suez Canal, arguing that the revenues from the canal would help construction of the dam.

On July 26, 1956, Nasser ordered an Egyptian blockade of the Gulf of Aqaba and nationalized the Suez Canal Company, in which the British government was a principal stockholder. In addition, Egypt convinced other Arab countries to resist joining the Baghdad Pact, and this strained British relations with Jordan. Eden in particular took a personal dislike to Nasser, likening his methods to those of the fascist dictators. Britain and France depended heavily on the canal for the transit of oil, and they considered Nasser a threat to their interests in the Middle East and in Africa.

France was also upset with Nasser, especially over the latter's support for the anti-French Front de Libération Nationale (National Liberation Front, FLN) in Algeria. In consequence, the government of Premier Guy Mollet entered into talks with Israel, which then were expanded to include the British government in discussions at Sèvres on October 24 concerning a military effort that would topple Nasser. After an attack on Egypt by Israeli forces on October 29, a joint Anglo-French military operation began against Egypt on October 31 with air attacks on Egyptian airfields. Apparently Eden had only reluctantly accepted in mid-October the idea of a joint invasion of Egypt after the failure of his efforts to resolve the situation peacefully.

Eden understood the postwar limitations on British power. In his memoirs, *Full Circle* (1960), he depicted the Anglo-French action as the culmination of a consistent policy undertaken from the beginning of the crisis rather than one that succumbed to increasing pressure to use force.

Eisenhower, caught by surprise at the Israeli-French-British military action, strongly opposed it. He believed that it was a mistaken policy that would only increase Soviet influence in the Middle East, and he had a stormy phone conversation with Eden over it. The U.S. government then applied heavy pressure on Britain as well as on France and Israel to withdraw. The final evacuation took place on December 22, with British and French forces being replaced by United Nations (UN) observers.

The Suez fiasco ruined Eden's reputation for political acuity and caused a sharp decline in his health. His foreign secretary, Harold Macmillan, despite having been one of the architects of the Suez enterprise, persuaded Eden to resign, succeeding him as prime minister in January 1957. Plagued by ill health in his later years, Eden also experienced a troubled marital life. Above all, he worried about his historical reputation. He nevertheless retained much of his personal popularity and was created Earl of Avon in 1961. In retirement he published personal and political memoirs, the latter in three volumes, *Full Circle* (1960), *Facing the Dictators* (1962), and *The Reckoning* (1965). Eden died in Alvediston, Wiltshire, on January 14, 1977.

PETER OVERLACK

See also

Aqaba, Gulf of; Arab Nationalism; Eisenhower, Dwight David; France, Middle East Policy; Macmillan, Maurice Harold; Mollet, Guy; Nasser, Gamal Abdel; Soviet Union and Russia, Middle East Policy; Suez Crisis; United Kingdom, Middle East Policy; United States, Middle East Policy

References

Dutton, David. *Anthony Eden: A Life and Reputation.* Oxford: Oxford University Press, 1997.

Eden, Anthony. *Facing the Dictators: The Memoirs of Anthony Eden, Earl of Avon.* Boston: Houghton Mifflin, 1962.

Pearson, Jonathan. *Sir Anthony Eden and the Suez Crisis: Reluctant Gamble.* New York: Palgrave Macmillan, 2003.

Thorpe, D. R. *Eden: The Life and Times of Anthony Eden, First Earl of Avon, 1897–1977.* London: Pimlico, 2004.

Egypt

An African and a Middle Eastern nation, Egypt encompasses 386,660 square miles and is bordered by the Mediterranean Sea to the north, Sudan to the south, Libya to the west, and the Red Sea to the east. Egypt is one of the world's oldest civilizations. Its documented history extends well back into the third millennium BC. Its strategic position and the fertility of its land have always attracted outside powers. This strategic importance only increased with the opening of the Suez Canal in 1869.

Although the canal company was predominantly French, Britain acquired the shares belonging to the Khedive of Egypt and a controlling interest in it. The British recognized the importance of the

Cairo skyline. This view is from the Citadel of Old Cairo and includes the ancient Al-Azhar University and mosque. (iStockPhoto.com)

canal as its imperial lifeline to India, and a nationalist uprising in Egypt gave Britain the excuse to seize control of Egypt in 1882. Within two decades, British authority was extended to the Sudan as well.

In December 1914 following the entry of the Ottoman Empire into World War I on the side of the Central Powers, Great Britain declared Egypt a protectorate. During the war Egypt became a major British military base for operations against Turkey on the Gallipoli Peninsula and in Palestine. Cairo was also the center for British diplomacy toward the Arabs.

In 1919, anti-British riots and labor unrest erupted in Egypt. In response, in February 1922 the British ended the protectorate and declared Egypt a sovereign, independent kingdom. This was window dressing only, for Britain continued to exercise real authority through its advisers, who controlled key departments including internal security. In April 1923 King Fuad promulgated a constitution that followed Western patterns but reserved considerable rights to the Crown. Anti-British demonstrations and agitation continued. Fuad died in April 1936 and was succeeded by his 16-year-old son Farouk. Meanwhile, the threat posed to the security of the region by Italy's invasion of Ethiopia in September 1935 and long-standing Egyptian grievances regarding British policy in Egypt and the Sudan had led to negotiations between the British and

Egyptian governments and a new treaty between the two nations signed on August 26, 1936.

Among the major terms of the 1936 treaty, Britain pledged to defend Egypt against outside aggression, while Egypt promised to place its facilities at Britain's disposal in case of war. Egypt agreed to a garrison of 10,000 British troops and 400 pilots in the Canal Zone and to provide their barracks. Britain was to evacuate all other bases except the naval base at Alexandria, which it would have for eight more years. British personnel in the Egyptian Army and the police were to be withdrawn (Britain had previously controlled the armed forces and the police), but a British military mission would advise the Egyptian army to the exclusion of other foreigners. Egyptian officers were to train abroad only in Britain. Britain also promised to allow unrestricted immigration of Egyptians into the Sudan, and Egyptian troops were also allowed to return there. Britain agreed to work for the removal of the capitulations and for most-favored nation commercial treaties, and its high commissioner was replaced by an ambassador. The treaty was to be of indefinite duration but with negotiations for any changes permitted after 20 years.

In effect, Britain retained its right to protect security through the canal and compromised on a number of other issues. Left unresolved was the question of the future of the Sudan. Egypt ratified the treaty, although there was much criticism of it. Egypt was then admitted to the League of Nations. Many of the treaty's terms, however, were set aside with the advent of World War II.

Before and during World War II, both the Egyptian Crown and Britain sought to break the power of the Wafd Party, which had been the main vehicle of Egyptian nationalism since its founding in 1919 and dominated the parliament. In February 1938, ignoring constitutional rights, the king dissolved the parliament. The Wafd remained out of power for the next four years.

During World War II there was some pro-Axis sentiment in Egypt, but the British requested and received full government cooperation against Germany. Egypt became the principal British, and later Allied, base in the Middle East with more than half a million troops stationed there, and Cairo was a center of intense diplomatic activity and the venue for a major Allied conference in the fall of 1943. During the war, the numbers of British, Australian, and New Zealand troops in the country went up dramatically, leading many Egyptians to conclude that their long struggle to escape Western dominance via negotiation was of little consequence. Wartime profiteering, increased prostitution, and alcohol and drug use accompanied the Commonwealth forces in the country.

The war set in motion profound economic changes in Egypt, and these helped prompt a dangerous increase in extremism, both leftist and rightist. On the Left the Egyptian Communist Party, although illegal, gained in influence, partly because of the heightened prestige of the Soviet Union from the war. The party sought to exploit legitimate labor grievances that had arisen from the war.

On the Right there was the powerful Muslim Brotherhood. Organized by Sheikh Hasan al-Banna in 1929, it was both staunchly pro-Islamic and anti-West and opposed the corruption of wealthy landowners in Parliament. In contrast to the small Communist Party of perhaps 5,000 members, the Muslim Brotherhood had a large following ranging from 500,000 to 3 million people according to different sources. It made no secret of its distaste for the Western use of the country to fight the Axis. In July 1946 the government moved against the Communists, arresting many of the party leaders and bringing them to trial in 1947. Most received prison terms.

The government also began a low-scale war with the Muslim Brotherhood in 1948 when it banned the organization following the assassination of a judge who had sentenced a member of the Brotherhood. The Muslim Brotherhood had developed a secret military organization since 1939 that was banned by General Guide Hasan al-Banna. After the ban, though, more violence broke out, and a member of the Brotherhood assassinated Prime Minister Mahmud al-Nuqrashi. The Egyptian secret police assassinated al-Banna in 1949 on the orders of the government, which refused to relegalize the Brotherhood.

In the January 1950 parliamentary elections, the Wafd won 228 of 319 seats in the Chamber, and Nahas Pasha again assumed the premiership. He persuaded King Farouk to remove 17 appointed senators, replacing them with Wafd nominees and giving that party an absolute majority in both chambers.

In foreign affairs, the Egyptian government was determined to revise the 1936 treaty with Britain. The two chief points of grievance for the Egyptians were the continued presence of British troops in the country and the matter of the future of the Sudan, which Egypt sought to regain or liberate from British control. There were strong historical, cultural, ethnic (in the case of the northern Sudan), and economic ties between Egypt and the Sudan, but Egypt was most concerned about the security of its critical water supply in the Nile River, which flowed north through the Sudan into Egypt.

In October 1946 Egyptian prime minister Sidqi Pasha concluded an agreement with British foreign secretary Ernest Bevin. It provided for the withdrawal of British forces from the Canal Zone and a formula regarding a settlement in the Sudan, by which the Sudanese themselves would determine their future government and whether the Sudan would be part of Egypt or independent.

In 1948 Egypt went to war against Israel. Egypt was able to send only a small military force to participate in the coalition of Arab states against the Jewish state, and Egyptian forces performed poorly, suffering a number of defeats. This was a source of embarrassment for Egyptians.

In the January 1950 general elections the Wafd was returned to power, resulting in talks with Britain in the winter of 1950–1951 over modification of the 1936 treaty. The Cold War produced British intransigence regarding revision, however, as Western nations regarded Egypt as their suitable base in the Middle East. As an indication of Egyptian attitudes, upon the beginning of the Korean War in June 1950 the Egyptian government announced that it would be neutral and not support the United Nations (UN) military effort there.

Discontent against the government and its policies had been steadily building. On January 19, 1952, rioting broke out at Ismailiyya, an important town and base at the north end of the Suez Canal. The British then occupied the town and evicted the local police. This led to major riots in Cairo in which hundreds of well-known establishments were put to the torch. The toll in a day of rioting on January 26 was 26 dead and 552 wounded. King Farouk, hostile to the Wafd, took advantage of this event to dismiss Nahas Pasha and his cabinet on January 27 and appoint Ali Mahir Pasha in his place.

All this created something of a political vacuum, which was filled on July 23, 1952, when a core of 13 army officers, representing a larger group that had formed in 1949, seized power in Egypt. They set up a Revolutionary Command Council (RCC) of 17 members. The chairmanship of the RCC went to Major General Mohammad Naguib, Ali Mahir headed the government, and a regency council acted for the son of King Farouk, Ahmad Fuad. The real leader of the Free Officers was Gamal Abdel Nasser, however. In 1953 when the monarchy was abolished, Nasser became deputy prime minister and minister of the interior in 1953, while Naguib became president and prime minister. The RCC made it clear that it sought to free Egypt from imperialism and feudalism and introduce a program of social justice, reform, and economic progress. On July 26, Naguib demanded that King Farouk renounce the throne and leave

Egypt forthwith. Farouk departed the same day, abdicating in favor of his infant son Ahmed Fuad II. This arrangement lasted for only one year until June 1953, when the military junta terminated the monarchy and declared Egypt a republic. While Naguib was the nominal head of the revolutionary government, the real authority rested in the hands of the RCC, which was dominated by Colonel Nasser. On April 17, 1954, Nasser pushed Naguib aside and assumed full power.

During the first years after the revolution, the military leaders perceived themselves as Egyptian nationalists with the twin missions of domestic social reform and ridding the country of foreign influence. The new government also moved against the Muslim Brotherhood, which had supported their coup. In January 1954 the government ordered it dissolved and arrested 78 of its leaders. Soon the Egyptian leader announced a broader movement known as Pan-Arabism (also called Nasserism), a mix of nationalism and Pan-Arab sentiments. Nasser supported improving the lot of the common man or peasants, and after 1961 he advocated greater Arab socialism. His regime moved to carry out land reform and nationalized most banks and many commercial and industrial enterprises. The centerpiece of Nasser's economic program was to be a new high dam at Aswan in southern Egypt. This, he believed, would provide electricity sufficient for Egyptian needs, halt the often costly Nile flooding, and open new lands for crops. Despite sweeping changes or due to their incomplete realization coupled with defense spending, the Egyptian economy underperformed during most of Nasser's years in power.

While the early years after the 1952 coup saw little participation by Egypt in Arab affairs, the Aswan High Dam project and the Suez Crisis soon changed that. On October 19, 1954, shortly after coming to power, Nasser had concluded a new treaty with Britain whereby the British gave up all rights to the Suez Canal base and agreed to evacuate the Canal Zone entirely within 20 months. In return, Egypt promised to keep the base in combat readiness and allow the British to return in case of an attack by an outside power against Turkey or any Arab state.

Meanwhile, the United States and Britain agreed to extend financial assistance to Egypt for the Aswan High Dam project. However, when these Western powers refused to sell Nasser advanced weaponry and he concluded a massive arms deal with Czechoslovakia for Soviet bloc weapons and then recognized the People's Republic of China (PRC), the United States cancelled its offer of aid for the dam construction. The British government followed suit. In response, on July 26, 1956, Nasser (elected president of Egypt on June 23) nationalized the Suez Canal. Nasser planned to use the revenues from the canal to pay for construction of the Aswan Dam.

In spite of the Egyptian assurances of compensation to the Suez Canal Company shareholders, Britain and France began a secret dialogue with Israel for an attack on Egypt to topple Nasser from power and reoccupy the Suez Canal Zone. The attack began on October 29, 1956, when Israelis troops invaded the Gaza Strip and the Sinai Peninsula. On October 31, 1956, British and French forces,

acting to protect the canal, joined the assault. These actions enraged U.S. president Dwight D. Eisenhower, who applied significant economic pressure to secure British withdrawal, which was followed by that of France and Israel. Meanwhile, during the fighting Nasser had ordered ships sunk in the canal to keep it from being used by the invaders. This resulted in the closure of the canal until April 1957.

There were several important ramifications of the Suez Crisis. First and foremost, it greatly bolstered Nasser's standing in the Arab world as a leader who could stand up to foreign powers, a position he would try to utilize to form Arab alliances for the remainder of his life. The conflict also resulted in the signing of a Treaty of Arab Solidarity among Egypt, Saudi Arabia, Syria, and Jordan in January 1957 as well as the Eisenhower administration's announcement of the Eisenhower Doctrine to provide both financial and military support to any nation in the Middle East in the struggle against communism.

Within a year, the solidarity movement from the Suez Crisis among the various Arab states was weakened. Some experts have called this the beginning of the Arab Cold War. However, Westerners might not appreciate Nasser's popularity throughout the region from Morocco to Iraq, not least because of his oratorical skills, which were heard over the radio. On February 1, 1958, Syria invited Nasser to join in a union known as the United Arab Republic (UAR). This created tensions in Syria, as one political faction had essentially preempted another with this invitation. Syrian opponents to the union complained of Egyptian dominance and economic changes not well suited to Syria (although the subsequent governments also embarked on land reform). Jordan also saw the UAR as a clear threat. In September 1961 the UAR dissolved after a coup swept the ruling faction in Syria out of office, and Nasser accepted the dissolution.

In the meantime, Egypt began to turn increasingly to the Soviet bloc for aid, beginning with Soviet assistance in construction of the Aswan Dam. Egypt began a war of words with Saudi Arabia that eventually emerged as a proxy struggle in Yemen. The Arab states agreed on the danger that Israel represented to them and the need to find justice for the Palestinian refugees. Egypt claimed leadership of the Pan-Arab movement in this regard and promoted cultural and intellectual expressions of Arab identity. Pan-Arabism remained very popular in the region among youths, workers, intellectuals, peasants, and professionals despite the difficulties of formally expressing it through political union. Nasser's strengthening of Egypt's political profile and regional leadership through Arabism was borne out in the country's continuing influence and mediation of crises in the region, from Jordan to Lebanon on up to the present day.

In December 1961 Nasser broke off relations with the monarchical government of Yemen and began clandestine support for a republican movement there. Saudi Arabia, meanwhile, supported the Yemeni monarchy. Finally, Egyptian armed forces intervened openly on the republican side. Egyptian troops remained in Yemen until 1967 and the Egyptian defeat in the Six-Day War. The Yemen

Mortuary temple of Hatshepsut at Deir el-Bahri, across the Nile River from Luxor, Egypt. The site is the location of the 1997 Luxor Massacre in which 62 tourists were killed by terrorists. (Corel)

war was both costly and deeply frustrating for Egypt. The People's Democratic Republic of Yemen was a highly progressive Marxist state that attempted modernization and reform, inspired in some ways by Nasser's Egypt. The country has since reunified.

Nasser signed a mutual defense treaty between Egypt and Syria on November 4, 1966. At the time, both Egypt and Syria were supporting guerrillas operating against Israel. Tensions in the region began to mount with this alliance, and they were exacerbated on November 13, 1966, when Israeli forces destroyed the Jordanian village of Samu, which Israel asserted had often served as a staging area for guerrilla strikes into its territory. This action escalated already high regional tensions.

On April 7, 1967, in response to an incident on the Golan Heights, Israeli aircraft shot down seven Syria fighter jets and concluded the action by a triumphant flight over Damascus itself. On May 16 Nasser promised to come to the aid of Syria if it was attacked, and he heightened tensions by ordering several divisions closer to the Israeli border in the Sinai. On May 18 Nasser demanded the removal of the UN Emergency Force (UNEF) along the ceasefire line with Israel, and UN secretary-general U Thant complied. Four days later, Nasser placed an Egyptian garrison at Sharm al-Sheikh and announced a blockade of the Straits of Tiran, effectively closing the Israeli port of Eilat. On May 30 Jordan's King Hussein signed a military alliance with Egypt.

On June 5, 1967, as tensions came to a head, Israel launched a series of well-coordinated peremptory strikes first against Egypt and then on Syria, Jordan, and Iraq. The centerpiece of this was a crippling air strike on the morning of June 5 that cost Egypt most of its aircraft destroyed on the ground. Soon, Israeli ground forces had driven deep into the Sinai. By June 8 after only four days of fighting, Egypt had suffered its most stunning modern military defeat. Still, the war continued for two more days. At its conclusion, the Israelis occupied the West Bank in Jordan, Syria's Golan Heights, and the entire Sinai Peninsula in Egypt. This last territorial acquisition brought Israeli troops to the Suez Canal.

In all, Egyptian losses included 10,000 enlisted men and 1,500 officers killed or wounded, with an additional 5,000 enlisted men and 500 officers taken prisoner. The Egyptians lost 600 tanks and virtually their entire air force.

The shock of the defeat lingered on for years. Nasser, stung by this sudden reversal, resigned the presidency on June 9. The Egyptian people took to the streets, however, refusing to accept his resignation and demanding that he remain in power, which he did. Indeed, Egypt's defeat in the 1967 Six-Day War led to the emergence of militant and revolutionary activity to protest the failures of the Arab states. While Egyptian political and military leaders took the first steps that might lead to the return of their lost territories, opposition groups and the Palestinians concluded that the Arab armies and governments might not be capable of victory and began planning smaller-scale military actions. Thus, the Six-Day War led directly to the War of Attrition (1968–1970).

In June 1968 Nasser's government, still smarting from the humiliation of the Six-Day War, began shelling Israeli positions on the east bank of the Suez Canal. In the meantime, the Israelis had fortified this forward position with a string of forts known as the Bar-Lev Line. The Israelis responded on October 30 with a commando raid that effectively destroyed Egypt's electrical generating facilities. In February 1969 Egypt again initiated a series of bombardments and counterbombardments across the canal. This time, the fighting led to superpower intervention when Nasser flew to Moscow in January 1970 seeking arms and military aid. This in turn precipitated a whole new set of difficulties. The United States became involved in negotiations that finally led to a cease-fire agreement on August 7, 1970. Nasser died suddenly the next month, on September 28, 1970, after negotiating a cease-fire in the Black September violence in Jordan. He was succeeded by his vice president, Anwar Sadat.

For a brief time, Sadat continued Nasser's policies toward both the Soviet Union and Israel as he dealt with internal opposition. But before long, Sadat began to replace Nasser's supporters in the government and initiated a major turn against his predecessor's policies, both foreign and domestic. Domestically, this included a move away from Nasser's state socialist economic policies, including changes in investment laws and import rules. These became known as the Infitah, or Economic Opening, by 1974. Sadat sent home the Soviet and Soviet bloc advisers in Egypt and sought increased economic aid from the West, including the United States. He also freed Islamist groups such as the Muslim Brotherhood and allowed Muslim student groups to meet in an effort to mobilize them against leftist students and elements who protested his new policies.

Sadat embarked on a concentrated program of rearmament and military reform. The new weaponry, which included large numbers of surface-to-air missiles (SAMs), was supplied mainly by the Soviet Union. After 1972, Egypt sought Western weapons and made efforts to upgrade older weapons systems. General Ismail Ali was the chief figure associated with these improvements in the Egyptian military. He undertook a series of changes in the Egyptian Army designed to take advantage of its strengths while at the same time minimizing its weaknesses. These resulted in the concentration of SAMs along the Suez Canal to counter the Israeli Air Force. Likewise, he drastically increased the proportion of antitank weapons to deal with Israeli armor.

By 1973 Sadat had agreed to participate with Syria in a daring preemptive strike against Israel as a way to reverse the outcome of the Six-Day War. The timing of the attack, around the Jewish holiday of Yom Kippur and the Muslim observance of Ramadan, was an attempt to maximize Arab chances. The overall strategy was for Egypt and Syria to launch a concerted attack on Israel, inflict a quick but serious defeat on the Jewish state, and thus influence the negotiations for the return of the lost territories.

For their part, the Israelis were clearly overconfident in their ability to repel any Arab attack after their easy victories in the Six-Day War and their continued success in the War of Attrition. Warnings of the impending attack fell on deaf ears, and the timing of the strike caught the Israelis by surprise. They were also certain that any Arab attack could be defeated from the air. In retrospect, the Arab attack was a great humiliation for the Israeli military and intelligence communities, for the Egyptians had practiced their attack in military exercises in plain view of the Israeli Army.

The actual attack began on October 13, 1973. The Egyptians were able to cross the Suez Canal and secure most of the forts of the vaunted Israeli Bar-Lev Line, while Syrian forces drove into the Golan Heights. The Egyptian plan had been to capture the Israeli defensive positions, destroy with their missiles the Israeli air and armor counterattacks, and wait for a negotiated settlement. But the success of the Egyptians in their crossing and their subsequent accomplishments in shooting down a number of aircraft and blunting the Israeli ground counterattack led Sadat to demand deeper offensive action. When the Egyptians deviated from the original plan, by October 15 the initiative had passed into the hands of the Israelis. The fighting raged on until October 22, when a cease-fire negotiated by the United States and the Soviet Union went into effect. From this point on, the negotiations began for a peace settlement.

Frustrated by the slow progress, Sadat decided on a radical change of course. On November 19, 1977, he flew to Israel, much to the astonishment of the world community. His move was condemned in most Arab capitals. By going to Israel, Sadat implicitly recognized its existence. He also became the first Arab leader to do so, and it proved the turning point in the negotiations. In September 1978, Sadat and Israeli prime minister Menachem Begin signed the Camp David Peace Accords. Negotiated in part with the assistance of U.S. president Jimmy Carter, the agreements returned the Sinai Peninsula to Egypt. In return, Egypt officially recognized Israel. This historic rapprochement in effect ended Egyptian involvement in the Arab-Israeli wars. The peace accords also solidified the growing Egyptian-American alliance.

Yet the Israeli-Egyptian peace deal had negative repercussions as well. Much of the Arab world was infuriated by Sadat's seeming capitulation to the Israelis. As such, the other states cut off aid, discouraged travel to Egypt, and expelled Egypt from the Arab League. Within Egypt, the bilateral agreement with Israel had not been popular. As time went on support for it steadily eroded, as many Egyptians blamed economic dislocations, rising factionalism, and dissatisfaction with the political scene on the Camp David settlement. Such public resentment also extended to Sadat, who had promised but not delivered political liberalization.

In 1980 a cultural agreement was signed between Egypt and Israel. Those intellectuals, journalists, physicians, athletes, and writers who braved boycotts in their professional syndicates in Egypt were disappointed to learn that even Israeli doves did not support Palestinian sovereignty. The Israeli Academic Center in Egypt brought little contact between Egyptians and Israelis. As a result, following Sadat's death the Egyptian government essentially stopped promoting cultural exchange.

As factionalism and extremism continued to rise in Egypt, Sadat's position became more difficult, and he arrested a large number of political opponents on the Left and the Right. On October 6, 1981, he was assassinated while in the reviewing stand during a military parade by members of the radical Islamic Jihad. Whereas Nasser was loudly and demonstrably mourned by the Egyptian public, Sadat was not.

Sadat was immediately succeeded by his vice president, Hosni Mubarak, who was also injured in the assassination. Mubarak, who has presided over Egyptian politics since 1981, continued Sadat's policies, although slowing economic rationalization and privatization. He also put the brakes on political liberalization that would strengthen any parts of government except for the executive or that might lead to free elections for all candidates and parties.

Under Sadat the Arab Socialist Union, the mass political party, had begun its transformation into the National Democratic Party. Only a few small opposition parties were allowed to operate openly, including the Wafd. Mubarak continued operating through the National Democratic Party in which his son, Jamal, is now a leader. Mubarak also continued Sadat's policy of cooperation with the West, and he maintained diplomatic relations with Israel except during several notable crises. Mubarak also sought to maintain a potent military establishment. He continued to modernize and upgrade it, and by 1992 the Egyptian Air Force was the largest in the Middle East.

Mubarak has come under increasing pressure from the international community to carry out significant political reform, including an end to the emergency laws that have been in place since Sadat's assassination and that prohibit political activity or gatherings not sanctioned by the government. He also refused to permit the holding of bona fide presidential and legislative elections or provide for judicial oversight of elections. In the past several years, he has taken only halting steps to address these issues. From the late 1980s to 1999 when a truce was forged, radical and fundamentalist groups within Egypt waged low-level terrorist activities against local and national officials as well as tourists. Since 2003, new extremist groups not participating in the truce have emerged. Many of these groups still decry the settlement with Israel.

During the 1991 Persian Gulf War, Mubarak joined the international coalition against the Iraqi invasion of Kuwait, and Egyptian troops were among the first to land in Kuwait at the beginning of the ground war in February 1991. As a result of its service to the coalition, Egypt received loan waivers from the United States, Western Europe, and several Persian Gulf states in excess of $20 billion.

In the late 1990s, the Egyptian economy entered a period of sluggish growth and high unemployment. The economy appears more favorable for big business, although tourism has been affected by terrorist attacks during 2004–2005. Unemployment and underemployment remain very high. Mubarak spoke out against the Anglo-American invasion of Iraq in 2003, believing that it would only further the growth of extremism in the region. He has since come under pressure from Washington to denounce both Hamas and Hezbollah, although Egyptians generally support them, and to rein in the Muslim Brotherhood, which is indeed his government's policy. Despite assassination attempts Mubarak has refused to designate a successor, and the opposition is concerned that this is because he intends to pass the presidency to his son Jamal following the completion of his fifth presidential term in 2011.

James McIntyre, Paul G. Pierpaoli Jr., Spencer C. Tucker, and Sherifa Zuhur

See also

Arab League; Arab Socialism; Attrition, War of; Camp David Accords; Egypt, Armed Forces; Eilat, Israel; Farouk I, King of Egypt; Mubarak, Hosni; Muslim Brotherhood; Naguib, Mohammad; Nasser, Gamal Abdel; Pan-Arabism; Sadat, Anwar; Sharm al-Sheikh; Sinai Campaign; Six-Day War; Strait of Tiran Crisis; Suez Canal; Suez Crisis; United Arab Republic; Yom Kippur War

References

Abdel-Malek, Anouar. *Egypt: Military Society, the Army Regime, the Left, and Social Change under Nasser.* New York: Random House, 1968.

Beattie, Kirk J. *Egypt during the Sadat Years.* New York: Palgrave, 2000.

Cooper, Chester L. *The Lion's Last Roar: Suez, 1956.* New York: Harper and Row, 1978.

Dawisha, A. I. *Egypt in the Arab World.* New York: Wiley, 1976.

Korn, David. A. *Stalemate: The War of Attrition and Great Power Diplomacy in the Middle East, 1967–1970.* Boulder, CO: Westview, 1992.

Lesch, Ann Mosely, and Mark Tessler. *Israel, Egypt, and the Palestinians: From Camp David to Intifada.* Bloomington: Indiana University Press, 1989.

Pollack, Kenneth M. *Arabs at War: Military Effectiveness, 1948–1991.* Lincoln: University of Nebraska Press, 2002.

Waterbury, John. *The Egypt of Nasser and Sadat: Political Economy of Two Regimes.* Princeton, NJ: Princeton University Press, 1983.

Zuhur, Sherifa. *The Middle East: Politics, History, and Neonationalism.* Carlisle, PA: Institute of Middle Eastern, Islamic, and Diasporic Studies, 2005.

Egypt, Armed Forces

The Egyptian armed forces that emerged following World War II were organized and equipped largely on the British model. At the beginning of the Israeli War of Independence in May 1948, the Egyptian Army was the largest of the Arab invading armies. The Egyptians fielded 40,000 men supported by more than 50 combat aircraft. Initially, the Egyptian expeditionary force included 10,000 troops in five infantry battalions and one armored battalion along with some field artillery. By the end of the war, the expeditionary force had grown to 20,000 men, more than 100 armored vehicles, and 90 artillery pieces.

Egyptian stamp from 1956 honoring Egyptian armed forces during the Suez Crisis of that year and specifically the fighting at Port Said. (iStockPhoto.com)

Despite the size of the Egyptian force, the heaviest fighting in the first months of the war occurred on Israel's northern and central fronts rather than in the south. The Egyptian military faced logistical difficulties in trying to move through the Sinai Peninsula and the Negev Desert. Although the Egyptians did capture several kibbutzim, they also sustained heavy losses in manpower and equipment and were eventually halted near Ashdod.

Following intervention by the United Nations (UN) on May 29, a truce went into effect on June 11, 1948. Folke Bernadotte, the UN mediator, proposed a partition of the region that would have placed the Negev Desert under Arab control. Egypt and Israel promptly rejected the plan, and Egyptian units resumed their advance on July 8, ending the cease-fire. During the first truce, Israel had obtained much-needed aircraft and weaponry, primarily from Czechoslovakia. The Israel Defense Forces (IDF) now concentrated most of their efforts in the Tel Aviv–Jerusalem corridor, but the Egyptian military failed to maintain the initiative in the south and only achieved a bloody stalemate by the time a second UN truce went into effect on July 18. After three months of negotiations the second cease-fire broke down, and the IDF initiated a series of operations to push the Arabs back.

On December 22, 1948, the IDF launched Operation HOREV, a massive push in the south to drive the Egyptian expeditionary force from Palestine. The operation succeeded in pushing the Egyptian Army out of the Negev and encircling it in the Gaza Strip. IDF forces also raided Egyptian territory in the Sinai, eventually obliging Egypt to accept a truce on January 7, 1949.

The two nations signed an armistice on February 24, 1949, the first between Israel and one of the Arab belligerents. According to the terms of the truce, the Gaza Strip remained under Egyptian occupation.

During the early 1950s, Egyptian and Israeli military units periodically raided and skirmished across the border, although no formal state of war existed. The Egyptian-Israeli armistice remained officially in place until 1956, when Egyptian president Gamal Abdel Nasser announced the nationalization of the Suez Canal. This action led to secret cooperation among Israeli, British, and French leaders in a plan to topple Nasser from power. Israel was to launch a drive

Estimated Combat Forces during the Arab-Israeli Wars

Country	Israeli War of Independence (1948)	Sinai Campaign (1956)	Six-Day War (1967)	Yom Kippur War (1973)
Britain	not a belligerent	2,000	not a belligerent	not a belligerent
Egypt	300,000	300,000	400,000	400,000
France	not a belligerent	1,000	not a belligerent	not a belligerent
Iraq	not a belligerent	not a belligerent	250,000	400,000
Israel	140,000	175,000	200,000	200,000
Jordan	60,000	not a belligerent	60,000	60,000
Syria	300,000	not a belligerent	300,000	350,000

Egyptian Army paratroopers perform static-line jumps from two C-141B Starlifter aircraft near Cairo West Air Base during a joint U.S.-Egyptian military exercise on November 14, 1996. (U.S. Department of Defense)

into the Sinai, whereupon the British and French would intervene to save the canal. The plan called for British and French forces to assume control of a buffer zone extending 10 miles from the Suez Canal. The intended consequences also included the fall of Nasser's government.

On October 29, 1956, Israeli troops attacked the Gaza Strip and the Sinai Peninsula, advancing quickly toward the Suez Canal. Britain and France offered to separate the warring armies, but Nasser refused. Two days later, British and French warplanes began bombing Egypt. Nasser thwarted the capture and reopening of the canal by ordering the sinking of 40 ships in the main channel. This forced the closure of the canal until 1957. The Soviet Union threatened to intervene on the side of Egypt, and the United States placed great diplomatic and economic pressure on Britain to withdraw its forces. The UN sent a peacekeeping force to the region, and by early 1957 all Israeli, British, and French forces had withdrawn from Egyptian soil. Nasser emerged from the Suez Crisis as a hero in the Arab world, which applauded his having stood up to Israel and the Western powers.

The UN Emergency Force (UNEF) remained in the Sinai, separating Israel and Egypt, until 1967, although the force gradually shrank in size over time. In 1967 Nasser began remilitarizing the Sinai. He also demanded and secured the complete withdrawal of

UNEF troops on May 18, 1967. He then announced that Egypt would close the Straits of Tiran to all Israeli shipping on May 23. On May 30, Egypt and Jordan signed a five-year mutual defense pact, joining an already-existing Egyptian-Syrian alliance. Jordan agreed to place its troops under Egyptian command, and the Jordanians were soon reinforced by Iraqi troops, also under temporary Egyptian control.

Once again, Egypt fielded the largest military force among the Arab belligerents arrayed against Israel. But almost half of Egypt's mobilized manpower of 200,000 was fighting in a civil war in Yemen and was thus unavailable for commitment against Israel. Egypt's air force consisted of more than 400 warplanes, most purchased from the Soviet Union. The force included a sizable number of medium-range bombers that could reach Israeli targets in a matter of minutes.

On June 5, 1967, in a masterful preemptive strike, the Israeli Air Force (IAF) attacked Egyptian airfields, committing virtually every Israeli warplane to the massive raid. More than 300 Egyptian aircraft were destroyed on the ground, almost completely wiping out the Egyptian Air Force. The Israelis lost only 19 aircraft. The air attack, followed by raids on Jordanian, Syrian, and Iraqi airfields, ensured Israeli air supremacy for the duration of the Six-Day War, which raged from June 5 to June 10, 1967.

The Egyptian army in the Sinai consisted of seven divisions, including four armored divisions, nearly 1,000 tanks, more than 1,000 armored personnel carriers, and 600 artillery pieces. They were opposed by three Israeli armored divisions with approximately 700 tanks. The Israelis, using combined-arms tactics and close-air support, quickly moved to encircle Abu Ageila and bypass Egyptian positions. When Abu Ageila fell, Egyptian forces attempted to retreat from the Sinai but were cut off by Israeli armor units in the mountain passes of the western Sinai. IAF warplanes continually attacked Egyptian ground troops, and although some units escaped, the Egyptian army was routed in only four days at a cost of hundreds of Egyptian combat vehicles. Following the cease-fire, the Sinai remained under Israeli occupation.

From 1968 to 1970, Egypt and Israel fought a limited war. Known as the War of Attrition, it consisted of a series of raids across the Suez Canal, Egyptian bombardments of Israeli positions in the Sinai, and Israeli commando raids against Egyptian targets. Hostilities began with an Egyptian artillery barrage against the Israeli-held east bank of the Suez Canal in June 1968. During the period of protracted struggle, Nasser sought assistance from the Soviet Union, which supplied surface-to-air missiles (SAMs), warplanes, and Soviet advisers and trainers. On August 7, 1970, a cease-fire went into effect that prohibited further military buildup in the Canal Zone. Egypt immediately violated the agreement by installing new SAM sites along the canal itself.

In 1973, Egyptian leader Anwar Sadat's effort to secure the Sinai brought the Yom Kippur War, fought during October 6–26, 1973. Egypt sought to regain control of the Sinai Peninsula and end the Israeli threat to the Suez Canal. At the same time, Syria hoped to regain the Golan Heights, seized by Israel in 1967. Egypt and Syria caught the Israelis by surprise, attacking without warning on October 6, 1973. The Egyptian assault force against the Bar-Lev Line, the Israeli system of fortifications along the Suez Canal, included a tremendous number of infantry antitank guided missiles, intended to neutralize Israel's armored vehicles.

The Egyptians had also established the most powerful air defenses in the region, which temporarily neutralized Israel's air superiority. Most of the air defense network consisted of fixed installations along the canal. The Egyptian Army initially did not intend to advance beyond its air defense umbrella. Instead, Egyptian forces breached the Israeli defenses along the Suez Canal and then dug in to repel the inevitable counterattack. When the attack came, Israeli commanders were stunned by the Egyptian antiair and antitank defenses. Egyptian SAMs exacted a heavy toll of Israeli aircraft.

On October 14 the Egyptians, in response to pleas from the Syrians, launched a massive offensive eastward into the Sinai. Although they advanced more than 10 miles, these forces suffered heavy losses when they moved beyond the range of their SAM batteries along the canal. They were soon battered by Israeli warplanes and antitank missiles. The next day, an Israeli counterattack crossed the Suez Canal, destroying Egyptian air defense emplacements and opening the skies to Israeli warplanes. As Israeli armored units

Military Expenditure as % of GNP among Selected Middle Eastern Countries (1975, 1995)

Country	Military Expenditures as % of GNP (1975)	Military Expenditures as % of GNP (1995)
Bahrain	2.1	7.7
Egypt	31.9	3.1
Iran	17.6	2.6
Iraq	17.4	7.1
Israel	29.2	10.3
Jordan	29.5	8.4
Kuwait	5.4	11.1
Lebanon	4.1	4.0
Oman	40.9	19.1
Qatar	3.5	10.4
Saudi Arabia	17.4	13.2
Syria	15.7	7.0

poured across the canal, they cut off Egyptian forces in the Sinai and inflicted yet another humiliating defeat upon the Egyptians. On October 22 a UN-mandated cease-fire went into effect, preventing further bloodshed but also trapping the Egyptian Third Army, now cut off without access to supplies. The Egyptians did not regard the Yom Kippur War as a defeat by any means but instead saw in it a psychological victory in that they had crossed the Suez. Indeed, as a direct result of the conflict, the Sinai was returned to Egypt.

The tremendous costs of war to Egypt, both in economic and human terms, convinced Sadat to do what no other Arab leader had done, both in traveling to Israel to meet with Israelis and in pursuing a peace agreement that culminated at Camp David in 1978. Ordinary Egyptians, while not favoring war and seeing it as a cynical outcome of debt and politics, had no political input into Sadat's decision. The Israel-Egypt Peace Treaty, signed in 1979, included provisions for an Israeli withdrawal from the Sinai and Egypt's recognition of Israel's right to exist. Egypt was subsequently expelled from the Arab League, and Sadat was assassinated in 1981 by army officers of the Islamic Jihad movement who opposed his policies, including his negotiations with Israel, and hoped to overthrow the government.

Assuming the Egyptian presidency upon Sadat's death, Hosni Mubarak, like all Egypt's presidents a military officer, has sought to maintain a modern military force that is ready for combat. The Egyptian military as of 2006 is one of the largest forces in the Middle East and the world. All adult men are obliged to serve three years (although many serve a lesser period) in the military, with conscripts making up about half of the Egyptian active duty force at any given time. After the 1978 Camp David Accords, Egypt reduced its defense ties to the Soviet Union and rearmed with American, French, and British equipment. Some of this modern weaponry, including the American M-1 Abrams main battle tank, is assembled under license in Egyptian factories.

The Egyptian Army has approximately 340,000 active duty troops and 375,000 reservists, augmented by the Egyptian Frontier Corps, a border security unit of some 12,000 Bedouin. Egypt's first-line armored and mechanized forces are equipped with almost 900 American M-1A1 and 1,700 M-60A3 main battle tanks and more than 2,600 M-113 armored personnel carriers. The Egyptians still operate a number of older Soviet armored vehicles, including 450 T-62 main battle tanks and more than 1,000 BTR-50 and BTR-60 armored personnel carriers. The Egyptian Army also maintains a substantial force of field artillery, including cannon, rockets, and missiles, as well as a continually upgraded arsenal of air defense systems. Egyptian field and air defense artillery remains a mixture of American and Soviet systems. Egyptian troops also continue to be armed with the Soviet AK-47 assault rifle.

As with all military forces built on the Soviet model, Egyptian decision making was rigid and highly centralized. The Egyptians, like their Soviet mentors, were capable of developing highly complicated and sophisticated plans, as they demonstrated so effectively when they crossed the Suez Canal in 1973. But once the initial phases of the plan unfolded, the Egyptians lacked the tactical flexibility and the lower-level command initiative to exploit any initial advantages. The Israelis took advantage of this weakness every time. Since moving away from the Soviet model, the Egyptians have made great strides in improving their command and operating systems. The United States and Egypt have also hosted biennial multinational military exercises in Egypt, known as BRIGHT STAR. The biggest Egyptian military handicap, however, remains the fact that a large number of the country's enlisted conscripts are illiterate and poorly equipped to learn how to operate modern, high-tech weapons systems.

The Egyptian Air Force, with some 580 fixed-wing aircraft and 121 armed helicopters, primarily flies American and French aircraft, including the Dassault Mirage 2000 and some 220 American General Dynamics F-16 Fighting Falcon fighters. It also continues to operate older fighter aircraft, including the American McDonnell F-4 Phantom and the Soviet Mikoyan Gurevich MiG-21. The primary Egyptian cargo aircraft is the ubiquitous American Lockheed four-engine turboprop EC-130E Hercules. Egyptian attack helicopters include the American Hughes (McDonnell Douglas/Boeing) AH-64 Apache.

The Egyptian Navy is a relatively small coastal force with some 20,000 personnel. It operates destroyers, submarines, missile boats, and patrol boats. It relies upon the air force for maritime aerial reconnaissance and all air support.

Egypt's various paramilitary groups include the Central Security Forces, which has about 250,000 troops, operates under the control of the Ministry of the Interior, and is used chiefly for law enforcement and intelligence; the National Guard, numbering between 50,000 and 60,000 men; the Border Guard Forces, with about 20,000; and the Coast Guard, with some 2,000 men.

In recent years Egypt has spent on average about $2.5 billion per year on defense, which translates roughly to 3.4 percent of the Egyptian gross domestic product (GDP). Egypt has remained at peace with Israel since 1973, which has reduced Egyptian standing in the Arab world. Nevertheless, Egypt has benefited significantly by improved ties with the United States and most of the members of the European Union (EU).

PAUL JOSEPH SPRINGER

See also

Arms Sales, International; Attrition, War of; Camp David Accords; Egypt; Israel-Egypt Peace Treaty; Israeli War of Independence, Israeli-Egyptian Front; Israeli War of Independence, Overview; Mubarak, Hosni; Naguib, Mohammad; Nasser, Gamal Abdel; Sadat, Anwar; Sinai Campaign; Six-Day War; Suez Crisis; Yom Kippur War

References

Abdel-Malek, Anouar. *Egypt: Military Society, the Army Regime, the Left, and Social Change under Nasser.* New York: Random House, 1968.

Bar-Siman-Tov, Yaacov. *The Israeli-Egyptian War of Attrition, 1969–1970: A Case-Study of Limited Local War.* New York: Columbia University Press, 1980.

Draper, Thomas. *Israel and the Middle East.* New York: H. W. Wilson, 1983.

El Shazly, Saad. *The Crossing of the Suez.* San Francisco: American Mideast Research, 1980.

Herzog, Chaim. *The Arab-Israeli Wars: War and Peace in the Middle East from the War of Independence to Lebanon.* Westminster, MD: Random House, 1984.

Quandt, William B. *The Middle East: Ten Years after Camp David.* Washington, DC: Brookings Institution, 1988.

Sacher, Howard Morkey. *Egypt and Israel.* New York: R. Marek, 1981.

Vatikiotis, P. J. *The Egyptian Army in Politics: Pattern for New Nations?* Westport, CT: Greenwood, 1975.

Egyptian-Soviet Arms Deal
Event Date: Summer of 1955

The first of many Egyptian-Soviet arms deals in which Egypt purchased tanks and other weapons systems from the Soviet Union. Because some of the purchases involved Czech-manufactured goods and given the fact that the Soviets hoped to obscure their involvement in the arms deal, this first Egyptian purchase of Soviet bloc military hardware was referred to as the Egyptian-Czechoslovakian arms deal. Nevertheless, it clearly had the Soviet imprimatur, and the Czechoslovakians could not have sold arms to Egypt without the prior and express consent of Moscow. The 1955 arms deal delivered to the Egyptians some 200 tanks and other weapons and amounted to about $325 million (in 1955 dollars).

The deal was consummated after several high-level Soviet figures visited Egypt in the summer of 1955. This marked the start of a major Soviet effort to insert its influence in the Middle East. It was also the beginning of an Egyptian-Soviet alliance that would last until the mid-1970s and paved the way for similar Soviet arms deals with Syria and Iraq.

The arms deal had implications far beyond that actual transfer of military goods to Egypt. First, it threatened to disrupt the regional Middle East military balance. In so doing, it essentially nullified the 1950 Tripartite Declaration, enunciated by the United

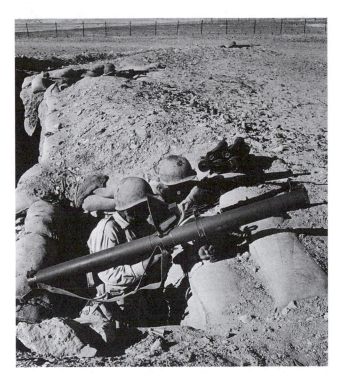

Egyptian soldiers test newly acquired Czech arms, including rifles and antitank rockets, near Cairo, Egypt, on March 2, 1956. (Bettmann/Corbis)

States, France, and Great Britain, that among other things instituted a virtual arms embargo against all nations in the Middle East. Second, it strengthened Egypt's Pan-Arab president Gamal Abdel Nasser's hand in the region and most certainly emboldened him to nationalize the Suez Canal less than a year later. Finally, from a larger geostrategic standpoint, the Egyptian-Soviet arms deal brought the Cold War rivalry to the Middle East in a very significant way. Indeed, the arms purchase helped induce both the United States and Great Britain to withdraw their financial support for the construction of the Aswan High Dam project in Egypt. This in turn precipitated Nasser's nationalization of the Suez Canal and the Suez Crisis of 1956 that followed.

When the Israelis learned of the arms purchases, they immediately began lobbying the West, and the United States in particular, to sell them arms as a countermeasure. The Americans stalled and then referred the Israeli government to France and other Western countries. Not until 1962, however, would the United States engage in an arms deal with the Israelis. The French were more than willing to oblige and sold about 200 tanks to Israel in early and mid-1956. Helping Israel was just one incentive to the French, however. They also saw the arms deal as retribution for Nasser's vocal support of Algerian nationalists fighting the French in the Algerian War, which had begun in earnest in 1954.

To pay for the arms shipment the Egyptians incurred considerable debt, and in 1956 nearly 40 percent of Egypt's cotton produc-

tion went to the Soviet Union as payment. Just two years earlier, only 15 percent of Egypt's cotton yield went to the Soviet Union.

PAUL G. PIERPAOLI JR.

See also

Arms Sales, International; Aswan High Dam Project; Egypt; France, Middle East Policy; Nasser, Gamal Abdel; Soviet Union and Russia, Middle East Policy; Suez Canal; Suez Crisis; Tripartite Declaration; United States, Middle East Policy

References

Jabber, Paul. *Not by War Alone: Security and Arms Control in the Middle East.* Berkeley: University of California Press, 1981.

Louis, William R., and Roger Owen, eds. *Suez, 1956: The Crisis and Its Consequences.* New York: Oxford University Press, 1989.

Varble, Derek. *The Suez Crisis, 1956.* London: Osprey, 2003.

Eichmann, Karl Adolf
Born: March 19, 1906
Died: June 1, 1962

German State Police official who oversaw the deportation of millions of Jews to extermination camps. Karl Adolf Eichmann was born on March 19, 1906, in Solingen, Germany, a small industrial city near Cologne. In 1913 his middle-class Protestant family moved to Linz, Austria, when his father was promoted at work. Because of his looks and dark complexion, Eichmann's classmates in Linz bullied him and accused him of being a Jew. Upon graduating from high school, he worked for a company organizing kerosene deliveries, where he proved himself detail-oriented.

In 1932 Eichmann joined the Austrian Nazi Party. In 1934 he became a member of the Schutzstaffel (SS) and served at the Dachau concentration camp. That September he joined the Sicherheitsdienst (SD), the powerful SS security service, and attracted the attention of Reinhard Heydrich and SS chief Heinrich Himmler, who appointed Eichmann to head the newly created SD Scientific Museum of Jewish Affairs.

In his new post, Eichmann became the Nazi authority on Jewish affairs. He became familiar with Zionism, studied Hebrew, and could even speak some Yiddish. Initially he supported the Zionist policy of Jewish emigration to Palestine, but this became impossible because of restrictive British quotas. After the German annexation of Austria (Anschluss) in March 1938, Eichmann, as head of the SS Office for Jewish Emigration, was sent to Vienna to promote Jewish emigration. In 1939, German leader Adolf Hitler appointed Eichmann to the directorship of Section IV B4, the Reich Central Office for Jewish Affairs and Evacuation. Eichmann was responsible for implementing the Nazi policy toward Jews in Germany and all of its occupied territories.

In July 1940 Eichmann proposed the Madagascar Plan to settle European Jews on an island off the east coast of Africa. The plan was never implemented, however. In January 1942 he and Heydrich organized the Wannsee Conference, which planned the Final Solution

Karl Adolf Eichmann, pictured here in a Jerusalem courtroom, was a principal figure in the so-called Final Solution, the murder of millions of Jews and other "undesirables" by the Third Reich. He was kidnapped in Latin America, brought to Israel, and tried and executed in 1962. (Library of Congress)

(Endlösung) to the so-called Jewish problem: the extermination of all European Jews. Eichmann efficiently coordinated the transport of European Jews to the extermination camps. As such, he was directly responsible for coordinating the slaughter of millions of Jews and other victims.

At the end of World War II, Eichmann was arrested and confined to a U.S. internment camp, but he escaped after a few months. In 1950, with the help of the SS underground, he fled to Argentina and there lived under the assumed name of Ricardo Klement for 10 years until Israeli Mossad agents, led by Isser Harel, kidnapped him on May 11, 1960. Heavily sedated, he was taken aboard an airliner to Israel disguised as a sick passenger. Brought to trial during April 2–August 14, 1961, Eichmann, who testified from a bullet-proof glass booth, used the defense that he was merely obeying orders. More than 100 witnesses, however, testified to Eichmann's willing participation in the Final Solution. The Eichmann trial aroused intense international interest and brought the Nazi atrocities to the forefront of world news. On December 2, 1961, the Israeli court sentenced him to death for crimes against the Jewish people and crimes against humanity. On June 1, 1962, he was executed by hanging. His body was cremated, and the ashes were spread at sea beyond Israel's territorial waters. The execution of Eichmann remains the only time that Israel has overtly carried out a judicial death sentence.

MICHAEL R. HALL

See also
Holocaust; Zionism

References
Gouri, Haim. *Facing the Glass Booth: The Jerusalem Trial of Adolf Eichmann.* Detroit, MI: Wayne State University Press, 2004.
Sachs, Ruth. *Adolf Eichmann: Engineer of Death.* New York: Rosen, 2001.

Eilat, Gulf of

See Aqaba, Gulf of

Eilat, Israel

Israel's southernmost city. Located on the Gulf of Aqaba, the eastern arm of the Red Sea, and near the Sinai region, Eilat has a population of approximately 55,000 people. Here the southernmost extensions of the Arabah savanna zone and the Negev Desert meet.

Eilat is a major port city with both economic and military significance. Dry savanna/desert flora and fauna that can withstand long periods of drought predominate. Indeed, the name "Eilat" is derived from the Hebrew word for "trees." Eilat's nearby neighbors are the Egyptian city of Taba and the Jordanian port of Aqaba, all providing access to Africa and the East.

Historically, Eilat is thought to be close to the site of Ezion-geber, a key port during the reign of King Solomon some 3,000 years ago. The city of Eilat was reestablished in 1949, and a modern deep-water harbor opened there in 1965.

Eilat enjoys a desert climate with predominantly warm and dry conditions, and tourism is a mainstay of the local economy. Other economic activities include port enterprises such as oil importation and specialized agriculture reliant on water-conservation techniques and rapid processing. Additional draws to the area include the impressive coral reefs of the Red Sea.

Eilat was strategically significant for Israel from the very inception of the Jewish state in 1948. When Egypt refused to allow passage of Israeli and non-Israeli ships headed for Israeli ports from traversing the Suez Canal, Eilat became the only viable entry port for the movement of goods into and out of Israel. The Egyptians had barred Israeli access to the canal as a result of the Israeli War of Independence (1948–1949). Essentially, Eilat became Israel's main artery. Especially critical were oil imports that now had to go through the city's port.

After the Egyptians shut off the Suez Canal to Israeli interests, Eilat became Israel's only direct way to access markets and resources

The city of Eilat, shown from the Gulf of Aqaba in 1995. (Moshe Milner/Israeli Government Press Office)

in Southeast Asia and East Africa. Indeed, were it not for Eilat, Israeli ships would have had to embark on a tortuous trip through the Mediterranean and around the African continent and the Cape of Good Hope to reach East Asia.

Keeping the port open became an absolute necessity. This became even more apparent in 1967 when the Egyptians blocked the Straits of Tiran to Israeli shipping. In so doing, they effectively blockaded Eilat. Among other provocations, the Israelis cited the closure of the straits as a reason for going to war against Egypt in 1967. Israel continues to take access to Eilat very seriously. Eilat became a free trade zone in 1985.

Antoinette Mannion

See also

Negev Desert; Red Sea; Six-Day War; Suez Canal

References

Orni, Ephraim. *Geography of Israel.* Philadelphia: Jewish Publication Society of America, 1977.

Parker, Richard B., ed. *The Six-Day War: A Retrospective.* Gainesville: University Press of Florida, 1996.

Eilat Sinking
Event Date: October 21, 1967

The sinking of the Israeli destroyer *Eilat* was the first time a warship was sunk by a missile. Beginning in 1962, Egypt received sev-

eral Osa- and Komar-class missile boats from the Soviet Union. Egypt did not deploy them in the 1967 Six-Day War, however. Armed with radar-guided Styx missiles that carried a 1,000-pound high-explosive, shaped charge warhead to a maximum range of 48 miles, these missile boats posed a serious threat to Israel's aging warships, but outside the Soviet bloc little was known about this new weapons system.

Following the Six-Day War, Israeli defense minister Moshe Dayan ordered Israeli military forces to demonstrate along the Sinai coast to assert Israeli possession of the newly occupied territory. Some of these warships approached Egypt's 12-mile territorial limit.

On July 11, 1967, while on patrol north of the Sinai desert, the Israeli destroyer *Eilat,* a veteran of World War II purchased from Britain, and two motor torpedo boats engaged and sank two Egyptian torpedo boats in a running gun battle. Fearing a missile attack, the *Eilat*'s captain, Commander Yitzhak Shoshan, engaged the Egyptians cautiously until lookouts determined that the Egyptian ships were older vessels armed with torpedoes rather than missiles.

This incident, however, encouraged Egyptian leaders to respond to Israel's naval patrols and test the Styx missile in combat. Three months later, on October 21, 1967, on another such patrol the *Eilat* approached Egypt's 12-mile territorial limit. At 5:30 p.m. local time roughly 13.5 miles north of Port Said, lookouts spotted an approaching missile. Shoshan ordered the engines full ahead and turned his ship to present its stern to the missile. The Israelis fired machine guns without effect at the missile, which struck the ship and severely damaged the engine room. While the crew fought the resulting fires, the damaged ship continued to turn broadside toward Port Said, whereupon lookouts spotted a second and then a third incoming missile. Both of these hit, leaving the *Eilat* severely damaged and listing. Two hours after the first missile hit, Shoshan ordered his crew to abandon ship and radioed for help. A fourth missile struck the ship as it sank, wounding many sailors struggling in the water. Rescue aircraft reached the survivors within the hour, and helicopters brought the survivors home. Of the 190-man crew, 47 died and 90 suffered injury.

The following May, Egyptian missile boats struck again, sinking the *Orit*, a small wooden fishing vessel, off El Arish. The attack demonstrated the effectiveness of the Styx against even very small ships. The sinking of the *Orit* convinced the Israeli Navy to develop electronic countermeasures against the Styx missile. They previously had thought the Styx's guidance system too primitive to locate small ships.

The sinking of the *Eilat* proved a rude awakening to naval officers around the world and gave new impetus to other nations to develop antiship guided missiles. Israel, already developing its Gabriel missile, rushed it to completion to equip its own French-built missile boats. Other nations also developed antiship missiles. These soon included the U.S. Harpoon, the French Exocet, and the Italian Otomat.

Israel retaliated for the attack on the *Eilat* by air strikes against Egyptian oil refineries at Suez. Egypt responded in kind, and raids along the Suez Canal soon escalated into the War of Attrition.

STEPHEN K. STEIN

See also

Attrition, War of; Dayan, Moshe; Six-Day War

References

Colvin, R. D. "Aftermath of the Eilat." *U.S. Naval Institute Proceedings* 95 (October 1969): 60–67.

Rabinovich, Abraham. *The Boats of Cherbourg: The Secret Israeli Operation That Revolutionized Naval Warfare.* New York: Seaver, 1988.

Tzalel, Moshe. *From Ice-Breaker to Missile Boat: The Evolution of Israel's Naval Strategy.* Westport, CT: Greenwood, 2000.

Einstein, Albert
Born: March 14, 1879
Died: April 18, 1955

German-born physicist, developer of the general and special theories of relativity, Nobel Prize laureate, prominent American Jew, and vocal post–World War II peace activist. Albert Einstein was born in Ulm, Württemberg, Germany, on March 14, 1879. When he was 15 years old, his family moved from Germany to escape a failed business venture. They settled in Pavia near Milan, Italy. At about the same time, Einstein renounced his German citizenship. In 1900

Theoretical physicist, Nobel Prize winner, and peace activist Albert Einstein. (Library of Congress)

he received his undergraduate degree from Zurich Polytechnic with majors in mathematics and physics. His first few years out of university were unhappy ones during which money was very tight. He became a Swiss citizen in 1901 and finally found work the next year in the Swiss Patent Office. In 1905 he was awarded his PhD in physics from his undergraduate alma mater.

That same year, Einstein authored a series of pioneering articles in physics that would revolutionize the field of science as a whole. In 1908 the physicist became an unsalaried university professor, and in 1911 he became an associate professor at the University of Zurich. From there, he enjoyed a storied academic career, holding teaching positions in Germany, Czechoslovakia, and Switzerland. By the early 1920s he had become perhaps the most famous scientist in the world. In 1921 he was awarded the Nobel Prize in Physics, although he earned this honor not for his theory of relativity but rather for his work on the photoelectric effect.

Einstein first became active in the Zionist movement in the 1920s when he met Zionist leader Chaim Weizmann. It is important to note, however, that Einstein did not support the nationalistic aspects of mainstream Zionism. He envisioned a place where Jews could be educated without prejudice and live in a community of shared values and ideas, not in a sovereign Jewish state per se.

Einstein was instrumental in the creation of the Hebrew University in Jerusalem, which opened in 1923. Later on he became disenchanted with the school, however, as it catered to wealthy Jews seeking an undergraduate education. Einstein had hoped that the school would become an elite university steeped in pathbreaking research. In 1929 he attended the Sixteenth Zionist Conference in Zurich, Switzerland, at which he spoke of the importance of maintaining Jewish cultural unity. He did not speak of the creation of a Jewish state. When the Arab riots broke out in Palestine in 1929, he urged accommodation with the Arabs instead of further confrontation.

Einstein had reapplied for German citizenship in 1914 to facilitate his work at the University of Berlin. However, the rise of the Nazi regime forced him to flee the country in 1933. He settled in the United States, where he became a professor of theoretical physics at Princeton University's Institute for Advanced Study. He retired from the post in 1945, although he remained active in the sciences and in various international causes until his death. Einstein was also famous for having given impetus to the Manhattan Project, which produced the world's first nuclear bomb. Using his fame and alarmed at the aggressiveness of the Axis powers, he wrote a letter to President Franklin D. Roosevelt in 1939 urging him to explore—for military purposes—the possibility of harnessing nuclear fusion to make bombs. By 1942, the Manhattan Project was in high gear.

After World War II, Einstein was active in both the Zionist movement and the incipient civil rights movement in America. As the United Nations (UN) debated the future of Palestine and finally announced its partition plan in 1947, Einstein spoke out fervently against the division of the area into Jewish and Arab states. He did not advocate the creation of a Jewish nation at all, in fact. Rather, he urged the establishment of a demilitarized nation in which both Arabs and Jews would live side-by-side in peace. In 1952 when Weizmann, Israel's first president, died, Prime Minister David Ben-Gurion asked Einstein to be the nation's second president. The famed physicist declined the offer, stating that he was not temperamentally suited to the position.

By the early 1950s, Einstein had come under scrutiny by right-wingers and acolytes of Sen. Joseph McCarthy for his left-leaning political views, which included world government, the advancement of socialist ideals, and the abolition of institutionalized racism. When the civil rights leader W. E. B. DuBois was accused of being a communist, an outraged Einstein stated that he would be a character witness in any potential trial. The charges against DuBois were unceremoniously dropped.

Ironically perhaps, Einstein also became an ardent proponent of nuclear disarmament after the war. Einstein joined with the social activist Bertrand Russell and the noted physician Albert Schweitzer to lobby hard for the abolition of nuclear tests and the immediate dismantlement of all nuclear weapons. Only a few days before his death, Einstein and Russell signed the Russell-Einstein Manifesto, which unambiguously called for a halt to all nuclear testing and worldwide nuclear disarmament. Einstein died in Princeton, New Jersey, on April 18, 1955.

PAUL G. PIERPAOLI JR.

See also

Weizmann, Chaim; Zionism

References

Clark, Ronald William. *Einstein: The Life and Times.* New York: Avon Books, 1999.

Einstein, Albert. *Albert Einstein, the Human Side: New Glimpses from His Archives.* Princeton, NJ: Princeton University Press, 1979.

Pais, Abraham. *Subtle Is the Lord: The Science and the Life of Albert Einstein.* New York: Oxford University Press, 1997.

Eisenhower, Dwight David
Born: October 14, 1890
Died: March 28, 1969

U.S. Army general and president of the United States (1953–1961). Born in Denison, Texas, on October 14, 1890, Dwight Eisenhower grew up in Abilene, Kansas, and graduated from the U.S. Military Academy at West Point in 1915. He did not see combat during World War I. Following the war, he remained in the army and served in a variety of assignments at home and overseas.

In 1939 Eisenhower became chief of staff of the newly established Third Army. Promoted to brigadier general in September 1941 and major general in April 1942, he transferred to London in June 1942 as commander of American and Allied forces in Britain and a month later was promoted to lieutenant general. In November 1942 he commanded the Allied invasion of North Africa. Promoted to full general in February 1943, he then oversaw the invasions of Sicily and Italy. In December 1943 he was named to command the Allied forces that invaded France in June 1944. In December 1944 he was promoted to the newly created rank of general of the army.

From 1945 to 1948 Eisenhower served as chief of staff of the U.S. Army. He was president of Columbia University from 1948 to 1952. During this time he was actively involved in foreign and military affairs and politics. He strongly endorsed President Harry S. Truman's developing Cold War policies, including intervention in Korea. In January 1951 Eisenhower took leave from Columbia to serve as the first supreme commander of the armed forces of the North Atlantic Treaty Organization (NATO).

In 1952 the Republican Party, desperate to choose a candidate who would be assured of victory, turned to Eisenhower. As a candidate, he promised to end the Korean War but otherwise continue Truman's Cold War policies. Eisenhower won the November 1952 elections.

Under Eisenhower, U.S. defense commitments around the world solidified into a network of bilateral and multilateral alliances. A fiscal conservative uncomfortable with high defense budgets, Eisenhower introduced the New Look strategy of relying heavily on nuclear weapons rather than conventional forces. Critics of the New Look complained that it left the United States unprepared to fight limited wars. As president, Eisenhower fulfilled his campaign pledge to end the Korean War, seemingly threatening to employ nuclear weapons unless an armistice agreement was concluded.

Dwight D. Eisenhower, U.S. Army general, was president of the United States during 1953–1961. (Library of Congress)

After Soviet dictator Joseph Stalin's death in March 1953, Eisenhower tried, unsuccessfully, to reach arms control agreements with the Soviets. In February 1956, Soviet leader Nikita Khrushchev repudiated much of Stalin's legacy, a move suggesting that potential existed for a Soviet-American rapprochement. Soon afterward, Khrushchev expressed his faith that it might be possible for the East and West to attain a state of peaceful coexistence. Progress toward this end was patchy, however. From 1958 until 1961, he made repeated attempts to coerce and intimidate the Western powers into abandoning control of West Berlin. The May 1960 U-2 spy plane fiasco all but quashed peaceful coexistence and torpedoed any chances at arms control between the two superpowers.

Eisenhower consistently sought to entice nations in the developing world into the Western camp. Nowhere was this more apparent than in the Middle East. Of course, the Eisenhower administration had other motives in the region, not the least of which was the protection of vital oil supplies. If anticommunism and protection of oil were absolutes in America's Middle East policies, the suppression of Pan-Arabism (often linked to radicalism) was not far behind. Fond of using covert operations via the Central Intelligence Agency (CIA), Eisenhower and Secretary of State John Foster Dulles used the CIA to overthrow a reputedly leftist regime in Iran in August 1953. When Iranian prime minister Mohammad Mosaddeq's policies began to go against the wishes of Mohammad Reza Shah Pahlavi—a staunch U.S. ally—Eisenhower came to suspect that Mosaddeq

had communist leanings at worst or Pan-Arab inclinations at best. Neither was acceptable to Washington. Operation AJAX, launched in August 1953, fomented violent street demonstrations in Iran and stirred up support for the shah, who had left the country only days earlier. Mosaddeq was forced to give up power and was arrested and detained. The shah was back in power by month's end. Pro-American stability had returned to the country, and its vast oil resources had been secured.

Three years later, another Middle East crisis embroiled the Eisenhower administration in the region's affairs. Egyptian president Gamal Abdel Nasser sought to purchase U.S. arms, and when the United States refused, Nasser brokered an arms barter deal with the Communist bloc. This was followed by Egyptian recognition of the People's Republic of China (PRC) and fierce anti-U.S. rhetoric in the government-controlled Egyptian press. In response, in July 1956 the Eisenhower administration, followed by the British government, rescinded an earlier offer to grant Egypt a substantial loan for Nasser's project to build a dam on the Nile south of Aswan.

Nasser then decided to nationalize the Suez Canal, a step that should not have surprised the Western powers. The British and French governments then conspired with the Israeli government for the latter to launch an attack against Egypt that would threaten the canal. Britain and France then planned to intervene militarily themselves and overthrow Nasser.

The resulting Suez Crisis unfolded at the end of October and in early November. Enraged that France and Britain had not consulted the United States and worried about a Soviet intervention, Eisenhower put heavy pressure on the three nations, especially Britain, to remove their forces back, which they did in November.

Responding to Soviet threats of interference in future Middle East crises, in January 1957 Eisenhower put forth the Eisenhower Doctrine, pledging American military and economic assistance to any Middle Eastern country that sought to resist communism. Except for Lebanon and Iraq (prior to Iraq's 1958 revolution), few nations welcomed this doctrine since most countries in the region believed that they had more to fear from Western imperialism than from Soviet expansionism. In April 1957 when Jordan's King Hussein came under intense pressure by indigenous socialists and Pan-Arabists, Eisenhower dispatched the Sixth Fleet to the eastern Mediterranean. His administration also provided the king with $10 million in economic aid.

The first significant test of the Eisenhower Doctrine came in 1958. In February of that year, Egypt and Syria whipped up Pan-Arab sentiments by their brief union in the United Arab Republic. This set the Eisenhower administration on edge, but it was events in Lebanon that activated the Eisenhower Doctrine. In May, Lebanon's Christian president, Camille Chamoun, who was opposed by a coalition of Muslim, Druze and Christians in the Lebanese National Front, appealed to Washington for assistance. Eisenhower's advisers decided to act in this instance, although too late to stave off revolution in Iraq or the Egyptian-Syrian political union. By July 15, the first contingent of some 15,000 U.S. marines landed on Beirut's beaches to restore order. Order was indeed restored, and U.S. forces departed Lebanon by the end of October. Miraculously, no Lebanese or Americans lost their lives during the intervention.

Despite Republican claims during the 1952 presidential campaign that they would roll back communism, when workers rose against Soviet rule in East Berlin in June 1953 and again when Hungarians attempted to expel Soviet troops in October 1956, Eisenhower refused to intervene. Although he would not recognize the PRC, he reacted cautiously in the successive Taiwan Straits crises of 1954–1955 and 1958. His administration encouraged the government of South Vietnam in its refusal to hold the elections mandated for 1956 and provided military and economic assistance to bolster its independence. Eisenhower justified these actions by citing the domino theory, which holds that if one noncommunist area were to become communist, the infection would inevitably spread to its neighbors.

Besides the 1953 covert coup in Iran, the CIA supported a successful coup in Guatemala in 1954. Eisenhower and Dulles encouraged it to undertake numerous other secret operations. These included plans for an ill-fated coup attempt against Cuba's communist leader, Fidel Castro.

After leaving office in 1961, Eisenhower backed American intervention in Southeast Asia, an area he specifically warned his successor John F. Kennedy not to abandon. Eisenhower died in Washington, D.C., on March 28, 1969.

PRISCILLA ROBERTS

See also

Decolonization; Dulles, John Foster; France, Middle East Policy; Hussein, King of Jordan; Israel; Khrushchev, Nikita; Lebanon; Nasser, Gamal Abdel; Soviet Union and Russia, Middle East Policy; Suez Crisis; United Kingdom, Middle East Policy; United States, Middle East Policy

References

Ambrose, Stephen E. *Eisenhower.* 2 vols. New York: Simon and Schuster, 1983–1984.
Bowie, Robert R., and Richard H. Immerman. *Waging Peace: How Eisenhower Shaped an Enduring Cold War Strategy.* New York: Oxford University Press, 1998.
Brands, H. W., Jr. *Cold Warriors: Eisenhower's Generation and American Foreign Policy.* New York: Columbia University Press, 1988.
Chandler, Alfred D., Jr., and Louis Galambos, eds. *The Papers of Dwight D. Eisenhower.* 21 vols. to date. Baltimore: Johns Hopkins Press, 1970–.
Perret, Geoffrey. *Eisenhower.* New York: Random House, 1999.

Eitan, Rafael

Born: January 11, 1929
Died: November 23, 2004

Israeli military officer and politician. Rafael "Raful" Eitan was born on January 11, 1929, in Afula in the British Mandate for Palestine. He was brought up and educated in the kibbutz Tel Adishim. In 1948 during the Israeli War of Independence (1948–1949), he

Chief of staff of the Israel Defense Forces (IDF) General Rafael Eitan, shown in 1978. Later active in politics, he was deputy prime minister during 1998–1999. (Israeli Government Press Office)

fought as a junior officer in the Palmach during the defense of Jerusalem and was wounded in the fight for the San Simon Monastery in April.

Eitan remained with the Israel Defense Forces (IDF) after the war, and in 1954 he was promoted to captain in command of a paratroop company in Unit 101. He was again wounded in Operation KINERETH, a 1955 raid on Syria. In 1956 he was a lieutenant colonel in command of the 890th Paratroop Battalion. On October 29, 1956, his paratroopers began the Sinai Campaign by securing the eastern approach to the strategic Mitla Pass in the Sinai Peninsula.

In 1967 during the Six-Day War, Colonel Eitan commanded the Paratroop Brigade on the Gaza front and received a severe head wound during the advance on the Suez Canal. Promoted to brigadier general in 1968, the next year he headed IDF infantry troops. He next commanded a division, and during the Syrian attack on the Golan Heights in the Yom Kippur War of October 1973, his division played a vital part in blunting the Syrian attack. During an advance of Syrian tanks, Eitan personally employed a bazooka to destroy several of the tanks himself. Immediately following the 1973 war, he was promoted to major general and assumed command of the northern front.

In April 1978 Eitan was promoted to lieutenant general and chief of staff of the IDF. In this role he approved the plans for Operation OPERA, which destroyed Iraq's nuclear facilities at Osiraq in June 1981, and he created the Raful Youth Project, which sought to encourage underprivileged Israelis to join the IDF and train there for professions. At the same time, he took measures to increase discipline and efficiency in the IDF. However, his most important role as chief of staff was to oversee the Israeli invasion of Lebanon in 1982. Despite some dramatic military successes, including the destruction of Syrian air defenses in the opening days of the conflict, the Israeli forces became bogged down in guerrilla warfare and were held responsible for the massacres at Sabra and Shatila Palestinian refugee camps near Beirut. Eitan received some of the blame for this in the report of the Kahan Commission, charged with investigating the events at Sabra and Shatila. This report ultimately compelled his resignation.

Eitan retired from the IDF in 1983, his military reputation now diminished by the failed Lebanese operation and refugee camp massacres. Nevertheless, he turned to politics and was elected to the Knesset (Israeli parliament) in 1984. A conservative, he formed his own party, Tsomet, that took a hard-line stance on national security and defense issues but a more liberal approach to domestic social issues. Between 1989 and 1991 he served as minister of agriculture. He published his memoirs, *A Soldier's Story,* in 1992.

Tsomet failed to gain in influence, even after the 1996 elections that brought conservative Benjamin Netanyahu to power. Between 1996 and 1998, Eitan served as the environment and agriculture minister, and he was deputy prime minister from 1998 to 1999. He retired from politics in 1999. On November 23, 2004, while on the breakwater at the Mediterranean port at Ashod where he was working on a port renewal project, Eitan drowned when a large wave swept him out to sea.

RALPH MARTIN BAKER

See also

Expellees and Refugees, Palestinian; Israel Defense Forces; Lebanon; Lebanon, Israeli Invasion of; Mitla Pass; Osiraq Raid; Palmach; Sinai Campaign; Six-Day War; Tsomet; Yom Kippur War

References

Eitan, Rafael. *A Soldier's Story: The Life and Times of an Israeli War Hero.* New York: S. P. I. Books, 1992.

Gabriel, Richard. *Operation Peace for Galilee: The Israeli-PLO War in Lebanon.* New York: Farrar, Straus and Giroux, 1985.

Rabinovich, Abraham. *The Yom Kippur War: The Epic Encounter That Transformed the Middle East.* New York: Schocken, 2005.

El Arish

Egyptian city located on the northeastern Sinai Peninsula along the Mediterranean Sea coast at 31″08′ north and 33″48′ east. El Arish (Al Arish) is approximately 30 miles southwest of the point where the boundaries of Israel, Egypt, and the Gaza Strip meet.

The Sinai Peninsula serves as the connection between Africa and Asia. As such, it has been an invasion route for armies since antiquity. Significant battles occurred there during the Arab-Israeli wars, including the Israeli War of Independence (1948–1949), the Sinai Campaign (1956), and the 1967 Six-Day War. Extensive sand dunes in the northern Sinai limit mobility, making the coastal road along the Mediterranean Sea an important target. El Arish lies at the crossroads of the coast road and the road leading southeast to Abu Ageila.

In late December 1948 during the closing days of the first Arab-Israeli war, Israel launched Operation HOREV (AYIN) in the Sinai-Gaza region. Initial successes brought Israeli troops to the airfield outside El Arish on December 29, 1948. Concerns for the security of the nearby Suez Canal prompted Britain to deliver an ultimatum on January 1, 1949, demanding that Israel withdraw from the Sinai or face British intervention. The Israelis complied on January 2, 1949, redirecting their forces in successful attacks against Egyptian units inside Israel proper.

The 1956 Suez Crisis and resultant Sinai Campaign consisted of an Anglo-French-Israeli offensive against Egypt. The war began on October 29, 1956, with an Israeli thrust that moved quickly toward the Suez Canal. Israeli forces reached the outskirts of El Arish on November 1, 1956, after bitter fighting at Abu Ageila and Rafah. That same day the Anglo-French attacks also started, which prompted Egyptian president Gamal Abdel Nasser to order his forces on the Sinai Peninsula to withdraw to reinforce the canal. Thus, the Israeli 27th Armored Brigade encountered only sporadic resistance when it captured El Arish on November 2, 1956. In accordance with the cease-fire brokered by the United Nations (UN), Israeli forces completed a phased withdrawal from the Sinai in January 1957.

In the 1967 Six-Day War, the preliminary Israeli ground offensive focused on the northern coastal road. During the fighting at El Arish, the Israeli 7th Armored Division attacked the Egyptian 7th Infantry Division. Bitter fighting occurred east of El Arish at the strategic Jiradi Pass, which changed hands repeatedly until Israeli paratroopers secured it after engaging in hand-to-hand combat. By the evening of June 5, 1967, the first day of the war, Israeli forces were on the outskirts of El Arish, and Israel Defense Forces (IDF) reconnaissance units were able to slip into the city under cover of darkness. The city fell to Israeli forces the following morning after a bitter but brief fight. Thus, for the second war in a row, Israeli forces captured El Arish without sustained urban combat. The city remained under Israeli control until 1979.

El Arish figured only briefly in the 1973 Yom Kippur War when the Egyptian Air Force conducted an air raid against Israeli installations there. Six Egyptian aircraft made attack runs from the sea, but the Israelis shot down three and drove off the remainder. El Arish was one of the first areas returned to the Egyptians as part of the 1979 Israel-Egypt Peace Treaty.

CHUCK FAHRER

An Israeli soldier guarding Egyptian prisoners of war at El Arish on July 6, 1967. (Shabtai Tal/Israeli Government Press Office)

See also

Egypt, Armed Forces; Israel Defense Forces; Israel-Egypt Peace Treaty; Israeli War of Independence, Israeli-Egyptian Front; Sinai; Sinai Campaign; Six-Day War; Yom Kippur War

References

Greenwood, Ned H. *The Sinai: A Physical Geography.* Austin: University of Texas Press, 1997.

Herzog, Chaim. *The Arab-Israeli Wars: War and Peace in the Middle East from the War of Independence to Lebanon.* Westminster, MD: Random House, 1984.

Pollack, Kenneth M. *Arabs at War: Military Effectiveness, 1948–1991.* Lincoln: University of Nebraska Press, 2002.

El Arish Scheme

Proposal for a Jewish settlement to be located in the Sinai Peninsula at Wadi El Arish. In October 1902, Zionist leader Theodor Herzl met with British secretary of state for the colonies Joseph Chamberlain. During that meeting Herzl asked for British government support to establish an autonomous Jewish settlement on Egypt's Sinai Peninsula. At the time, there was considerable world outrage over the persecution of Jews in Russia. Herzl's plan became known as the El Arish Scheme.

According to Herzl's diaries, Chamberlain supported the idea providing it also have the support of Foreign Secretary Lord Lansdowne and be proposed by Lord Cromer, British consul general in Egypt who was in effect running Egypt, then under British control. Although Lansdowne also told Herzl that he supported the plan, he said that the plan must have the backing of Cromer and the Egyptian government.

At Cromer's request, Herzl sent an investigating committee to El Arish. The committee was headed by South African Zionist and engineer Leopold Kessler and included experts in various fields as well as a representative of the Egyptian government. The committee was to report on the suitability of the land to support construction and agricultural development. At the same time, Herzl worked to solicit funds for the proposed settlement.

While the committee reported back that El Arish would be suitable for such a settlement provided that water could be brought to the area, in May 1903 the Egyptian government concluded that water from the Nile could not be spared for the El Arish Scheme and formally turned down the plan. Cromer also had second thoughts, concluding that it would not be wise for Britain to encumber the Egyptian government with yet another problem.

Meanwhile, in April 1903, Chamberlain had again met with Herzl and informed him of opposition to the plan. At that time

Chamberlain suggested instead a self-governing Jewish settlement for immigrants in Uganda in British East Africa. This became known as the East Africa Scheme. That October at the Sixth Zionist Congress in Basle, Switzerland, Herzl reported to the delegates the failure of the El Arish Scheme and also the new plan for an East Africa settlement. Much more controversial for the delegates, it too failed.

SPENCER C. TUCKER

See also
Chamberlain, Joseph; East Africa Scheme; Herzl, Theodor; Zionism

References
Bein, Alex. *Theodor Herzl: A Biography.* London: Jewish Publication Society of America, 1943.
Brenner, Michael. *Zionism: A Brief History.* Translated by Shelley Frisch. Princeton, NJ: Markus Wiener, 2003.
Laqueur, Walter. *A History of Zionism: From the French Revolution to the Establishment of the State of Israel.* Reprint ed. New York: Schocken, 2003.
Pappe, Ilan. *A History of Modern Palestine: One Land, Two Peoples.* Cambridge: Cambridge University Press, 2003.
Sanders, Ronald. *The High Walls of Jerusalem: A History of the Balfour Declaration and the Birth of the British Mandate for Palestine.* New York: Holt, Rinehart and Winston, 1983.

Elazar, David
Born: August 27, 1925
Died: April 22, 1976

Israel Defense Forces (IDF) general and chief of staff from 1971 to 1974. David Elazar (nicknamed "Dado") was born of Sephardic heritage on August 27, 1925, in Sarajevo, Yugoslavia (now Bosnia). In 1940 he immigrated to Palestine. He was briefly sent to a British internment camp where he was confined until March 1941, after which he was released to work on Kibbutz Ein Shemer. He joined Palmach, the Jewish underground military organization, in 1946 and was initially assigned to a scout company. He saw action in a number of important engagements in the 1948–1949 Israeli War of Independence including the Battle of San Simon Monastery in Jerusalem, where he saw extremely heavy combat. In July 1948 he rose to become the commander of the 4th Battalion (Raiders) and a major in the new IDF.

Following the war, Elazar elected to remain in the IDF. He attended a battalion commanders' course and then served in the Training Command as an instructor. He was promoted to lieutenant colonel and appointed as a senior military instructor in 1950.

Israel Defense Forces (IDF) chief of staff Lieutenant General David Elazar during a press statement after the signing ceremony of the disengagement agreement following the Yom Kippur War, January 18, 1974. (Israeli Government Press Office)

In June 1952 he was appointed operations officer at the IDF's Central Command. In 1954 he became head of the Combat Doctrine Department of the Training Branch, and in late 1955 he received a secondary appointment as the commander of a reserve unit, the reinforced 12th Infantry Brigade. In June 1956 he was appointed commander of the Infantry School and promoted to the rank of colonel.

Elazar fought in the Gaza Strip during the 1956 Suez Crisis and Sinai Campaign as the commander of the 12th Infantry Brigade, which had been mobilized for the fighting. He transferred to the newly created armor corps in July 1957 at his own request out of a belief that tank warfare was the wave of the future for the IDF. In March 1958 he was appointed commander of the 7th Armored Brigade, the IDF's regular armor unit. In April 1959 he left brigade command and became deputy commander of the Armored Corps. In June 1961 he was promoted to major general and appointed as commander of the Armored Corps.

In 1964 Elazar was appointed as officer in charge of Israel's Northern Command, where he remained for five years. During the June 1967 Six-Day War, he led Israeli troops to victory over the Syrians and seized the Golan Heights in the last major campaign of the war. In 1969 he was appointed chief of the General Staff's Operations Division, the traditional stepping stone to becoming chief of staff.

Elazar became a lieutenant general and chief of staff of the Israeli Army in December 1971. He spent the first part of his tenure focused on fighting terrorists and Palestinian guerrillas. During his watch the 1972 Munich Olympics massacre took place. In retaliation, Elazar ordered the largest Israeli attack on terrorist enclaves in the country's history to that point. Artillery and air attacks pounded terrorist camps in both Lebanon and Syria. Operation SPRING OF YOUTH resulted in the deaths of dozens more terrorists in Beirut in April 1973.

Elazar's career and reputation suffered a crippling setback as a result of the 1973 Yom Kippur War when the Israeli military was caught off guard by the Egyptian and Syrian attack. Although Elazar became convinced at 5:00 a.m. on October 6 (Yom Kippur) that an attack would occur that day, the chief of Israeli military intelligence, Major General Eli Zeira, and the minister of defense, Moshe Dayan, did not believe it likely. That morning Elazar requested both a general mobilization and a preemptive attack by the Israeli Air Force against Syria scheduled for 11:00 a.m., but Dayan rejected both, although he agreed to take Elazar's recommendations to Prime Minister Golda Meir. On his own authority, Elazar ordered a partial mobilization of several thousand essential army and air force reservists.

Elazar was nevertheless held responsible for the early Israeli reverses in the war. In April 1974 the Agranat Commission board of inquiry recommended his dismissal. Elazar resigned from the Israeli Army shortly after the report's release. Later historians have been much kinder to Elazar than the Agranat Commission, noting that he remained calm and effective during the early stages of the

war, in sharp contrast to both Dayan and the Israeli political leadership. Meir depended heavily on Elazar and stated that "he was a rock" during the 1973 war. Nevertheless, he was at least partially responsible for accepting and propagating a military doctrine that was largely dismissive of Arab military capabilities prior to the attack.

After he left the army, Elazar became director-general of the Israeli Navigation Company (ZIM). He died in Tel Aviv on April 22, 1976, of heart failure.

W. Andrew Terrill and Mary J. Elias

See also

Gaza Strip; Golan Heights; Israel Defense Forces; Munich Olympic Games; Palmach; Sinai Campaign; Six-Day War; Yom Kippur War

References

Bartov, Hanoch. *Dado: 48 Years and 20 Days.* New York: Ma'ariv Book Guild, 1981.

Herzog, Chaim. *The War of Atonement: October, 1973.* Boston: Little, Brown, 1975.

Insight Team of the Sunday Times. *The Yom Kippur War.* New York: Simon and Schuster, 2002.

Rabinovich, Abraham. *The Yom Kippur War: The Epic Encounter That Transformed the Middle East.* New York: Schocken, 2005.

ElBaradei, Mohamed
Born: June 17, 1942

United Nations (UN) official and director-general of the International Atomic Energy Agency (IAEA). Mohamed M. ElBaradei was born in Cairo, Egypt, on June 17, 1942. His father was Mostafa ElBaradei, a lawyer and former president of the Egyptian Bar Association. The younger ElBaradei earned a bachelor's degree in law from the University of Cairo and a master's degree (1971) and doctorate (1974) in international law from the New York University School of Law.

ElBaradei joined the Egyptian Ministry of Foreign Affairs in 1964. He was twice in the Egyptian permanent missions to the UN in New York and Geneva with responsibilities for political, legal, and arms control issues. In between these postings, during 1974–1978 he was a special assistant to Egypt's foreign minister. ElBaradei became the senior fellow in charge of the International Law Program at the UN Institute for Training and Research in 1980, and in 1984 he became a senior staff member of the IAEA Secretariat, where he served as its legal adviser (1984–1993).

During 1984–1987 ElBaradei was also the representative of the IAEA director-general to the UN in New York. During 1981–1987 he also taught as an adjunct professor of international law at the New York University School of Law. He served as the assistant director-general for external relations for the UN during 1993–1997. In January 1997 he accepted the position of director-general of the IAEA.

Prior to the beginning of the 2003 Iraq War, ElBaradei and Hans Blix, the Swedish diplomat who headed the UN Monitoring, Verification, and Inspection Commission from January 2000 to June 2003, led the UN inspection team in Iraq. He and Blix asserted that Iraq had no weapons of mass destruction (WMDs).

ElBaradei has since publicly questioned the WMDs rationale used by the George W. Bush administration to initiate the Iraq War. ElBaradei has also served as the point man for the UN in the controversy over Iran's alleged drive to develop nuclear weapons. In September 2005, despite U.S. opposition, ElBaradei was appointed to his third term as director of the IAEA. The Bush administration contended that ElBaradei had been reluctant to confront Iran on its ability to turn nuclear material into weapons grade fissionable material. In October 2005, ElBaradei and the IAEA were jointly awarded the Nobel Peace Prize for efforts "to prevent nuclear energy from being used for military purposes and to ensure that nuclear energy for peaceful purposes is used in the safest possible way."

ElBaradei favored a diplomatic solution to Iran's developing nuclear weapons capability and worked through European and Russian diplomats along with the UN Security Council to limit Iran's nuclear capability. He also favored the imposition of diplomatic and economic sanctions on Iran sufficient to bring it into compliance with the Nuclear Non-Proliferation Pact (NNPP) and the IAEA mission of Atoms for Peace.

RICHARD M. EDWARDS

See also
Iraq War; Nuclear Weapons

References
Kile, Shannon N., ed. *Europe and Iran: Perspectives on Non-Proliferation.* SIPRI Research Reports. Oxford: Oxford University Press, 2006.
Timmerman, Kenneth R. *Countdown to Crisis: The Coming Nuclear Showdown with Iran.* New York: Three Rivers, 2006.
United Nations, ed. *Basic Facts about the United Nations.* New York: United Nations, 2004.

El Hassan bin Talal, Prince
Born: March 20, 1947

Younger brother of King Hussein of Jordan. Born in Amman on March 20, 1947, the youngest son of then Crown Prince Talal ibn Abdullah and Princess Zayn El Sharaf bint Jamal, El Hassan bin Talal was a direct 42nd-generation descendant of the Prophet Muhammad. Hassan received his primary education in Amman, largely with tutors, and then attended the Summer Fields School and Harrow in England. He then went on to Christ Church College, Oxford University, where he earned both BA and MA degrees in Oriental studies from Oxford University.

Hassan was named crown prince at age 18 in 1965 by King Hussein, who amended the 1952 constitution to permit brothers along

Prince Hassan of Jordan. The younger brother of Jordan's late King Hussein, Hassan was Hussein's designated successor for more than three decades until Hussein abruptly stripped him of the title in January 1999 and named his own eldest son, Prince Abdullah ibn al-Hussein (now King Abdullah II) as his successor. (European Community)

with sons of the king to ascend to the throne. At the time, the king, having survived a series of assassination attempts, chose Hassan as regent in preference to his own son Prince Abdullah, who was just 3 years old.

For 34 years, Hassan played a significant role in the Jordanian government, acting as regent during the absences of the king. As King Hussein's closest political adviser, Hassan was a proponent of scientific education in Jordan and helped to promote integration of the regional economy. He participated in the negotiations with Israel that led to the historic 1994 Israeli-Jordanian Peace Accord, all the while maintaining a close relationship with many Arab leaders. In 1970 he founded the Royal Scientific Society of Jordan and was made ombudsman for National Development in 1971. He was also an honorary army general.

Throughout the 1990s, Jordanian rule reverted to Prince Hassan during several prolonged absences of the king, who was diagnosed with cancer in 1992 and underwent several rounds of medical treatment in the United States. Upon his return to Jordan after a six-month medical absence in late 1998, King Hussein publicly criticized the way in which Hassan had been handling Jordanian affairs and accused his brother of abusing his power as regent and crown prince. Over the course of a few days just before his death on February 7, 1999, the king abruptly shifted the line of succession, naming his eldest son Abdullah ibn Hussein as heir to the throne. There is speculation about Hussein's actual reasons for doing so.

Hassan continues to serve as a close adviser to his nephew, King Abdullah II, and has written seven books, some of which have been translated into English.

SPENCER C. TUCKER

See also
Abdullah II, King of Jordan; Hussein, King of Jordan; Jordan

References
Hassan Bin Talal. *Palestinian Self-Determination: A Study of the West Bank and Gaza Strip.* New York: Quartet, 1981.

Robbins, Philip. *A History of Jordan.* Cambridge: Cambridge University Press, 2004.

Salibi, Kamal S. *The Modern History of Jordan.* New ed. London: Tauris, 1998.

Wagner, Heather Lehr. *King Abdullah II.* New York: Chelsea House, 2005.

Emancipation of the Jewish Population

Movement in Europe to free Jews from traditional restrictions and to make them equal to other members of European societies. The emancipation of the Jewish population in Europe began to be debated during the 18th-century Enlightenment. The success or failure of emancipation influenced the future of the Jews in Europe. If they were able to become the true equals of Christians in all things, then there would be little need for them to establish a Jewish homeland. If emancipation was ultimately unable to allow them to fully assimilate into Christian society, then a separate Jewish homeland would become the goal of many.

During most of the Common Era, Jews in Europe were discriminated against and persecuted. Various countries, including England and Spain, routinely expelled Jews from their lands. Even in countries that allowed Jewish communities, many professions were closed to Jews. They were often forced to live in certain areas, and their rights were restricted as compared to Christians. The close identification between the Christian religion and the secular state promoted the image of the Jew as outsider in both social and legal aspects.

After the Reformation of the 16th century, when diversity in religious beliefs became more common, the idea of a split between a secular society and church gained more support. By the 17th century, serious proposals were appearing for the removal of restrictions on Jews. In 1638, an Italian rabbi named Simon Luzzatto argued that greater tolerance for Jews would result in mutual economic benefit for both Jews and Christians. Less than 20 years later, Rabbi Manasseh ben Israel wrote a proposal that the English government allow Jews to return to that country. In European societies where one's religion was seen as a personal choice, Jews were able to argue that they were set apart only because of their faith.

The Enlightenment brought more publications that called for Jews to have the same rights as other individuals. Thinkers such as Honoré Gabriel Riqueti, Comte de Mirabeau (1749–1791), believed that an end to restrictions would benefit everyone in society. Laws limiting Jews in their activities were prompted by religious intolerance rather than reason, they asserted. They admitted that some defects existed but blamed the effects of centuries of discrimination and persecution.

Governments responded slowly to these arguments. In 1740, for example, the British Parliament passed legislation allowing Jews to be naturalized in the British colonies if they had lived there for seven years. In other states, Jews were given the right to elect representatives to local governing bodies and institutions. The influential work calling for Jewish emancipation was written by the Christian Prussian bureaucrat Wilhelm von Dohm in 1781. In *On the Civic Improvement of the Jews,* von Dohm called for the integration of Jews into European society.

The Age of Emancipation is considered to have begun in 1781 with von Dohm's book and with the Edicts of Toleration, proclaimed by Austrian emperor Joseph II. The edicts were intended to encourage the integration of Jews into Habsburg society and were followed by the repeal of some taxes imposed on Jews, both in Austria and France. In the newly independent United States, freedoms of conscience and religion included Jews as well as other religious groups. Perhaps the most prolific writer in support of Jewish emancipation and integration into the broader European society was Moses Mendelssohn (1729–1786).

The French Revolution, which began in 1789, was an important milestone in Jewish emancipation because it made emancipation a reality in France and led to emancipation in countries conquered by France and Napoleon Bonaparte. When the French National Assembly issued the Declaration of the Rights of Man in 1789, many

Lithograph of delegates to the Congress of Berlin in 1878. German chancellor Otto von Bismarck is shown second from the right in the foreground, shaking hands. Among other decisions of the congress was a declaration of equality for Jews as a principle of international law. (Bettmann/Corbis)

assumed that it would apply to Jews as well as Christians. Equal rights for Jews were explicitly proclaimed in "The Law Relating to Jews," issued on November 13, 1791. It stated that every man who satisfies the constitutional requirements for citizenship and fulfills its duties was eligible to all the benefits of citizenship. The law also repealed any special privileges previously granted to individual Jews. Emancipation for Jews was later proclaimed in states such as Rome, Westphalia, and the Duchy of Warsaw. Even so, discrimination against Jews remained, and Emperor Napoleon I proclaimed special regulations for Jews that reduced their rights compared to Christians.

The defeat of Napoleon I in 1815 marked the beginning of a reactionary period, and legitimist and conservative governments tried to dampen liberal ideas and movements. Local populations across Europe also responded to change in the status of Jews. In 1819 bloody pogroms, known as the Hep-Hep Riots, against Jews took place from Alsace in France to Riga in Russia. Even so, liberalism slowly made headway against conservative ideas, and most educated Jews recognized that they could find common cause with liberalism. Ideas such as nationalism and self-determination were adopted by Jewish intellectuals.

Jews took prominent roles in the revolutions that occurred after 1848 in Europe. New legislation granted them further rights, and Jews were elected to parliaments. Although a conservative backlash took away many of those rights, liberalism remained a driving force. By the 1860s, Jewish emancipation was formalized in most of Europe.

At the Congress of Berlin in 1878, equality for Jews was declared a principle of international law. Russia remained the only country in Europe to have restrictions on Jews.

During the last quarter of the 19th century, a growing anti-Semitism movement swept Europe. Whereas earlier persecutions had been based upon religion, the new persecution claimed that Jews were a separate race. As such, they could never be fully integrated into broader society. Jews who supported Haskalah, or integration into European society, realized that they would always remain outsiders for many Europeans. This was disillusioning to many Jews, who considered themselves good citizens of the country in which they lived. They had come to believe that the calls for a return to Zion were for a spiritual rebirth, not a physical emigration. As a result of this disappointment, large numbers turned to Zionism and the belief that only a separate Jewish society would guarantee them equality and freedom from persecution.

Zionism was strongest in those areas in which emancipation was least complete. In Great Britain and France, for example, emancipation had resulted in the removal of all formal restrictions on Jewish rights. In Russia, however, groups such as the Hoveve Zion (Lovers of Zion) promoted emigration to Palestine. Other Jews continued to work for real emancipation and change in Russian society, including those who were active in revolutionary parties such as the Bolsheviks.

TIM J. WATTS

See also

Anti-Semitism; Haskalah; Hoveve Zion; Zionism

References

Birnbaum, Pierre, and Ira Katznelson. *Paths of Emancipation: Jews, States, and Citizenship*. Princeton, NJ: Princeton University Press, 1995.

Frankel, Jonathan, and Steven J. Zipperstein. *Assimilation and Community: The Jews in Nineteenth-Century Europe*. New York: Cambridge University Press, 1992.

Katz, Jacob. *Jewish Emancipation and Self-Emancipation*. Philadelphia: Jewish Publication Society, 1986.

Sorkin, David Jan. *Moses Mendelssohn and the Religious Enlightenment*. Berkeley: University of California Press, 1996.

Emergency Committee for Zionist Affairs

Pro-Zionist organization created to coordinate worldwide Zionism in the shadow of World War II. In the late 1930s, Zionist activities in the world were primarily centered in two locations: London and Jerusalem. As the possibility of war increased at the end of the decade, however, both locations seemed likely to become dangerous war zones where Zionist organizations would be considered an unwelcome distraction to the British Empire at best and potentially disloyal forces at worst. As such, the Emergency Committee for Zionist Affairs (ECZA) was created in the United States to temporarily assume the lead role in Zionist activism. Although the ECZA was intended as an umbrella organization, coordinating the efforts of multiple agencies, it was dominated by the Zionist Organization of America (ZOA). The ZOA's massive influence promulgated intense rivalry within the ECZA, which exacerbated the problems caused by the disorganized nature of the institution. The ECZA's ability to influence public opinion and arouse sympathy for the Zionist cause was further hindered by a lack of effective fund-raising methods and an unwillingness among ECZA leadership to criticize the policies of Great Britain during wartime.

This hesitation came in spite of the fact that the Zionist cause was directly contradictory to the practices of the British Mandate for Palestine. It was perceived that Nazi Germany represented a much greater threat to the worldwide Jewish population and the Zionist cause than the British government could possibly create. As such, all strident criticism of British policies in Palestine was virtually halted for the duration of World War II.

In 1941 the ECZA hired Emanuel Neumann to serve as the public relations director for the committee. Neumann had been born in the United States but spent most of the 1930s living in Palestine, working for various Zionist institutions. He founded the American Palestine Committee (APC) in 1932 as a means of enlisting non-Jews in support of the Zionist cause. Upon his return to the United States, he refounded the organization and created the Christian Council on Palestine (CCP) to appeal to Christian clergy who wished to assist the Zionist cause. Neumann quickly energized the ECZA, pushing for a massive Zionist gathering of international supporters. In May 1942 he orchestrated the Biltmore Conference, a meeting of 600 delegates who called for the creation of a Jewish commonwealth via the Biltmore Program.

Neumann's aggressive approach to public relations irritated the chairman of the ECZA, Rabbi Stephen Samuel Wise. Wise opposed any action that confronted President Franklin Delano Roosevelt's Palestine policies. Indeed, Wise feared that provoking Roosevelt during wartime might trigger a backlash against the Jewish community in America and could ruin the Zionist dream of a Jewish national homeland. When Wise and Neumann could not agree on a coherent strategy for the ECZA, Neumann resigned his position, leaving the organization late in 1942.

Shortly after the United States entered World War II, the ECZA changed its name to the American Emergency Council for Zionist Affairs (AECZA). This change was specifically designed to emphasize the patriotic nature of AECZA's participants, who professed to view themselves as Americans first and Zionists second. Late in 1942 the name was changed again, this time to the American Zionist Emergency Council (AZEC), and the organization began to grow in both size and ambition. The resignation of Neumann did not end the possibility of aggressive leadership, however, as shortly after his departure Rabbi Abba Hillel Silver became Wise's cochair for the organization.

Silver and Wise did not cooperate well together, and in addition to an adamant personal antipathy, the two differed fundamentally on the proper course for the AZEC. Wise wished to continue the nonconfrontational approach for the duration of the war, while Silver pushed for a much more forthright approach. Unlike Wise, Silver saw the war as creating an unprecedented opportunity for the establishment of a Jewish state in Palestine, possibly in exchange for increased Jewish support of the Allied cause. Silver's passionate advocacy led to renewed fund-raising efforts, the additional finances of which were used to hire lobbyists, publicists, and organizers who could expand the AZEC's efforts at the state and national levels. The AZEC's membership expanded, as did a nationwide network of activists who lobbied both Democratic and Republican members of Congress. The organization hoped that legislative pressure could influence Roosevelt, who in turn could pressure the British government for changes in the governance of Palestine.

In 1944, Silver proposed a pro-Zionist Congressional resolution, to formally offer public support for the development of an autonomous Jewish state in Palestine. Wise opposed the resolution, and the resulting struggle caused Silver to resign his position. This proved to be a Pyrrhic victory for Wise, however, because the AZEC membership overwhelmingly favored the measure. The backlash from Wise's obstructionism drove him from his position, which handed sole chairmanship of the AZEC to Silver in the spring of 1945.

From 1945 until 1948, the AZEC engaged in a massive propaganda campaign directed primarily at President Harry S. Truman. The U.S. Department of State attempted to counter Zionist activists, urging Truman to remain aloof from the dispute or even to push for an independent Palestinian state under Arab leadership. However, the AZEC gradually won over congressional and public support for the Zionist cause, preventing Truman from following the advice of Secretary of State George C. Marshall, who did not favor a Jewish state in Palestine.

After Israel proclaimed its independence on May 15, 1948, the AZEC shortened its title to the American Zionist Committee (AZC) and adopted a new role as an umbrella organization for pro-Israel groups in the United States. In the first decade of Israel's existence, the AZC established two new organizations: the American Israel Public Affairs Committee (1954) and the Conference of Presidents of Major American Jewish Organizations (1955). After two decades of coordination and fund-raising, the AZC was reorganized in 1970 as the American Zionist Federation (AZF). It began with 11 member organizations and had grown to 16 groups by 1990. In 1993 it became the American Zionist Movement (AZM), and began soliciting individual members as well as organizational affiliations. Over the next two years, the AZM lost its association with 6 member organizations. Three departed after a dispute regarding religious pluralism. The other 3 left following the AZM's refusal to denounce the Oslo Accords of 1993. The AZM membership in 2006 includes 15 member organizations and 5 affiliated nonmember organizations.

PAUL J. SPRINGER

See also

American Israel Public Affairs Committee; American Palestine Committee; Biltmore Program; Zionism

References

Brenner, Lenni. *Zionism in the Age of the Dictators.* Westport, CT: Lawrence Hill, 1983.

Cohn-Sherbok, Dan, and Dawoud El-Alami. *The Palestine-Israeli Conflict: A Beginner's Guide.* Oxford, UK: Oneworld, 2001.

Laqueur, Walter. *A History of Zionism: From the French Revolution to the Establishment of the State of Israel.* Reprint ed. New York: Schocken, 2003.

Peretz, Don. *The Government and Politics of Israel.* Boulder, CO: Westview, 1979.

Entebbe Hostage Rescue

Start Date: July 3, 1976
End Date: July 4, 1976

Rescue of hostages aboard a French jetliner in Entebbe, Uganda, by the Israel Defense Forces (IDF) on July 3–4, 1976. Around noon on June 27, 1976, hijackers commandeered Air France Flight 139, in route from Tel Aviv to Paris. The hijacking occurred shortly after a brief stopover in Athens, Greece. The plane carried 246 passengers and 12 crew members. Four hijackers had boarded the aircraft in Athens. The hijackers were led by Wilfred Bose, a West German Red Army Faction terrorist, and Fayez Abdul-Rahim Jaber. The operation was carried out in the name of the Popular Front for the Liberation of Palestine (PFLP).

The hijacked plane left the Athens radar screen and flew to a preplanned stop in Libya, a nation that had long harbored terrorists. As the aircraft refueled at the Benghazi airport, one passenger, an Israeli woman claiming to be pregnant, was freed. Departing Libya around 9:30 p.m., Flight 139 flew to Entebbe Airport in Uganda, in accordance with the hijacking plan. It arrived at Entebbe 3:15 a.m. on June 28. Three additional terrorists joined the hijackers at Entebbe.

All evidence suggests that the Ugandan government was complicit in the hijacking of Flight 139 from the very beginning. It also clearly demonstrates that Ugandan president Idi Amin Dada assisted the terrorists once the hijacked plane had arrived. Uganda had long been friendly to Israel, and Amin had once been tutored by the Israelis. In 1972, however, the mercurial Amin turned on the Israelis and ordered all Jews out of Uganda. He then promptly turned Uganda into a Palestinian terrorist training ground. Although Amin visited the hostages several times during their ordeal, he did not discourage the hijackers' actions and seemed to be pushing their demands. Throughout the crisis, Ugandan troops at Entebbe Airport assisted the terrorists in guarding the Jewish hostages.

On June 29 the hijackers issued their demands, which included the release of 40 terrorists held by the Israelis and another 13 terrorists languishing in jails in France, Germany, Switzerland, and Kenya. In two stages the hijackers released many hostages, almost all non-Jews, who were flown to Paris. The hijackers continued to hold the remaining 105 hostages, all identified as Jews. The entire French air crew bravely refused to take advantage of the release and stayed behind with the remaining hostages.

An extremely distressed Israeli cabinet initially rejected any hope of mounting a military rescue operation. It did so chiefly because of the great distance between Israel and Entebbe, more than 2,000 air miles one way. Instead, Prime Minister Yitzhak Rabin's government concentrated on negotiations that they hoped would free the hostages. Because the hijacked aircraft was French owned, Israeli diplomats traveled to Paris to arrange a trade of terrorists for hostages, most likely in either Paris or Djibouti. The Israeli cabinet faced added pressure from relatives of the hostages, who demanded that the government seek a deal at the earliest opportunity.

Israeli defense minister Shimon Peres subsequently ordered the IDF General Staff to review any reasonable military option. Peres's military staff was nearly as pessimistic as the cabinet about a successful rescue operation. Under the direction of IDF chief of staff Mordechai Gur and Israeli Air Force chief Benny Peled, a planning committee led by General Dan Shomron began to plot the suitability of any and all military options. The military planning was done in great secrecy, while Rabin continued to use diplomatic channels to negotiate a possible end to the situation.

The intense planning and training period for Israeli military personnel was backed by a massive intelligence collection effort to learn everything possible about Entebbe Airport. Military planning was enhanced by the Israelis' knowledge of the construction of Entebbe Airport, which they had built years before. Israeli agents traveled to Paris to interview the released hostages, which provided sharp insights into both the hostage and the terrorist situation. On July 1 a final plan was presented to the IDF General Staff and Defense Minister Peres, and the plan was approved. A reluctant

One of the injured hostages from a hijacked Air France flight being transported by the Israeli military to Tel Aviv on July 7, 1976. The plane had been hijacked by pro-Palestinian terrorists on June 27 and landed at Entebbe in Uganda. Non-Jewish passengers were released, but 103 Jewish people were held captive until a daring rescue raid by the Israel Defense Forces (IDF) on July 4. (AFP/Getty Images)

Rabin, appalled by the possibility of having to yield to terrorism, agreed to the plan, subject to cabinet approval. He convened a cabinet meeting for the afternoon of July 3 while military rehearsals continued.

In order to arrive at Entebbe at the desired time of 11:00 p.m. on July 3, the rescue operation left Israeli airspace in midafternoon prior to final approval by the cabinet. When the cabinet unanimously backed the plan, the rescue operation proceeded. Four C-130 aircraft carrying approximately 200 IDF personnel landed on schedule at Entebbe. The rescue force was commanded by Lieutenant Colonel Jonathan Netanyahu, brother of future prime minister Benjamin Netanyahu.

The initial assault team was charged with seizing the old terminal building and releasing the hostages. Netanyahu, on the lead aircraft, drove up to the old terminal in a black Mercedes-Benz, an exact replica of the official car of the Ugandan dictator. The Ugandan troops guarding the terminal were initially duped into believing it was a surprise late-night arrival of Amin. One assault element commandeered the air traffic center at the new terminal while another team prepared emergency beacons for the runways. A fourth team refueled the Israeli aircraft using Entebbe's own fuel tanks. A final assault team was to destroy Ugandan aircraft on the ground that might threaten the Israelis' escape. One Israeli aircraft was dispatched to Nairobi, Kenya, to assist in the medical care for the hostages and IDF personnel, while another aircraft flew over Lake Victoria providing electronic support to rescuers.

The IDF force secured the hostages after a brief firefight, during which Netanyahu was fatally wounded. The first C-130, carrying the hostages, left the airport within 40 minutes. The entire operation lasted less than an hour on the ground. The Israelis destroyed 11 MiG-17 and MiG-21 aircraft, probably half of the Ugandan Air Force. The Kenyans welcomed the IDF planes to the Nairobi airport largely because of their hatred for Amin. The planes then refueled before returning to Israel. By midday on July 4, even before the former hostages had reached Israel, most of the world was aware of the successful rescue.

At least 6 terrorists involved in the hijacking were killed, and approximately 20 to 40 Ugandan soldiers supporting the terrorists were believed killed resisting the Israeli rescuers. One IDF soldier was wounded, while the number of wounded terrorists and Ugandan soldiers remains unknown. Three hostages were either killed during the operation or died of wounds later on. One hostage, Dora Bloch, had been removed from the Entebbe old terminal prior to the rescue operation because of illness and was taken to a local hospital and is believed to have been murdered by 2 army officers on Amin's orders. Bloch and 4 Ugandan air traffic controllers from the airport were executed by order of Amin after the rescue operation's success had been revealed to the world.

RALPH MARTIN BAKER

See also

Allon, Yigal; Gur, Mordechai; Netanyahu, Jonathan; Peres, Shimon; Popular Front for the Liberation of Palestine; Rabin, Yitzhak; Shomron, Dan

References

Ben-Porat, Yeshayahu, Eitan Haber, and Zeev Schiff. *Entebbe Rescue.* New York: Delacorte, 1977.

Herzog, Chaim. *Heroes of Israel: Profiles of Jewish Courage.* London: Little, Brown, 1989.

Stevenson, William. *90 Minutes at Entebbe.* New York: Bantam, 1976.

Eshkol, Levi
Born: October 25, 1895
Died: February 26, 1969

Israel's first minister of defense (1948–1951) and its minister of finance (1952–1963) and prime minister (1963–1969). Levi Eshkol was born Levi Shkolnik on October 25, 1895, in the Ukrainian village of Oratova, near Kiev. Following a traditional Jewish education in Oratova, he attended a Hebrew high school in Vilna, Lithuania. At the age of 16 he joined the Zionist youth group Tzeirei Tzion (Youth of Zion). In 1914 he immigrated to Palestine, where he worked as an agricultural laborer and political activist.

In 1918 Eshkol joined the Jewish Legion of the British Army. After World War I he helped found Degania Beth, one of the first kibbutzim in Palestine. He was elected to the first three sessions of the Assembly of Palestine Jewry. In 1921 he took part in the founding of Histadrut (the General Confederation of Labor). He joined the Mapai, the left-of-center workers' party, in 1929, eventually becoming a member of its central committee. During the 1930s he worked to bring Jewish immigrants from Germany to Palestine. He also helped found the Mekorot Water Company, Israel's water utility, in 1937 and served as its chief executive until 1951.

In 1940 Eshkol joined the Haganah, the Jewish self-defense military organization. In 1947 he was responsible for recruiting what became the Israel Defense Forces (IDF). He became the first director-general of the Ministry of Defense when Israel gained independence in 1948. He was appointed minister of agriculture and development in 1951 and became minister of finance in 1952, holding that post for 12 years. In this key position he helped secure funds

Israeli prime minister Levi Eshkol shown visiting the Ein-Gev settlement on the Sea of Galilee on April 8, 1967. (Library of Congress)

for economic development, absorb the many Jewish refugees who immigrated to Israel, and secure modern military equipment for the IDF. He served briefly as deputy prime minister and was favored by many Israelis to replace Prime Minister David Ben-Gurion when the latter temporarily retired from the government in late 1953. The Mapai Party chose Moshe Sharett as party leader instead.

Ben-Gurion returned as prime minister following the 1961 elections but resigned on June 16, 1963. Eshkol followed him as Israeli prime minister and remained in the post until his death in 1969. Among his accomplishments was the opening of diplomatic relations with West Germany. He also established cultural ties with the Soviet Union, which then allowed some Jews to immigrate to Israel. In May 1964, Eshkol was the first Israeli prime minister to visit the United States.

Eshkol's most important accomplishment was undoubtedly that of guiding the nation through the period just before and during the 1967 Six-Day War. His initial reluctance to accept his own military leaders' calls for a preemptive strike was at the time seen as timid. His decision to delay proved prescient, however, for it served to increase Egyptian president Gamal Abdel Nasser's provocations and created diplomatic support for Israel's position, especially in the United States, when the government did indeed launch the war. On the commencement of the June 1967 war, Eshkol created a government of national unity by giving the post of minister of defense to Moshe Dayan and by bringing Menachem Begin of the Herut Party into the cabinet. Eshkol also worked to find new sources of supplies after France initiated a military boycott of Israel. Eshkol died of a heart attack in the prime minister's residence in Jerusalem on February 26, 1969.

DAVE RAUSCH AND SPENCER C. TUCKER

See also

Begin, Menachem; Ben-Gurion, David; Haganah; Labor Party; Nasser, Gamal Abdel; Six-Day War

References

Hammel, Eric. *Six Days in June: How Israel Won the 1967 Arab-Israeli War.* New York: Scribner, 1992.

Oren, Michael B. *Six Days of War: June 1967 and the Making of the Modern Middle East.* Novato, CA: Presidio, 2003.

Prittie, Terence. *Eshkol: The Man and the Nation.* New York: Pitman, 1969.

Etzel

See Irgun Tsvai Leumi

European Union and the Arab-Israeli Conflict

From the outset, the European Economic Community (EEC), later renamed the European Community (EC) and currently known as the European Union (EU), has had problematic relations with Israel. There are several reasons for this. First, member states of the EU have often acted unilaterally, reflecting individual rather than group priorities. Second, international developments, especially in the context of Arab-Israeli conflicts, have shifted, triggering changes in policy. Third, both Israel and its major supporter, the United States, have objected to the European body's perceived pro-Arab stance and have therefore been hesitant to allow the EU an active role in the Middle East peace process.

The EU's Israeli policies thus need to be viewed in an evolving context. By and large, however, they reflect a movement from an initially passive to a more active role in the peace process, alongside increasing efforts to consolidate economic and cultural links with both Israel and the Arab world. Central to these initiatives are the EU's Euro-Mediterranean Partnership (EMP), otherwise known as the Barcelona Process, and the European Neighborhood Policy (ENP).

The Treaty of Rome (1957), which founded the EEC, included no formal foreign policy provisions, leaving key aspects up to individual member states. Although the EEC recognized Israel as early as 1959 and by 1964 had drawn up a limited European-Israeli trade agreement, its more active role in the Middle East developed slowly. During the 1967 Six-Day War, EEC policy largely reflected that of the United States, focusing on curtailing the Soviet presence and its influence on the spread of Arab nationalism. Nevertheless, the policy of individual EEC members reflected a growingly critical stance,

as in 1965 when West German chancellor Ludwig Erhard proclaimed his country's neutrality in future Arab-Israeli conflicts and in 1967 when French president Charles de Gaulle condemned Israel's decision to wage war, terminating Franco-Israeli military cooperation.

Nevertheless, it was not until the Yom Kippur War of 1973 and the subsequent Organization of Petroleum Exporting Countries (OPEC) oil embargo that the European body, now renamed the European Community, began to abandon its passive role toward Israel and the Middle East. OPEC's October 13, 1973, announcement that 11 Arab oil-producing countries would reduce oil production by 5 percent monthly, an action that would target countries viewed as supporters of Israel, created panic in Western Europe, which then depended on Arab countries for about 70–80 percent of its oil. This development led the EC to its first major collective action when on October 28, 1973, it released a communiqué calling for Israel to recognize Palestinian rights and withdraw from all territories it had occupied since the June 1967 Six-Day War.

This increasingly critical stance toward Israel continued with the EC's 1979 condemnation of Israeli settlement policy and culminated in the Venice Declaration of 1980, issued in the wake of the U.S.-sponsored Camp David Accords between Egypt and Israel. This declaration voiced EC support of United Nations (UN) Security Council Resolutions 242 and 338. While the UN resolutions, however, viewed the Palestinian problem primarily from a refugee perspective, the European declaration emphasized that the Palestinian people should be allowed to exercise their right to self-determination and that the Palestine Liberation Organization (PLO) should take part in peace negotiations. Israel strongly objected to Europe's demand that it deal with a "terrorist organization" and denounced Europe's "Munich-like capitulation to totalitarian blackmail."

The crises of 1973 further spurred the EC's foreign involvement by highlighting the importance of diplomatic exchange and trade agreements. To serve these ends, the EC expanded its political relationship with Middle Eastern countries via the Euro-Arab dialogue and set in motion its long-term goal of creating a free trade area in the Mediterranean region by implementing the Global Mediterranean Policy (GMP). The 1975 Co-operation Agreement with Israel aimed at mutually eliminating all custom duties on industrial goods and establishing a cooperative in the areas of finance, agriculture, and industry. By the beginning of 1977, the EC provided free access for Israeli industrial products. Correspondingly, Israel removed duties on comparable EC goods by 1989. In short, Israel had achieved a preferential status as an EC trading partner.

Nevertheless, the ongoing Arab-Israeli conflict left its mark on trade relations between Israel and Europe. In 1982 the EC condemned Israel's invasion of Lebanon as a violation of international law and placed the 1975 trade agreement on hold for a year. Similarly, the First Intifada of 1987 led the European Parliament to delay finalization of three financial and trade protocols with Israel in March 1988. These were passed only when Israel agreed to permit agricultural and manufactured goods stemming from the occupied

Palestinian president Yasser Arafat (*left*) and Miguel Moratinos (*right*), European Union (EU) special envoy for the peace process, after their meeting at Arafat's office in Gaza City, May 6, 2001. (Reuters/Corbis)

territories to pass unobstructed through Israeli ports en route to Europe. Before the introduction of the Single Market in 1992, the EC placed further pressure on Israel by delaying negotiations on a new bilateral trade agreement. Progress was made dependent upon breakthroughs in the Madrid peace process, begun in 1991. Only with the signing of the Oslo Accords in 1993 did the European body, now known as the EU, proceed with negotiations, which officially resumed in November 1995.

In spite of the EU's growing economic and political importance, however, Israel and the United States were reluctant to assign Europe a more active role in peace negotiations, as when the EU secured merely observer status in the Madrid Conference of 1991, convened by the United States and Russia. The EU nevertheless began to play a leading role in multilateral working groups set up to channel financial aid to the Middle East and coordinate economic, infrastructural, social, and environmental projects. Most importantly, it headed the Regional Economic Development Working Group (REDWG) that, after the Oslo Accords and the Washington Agreements were signed in 1993, was delegated with initiatives for

economic rebuilding in the occupied territories. The EU soon became the main financial supporter of the Palestinian Authority (PA), contributing more than $2 billion from 1994 to 1999.

Subsequent developments caused further deterioration in EU-Israeli relations and highlighted disunity within the EU. After the failure of the Oslo Accords, French president Jacques Chirac paid a controversial visit to East Jerusalem in 1996 and sent French delegates to negotiate a cease-fire after the Israeli shelling of southern Lebanon in April 1996. Critical of the French action, the EU reluctantly sent its own negotiating team and held talks with PLO leader Yasser Arafat and Israeli foreign minister David Levy. Israel rebuffed the European move, while U.S. secretary of state Warren Christopher warned EU members to refrain from interfering in the peace process at such a delicate time.

The EU's next move, appointing a special envoy to the peace process, was more successful. Miguel Moratinos, the former Spanish ambassador to Israel, received a mandate to facilitate dialogue among Israelis, Palestinians, and other Arabs. Not only did he arrange a meeting between Arafat and the Israeli foreign minister in Brus-

ALLIANCES IN EUROPE, 1945 – 1990

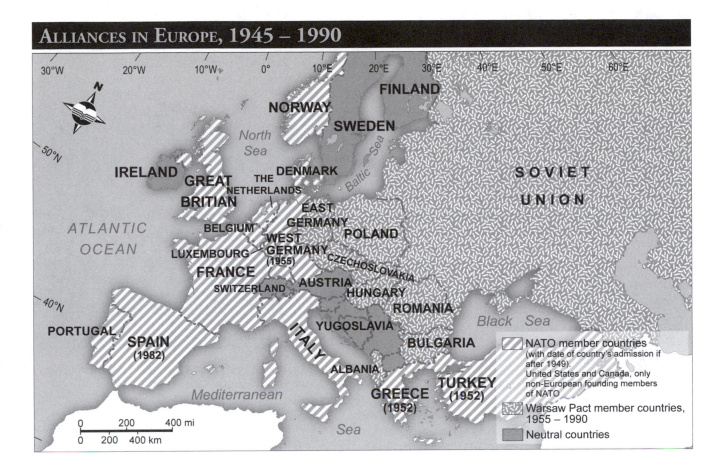

sels, but he was also instrumental in Israel's agreement to withdraw its troops from Hebron, where they had been stationed since the massacre of 1994. Late in 1997, Moratinos presented a code of conduct to Palestinian and Israeli representatives, calling upon the Israeli government of Benjamin Netanyahu to adhere to previous commitments and the Palestinians to combat terrorism. As another signal of increasing European involvement, in March 1998 an EU delegation headed by British foreign minister Robin Cook highlighted concerns with Israeli settlement policy and protested the Netanyahu government's refusal to open an EU-funded airport in Gaza.

Yet the EU took no part in the U.S.-led diplomacy culminating in the Wye River Memorandum of October 1998, whereby Israel agreed to withdraw from 13 percent of West Bank territory. The Washington Donors' Conference of November 30, 1998, whereby the EU and member states pledged 3.2 billion European currency units (ECUs) in support of the PA, reconfirmed Europe's role as a payer and not a major player in the Middle East peace process.

The failure of the Camp David Summit in September 2000 marked a new low in the Middle East peace process, exacerbated by the shift of focus from Palestine to Iraq in the wake of the September 11, 2001, terror attacks on the United States. Nevertheless, the Mitchell Report of April 2001, cosponsored by the United States and the EU, made recommendations for resuming negotiations, and a new diplomatic initiative resulted in the creation of the Quartet—

the United States, Russia, the UN, and the EU—as a forum for advancing the peace process. By the end of 2002, the Quartet, upon European urging, had established the Road Map to Peace for a Palestinian-Israeli settlement that would lead to the establishment of two states. On April 30, 2003, the plan was presented to Israeli prime minister Ariel Sharon and Mahmoud Abbas, newly elected PA prime minister.

The first years of the 21st century, however, have highlighted the EU's impotence and disunity in the ongoing conflict. Europe's credibility suffered from its failure to take a unified stand on sanctions against Israel in the wake of its renewed occupation of West Bank territory. Nevertheless, in November 2005 Israel agreed to allow the EU to maintain a Border Assistance Mission at the Rafah crossing between the Gaza Strip and Egypt. Similarly, Israel also welcomed the presence of European countries as peacekeepers after the Israeli-Hezbollah War (July–August 2006).

EU-Israeli relations underwent yet another shift with the PA's election of a Hamas government on January 25, 2006. On April 10, 2006, the EU decided to suspend direct aid to the PA, announcing that in coordination with the Middle East Quartet it would cut $600 million, which had comprised some 25 percent of the PA's total foreign aid. The United States also cut $420 million at this time, and Israel withheld about $60 million per month, also using $15 million to pay the PA's water and electricity bills, which the PA will not pay directly. The EU instead allowed an emergency aid package of $140 million to keep the PA from collapsing, although this has meant a barely functioning state.

Other indications of a possible rapprochement between the EU and Israel include the endorsement of a three-year European Neighborhood Policy Action Plan in December 2004 and its implementation in April 2005. As part of the Euro-Mediterranean Partnership (Barcelona Process), the agreement incorporates free trade arrangements for industrial goods, concessionary arrangements for trade in agricultural products, and the possibility for Israel to participate increasingly in key aspects of EU policies and programs. Since June 2006 the EU has provided direct assistance to the Palestinians through the Temporary International Mechanism (TIM). Created at the request of the Quartet and the European Council (EC), the TIM works closely with the PA Ministry of Finance to facilitate need-based assistance by international donors to the Palestinian people. Aid emphasis is in the public social services sector. In 2007 the EC committed £265 million through the TIM.

ANNA WITTMANN

See also

Arab Oil Embargo; Camp David Accords; France, Middle East Policy; Germany, Federal Republic of, Middle East Policy; Hamas; Intifada, First; Israel; Madrid Conference; Oil As an Economic Weapon; Organization of Petroleum Exporting Countries; Oslo Accords; Palestine Liberation Organization; Palestinian Authority; Settlements, Israeli; Six-Day War; United Kingdom, Middle East Policy; United States Coordinating and Monitoring Mission; Wye River Agreement; Yom Kippur War

References

Aoun, Elena. "European Foreign Policy and the Arab-Israeli Dispute: Much Ado About Nothing?" *European Foreign Affairs Review* 8 (2003): 289–312.

Dannreuther, Roland, ed. *European Union Foreign and Security Policy: Towards a Neighbourhood Strategy.* London: Routledge, 2004.

Gomez, Ricardo. *Negotiating the Euro-Mediterranean Partnership: Strategic Action in EU Foreign Policy?* Aldershot, UK: Ashgate, 2003.

Gorce, Paul-Marie de la. "Europe and the Arab-Israel Conflict: A Survey." *Journal of Palestine Studies* 26(3) (Spring 1997): 5–16.

Hollis, Rosemary. "Europe and the Middle East: Power by Stealth?" *International Affairs* 73(1) (January 1997): 15–29.

Executive, World Zionist Organization

See World Zionist Organization Executive

Exodus Incident

Start Date: July 11, 1947
End Date: August 22, 1947

The ill-fated voyage of the ship *Exodus 1947* (July 11–August 22, 1947) highlighted the plight of Jewish refugees attempting to immigrate to Palestine after World War II. The British government had from 1939 continued to limit Jewish immigration to Palestine. Indeed, during the war and in the midst of the Holocaust Britain

The ship *Exodus 1947,* filled with Jewish refugees to Palestine, at Haifa on July 18, 1947. (Pinn Hans/Israeli Government Press Office)

had maintained warships off Palestine to intercept ships bound for Palestine carrying Jewish refugees fleeing the Holocaust.

British policies of blocking illegal Jewish immigration to Palestine continued after the war. Jewish leaders responded by encouraging and facilitating illegal immigration (Aliya Bet). From 1945 to 1948, Mossad Le-Aliya Bet, a branch of the Haganah headed by Shaul Avigur, organized 65 voyages transporting in all some 70,000 displaced Jews to Palestine. One of the vessels involved in this effort was the former *President Warfield.*

The *President Warfield* was a Chesapeake Bay ferry that had been transferred to the British under Lend-Lease and had participated in ferrying operations to Normandy after the June 6, 1944, invasion. It had been returned to the United States after the war. This worn-out ship was then sold as scrap to the Jewish immigration effort for slightly more than $8,000.

Renamed the *Exodus 1947* and packed with 4,515 refugees for Palestine, the ship departed Sète, France, on July 11, 1947. Eight British warships—the cruiser *Ajax,* five destroyers, and two minelayers—eventually trailed the *Exodus 1947.* Twelve miles beyond Palestinian territorial waters, the British surrounded the *Exodus 1947* on July 18 and boarded it.

Hand-to-hand fighting ensued. In the melee that extended over several hours, the British finally resorted to small arms fire. Two passengers and 1 crewman died, and 32 others were injured. The crewmen surrendered only when the British began ramming the *Exodus 1947,* threatening to sink it.

The British towed the *Exodus 1947,* now listing badly, to Haifa. Ordinarily, the refugees would have been sent to camps in Cyprus, but these were now packed with 26,000 people, and the British sought to make an example. They embarked the passengers on three troopships and sent them to the port of Marseille, France, in effect returning them to their point of debarkation. There the deportees rejected orders to go ashore, and French officials, who were willing to see them reenter France, refused to remove them by force. Only 130 passengers, most of them sick or pregnant, disembarked.

The remaining passengers, including many orphaned children who were Holocaust survivors, began a hunger strike. French authorities offered supplies, which the refugees rejected despite desperate sanitary conditions and extreme heat.

After 24 days and fearing the outbreak of an epidemic, the French ordered the three ships to depart. The British government, reeling from growing adverse worldwide public outrage over what had transpired, ordered the ships on to Hamburg in their zone of Germany. There, British soldiers forcibly removed the refugees, who were then sent on to two displaced persons (DP) camps near Lübeck. Demonstrations and protests occurred in DP camps throughout Europe over the events.

The British then changed their policy, ending the effort to return illegal immigrants to Palestine to their port of origin. Instead, they sent them to Cyprus. Media coverage of the events also led to a swing in public opinion in favor of the Jews and establishment of a Jewish state in 1948.

Many of the passengers on the *Exodus 1947* continued to try to reach Palestine. Although some gained illegal entry, more than half of them were detained again and deported to Cyprus. There they remained until they were allowed to immigrate to Israel after its founding in May 1948. The *Exodus 1947* itself burned at Haifa in August 1952 and was scrapped in 1963.

Writer Leon Uris loosely based his novel *Exodus* (1958) on the *Exodus 1947* incident and the lives of David Ben-Gurion and Menachem Begin. Paul Newman received an Academy Award for Best Actor for his portrayal of the fictional Ari Ben Canaan in the film *Exodus* (1958), directed by Otto Preminger.

RICHARD EDWARDS AND SPENCER C. TUCKER

See also

Haganah; Immigration to Palestine/Israel; Zionism

References

Gruber, Ruth. *Exodus 1947: The Ship That Launched a Nation*. New York: Crown, 1999.

Halamish, Aviva. *The Exodus Affair: Holocaust Survivors and the Struggle for Palestine (Religion, Theology and the Holocaust)*. Translated by Ora Cummings. Syracuse, NY: Syracuse University Press, 1998.

Kaniuk, Yoram. *Commander of the Exodus*. New York: Grove, 2001.

Uris, Leon. *Exodus*. New York: Wings, 2000.

Expellees and Refugees, Palestinian

The plight of the Palestinian refugee community remains one of the most tragic and controversial aspects of the Israeli-Palestinian conflict since the Israeli War of Independence (1948–1949). In the violent events of that time, hundreds of thousands of Palestinians within what was to become the Green Line of Israel fled or were driven from their homes to escape the encroaching violence. This event is known as the Nakba (Catastrophe). The United Nations (UN) General Assembly Resolution 194 of 1948 called in vain for the restoration of these exiles to their homes.

According to the UN Relief and Works Agency for Palestine Refugees in the Near East (UNRWA), more than 914,000 individuals became refugees during this time. Put another way, from 1.4 million Palestinians in 1948, only 60,000 were counted in the first Israeli census inside Israel. Some 360,000 refugees settled in the West Bank, and 200,000 went to the Gaza Strip. They also went to surrounding Arab states, including Jordan (100,000), Lebanon (104,000), Syria (82,000), and Iraq, Egypt, Saudi Arabia and Kuwait. Most of the remaining two-thirds settled either in or around major cities of their host countries or near the camps themselves. Following the 1967 Six-Day War in which Israel took administrative and military control of East Jerusalem, the West Bank, and Gaza, the refugee camps swelled with a new influx of displaced persons.

In the decades since the creation of the Palestinian refugee crisis, the status of the community has changed dramatically even as its future has remained consistently uncertain. The most obvious shift in the refugees' plight has been the gradual acknowledgment of a semipermanent status to what was once assumed a temporary issue. Shabby concrete blocks have replaced tent city camps around the region, while most of the refugees' former homes have been razed or subsumed and reinhabited within Israeli townships.

The number of registered refugees grew to more than 4.1 million people in 59 official camps by 2004. More than 1.7 million are in 10 camps in Jordan alone. Jordan remains the only primary host country to offer some Palestinian refugees national citizenship. Many but by no means all of the refugees in Jordan have managed to participate in wider national socioeconomic life, often successfully. In the remaining areas, including camps in the West Bank and Gaza, refugees linger in semipermanent ghettos that tend to be overcrowded, with poor sanitation and infrastructure, extremely high unemployment, and a general situation of grinding poverty and malaise. This state of affairs has played a key role in significant regional events of the past several decades, including Jordan's Black September uprising (1970), the Lebanese Civil War (1975–1991), and the First and Second Intifadas in the West Bank and Gaza (1987–1993 and 2000–2004, respectively).

Initially, relief functions were undertaken by Palestinian charitable organizations. UNRWA, created in 1948 (although its operations in the area did not effectively commence until 1951), has been responsible for the refugees' education, health, and general social services. Its specific mandate has been to assist this population, an acknowledgment by the international community of the scale of the humanitarian crisis.

Behind such statistics, the fact remains that the status of Palestinian refugees, past and future, is still an issue as contentious and politically complex as the future status of East Jerusalem and the fate of Jewish settlements. For the tenuous Palestinian leadership,

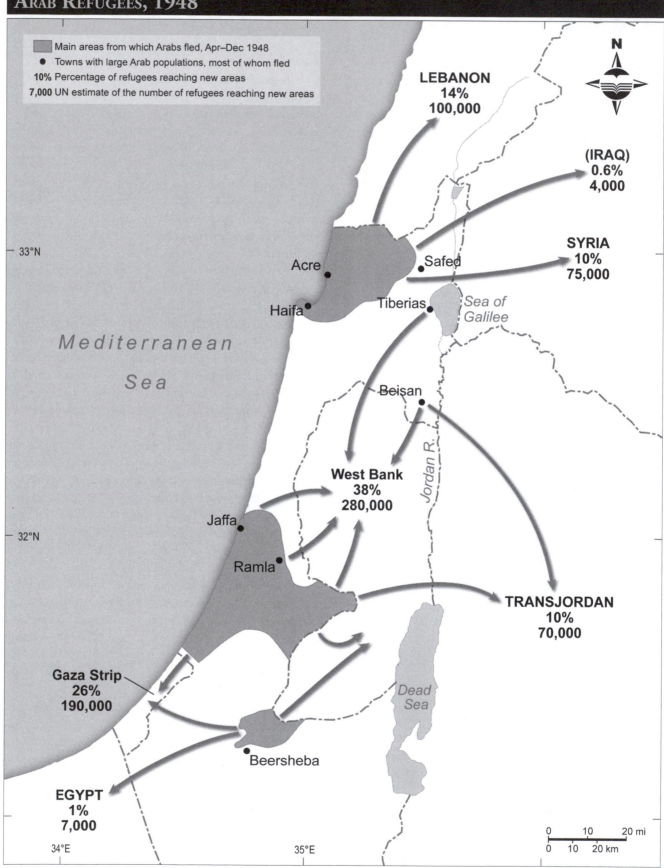

ARAB REFUGEES, 1948

Main areas from which Arabs fled, Apr–Dec 1948
● Towns with large Arab populations, most of whom fled
10% Percentage of refugees reaching new areas
7,000 UN estimate of the number of refugees reaching new areas

N

LEBANON
14%
100,000

(IRAQ)
0.6%
4,000

Acre

Safed

SYRIA
10%
75,000

Haifa

Tiberias

Sea of Galilee

Mediterranean Sea

Beisan

Jordan R.

West Bank
38%
280,000

Jaffa

Ramla

TRANSJORDAN
10%
70,000

Dead Sea

Gaza Strip
26%
190,000

Beersheba

EGYPT
1%
7,000

33°N

32°N

34°E

35°E

0   10   20 mi
0   10   20 km

Palestinian Arabs in the Egyptian prison camp of Abu Ageila on December 15, 1948. (Israeli Government Press Office)

the refugees make up a majority of its wider constituency and, more importantly, their claim of the right of return represents a call for the acknowledgment of and restitution for their wrongful exile during the Nakba of 1947–1948. They point out that the Palestinians who fled their homes at that time were the victims of a Zionist strategy designed to make way for a clear Jewish majority. Many of the refugees themselves cling to keys, deeds, identity cards, and other remnants of their ancestral claims within Israel in the hopes that any eventual final status agreements will allow them to return or receive compensation. Although there have been a number of legal rulings on the illegal seizure of lands and property, finding in favor of Palestinians, no land has been returned.

For Israel to accept a role of responsibility in the refugee crisis would imply by extension that Palestinian exiles have ancestral rights within what is now Israel, therefore weakening the long-standing argument that these refugees should be subsumed into their sister ethnic communities within the Arab states. Furthermore, accepting a right of return for these refugees would shake the foundations of the Israeli state. For its population of 6.7 million, ideologically dependent on a clear Jewish majority of 73 percent (5.1 million people), the addition of 4.1 million Palestinian Arabs would mean a practical end to modern Zionism.

The fate of the Palestinian refugee community, then, represents more than a present humanitarian crisis. It is also a linchpin of the Israeli-Palestinian conflict around which turn some enormously complex issues. Any proposed solution will have real and significant ideological, demographic, and humanitarian consequences. It is thus unsurprising that by the time of this writing, few genuine solutions to the refugee issue have been seriously considered or approached.

Kurt Werthmuller

See also

Black September; Gaza Strip; Intifada, First; Intifada, Second; Israel; Israeli War of Independence, Overview; Lebanon, Civil War in; Palestinian Refugee Camps; Right of Return, Palestinian; United Nations General Assembly Resolution 194; West Bank; Zionism

References

Ateek, Naim, Hilary Rantisi, and Kent Wilkens. *Our Story: The Palestinians.* Jerusalem: Sabeel Ecumenical Liberation Theology Center, 2000.

Fischbach, Michael R. *Records of Dispossession: Palestinian Refugee Property and the Arab-Israeli Conflict.* New York: Columbia University Press, 2003.

Masalha, Nur. *Expulsion of the Palestinians: The Concept of "Transfer" in Zionist Political Thought, 1882–1948.* Washington, DC: Institute for Palestine Studies, 1992.

Morris, Benny. *The Birth of the Palestinian Refugee Problem Revisited.* 2nd ed. Cambridge: Cambridge University Press, 2004.

Shlaim, Avi. *The Iron Wall: Israel and the Arab World.* New York: Norton, 2001.

Smith, Charles D. *Palestine and the Arab-Israeli Conflict: A History with Documents.* 6th ed. New York: Bedford/St. Martin's, 2006.

United Nations Relief and Works Agency. *UNRWA: The United Nations Relief and Works Agency for Palestine Refugees.* Pamphlet. Amman, Jordan: UNRWA Public Information Office, 2003.

———. *UNRWA in Figures.* Pamphlet. Gaza City: UNRWA Public Information Office, March 2004.

EZRA AND NEHEMIA, **Operation**
Start Date: March 1951
End Date: 1952

Operation EZRA AND NEHEMIA (also known as Operation ALI BABA) involved the airlifting of nearly 130,000 Jews from Iraq to Israel in 1951 and 1952. The operation was named for the Jewish biblical leaders who brought the Jews back from Babylonian captivity and rebuilt the temple in Jerusalem. It was the largest and most successful Israeli effort to remove a Jewish community from a hostile nation and bring it to Israel. The operation was a prime example of the Jewish state's commitment to the aliya, or ingathering of Jewish exiles.

The Jewish community in Iraq was one of the oldest in the world, dating back to the Babylonian exile of the sixth century BC. Iraq was a center of Jewish learning and culture as well as having one of the largest Jewish communities outside of Europe. By 1947 it had peaked at 150,000 people. Under some Muslim rulers, members of the community were given high-ranking positions in the Iraqi government. At other times, however, Jews were forced to live in restricted areas and could work only in approved occupations.

During the British administration of Iraq after World War I, conditions in the Jewish community were very good. After Iraqi independence in 1932, however, many Jews were persecuted. Some were killed in mob violence, and synagogues and businesses were destroyed.

At the end of World War II, the dispute over the future of Palestine caused more violence and restrictions against Jews. When the proposed partition of Palestine was announced in 1947, hundreds of young Jews were arrested throughout Iraq. Emigration from Iraq to Palestine was made illegal, although hundreds managed to make

the trip anyway. When Israeli independence was officially declared in May 1948, the Iraqi government made Zionism a capital offense.

The declaration of the State of Israel included a promise that all Jews were welcome to immigrate to the Jewish state. The Law of Return, passed in 1950 by the Knesset (Israeli parliament), promised all Jews the right to come to Israel and immediately receive citizenship. This promise was considered very important, and the Israeli government was determined to do everything possible to gather in the exiled communities. After a series of negotiations, the Iraqi government passed a law in March 1950 legalizing Jewish immigration to Israel. By registering to emigrate, Jews surrendered their Iraqi citizenship. Their assets were also frozen. Property owners were forced to sell their property at a fraction of its true value. Immigrants could take funds only in the form of Ottoman Bank checks. Each adult was limited to $140, while children received about half that. Only 66 pounds of luggage was allowed for each person, and no jewelry could be taken from Iraq.

Despite these conditions, thousands of Jews registered to leave Iraq. While the Iraqi government expected around 8,000 to leave, nearly 105,000 Jews registered to emigrate by March 1951. The Israeli government contracted with the Near East Transport Company to fly the Iraqi Jews to Israel. At first, the former Iraqi Jews had to fly to Nicosia, Cyprus, before transferring to planes that took them to Lod Airport in Israel. After March 1951, the Iraqi government allowed the planes to fly directly to Israel.

By the end of the operation in early 1952, nearly 130,000 Jews had emigrated from Iraq. Besides those who flew out, another 25,000 made their way out illegally via Iran. Special camps were prepared to ease their transition into Israeli society. The Israeli government did all it could to integrate the new arrivals into the fabric of the nation. Operation EZRA AND NEHEMIA served as the model of smaller operations to bring other Jewish groups from Middle Eastern countries into Israel.

TIM J. WATTS

See also

Anti-Semitism; Diaspora; Iraq; Israel

References

Gat, Moseh. *The Jewish Exodus from Iraq, 1948–1951.* London: Frank Cass, 1997.

Hillel, Shlomo. *Operation Babylon.* Garden City, NY: Doubleday, 1987.

Shiblak, Abbas. *Iraqi Jews: A History of the Mass Exodus.* London: Saqi, 2005.

F

Fahd, King of Saudi Arabia
Born: 1922 or 1923
Died: August 1, 2005

King of Saudi Arabia (1982–2005) and 11th son of the founder of Saudi Arabia, Abd al-Aziz ibn Abd al-Rahman al-Saud (commonly known as Ibn Saud). Fahd ibn Abdel Aziz al-Saud was born in 1922 or 1923 in Riyadh, the current capital of Saudi Arabia. At the time of his birth, his father was in the process of building modern Saudi Arabia, and during the 1920s Ibn Saud gained control over the Hejaz, the western region where the Holy Cities of Mecca and Medina are located.

Fahd was one of Ibn Saud's 37 officially recognized sons. According to the Kingdom of Saudi Arabia's 1992 Basic Law, only sons and grandsons of monarchs are eligible to be kings of Saudi Arabia. Fahd was the eldest of the so-called Sudayri Seven, the seven sons fathered by Ibn Saud with his favorite wife, Hussah bint Ahmad al-Sudayri. These seven brothers formed a close-knit group within the Saudi royal family. Fahd's full brothers include Sultan bin Abd al-Aziz, the minister of defense since 1963 and crown prince since August 1, 2005; Nayif bin Abd al-Aziz, the interior minister since 1975; and Salman bin Abdul Aziz, the governor of Riyadh. All of his brothers are considered potential future kings of Saudi Arabia.

Fahd was educated at the Princes' School, an educational institution established by Ibn Saud to educate members of the royal family. In 1945, Fahd accompanied his half brother Faisal to New York City to attend the first session of the General Assembly of the United Nations (UN). At the time Faisal, who eventually became Saudi Arabia's third king, was the foreign minister.

From 1953 to 1960, Fahd served as the minister of education. In 1959, he led the Saudi delegation to the meeting of the League of Arab States. In 1964, he became interior minister. In this capacity, he ordered mass arrests after several terrorist attacks on oil facilities and government ministries. He also reportedly put down a coup attempt in 1968. Later he assumed the post of second deputy prime minister.

Following the assassination of King Faisal by his nephew on March 25, 1975, Fahd was named crown prince of Saudi Arabia. By 1981, because of King Khalid's incapacitating illness, Fahd became the de facto ruler of Saudi Arabia. In August 1981, Crown Prince Fahd advanced an eight-point plan to solve the Israeli-Palestinian-Arab dispute consisting of Israeli withdrawal from 1967 to 1948 boundaries, dismantling of post-1967 Israeli settlements, guaranteed freedom of worship for all religious groups at the holy sites, affirmation of the right of return for Palestinians and compensation for those who did not wish to return, and a transitional UN authority over the West Bank and Gaza Strip leading to an independent Palestinian state with Jerusalem as its capital, a guarantee of peace for all nations in the region, and a guarantee of the agreements by the UN or selected UN member states. Israel rejected the proposal.

Following the death of King Khalid on June 13, 1982, Fahd formally assumed the throne. During his reign, Fahd pursued a policy of open friendship with the United States while also attempting to take a leading role in Islamic and Arab issues in the Middle East. He encouraged fairly aggressive economic development policies in Saudi Arabia based on the nation's vast oil wealth and consistently sought to develop plans for economic diversification. Although Saudi Arabia remained one of the most traditional Islamic societies during Fahd's rule, advancements were nevertheless realized in technology, infrastructure, and education. Within Saudi Arabia, Islamic fundamentalists were the king's greatest critics.

King Fahd of Saudi Arabia (1982–2005), January 1987. (Peter Turnley/ Corbis)

On November 22, 1979, heavily armed ultra-Wahhabists, led by Juhayman Utaybi, seized the Kaaba holy shrine within the Grand Mosque at Mecca and held hostages there for two weeks until the Wahhabists were ousted. Utaybi and 62 others were subsequently beheaded. The rebels had accused the Saudi royal family of bowing to secularism. Later, Iranian Islamic revolutionaries made similar claims in a propaganda war against the Saudis.

In August 1990, after Saddam Hussein's forces invaded and occupied Kuwait, Fahd agreed to allow U.S. and allied troops into Saudi Arabia. He did this mainly out of concern that Hussein also had his eye on Saudi Arabia and its vast oil reserves. Fahd's decision earned him the condemnation of many Islamic extremists, including the terrorist Osama bin Laden. Bin Laden himself was from a wealthy Saudi family.

After 1990, Fahd and Hussein became implacable enemies. Fahd was an avid supporter of the UN. Indeed, that organization's backing of the plan to expel Iraqi forces from Kuwait helped Fahd in his decision to allow U.S. troops access to his country. He also supported the Palestinian cause and repeatedly criticized the Israeli government's policies toward the Palestine Liberation Organization (PLO).

After Fahd suffered a debilitating stroke in 1995, many of his official duties as monarch were delegated to his brother, Crown Prince Abdullah. Although Fahd still attended government meetings, he spent increasing amounts of time on his 200-acre estate in Marbella, Spain. After the terrorist attacks of September 11, 2001, Fahd's government fully supported the so-called war on terror and mounted its own counterterrorism campaign against Al Qaeda operatives in Saudi Arabia. Fahd died of pneumonia in Riyadh on August 1, 2005. At the time of his death, he was considered one of the richest men in the world, with a personal fortune worth more than $20 billion. He was succeeded by his brother Abdullah.

MICHAEL R. HALL

See also

Abdullah, King of Saudi Arabia; Faisal, King of Saudi Arabia; Ibn Saud, King of Saudi Arabia; Iran-Iraq War; Persian Gulf War; Saudi Arabia

References

Farsy, Fouad. *Custodian of the Two Holy Mosques: King Fahd bin Abdul Aziz.* New York: Knight Communications, 2001.
Henderson, Simon. *After King Fu'ad: Succession in Saudi Arabia.* Washington, DC: Washington Institute for Near East Policy, 1994.

Faisal, King of Saudi Arabia
Born: 1903 or 1906
Died: March 25, 1975

Third king of Saudi Arabia, reigning from 1964 to 1975. King Faisal ibn Abd al-Aziz al-Saud was born in Riyadh in 1903 (some sources claim 1906), the fourth son of King Abd al-Aziz ibn Saud, founder of the Saudi dynasty. In 1925 Faisal, in command of an army of Saudi loyalists, won a decisive victory over Hussein ibn Ali in the Hejaz region of western Arabia. In reward Faisal was made the governor of Hejaz the following year. After the new Kingdom of Saudi Arabia was formalized, he was named minister of foreign affairs in 1932, a post he would hold until 1964.

During the first oil boom of 1947–1952, Faisal played a key role in shaping Saudi policies. In 1953 when his elder half brother Saud became king, Faisal was declared crown prince and continued as foreign minister. In 1958 during an economic and internal political crisis, a council of princes within the Saud family sought to oust Saud and replace him with Faisal. Faisal was unwilling to endorse this political change. Instead, Faisal received full executive powers as president of the reconstituted council of ministers. Saud and some supporters seized executive authority again in 1960 when Faisal was out of the country, and in response Faisal resigned.

Faisal returned to the government in 1962, when he assumed virtually full executive authority. When Saud's health began to fail, Faisal was appointed regent, assuming office on March 4, 1964. On November 2 of that year, he became king after his brother Saud was finally officially forced to abdicate by the ruling family and left for Greece.

Faisal, king of Saudi Arabia during 1964–1975. (Library of Congress)

Although a traditionalist in many ways, King Faisal proved to be a farsighted innovator and administrator who modernized the ministries of government and established for the first time an efficient bureaucracy. In the course of his reign, he also initiated a number of major economic and social development plans. Under Faisal, the industrial development of the Kingdom of Saudi Arabia began in earnest.

Using Saudi Arabia's vast oil revenues, which grew from $334 million in 1960 to $22.5 billion in 1974, Faisal established state benefits, including medical care and education to the postgraduate level. His government subsidized food, water, fuel, electricity, and rents. Faisal also introduced reforms such as girls' schools and television, which was hotly protested. Indeed, these reforms were opposed by many Saudis including members of the royal family, who saw them as counter to the tenets of Islam.

Saudi Arabia joined the Arab states in the Six-Day War of 1967, but Faisal was devastated when Israel won the conflict. In 1973 he began a program intended to increase the military power of Saudi Arabia. On October 17 he withdrew Saudi oil from world markets, quadrupling the price of oil worldwide. Reacting to U.S. assistance to Israel during the 1973 Yom Kippur War, Faisal's action was the primary force behind the 1973 oil crisis, which limited American and European access to Saudi oil. It also empowered the Organization of Petroleum Exporting Countries (OPEC), which was further

empowered to set the supply and price of oil supplies. In 1974 Faisal was named *Time* magazine's Man of the Year.

On March 25, 1975, Faisal was shot and killed by his nephew, Prince Faisal ibn Musad. It is generally believed that the prince wanted to avenge his elder brother, who was killed by security forces in a clash over the introduction of television into the kingdom in 1966. Ibn Musad's father had sought vengeance against his son's killer, but the ruler had deemed that the authorities were in the right. Some speculated that when the younger Faisal was in the United States, drug use might have further impaired his judgment. Ibn Musad was captured shortly after the attack. Declared sane, he was tried and found guilty of regicide and was beheaded in a public square in Riyadh in June 1975. King Faisal was succeeded by his half brother, Crown Prince Khalid.

JAMES H. WILLBANKS

See also

Organization of Petroleum Exporting Countries; Saudi Arabia; Six-Day War; Yom Kippur War

References

Beling, William A., ed. *King Faisal and the Modernization of Saudi Arabia.* Boulder, CO: Westview, 1980.

De Gaury, Gerald. *Faisal: Biography of a King.* New York: Praeger, 1967.

Holden, David, and Richard Johns. *The House of Saud.* New York: Holt, Rinehart and Winston, 1982.

Faisal I, King of Iraq
Born: May 20, 1885
Died: September 8, 1933

Arab Revolt and nationalist leader, later king of Syria and Iraq. Born on May 20, 1885, in Taif near Mecca, Prince Faisal ibn Hussein of the Kingdom of Hejaz was the third son of Hussein ibn Ali. Faisal's early childhood was spent in Arabia. From 1891 he was educated in Constantinople, where his father lived under house arrest at the order of the Ottoman sultan, who was trying to control Arab nationalist leaders. In 1908 his family returned to Mecca after his father had been appointed sharif of Mecca. Gathering support from nationalists and the British, Sharif Hussein proclaimed the Arab Revolt against the Ottoman Empire on June 10, 1916.

As part of that revolt, Faisal served as his father's principal military commander. His brother Ali ibn Hussein attacked Medina. That attack and another on Wadi Safra were both repulsed. Faisal moved with the Northern Arab Army, utilizing Bedouin irregular forces as well as deserters from the Ottoman Army. Lieutenant Colonel T. E. Lawrence described Faisal as an excellent Arab chieftain, or emir. By dint of personal courage and leadership, Faisal received the fierce loyalty of the Arab fighters drawn to his cause.

In early 1917 Faisal led the Northern Arab Army of some 10,000 men north to Wajh. With Faisal's authorization, Lawrence then led the raid that captured Aqaba, which became the next staging area for the army. In the autumn of 1917 Faisal was made a British general under the commander of Egyptian Expeditionary Force, General Edmund Allenby, who had been charged with carrying the campaign from the Transjordan region to Damascus.

As the fighting in 1918 progressed, Faisal moved his headquarters from Aqaba northward and then to Azraq. Meanwhile, the Southern Division of the Arab Army immobilized the Turkish garrisons at Medina. The Arab forces were also successful in the north at Maan and easily triumphed over the remaining resistance blocking the way to Damascus. Faisal entered Damascus in triumph on October 3, 1918, then headed a provisional government. Because the British had promised him a united Arab state, he was angered to learn that Britain had agreed to the French Mandate for Syria. At the 1919 Paris Peace Conference he declared, "We desire, passionately, one thing—independence."

In March 1920 the Syrian National Congress proclaimed Faisal king, but the French expelled him, defeating his forces in the Battle of Maysalun. With British intervention, he was made king of Iraq in 1921. King Faisal died on September 8, 1933, in Bern, Switzerland, while undergoing treatment for heart problems.

ANDREW J. WASKEY

See also

Allenby, Sir Edmund Henry Hynman, 1st Viscount; Arab Revolt of 1916–1918; Bedouin; Hussein ibn Ali, Sharif of Mecca; Iraq; Lawrence, Thomas Edward

References

Erskine, Beatrice. *King Faisal of Iraq*. London: Hutchinson, 1933.
Lawrence, T. E. *Revolt in the Desert*. Herefordshire, UK: Wordsworth Editions, 1997.

Faisal II, King of Iraq
Born: May 2, 1935
Died: July 14, 1958

King of Iraq from 1939 to 1958. Faisal was born in Baghdad on May 2, 1935. He was the only son of the second king of Iraq, Ghazi II, who died in an automobile accident in 1938. Until Faisal turned 18 in 1953, his uncle, Abd al-Ilah, served as regent of Iraq and de facto head of state.

Faisal meanwhile studied at the Harrow School in Great Britain with his cousin, the future King Hussein of Jordan. The two men enjoyed a close relationship, and both would subsequently face growing militant Pan-Arab nationalism in the Middle East. In 1952, Faisal graduated and returned to Iraq.

Following World War I, the British received a League of Nations mandate over Iraq. The British were soon confronted with a fierce rebellion against their rule during 1920–1922, however. In restoring order and stability in Iraq, they installed on the Iraqi throne a member of the Hashemite family, Faisal I (the grandfather of Faisal II), to whom they had earlier promised the throne of Syria. Some

Faisal II, king of Iraq (1939–1958), shown during a state visit to London, July 17, 1956. (Bettmann/Corbis)

Iraqis viewed the members of the Iraqi royal family as foreigners, as they hailed from the Hejaz, a western area of the Arabian Peninsula. Others supported Faisal I, who had symbolized the Arab cause for independence in the Arab Revolt. Many political followers of Faisal I accompanied him from Syria to Iraq, including Iraqi former Ottoman Army officers who provided a base of power for him. His son Ghazi was popular with Iraqis but was not an adept ruler. The royal family's pro-British policies and those of Nuri al-Said Pasha, who had held as many as 48 cabinet positions, including repeated stints as prime minister, caused Faisal II and the regent to be viewed by Iraqis as puppets of the British government.

By 1940 the most powerful group in Iraqi politics was the Golden Square of four army colonels, led by Colonel Salah al-Din al-Sabagh, an Arab nationalist who supported the Palestinian cause. The British regarded the Golden Square as a distinct threat and sympathetic to the Axis cause. In April 1941 Colonel Rashid Ali al-Gaylani, part of this group, engineered a military coup in Iraq, sent Abd al-Ilah into exile, and proclaimed himself regent. Rashid Ali sought to pursue a foreign policy independent of the United Kingdom. The young King Faisal went into seclusion outside of Baghdad. Within a month, however, a combined force of the Royal Iraqi Air Force, Jordan's Arab Legion, and a contingent of British troops defeated Rashid Ali's forces and restored Abd al-Ilah as regent. Faisal II then returned to Baghdad. In May 1953, upon his 18th birthday, he assumed full governing responsibility over Iraq.

In his policies, Faisal II was guided by his mentor and uncle, Abd al-Ilah, and pro-British prime minister Nuri al-Said. Many Iraqis became disillusioned with Faisal's foreign policy during the 1950s, however. Arab nationalists opposed the government's pro-Western stance on diplomatic issues. In 1955, Iraq joined the U.S.-inspired anti-Soviet Middle East Treaty Organization (also known as the Baghdad Pact). Its members included Iraq, the United States (as an associate member), the United Kingdom, Turkey, Pakistan, and Iran. The Arab nationalist president of Egypt, Gamal Abdel Nasser, strongly opposed the pact, arguing that threats to the Middle East originated in Israel, not from the Soviet Union. During the 1956 Suez Crisis, Iraqis supported Egypt's resistance to the coordinated attack undertaken by Great Britain, France, and Israel. The Iraqi government's relationship with Great Britain, however, caused tensions concerning the rise of Nasserists and Pan-Arabists in Iraq after this crisis.

In response to Egypt's February 1, 1958, union with Syria known as the United Arab Republic (UAR), the Hashemite monarchs of Jordan and Iraq created the Arab Federation of Iraq and Jordan on February 14, 1958. Faisal II became head of state of the new federation.

In June 1958, King Hussein of Jordan requested military assistance from Iraq to quell disturbances fueled by Arab nationalists. Faisal ordered troops to Jordan, including a division of the Iraqi Army under the command of General Abdul Karim Qassem, a staunch opponent of British ambitions in the Middle East. On July 14, 1958, using the troop movements as a cover, Qassem overthrew the monarchy and proclaimed a republic. Members of the royal family, including King Faisal II, were murdered and their bodies mutilated. Prince Zayid, the youngest brother of Faisal I, was in London at the time of the coup and became the heir-in-exile to the Iraqi throne. When Zayid died in 1970, he was succeeded as heir-in-exile by his son, Raad, an adviser to Jordan's King Abdullah.

MICHAEL R. HALL AND SHERIFA ZUHUR

See also

Arab Legion; Baghdad Pact; Hussein, King of Jordan; Iraq; Iraq, Armed Forces; Nasser, Gamal Abdel; Said, Nuri al-; Suez Crisis

References

Eppel, Michael. *Iraq from Monarchy to Tyranny: From the Hashemites to the Rise of Saddam.* Gainesville: University Press of Florida, 2004.
Marr, Phebe. *The Modern History of Iraq.* 2nd ed. Boulder, CO: Westview, 2003.

Falwell, Jerry
Born: August 11, 1933
Died: May 15, 2007

Conservative American fundamentalist Baptist pastor, educator, author, televangelist, and pro-Israel activist. Jerry Lamon Falwell was born in Lynchburg, Virginia, on August 11, 1933, and graduated with a degree in Bible studies from the Baptist Bible College in Springfield, Missouri, in 1956. That same year he returned to Lynchburg and founded the Thomas Road Bible Church (TRBC). Church membership grew from the original 35 members in 1956 to 24,000 by 2006. Falwell also founded the Lynchburg Baptist College (now Liberty University) in 1971.

In 1979 Falwell and Ed McAteer founded the Moral Majority, a conservative Christian lobbying group that stood against abortion, pornography, feminism, and homosexuality and advocated the increased role of religion in public schools and traditional family values. The Moral Majority was highly influential in the election of Republican Ronald Reagan to the presidency in 1980 and also championed continued American support of Israel. Meanwhile, Falwell had developed a national following through his television and radio programming. The *Old Time Gospel Hour,* still in production, broadcasts the TRBC's Sunday morning services, and *Listen America Radio* produces three-minute news and commentary segments featuring the opinions of various conservatives.

During the 1990s, Falwell was a vehement opponent of President Bill and First Lady Hillary Clinton. Falwell actively promoted a video titled *The Clinton Chronicles* that preposterously accused the Clintons of complicity in the suicide death of White House counsel Vincent Foster.

Falwell's resolute support of Israel has been referred to as Christian Zionism. He and other American Christian Zionists contend that conservative American Christians are the staunchest and most loyal supporters of Israel and that this 70-million-strong bloc will closely monitor American policies toward Israel. In January 1998 Falwell stated that if need be he could contact 200,000 evangelical pastors on behalf of Israel. He proved this point when he responded to President George W. Bush's April 2002 prodding of Israel to remove its tanks from Palestinian towns on the West Bank with a personal letter of protest followed by more than 100,000 e-mails from Christian conservatives. The tanks remained, and Bush issued no follow-up call for their withdrawal.

Falwell believed that the return of the Jews to their homeland resumed a prophetic cycle that had ended with the destruction of Jerusalem and the temple in AD 70. The formation of the State of Israel in 1948 was the necessary component that restarted the prophetic cycle, which will end with the Second Coming of Jesus. Israel's retaking of the Western (Wailing) Wall, the only remaining wall of Solomon's original temple, and of the Temple Mount during the 1967 Six-Day War was seen as a further progression of the

Rev. Jerry Falwell, American fundamentalist Baptist pastor, educator, author, televangelist, and pro-Israel activist, January 1986. (Bettmann/Corbis)

cycle that would ultimately lead to the end of the world. Falwell viewed the continued war and upheaval in the Middle East as drawing the world closer to Armageddon, the final battle played out as prophesied in the Revelation of John.

Falwell viewed Israel as the catalyst necessary for the completion of this cycle. To this end, he agreed with former Israeli prime minister Menachem Begin that the boundaries of ancient Judea and Samaria must be maintained at all costs. Falwell therefore opposed all land concessions to the Palestinian Authority (PA), including the West Bank and Gaza. He thus saw Prime Minister Yitzhak Rabin's signing of the 1993 Oslo Accords and offer to trade land for peace as a terrible sin.

Falwell also asserted that Islam is not a religion of peace and that the Prophet Muhammad was a terrorist. A fatwa encouraging the murder of Falwell was promptly issued by Iranian clerics on October 11, 2002, after Falwell's incendiary characterization was aired on CBS on national television in October 2002. Falwell continued to lobby for the interests of the far Christian Right and remained an important emblem to advance their agenda until his death in Lynchburg on May 15, 2007.

RICHARD M. EDWARDS

See also

Begin, Menachem; Haram al-Sharif; Oslo Accords; Rabin, Yitzhak; Western Wall

References

Falwell, Jerry. *Falwell: An Autobiography.* New York: Liberty House, 1996.

Gorenberg, Gershom. *The End of Days: Fundamentalism and the Struggle for the Temple Mount.* New York: Oxford University Press, 2000.

Harding, Susan Friend. *The Book of Jerry Falwell: Fundamentalist Language and Politics.* Princeton, NJ: Princeton University Press, 2001.

Simon, Merrill. *Jerry Falwell and the Jews.* New York: Jonathan David, 1999.

Farouk I, King of Egypt
Born: February 11, 1920
Died: March 18, 1965

Farouk I was the king of Egypt from 1936 to 1952, when a military coup forced him to abdicate. Born on February 11, 1920, in Cairo, Egypt, he was the only surviving son of King Fuad I (1868–1936).

Farouk I, the last king of Egypt, succeeded his father in 1936. Forced to abdicate in 1952, Farouk lived in exile until his death in 1965. (Library of Congress)

Farouk was the penultimate monarch of a family of Albanian and Turko-Circassian origin that had ruled Egypt since 1801, when the Ottoman sultan appointed Muhammad Ali Pasha the viceroy, or khedive, of Egypt. Whereas Muhammad Ali was a strong and competent ruler, his heirs proved to be both weak and corrupt.

Technically, the Ottoman Empire continued to rule Egypt until 1922, when the British granted Egypt independence. Educated in Egypt and England, Farouk ascended the throne at age 16. It was not until 1938, however, when he turned 18 that he was vested with complete royal authority. Unlike his father, who was regarded as a strong personality, Farouk proved a great disappointment.

A member of one of the world's wealthiest families, Farouk was enamored with the glamorous royal lifestyle and corrupted by those around him who catered to his whims. He owned dozens of palaces, hundreds of cars, and vast estates and also managed to offend many with his indiscreet behavior. Despite the hardships faced by the Egyptian people during World War II, Farouk continued to lavishly entertain his guests in his royal palaces. His fondness for European casinos, night clubs, and women was criticized by pious Muslims in Egypt.

There was strong sentiment in Egypt in favor of the Axis side during World War II, if only for the hope that this might bring inde-

pendence from the British. Although Farouk tried to keep Egypt neutral during the war, Egypt's treaty obligations with Britain forced him to support the Allied cause. In 1942 the British also forced Farouk, by surrounding his palace with tanks, to appoint a pro-British prime minister, which greatly undermined the king's legitimacy in the eyes of his people. In an attempt to regain legitimacy, Farouk supported the creation of the Arab League in 1945. Although that organization came to be headquartered in Cairo, resentment against the king among rank-and-file Egyptians continued to grow.

Egypt's humiliating defeat in the Israeli War of Independence (1948–1949) caused heightened Arab nationalism and resentment against Farouk in Egypt. Although Farouk was not directly involved in the planning of Egypt's military strategy, many Egyptians argued that the monarch's wealth should have been used to assist the Egyptian military effort.

Attacks by the British in the Suez Canal Zone on Egyptian police, together with the king's blatant corruption, led to his overthrow in the July Revolution of 1952. Egypt's new leaders forced Farouk to abdicate on July 26. Although his infant son Fuad II was nominally king for one year after his abdication, a republic was declared in 1953.

Farouk then took up residence in Monaco, where he obtained citizenship in 1959. The 300-pound former monarch, who had a penchant for heavy meals, died of a heart attack on March 18, 1965, while at dinner in Rome.

MICHAEL R. HALL

See also
Arab League; Egypt; Muslim Brotherhood; Nasser, Gamal Abdel

References
McLeave, Hugh. *The Last Pharaoh: Farouk of Egypt.* New York: McCall, 1970.
Sabit, Adel M. *A King Betrayed: The Ill-Fated Reign of Farouk of Egypt.* London: Quartet, 1989.
Stadiem, William. *Too Rich: The High Life and Tragic Death of King Farouk.* New York: Carroll and Graf, 1991.

Fatah

Highly influential political, military, and governing faction within the Palestine Liberation Organization (PLO). Fatah, meaning "victory" or "conquest" in Arabic, is a reverse acronym of Harakat al-Tahrir al-Watani al-Falastini (Palestinian National Liberation Movement) and was formally organized on December 31, 1964.

For much of its official history, Yasser Arafat (also PLO chairman from 1969 until his death in 2004) served as the party chief, although the beginnings of Fatah date to the late 1950s when Palestinian groups began fighting the Israelis during their occupation of the Gaza Strip. Fatah's founders include Arafat, Salah Khalaf, Khalil al-Wazir (Abu Jihad), and Khalid Hassan. Fatah was a combination of a political organization (al-Tanzim) and paramilitary cells, the objective of which was the liberation of Palestine, armed resistance

Fatah militiamen rest under a tent close to the Jordan River at Baquar, Jordan, on November 4, 1969. (AFP/Getty Images)

to Israel, and the creation of a Palestinian state. From the late 1960s, Fatah was larger than many of the other groups under the umbrella of the PLO because it did not avidly espouse their Marxist-Leninist doctrines. Consequently, Fatah has experienced a larger Muslim-to-Christian ratio than the small progressive parties. And because Fatah controlled much of the monetary resources of the PLO, it wielded considerable influence.

Fatah has undergone many transformations over the years and until very recently hardly resembled a political party in the traditional sense. In its first years, the group eschewed the establishment of a formal organizational structure and indirectly appealed to the Palestinian Diaspora in Syria, Jordan, Egypt, Lebanon, Iraq, the Gulf States, and Western countries. Fatah had a following not only in the Diaspora but also in the important structures such as the General Union of Palestinian Students, the General Union of Palestinian Workers, and the General Union of Palestinian Women. Fatah published an occasional periodical titled *Filastinuna* (Our Palestine).

Early on and from the 1967 defeat until about 1974, Fatah embraced the concept of armed confrontation as the primary means of achieving a unified, independent Palestine. Fatah's pragmatism

ensured it a large base of support and also created a de facto ideology that stressed Palestinian unity, with the idea that although Palestinians might have varied approaches to their problems, they could all be united in their three major goals: the destruction of Israel, political freedom from Arab nations, and the creation of a Palestinian state.

Although Fatah did not initially maintain an organizational hierarchy (it was more along the lines of an uncoordinated series of factions, each led by a different head), it did quickly establish a coherent military force capable of harassing the Israelis. Several militant groups based in Jordan were involved in attacks on Israel, among them the Asifah group, and their actions and the Israeli response caused a crackdown and their expulsion by King Hussein of Jordan. That expulsion in 1970, known as Black September, did, however, create fissures between the rightists and leftists within Fatah and with the broader Palestinian movement. When Fatah reconstituted itself in Lebanon beginning in 1970, it found that resisting involvement in the internal machinations of its host country was impossible. This diminished its effectiveness and made it more prone to pressure from other Arab states. Soon enough, conflict among Fatah members surfaced when some in the group began to espouse a two-state solution to the Palestinian-Israeli conflict, which outraged many.

Soon embroiled in the Lebanese Civil War that began in 1975, Fatah continued to sponsor attacks against Israeli interests, including two massive assaults on Israeli territory in 1975 with the loss of many lives. In 1982, the PLO (and thus Fatah) was forced out of Lebanon by the Israeli invasion of that country. From 1982 to 1993 Fatah, along with the PLO, was located in Tunisia. In 1983 an anti-Arafatist revolt occurred that was led by Said Muragha (Abu Musa). He created a splinter group known as Fatah Uprising, which was backed by Syrian officials. Meanwhile, Fatah's Revolutionary Council and the Revolutionary Council Emergency Command both broke with Fatah over policy issues. Despite these setbacks, Fatah remained the preeminent Palestinian faction, and Arafat maintained an iron grip over Fatah.

Many in Fatah's leading group had supported a two-state solution ever since the Rabat conference of 1974 and realized that this meant tacit recognition of Israel. Fatah's leadership also concluded that armed conflict was not moving the organization any closer to its goal of a Palestinian state. By 1988 Arafat had recognized Israel's right to exist explicitly in meetings and proposed the pursuit of diplomacy and a land-for-peace arrangement.

Arafat supported Saddam Hussein in the 1991 Persian Gulf War because of Hussein's support of Fatah. This support, however, led to the mass exile of Palestinians from Kuwait after the war and difficult economic times for the Palestinians in general. Consequently, as the effort to reach a comprehensive accord in Madrid was occurring, Arafat had agreed to a secret Palestinian-Israeli track in Oslo, Norway.

The 1993 Oslo Accords and the 1994 creation of the Palestinian Authority (PA) witnessed the relocation of the PLO and Fatah to Gaza and the West Bank. This finally centered the Palestinian power base in Palestine after almost 50 years of transience. But by this time, the Palestinians were no longer entirely represented by the Tunisian old guard of Fatah. Younger leaders were frustrated with the policies of the longtime exiles and with major financial difficulties and corruption. Also, Islamist organizations such as Islamic Jihad of Palestine and especially Hamas had begun to attract far more support from the Palestinian population than Fatah. Arafat clung to power, still recognized for his many years of devotion to the Palestinian cause. In January 1996 he was elected as the PA's first president. He now simultaneously held the positions of PLO chairman, PA president, and leader of Fatah.

Fatah essentially controlled the PA bureaucracy, although the fissures within the organization began to grow deeper. While Fatah

A Palestinian woman passes under Hamas and Fatah flags as she arrives to vote at a polling station in the West Bank village of Hawarra, January 25, 2006. (David Silverman/Getty Images)

attempted to push ahead with the Palestinian-Israeli peace process, certain members who were opposed to it began to sabotage Arafat. Now the group was divided by hard-liners versus peace proponents, old guard versus youths, and bureaucrats versus revolutionaries. The Second (al-Aqsa) Intifada, which broke out in September 2000, saw the embattled Fatah become even more divided against itself. Fatah member Marwan Barghuti organized a militia called al-Tanzim, whose goal was attacking Israeli forces. And in 2002, the al-Aqsa Martyrs Brigades, another faction consisting of local militias and theoretically aligned with Fatah, began launching major attacks against Israeli forces as well. To punish the PA for a particularly heinous suicide bombing in the spring of 2002, the Israelis reoccupied much of the West Bank. Arafat was trapped in his own headquarters, and much of the rebuilding and the infrastructure in the West Bank were destroyed. Israeli officials had periodically launched campaigns against Arafat's leadership, and these were now revived.

Now under enormous pressure from Israel and the United States, Arafat reluctantly acquiesced to the creation of a new position within the PA, that of prime minister. In April 2003 he named Mahmoud Abbas to the post. However, after months of infighting, Abbas resigned from office in September 2003. Then in February 2004, 300 Fatah members resigned in unison to show their contempt for their leadership. A hasty convening of Fatah's Revolutionary Council was called, but the meeting accomplished nothing and resulted in bitter recriminations from all sides.

Arafat died on November 11, 2004, and this threw Fatah and the PA into more turmoil. Days after Arafat's death, Fatah's Central Committee named Farouk Qaddumi to replace him. This was in itself problematic because Qaddumi, unlike his predecessor, did not support the peace process. Meanwhile, Abbas was named to succeed Arafat as PLO chairman. For the first time, Fatah and the PLO were not controlled by the same person. After bitter political machinations, Fatah decided to put Abbas up as its presidential candidate in the January 2005 election. Abbas was strongly challenged in this by Barghuti, who vowed to run as an independent from a jail cell in Israel. Barghuti, who came under intense pressure to bow out, finally did so, opening the way for Abbas's victory in January 2005.

Abbas's victory, however, was not a harbinger of a resurgent and unified Fatah. In the December 2004 municipal elections for the PA, Hamas had racked up impressive gains. Then, in December 2005, Barghuti formed a rival political alliance, al-Mustaqbal, vowing to run a new slate of candidates for the January 2006 PA legislative elections. At the last moment, the two factions decided to run a single slate, but this temporary rapprochement was not enough to prevent a stunning victory for Hamas. In fact, Hamas's strength did not rest simply on the divisions within Fatah. Indeed, Hamas won 74 seats to Fatah's 45, although Hamas had captured only 43 percent of the popular vote. The election allowed Hamas to form its own government and elect a prime minister, Ismail Haniyeh, who assumed the premiership in February 2006. As a result of the Hamas victory, the United States and some European nations cut off funding to the PA in protest of the group's electoral success. This placed the PA in a state of crisis, as no civil servants could be paid, and hospitals and clinics had no supplies. For more than a year, and despite an agreement between Hamas and Fatah, the U.S. government continued to state that only if Hamas renounced its violent intentions against Israel in a format satisfactory to Israel and the United States would any funds be allowed into the PA.

On March 17, 2007, Abbas brokered a Palestinian unity government that included both Fatah and Hamas, with Hamas leader Haniyeh becoming prime minister. Yet in May, violence between Hamas and Fatah escalated. Following the Hamas takeover of Gaza on June 14, Abbas dissolved the Hamas-led unity government and declared a state of emergency. On June 18, having been assured of European Union (EU) support, Abbas also dissolved the National Security Council and swore in an emergency Palestinian government. That same day, the United States ended its 15-month embargo on the PA and resumed aid in an effort to strengthen Abbas's government, which was now limited to the West Bank. On June 19 Abbas cut off all ties and dialogue with Hamas, pending the return of Gaza. In a further move to strengthen the perceived moderate Abbas, on July 1 Israel restored financial ties to the PA.

Today, Fatah is recognized by Palestinians as a full-fledged political party, with the attendant organizational structures that have in fact been in place for several decades. Competition between its four major parties caused problems in the past, but today it is the competition with Hamas that appears more pressing. Fatah can either purge itself of the rampant corruption among its ranks or risk the status quo and the mass exodus of disaffected party members that will likely follow.

PAUL G. PIERPAOLI JR. AND SHERIFA ZUHUR

See also

Abbas, Mahmoud; Al-Aqsa Martyrs Brigades; Arafat, Yasser; Barghuti, Marwan; Black September; Hamas; Intifada, Second; Islamic Jihad, Palestinian; Lebanon, Civil War in; Oslo Accords; Palestine Liberation Organization; Palestinian Authority; Ramallah

References

Aburish, Said K. *Arafat: From Defender to Dictator.* New York: Bloomsbury, 1998.

Hart, Alan. *Arafat: A Political Biography.* Rev. ed. London: Sidgwick and Jackson, 1994.

Jamal, Amal. *The Palestinian National Movement: Politics of Contention, 1967–2005.* Bloomington: Indiana University Press, 2005.

Kurz, Anat N. *Fatah and the Politics of Violence: The Institutionalization of a Popular Struggle.* Eastbourne, East Sussex, UK: Sussex Academic, 2006.

Rubin, Barry. *The Transformation of Palestinian Politics: From Revolution to State-Building.* Cambridge: Harvard University Press, 2001.

Said, Edward W. *Peace and Its Discontents: Essays on Palestine in the Middle East Process.* New York: Vintage Books, 1995.

Fatwa

The fatwa (singular, *responsa*) or fatawa (plural, *responsae*) is a question and answer process referred to in the Koran (4:127, 176)

An Afghani shows a copy of an Islamic decree, or fatwa, in Spin Boldak on the southern Afghan border, December 11, 2005. (Saeed Ali Achakzai/Reuters/Corbis)

that began in early Islam as a means to impart knowledge about theology, philosophy, hadith, legal theory, religious duties, and, later and more specifically, Sharia, or Islamic law. Fatawa may deal with a much broader series of subjects than did the Islamic courts, and a fatwa, unlike a court ruling, is not binding. The reason it is not binding is that in a court, a qadi (judge) is concerned with evidentiary matters and may actually investigate these and hear two sides to an argument, but a cleric or authority issuing a fatwa is responding instead to just one party, should the question involve a dispute, and thus the question might be formulated in a particular way.

In modern times, a fatwa is usually defined as a legal opinion given by someone with expertise in Islamic law. However, so long as a person mentions the sources he uses in a legal opinion, other Muslim authorities or figures may issue fatawa. A modern fatwa usually responds to a question about an action, form of behavior, or practice that classifies it as being obligatory, forbidden, permitted, recommended, or reprehensible. Traditionally, a fatwa could be issued by a Muslim scholar knowledgeable of both the subject

and the theories of jurisprudence. These persons might be part of or independent from the court systems. However, other persons might issue fatawa as well. Muslim governments typically designated a chief mufti who had the role of the sheikh of Islam in the Ottoman Empire.

In the colonial period, the Islamic madrassas, or institutes of Islamic education, began to include a fatwa-issuing office, dar al-ifta, in some cases. Muslim governments continued in efforts to control and limit the issuing of fatawa, as in the Higher Council of Ulama or Permanent Council for Scientific Research and Legal Opinions in Saudi Arabia or the Council of Islamic Ideology in Pakistan. However, many Muslim authorities—from lesser-trained sheikhs to political figures to legal specialists classified as fuqaha (specialists in jurisprudence), mujtahids, and muftis—issue fatawa. Some are no more than a short response to the inquiry, whereas others are recorded, published, or circulated along with explanations.

For many reasons, including the development of differing legal schools within Islam and the history of opinions concerning religious requirements as opposed to mere duties, fatawa may conflict with each other. For example, the legal opinions concerning women's inheritance under Jafari, or Twelver Shia law, and that given by a Hanafi Sunni jurist would differ. At times, even councils of jurists from a single sect may issue a complex opinion with, for instance, each indicating their agreement with or reservations about different implications or subquestions of a fatwa. Muslim countries today may govern with civil laws that are partially dependent on principles of Islamic law or are derived in part from Ottoman law. When matters of civil legal reform are discussed, then the opinions of religious authorities might be consulted. Or a fatwa may be issued by popular figures outside of the venue of civil authorities. Other countries, however, operate on the basis of uncodified Islamic law. At the supranational level, there is no single authoritative person or body that can settle conflicting issues or declare binding fatawa in Islamic law (as the pope and the Vatican issue religious decrees for Roman Catholicism).

In 1933 clerics in Iraq issued a fatwa that called for a boycott of all Zionist-made products. In 2004 the very popular Egyptian Sunni Muslim cleric and scholar Yusuf al-Qaradawi declared a fatwa similarly calling for a boycott of goods manufactured in Israel or the United States.

Other much-disputed questions have concerned the necessary resistance of Palestinians to Israeli rule or the actual status of Palestine. One set of questions, mainly affecting the right to wage jihad (holy war), concerns the land's status (dar al-Islam) or an Islamic territory that is the generally agreed condition resting on the presence of the Bayt al-Maqdis, the holy sites at the al-Aqsa Mosque complex, from which the Prophet Muhammad experienced the Miraj and the Isra (the Night Journey and Ascent to Heaven). Because the country is an Islamic land and Muslims cannot visit their holy sites or practice their religion and have had their lands and properties seized, some fatawa assert that jihad is an individual duty, incumbent on Muslims. Divergent fatawa say the country, now Israel, is *dar al-kufr,* a land of unbelief (somewhat like India under British rule) from which Muslims should flee, as in a highly disputed fatwa by Sheikh Muhammad Nasir al-Din al-Albani. While Palestinian Islamic Jihad issued a lengthy fatwa in 1989 that legitimated suicide attacks by Palestinians in the context of jihad, no leading clerics actually signed this document. It could be countered by a statement by the grand mufti of Saudi Arabia, made on April 21, 2001, that Islam forbids suicide attacks, which is referred to as if it were a formal fatwa. Sheikh Qaradawi issued a fatwa in 2002 that said women could engage in martyrdom operations in conditions when jihad is an individual duty.

PAUL G. PIERPAOLI JR. AND SHERIFA ZUHUR

See also

Al-Aqsa Mosque; Haram al-Sharif; Khomeini, Ruhollah; Religious Sites in the Middle East, Muslim; Shia Islam; Sunni Islam

References

Coulson, Noel J. *A History of Islamic Law.* Edinburgh, UK: Edinburgh University Press, 1994.

Esposito, John L. *Islam: The Straight Path.* New York: Oxford University Press, 1991.

Messick, Brinkley. *The Calligraphic State: Textual Domination and History in a Muslim Society.* Berkeley: University of California Press, 1993.

Nawawi, Abu Zakariyya Yahya Ibn Sharaf al-. *Adab al-fatwa wa-al-mufti wa al-mustafi.* Damascus: Dar al-Fikr, 1988.

Fayruz
Born: November 21, 1935

Lebanese singer, beloved throughout the Arab world. Fayruz was born Nuhad Haddad on November 21, 1935, in Beirut. She later adopted the stage name Fayruz, which means "turquoise," after an early teacher described her voice as a rare gem. Fayruz attended public school, where she was discovered at age 14 by the founder of Lebanon's music conservatory, Muhammad Flayfal, who was searching for new talent to sing national songs on the newly established Lebanese Radio Station. As a chorus member at the radio station, Fayruz made the acquaintance of Assi Rahbani, a composer who would become her husband, and his brother Mansur, who wrote the lyrics for many of her subsequent hit songs and a series of musical plays that established the success of this musical partnership. By combining Arab folkloric traditions with European and Arab instruments and Fayruz's lucid soprano tones, the trio created a volume of compositions that helped to transform Middle Eastern music, drawing on historical themes and poetry as well as modern love songs.

Fayruz became known to the Lebanese through the Rahbani musical plays, masrahiyat, that were comedic, light, and featured exciting dance sequences. She also recorded love songs such as the "Itab" (Blame).

After marrying Assi Rahbani in 1953, Fayruz appeared in yearly musical plays and in several films. She did not, like the majority of singers of her era, move to Cairo to launch her career from that recording capital of the Arab world. She therefore became far more identified with a Lebanese repertoire and was popular in the Arab Diaspora, with its large community of Lebanese exiles. Her songs, backed up by violins and such Arab instruments as the qanun (long-necked lute that is specific to Lebanon), the buzuq (a long-necked fretted lute), the ud (a stringed instrument slightly smaller than a guitar with 11 strings in 7 courses), and the nay (reed flute), included ballads, Christmas carols, and odes to Jerusalem and other holy cities. Fayruz and the Rahbani brothers' musical plays were the centerpiece of an annual Lebanese cultural event known as the Baalbek Festival, a format that was repeated elsewhere in Lebanon, Jordan, Syria, Tunisia, and elsewhere, where Western performers could be showcased alongside talented local or other Arab singers, dancers, and performers.

During Lebanon's civil war, which lasted from 1975 to 1990, Fayruz's career suffered, but her songs came to represent the intense longing of the Lebanese for their old prewar lifestyle. Several songs,

Fayruz, one of the Arab world's most popular singers, performing before thousands of fans during a sold-out concert at the mountain resort of Beiteddine, Lebanon, July 27, 2001. (Hussein Malla/AP/Wide World Photos)

such as "Bahhabak Ya Lubnan" (I Love You Lebanon), were sung at every gathering, and another song, "To Beirut," became an anthem to the city's residents, who holed up in their basements as artillery fire raged in the streets above. In the years following the war, her performances of such songs evoked strong emotional responses from audience members, who often wept and applauded as she sang.

Fayruz has received numerous awards for her talents. In 1957 she was honored by Lebanese president Camille Chamoun with the Cavalier Medal, the highest award ever given to a Lebanese artist. In 1969 she was honored on a Lebanese postage stamp. In 1961 she received the symbolic key to the city of Jerusalem, as Palestine was the subject of one of her more memorable record albums. Jordan's King Hussein presented Fayruz with a Medal of Honor in 1963 and His Majesty's Gold Medal in 1975.

One reason Fayruz has been so highly praised is that her voice is aesthetically pleasing to those who like a more Western sound, yet she is capable of the very demanding vocal capacity, ornamentation, and power of a vocalist of Arabic song. Her coloratura abilities are also complemented by clear diction and a wide vocal range.

Fayruz's son Ziyad Rahbani recorded an album with his mother during the war years that included new types of compositions that reflected a shift away from the past. In 1998 Fayruz returned to the festival in Baalbek, a nostalgic event. In 1999 she released her first new album since 1988, *Mish Kan Hayk Tkun.*

Ziyad has introduced more influences of Western jazz in Fayruz's songs, and he, himself a talented performer, has tried to speak out against what he considers a smothering old style of nostalgia for the past. His mother, like other Arab singers such as Sabah, who utilized folklore and Arab identity in their heyday in the 1950s and 1960s, is still beloved, but several generations of younger singers are now much more the face of Arabic music.

Spencer C. Tucker and Sherifa Zuhur

See also

Chamoun, Camille; Lebanon; Lebanon, Civil War in; Music

References

Boullata, Kamal, and Sargon Boulus, eds. *Fayrouz: Legend and Legacy.* Washington, DC: Forum for International Art and Culture, 1981.

Racy, Ali Jihad. *Making Music in the Arab World.* Cambridge: Cambridge University Press, 2004.

Zuhur, Sherifa, ed. *Colors of Enchantment: Theater, Music, Dance, and Visual Arts of the Middle East.* Cairo: American University in Cairo Press, 2001.

Fayyad, Salam
Born: 1952

Palestinian politician and prime minister of the Palestinian Authority (PA) since June 2007. Born in 1952 in Deir al-Ghasun, Jordan, Salam Fayyad grew up near Tulkarm in the West Bank. He graduated from Beirut University in 1975 and went on to earn a doctorate in economics from the University of Texas at Austin. He then worked for the Federal Reserve Bank of St. Louis, Missouri; taught economics at Yarmuk University in Jordan; and joined the staff of the World Bank in 1987. He lived in the United States until 1995, when he became the representative of the International Monetary Fund to the PA, a post he held until 2001. In June 2002 PA president Yasser Arafat, pressed by Western governments to clean up the vast corruption in Palestinian finances, appointed the internationally respected Fayyad to be finance minister. He held the position until December 2005, when he resigned over what he believed was an unwarranted pay increase granted to the already bloated Palestinian civil service.

Fayyad ran in the January 2006 Palestinian legislative elections as a member of a new political party, the Third Way, that won only 2.4 percent of the vote and elected only its two leaders, Fayyad and Hanan Ashrawi. When Mahmoud Abbas formed a unity government with Hamas, Fayyad agreed to become finance minister in March 2007. In this post he urged Israel to release tax revenues it was withholding.

After the outbreak of fighting in the Gaza Strip and the Hamas seizure of that territory, President Abbas carried out a questionable

Salam Fayyad, attending a conference on the Middle East conflict during the World Economic Forum in Davos, Switzerland, January 24, 2003. Fayyad became prime minister of the Palestinian Authority (PA) in 2007. (Fabrice Coffrini/epa/Corbis)

firing of the Hamas-led ministry and on June 15, 2007, appointed the technocrat Fayyad as head of the new emergency government. A reformer who believes that ideology will not solve problems, Fayyad is in effect not only prime minister but also foreign minister and finance minister. He has expressed the conviction that armed resistance is counterproductive and has sought to bar anyone from carrying arms except members of the uniformed security services, a position opposed by many Palestinians. He has also trimmed a number of political appointees from the bloated government payroll.

Fayyad believes that while the peace process should be ongoing, it must parallel efforts to create jobs, improve security, and loosen Israeli security restrictions that are stifling the Palestinian economy. Still, he believes that the main issue remains the Palestinians gaining their freedom and that this can be resolved only by political means. Fayyad hopes to create in the West Bank a model of stability that will inspire Palestinians and defeat the challenge posed by Hamas.

SPENCER C. TUCKER

See also

Abbas, Mahmoud; Arafat, Yasser; Ashrawi, Hanan Mikhail; Fatah; Hamas; Palestinian Elections of 2006

References

Gelvin, James L. *The Israel-Palestine Conflict: One Hundred Years of War.* Cambridge: Cambridge University Press, 2005.

Parson, Nigel Craig. *The Politics of the Palestinian Authority: From Oslo to al-Aqsa.* London: Routledge, 2005.

Fedayeen

Term used to refer to various (usually Arab) groups that have engaged in either armed struggle or guerrilla tactics against civilians and, sometimes, governments. The term "fedayeen" is the plural of the Arabic word meaning "one who is ready to sacrifice his life" and has for centuries referred to Muslim fighters, including Egyptians who fought against the British in the Suez Canal Zone, Palestinians who waged attacks against Israelis in the 1950s and 1960s, Iranian guerrillas opposed to Mohammad Reza Shah Pahlavi's regime in the 1970s, and a force loyal to Iraqi dictator Saddam Hussein during the Iraq War of 2003.

Following the rejection by Arab leaders of the 1947 United Nations (UN) partition plan that would have created a Palestinian state in the West Bank and Gaza Strip and the resulting declaration of the State of Israel the following year, Palestinian refugees were driven from their homes and flooded into the areas surrounding the new Jewish state. Anti-Israel activity became prevalent, particularly in West Bank and Gaza Strip areas. Supported by money and arms from a number of Arab states, Palestinians carried out attacks against Israeli military forces and also Israeli settlers, and in 1951 the raids became more organized. These fighters were referred to as fedayeen since they were an irregular rather than a government force. The fighters created bases in Egypt, Jordan, and Lebanon, with Egyptian intelligence training and arming many of them. Between 1951 and 1956, the fedayeen orchestrated hundreds of raids along the Israeli border, killing an estimated 400 Israelis and injuring 900 others.

The fedayeen operated primarily out of Jordan, and this caused that country to bear the brunt of the retaliation campaign carried out by the Israel Defense Forces (IDF) and paramilitary groups. Fedayeen attacks and subsequent retaliations were significant factors in the outbreak of hostilities during the 1956 Suez Crisis. The fedayeen continued to be active after that, now launching attacks into Israel from Jordanian territory. The fighters included those associated with the Palestine Liberation Organization (PLO), the Popular Front for the Liberation of Palestine (PFLP), and various other militant groups.

King Hussein of Jordan was initially supportive of the groups, but by 1970 he deemed their presence detrimental to Jordan and a threat to his own political power. Although based in refugee camps, the fedayeen were able to obtain arms and financial support from other Arab countries and therefore clashed with Jordanian government troops who attempted to disarm them beginning in 1968. The civil war that erupted in 1970 during what has been called Black September saw the eventual defeat and removal of the fedayeen from Jordanian soil.

The fedayeen were forced to recognize Jordanian sovereignty via an October 13, 1970, agreement between PLO leader Yasser Arafat and King Hussein. Although PLO members often participated in fedayeen raids, the PLO denied playing a role in several terrorist attacks. After being ousted from Jordan, the PLO and the fedayeen relocated to Lebanon, where they continued to stage attacks on Israel. At present, the term "fedayeen" is still used by many Palestinian militants who see them as freedom fighters seeking the establishment of a Palestinian state in the region.

Fedayeen-e Khalq was the name taken by a radical Islamic group opposed to the reign of Reza Pahlavi of Iran. Between 1971 and 1983, these Iranian fedayeen carried out numerous attacks, including political assassinations, against people supportive of the shah. Most recently, the name was used for a group loyal to ousted Iraqi leader Saddam Hussein. The Fedayeen Saddam was most likely named to imply association with anti-imperialism and freedom fighters as well as the example of the Palestinians. Although established by Hussein's son, Uday, in 1995, the group drew international attention only with the outbreak of the 2003 Iraq War. Like their Palestinian counterparts, members of the Fedayeen Saddam were mostly young unemployed men and did not constitute part of Iraq's regular army. These irregular soldiers became part of the Iraqi resistance, or *muqawama*. Following the March 2003 U.S.- and British-led invasion, the fedayeen turned their attention to coalition troops, attacking them with rocket-propelled grenades, machine guns, and mortars.

SPENCER C. TUCKER

See also

Black September; Expellees and Refugees, Palestinian; Gaza Strip; Hussein, King of Jordan; Hussein, Saddam; Iran; Iraq; Israel; Jordan; Palestine Liberation Organization; Popular Front for the Liberation of Palestine; Reza Pahlavi, Mohammad, Shah of Iran; Suicide Bombings; Terrorism; West Bank

References

Laqueur, Walter, and Barry Rubin, eds. *The Israel-Arab Reader: A Documentary History of the Middle East Conflict.* London: Penguin, 2001.

Nafez, Nazzal, and Laila A. Nafez. *Historical Dictionary of Palestine.* Lanham, MD: Scarecrow, 1997.

O'Neill, Bard E. *Revolutionary Warfare in the Middle East: The Israelis vs. the Fedayeen.* Boulder, CO: Paladin, 1974.

Rubin, Barry. *Revolution until Victory? The Politics and History of the PLO.* Reprint ed. Cambridge: Harvard University Press, 2003.

Fifth Aliya

See Aliya, Fifth

Film and the Arab-Israeli Conflict

The portrayal of the Arab-Israeli conflict in motion pictures has traditionally favored Israel. Most films produced in the United States and Europe, particularly those revolving around the theme of ter-

Films about the Arab-Israeli Conflict and Middle Eastern Terrorism

Title	Date	Director
Exodus	1960	Otto Preminger
Victory at Entebbe	1976	Marvin J. Chomsky
Twenty-One Hours at Munich	1976	William A. Graham
Black Sunday	1977	John Frankenheimer
Little Drummer Girl	1984	George Roy Hill
True Lies	1994	James Cameron
Executive Decision	1996	Stuart Baird
The Siege	1998	Edward Zwick
Rules of Engagement	2000	William Friedkin
Paradise Now	2005	Hany abu-Assad
Munich	2006	Steven Spielberg

rorism, have tended to portray Americans and Israelis as heroic agents of Western or Israeli intelligence services trying to prevent fanatical Arab terrorists from carrying out mass and wanton acts that might kill thousands of people. More recently, some films have shown Arabs in a more positive light. Some have also given more screen time to the Arab-Muslim perspective. However, the predominant trend is still one that favors the Israeli-American-European perspective. In light of the September 11, 2001, terrorist attacks on the United States, this trend is likely to continue.

The pro-Israel slant in post–World War II films about the Arab-Israeli dispute has been influenced by sympathy toward the Jews and Israel growing out of the shock and guilt over the Holocaust. It has also been affected by cultural differences between the West and the Muslim world that have grown more pronounced with the rise of Arab nationalism and Islamic fundamentalism and with high-profile acts of terrorism by Arabs and European sympathizers against U.S. and Western interests. As a result, there has been a tendency to reduce Arab characters in war or terrorist movies to raving maniacal killers lacking decency or morality.

The negative stereotyping of Arabs and of Middle Eastern and Islamic culture in film predates World War II and the emergence of the Arab-Israeli conflict. It was present in earlier films romanticizing the Western presence in the Middle East such as *Beau Geste* (1926) and *The Lost Patrol* (1934). During World War II, films set in the Middle East, such as *A Yank in Libya* (1942), portrayed Arabs as treacherous collaborators with the Germans. This trend continued in the postwar period. *Lawrence of Arabia* (1961) portrayed the life of T. E. Lawrence, a British officer credited with leading the Arab uprising against the Ottoman Turks during World War I. Although sympathetic to the Arabs, the film portrayed the Arabs as fractious, unpredictable, violent, and ignorant tribesmen open to exploitation by unscrupulous British and French imperialists.

The first movie to directly address the Arab-Israeli dispute was *Exodus* (1960). Set during the post–World War II period in the last days of the British Mandate for Palestine, *Exodus* was openly sympathetic to the Israelis. The Jewish protagonists (led by Paul Newman as Ari Ben Canaan) were all portrayed in a heroic light. While the film did portray harmonious relations between a kibbutz and a

Paul Newman, as Ari Ben Canaan, in the 1960 film *Exodus.* (Sunset Boulevard/Corbis)

local Arab village, most Arabs were seen as treacherous extremists who killed and mutilated innocent Jews in the dark. These images were in stark contrast with the perception of Israel as an enlightened Western-style democracy. The idea of portraying Arabs and Muslims as the others, of course, was first investigated by Edward Said.

This pattern continued and emerged as a major theme in the terrorist movie genre that flourished in the late 1970s and early 1980s and again from the mid-1990s to the present. These films were produced in the context of major political events related to the Middle East: the Palestinian terrorist acts against Israel, particularly the rash of attacks on American and European airliners in August and September 1970; the attack on Israeli athletes at the Munich Olympics in 1972; the Arab oil embargo following the outbreak of the 1973 Yom Kippur War; and the successful Israeli raid at Entebbe Airport (Uganda) in 1976. These events were reflected in at least nine films (both historical and fictional) made between 1972 and 1977. They dealt with the threat posed by Arab terrorists seeking to carry out strikes against the United States and Israel. The films include *Victory at Entebbe* (1976) and *Twenty-One Hours at Munich* (1976).

Of these films, the most successful was *Black Sunday* (1977). *Black Sunday* qualifies as a landmark motion picture around which others in the genre coalesced. The story line centers around a plot by a disgruntled blimp pilot and former Vietnam prisoner of war (played by Bruce Dern) who has lost his family and his career and wants to get even. The other major character is a young German Palestinian woman (played by Marthe Keller) who is an agent for the Black September terrorist organization. Their protagonist is an

Israeli Mossad agent (played by Robert Shaw) who is weary of his work and beginning to show sympathy for the plight of the Palestinians. The act that the terrorists are planning is to occur not in Europe or the Middle East but rather in the United States and is aimed at that most defining of American rituals, the Super Bowl. The young woman is defined by her single-minded determination to make the Americans suffer for their support for Israel. The goal is to hijack the Goodyear Blimp, rig a bomb to its undercarriage, and set it off over the Orange Bowl, scattering thousands of tiny needles that would kill many thousands of people in the stadium, including the president of the United States. *Black Sunday* is consistent with earlier films portraying the Arabs as marginal fanatics, as opposed to Shaw's tough but compassionate Israeli.

The 1980s and 1990s gave rise to an even greater number of films with themes revolving around Arab or Middle Eastern terrorists. Not all centered on acts of terror against Israel, however. Indeed, most were concerned with acts targeting the United States. But all of them reinforced to varying degrees sympathy for Israel and negative Arab stereotypes. This trend was again reinforced by international events, among them the Iran hostage crisis of 1979–1981, the Lebanon hostage imbroglio that eventually resulted in the Iran-Contra Scandal during President Ronald Reagan's second term, and the bombing of the U.S. marine barracks at Beirut International Airport in 1983.

Among the more representative of these films was *Little Drummer Girl* (1984). The plot revolves around an operation mounted by the Mossad and led by a ruthless spymaster (played by Klaus Kinski) aimed at destroying a Palestinian terrorist cell responsible for the bombings of a number of Israeli diplomatic posts and Jewish facilities in Europe. They bait the trap with a naive American student (played by Diane Keaton). In the end, the Israelis succeed in destroying the cell, but only after causing severe psychological trauma to a number of innocent people (including Keaton's character). The movie was unique in that it gave more than the usual amount of screen time to Palestinians (many of whom were sympathetically portrayed). In the film, the Palestinians talked about the reasons for the pain and rage over their refugee status and the loss of their homeland. Nevertheless, the film still maintained the image of the Arab terrorist as dangerous, fanatical, and unable to see any perspective except his or her own.

A recent effort, presented along the same lines as *Little Drummer Girl* in its portrayal of the brutalizing effect of counterterrorist work and in its willingness to present Arabs more sympathetically, is *Munich* (2006), directed by Steven Spielberg. Set in the aftermath of the Black September attack on the Israeli athletes at the 1972 Munich Olympics, the film focuses on the team of undercover agents sent by the Israeli government to hunt down and kill the perpetrators. The work is physically and emotionally draining and begins to take a toll on the agents involved. The central characters are Avner (played by Eric Bana) and his handler Ephraim (played by Tony Kushner). As the hunt goes on, Avner begins to question if the Palestinians they have been ordered to kill are really culpable.

Eric Bana as Avner (*left*) and Geoffrey Rush as Ephraim (*right*) star in Steven Spielberg's film *Munich*. (Karen Ballard/Universal Pictures/Zuma/Corbis)

Ephraim's refusal to give Avner more information sharpens the conflict between the two men and complicates the operation further. The film ends with Avner resigning from the team and leaving Israel to live in New York. *Munich* is unique in its balanced portrayal of both Arabs and Israelis and its unromantic view of both Palestinians and Israelis.

Munich stands virtually alone among recent films in its even-handedness in sympathy for both sides in the Arab-Israeli dispute. Probably the best example in the 1990s of the terrorist genre (and the most successful commercially) is James Cameron's *True Lies* (1994). Although not directly concerned with the Arab-Israeli dispute, it did make reference to a wide range of conventions used in Middle Eastern terrorist films to reinforce the image of the Arab as the outsider/other who threatens Western notions of order and stability. *True Lies* is an entertaining mix of espionage, action, and romantic comedy. It revolves around Harry Tasker (played by Arnold Schwarzenegger), a counterterrorist operative who poses as a businessman, and his loving but bored wife (played by Jamie Lee Curtis), who is unaware of his double life. Tasker is hunting an Arab terrorist cell, Crimson Jihad, that has carried out numerous car and café bombings and is seeking to detonate nuclear weapons throughout the United States. Schwarzenegger's antagonists are a shady Arab businessman who is bankrolling Crimson Jihad's operations and that

group's hateful and fanatical chieftain, Selim Abu Aziz (played by Art Malik). The other Arab characters in the film are rather bumbling terrorists whose main purpose is to act as targets for Schwarzenegger and the high-tech weaponry of the U.S. military. In a tangled plot full of outlandish chase scenes, Schwarzenegger's character foils the terrorist plot and redeems his family. Although entertaining, the film did nothing to enhance the image of the Arabs or create any sympathy for the Arab perspective in the Arab-Israeli conflict.

The prevailing pattern of showing Arabs and Muslims in roles as fanatical, homicidal terrorists or shady terrorist sympathizers continued in the 1990s in films such as *Executive Decision* (1996), *The Siege* (1998), and *Rules of Engagement* (2000). All these films featured lurid portrayals of Arabs as alien, violent strangers intent on inflicting violence and suffering on nonbelievers throughout the world. The makers of *The Siege* went to some length to create sympathetic roles for some Arab characters and actually developed a significant sympathetic Arab in a leading role, the main character's trusted partner (played by Tony Shaloub). Nevertheless, the net effect of the film is to reinforce negative images of Arabs. The main character, a Federal Bureau of Investigation (FBI) agent (played by Denzel Washington), is trying to stop a series of terrorist bombings that have terrorized New York City before a hawkish U.S. Army Special Forces colonel (played by Bruce Willis) places

New York City under martial law. The terrorists nearly succeed, largely because an Arab American whom the FBI agents mistakenly trusted as an information source turns out to be a suicide bomber.

While films such as *True Lies* and *The Siege* have reinforced negative stereotypes of Arabs, to loud and growing protests from the Arab American community, there have been efforts among filmmakers to portray Arabs and the Arab side of the dispute with Israel more sympathetically. *Paradise Now* (2005), directed by Hany abu-Assad, is a critically acclaimed film written and produced by a Palestinian that portrays what may be the last 48 hours in the lives of two young Palestinian men who have been recruited as suicide bombers. The film shows their fear and anguish as they prepare to go on their mission and explores how the brutality of life in the Israeli-occupied Arab territories propels them to commit such an act. When they are intercepted at the Israeli border, a young woman who discovers their intentions causes them to reconsider their plan. *Paradise Now* won a Golden Globe for best foreign film in 2005 and was nominated for an Academy Award that same year. The film's impact, however, has been limited. It was not shown widely in theaters but has been extensively distributed on DVD.

The general direction of the treatment of the Arab-Israeli dispute in film at this point remains somewhat unclear. The terrorist attacks of September 11 have focused attention on the threat of Arab terrorism in the United States and other Western countries, diverting attention away from the Arab-Israeli dispute per se. Although a number of films have appeared that differentiate between Arab/Islamic moderates and extremists, the prevailing image of Arabs and Muslims in film is still negative. Similarly, the portrayal of Israelis in films such as *Munich,* although not as romanticized as in earlier films such as *Exodus* and *Black Sunday,* is still largely sympathetic. The most sympathetic leading characters are still Israelis and Americans. In the present atmosphere of Western suspicion and distrust of Arabs and Muslims, these trends are likely to continue.

WALTER F. BELL

See also

Black September Organization; Entebbe Hostage Rescue; Expellees and Refugees, Palestinian; Literature of the Arab-Israeli Wars; Lobbies, Arab; Mossad; Munich Olympic Games; Said, Edward; Suicide Bombings; Terrorism; Yom Kippur War

References

Bernstein, Matthew, and Gaylyn Studler, eds. *Visions of the East: Orientalism in Film.* New Brunswick, NJ: Rutgers University Press, 1997.

Eisele, John C. "The Wild East: Deconstructing the Language of Genre in the Hollywood Eastern." *Cinema Journal* 41(4) (Summer 2002): 68–94.

Mandel, Daniel. "Muslims on the Silver Screen." *Middle East Quarterly* 8(2) (Spring 2001): 19–30

Semmerling, Tim Jon. *Evil Arabs in American Popular Film: Orientalist Fear.* Austin: University of Texas Press, 2006.

First Aliya

See Aliya, First

Fortifications

Forts, fortifications, fortified positions, and defensive lines have been built and employed by a number of nations in the Middle East over the past six decades. Among others, Syria and Egypt especially have used various fortifications. But it has been the Israelis who have employed fortifications the most, mainly the consequence of their strategic positioning and precarious geopolitical situation in the volatile Middle East.

The Syrians had a large number of fortified strong points on the Golan Heights. These proved vulnerable to helicopter-borne commando attacks and were quickly neutralized at the onset of the 1967 Six-Day War.

Egypt had a heavily fortified position called Green Island at the southern end of the Suez Canal that was a symbol of Egyptian military prestige. In 1969 the Israelis planned to assault the position, as it had been used to launch numerous commando assaults against Israel during the War of Attrition in the wake of the Six-Day War.

Green Island had been built by the British and then turned over to Egypt upon independence. The fort was built at the mouth of the canal and was 450 feet long and 240 feet wide. It was a large concrete fort that had 12 heavy machine-gun positions along the roof and a large fortified tower with multiple 40-mm antiaircraft guns. The walls were more than a yard thick. Made of reinforced concrete, they rose straight out of the water. These fortifications were supplemented by generous amounts of barbed wire entanglements. Entrenchments and bunkers covered all approaches to the island. The position was occupied by 100 crack Egyptian troops, including an elite marine commando unit, the al-Saiqa Commando Brigade. The Egyptians considered the fort impregnable.

On July 20, 1969, after Egyptian commandos had launched a brutal attack against the Israelis 10 days earlier, the elite Israeli marine commando force Flotilla 13 sent combat swimmers to neutralize Egyptian guards on the sea approach to Green Island. Forty commandos in inflatable boats landed at the tip of the island, and in the space of a few hours the entire Egyptian garrison had been killed or captured. The Israelis then sabotaged the facilities.

Israel, however, built the most extensive defensive system of fortifications. This is ironic, for Israel had traditionally relied on mobile warfare. Israel has always been highly vulnerable to attack. It is a nation with few natural barriers and surrounded by enemies. From 1948 on, Israel had relied on mobile warfare. Some defensive fortifications were employed before 1973, but they were usually makeshift and temporary. Israel has relied primarily on speed and maneuver to win its wars, and the Israel Defense Forces (IDF) has traditionally viewed static defenses as less important. When the Israelis have placed faith in fortified positions such as the Bar-Lev Line, they have been sorely disappointed.

The most rudimentary types of fortifications consist of trench networks bolstered by bunkers, barbed wire, and artillery support. Trench systems were not practical for the Israelis in the southern

Israeli soldiers inside a bunker near the Suez Canal at Kantara, during the War of Attrition, on November 26, 1970. (Moshe Milner/Israeli Government Press Office)

and eastern desert regions, where digging trenches was problematic. In the north prior to 1967, the Israelis were threatened by Syrian positions along the Golan Heights. Fortified positions under direct observation and threat from high ground are virtually useless. Nevertheless, many kibbutzim in the north had built fortified shelters and temporary gun positions constructed from wood and sandbags. But there were no truly fortified positions facing Syria or Lebanon before the Six-Day War.

The Six-Day War enabled the Israelis to capture and occupy territory belonging to Syria and Egypt. In these forward positions, the Israelis erected fortified systems. On the Golan Heights the Israelis constructed a number of bunker complexes to support trench networks. In many cases they merely occupied Syrian fortifications that were already existent. In the south, the Israelis occupied the Sinai Peninsula and constructed the longest and most thorough and powerful chain of fortifications they had ever attempted. They did so at a staggering cost of $500 million. The Bar-Lev Line, named after the then chief of staff of the army, Lieutenant General Chaim Bar-Lev, was believed to be impenetrable and impervious to everything short of a nuclear strike.

The cornerstone of the Bar-Lev defensive system consisted of enormous sand barriers 20–25 meters in height and inclined at a 45 degree angle that came down to the water's edge along the Suez Canal. Approximately every 6 miles, a concrete observation platform was erected. Each platform housed some 15 soldiers whose task was to give early warning of attempted crossings of the canal and direct artillery fire from support batteries to the rear. Extensive systems of strong points, some 20 in all, were placed behind the rampart. These strong points were independently functioning fire bases that could mutually support each other. The largest was called Budapest. Other large ones were named Nisan, Orcal, and Tasa.

Garrison troops occupying the strong points were backed up by mobile armored forces. Further to the rear were large supply dumps of ammunition and other crucial supplies. Unfortunately, the defensive system rested on reserves reaching the front in a timely manner.

Many in the Israeli military were critical of this barrier. They were worried that planners had succumbed to the Maginot Syndrome (named for the French concentration on a defensive mindset prior to World War II) and were too reliant on forts that might not hold. Critics of the Bar-Lev would be vindicated during the Yom Kippur War in 1973.

On October 24, 1973, the Israeli observation platforms were lightly manned because of the Yom Kippur holiday. Carefully planned

Egyptian artillery and air strikes quickly severed all but radio communications with the rear. The observation platforms were soon neutralized, and the Egyptians, using pontoons, bridged the canal in 81 places. Confronted with the massive earthen and sand ramparts, the Egyptian engineers employed high-pressure hoses drawing water from the canal to breach the barriers. Caught off guard, the strong points behind the barrier were overwhelmed one after another. All fell within the first day of the war except Budapest, which held throughout the duration of the conflict.

Since the Yom Kippur War, the Israelis have reverted to their tried-and true tactics of mobile defensive warfare. But there has been a large series of fortifications including bunkers and massive razor-wire entanglements set up along the Lebanese border since the 1980s. This included a demilitarized zone inside Lebanon proper, which is designed to prevent infiltration of Hezbollah guerrillas into Israel. Israel is also constructing a fortified wall between much of the West Bank and Israel designed to prevent infiltration of Palestinian terrorists from the Palestinian territories. A similar barrier is planned to isolate the Gaza Strip. The Egyptians learned then the same lesson the Israelis would learn in 1973, that there is no such thing as an impregnable fortification.

ROD VOSBURGH

See also

Attrition, War of; Bar-Lev, Chaim; Bar-Lev Line; Egypt, Armed Forces; Israel Defense Forces; Six-Day War; Syria, Armed Forces; Yom Kippur War

References

Blum, Howard. *The Eve of Destruction: The Untold Story of the Yom Kippur War.* New York: Perennial Books, 2004.

Dunstan, Simon. *The Yom Kippur War, 1973.* 2 vols. Westport, CT: Praeger, 2005.

Rabinovich, Abraham. *The Yom Kippur War: The Epic Encounter That Transformed the Middle East.* New York: Schocken, 2005.

Shapiro, Stephen, et al. *Battle Stations! Fortifications through the Ages.* Toronto: Annick, 2005.

Waterbury, John. *The Crossing: From The Bar-Lev Line to Geneva.* Hanover, NH: American Universities Field Staff Reports, 1973.

Fourth Aliya

See Aliya, Fourth

France, Middle East Policy

France, whose interests in the Middle East date back many centuries, acquired extensive imperial interests in the region during the 19th century, gradually annexing or acquiring protectorates or special rights in Lebanon, Egypt, Algeria, Tunisia, and Morocco. During the 1854–1856 Crimean War, France protected Ottoman Turkey against Russian incursions, while French capital and engineers built the Suez Canal, and, until 1882 when Britain occupied Egypt, helped to administer that country. France's stake in the former Ottoman Empire expanded under the World War I Sykes-Picot Agreement (1916) whereby France eventually gained mandates over the Levant (present-day Syria and Lebanon). It effectively administered the regions as colonial territories until World War II began in 1939.

After World War II, France maintained substantial cultural influence in its former territories, but the French Middle Eastern empire rapidly shrank as its former colonies demanded and—sometimes humiliatingly for France, as in Algeria—gained independence. Meanwhile, France's 1956 effort with Britain and Israel to regain the Suez Canal ended in a fiasco. Over time, traditional ties to former colonies and economic self-interest made France broadly pro-Arab in the protracted Arab-Israeli conflict.

French interest in the Middle East dates back to the Crusades of 1096–1291, which received major backing and participation from the French monarchy. By the 16th century, French leaders considered the Ottomans a valuable counterbalance to rival Habsburg power in Europe. In 1535 Francis I of France and Ottoman sultan Suleiman I signed a Treaty of Friendship whereby the latter effectively recognized France as the protector of Latin Christians in the Ottoman Empire. Suleiman granted France economic and legal privileges known as capitulations whereby France exercised legal jurisdiction over French merchants and received other commercial rights in Ottoman territories, which were further extended by King Louis XV in 1740 and Napoleon I in 1802. Until well into the mid-18th century, French commerce dominated the Mediterranean.

By the late 18th century, French leaders also viewed the eastern Mediterranean as an arena for imperial competition with Great Britain and other powers, usually at the expense of the increasingly crumbling Ottoman Empire. Seeking to take over Britain's Indian territories, in 1798 Napoleon (then still General Bonaparte) invaded and briefly conquered Mamluk-administered Egypt, then under Ottoman sovereignty. Napoleon's subsequent advances into Palestine and Syria halted when he failed to take the city of Acre. He returned to France in 1799, while the remaining French troops in Egypt surrendered to Britain in 1801, ending the unpopular French occupation.

Throughout the 19th century, Ottoman weakness provided opportunities for France and other European powers to acquire colonial possessions and quasi-imperial rights and privileges in the Middle East. Early-19th-century British ties with the Ottoman government were a major reason that during the 1820s and 1830s, France backed efforts by independent-minded Muhammad Ali Pasha of Egypt to gain greater autonomy from his Ottoman overlord, although in 1840 the French declined to assist him when Britain and other European powers curbed his power.

The Anglo-French entente that characterized Napoleon III's reign during the 1850s and 1860s led France and Britain to cooperate extensively in the Middle East. Seeking to restrain Russian ambitions against Ottoman territory, the two joined forces against Russia in the 1854–1856 Crimean War. In Lebanon, France claimed special rights as protector of the substantial Maronite Christian

The Palais Bourbon in Paris, seat of the French National Assembly. (PhotoDisc)

community and intervened to assist its clients during 1842–1845 and again in 1860 when it collaborated with Britain to end major civil strife.

The Anglo-French entente was not permanent, as France's weakness after its 1870 defeat by Germany encouraged other powers to encroach upon its sphere. In 1854 and 1856 French engineer Ferdinand de Lesseps obtained concessions from the Egyptian government to build a canal across the Isthmus of Suez separating Africa from Egypt, a waterway that would enable merchant and military shipping traveling between Asia and Europe to avoid circumnavigating the African continent. The French and Egyptian governments provided the capital for the Suez Canal Company, which would own and operate the canal for 99 years. Built with French expertise, it opened with great fanfare in 1869.

At this time, French and British nationals jointly administered Egypt's debts. In 1875, however, financial difficulties forced Viceroy (Khedive) Ismail Pasha of Egypt to sell the Egyptian stake in the Suez Canal shares to the British government. Seven years later, to bitter French resentment, Britain occupied Egypt and took over its administration. This had been planned as a joint British-French venture, but the fall of the French cabinet led the French to renege, and the British then went in alone. In the latter 19th and early 20th centuries, French bankers lent money to the Ottoman government,

loans under whose terms French nationals and other Westerners supervised and administered some Ottoman revenues.

During the 19th century, France also acquired a North African empire at Ottoman expense. In 1830 France conquered Algeria in the Maghrib, which was incorporated outright into France, to become three French departments. Four decades of sporadic military operations against the Muslim Arab and Berber populations ensued before French control was assured, and numerous French colonists settled in Algeria. During 1881–1883 France made neighboring Tunisia a protectorate. In 1912 Morocco also became a French protectorate. In East Africa, the French acquired Djibouti during the 1880s and sought to expand their African possessions into the southern Sudan, provoking the 1898 Fashoda Crisis with Great Britain, which considered the Sudan part of Egypt. In the aftermath of the crisis, France finally renounced all designs on the Sudan. The net effect of this was to concentrate French imperial efforts in Africa and make possible an entente with Britain.

World War I intensified French appetites for colonial concessions in Ottoman-administered territory. In early 1915 Britain agreed to allow Russia to acquire Constantinople, the Ottoman capital that commanded the strategic Dardanelles Straits connecting the Black Sea to the Mediterranean. France responded by claiming much of the Levant and in 1916 concluded the Sykes-Picot Agreement with

French troops in Port Said prior to leaving the Suez Canal Zone following the Anglo-French intervention in Egypt, December 27, 1956. (AFP/Getty Images)

Britain. This allocated French rule over coastal Syria and Lebanon and much of the Anatolian province of Cilicia, a sphere of influence that would include the remainder of Syria and the Mesopotamian province of Mosul. The agreement also guaranteed French participation in an international administration of Palestine.

The 1919 Paris Peace Conference modified these provisions, and France abandoned Mosul and Palestine to be ruled as British mandates. In return, the French received a mandate that gave it full control over all the Levant, essentially present-day Syria and Lebanon. Growing Turkish nationalism meant that although the 1920 Treaty of Sèvres recognized French control of Cilicia, France could not enforce its rule and abandoned this claim under the subsequent 1923 Treaty of Lausanne.

French rule over Syria and Lebanon proved contentious. During 1925–1926 French forces suppressed an armed rebellion in Syria.

In 1936 France signed treaties granting both Syria and Lebanon independence within three years, although France retained military base rights in both states. But the treaties were never ratified or implemented, and instead in 1939 France restored colonial rule. After France's defeat by Germany in June 1940, French administrators in Syria and Lebanon supported the Vichy government that negotiated an armistice with Germany. In June 1941, however, British and Free French forces took over the areas, and Free French representative General Georges Catroux promised independence to both. After a number of military and political clashes between French officials and Lebanese and Syrians, France withdrew all its forces from the two states, which became fully independent in 1946.

The French position in North Africa was almost equally precarious. During the 1920s General Louis-Hubert Lyautey suppressed two insurgencies in Morocco, but nationalist forces nonetheless burgeoned. Serious nationalist unrest occurred in Tunisia in 1938, and despite having been banned in the late 1930s, nationalist parties existed in Algeria. In June 1940, administrators in France's North African colonies backed the Vichy regime, but in November 1942 Allied forces launched a successful invasion. Despite strong French opposition in all three states, Allied and Axis wartime propaganda alike encouraged independence movements.

Morocco's sultan adeptly headed his nationalist forces, eventually winning independence in 1956. A guerrilla war led by activist Habib Bourguiba began in Tunisia in 1952, bringing autonomy in 1955 and full independence in 1956. In the province of Algeria, politically influential French settlers, or colons, adamantly opposed independence, and a brutal eight-year conflict began in 1954 that killed between 300,000 and 1 million Algerians before French president Charles de Gaulle finally granted the country independence in 1962.

Most colons thereupon hastily returned to France, whose population split bitterly over the war. Under agreements reached in 1965, French companies retained control of Algerian oil and gas resources, but after repeated disputes, in 1971 the Algerian government nationalized majority holdings in these companies.

Despite a vaunted close identification with Arab interests, in 1947 France voted to partition Palestine and in 1949 recognized the new State of Israel. In 1950 France joined Britain and the United States in the Tripartite Declaration, imposing an arms embargo on all parties in the Middle East conflict. This effectively preserved the existing status quo, and by 1955 France had become a major arms supplier to the Israeli military. Resentment of Arab nationalism in North Africa was one reason that France, alarmed by Egyptian president Gamal Abdel Nasser's nationalization of the Suez Canal in July 1956, joined Britain and Israel in October 1956 in an abortive military expedition to Egypt intended to retake control of the canal. Within 10 days, American economic pressure forced Britain and then France and Israel into a humiliating and much resented withdrawal.

In the late 1950s France helped Israel develop a nuclear capability, but once Algeria won independence, Franco-Arab tensions relaxed, and French strategic and economic interests brought a tilt away from Israel. Before the 1967 Six-Day War, de Gaulle sought to restrain Israel from launching a preemptive strike and in June imposed a complete arms embargo on all parties to the conflict, a measure that primarily affected Israel. He subsequently urged unconditional Israeli withdrawal from all occupied Arab territories. From late 1969 onward, France became a major arms supplier to several Arab states. During and after the 1973 Yom Kippur War, France heeded Arab demands, reinforced by an oil embargo on offending nations, to cease supplying arms to Israel. French officials promoted a pro-Arab stance in the European Economic Community (EEC), urged admission of the Palestine Liberation Organization (PLO) to international bodies, and in October 1981 endorsed the Palestinian call for a national homeland.

During the 1980s, French policies toward the Middle East conflict became more evenhanded as France became a target for assorted Lebanese, Iraqi, Iranian, Palestinian, and other terrorists. Although France had sheltered the exiled Iranian ayatollah Ruhollah Khomeini, who became head of the revolutionary Iranian government in 1979, French arms supplies to Iraq during the subsequent Iran-Iraq War (1980–1988) and the asylum France afforded various post-1979 Iranian political exiles strained relations with the new regime.

France still felt special responsibility for Lebanon and in July 1982 contributed troops to a multinational United Nations (UN) task force to oversee the evacuation of Syrian and PLO fighters first from Beirut and later, in December 1983, from Tripoli. In 1984 France also sent observers to monitor the Lebanese cease-fire, but heavy casualties brought their withdrawal two years later. From 1980 until 1987 when Libyan forces withdrew, France sought with only moderate success to exert political and military pressure on Libya to cease its incursions against neighboring Chad.

France acquiesced and participated in the 1991 Persian Gulf War when a U.S.-led international coalition drove Iraq out of oil-rich Kuwait, which Saddam Hussein had forcefully annexed. In 1993 France along with Britain and the United States also launched air strikes against Iraq to protest Hussein's infractions of UN sanctions, operations that recurred frequently throughout the 1990s. During the 1990s and early 2000s, French sales of arms and other goods to Iraq, Iran, and other regimes that the United States found unpalatable nonetheless provoked considerable U.S. rhetorical condemnation.

In the late 1990s, the presence of several million North African immigrants and migrant workers in France contributed to the growing strength of extremist right-wing political groups who resented and campaigned against their arrival. After the extremist Al Qaeda organization launched the September 11, 2001, terrorist attacks against the United States, the French government expressed full support for the United States in moves to track down terrorists and the subsequent invasion of Afghanistan, Al Qaeda's territorial base. France feared that fundamentalist Muslims might launch similar attacks on French soil. With anti-Semitism burgeoning dramatically in France, in 2004 the French government banned Muslim girls in state-run schools from wearing the hijab (or headscarf) in class, a measure that provoked spirited national and international debate.

French leaders nonetheless deplored and refused to endorse the spring 2003 U.S. invasion of Iraq, and for at least a year French and American officials engaged in bitter and highly undiplomatic attacks on each other's countries. The July 2005 Muslim terrorist attacks on London transportation systems raised new fears that France would soon become a terrorist target and that French Muslims might become objects of popular suspicion and harassment. French Muslims for their part were thoroughly angered by official neglect, discrimination, and rising racist sentiment encouraged by leaders such as Étienne Le Pen.

PRISCILLA MARY ROBERTS

See also

Algeria; De Gaulle, Charles; Egypt; Iran; Iran-Iraq War; Israel; Khomeini, Ruhollah; Kuwait; Lebanon; Lebanon, Israeli Invasion of; Libya; Morocco; Nasser, Gamal Abdel; Six-Day War; Suez Crisis; Syria; Terrorism; Tripartite Declaration; Tunisia; Turkey, Middle East Policy; United Kingdom, Middle East Policy; United States, Middle East Policy; Yom Kippur War

References

Brown, L. Carl, and Matthew S. Gordon, eds. *Franco-Arab Encounters: Studies in Memory of David C. Gordon.* Beirut, Lebanon: American University of Beirut, 1996.

Gaunson, A. B. *The Anglo-French Clash in Lebanon and Syria, 1940–1945.* New York: St. Martin's, 1987.

Marlowe, John. *Perfidious Albion: The Origins of Anglo-French Rivalry in the Levant.* London: Elek, 1971.

Tal, David, ed. *The 1956 War: Collusion and Rivalry in the Middle East.* Portland, OR: Frank Cass, 2001.

Thomas, Martin. *The French North African Crisis: Colonial Breakdown and Anglo-French Relations, 1945–62.* Basingstoke, UK: Macmillan, 2000.

Wall, Irwin M. *France, the United States, and the Algerian War.* Berkeley: University of California Press, 2001.

Watson, William E. *Tricolor and Crescent: France and the Islamic World.* Westport, CT: Praeger, 2003.

Williams, Ann. *Britain and France in the Middle East and North Africa, 1914–1967.* London: Macmillan, 1968.

Franco-Lebanese Treaty
Event Date: November 13, 1936

A mutual agreement of friendship negotiated between the government of France and the mandate government of Lebanon that granted Lebanon considerable autonomy. The Franco-Lebanese Treaty was signed on November 13, 1936, and was intended to clarify France's relationship to Lebanon in light of the Franco-Syrian Treaty of September 1936 that had essentially begun Syria's course toward independence. At the time, both Lebanon and Syria were part of a French mandate authorized by the League of Nations. The French parliament, however, did not ratify the treaty. Coming so close on the heels of the treaty with Syria, many French politicians were leery of setting Lebanon on its own course of independence. Be that as it may, the spirit of the treaty guided Franco-Lebanese relations right up until the fall of France in 1940.

Most notably, the Franco-Lebanese Treaty granted to the Christian Maronites preferential treatment in terms of politics and economic matters. Indeed, the Maronites had enjoyed a long and beneficial connection with the French that had furthered France's commercial interests, and the French hoped to capitalize on this. The privileges granted within an unwritten document known as the Mithaq al-Watani (the National Pact) angered the Muslim and Druze populations, however, and created animosities that would plague Lebanon into the 21st century. Indeed, by the early 1930s the Maronites no longer constituted a majority of the Lebanese population. There was a rough parity between Christians and Muslims.

(Druze can also be included in this category, although they are not actually Muslim.)

The Muslims decried the continuation of French rule via the mandate and did not wish to be part of a secular, independent Lebanon. Rather, they hoped to either form their own Arab Muslim state or become part of a greater Syrian state. Needless to say, Lebanon's Muslims and Druze were not enamored of the treaty with the French.

When France fell to invading Nazi German armies in June 1940, the Lebanese mandate fell under the control of the collaborationist Vichy government. In 1941, however, Free French troops occupied Lebanon and took control of the country politically and militarily. Soon thereafter, Free French officials proclaimed Lebanese and Syrian independence, which the British underwrote. Nevertheless, Free French policymakers were reluctant to hand over complete control to the Lebanese. And in 1943 when the new democratically elected Lebanese government moved to purge Lebanon of any French influences, Free French forces promptly jailed most of the Lebanese officials, including President Bishara al-Khuri. This precipitated a Lebanese rebellion that had to be handled via diplomatic intervention on the part of the British. Not until 1946 would the last of French (and British) troops be withdrawn from Lebanon. That same year, the Lebanese achieved complete independence. French preferential treatment of the Maronites via the treaty and their heavy-handedness during World War II most certainly led to the balkanization of Lebanese politics in the postwar era.

PAUL G. PIERPAOLI JR.

See also

France, Middle East Policy; Lebanon

References

Gaunson, A. B. *The Anglo-French Clash in Lebanon and Syria, 1940–1945.* New York: St. Martin's, 1987.

Odeh, J. B. *Lebanon, Dynamics of Conflict: A Modern Political History.* London: Zed, 1985.

Franco-Syrian Treaty
Event Date: September 9, 1936

Treaty signed on September 9, 1936, between the French government and the Syrian government, which at the time was under a French-administered League of Nations mandate. Like the Franco-Lebanese Treaty of November 1936, the Syrian treaty was not ratified by the French parliament. The treaty was designed to begin the process toward Syrian independence and pledged both governments to mutual friendship and alliance. The treaty also stipulated that Syria and Lebanon would retain their separate statuses and that Syria would attain its independence by the close of 1939. At that point, it would join the League of Nations as an independent state.

This was not the first time that the French had attempted to negotiate an independence treaty with the Syrians. Two years earlier, in 1934, the French had tried to impose a treaty on the Syrian

Officials sign the Franco-Syrian Treaty on September 9, 1936. The photograph shows (*right to left*) Camille Chautemps, Léon Blum, Paul Vienot, and Hachem Bey Stassi. (Bettmann/Corbis)

government, which at the time was headed by pro-French president Muhammad Ali Bey al-Abid. Al-Abid was extremely pro-French, in sharp contrast to many of the Syrian leaders who were nationalists. When word of the proposed treaty leaked out, Syrian nationalists were outraged. The treaty was heavily pro-French, and while eventual independence would have been granted, the French wanted to control the Syrian Mountains themselves, apparently in perpetuity.

Syrian nationalist leader and parliament member Hashim al-Atasi almost immediately mobilized his forces to stage countrywide protests. These included a 60-day general strike that soon crippled the economy. Mass protests ensued, as did several riots in urban areas. Within weeks, al-Atasi's National Bloc had seized the upper hand, and the proposed 1934 treaty was scrapped.

When al-Atasi and the National Bloc had proven themselves to the favored ruling coalition in Syria, France's recently inaugurated Popular Front government agreed to enter into negotiations with al-Atasi. On March 22, 1936, al-Atasi arrived in Paris to begin talks with the Paris government. For almost six months al-Atasi, who had not yet assumed the Syrian presidency (he would do so in Decem-

ber), led the Syrian delegation in the negotiations. The final treaty draft guaranteed immediate recognition of a Syrian Republic and a 25-year transition to complete independence. It also stipulated that the Syrian government would control both the Druze and Alawite populations, that France would gradually reduce its military presence in Syria, and that Paris would not involve itself in the internal political affairs of the Syrian Republic.

Although the treaty was less than al-Atasi and other nationalists had hoped, it was nevertheless an important step toward independence and was far less slavish to French interests than the aborted 1934 treaty. The treaty bolstered the National Bloc and the political fortunes of al-Atasi, who was elected to the presidency in late November 1936. He is considered Syria's first modern head of state.

The French soon proved recalcitrant, however. The treaty was put before the French parliament on more than one occasion, and each time it came up for a vote the treaty fell short of the required majority. There were two major factors driving France's backtracking on the Franco-Syrian Treaty. First, as Nazi Germany became stronger as the 1930s progressed, French policymakers became increasingly reluctant to cede any of France's colonial territories. The fear, of course, was that Germany would move against the Middle East and gain access through weak ex-colonial holdings there. Also driving French hesitance was a rising tide of procolonial forces in French politics. These individuals vowed not to relinquish any of France's colonial possessions.

As 1939 dawned, it had become patently obvious that the French were indeed not going to ratify the treaty. By the spring of 1939, protests and riots again wracked Syria as the public grew resentful of what they considered to be French duplicity. Al-Atasi was greatly angered and embarrassed by the turn of events but was in no position to alter the situation in any meaningful way. When France unilaterally ceded to Turkey the Syrian province of Alexandretta, which the French had guaranteed would stay under Syrian control, Syrian nationalists had had enough. After mobilizing more demonstrations and strikes, they were successful in driving al-Atasi and the National Bloc from office. Al-Atssi resigned the presidency on July 9, 1939. Thereafter, several years of political unrest and French military engagements ensued. Syria would finally achieve independence in 1946.

PAUL G. PIERPAOLI JR.

See also

France, Middle East Policy; Franco-Lebanese Treaty; Lebanon; Syria; World War I, Impact of; World War II, Impact of

References

Harvey, John. *With the French Foreign Legion in Syria.* London: Greenhill, 1995.

Pipes, Daniel. *Greater Syria: The History of an Ambition.* New York: Oxford University Press, 1990.

Shambrook, Peter A. *French Imperialism in Syria, 1927–1936.* Reading, Berkshire, UK: Garnet Publishing/Ithaca Press, 1999.

Categorical Index

Events

Groups and Organizations

Index